Lecture Notes in Computer Science 1894

Edited by G. Goos, J. Hartmanis and J. van Leeuwen

T0191674

Rina Dechter (Ed.)

Principles and Practice of Constraint Programming – CP 2000

6th International Conference, CP 2000
Singapore, September 18-21, 2000
Proceedings

 Springer

Series Editors

Gerhard Goos, Karlsruhe University, Germany
Juris Hartmanis, Cornell University, NY, USA
Jan van Leeuwen, Utrecht University, The Netherlands

Volume Editor

Rina Dechter
University of California at Irvine
Department of Computer Science
Irvine, CA 92697, USA
E-mail: dechter@ics.uci.edu

Cataloging-in-Publication Data applied for

Die Deutsche Bibliothek - CIP-Einheitsaufnahme

Principles and practice of constraint programming : 6th international
conference ; proceedings / CP 2000, Singapore, September 18 - 21,
2000. Rina Dechter (ed.). - Berlin ; Heidelberg ; New York ; Barcelona ;
Hong Kong ; London ; Milan ; Paris ; Singapore ; Tokyo : Springer, 2000
   (Lecture notes in computer science ; Vol. 1894)
   ISBN 3-540-41053-8

CR Subject Classification (1998): D.1, D.3.2-3, I.2.3-4, F.3.2, F.4.1, I.2.8

ISSN 0302-9743
ISBN 3-540-41053-8 Springer-Verlag Berlin Heidelberg New York

Springer-Verlag Berlin Heidelberg New York
a member of BertelsmannSpringer Science+Business Media GmbH
© Springer-Verlag Berlin Heidelberg 2000
Printed in Germany

Typesetting: Camera-ready by author, data conversion by DA-TeX Gerd Blumenstein
Printed on acid-free paper   SPIN 10722557   06/3142   5 4 3 2 1 0

Preface

As computer science enters the new millennium, methods and languages for reasoning with constraints have come to play an important role, with both theoretical advances and practical applications. Constraints have emerged as the basis of a representational and computational paradigm that draws from many disciplines and can be brought to bear on many problem domains, including artificial intelligence, databases, and combinatorial optimization. The conference is concerned with all aspects of computing with constraints including algorithms, applications, environments, languages, models and systems.

The Sixth International Conference on Principles and Practice of Constraint Programming (CP2000) continues to provide an international forum for presenting and discussing state-of-the-art research and applications involving constraints. After a few annual workshops, CP'95 took place in Cassis, France; CP'96 in Cambridge, USA; CP'97 in Schloss Hagenberg, Austria; CP'98 in Pisa, Italy and CP'99 in Alexandria, USA. This year the conference is held in Singapore, from 18 through 21 September 2000.

This volume comprises the papers that were accepted for presentation at CP2000. From the 101 papers that were submitted, 31 papers were accepted for presentation in the plenary session and 13 papers were selected as posters and have a short version (five pages) in this volume. All papers were subjected to rigorous review three program committee members (or their designated reviewers) refereed each paper. Decisions were reached following discussions among reviewers and, in some instances, by e-mail consultation of the entire program committee. I believe the reader will find these articles to be of the highest quality, representing a significant contribution to the field.

Apart from the presentation of the technical papers and posters, we are very pleased to have three distinguished invited speakers: Alan Mackworth (University of British Columbia), David McAllester (AT&T Labs Research) and Alan Borning (University of Washington). The program included four tutorials presented by (1) George Gottlob and Francesco Scarello, (2) Thom Fruehwirth, (3) Michela Milano and (4) Joao Marques-Silva. The technical program was followed by five post-conference workshops on a variety of topics.

Last, but certainly not least, much is owed to the organizational skills of the CP2000 General Chairman Roland Yap. We are also indebted to Martin Henz, the Publicity Chair, and Toby Walsh, the Workshops and Tutorials Chair. Finally, I would like to thank Hong Zhao who was instrumental in setting up and running the web-based conference software and to Mario Espinoza for his dedicated help in assembling this volume.

Irvine, June 2000

Rina Dechter
Program Chair
CP2000

Conference Organization

Program Chair: Rina Dechter, University of California, USA
General Chair: Roland Yap, National University of Singapore
Publicity Chair: Martin Henz, National University of Singapore
Workshop and
Tutorial Chair: Toby Walsh, The University of York

Program Committee

Krzysztof Apt, CWI, The Netherlands
Roberto Bayardo, IBM Almaden Research Center, USA
Peter van Beek, University of Alberta, Canda
Alexander Bockmayr, LORIA, France
Alex Brodsky, George Mason University, USA
Philippe Codognet, University of Paris 6, France
Boi Faltings, LIA-EPFL, Switzerland
Ian Gent, University of St. Andrews, Scotland
John Hooker, Carnegie Mellon University, USA
Joxan Jaffar, National University of Singapore, Singapore
Peter Jeavons, Oxford University, England
Henry Kautz, AT&T Labs, USA
Manolis Koubarakis, Technical University of Crete, Greece
Michael Maher, Griffith University, Australia
Jean-François Puget, ILOG, France
Francesca Rossi, University of Padova, Italy
Christian Schulte, University of the Saarland, Germany
Helmut Simonis, Cosytec, France
Barbara Smith, University of Leeds, UK
Mark Wallace, IC-Parc, Imperial College, London
Makoto Yokoo, NTT,

Referees

Slim Abdennadher
Krzysztof Apt
Roberto Bayardo
Chris Beck
Peter Van Beek
Frédéric Benhamou
Alexander Bockmayr
Alex Brodsky
Matz Carlson
Hoong Chuin Lau
Philippe Codognet
David Cohen
Yannis Dimopoulos
J.S. Dong
Fredrich Eisenbrand
François Fages
Boi Faltings
Sarah Fores
Dan Frost
Richard Gault
Rosella Gennari
Ian Gent
Philippe Gerards
Nam Gi-Joon
Dina Goldin
Warwick Harvey
Nevin Heintze

Martin Henz
John Hooker
Joxan Jaffar
Peter Jeavons
Olli Kamarainen
Kalev Kask
Thomas Kasper
Henry Kautz
Hak-Jin Kim
Manolis Koubarakis
Javier Larrosa
Jonathan Lever
Andrew Lim
Michael Maher
Kim Marriott
Shigeo Matsubara
David McAllester
Pedro Meseguer
Bernd Meyer
Michela Milano
Eric Monfroy
Tobias Muller
Joachim Niehren
Stefano Novello
Greger Ottosson
Leszek Pacholski
Patrick Prosser

Jean-François Puget
Tom Richards
Christophe Ringeissen
Isla Ross
Gianfranco Rossi
Hani El Sakkout
Taisuke Sato
Abdul Sattar
Joachim Schimpf
Christian Schulte
Marius Silaghi
Josh Singer
Barbara Smith
J.-C. Sogno
Kostas Stergiou
Peter Stuckey
John Thornton
E. Thorsteinsson
Edward Tsang
Mark Wallace
Toby Walsh
Limsoon Wong
Roland Yap
Makoto Yokoo
Y.L. Zhang
Yuanlin Zhang

CP Organizing Committee

Alan Borning, University of Washington, USA
Alex Brodsky, George Mason University, USA
Jacques Cohen, Brandeis University, USA
Alain Colmerauer, University of Marseille, France
Eugene Freuder, Chair, University of New Hampshire, USA
Hervé Gallaire, Xerox, France
Joxan Jaffar, National University of Singapore, Singapore
Jean-Pierre Jouannaud, University of Paris-Sud, France
Jean-Louis Lassez, New Mexico Institute of Technology, USA
Michael Maher, Griffith University, Australia
Ugo Montanari, University of Pisa, Italy
Anil Nerode, Cornell University, USA
Jean-François Puget, ILOG, France
Francesca Rossi, University of Padova, Italy
Vijay Saraswat, AT&T Research, USA
Gert Smolka, DFKI and University of the Saarland, Germany
Ralph Wachter, Office of Naval Research, USA

Sponsors

Support from the following institutions is gratefully acknowledged.

Advanced Object Technologies Ltd, Hong Kong
COSYTEC SA, France
ILOG Singapore, Singapore
National University of Singapore, Singapore
Office of Naval Research, USA
PSA Corporation Ltd, Singapore

Table of Contents

Poster Papers

Constraint-Based Agents:
The ABC's of CBA's

Alan K. Mackworth

Laboratory for Computational Intelligence, Department of Computer Science
University of British Columbia, Vancouver, B.C. V6T 1Z4, Canada
mack@cs.ubc.ca
http://www.cs.ubc.ca/spider/mack

Abstract. The Constraint-Based Agent (CBA) framework is a set of
tools for designing, simulating, building, verifying, optimizing, learning
and debugging controllers for agents embedded in an active environment.
The agent and the environment are modelled symmetrically as, possibly
hybrid, dynamical systems in Constraint Nets, as developed by Zhang
and Mackworth. This paper is a tutorial overview of the development
and application of the CBA framework, emphasizing the important special case where the agent is an online constraint-satisfying device. Here
it is often possible to verify complex agents as obeying real-time temporal constraint specifications and, sometimes, to synthesize controllers
automatically. The CBA framework demonstrates the power of viewing
constraint programming as the creation of online constraint-solvers in
dynamic environments.

1   Introduction

Constraint programming has evolved several powerful frameworks for building
problem-solvers as constraint-satisfying devices. Primarily, these devices are offline problem-solvers. For example, the Constraint Satisfaction Problem (CSP)
paradigm has evolved and matured over the last twenty-five years. The algorithms developed in the CSP paradigm were made more available and more
useful when they were incorporated into the Constraint Programming (CP) language paradigms. Despite this success, however, a major challenge still facing
the constraint research community is to develop useful theoretical and practical
tools for the constraint-based design of embedded intelligent systems. Many applications require us to develop online constraint-satisfying systems that function
in a dynamic, coupled environment [6]. An archetypal example of an application
in this class is the design of controllers for sensory-based robots [13,10,7]. If we
examine this problem we see that almost all the tools developed to date in the
CSP and CP paradigms are inadequate for the task, despite the superficial at-
traction of the constraint-based approach. The fundamental difficulty is that, for
the most part, the CSP and CP paradigms still presume a disembodied, offline
model of computation.

R. Dechter (Ed.): CP 2000, LNCS 1894, pp. 1–10, 2000.

Consider an agent coupled to its active environment as shown in Figure 1. Each is an open dynamic system in its own right, acting on, and reacting to, the other. The coupled pair form a closed system that evolves over time.

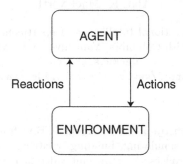

Fig. 1. An agent interacting with its environment

To deal with such embedded applications, we must radically shift our perspective on constraint satisfaction from the offline model in which a solution is a function of pre-given static inputs to an online model where a solution is a temporal trace of values, a transduction of the input trace over time. Values in the input trace may depend on earlier values in the output trace. In fact, the input trace for the agent is itself a mapping of its output trace, representing the dynamics of the environment, as shown in Figure 1.

Intelligent systems embedded as controllers in real or virtual systems must be designed in an online model based on various time structures: continuous, discrete and event-based. The requisite online computations, or transductions, are to be performed over various type structures including continuous and discrete domains. These hybrid systems require new models of computation, constraint satisfaction and constraint programming. To this end, we have defined constraint satisfaction as a dynamic system process that approaches asymptotically the solution set of the given, possibly time-varying, constraints [12]. Under this view, constraint programming is the creation of a dynamic system with the required property.

In this paper I present a tutorial overview of our approach, called Constraint-Based Agents (CBA), the ABC's of CBA's, if you like. The CBA model consists, at its simplest, of a symmetrical coupling of an agent and its active environment. As we'll see later, we say the agent is constraint-based if its behaviour satisfies a specification in a constraint-based temporal logic.

2   Agents in the World

The most obvious artificial agents in the world are robots. But the CBA approach applies equally to embedded devices, pure software agents and natural animate agents. There are many ways of using a CBA model, including the embedded mode, simulation mode, verification mode, optimization mode, learning mode and design mode [8, p. 449]. The agent design problem is formidable, regardless of whether the agent is designed or modified by a human, by nature (evolution), by another agent (bootstrapping), or by itself (learning). An agent is, typically, a hybrid intelligent system, consisting of a controller coupled to its body as shown in Figure 2.

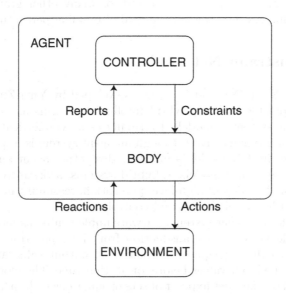

Fig. 2. The structure of a constraint-based agent system

The controller and the body both consist of discrete-time, continuous-time or event-driven components operating over discrete or continuous domains. The controller has perceptual subsystems that can (partially) observe, or infer, the state of the body and, through it, the state of the environment.

Parenthetically, the 'body' of an agent is simply the direct interface of the agent to its environment. The body executes actions in the environment, senses the state of the environment, which may well cause state changes in the body, and reports to the controller. In the case of a robotic agent the body consists of one or more physical systems but in the case of an embedded software agent, the body is simply the software module that directly interfaces to the virtual or physical environment. Control theorists typically call the body the 'plant'. Some models do not differentiate between the body and the environment; we prefer to make that differentiation, based on the distinction between what is directly, and what is indirectly, controlled.

Agent design methodologies are evolving dialectically [4]. The symbolic methods of 'Good Old Fashioned Artificial Intelligence and Robotics' (GOFAIR) constitute the original thesis. The antithesis is reactive 'Insect AI' and control theory. The emerging synthesis, Situated Agents, has promise, but needs formal rigor and practical tools [9,3,2,4,13,7].

In 1992, I proposed robot soccer as a grand challenge problem [4] since it has the task characteristics that force us to confront the fundamental issues of agent design in a practical way for a perceptual, collaborative, real-time task with clear performance criteria. At the same time, I described the first system for playing robot soccer. Since then it has been a very productive testbed both for our laboratory [1,10,5,16,18,17,20] and for many other groups around the world, stimulating research toward the goal of building perceptual agents.

3   The Constraint Net Model

The Constraint Net (CN) model [14] was developed by Ying Zhang and Mackworth as a model for building hybrid intelligent systems as Situated Agents. In CN, an agent system is modelled formally as a symmetrical coupling of an agent with its environment. Even though an agent system is, typically, a hybrid dynamic system, its CN model is unitary. Most other agent and robot design methodologies use hybrid models of hybrid systems, awkwardly combining off-line computational models of high-level perception, reasoning and planning with online models of low-level sensing and control.

CN is a model for agent systems software implemented as modules with I/O ports. A module performs a transduction from its input traces to its output traces, subject to the principle of causality: an output value at any time can depend only on the input values before, or at, that time. The model has a formal semantics based on the least fixpoint of sets of equations [14]. In applying it to an agent operating in a given environment, one separately specifies the behaviour of the agent body, the agent control program, and the environment. The total system can then be shown to have various properties, such as safety and liveness, based on provable properties of its subsystems. This approach allows one to specify and verify models of embedded control systems. Our goal is to develop it as a practical tool for building real, complex, sensor-based agents. It can be seen as a formal development of Brooks' subsumption architecture [2] that enhances its reliability, modularity and scalability while avoiding the limitations of the augmented finite state machine approach, combining proactivity with reactivity.

An agent situated in an environment can be modelled as three machines: the agent body, the agent controller and the environment, as shown above in Figure 2. Each can be modelled separately as a dynamical system by specifying a CN with input and output ports. The agent is modelled as a CN consisting of a coupling of its body CN and its controller CN by identifying corresponding input and output ports. Similarly the agent CN is coupled to the environment CN to form a closed agent-environment CN, as shown above in Figure 1

The CN model is realized as an online dataflow-like distributed programming language with a formal algebraic denotational semantics and a specification language, a real-time temporal logic, that allows the designer to specify and prove properties of the situated agent by proving them of the agent-environment CN. We have shown how to specify, design, verify and implement systems for a robot that can track other robots [11], a robot that can escape from mazes and a two-handed robot that assembles objects [13], an elevator system [19] and a car-like robot that can plan and execute paths under non-holonomic constraints [16].

Although CN can carry out traditional symbolic computation online, such as solving Constraint Satisfaction Problems and path planning, notice that much of the symbolic reasoning and theorem-proving may be outside the agent, in the mind of the designer, for controller synthesis and verification. GOFAIR does not make this distinction, assuming that such symbolic reasoning occurs explicitly in, and only in, the mind of the agent.

The question "Will the agent do the right thing?" [13] is answered positively if we can:

1. model the coupled agent system at a suitable level of abstraction,
2. specify the required global properties of the system's evolution, and
3. verify that the model satisfies the specification.

In CN the modelling language and the specification language are totally distinct since they have very different requirements. The modelling language is a generalized dynamical system language. Two versions of the specification language, Timed Linear Temporal Logic [16] and Timed ∀-automata [12], have been developed with appropriate theorem-proving and model-checking techniques for verifying systems. In [8, Chapter 12] we describe how to build a situated robot controller using CN as realized in a logic program.

4 Constraint-Satisfying Agents

Many agents can be designed as online constraint-satisfying devices [12,15,16]. A robot in this restricted scheme can be verified more easily. Moreover, given a constraint-based specification and a model of the body and the environment, automatic synthesis of a correct constraint-satisfying controller sometimes becomes feasible, as shown for a simple goal-scoring robot in [16].

As a simple example, in Figure 2 suppose the CONTROLLER is a thermostat turning on or off a furnace, the BODY, that is heating the ENVIRONMENT. The goal of the system is to make the temperature of of the ENVIRONMENT, T_E, equal to a desired temperature, T_D. In other words the CONTROLLER of the AGENT is trying to solve the constraint $T_E(t) = T_D(t)$. One version of CONTROLLER correctness is established if we can prove that the (thermal) dynamics of the coupled AGENT-ENVIRONMENT system satisfy the temporal logic formula $\Diamond \Box |T_E - T_D| < \epsilon$ where $\Diamond$ can be read as 'eventually' and $\Box$ can be read as 'always'. In other words, the system will, no matter how it is disturbed, eventually enter, and remain within, an ϵ-neighborhood of the solution manifold of the constraint. A less restrictive form of correctness corresponds to the specification $\Box \Diamond |T_E - T_D| < \epsilon$ which is to say that the system will always return, asymptotically, to the constraint solution manifold if it should happen to leave it.

A constraint is simply a relation on the phase space of the agent system, which is the product of the controller, body and environment spaces. A controller is defined to be *constraint-satisfying* if it, repeatedly, eventually drives the system into an ϵ-neighborhood of the constraint using a constraint satisfaction method such as gradient descent or a symbolic technique.

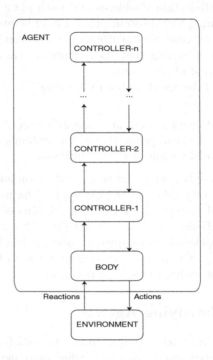

Fig. 3. A hierarchical agent controller

A constraint-satisfying controller may be *hierarchical* with several layers of controller above the body, as shown in Figure 3. In this case, each layer must satisfy the constraints, defined on its state variables, appropriate to the layer, as, typically, set by the layer above. The layers below each layer present to that layer as a virtual agent body, in a suitably abstract state space [16,17]. The lower layers are, typically, reactive and synchronous (or in continuous time) on continuous state spaces; the upper layers are more deliberative and asynchronous (or event-triggered) in symbolic, discrete spaces.

A typical layer in a hierarchical controller is shown in Figure 4.

Each layer has two external inputs: the trace of constraint requests coming from above *ConstraintsIn* (*CI*) and the reports coming from below *ReportsIn* (*RI*). Its two outputs are its reports to the level above *ReportsOut* (*RO*) and its constraint requests to the level below *ConstraintsOut* (*CO*). These traces arise from *causal transductions* of the external inputs:

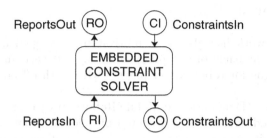

Fig. 4. A layer in a constraint-based controller

$$CO = C_t(CI, RI) \tag{1}$$
$$RO = R_t(CI, RI) \tag{2}$$

If the constraint-solver can be represented as a state-based solver then the layer may be represented as shown in Figure 5.

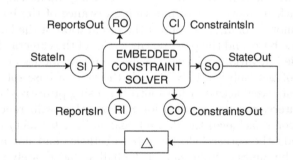

Fig. 5. A layer with state in a constraint-based controller

Here, for simplicity, a discrete-time state-based layer is shown. It produces an extra output *StateOut (SO)* that is consumed as an extra input *StateIn (SI)* after a unit delay (Δ). In this case the behaviour of the layer may be represented by computing the values of the three outputs as *transliterations* (functions) of the current values of the three inputs:

$$co(t) = c_f(ci(t), ri(t), si(t)) \tag{3}$$
$$ro(t) = r_f(ci(t), ri(t), si(t)) \tag{4}$$
$$so(t) = s_f(ci(t), ri(t), si(t)) \tag{5}$$
$$si(t+1) = so(t) \tag{6}$$

5   Robot Soccer Players

The CBA framework has also been motivated, developed and tested by application to the challenge of designing, building and verifying controllers with perceptual systems for robot soccer players with both off-board and on-board vision systems.

In the Dynamo (Dynamics and Mobile Robots) project in our laboratory, we have experimented, since 1991, with multiple mobile robots under visual control. The Dynamite testbed consists of a fleet of radio-controlled vehicles that receive commands from a remote computer. Using our custom hardware and a distributed MIMD environment, vision programs are able to monitor the position and orientation of each robot at 60 Hz; planning and control programs generate and send motor commands at the same rate. This approach allows umbilical-free behaviour and very rapid, lightweight fully autonomous robots. Using this testbed we have demonstrated various robot tasks [1], including playing soccer [10] using a 2-layer deliberative/reactive controller architecture.

One of the Dynamo robots, Spinoza, is a self-contained robot consisting of an RWI base with an RGB camera on a pan-tilt platform mounted as its head and a trinocular stereo camera in its base. As a illustration of these ideas, consider the task for Spinoza of repeatedly finding, tracking, chasing and kicking a soccer ball, using the pan-tilt camera. After locating the moving ball Spinoza is required to track it, move to within striking distance of the ball and strike it. The available motor commands control the orientation of the base, the forward movement of the base, and the pan and tilt angles of the camera. The parameters can be controlled in various relative/absolute position modes or rate mode. The available rate of pan substantially exceeds the rate of base rotation. A hierarchical constraint-based active-vision controller, using prioritized constraints and constraint arbiters, can be specified for Spinoza that will, repeatedly, achieve and maintain (or re-achieve) the desired goal subject to safety conditions such as staying inside the soccer field, avoiding obstacles and not accelerating too quickly. If the dynamics of Spinoza and the ball are adequately modelled by the designer then this constraint-based vision system will be guaranteed to achieve its specification.

Yu Zhang and Mackworth have extended these ideas to build three-layer constraint-satisfying controllers for a complete soccer team [20]. The controllers for our softbot soccer team, UBC Dynamo98, are modelled in CN and implemented in Java, using the Java Beans architecture [17]. They control the soccer players' bodies in the Soccer Server developed by Noda Itsuki for RoboCup. These experiments provide evidence that the constraint-based CN approach is a clean and practical design framework for perceptual robots.

6   Conclusions

The Constraint-Based Agent approach is a framework for the specification, design, analysis, implementation and validation of artificial and natural agent systems. It requires a new model of online and embedded computation for Constraint Programming, Constraint Nets.

Acknowledgments

I am most grateful to Ying Zhang and Yu Zhang for our collaborations. I also thank Rod Barman, Cullen Jennings, Stewart Kingdon, Jim Little, Valerie McRae, Don Murray, Dinesh Pai, David Poole, Michael Sahota, and Vlad Tucakov for help with this. This work is supported, in part, by the Natural Sciences and Engineering Research Council of Canada and the Institute for Robotics and Intelligent Systems Network of Centres of Excellence.

References

1. R. A. Barman, S. J. Kingdon, J. J. Little, A. K. Mackworth, D. K. Pai, M. Sahota, H. Wilkinson, and Y. Zhang. Dynamo: Real-time experiments with multiple mobile robots. In *Intelligent Vehicles Symposium*, pages 261–266, Tokyo, July 1993. 4, 8
2. R. A. Brooks. Intelligence without reason. In *IJCAI-91*, pages 569–595, Sydney, Australia, Aug. 1991. 4
3. J. Lavignon and Y. Shoham. Temporal automata. Technical Report STAN-CS-90-1325, Stanford University, Stanford, CA, 1990. 4
4. A. K. Mackworth. On seeing robots. In A. Basu and X. Li, editors, *Computer Vision: Systems, Theory, and Applications*, pages 1–13. World Scientific Press, Singapore, 1993. 3, 4
5. A. K. Mackworth. Quick and clean: Constraint-based vision for situated robots. In *IEEE Int'l. Conf. on Image Processing*, pages 789–792, Lausanne, Switzerland, Sept. 1996. 4
6. A. K. Mackworth. Constraint-based design of embedded intelligent systems. *Constraints*, 2(1):83–86, 1997. 1
7. A. K. Mackworth. The dynamics of intelligence: Constraint-satisfying hybrid systems for perceptual agents. In *Hybrid Systems and AI: Modeling, Analysis and Control of Discrete and Continuous Systems*, number SS-99-05 in AAAI, Spring Symposium Series, pages 210–214, Stanford, CA, Mar. 1999. 1, 4
8. D. L. Poole, A. K. Mackworth, and R. G. Goebel. *Computational Intelligence: A Logical Approach*. Oxford University Press, New York, 1998. 3, 5
9. S. J. Rosenschein and L. P. Kaelbling. The synthesis of machines with provable epistemic properties. In Joseph Halpern, editor, *Proc. Conf. on Theoretical Aspects of Reasoning about Knowledge*, pages 83–98. Morgan Kaufmann, Los Altos, CA, 1986. 4
10. M. Sahota and A. K. Mackworth. Can situated robots play soccer? In *Proc. Artificial Intelligence 94*, pages 249 – 254, Banff, Alberta, May 1994. 1, 4, 8
11. Y. Zhang and A. K. Mackworth. Modeling behavioral dynamics in discrete robotic systems with logical concurrent objects. In S. G. Tzafestas and J. C. Gentina, editors, *Robotics and Flexible Manufacturing Systems*, pages 187–196. Elsevier Science Publishers B. V., 1992. 5
12. Y. Zhang and A. K. Mackworth. Specification and verification of constraint-based dynamic systems. In A. Borning, editor, *Principles and Practice of Constraint Programming*, number 874 in Lecture Notes in Computer Science, pages 229 – 242. Springer-Verlag, 1994. 2, 5

13. Y. Zhang and A. K. Mackworth. Will the robot do the right thing? In *Proc. Artificial Intelligence 94*, pages 255 – 262, Banff, Alberta, May 1994. 1, 4, 5
14. Y. Zhang and A. K. Mackworth. Constraint Nets: A semantic model for hybrid dynamic systems. *Theoretical Computer Science*, 138:211 – 239, 1995. 4
15. Y. Zhang and A. K. Mackworth. Constraint programming in Constraint Nets. In V. Saraswat and P. Van Hentenryck, editor, *Principles and Practice of Constraint Programming*, chapter 3, pages 49–68. The MIT Press, Cambridge, MA, 1995. 5
16. Y. Zhang and A. K. Mackworth. Synthesis of hybrid constraint-based controllers. In P. Antsaklis, W. Kohn, A. Nerode, and S. Sastry, editors, *Hybrid Systems II*, Lecture Notes in Computer Science 999, pages 552 – 567. Springer Verlag, 1995. 4, 5, 6
17. Y. Zhang and A. K. Mackworth. A constraint-based controller for soccer-playing robots. In *Proceedings of IROS '98*, pages 1290 – 1295, Victoria, BC, Canada, Oct. 1998. 4, 6, 8
18. Y. Zhang and A. K. Mackworth. Using reactive deliberation for real-time control of soccer-playing robots. In H. Kitano, editor, *RoboCup-97: Robot Soccer World Cup 1*, pages 508–512. Springer-Verlag, Aug. 1998. 4
19. Y. Zhang and A. K. Mackworth. Modelling and analysis of hybrid systems: An elevator case study. In H. Levesque and F. Pirri, editors, *Logical Foundations for Cognitive Agents*, pages 370–396. Springer, Berlin, 1999. 5
20. Y. Zhang and A. K. Mackworth. A multi-level constraint-based controller for the Dynamo98 robot soccer team. In Minoru Asada and Hiroaki Kitano, editor, *RoboCup-98: Robot Soccer World Cup II*, pages 402–409. Springer, 1999. 4, 8

Constraints for Interactive Graphical Applications

Alan Borning

Dept. of Computer Science & Engineering, University of Washington
PO Box 352350, Seattle, Washington 98195, USA
borning@cs.washington.edu

Extended Abstract

Constraints have been used in interactive graphical applications since Sketchpad in the early 60's [8]. Constraints in this domain, as in others, provide a declarative way for the user to specify what is desired rather than how to achieve it. Two particular features of this domain, however, stem from interactivity: the need to handle state and change properly as a graphical figure is manipulated, and the need for efficient incremental algorithms for satisfying the constraints to preserve interactive response.

In the talk I will first describe Cassowary [2,6], an algorithm for satisfying sets of linear equality and inequality constraints. Cassowary is a version of the simplex algorithm that incrementally solves hierarchies of hard and soft constraints [5], with special treatment of the *edit* and *stay* constraints that can be used to express the semantics of editing and updating a graphical figure. Two important properties of Cassowary are that it is very efficient (the constraint solving time is normally dominated by the graphics refresh time), and that it handles simultaneous equations, simultaneous inequalities, and over- and under-constrained systems without difficulty. The Cassowary toolkit is freely available under the GNU Library General Public License, and has been used for a number of applications, including those mentioned below and others.

I will then describe several recent applications. One application is constraint-based web layout [3]. Here, we extend the Cascading Style Sheet standard [7] to include constraints. For example, we can constrain two columns in a table to have the same width, and to be at least 10 times as wide as the gutter between them, or constrain a heading font to be 2 points larger than the body font. These constraints can be preferences as well as requirements, and can come from the viewer as well as the page author. (For example, the viewer might insist on a minimum of 12 point font sizes, or a particular browser width.) The final appearance of the web page is thus the result of an arbitration between the desires of the author and viewer, where this arbitration is performed by solving the combined set of constraints.

A second application is the Scheme Constraints Window Manager [4]. This window manager allows users to express their intentions using both direct manipulation and with persistent constraints, e.g. that one window be always to the

R. Dechter (Ed.): CP 2000, LNCS 1894, pp. 11–12, 2000.
© Springer-Verlag Berlin Heidelberg 2000

left of another and of the same height. A number of other features support the ready use of constraints in the window manager, including a graphical toolbar for applying constraints, a recorder for defining new compound constraints using a simple programming-by-demonstration technique, and a graphical constraint investigator for visually display the current set of constraints when desired.

Finally, a third application extends the Scalable Vector Graphics (SVG) standard for the web [1] to allow constraints on the positions of graphical elements. SVG is an important advance over including bitmap images in web pages, since the image is resolution-independent. However, the internal geometry of an SVG image is fixed. Constraint Scalable Vector Graphics generalizes SVG, so that a given illustration can be resized and reformatted appropriately for the available space, while still satisfying its constraints. In addition, constraints on a read-only "time" variable provide a simple animation facility.

Papers and source code are available from our web site at
www.cs.washington.edu/research/constraints

This research has been funded in part by U.S. National Science Foundation Grant No. IIS-9975990.

References

1. Greg Badros. *Extending Interactive Graphical Applications with Constraints*. PhD thesis, Department of Computer Science & Engineering, University of Washington, June 2000. 12
2. Greg Badros and Alan Borning. The Cassowary linear arithmetic constraint solving algorithm: Interface and implementation. Technical Report 98-06-04, Dept. of Computer Science and Engineering, University of Washington, Seattle, WA, June 1998. 11
3. Greg Badros, Alan Borning, Kim Marriott, and Peter Stuckey. Constraint cascading style sheets for the web. In *Proceedings of the 1999 ACM Symposium on User Interface Software and Technology*, pages 73–82, November 1999. 11
4. Greg Badros, Jeffrey Nichols, and Alan Borning. SCWM—the scheme constraints window manager. In *Proceedings of the AAAI 2000 Spring Symposium Series on Smart Graphics*, March 2000. 11
5. Alan Borning, Bjorn Freeman-Benson, and Molly Wilson. Constraint hierarchies. *Lisp and Symbolic Computation*, 5(3):223–270, September 1992. 11
6. Alan Borning, Kim Marriott, Peter Stuckey, and Yi Xiao. Solving linear arithmetic constraints for user interface applications. In *Proceedings of the 1997 ACM Symposium on User Interface Software and Technology*, October 1997. 11
7. Håkon Wium Lie and Bert Bos. *Cascading Style Sheets: Designing for the Web*. Addison-Wesley, 1997. 11
8. Ivan Sutherland. *Sketchpad: A Man-Machine Graphical Communication System*. PhD thesis, Department of Electrical Engineering, MIT, January 1963. 11

Meta-complexity Theorems: Talk Abstract

Kavid / cZllester

AT&T Labs-Research
180 Park Ave, Florham Park NJ 07932
dmac@research.att.com
http://www.research.att.com/~dmac

1 Overview

Z variety of authors have argued that bottom-up logic programs provide a clear presentation of a wide variety of algorithms, e.g.,[6,Ŋ5,2,j]. Recently meta-complexity theorems have been given that allow, in many cases, the running time of a bottom-up logic program to be determined by inspection [1]. This talk abstract presents the fundamental meta-complexity theorem. ı ew meta-compleixty theorems useful for optimization algorithms were presented in the talk.

Z bottom-up logic program is a set of inference rules. To give theorems about inference rules in general, we formally define an inference rule to be a first order , orn clause, i.e. a first order formula of the form $A_1 \wedge \ldots \wedge A_n \to C$ where C and each A_i is a first order atom, i.e., a predicate applied to first order terms. ffirst order , orn clauses form a Turing complete model of computation and can be used in practice as a general purpose programming language. The atoms A_1, ..., A_n are called the antecedents of the rule and the atom C is called the conclusion.

There are two basic ways to view a set of inference rules as an algorithm — the backward chaining approach taken in traditional ¨ rolog interpreters and the forward chaining, or bottom-up approach common in deductive databases [6,5,2]. / eta-complexity analysis derives from the bottom-up approach. Zs a simple example consider the rule $P(x,y) \wedge P(y,z) \to P(x,z)$ which states that the binary predicate P is transitive. Ǫet D be a set of assertions of the form $P(c,d)$ where c and d are constant symbols. / ore generally we will use the term *assertion* to mean a ground atom, i.e., an atom not containing variable, and use the term *database* to mean a set of assertions. ffor any set R of inference rules and any database D we let $R(D)$ denote the set of assertions that can be proved in the obvious way from assertions in D using rules in R. If R consists of the above rule for transitivity, and D consists of assertions of the form $P(c,d)$, then $R(D)$ is simply the transitive closure of D. In the bottom-up view a rule set R is taken to be an algorithm for computing output $R(D)$ from input D. Z rule set will be called terminating if for every finite database D we have that $R(D)$ is finite.

, ere we are interested in methods for quickly determining the running time of a rule set R, i.e., the time required to compute $R(D)$ from D. ffor example, consider the following "algorithm" for computing the transitive closure of

R. Dechter (Ed.): CP 2000, LNCS 1894, pp. 13–17, 2000.

a predicate EDGE defined by the bottom-up rules $\text{EDGE}(x,y) \to \text{PATH}(x,y)$ and $\text{EDGE}(x,y) \wedge \text{PATH}(y,z) \to \text{PATH}(x,z)$. If the input graph contains e edges this algorithm runs in $O(en)$ time — significantly better than $O(n^3)$ for sparse graphs. ı ote that the $O(en)$ running time can not be derived by simply counting the number of variables in any single rule.

The fundamental theorem states that, for any terminating rule set R, the database $R(D)$ can be computed in time proportional to the number of assertions in D plus the number of "prefix firings" of the rules in R — the number of derivable ground instances of prefixes of rule antecedents. This theorem holds for arbitrary terminating rule sets, no matter how complex the antecedents or how many antecedents rules have. The fundamental meta-complexity theorem immediately implies the $O(en)$ running time of the sparse transitive closure algorithm given above — there are e ways of instantiating the first antecedent and, for given values of x and y, at most n ways of instantiating z. ffor this simple rule set the $O(en)$ running time may seem obvious, but the meta-complexity theorem can be used in many more complex rule sets where a completely rigorous treatment of the running time would be otherwise tedious.

2   The Fundamental Theorem

Z ground substitution is a mapping from a finite set of variables to ground terms. ₂ ere we consider only ground substitutions. If σ is a ground substitution defined on all the variables occurring in a term t then $\sigma(t)$ is defined in the standard way as the result of replacing each variable by its image under σ. We also assume that all expressions — both terms and atoms — are represented as interned dag data structures. This means that the same term is always represented by the same pointer to memory so that equality testing is a unit time operation. ffurthermore, we assume that hash table operations take unit time so that for any substitution σ defined (only) on x and y we can compute (the pointer representing) $\sigma(f(x, y))$ in unit time. ı ote that interned expressions support indexing. ffor example, given a binary predicate P we can index all assertions of the form $P(t,w)$ so that the data structure representing t points to a list of all terms w such that $P(t,w)$ has been asserted and, conversely, all terms w point to a list of all terms t such that $P(t,w)$ has been asserted.

We will say that a database E is closed under a rule set R if $R(E) = E$. It would seem that determining closedness would be easier than computing the closure in cases where we are not yet closed. The meta-complexity theorem states, in essence, that the closure can be computed quickly — it can be computed in the time needed to merely check the closedness of the final result. Consider a rule $A_1 \wedge \ldots \wedge A_n \to C$. To check that a database E is closed under this rule one can compute all ground substitutions σ such that $\sigma(A_1), \ldots \sigma(A_n)$ are all in E and then check that $\sigma(C)$ is also in E. To find all such substitutions we can first match the pattern A_1 against assertions in the database to get all substitutions σ_1 such that $\sigma_1(A_1) \in D$. Then given σ_i such that $\sigma_i(A_1), \ldots, \sigma_i(A_i)$ are all in E we can match $\sigma_i(A_{i+1})$ against the assertions in the database to get all extensions σ_{i+1} such that $\sigma_{i+1}(A_1)$, ..., $\sigma_{i+1}(A_{i+1})$ are in E. Each substitution σ_i determines a "prefix firing" of the rule as defined below.

Definition 1. *We define a* prefix firing *of a rule* A_1, ..., $A_n \rightarrow C$ *in a rule set* R *under database* E *to be a ground instance* B_1, ..., B_i *of an initial sequence* A_1, ..., A_i, $i \leq n$, *such that* B_1, ..., B_n *are all contained in* D. *We let* $P_R(E)$ *be the set of all prefix firings of rules in* R *for database* E.

ı ote that the rule $P(x, y) \wedge P(y, z) \wedge R(z) \rightarrow P(x, z)$ might have a large number of firings for the first two antecedents while having no firings of all three antecedents. The simple algorithm outlined above for checking that E is closed under R requires at least $|P_R(E)|$ steps of computation. Zs outlined above, the closure check algorithm would actually require more time because each step of extending σ_i to σ_{i+1} involves iterating over the entire database. The following theorem states that for any terminating rule set R we can compute $R(D)$ in time proportional to $|D|$ (the number of distinct assertions in D) plus $|P_R(R(D))|$ (the number of prefix firings).

Theorem 1 (McAllester[1]). *For any terminating rule set* R *there exists an algorithm for mapping* D *to* $R(D)$ *which runs in* $O(|D| + |P_R(R(D))|)$ *time.*

Eefore proving theorem 1 we consider a simple application. Consider the algorithm for context free parsing shown in figure 1. The grammar is given in Chomsky normal form and consists of a set of assertions of the form $X \rightarrow a$ and $X \rightarrow YZ$. The input sting is represented as a "lisp list" of the form CONS(a_1, CONS(a_2, ... CONS(a_n, NIL))) and the input string is specified by an assertion of the form INPUT(s). Qet g be the number of productions in the grammar and let n be the length of the input string. These rules terminate and theorem 1 immediately implies that this algorithm runs in $O(gn^3)$ time. ı ote that there is a rule with six variables — three string index variables and three grammar nonterminal variables.

We now give a proof of theorem 1. ffirst, we say that a rule has unbound variables if some variable in the conclusion of the rule does not appear in any antecedent of the rule. Suppose that R contains an rule with unbound variables and consider a D such that $R(D)$ contains an instance of the antecedents of that rule. Since an unbound variable in the conclusion can be instantiated with any term, we must have that $R(D)$ is infinite. Therefore, if R is terminating, then no rule in R with unbound variables can ever be used in computing $R(D)$. So, if R is terminating, then R is equivalent (as a mapping from input database to output database) to the subset of R consisting of just the rules without unbound variables. So we can assume without loss of generality that no rule in R has unbound variables.

---

[1]   The theorem proved in [1] is stated slightly differently — rather than consider an arbitrary terminating rule set the theorem presented there requires that every variable in the conclusion of a rule appear in some antecendent of that rule. However, the proofs of these two variants of the theorem are essentially identicle.

$$\frac{\begin{array}{l} U \to a \\ \texttt{INPUT(CONS}(a,\ j)) \end{array}}{\texttt{PARSES}(U,\ \texttt{CONS}(a,\ j),\ j)}$$

$$\frac{\begin{array}{l} A \to BC \\ \texttt{PARSES}(B,\ i,\ j) \\ \texttt{PARSES}(C,\ j,\ k) \end{array}}{\texttt{PARSES}(A,\ i,\ k)}$$

$$\frac{\texttt{INPUT(CONS(X, Y))}}{\texttt{INPUT(Y)}}$$

Fig. 1. The Cocke-Xasimi-Younger (CXY) parsing algorithm. $\texttt{PARSES}(u,\ i,\ j)$ means that the substring from i to j parses as nonterminal u7

ffiiven that no rule has unbound variables6 the proof is based on a source to source transformation of the given program7 We note that each of the following source to source transformations on inference rules preserve the quantity $|D|$ + $|P_R 9R9D55|$ 9as a function of $D5$ up to a multiplicative constant7 Vh the second transformation note that there must be at least one element of D or $P_r 9R9D55$ for each assertion in $R9D57$ ̦ ence adding any rule with only a single antecedent and with a fresh predicate in the conclusion at most doubles the value of $|D|$ + $|P_R 9R9D55|$7 The second transformation can then be done in two steps — first we add the new rule and then replace the antecedent in the existing rule7 Z similar analysis holds for the third transformation7

$$A_1,\ A_2,\ A_3,\ \ldots A_n \to C \quad \Rightarrow$$

$$A_1,\ A_2 \to P9x_1,\ \ldots,\ x_n 5, \quad P9x_1,\ \ldots,\ x_n 5,\ A_3,\ \ldots,\ A_n \to C$$

where $x_1,\ \ldots, x_n$ are all free variables in A_1 and $A_2$7

$$A_1,\ \ldots,\ P9t_1,\ \ldots,\ t_n 5,\ \ldots, A_n \to C \quad \Rightarrow$$

$$P9t_1,\ \ldots,\ t_n 5 \to Q9x_1,\ \ldots,\ x_m 5, \quad A_1,\ \ldots,\ Q9x_1,\ \ldots,\ x_m 5,\ \ldots, A_n \to C$$

where at least one of t_i is a non͡variable and $x_1,\ \ldots,\ x_m$ are all the free variables in $t_1,\ \ldots,\ t_n$7

$$P9x_1,\ \ldots,\ x_n 5,\ Q9y_1,\ \ldots,\ y_m 5 \to C \quad \Rightarrow$$

$$P9x_1,\ \ldots,\ x_n 5 \to P'9f9z_1,\ \ldots,\ z_k 5,\ g9w_1,\ \ldots w_h 55$$

$$Q9y_1,\ \ldots,\ y_n 5 \to Q'9g9w_1,\ \ldots,\ w_h 5,\ u9v_1,\ \ldots v_j 55$$

$$P'9x, y5,\ Q'9y, z5 \to R9x, y, z5$$

$$R9f9x_1,\ \ldots,\ x_n 5,\ g9w_1,\ \ldots,\ w_h 5,\ u9v_1,\ \ldots,\ v_m 55 \to C$$

where $z_1, \ldots, z_k$ are those variables among the x_is which are not among the y_isR$w_1, \ldots, w_h$ are those variables that occur both in the x_is and y_isR and $v_1, \ldots v_i$ are those variables among the y_is that are not among the x_is7

These transformations allow us to assume without loss of generality that the only multiple antecedent rules are of the form $P9x, y5, Q9y, z5 \to R9x, y, z57$ ffor each such multiple antecedent rule we create an index such that for each y we can enumerate the values of x such that $P9x, y5$ has been asserted and also enumerate the values of z such that $Q9y, z5$ has been asserted7 When a new assertion of the form $P9x, y5$ or $Q9y, z5$ is derived we can now iterate over the possible values of the missing variable in time proportional to the number of such values7

References

1. David McAllester. The complexity analysis of static analyses. In *Symposium on Static Analysis*. Springer Verlag, 1999.   13, 15
2. Jeff Naughton and Raghu Ramakrishnan. Bottom-up evaluation of logic programs. In Jean-Louis Lassez and Gordon Plotkin, editors, *Computational Logic*. MIT Press, 1991.   13
3. Thomas Reps. Demand interprocedural program analysis using logic databases. pages 163–196, 1994.   13
4. J. Ullman. *Principles of Database and Knowledge-Base Systems*. Computer Science Press, 1988.   13
5. J. Ullman. Bottom-up beats top-down for datalog. In *Proceedings of the Eigth ACM SIGACT-SIGMOD-SIGART Symposium on the Principles of Database Systems*, pages 140–149, March 1989.   13
6. M. Vardi. Complexity of relational query languages. In *14th Symposium on Theory of Computation*, pages 137–146, 1982.   13

Automatic Generation of Propagation Rules for Finite Domains

Slim Abdennadher[1] and Christophe Rigotti[2]*

[1] Computer Science Department, University of Munich
Oettingenstr. 67, 80538 München, Germany
Slim.Abdennadher@informatik.uni-muenchen.de
[2] Laboratoire d'Ingénierie des Systèmes d'Information
Bâtiment 501, INSA Lyon, 69621 Villeurbanne Cedex, France
Christophe.Rigotti@insa-lyon.fr

Abstract. A general approach to specify the propagation and simplification process of constraints consists of applying rules over these constraints. In this paper, we propose a method for generating propagation rules for constraints over finite domains defined extensionally by e.g. a truth table or their tuples. Using our algorithm, the user has the possibility to specify the admissible syntactic forms of the rules. The generated rules will be implemented as rules of the language Constraint Handling Rules (CHR).
Furthermore, we show that our approach performs well on various examples, including Boolean constraints, three valued logic, Allen's qualitative approach to temporal logic and qualitative spatial reasoning with the Region Connection Calculus.

1 Introduction

Rule-based formalisms are ubiquitous in computer science, and even more so in constraint reasoning and programming. In constraint reasoning, algorithms are often specified using inference rules, rewrite rules, sequents, or first-order axioms written as implications. Advanced programming languages like ELAN [9] and Constraint Handling Rules (CHR) [8] allow to implement constraint solvers in a rule-based formalism. This approach makes it easy to modify a solver or build a solver over a new domain. Furthermore, it is easy to reason about and analyze a constraint solver.

A difficulty that arises frequently when writing a constraint solver is to determine the constraint propagation algorithm. In [6] a first step has been done to solve finite constraint satisfaction problems by means of automatically generated constraint propagation algorithms. I n this paper, we continue this line of work.

A constraint over a finite domain can be defined extensionally by a truth table or equivalently by all the tuples of the constraint. For example, let $c1$ be a constraint defined by the following truth table:[1]

---

* The research reported in this paper has been supported by the Bavarian-French Hochschulzentrum.
[1] The following two examples are taken from [17].

R. Dechter (Ed.): CP 2000, LNCS 1894, pp. 18–34, 2000.

c1	X_1	X_2	X_3
0	0	0	0
1	0	0	1
0	0	1	0
0	0	1	1
0	1	0	0
0	1	0	1
0	1	1	0
1	1	1	1

The constraint $c1$ can also be represented by its tuples $\{(0,0,1),(1,1,1)\}$.

The approach we have taken is to develop an automatic method to generate general rules defining some properties of constraints given their extensional definition. Using our method inspired by techniques used in the field of knowledge discovery the user has the possibility to specify the form of the rules she/he wants to generate. The method allows any kind of constraints in the left hand side of rules and in their right hand side as well.

For the constraint $c1$ our algorithm described in Section 2 generates the following single rule, if the user specifies that the right hand side of the rules may consist of a conjunction of equality constraints:

$$c1(X_1, X_2, X_3) \rightarrow X_1{=}X_2 \wedge X_3{=}1$$

For a constraint $c2$ defined by its tuples $\{(0,1,0),(0,1,1),(1,0,0),(1,1,0)\}$, our algorithm can generate the following rule provided the user specifies the right hand side of the rule to be the logical disjunction, defined by the ternary constraint or (whose last argument is the disjunction of the first and second):

$$c2(X_1, X_2, X_3) \rightarrow or(X_2, X_3, X_2).$$

Note that this rule expresses only a necessary property of $c2$ but not a definition that is equivalent to $c2$. In the previous example, the right hand side of the rule happened to be also sufficient for $c1$.

The generated rules are implemented as rules of the language Constraint Handling Rules [8].

Related Work

In the pioneering paper [6], K. Apt and E. Monfroy proposed two algorithms: One generates the so-called inclusion rules ensuring arc-consistency, whereas the second one generates propagation rules ensuring a weaker notion of local consistency, rule consistency. In contrast to our approach the user has no possibility to affect the form of the generated rules.

Let C be an atomic constraint. The algorithm presented in [6] generates propagation rules of the following form

$$X_1{=}v_1 \wedge \ldots \wedge X_k{=}v_k \rightarrow Y{\neq}v,$$

where $X_1, \ldots, X_k$ are some variables occurring in C, and $v_1, \ldots v_k, v$ are elements of the domain associated to variables of C, and Y is a variable occurring in C but not in $X_1, \ldots, X_k$.

For the constraint $c1(X_1, X_2, X_3)$ defined above the following propagation rules are generated by the algorithm presented in [6]:

$$
\begin{aligned}
true &\rightarrow X_3 \neq 0 \\
X_1 = 1 &\rightarrow X_2 \neq 0 \\
X_1 = 0 &\rightarrow X_2 \neq 1 \\
X_2 = 1 &\rightarrow X_1 \neq 0 \\
X_2 = 0 &\rightarrow X_1 \neq 1
\end{aligned}
$$

true denotes an empty left hand side, i.e. there is no further assignment of variables.

The algorithm presented in [17] is a combination of the one described in [6] and unification in finite algebra [16]. Similar to [6] the user has here no possibility to specify the form of the rules. The rules generated by this algorithm have the following form:

$$X_1 = v_1 \wedge \ldots \wedge X_k = v_k \rightarrow B,$$

where now $v_1, \ldots v_k$ are either elements of the domain or free constants to represent symbolically any element of the domain as used in unification in finite algebra [10]. B is a conjunction of equality constraints and membership constraints (e.g. $X \in D$).

With the notion of free constants, equality between variables in the right-hand side of rules can be deduced. For the constraint $c1(X_1, X_2, X_3)$, the algorithm presented in [17] generates the following rules:

$$
\begin{aligned}
true &\rightarrow X_1 \in \{0, 1\} \wedge X_2 \in \{0, 1\} \wedge X_3 = 1 \\
X_1 = x_1 &\rightarrow X_2 = x_1 \wedge X_3 = 1 \\
X_2 = x_2 &\rightarrow X_1 = x_2 \wedge X_3 = 1
\end{aligned}
$$

In contrast to the algorithms presented in [6] and [17] our algorithm leads to a more compact and more expressive set of rules. With the rules generated by the algorithm presented in [6], one propagates from $c1(X_1, X_2, X_3)$ that $X_3 = 1$. With our generated rule we also propagate that $X_1 = X_2$. This can also be deduced from the rules generated by the algorithm presented in [17]. However, for the constraint $c2$ our algorithm can also generate the following rule

$$c2(X_1, X_1, X_3) \rightarrow X_1 = 1 \wedge X_3 = 0$$

Using this rule, one can deduce from $c2(X_1, X_1, X_3)$ that $X_1 = 1 \land X_3 = 0$. This cannot be deduced neither by the algorithm presented in [6] nor by the one presented in [17].[2]

Furthermore, we will show that in contrast to the algorithms presented in [6] and [17] our algorithm is able to generate rules with a conjunction of constraints in the left hand side of the rules which is an essential feature for non-trivial constraint handling.

Our approach is orthogonal to the work in Inductive Logic Programming [12] (ILP), where one is interested to find out logical clauses from examples rather than general rules that are useful for constraint solving. Nevertheless, our method is inspired by techniques used in this field.

Organization of the Paper

In section 2, we present our algorithm for the generation of propagation rules and give some soundness, correctness and termination results. I n Section   3, we give more examples for the use of our algorithm. Finally, we conclude with a summary and directions for future work.

2   Generation of Propagation Rules

In this section, we describe the algorithm, RULEMINER, for generating propagation rules.

2.1   Class of Generated Rules

We call an atomic formula with a constraint symbol an *atomic constraint*. An inconsistent atomic constraint is represented by   *false*.

A *constraint* over a set of atomic constraints $\mathcal{A}$ is a finite subset of $\mathcal{A}$. A constraint $C \subseteq \mathcal{A}$ is interpreted as the conjunction of the atomic constraints in C. The set of all constraints over $\mathcal{A}$, i.e. the set of all non-empty finite subsets of $\mathcal{A}$, is noted $\mathcal{L}(\mathcal{A})$. The set of variables appearing in $\mathcal{A}$ is denoted by $Var(\mathcal{A})$.

Let CT be a constraint theory defining a constraint C and let σ be a ground substitution. σ is a *solution* of C if and only if $CT \models \sigma(C)$.

A *propagation rule* is a rule of the form $C_1 \Rightarrow C_2$, where C_1 and C_2 are constraints. C_1 is called the left hand side (lhs) and C_2 the right hand side (rhs) of the rule.

Definition 1. Let $\mathcal{A}_{lhs}$ and $\mathcal{A}_{rhs}$ be two sets of atomic constraints not containing *false*[3]. The set of *propagation rules* over $\langle \mathcal{A}_{lhs}, \mathcal{A}_{rhs} \rangle$ is the set of all rules of the form $C_1 \Rightarrow C_2$, where $C_1 \in \mathcal{L}(\mathcal{A}_{lhs})$ and $C_2 \in \mathcal{L}(\mathcal{A}_{rhs}) \cup \{\{false\}\}$ and $C_1 \cap C_2 = \emptyset$. A *failure rule* is a propagation rule of the form $C_1 \Rightarrow \{false\}$.

---

[2] Personal communication with E. Monfroy, Email, March 2000.

[3] *false* will be used as a particular rhs for the rules.

Definition 2. A propagation rule $C_1 \Rightarrow C_2$ is *valid* if and only if for any ground substitution σ, if σ is a solution of C_1 then σ is a solution of C_2. The rule $C_1 \Rightarrow \{false\}$ is *valid* if and only if C_1 has no solution.

Since the number of valid rules may become quite large, we considered that the rules that are in some sense the most general will be the most interesting to build a solver. We consider only a syntactical notion of rule generality which is inspired by the notion of structural covering used in association rule mining [18].

Definition 3. Let $\mathcal{R}$ and $\mathcal{R}'$ be two sets of propagation rules. $\mathcal{R}'$ is a *lhs-cover* of $\mathcal{R}$ if and only if for all $(C_1 \Rightarrow C_2) \in \mathcal{R}$ there exists $(C_1' \Rightarrow C_2') \in \mathcal{R}'$, such that $C_1' \subseteq C_1$ and $C_2 \subseteq C_2'$.

Note that this is a form of subsumption in the ground case and that if $\mathcal{R}'$ is a lhs-cover of $\mathcal{R}$, then every rule in $\mathcal{R}$ is logically entailed in CT by some rule in $\mathcal{R}'$.

Example 1. Let *and* be a ternary constraint defining the Boolean conjunction. $\{\{and(X,Y,Z),\ X{=}0\} \Rightarrow \{Z{=}0\}\}$ is a lhs-cover of $\{\{and(X,Y,Z),\ X{=}0\} \Rightarrow \{Z{=}0\}, \{and(X,Y,Z),\ X{=}0,\ Y{=}0\} \Rightarrow \{Z{=}0\}\}$.

The algorithm RuleMiner generates a lhs-cover of the set of *valid propagation rules* over $\langle \mathcal{A}_{lhs}, \mathcal{A}_{rhs} \rangle$. However, many lhs are of little interest to build solvers based on propagation rules. We used a syntactic bias to restrict the generation to a particular set of rules called *relevant propagation rules*.

Definition 4. Let $Base_{lhs}$ be a set of atomic constraints. A set of atomic constraints $\mathcal{A}$ is an *interesting pattern* wrt. $Base_{lhs}$ if and only if the following conditions are satisfied:

1. $Base_{lhs} \subseteq \mathcal{A}$.
2. the graph defined by the relation $join_{\mathcal{A}}$ is connected, where $join_{\mathcal{A}}$ is a binary relation that holds for pairs of atomic constraints in $\mathcal{A}$ that share at least one variable, i.e., $join_{\mathcal{A}} = \{\langle c_1, c_2 \rangle \mid c_1 \in \mathcal{A}, c_2 \in \mathcal{A}, Var(\{c_1\}) \cap Var(\{c_2\}) \neq \emptyset\}$.

Definition 5. The set of *relevant propagation rules* over $\langle Base_{lhs}, \mathcal{A}_{lhs}, \mathcal{A}_{rhs} \rangle$ is the set of propagation rules over $\langle \mathcal{A}_{lhs}, \mathcal{A}_{rhs} \rangle$ without the rules with a left hand side that is not an interesting pattern wrt. $Base_{lhs}$ and without the rules of the form $C_1 \Rightarrow C_2$, where $C_1 \in \mathcal{L}(\mathcal{A}_{lhs})$ and $C_2 \in \mathcal{L}(\mathcal{A}_{rhs})$ and C_1 has no solution.

Note that the second restriction ensures that propagation rules with an inconsistent lhs and with a rhs different from *false* are not relevant.

Example 2. Assume we want to generate interaction rules between the Boolean operations conjunction (*and*) and negation (*neg*), then $Base_{lhs}$ has the following form $\{and(X,Y,Z),\ neg(A,B)\}$. $\{and(X,Y,Z),\ neg(A,B),\ A{=}X,\ B{=}Y\} \Rightarrow \{Z{=}0\}$ is then a relevant propagation rule, while the rule $\{and(X,Y,Z),\ Y{=}1\} \Rightarrow \{Z{=}X\}$ and the rule

$\{and(X,Y,Z), \ neg(A,B), \ X{=}0\} \Rightarrow \{Z{=}0\}$ are not. However, it should be noticed that the first one will be relevant for the constraint *and* alone (i. e. , when $Base_{lhs} = \{and(X,Y,Z)\}$).

The generation algorithm will discard any rule which is not a relevant propagation rule over a given $\langle Base_{lhs}, \mathcal{A}_{lhs}, \mathcal{A}_{rhs} \rangle$. We present in Section 2.3 additional simplifications of the set of rules generated to remove some redundancies.

2.2   The RULEMINER Algorithm

Principle Using RULEMINER the user has the possibility to specify the admissible syntactic forms of the rules. The user determines the constraint for which rules have to be generated (i.e. $Base_{lhs}$) and chooses the candidate constraints to form conjunctions together with $Base_{lhs}$ in the left hand side (noted $Cand_{lhs}$). Usually, these candidate constraints are simply equality constraints. For the right hand side of the rules the user specifies also the form of candidate constraints she/he wants to see there (noted $Cand_{rhs}$). Finally, the user determines the semantics of the constraint $Base_{lhs}$ by means of its extensional definition (noted $SolBase_{lhs}$) which must be finite, and provides the semantics of the candidate constraints $Cand_{lhs}$ and $Cand_{rhs}$ by two constraint theories CT_{lhs} and CT_{rhs}, respectively. Furthermore, we assume that the constraints defined by CT_{lhs} and CT_{rhs} are handled by an appropriate constraint solver.

To compute the propagation rules the algorithm generates each possible lhs constraint (noted C_{lhs}) and for each determines the corresponding rhs constraint (noted C_{rhs}).

For each lhs C_{lhs} the corresponding rhs C_{rhs} is computed in the following way:

1. if C_{lhs} has no solution then $C_{rhs} = \{false\}$ and we have the failure rule $C_{lhs} \Rightarrow \{false\}$.
2. if C_{lhs} has at least one solution then C_{rhs} is the set of all atomic constraints that are candidates for the rhs part and are true for all solutions of C_{lhs}. If C_{rhs} is not empty we have the rule $C_{lhs} \Rightarrow C_{rhs}$.

During the exploration of the search space, the algorithm uses two main pruning strategies:

1. (*Pruning1*) if a rule $C_{lhs} \Rightarrow \{false\}$ is generated then there is no need to consider any superset of C_{lhs} to form other rule lhs.
2. (*Pruning2*) if a rule $C_{lhs} \Rightarrow C_{rhs}$ is generated then there is no need to consider any C such that $C_{lhs} \subset C$ and $C \cap C_{rhs} \neq \emptyset$ to form other rule lhs.

The condition $C \cap C_{rhs} \neq \emptyset$ in the strategy *Pruning2* is needed to reduce the number of the propagation rules generated, as shown in the following example.

Example 3. After generating the relevant propagation rule of example 2:
$\{and(X,Y,Z), \ neg(A,B), \ A{=}X, \ B{=}Y\} \Rightarrow \{Z{=}0\}$, the possible lhs
$\{and(X,Y,Z), \ neg(A,B), \ A{=}X, \ B{=}Y, \ B{=}1, \ Z{=}0\}$ is not considered using

Pruning2, while $\{and(X,Y,Z),\ neg(A,B),\ A{=}X,\ B{=}Y,\ B{=}1\}$ remains a lhs candidate and may lead to the following rule
$\{and(X,Y,Z),\ neg(A,B),\ A{=}X,\ B{=}Y,\ B{=}1\} \Rightarrow \{Z{=}0,\ A{=}0,\ X{=}0,\ Y{=}1\}$.

These pruning strategies are much more efficient if during the enumeration of all possible rule lhs, a given lhs is considered before any of its supersets. So a specific ordering for this enumeration is imposed in the algorithm. Moreover, this ordering allows to discover early covering rules avoiding then the generation of many uninteresting covered rules.

To simplify the presentation of the algorithm we consider that all possible lhs are stored in a list L and that unnecessary lhs candidates are simply removed from this list. For efficiency reasons the concrete implementation is not based on a list but on a tree containing lhs candidates on its nodes. More details are given in Section 2.4.

We now give an abstract description of the RULEMINER algorithm. The algorithm is given in Figure 1. It takes as input:

- $Base_{lhs}$: a constraint that must be included in any lhs of the rules.
- $SolBase_{lhs}$: the finite set of ground substitutions that are solutions of $Base_{lhs}$. Note that this defines the constraint $Base_{lhs}$ extensionally.
- $Cand_{lhs}$: a finite set of atomic constraints that are candidates to form lhs of the rules such that $Var(Cand_{lhs}) \subseteq Var(Base_{lhs})$.
- $Cand_{rhs}$: a finite set of atomic constraints that are candidates to form rhs of the rules such that $Var(Cand_{rhs}) \subseteq Var(Base_{lhs})$.
- CT_{lhs}: a constraint theory defining $Cand_{lhs}$.
- CT_{rhs}: a constraint theory defining $Cand_{rhs}$.

And it produces the following output: a lhs-cover of the valid relevant propagation rules over $\langle Base_{lhs}, Cand_{lhs}, Cand_{rhs} \rangle$

We require the constraint theories CT_{lhs} and CT_{rhs} to be ground complete for $\langle Cand_{lhs}, SolBase_{lhs} \rangle$ and $\langle Cand_{rhs}, SolBase_{lhs} \rangle$, respectively[4].

Definition 6. Let CT be a constraint theory, let Γ be a set of ground substitutions and $\mathcal{A}$ be a set of atomic constraints. CT is *ground complete* for $\langle \mathcal{A}, \Gamma \rangle$ if and only if for every $c \in \mathcal{A}$ and for any substitution $\sigma \in \Gamma$ we have either $CT \models \sigma(c)$ or $CT \models \neg\sigma(c)$.

In RULEMINER the list L of possible lhs is initialized to be a finite list. Each iteration of the while loop removes at least one element in L. This ensures the following property.

Theorem 1 (Termination). The algorithm RULEMINER terminates and yields a finite set of propagation rules.

The following results establish soundness and correctness of the algorithm.

---

[4] Note that this restriction is very weak, since the property holds for almost all useful classes of constraint theories.

begin

    Let $\mathcal{R}$ be an empty set of rules.
    Let L be a list containing the elements of $\mathcal{L}(Base_{lhs} \cup Cand_{lhs})$ in any order.

    Remove from L any element which is not an interesting pattern wrt. $Base_{lhs}$.
    Order L with any total ordering compatible with the subset partial ordering
    (i.e., for all C_1 in L if C_2 is after C_1 in L then $C_2 \not\subset C_1$).

    while L is not empty **do**
        Let C_{lhs} be the first element of L.
        Remove from L its first element.
            if for all $\sigma \in SolBase_{lhs}$ we have
            $CT_{lhs} \models \neg\sigma(C_{lhs} \setminus Base_{lhs})$ **then**
                add the failure rule $(C_{lhs} \Rightarrow \{false\})$ to $\mathcal{R}$
                and remove from L each element C such that $C_{lhs} \subset C$.
        else
            compute C_{rhs} the rule rhs, defined by
            $C_{rhs} = \{c | c \in (Cand_{rhs} \setminus Cand_{lhs})$ and for all $\sigma \in SolBase_{lhs}$
                when $CT_{lhs} \models \sigma(C_{lhs} \setminus Base_{lhs})$ we have $CT_{rhs} \models \sigma(c)\}$.
            if C_{rhs} is not empty **then**
                add the rule $(C_{lhs} \Rightarrow C_{rhs})$ to $\mathcal{R}$
                and remove from L each element C such that
                    $C_{lhs} \subset C$ and $C \cap C_{rhs} \neq \emptyset$.
            endif
        endif
    endwhile

    output $\mathcal{R}$

end

Fig. 1. The RuleMiner Algorithm

Theorem 2 (Soundness). RuleMiner computes valid relevant propagation rules over $\langle Base_{lhs}, Cand_{lhs}, Cand_{rhs} \rangle$.

Proof. (*Sketch*) All C_{lhs} considered are interesting pattern wrt. $Base_{lhs}$, thus only relevant rules can be generated. Let $C'_{lhs} = C_{lhs} \setminus Base_{lhs}$. A rule of the form $C_{lhs} \Rightarrow \{false\}$ can be generated only if all solutions of $Base_{lhs}$ are not solutions of C'_{lhs}. So any rule $C_{lhs} \Rightarrow \{false\}$ generated is valid. A rule of the form $C_{lhs} \Rightarrow C_{rhs}$, where $C_{rhs} \neq \{false\}$ can be generated only if all solutions of $Base_{lhs}$ that are solutions of C'_{lhs}, are also solutions of all atomic constraints in C_{rhs}. Hence all generated rules of the form $C_{lhs} \Rightarrow C_{rhs}$ are valid.

$\square$

Theorem 3 (Correctness). RULEMINER computes a lhs-cover of the valid relevant propagation rules over $\langle Base_{lhs}, Cand_{lhs}, Cand_{rhs} \rangle$ when $Var(Cand_{lhs}) \subseteq Var(Base_{lhs})$ and $Var(Cand_{rhs}) \subseteq Var(Base_{lhs})$.

Proof. (Sketch) First, we do not consider the two pruning strategies *Pruning1* and *Pruning2*. Then the algorithm enumerates all possible rule lhs that are interesting pattern wrt. $Base_{lhs}$. So it generates all valid relevant failure rules. Moreover for any valid relevant rule of the form $C_1 \Rightarrow C_2$, where $C_2 \neq \{false\}$ the algorithm consider C_1 as a candidate lhs. Then it computes C_{rhs} containing all atomic constraints c such that all solutions of C_1 are solutions of c. Thus $C_2 \subseteq C_{rhs}$. So if we do not consider the two pruning strategies *Pruning1* and *Pruning2* the algorithm output a lhs-cover of the valid relevant propagation rules.

Now we show that the two pruning criteria are safe.

(Pruning1) When a rule of the form $C_1 \Rightarrow \{false\}$ is generated all candidate lhs $C_{lhs} \supset C_1$ are discarded. However since $C_1 \Rightarrow \{false\}$ is valid, C_1 has no solution, and thus any $C_{lhs} \supset C_1$ have no solution too, and can only leads to a rule of the form $C_{lhs} \Rightarrow \{false\}$ which will be lhs-covered by $C_1 \Rightarrow \{false\}$.

(Pruning2) When a rule of the form $C_1 \Rightarrow C_2$, where $C_2 \neq \{false\}$ is generated all candidates lhs C_{lhs} such that $C_1 \subset C_{lhs}$ and $C_{lhs} \cap C_2 \neq \emptyset$ are discarded.

The key idea of the safety of this pruning criterion is the following:

Consider a C_{lhs} discarded and any valid relevant rule of the form $C_{lhs} \Rightarrow C_3$, where $Var(C_3) \subseteq Var(C_{lhs})$. There is another lhs candidate $C'_{lhs} = C_{lhs} \setminus C_2$ that has not been discarded, such that $C_1 \subseteq C'_{lhs}$. Any ground substitution σ solution of C'_{lhs} is a solution of C_1 and thus of C_2 because $C_1 \Rightarrow C_2$ is valid. Then σ is a solution of C_{lhs} and also of C_3 since $C_{lhs} \Rightarrow C_3$ is valid. Hence the candidate C'_{lhs} will generate a rule $C'_{lhs} \Rightarrow C_4$ with $C_3 \subseteq C_4$ that lhs-covers rule $C_{lhs} \Rightarrow C_3$.

$\square$

For convenience, we introduce the following notation. Let c be a constraint symbol of arity 2 and D_1 and D_2 be two sets of terms. We define $atomic(c, D_1, D_2)$ as the set of all atomic constraints built from c over $D_1 \times D_2$. More precisely, $atomic(c, D_1, D_2) = \{c(\alpha, \beta) \mid \alpha \in D_1 \text{ and } \beta \in D_2\}$.

If $Base_{lhs}$ consists of an atomic constraint and if we allow equality constraints (between a variable and a constant) in lhs and disequality constraints (between a variable and a constant) in rhs, then we can easily see that the class of rules generated by RULEMINER corresponds to the class of *rules* defined in [6]. Then according to Theorem 3 the rules generated enforce the same kind of consistency. So we have the following property:

Theorem 4. Let $C(X_1, \dots, X_n)$ be an atomic constraint and let $v_1, \dots, v_k$ be elements of the domain associated to $X_1, \dots, X_n$, where the three following conditions are satisfied:

$$Base_{lhs} = \{C(X_1, \ldots, X_n)\}$$
$$Cand_{lhs} = atomic(=, \{X_1, \ldots, X_n\}, \{v_1, \ldots, v_k\})$$
$$Cand_{rhs} = atomic(\neq, \{X_1, \ldots, X_n\}, \{v_1, \ldots, v_k\})$$

then the propagation rules generated by RULEMINER enforce rule consistency, i.e. the local consistency notion presented in [6] which is equivalent to arc consistency for unary and binary domains.

2.3   Rule Simplification

Even though RULEMINER computes a lhs-cover of the valid relevant propagation rules over $\langle Base_{lhs}, Cand_{lhs}, Cand_{rhs}\rangle$, this cover may contain some kind of redundancies.

Example 4. RULEMINER as presented in Figure 1 can produce the following rule $\{and(X, Y, Z),\ Z{=}1\} \Rightarrow \{X{=}Y,\ X{=}Z,\ Y{=}Z,\ X{=}1,\ Y{=}1\}$. If we have already a solver to handle equality constraints, then this rule can be simplified into $\{and(X, Y, 1)\} \Rightarrow \{X{=}1,\ Y{=}1\}$.

On another input RULEMINER can produce the following rules for the logical operation exclusive-or (*xor*): $\{xor(X, Y, Z),\ X{=}Y\} \Rightarrow \{Z{=}0\}$ and the rule $\{xor(X, Y, Z),\ X{=}0,\ Y{=}0\} \Rightarrow \{Z{=}0\}$. The second rule cannot propagate new atomic constraints wrt. the first rule, and thus can be discarded.

We use an ad-hoc technique to simplify the rule lhs and rhs, and to suppress some redundant rules. This process does not lead to a precisely defined canonical representation of the rules generated, but in practice (see Section 3) it produces small and readable sets of rules.

This simplification technique is incorporated in RULEMINER and performed during the generation of the rules. For clarity reasons it is presented apart from the algorithm given in Figure 1. The simplification principle is as follows:

- For each rule generated by the algorithm of Figure 1 the equality constraints appearing in the lhs are transformed into substitutions that are applied to the lhs and the rhs, and then the completely ground atomic constraints are removed from lhs and rhs (e.g., $\{and(X, Y, Z),\ Z{=}1\} \Rightarrow \{X{=}Y,\ X{=}Z,\ Y{=}Z,\ X{=}1,\ Y{=}1\}$ will be simplified to $\{and(X, Y, 1)\} \Rightarrow \{X{=}Y,\ X{=}1,\ Y{=}1\}$).
- The new rules are then ordered in a list L' using any total ordering on the rule lhs compatible with the θ-subsumption ordering [14] (i.e., a rule having a more general lhs is placed before a rule with a more specialized lhs).
- Let S be a set of rules initialized to the empty set. For each rule $C_1 \Rightarrow C_2$ in L' (taken according to the list ordering) the constraint C_2 will be simplified to an equivalent constraint C_{simp} by the already known solver for $Cand_{rhs}$ and by the rules in S. If C_{simp} is empty then the rule can be discarded, else add the rule $C_1 \Rightarrow C_{simp}$ to S. (e.g., $\{and(X, Y, 1)\} \Rightarrow \{X{=}Y,\ X{=}1,\ Y{=}1\}$ will be simplified to $\{and(X, Y, 1)\} \Rightarrow \{X{=}1,\ Y{=}1\}$)
- Output the set S containing the simplified set of rules.

2.4   Implementation Issues

The RULEMINER algorithm has been developed based on previous work done in the field of *knowledge discovery*. More precisely, we combine several techniques stemming from two domains: *association rule mining* [4] and ILP [12].

As described in Section 2.2, RULEMINER needs to enumerate lhs constraints. Our implementation follows the idea of direct extraction of association rules by exploring a tree corresponding to the lhs search space as described in [7]. This tree is expanded and explored using a depth first strategy, in a way that constructs only necessary lhs candidates and allows to remove uninteresting candidates by cutting whole branches of the tree. The branches of the tree are developed using a partial ordering on the lhs candidates such that the more general lhs are examined before more specialized ones. The partial ordering used in our implementation is the θ-subsumption [14] ordering commonly used in ILP to structure the search space [12]. To prune branches in the tree, one of the two main strategies (*Pruning2*) has been inspired by the CLOSE algorithm [13] devoted to the extraction of frequent *itemsets* in dense[5] data sets.

The running prototype is implemented in SICStus Prolog 3.7.1 and takes advantage of the support of CHR in this environment in the following way. During the execution of RULEMINER we build incrementally a CHR solver with the propagation rules generated and this solver is used to perform the rule simplification according to Section 2.3.

Example 5. Let $\{and(X, Y, 1)\} \Rightarrow \{X = 1, Y = 1\}$ be a rule in the current CHR solver. Then the rule $\{and(0, Y, 1)\} \Rightarrow \{false\}$ will be discarded since $and(0, Y, 1)$ leads already to a failure using the current CHR solver.

3   Applications

This section shows with examples that a practical application of our method lies in software development. Our algorithm can be used to build constraint solvers automatically. The rules generated by RULEMINER will be implemented as rules of the language Constraint Handling Rules [8].

Constraint Handling Rules (CHR) is essentially a committed-choice language consisting of multi-headed guarded rules that rewrite constraints into simpler ones until they are solved. There are basically two kinds of rules[6]: CHR Simplification rules replace constraints by simpler constraints while preserving logical equivalence. CHR Propagation rules add new constraints which are logically redundant but may cause further simplification. Repeatedly applying the rules incrementally solves constraints. Due to space limitations, we cannot give a formal account of syntax and semantics of CHR in this paper. An overview on CHR can be found in [8]. Detailed semantics results for CHR are available in [2].

---

[5] e.g., data sets containing many strong correlations.
[6] There is a third hybrid kind of rule called CHR simpagation rule.

In the following, the generated rules are modelled by means of CHR propagation rules. While we cannot – within the space limitations – introduce the whole generated constraint solver, we still give a fragment of it. The complete solvers are available in [1] and can be executed online.

In the following, we assume that the constraint theories define among other constraints equality ("=") and disequality ("≠") as syntactic equality and disequality. Furthermore, we assume that these constraints are handled by an appropriate constraint solver. We denote the disequality constraint by **ne**.

We will compare our results only to the ones presented in [6], since experiments with practical applications are still missing in [17]. One can remark that the times for the generation of rules are in the same order of magnitude. We have used the following software and hardware: SICStus Prolog 3.7.1, PC Pentium 3 with 256 MBytes of memory and a 500 MHZ processor.

3.1 Boolean Constraints

Boolean primitive constraints consist of Boolean variables which may take the value 0 for falsity or 1 for truth, and Boolean operations such as conjunction (**and**), disjunction (**or**), negation (**neg**) and exclusive-or (**xor**), modeled here as relations.

For the conjunction constraint **and(X,Y,Z)** the algorithm RULEMINER with the following input

$$Base_{lhs} = \{\text{and(X,Y,Z)}\}$$
$$Cand_{lhs} = Cand_{rhs} = atomic(=, \{\text{X,Y,Z}\}, \{\text{X,Y,Z,0,1}\})$$

generates the following rules in 0.05 seconds:

```
and(X,X,Z) ==> X=Z.
and(X,Y,1) ==> X=1, Y=1.
and(X,1,Z) ==> X=Z.
and(X,0,Z) ==> Z=0.
and(1,Y,Z) ==> Y=Z.
and(0,Y,Z) ==> Z=0.
```

For example, the first rule says that the constraint **and(X,Y,Z)**, when it is known that the first input argument **X** is equal to the second input argument **Y**, can propagate the constraint that the output **Z** must be equal to **X**. Hence the goal **and(X,X,Z)** will result in **and(X,X,Z), X=Z**.

Goals of the form **and(X,X,Z)** cannot be handled using the rules generated by the algorithm presented in [6], since the first rule is not present there. One can easily see that the propagation rules generated by RULEMINER correspond to the implementation of **and** using CHR [8].

For the negation constraint **neg(X,Y)**, RULEMINER generates among other rules the following failure rule:

```
neg(X,X) ==> fail.
```

The algorithm RULEMINER can generate propagation rules defining interactions between constraints. With the following input

$$Base_{lhs} = \{\texttt{and(X,Y,Z)}, \texttt{ neg(A,B)}\}$$
$$Cand_{lhs} = Cand_{rhs} = atomic(\texttt{=}, \{\texttt{X,Y,Z,A,B}\}, \{\texttt{X,Y,Z,A,B,0,1}\})$$

the following rules defining interaction between **neg** and **and** are generated:

```
and(X,Y,Z), neg(X,Y) ==> Z=0.
and(X,Y,Z), neg(Y,X) ==> Z=0.
and(X,Y,Z), neg(X,Z) ==> Z=0, Y=Z.
and(X,Y,Z), neg(Z,X) ==> X=1, Y=Z.
and(X,Y,Z), neg(Y,Z) ==> X=Z.
and(X,Y,Z), neg(Z,Y) ==> X=Z.
```

The rules generated by RULEMINER are slightly different than the ones implemented manually [1]. However, one can easily show that both programs[7] are operationally equivalent [3].

With our algorithm, propagation rules with a right hand side consisting of more complex constraints than equality constraints can also be generated. The user can specify the form of the right hand side of the rules. Using RULEMINER with the following input

$$Base_{lhs} = \{\texttt{xor(X,Y,Z)}\}$$
$$Cand_{lhs} = atomic(\texttt{=}, \{\texttt{X,Y,Z}\}, \{\texttt{X,Y,Z,0,1}\})$$
$$Cand_{rhs} = Cand_{lhs} \cup atomic(\texttt{neg}, \{\texttt{X,Y,Z}\}, \{\texttt{X,Y,Z,0,1}\})$$

6 rules, analogous to the ones for **and**, and the following 3 rules for the constraint **xor** are generated in 0.1 seconds:

```
xor(X,Y,1) ==> neg(X,Y).
xor(X,1,Z) ==> neg(X,Z).
xor(1,Y,Z) ==> neg(Y,Z).
```

3.2 Full-Adder

One important application of Boolean constraints is for modeling logic circuits. A full-adder can be built using the following logical gates (see, e.g. [19,8]):

```
fulladder(X,Y,CI,S,C) :-
        and(X,Y,I1),
        xor(X,Y,I2),
        and(I2,CI,I3),
        xor(I2,CI,S),
        or(I1,I3,C).
```

---

[7] After rewriting the manually implemented rules as CHR propagation rules, i.e. transformation of CHR simplification and CHR simpagation rules into CHR propagation rules.

Using the RULEMINER algorithm 28 rules within 0.68 seconds are generated for the `fulladder` constraint. These rules enforce the same local consistency notion as the 52 rules generated by the algorithm presented in [6] within 0.27 seconds. Typical rules are:

```
fulladder(X,Y,CI,S,S) ==> X=S, Y=S, CI=S.
fulladder(X,Y,CI,CI,C) ==> X=C, Y=C.
fulladder(0,Y,CI,S,1) ==> S=0.
```

The first rule says that the constraint `fulladder(X,Y,CI,S,C)`, whenever the output bit S is equal to the output carry bit C, can propagate the information that the bits to be added X and Y and the input carry bit CI are equal to the output bit S. This kind of propagation cannot be performed using the rules generated by the algorithm presented in [6].

3.3   Three Valued Logics

We consider the equivalence relation defined by the truth table given in [11], where the value t stands for true, f for false and u for unknown.

X	Y	X ≡ Y
t	t	t
t	f	f
t	u	u
f	t	f
f	f	t
f	u	u
u	t	u
u	f	u
u	u	u

RULEMINER generates for the ternary equivalence constraint `eq3val` 16 rules within 0.3 seconds, e.g.

```
eq3val(X,X,X) ==> X ne f.
eq3val(X,Y,t) ==> X ne u, X=Y.
eq3val(X,f,X) ==> X = u.
```

The first rule says that the constraint `eq3val(X,Y,Z)`, when it is known that the input arguments X and Y and the output Z are equal, can propagate that X is different from f.

3.4   Temporal Reasoning

In [5] an interval-based approach to temporal reasoning is presented. Allen's approach to reasoning about time is based on the notion of time intervals and binary relations on them. Given two time intervals, their relative positions can be described by exactly one of thirteen primitive interval relations, where each primitive relation can be defined in terms of its endpoint relations, i.e. equality and 6 other relations (*before*, *during*, *overlaps*, *meets*, *starts* and *finishes*) with their converses.

In [5] different ordering relations between intervals are introduced. There is a 13×13 table defining a "composition" constraint between a triple of events X, Y and Z, e.g. if the temporal relations between the events X and Y and the events Y and Z are known, what is the temporal relation between X and Z. The composition constraint, denoted by *allenComp*, can be defined as follows:

$$allenComp(R_1, R_2, R_3) \leftrightarrow (R_1(X,Y) \wedge R_2(Y,Z) \rightarrow R_3(X,Z)),$$

where R_1, R_2, R_3 are primitive interval relations.

Our algorithm generates for *allenComp* 489 rules within 83.12 seconds, provided the user specifies that the right hand side of the rules may consist of a conjunction of equality and disequality constraints. Analogous to [6] we denote the 6 relations respectively by b,d,o,m,s,f, their converses by b-,d-,o-,m-,s-,f- and the equality relation by e. Typical rules are:

```
allenComp(X,X,X) ==> X ne m, X ne m-.
allenComp(X,X,e) ==> X=e.
allenComp(o,b,Z) ==> Z=b.
```

The algorithm presented in [6] generates 498 rules within 31.16 seconds. The right hand side of rules consists only of disequality constraints. Furthermore, rules with multiple occurrences of variables cannot be generated. Thus, no information can be propagated from a constraint of the form `allenComp(X,X,X)`.

3.5   Spatial Reasoning

The Region Connection Calculus (RCC) is a topological approach to qualitative spatial representation and reasoning where spatial regions are subsets of topological space [15]. Relationships between spatial regions are defined in terms of the relation $C(X,Y)$ which is true iff the topological closures of regions X and Y share at least one point.

In [15] a composition table for the set of eight basic relations is presented. The relations are dc (*disconnected*), ec (*externally connected*), po (*partial overlap*), eq (*equal*), tpp (*tangential proper part*) and ntpp (*nontangential proper part*). The relations tpp and ntpp have inverses (here symbolized by tpp- and ntpp-).

For the composition constraint rccComp, our algorithm generates 178 rules in 24 seconds. Examples of rules are:

```
rccComp(X,X,eq) ==> X ne ntpp-, X ne tpp-, X ne ntpp, X ne tpp.
rccComp(X,eq,Z) ==> X=Z.
rccCom(dc,Y,ntpp-) ==> Y=dc.
```

4   Conclusion and Future Work

We have presented a method for generating propagation rules for finite constraints given their extensional representation. This method has been developed based on several techniques used in association rule mining [4] and ILP [12]. Compared to the algorithms described in [6] and [17] our algorithm, RULEMINER, is able to generate more general and more expressive rules. On one hand, we allow multiple occurrences of variables and conjunction of constraints with shared variables in the left hand side of rules. On the other hand the user has the possibility to specify the form of the right hand side of rules which can consist of more complex constraints than (dis-)equality constraints.

We also gave termination, soundness and correctness results for our algorithm. Furthermore, we showed that our algorithm is able to generate rules ensuring the rule consistency notion presented in [6], a local consistency notion which coincides with arc consistency for domains consisting of at most two elements.

Then we gave various examples to show that our approach can be used as a method to derive new constraint solvers. Due to the generality of the extracted rules, our method can be seen as a further step towards a tool for automatic generation of constraint solvers.

Our algorithm generates rules which are implemented by means of CHR propagation rules. Often some generated rules can be modelled as CHR simplification rules. Thus, we are currently searching for some criteria to perform such a transformation. A simple criteria could be the following: whenever a right hand side of a rule propagates information making its left hand side ground, then this rule can be implemented by means of a CHR simplification rule.

We intend to investigate the notion of local consistency which is enforced by the generated rules. In general, the rules ensure a stronger local consistency notion than rule consistency. First experiments turn out that our algorithm is able to generate rules which are equivalent to the inclusion rules defined in [6] (i.e. rules of the form $X_1 \subseteq S_1 \wedge \ldots \wedge X_k \subseteq S_k \rightarrow Y \neq v$). This can be achieved by allowing disequality constraints in the left hand side of rules and in their right hand side.

References

1. Constraint Handling Rules Online,
   http://www.pms.informatik.uni-muenchen.de/~webchr/ 29, 30
2. S. Abdennadher. Operational semantics and confluence of constraint propagation rules. In *Third International Conference on Principles and Practice of Constraint Programming, CP'97*, LNCS 1330. Springer-Verlag, Nov. 1997. 28
3. S. Abdennadher and T. Frühwirth. Operational equivalence of CHR programs and constraints. In *5th International Conference on Principles and Practice of Constraint Programming, CP'99*, LNCS 1713. Springer-Verlag, 1999. 30

34   Slim Abdennadher and Christophe Rigotti

4. R. Agrawal, T. Imielinski, and A. N. Swami. Mining association rules between sets of items in large databases. In *Proceedings of the 1993 ACM SIGMOD International Conference on Management of Data*, pages 207–216. ACM Press, 1993. 28, 33
5. J. F. Allen. Maintaining knowledge about temporal intervals. *Communications of ACM*, 26(11):832–843, 1983. 31, 32
6. K. Apt and E. Monfroy. Automatic generation of constraint propagation algorithms for small finite domains. In *5th International Conference on Principles and Practice of Constraint Programming, CP'99*, LNCS 1713. Springer-Verlag, 1999. 18, 19, 20, 21, 26, 27, 29, 31, 32, 33
7. R. J. Bayardo, R. Agrawal, and D. Gunopulos. Constraint-based rule mining in large, dense databases. In *Proceedings of the 15th International Conference on Data Engineering*, pages 188–197. IEEE Computer Society, 1999. 28
8. T. Frühwirth. Theory and practice of constraint handling rules, special issue on constraint logic programming. *Journal of Logic Programming*, 37(1-3):95–138, October 1998. 18, 19, 28, 29, 30
9. C. Kirchner, H. Kirchner, and M. Vittek. Implementing computational systems with constraints. In *Proceedings of the First Workshop on Principles and Practice of Constraints Programming*. MIT Press, Apr. 1993. 18
10. H. Kirchner and C. Ringeissen. A constraint solver in finite algebras and its combination with unification algorithms. In *Proc. Joint International Conference and Symposium on Logic Programming*, pages 225–239. MIT Press, 1992. 20
11. S. Kleene. *Introduction to Metamathematics*. Van Nostrand, Princeton, New Jersey, 1950. 31
12. S. Muggleton and L. De Raedt. Inductive Logic Programming : theory and methods. *Journal of Logic Programming*, 19,20:629–679, 1994. 21, 28, 33
13. N. Pasquier, Y. Bastide, R. Taouil, and L. Lakhal. Efficient mining of association rules using closed itemset lattices. *Information Systems*, 24(1):25–46, 1999. 28
14. G. Plotkin. A note on inductive generalization. In *Machine Intelligence*, volume 5, pages 153–163. Edinburgh University Press, 1970. 27, 28
15. D. A. Randell, Z. Cui, and A. G. Cohn. A spatial logic based on regions and connection. In *Proceedings of the 3rd International Conference on Principles of Knowledge Representation and Reasoning*, pages 165–176, Cambridge, MA, Oct. 1992. Morgan Kaufmann. 32
16. C. Ringeissen. Etude et implantation d'un algorithme d'unification dans les algèbres finies. Rapport de DEA, Université de Nancy I, 1990. 20
17. C. Ringeissen and E. Monfroy. Generating propagation rules for finite domains via unification in finite algebra. In *ERCIM Working Group on Constraints / CompulogNet Area on Constraint Programming Workshop*, 1999. 18, 20, 21, 29, 33
18. H. Toivonen, M. Klemettinen, P. Ronkainen, K. Hätönen, and H. Mannila. Pruning and grouping of discovered association rules. In *Workshop Notes of the ECML-95 Workshop on Statistics, Machine Learning, and Knowledge Discovery in Databases*, pages 47–52, Apr. 1995. 22
19. P. van Hentenryck. Constraint logic programming. *The Knowledge Engineering Review*, 6, 1991. 30

Extending Forward Checking*

Fahiem Bacchus

Department. of Computer Science, 6 Kings College Road, University Of Toronto,
Toronto, Ontario, Canada, M5S 1A4
fbacchus@cs.toronto.edu

Abstract. Among backtracking based algorithms for constraint satisfaction problems (CSPs), algorithms employing constraint propagation,
like forward checking (FC) and MAC, have had the most practical impact. These algorithms use constraint propagation during search to prune
inconsistent values from the domains of the uninstantiated variables. In
this paper we present a general approach to extending constraint propagating algorithms, especially forward checking. In particular, we provide
a simple yet flexible mechanism for pruning domain values, and show
that with this in place it becomes easy to utilize new mechanisms for
detecting inconsistent values during search. This leads to a powerful and
uniform technique for designing new CSP algorithms: one simply need
design new methods for detecting inconsistent values and then interface
them with the domain pruning mechanism. Furthermore, we also show
that algorithms following this design can proved to be correct in a simple
and uniform way. To demonstrate the utility of these ideas five "new"
CSP algorithms are presented.

1 Introduction

Many of the most useful backtracking based (systematic) CSP algorithms utilize constraint propagation to detect inconsistent values during search. These
inconsistent values can then be temporarily pruned from the domains of those
variables, and restored when the search backtracks and nullifies the reason the
values became inconsistent. In terms of simplicity and historical precedence the
most basic algorithm in this class is Haralick and Elliott's forward checking
algorithm (FC) [1].

Although conceptually simple, pruning values during search has rather pro-
found computational effects. Different amounts of computation can be devoted
to detect inconsistent values. But, once a value is known to be inconsistent it
is easy to prune it (e.g., it can be delinked from a linked list containing the
variable's current values), and this can yield exponential savings in the search of
the subtree below— if we had not pruned it we might have had to, e.g., process
this value an exponential number of times in subtree below. Perhaps an even
more important benefit is that domain pruning causes the domain sizes of the

---

* This research was supported by the Canadian Government through their NSERC
program.

R. Dechter (Ed.): CP 2000, LNCS 1894, pp. 35–51, 2000.

uninstantiated variables to vary dynamically, and this provides invaluable input to dynamic variable order (DVO) heuristics [2].

However, popular algorithms like FC and MAC employ domain pruning in a fairly restricted way. In both of these algorithms pruning is done in lock step with search. That is, every time a new assignment $\mathcal{A}$ is made these algorithms perform constraint propagation, detect some set of inconsistent values, and prune those values to the *current* level. Hence, when we undo $\mathcal{A}$, all of these values are restored. As a result the domains of the uninstantiated variables are in the same state when we backtrack from the current level as when we first entered it.

In this paper we show that there are other opportunities for detecting and pruning inconsistent values, and we use these new opportunities to develop an interesting range of extensions to the standard algorithms. It is very simple to implement a more general domain pruning and restoring mechanism that allows one to prune a value to an arbitrary level of the search tree. With this extra flexibility in place, one can set to the task of developing ways in which to use it. And as we will demonstrate in this paper there are a number of ways to do so. That is, there are ways of detecting that a value is inconsistent with levels higher than the current level, and thus pruning it above the current level.

In the sequel we present a generic template for extending constraint propagation algorithms. This template has an abstract interface to a domain pruning mechanism (that mechanism must do at least as much pruning as would FC). By designing and implementing new pruning mechanisms we can combine them with this template to obtain new CSP algorithms that extend FC. We then present a theorem which shows that as long as the new pruning mechanism satisfies a simple soundness criteria, the algorithm that arises from combining it with the template is both sound and complete. This means we can easily verify the correctness of our new algorithms (or any future algorithms that employ the same design technique). We then present five "new" CSP algorithms, all of which extend forward checking by taking advantage of various insights into when we can detect that values have become inconsistent. We are still working on evaluating these new algorithms empirically, but we present some preliminary results indicating potential in terms of improved search efficiency.

Given the intensity of research into new CSP algorithms, it should not be too surprising that some of these new algorithms end up being similar to previous proposals. However, an important contribution of our approach is that it provides a unification and simplification of a number of these previous proposals. This in itself has important practical significance: methods for cleanly designing and implementing CSP algorithms have as much of a role to play in practice as improved algorithmic efficiency. Furthermore, despite the relationship with previous proposals, some of the algorithms we present are novel and they all have novel features. Our approach also opens the door for the discovery of further improvements: any sound new method for discovering value inconsistencies can easily be plugged into our template to yield a new CSP algorithm.

2   Notation and Background

A CSP consists of a set of variables $\{V_1, \ldots, V_n\}$ and a set of constraints $\{C_1, \ldots, C_m\}$. Each variable V has a domain of values $Dom[V]$, and can be assigned any value $v \in Dom[V]$, indicated by $V \leftarrow v$.

Let $\mathcal{A}$ be any set of assignments. A variable can only be assigned a single value, hence the cardinality of $\mathcal{A}$ is at most n, $\|\mathcal{A}\| \leq n$. When $\|\mathcal{A}\| = n$ we call it a *complete* set of assignments. Associated with $\mathcal{A}$ is a set $VarsOf(\mathcal{A})$, the set of variables assigned values in $\mathcal{A}$.

Each constraint C is over some set of variables $VarsOf(C)$, and its arity is $\|VarsOf(C)\|$. A constraint is a set of sets of assignments: if the arity of C is k, then each element of C is a set of k assignments, one for each of the variables in $VarsOf(C)$. We say that a set of assignments $\mathcal{A}$ *satisfies* a constraint C if $VarsOf(C) \subseteq VarsOf(\mathcal{A})$ and there exists an element of C that is a subset of $\mathcal{A}$. Furthermore, we say that $\mathcal{A}$ is *consistent* if it satisfies all constraints C such that $VarsOf(C) \subseteq VarsOf(\mathcal{A})$. That is, it satisfies all constraints it *fully instantiates*. A *solution* to a CSP is a complete and consistent set of assignments.

An assignment $V \leftarrow v$ is *consistent* with a set of assignments $\mathcal{A}$ if $\mathcal{A} \cup \{V \leftarrow v\}$ is consistent. A *value* v (of some variable V) is consistent with $\mathcal{A}$ when $V \leftarrow v$ is consistent with $\mathcal{A}$, otherwise it is *inconsistent*. Finally, if we have a constraint C with $\{V, V'\} \subseteq VarsOf(C)$ then two values $v \in Dom[V]$ and $v' \in Dom[V']$ are said to be *compatible* (given some set of assignments $\mathcal{A}$ to the other variables of C) if $\{V \leftarrow v, V' \leftarrow v'\} \cup \mathcal{A} \in C$, in this case we also say that v *supports* v' (given $\mathcal{A}$) and vice versa.

3   A Template for Extending Forward Checking

FC+Prune is template for constraint propagating algorithms that find solutions by searching in a tree of variable assignments. It utilizes the following data structures. *FutureVars*, the set of uninstantiated variables. *asgnVal*, a map from a variable to its currently assigned value. *VarAtLevel*, a map from a level of the search tree to the variable assigned at that level. *CurDom*, a map from a variable to a set containing all of the values still available for it at this point of the search (i.e., the set of unpruned values of the variable). *Dom*, a map from a variable to its original domain of values. *PrunedVals*, a map from a level of the search tree to a set of values that have been pruned to this level.

In order to more flexibly prune and restore values at different levels of the tree we represent each value, v, by a structure that includes the fields $v.val$, the actual numeric or symbol value associated the value, $v.Var$, the variable the value is for, $v.prlevel$, the level to which v has been pruned back to, and $v.CF$ the conflict associated with v. How these data structures are used during search is explained below.

Search is initiated by the call **FC+Prune**(1). At every level the next variable to assign is selected (heuristically) by `picknextVar`. `picknextVar` returns NIL if there are no more future variables. Given the conditions specified below, this

FC+Prune(level)
1. Var := picknextVar();
2. *if*(Var == NIL)
3.   processSolution();
4.   *if*(FINDALL)
5.   **Prune::FoundSoln**(level);
6.   unassignlevels(level-1,level-1);
7.   *return*(level-1);
8.   *else*
9.   *return*(0);
10. *foreach* val ∈ *CurDom*[Var]
11.   assign(Var,val,level);
12.   **Prune::Asgn**(Var,val,level);
13.   jbl := **FC+Prune**(level+1);
14.   *if*(jbl != level)
15.   *return*(jbl);
16. jbl := maxprlevel(Var);
17. **Prune::Backup**(jbl,Var,level);
18. unassignlevels(level,jbl);
19. *return*(jbl);

picknextVar()
1. *if*(*FutureVars* == {})
2.   Var := NIL;
3. *elseif* ∃ *V.V* ∈ *FutureVars* ∧ *CurDom*[V] == {}
4.   Var := pick *V* ∈ *FutureVars* **such that**
             CurDom[V]={}
5. *else*
6.   Var := pick some *V* ∈ *FutureVars*;
7. *return*(Var);

assign(Var,val,level)
1. *FutureVars* := *FutureVars* - {**Var**};
2. *asgnVal*[Var] := val;
3. *VarAtLevel*[level] := Var;

unassignlevels(l1,l2)
1. *for* i := l1 *to* l2
2.   Var := *VarAtLevel*[i];
3.   *VarAtLevel*[i] := NIL;
4.   *asgnVal*[Var] := NIL;
5.   *FutureVars* := *FutureVars* ∪ {**Var**};
6.   *foreach* v ∈ *PrunedVals*[i]
7.   *CurDom*[v.Var] := *CurDom*[v.Var] ∪ {v};
8.   v.prlevel = NIL;
9.   v.CF = {0};
10.   *PrunedVals*[i] := {};

maxprlevel(Var)
1. m := 0
2. *foreach* v ∈ *Dom*[Var]
3.   m := max(m,v.prlevel);

prune(v,level)
1. *CurDom*[v.Var] := *CurDom*[v.Var] - {v};
2. *PrunedVals*[level] := *PrunedVals*[level] ∪ {v};
3. v.prlevel := level;

Fig. 1. A Template for Extending Forward Checking

will mean that the current set of assignments, *CurAsgns*, is a solution, the last assignment of which was made at the previous level. The solution will be enumerated by `processSolution` (line 3). If we want to enumerate all solutions `FINDALL` is set to be true which will cause a return to the previous level to search for more solutions. Otherwise 0 will be returned (line 9) causing the recursion to unwind and terminate.

If we haven't found a solution, we proceed to examine every value in the current domain of the selected variable (line 10). For each value `val` we augment *CurAsgns* by making the assignment `Var ← val` using `assign`. (`assign` updates the *FutureVars*, *asgnVal*, and *VarAtLevel* data structures). We then recursively examine the search tree under this assignment. The recursion will return a jump back level, and if that level is above the current level, we return to a previous invocation of **FC+Prune** higher up the search tree. Otherwise we continue with the *foreach* loop to test `Var`'s next value.

Once we have exhausted all possible values, we compute the deepest level to which we can backtrack so as to restore at least one value of `Var`'s domain (line 16),[1] undo all of assignments in between these levels (`unassignlevels` updates the same data structures as `assign`), and then jump back. One important feature of our version of tree search is that this method of computing the level to backtrack to is uniformly applied even when sophisticated forms of backjumping are used.[2]

Flexible domain pruning is implemented by the simple device of maintaining the sets *PrunedVals* and *CurDom*. Given that we have detected that a value has become inconsistent with the assignments made at some prior level ℓ, we can prune that value by removing it from the *CurDom* of its variable, and placing it in the set *PrunedVals*[ℓ]. When search backtracks to level ℓ (thus nullifying the reason the value became inconsistent) it restores all of the values in *PrunedVals*[ℓ] by moving these values back into the *CurDom* set of their associated variable. This processing is done by the functions `prune` and `unassignlevels`. It can also be noted that in some cases we might detect that a value has become inconsistent back to level 0 (the level above the first assignment). In this case we put the value in *PrunedVals*[0] and it will never be restored.

One simplification used in **FC+Prune** is that it does not immediately check the result of pruning the future domains. If some future variables has its domain entirely deleted by **Prune::Asgn** (line 12), i.e., if a DWO has occurred, **FC+Prune** will detect this in its next recursive invocation: `picknextVar` always returns a variable with an empty domain if one exists. By doing this we simplify the code and the interface to the domain pruning mechanism.

FC+Prune allows for an interaction with an arbitrary domain pruning mechanism in three different locations: when we have found a solution

---

[1] The code maintains the invariant that if a value is a member of *PrunedVals*[i] its *.prlevel* field has been set to i (all values are pruned by calling the function `prune`). Thus if we jump back to the maximum of these values (computed by `maxprlevel`), we will restore at least one value.

[2] Sophisticated backwards moves are handled by sophisticated ways of doing domain pruning.

Prune::FoundSoln (line 5), when we assign a value **Prune::Asgn** (line 12) and when we backtrack after having exhausted the domain of a variable **Prune::Backup** (line 17). At these three locations new inconsistent values can be discovered and pruned. All of the algorithms we present can be implemented by combining the **FC+Prune** template with an instantiation of these three subroutines.

3.1   Soundness and Completeness

Subject to two simple conditions we can show that any CSP algorithm generated by combining **FC+Prune** with an instantiation of the domain pruning subroutines is both sound and complete.

1. **Prune::Asgn** must remove all values of the future variables that are inconsistent with $CurAsgns$. This means we can consistently extend $CurAsgns$ by assigning any future variable any value from its current domain.[3]
2. The domain pruning process must be *sound*. That is, at every stage of the search if a value v from the domain of variable V is in $PrunedVals[\ell]$ for some ℓ, then there can be no *unenumerated* solution in the subtree below level ℓ containing $V \leftarrow v$. That is, pruning can only eliminate a value from a subtree when it is certain that the value cannot participate in any further solutions in that subtree.[4]

Theorem 1. *Subject to these conditions on the pruning subroutines* **FC+Prune** *is sound, i.e., all solutions it reports are in fact solutions, and complete, i.e., it will enumerate all solutions if* FINDALL *is true and it will enumerate one solution if* FINDALL *is false and there exists a solution. It will not enumerate any solutions if and only if none exist.*

All of the algorithms we present here satisfy the first condition (they all extend forward checking), and thus all we have to do to show them to be sound and complete is to demonstrate the second condition.

4   Some New CSP Algorithms

All of our new algorithms are developed by insights into new sound ways of detecting inconsistent values and detecting the level at which they became inconsistent (which might be above the current level). Inconsistent values can then be pruned back to their level of inconsistency. These algorithms can all be implemented by simply specifying the three pruning routines. In this section we

---

[3] For binary CSPs this means that the domain pruning mechanism must do at least as much pruning as FC. For n-ary CSPs, it must do at least as much pruning as the version of FC defined by van Hentenryck [3].

[4] Note that we define soundness with respect to the set of unenumerated solutions. By doing this we obtain a uniform way of treating the case where the algorithm is searching for all solutions.

present five new CSP algorithms designed in this way. All of these algorithms can be formalized to deal with n-ary CSPs. However, we will restrict our presentation to binary versions of the algorithms. The binary versions are easier to understand and more concise to present.

4.1   Extending FC

The first two algorithms we present are simple extensions of FC. After a new assignment $V' \leftarrow v'$ is made at level ℓ, FC prunes all values of the future variables that are inconsistent with this assignment. In FC these inconsistent values are pruned to level ℓ (i.e., placed in $PrunedVals[\ell]$). Thus these values will be restored as soon as we backtrack to level ℓ. One way of extending FC is illustrated by the following example.

Example 1. Say that we have two variables A and B, each with the domain of values $\{1, 2, 3\}$ and the constraint $A \geq B$. Further, say that along the current path of the search tree we instantiate A at level 5, that the value 3 of A has already been pruned by a prior assignment at level 1, and that no other values of A have been pruned. Hence at level 5 $CurDom[A] = \{1, 2\}$, $3 \in PrunedVals[1]$, and $3.prlevel = 1$.

Say that we next make the assignment $A \leftarrow 1$, and then forward check the unassigned variables. When we forward check B we find that its values 2 and 3 are both inconsistent with $A \leftarrow 1$. Forward checking would prune both of these values to level 5. However, closer examination shows that $B \leftarrow 3$ became inconsistent at level 1, four levels above the current level. We cannot make the assignment $B \leftarrow 3$ until we can make the assignment $A \leftarrow 3$, which we cannot do until we restore that value by backtracking to level 1: all of the supports $B \leftarrow 3$ has on the domain of A were pruned away at level 1.

The following routine computes the value at which it is safe to prune a future value v given that we have just instantiated Var. In this routine *compat*(val,v) is true if and only the two values val and v are compatible, i.e., they satisfy the constraint between val.Var and v.Var or there is no constraint between their variables.

findDS(v,Var)
```
1. ds := 0;
2. foreach val ∈ Dom[Var] ∧ compat(val,v)
3.    ds := max(ds,val.prlevel);
4. return(ds);
```

In the above example, when we call findDS with v equal to 3 of B and Var equal to A, it will correctly return the level 1: only 3 of A is compatible with 3 of B, and this value was pruned at level 1 ($3.prlevel = 1$).

What about $B \leftarrow 2$? This value is also inconsistent with the assignment $A \leftarrow 1$, but unlike $B \leftarrow 3$ it is consistent with the as yet unpruned value 2 of A. Hence, when we undo $A \leftarrow 1$ we must also restore 2 of B so that it is available when we try $A \leftarrow 2$. That is, it is only sound to prune 2 of B to level 5, the current level. We can get findDS to compute a sound pruning level in this case also by simply pruning all of the other values in $CurDom[A]$ to the current level whenever we make an assignment to A. Clearly we cannot use these other values until we undo the current assignment to A, so it is sound to prune them to the current level. With this modification, findDS will find that A's compatible values for $B \leftarrow 2$, 2 and 3, have been pruned at levels 5 and 1 respectively, and thus that it is sound to prune 2 of B to level 5.

EFC—Extended Forward Checking Our first algorithm EFC is based on using findDS when doing pruning after an assignment. In particular, it uses the following instantiation:

```
Prune::Asgn(Var,val,level)
 1. foreach v ∈ CurDom[Var] ∧ v != val
 2.     prune(v,level);
 3. foreach V ∈ FutureVars ∧ constrained(Var,V)
 4.     foreach v ∈ CurDom[V];
 5.        if(¬compat(val,v));
 6.            prune(v,findDS(v,Var));
```

This routine is called whenever we assign variable Var the value val at the current level level. It operates just like FC except (1) it prunes all other values in $CurDom[\texttt{Var}]$ to level and (2) instead of pruning inconsistent future values to level it prunes them to the perhaps higher level returned by findDS. Hence, when we backtrack back to level we can save work by not having to reconsider some of these future values until we backtrack to an even higher level.

We can apply the same insight when we backtrack. Extending our previous example, say that at level 5 in addition to $CurDom[A] = \{1,2\}$ and $3.prlevel = 1$ we also have that 1 of B has been pruned by a previous assignment at level 2. Hence, $CurDom[B] = \{2,3\}$ and value 1 of B has $1.prlevel = 2$. Now we make the assignment $A \leftarrow 1$ at level 5 as before. The remaining values of B are inconsistent with the new assignment, and thus $A \leftarrow 1$ will cause a wipeout of B. B will then be the next variable selected at level 6 (variables with empty domains must be selected first by picknextVar), and at that level the values of B will have $1.prlevel = 2$, $2.prlevel = 5$, and $3.prlevel = 1$ (with 3 having been pruned back to level 1 by **Prune::Asgn**). This will cause a backtrack to level 5 to try a different assignment to A. Say that search continues, eventually backtracking to level 4 and then descending again. On the new descent we might again explore the assignment $A \leftarrow 1$. However, it is obvious that this assignment cannot succeed, in fact it cannot succeed until we ascend to level 2 and there restore the value 1 of B: $A \leftarrow 1$ lost its last support on B at level 2.

Hence, at the moment we backtrack from level 6, we can detect that the assignment $A \leftarrow 1$ made at the level we are backtracking to (level 5) is in fact inconsistent back to level 2 and prune this value to that level. This yields the following version of

```
Prune::Backup(jbl,Var,level)
 1. jbval := asgnVal[VarAtLevel[jbl]]
 2. prlevel := min(findDS(jbval,Var),jbl-1);
 3. prune(jbval,prlevel);
```

In this routine, Var is the variable causing the backtrack—the variable whose domain has been exhausted, level is the current level, and jbl is the level we are about to jumpback to. The routine prunes the value assigned at jbl, i.e., jbval: we find the deepest support jbval, has on the exhausted variable Var, and prune it back to that level. In our example, this routine will be called with jbl equal to 5, Var equal to B, level equal to 6, thus 1 of A (jbval), will be pruned back to level 2.

Note however, that we have just completed the search of the subtree below jbval, so we also know that we do not need to try jbval again until we undo at least the previous assignment made at level jbl-1. Hence, it is always sound to prune jbval to the previous level jbl-1. Hence, we can prune it to the minimum of jbl-1 and its deepest support.

Finally, **FC+Prune** delays checking whether on not it has found a solution until it recurses to the next level. Thus when a solution is enumerated its last assignment was made at the previous level level-1. **Prune::FoundSoln** simply prunes the last value assigned *asgnVal*[*VarAtLevel*[level-1]] back to the previous level, level-2. This pruning is sound: no *unenumerated* solution can contain this value until at least one other assignment in the current solution is undone (i.e., the assignment at level-2):

Prune::FoundSoln(level)
 1. val := *asgnVal*[*VarAtLevel*[level-1]];
 2. prune(val,level-2);

It is not difficult to turn the discussion above into a proof that the domain pruning used by EFC is *sound*, and thus to show by Theorem 1 that EFC is sound and complete.

EFC- It is often not worth the extra computation to backprune forward checked values (line 6 of **Prune::Asgn**).[5] So we could restrict ourselves to the extra pruning done by **Prune::Backup**. Thus we can define a new algorithm EFC-, by substituting on line 8 of **Prune::Asgn** the call prune(v,level), which simply prunes forward checked values to the current level exactly like FC does.

Observations and Some Empirical Results Both algorithms have the ability to prune values back beyond the current level, whereas FC only prunes values to the current level. This means that there will be cases where at level i we find that all of the values of the current variable have been pruned above level $i - 1$. This will cause a backjump as we always backtrack to a level were we can restore at least one value of the exhausted variable. Furthermore, by pruning back the assignment we backtrack to, it is possible that we might backtrack to a variable and there discover that all of its values have been pruned back even further. This will generate another backjump. That is, multiple backjumps are possible. Both

---

[5] In particular, there are often a large number of values removed by forward checking, and computing the deepest support for all of them can be more costly than is worthwhile.

algorithms also have the ability to discover arc-inconsistent values and prune those values back to the level they became arc-inconsistent (including pruning values that were initially arc-inconsistent back to level 0 where they will never be restored).[6]

For binary CSPs it can be shown that if EFC is able to prune a value v back to level i, then MAC would have pruned v at level i (or less). This means that on binary CSPs, except for heuristic reasons, EFC/EFC- cannot offer a savings in the number of nodes explored over MAC. Hence the potential for savings in these algorithms over MAC on binary CSPs is limited. In our experiments with random binary CSP problems generated by the CT model we have found EFC/EFC- to be mostly inferior to MAC. EFC/EFC- may still have some potential on n-ary CSPs.[7]

Nevertheless, in the binary case both EFC and EFC- can be, like conflict directed backjumping (CBJ) [6], of considerable assistance to standard FC. Table 1 shows a typical example using 50 random binary CSPs. Each CSP is generated using the standard random CT model, and has 200 variables each having 10 possible values, and 200 constraints with 76 incompatible pairs.[8] In the experiment (and the experiment reported in the next section) we are searching for the first solution using a 500MHz Pentium III machine. We utilize dynamic variable ordering with the fail-first heuristic (minimum remaining values), and using the variable's current degree as a tie-breaker.[9]

MAC on this problem suite outperforms EFC/EFC-. It also performs better on many other parameter settings the CT model. But interestingly we have not found a case where there are orders of magnitude difference in performance, as can occur when we compare MAC with FC (or even FCCBJ). MAC's superiority on these problems is not surprising. Achlioptas et al. have shown that the random CT model generates problems that are highly biased in favor of MAC [8], especially as the number of constraints grows (irrespective of tightness as long as the number of incompatible pairs is greater than the domain size). With 200 constraints and a high tightness of 76% the problems being generated are either initially arc-inconsistent or become arc-inconsistent after only a few variables have been assigned (MAC visits only a average of 29.6 nodes on these problems). Furthermore these problems have a large number of arc-inconsistent

---

[6] Prosser's FC-D2C algorithm [4] uses a special test to recognize the case when a value can be pruned back to level 0. This special case is achieved automatically in EFC/EFC-.

[7] It is not hard to define EFC for n-ary CSPs, and it should be feasible to extend all of the new n-ary versions of FC defined in [5] using these ideas. Further empirical evaluation is needed to determine how useful such extensions would be.

[8] The particular, in the random CT model the 200 constraints are chosen at random from the (200*199/2) possible binary constraints, and the 76 incompatible pairs are chosen at random from the 100 possible pairs.

[9] We also tried the current domain size divided by degree as a heuristic [7]. FC showed somewhat better performance with this heuristic but it still failed on many problems, otherwise the results were very similar with both EFC and EFC- still performing better than FCCBJ.

Table 1. Performance on 50 <200,10,200,76> random binary CSPs

	Time in CPU sec.		Nodes Visited	
	Ave.	Max.	Ave.	Max.
MAC	0.012	0.030	29.64	275
EFC	0.033	0.190	1507	12584
EFC-	0.274	5.910	31306	66121
FCCBJ	5.105	194.680	404308	15819402
FC	FC is able to solve only some of these problems within a 250 sec. time bound			

values, so the fail-first heuristic works particularly well for MAC. Nevertheless, the results (and many other similar parameter settings of the CT model) do serve to demonstrate that there exist classes of problems for which EFC is a significant assist to FC.

One final point is that EFC- is identical to the algorithm FC-BM described by Prosser in [9]. In particular, Prosser identified that when backing up from a DWO the gains of **Prune::Backup** could be achieved. However, the algorithm he described utilized backmarking style data structures as well as domain pruning data structures. The result was very complex as it was difficult to keep these two data structures synchronized. The relative simplicity of EFC- helps to demonstrate the advantages of our design.[10]

4.2   Conflict Directed Pruning

Our other new CSP algorithms are based on using conflicts or no-goods to detect inconsistent values. Conflicts have appeared many times before in CSP algorithms, e.g., in Conflict Directed Backjumping (CBJ) [6] and in no-good learning [11]. One difference here is that we maintain conflicts for values rather than variables.

A *conflict* C for the value v is a set of assignments $\{V_1 \leftarrow v_1, \ldots, V_k \leftarrow v_k\}$ such that no *unenumerated* solution contains both $v.Var \leftarrow v$ and C.[11] All of the conflicts manipulated by our algorithms will be subsets of *CurAsgns*, and thus they can be represented as a set of levels: the set of assignments made at those levels is the conflict proper. For a conflict CF, $\max(CF)$ will denote its maximum level.

The three algorithms we present are all based on a pruning mechanism that prunes the value v back to $\max(CF)$ once we detect that CF is a conflict for v.

---

[10] That backmarking (BM) type savings can be a achieved with a domain pruning mechanism is not so surprising given the close relationship between BM and FC demonstrated in [10].

[11] We are using the set of *unenumerated* solutions to define conflicts. This again allows us to provide a uniform treatment of the case when our algorithms are searching for all solutions.

It is clear that such a pruning mechanism is *sound*: $V \leftarrow v$ cannot participate in any solution until the assignment at max(CF) is undone. Hence, all that we have to do to prove these algorithms sound and complete is to ensure that the sets they identify as being conflicts are in fact conflicts.

Say we have a value $v \in Dom[V]$, we can compute a conflict for v given conflicts for the values of another variable V'. Let $\{v'_1, \ldots, v'_k\}$ be the values of V' that are *compatible* with v, then it can be shown that the union of the conflicts for the v'_i is a conflict for v. The following algorithm computes a conflict for a value v given that we have conflicts for the values of the variable Var.[12]

computeCF(v,Var)
```
1. cf := {0};
2. foreach val ∈Dom[Var] ∧ compat(val,v)
3.    cf := cf ∪ val.CF;
4. return(cf);
```

CFFC—Conflict Based Forward Checking The algorithm CFFC uses the same structure as EFC. When we make a new assignment $A \leftarrow a$, we prune all other values in $CurDom[A]$, setting their conflict set to be the current level. Then we do forward checking. When we find an inconsistent future value, we compute a conflict for it by unioning all the conflicts of its compatible values on A, and prune that future value back to the maximum of its new conflict set. This yields **Prune::Asgn**

Prune::Asgn(Var,val,level)
```
1. foreach v ∈ CurDom[Var] ∧ v != val
2.    v.CF := {level};
3.    prune(v,max(v.CF));
4. foreach V ∈ FutureVars ∧ constrained(Var,V)
5.    foreach v ∈ CurDom[V];
6.      if(¬compat(val,v));
7.        v.CF := computeCF(v,Var);
8.        prune(v,max(v.CF));
```

Similarly, when we backtrack to level jbl because we have exhausted all the values of Var at level level, we can compute a conflict for jbval, the value assigned at the jumpback level. This conflict is the union of the conflicts of the values of the exhausted variable Var that are compatible with jbvar, except that in this case we can remove jbl from these conflicts. We can then prune jbval back to the maximum of its conflict.[13]

Prune::Backup(jbl,Var,level)
```
1. jbval := asgnVal[VarAtLevel[jbl]]
2. jbval.CF := computeCF(jbval,Var) - {jbl};
3. prune(jbval,max(jbval.CF));
```

---

[12] The initial 0 in the conflict facilitates pruning values back to level 0 by allowing max(CF) to take on the value 0. For example, if v has no compatible values on Var, the conflict $\{0\}$ will be computed. In this case we can permanent prune v by pruning it back to level 0.

[13] Since 0 might be the maximum of a conflict set, this process automatically achieves the special case permanent pruning of Prosser's CBJ-DkC algorithm [4].

Finally, when we find a solution and we wish to enumerate more, we have discovered that all of the previous levels are a conflict for the last assigned value (assigned at level `level-1`).

Prune::FoundSoln(`level`)
```
1. val := asgnVal[VarAtLevel[level-1]];
2. val.CF := {1,...,level-2};
3. prune(val,max(val.CF));
```

The basic algorithm CFFC has some similar features to conflict directed backjumping (CBJ) [6], dead-end driven learning [12], and the no-goods used in dynamic backtracking [13]. The conflicts used here are, however, more fine grained: they are value specific conflicts.

In addition to CFFC we can define CFFC-. In analogy with EFC-, CFFC- is identical to CFFC except that instead of computing a conflict for each value that is pruned by forward checking in **Prune::Asgn**, we simply set its conflict to be the single level of the current assignment (much like FC). Specifically, we replace line 7 of the routine with line `v.CF := {level}`. CFFC- is generally faster that CFFC as computing the conflict sets for all values pruned by forward checking can take more time than it saves. We have also found that on some problems the extra pruning performed by CFFC can seriously degrade backjumping [4].

Finally we can define our fifth algorithm CFMAC. In this routine instead of doing forward checking we enforce arc-consistency. As in the forward checking case, whenever we discover that a value v can be pruned because it has lost all of its support on some variable V' we set v's conflict to the union of the conflicts of its supports on V' (again using the routine `computeCF`) and prune it to the max of this conflict set. In standard MAC, v would only be pruned to the current level. (In CFMAC we prune on backup just as with CFFC).

Observations and Some Empirical Results CFFC is a very powerful CSP algorithm. In particular, its backjumping ability is more powerful than CBJ. CBJ maintains one conflict per variable. This conflict is simply the union of the conflicts maintained by CFFC over all the values of the variable.[14] The higher level of detail maintained by CFFC allows for larger backjumps.

For simplicity, assume that we are using CFFC- (i.e., no backpruning of forward checked values occurs). Say that we have two variables A and B both with domain $\{a, b, c\}$ and the constraint $A = B$. And that at level 7 we have that $CurDom[B] = \{c\}$, with conflicts for its other two values $a.CF = \{1\}$, and $b.CF = \{6\}$. Furthermore, say that $CurDom[A] = \{a\}$, with the conflicts for its other two values $b.CF = \{1\}$ and $c.CF = \{2\}$. If at level 7 we next attempt to assign A we have only value to try: $A \leftarrow a$. This causes a DWO of B.

---

[14] Of course CFFC requires more storage, in the worst case $N^2 * D$ space to store all of the conflicts (where N is the number of variables and D is the maximum size of their domains). However, in practice, we can store conflicts as lists of elements, and we can reuse these elements when we backtrack and empty these sets (line 9 of `unassignlevels`). In our implementation we have never found space to be a critical issue.

Table 2. Performance on 100 3-SAT instances with an embedded unsatisfiable subproblem

	Size	Ave CPU time sec.	Ave. Nodes		Size	Ave CPU time sec.	Ave. Nodes
MAC	85	160.523	2241218	MAC	90	328.825	4824044
MACCBJ	85	44.130	263010	MACCBJ	90	66.305	352838
CFFC-	85	0.078	3318	CFFC-	90	0.067	2719
CFFC	85	4.702	137418	CFFC	90	4.343	120536
CFMAC	85	4.242	24546	CFMAC	90	5.818	28966

Search will descend to level 8 where it will examine B. At this point we have for the values of B, $a.CF = \{1\}$, $b.CF = \{6\}$, and $c.CF = \{7\}$ (the last having been computed by forward checking from $A \leftarrow a$). These conflicts cause a backtrack to level 7 to try a different value for A. Standard CBJ will at this point union $\{1,6\}$ into A's conflict set: i.e., all of the conflicts of B except level 7. Since there are no more values for A, the search will then backstep to level 6. CFFC, on the other hand, will set a value specific conflict for the value a of A: a of A will only inherit the conflict set associated with a of B due to the constraint between A and B. Thus, on backtrack to level 7, the individual value conflicts associated with A will be $a.CF = \{1\}$, $b.CF = \{1\}$ and $c.CF = \{2\}$, and the search will backjump all the way to level 2. This kind of behavior multiplies. On backtrack we can pass back a shorter conflict, and this in turn can pass back shorter conflicts and generate better backtracks at the higher levels.

Another feature of CFFC is its ability to detect and prune values that have become i-inverse inconsistent [14] for arbitrary i. Thus, CFFC has the potential to achieve exponential savings over an algorithm that continually enforces k-inverse consistency on the values of the future variables for any fixed k. However an algorithm that enforces k-inverse consistency does the work required to discover all k-inverse inconsistent values prior to continuing its search, whereas CFFC might not discover some of these inconsistencies until after it has performed a search exponential in j for some $j > k$. Thus, the potential for exponential savings exists the other way around as well. On the other hand, CFFC is "getting" on with the search while it discovering these k-inverse inconsistent values.[15] CFMAC, takes the approach that it is useful to discover all 2-inconsistencies prior to continuing search by always enforcing arc-consistency. Conflict based pruning can then be used to take advantage of any higher order inconsistencies discovered during search.

CFFC and its variants do not perform very well on problems drawn from the random CT class. It is almost always outperformed by either MAC or on smaller

---

[15] In an interesting recent paper, it has been shown that search is a generic way of implementing k-inverse consistency checking [15]. CFFC can be viewed as an algorithm that does both at the same time.

problems by FC. Again this is to be expected from the results of Achlioptas et al. [8]. The problems generated by the random CT model are likely to contain many arc-inconsistent values (thus MAC has an advantage on these problems), and more telling, these problems are unlikely to contain any values that are k-inverse inconsistent for large k while being $k-1$-inverse consistent.[16] Thus the expense of using conflicts to detect k-inconsistent values for larger k is hardly ever beneficial: simple arc-consistency will immediately detect almost all inconsistent values. Furthermore, this also means that conflicts are unlikely to generate powerful backtracks. Thus, CBJ hardly helps (over MAC) on these problems either [17].

Nevertheless, there are problems on which CFFC is superior. One example, are problems that have a small group of variables participating in an unsolvable subproblem. On these kinds of problems the CFFC algorithms perform exponentially better than MAC and MACCBJ. This behavior arises from the fact that the CFFC algorithms are able to prune away the values of these inconsistent variables so that it does not need to keep on trying them, and is also able to generate more powerful backjumps than CBJ. Although a perfect heuristic could instantiate these "bad" variables at the top of the tree any heuristics can be foiled by the structure of the problem.

Table 2 shows one type of embedded problem. These problems originated in the work of Bayardo and Schrag and were used to illustrate their CBJ based satisfiability solver RelSat [18]. They took relatively easy random 3-sat problems and embedded in them a small unsatisfiable sat problem. We took the random SAT problems produced by their generator and converted them to binary CSPs so that we could test them with our (currently binary) algorithms. The results are shown in Table 2.[17] One surprising result is the performance of CFFC-, which explores significantly fewer nodes than the CFFC and CFMAC both of which do more pruning than CFFC-. In these problems the extra pruning is significantly degrading backtracking [4]. In the experiment we used the same hardware as before, and DVO with the fail-first heuristic and the variable's current degree as a tie-breaker. The MAC algorithm we used was based on AC3, and in our

---

[16] This follows from Mitchell's recent results showing that these problems have short refutation resolutions [16].

[17] In more detail, the RelSat generator took easy random 3-SAT problems with N variables (85 and 90 in our experiment) and $3.5N$ clauses and added an unsatisfiable subproblem with 10 variables and 40 clauses. We took each 3-clause and converted it to a variable with domain size 7. Each value for this clause/variable corresponds to a truth assignment to the 3 variables in the clause (there are 7 satisfying truth assignments for a 3-clause), and two clauses sharing variables became variables constrained so that they have compatible truth assignments. This is the dual construction [19]. Although this is not a particularly effective way of solving SAT problems, it does have the nice feature that it preserves the small unsatisfiable subproblem: the subproblem generates a set of variables in the CSP for which there is no consistent set of values.

benchmarking it ran at about 65% of the speed of the more sophisticated AC7
based implementation of J.C. Regin [20][18]

We have also experimented with a preliminary implementation of n-ary versions of CFFC, CFFC-, and CFMAC algorithms. The implementation was built
on top of van Beek's CPLAN system [21]. In these experiments we found that on
harder logistics, blocks, and grid world planning problem CFMAC out performs
the base GAC-CBJ (generalized arc consistency with conflict directed backtracking) implemented in CPLAN (CFMAC can run 2 to 5 times faster on some of the
harder problems). Plain GAC is completely outclassed by these two algorithms—
it can take more than two hours of CPU time on some problems that are solved
in less than 10 seconds by CFMAC and GAC-CBJ. In comparision with CFFC-
and CFFC, plain GAC is sometimes inferior sometimes superior. We also tried
an n-ary version of the Golomb ruler problem (using quaternary constraints). In
contrast with the planning problems on the Golomb ruler CFFC- is the fastest
algorithm, being about 10 times faster than CFMAC and GAC-CBJ on the 10
marks ruler problem (length 55). We plan to report in more detail on these
experiments in the near future.

In conclusion, the work presented here makes the following contributions: (1)
it unifies a number of ideas that have appeared previous work, (2) it provides a
clean design for a range of extensions to constraint propagating algorithms, and
(3) it provides a clean way to implement and prove correct these new extensions.
We have also presented some sample extensions that demonstrate the approach,
and some evidence that these extensions might have potential for practical use.
More work needs to be done to get a true picture of the empirical properties of
these extensions.

References

1. R. M. Haralick and G. L. Elliott. Increasing tree search efficiency for constraint
   satisfaction problems. *Artificial Intelligence*, 14:263–313, 1980. 35
2. Fahiem Bacchus and Paul van Run. Dynamic variable reordering in CSPs. In
   Principles and Practice of Constraint Programming (CP95), number 976 in LNCS,
   pages 258–275. Springer-Verlag, New York, 1995. 36
3. Pascal van Hentenryck. *Constraint Satisfaction for Logic Programming*. MIT Press,
   1989. 40
4. Patrick Prosser. Domain filtering can degrade intelligent backtracking search. In
   *Procceedings of the International Joint Conference on Artifical Intelligence (IJ-
   CAI)*, pages 262–267, 1993. 44, 46, 47, 49
5. Christian Bessière, Pedro Meseguer, Eugene C. Freuder, and Javier Larrosa. On
   forward checking for non-binary constraint satisfaction. In *Principles and Practice of Constraint Programming (CP99)*, number 1713 in LNCS, pages 88–102.
   Springer-Verlag, New York, 1999. 44

---

[18] Thus using the AC7 version of MAC would not have altered our results. We did
not use Regin's implementation because it only ran on SUN SPARCs, and our main
computational resource was an Intel based PC. We also tried the current domain
size divided by degree heuristic. In this case all of the algorithms performed slightly
worse, but the relative performance was the same.

6. P. Prosser. Hybrid algorithms for the constraint satisfaction problem. *Computational Intelligence*, 9(3), 1993. 44, 45, 47

7. C. Bessiere and J.-C. Regin. MAC and combined heuristics: Two reasons to forsake FC (and CBJ?) on hard problems. In *Principles and Practice of Constraint Programming (CP96)*, number 1118 in LNCS, pages 61–75. Springer-Verlag, New York, 1996. 44

8. L. M. Achlioptas, L. Kirousis, E. Kranakis, D. Krizanc, M. Molloy, and Y. Stamatiou. Random constraint satisfaction: A more accurate picture. In *Principles and Practice of Constraint Programming (CP97)*, number 1330 in LNCS, pages 107–120. Springer-Verlag, New York, 1997. 44, 49

9. P. Prosser. Forward checking with backmarking. In M. Meyer, editor, *Constraint Processing*, LNCS 923, pages 185–204. Springer-Verlag, New York, 1995. 45

10. Fahiem Bacchus and Adam Grove. On the Forward Checking algorithm. In *Principles and Practice of Constraint Programming (CP95)*, number 976 in LNCS, pages 292–309. Springer-Verlag, New York, 1995. 45

11. R. Dechter. Enhancement schemes for constraint processing: Backjumping, learning and cutset decomposition. *Artificial Intelligence*, 41:273–312, 1990. 45

12. Daniel Frost and Rina Dechter. Dead-end driven learning. In *Proceedings of the AAAI National Conference*, pages 294–300, 1994. 47

13. Matthew L. Ginsberg. Dynamic backtracking. *Journal of Artificial Intelligence Research*, 1:25–46, 1993. 47

14. E. Freuder and C. D. Elfe. Neighborhood inverse consistency preprocessing. In *Proceedings of the AAAI National Conference*, pages 202–208, 1996. 48

15. Gérard Verfaillie, David Martinez, and Christian Bessière. A generic customizable framework for inverse local consistency. In *Proceedings of the AAAI National Conference*, pages 169–174, 1999. 48

16. David Mitchell. Some random csps are hard for resolution. http://http://www.cs.toronto.edu/~mitchell/papers/some.ps, 2000. 49

17. S. A. Grant and B. M. Smith. The phase transition behaviour of maintaining arc consistency. Technical report, University of Leeds, School of Computer Studies, 1995. Technical Report 95:25, available at http://www.scs.leeds.ac.uk/bms/papers.html. 49

18. R. J. Jr. Bayardo and R. C. Schrag. Using csp look-back techniques to solve exceptionally hard sat instances. In *Principles and Practice of Constraint Programming (CP-96)*, pages 46–60, 1996. 49

19. Fahiem Bacchus and Peter van Beek. On the conversion between non-binary and binary constraint satisfaction problems. In *Proceedings of the AAAI National Conference*, pages 311–318, 1998. 49

20. J.-C. Regin. *Developpement d'outils alogorithmiques pour l'Intelligence Artificielle. Application a la chimie.* PhD thesis, Universite Montpellier II, France, 1995. 50

21. Peter van Beek and Xinguang Chen. A constraint programming approach to planning. In *Proceedings of the AAAI National Conference*, pages 585–590, 1999. 50

Global Constraints as Graph Properties on a Structured Network of Elementary Constraints of the Same Type

Nicolas Beldiceanu

SICS, Lägerhyddvägen 18, SE-75237 Uppsala, Sweden
nicolas@sics.se

Abstract. This paper introduces a classification scheme for global constraints. This classification is based on a small number of basic ingredients from which one can generate almost all existing global constraints and come up with new interesting constraints. Global constraints are defined in a very concise way, in terms of graph properties that have to hold, where the graph is a structured network of same elementary constraints.

1   Introduction

Over the past ten years a variety of useful constraints have gradually been introduced in the finite domain constraint field [2], [13], [14], [17] in order to tackle scheduling, timetabling and vehicle routing problems. Quite often it appears that similar constraints were introduced with different naming schemes and different ways of presenting their arguments, this within different frameworks such as logic programming or object oriented programming.

If one looks to the operation research community, classifications have already been established in different areas. For example, if we consider scheduling, an early classification was settled by [10] and updated by [11]. One common feature of all these classifications is that they are problem oriented. It means that they try to capture the description a complete family of problems from a specific area with a general unambiguous classification scheme. For this purpose they use high-level domain dependent abstractions like non-renewable resource that are not derived from some kind of "first principle". This was motivated by the fact that persons wanted to characterize the complexity of the corresponding problems. However, from a constraint perspective one is more interested in classifying all the constraints that occur in different problems, rather than to classify the problems themselves. This is perhaps due to the fact that one hopes that the mathematical insight gained for one category of constraints will be relevant for all problems that mention this category of constraints. One other reason for trying to classify the constraints rather than the problems themselves is that the number of constraints should be in some sense "lower" than the number of problems.

R. Dechter (Ed.): CP 2000, LNCS 1894, pp. 52-66, 2000.
© Springer-Verlag Berlin Heidelberg 2000

The goal of this paper is to come up with a classification that is more related to the internal structure of the constraints rather than to specific problems areas. In the long term, one should be able to link the characteristics of a constraint to the algorithms that have to be used in order to perform test and pruning for that constraint. This classification is based on the following basic ingredients from which one can reconstruct almost all existing finite domain global constraints and come up with new interesting global constraints:

- basic data structures that are used in order to pass parameters to the constraints,
- elementary constraints (mainly unary and binary constraints),
- graphs with a regular structure (*i.e.* clique, grid, cycle, ..),
- properties on graphs structures (*i.e.* strongly connected component, source, ..).

We introduce the following two types of global constraints:

- simple global constraints are constraints for which one initially knows all variables that will be linked by a given condition.
- dynamic global constraints are constraints for which one has to enforce a condition on different sets of variables that are not initially explicitly known.

Sections 2, 3, 4 and 5 explain each ingredient separately, while sections 6 and 7 describe simple and dynamic global constraints in terms of these basic ingredients. Finally, section 8 presents different categories of global constraints.

2   Basic Data Types

Since constraints have to receive their arguments in some form, we first start to describe the abstract data types that we use in order to pass arguments to the constraints. The data types are not related to a specific programming language. If one wants to consider a specific language, then one has to map these abstract data types to the data types that are available within the considered programming language. This allows describing constraints in a way that is not related to any specific language.

We provide the following 3 basic data types "int", "atom" and "dvar" that respectively corresponds to an integer, to an atom and to a domain variable. In addition, we provide the following compound data types:

- $\text{list}(T)$: a list of elements of type T.
- $\text{term}(t,T_1,...,T_n)$: a term of arity n with a functor t and n arguments of given types $T_1,...,T_n$.
- $c:\text{collection}(A_1,...,A_n)$: a collection with name c of ordered items, each item having a set of attributes $A_1,...,A_n$; each attribute is described by one of the following expression $a\text{-}T$ or $a\text{-}T\text{-}d$ where a is the name of the attribute, T the type of the attribute and d a default value for the attribute.
- $T_1|...|T_n$: one of the specified types $T_1,...,T_n$; all the types $T_1,...,T_n$ should be pairwise exclusive: one should be able to decide for any instantiated data structure its type.

We use the following notation to describe instantiated data structures of the previous types:

- a list of elements $e_1,...,e_n$ is denoted $[e_1,...,e_n]$,
- a term with functor t and arguments $a_1,...,a_n$ is denoted $t(a_1,...,a_n)$,
- a collection of n items, each item having m attributes, is denoted $\{a_1 - v_{11}...a_m - v_{1m},...,a_1 - v_{n1}...a_m - v_{nm}\}$; each item is separated from the previous item by a comma.

3   Elementary Constraints

Examples of elementary constraints are described in the next table by using the following entries:
- Name provides a symbolic name for the constraint,
- Arity indicates the arity of the constraint; we use the letter "n" to show that a constraint can be used on any arity,
- Arguments describes the type of each argument,
- Parameters describes the type of each parameter (*i.e.* fixed values),
- Purpose explains what is the purpose of the constraint.

Table 1. Examples of elementary constraints between variables

NAME	ARITY	ARGUMENTS	PARAMETERS	PURPOSE
Eq	1	X:dvar	VAL:int	X = VAL
Equal	2	X,Y:dvar		X = Y
Diff	2	X,Y:dvar		X ≠ Y
Sum	n	Xi:dvar	INF:int SUP:int	INF ≤ΣXi ≤SUP
Card	n	Xi:dvar	VALS:collection(val-int) INF:int SUP:int	INF ≤ Σ(Xi in VALS) ≤SUP
SameDiff	2	X,Y:collection(p-dvar,q-dvar)		X.p-X.q = Y.p-Y.q[1]
Succ	2	X,Y:item[2] of NODES NODES:collection(index-int,succ-dvar)		X.succ = Y.index

4   Regular Structures

The purpose of this section is to describe the third basic ingredient that we use in order to define global constraints. This ingredient corresponds to directed hypergraphs [9], which have a very regular structure. They are defined in the following way. We consider c collections of items. Each collection denoted C_i $(1: i: c)$ has the same type of item and each attribute of an item is an integer or a domain variable.
- the vertices of the directed hypergraph are generated by a vertex generator, which takes as input the different collections of items C_i $(1: i: c)$ and produces one or

---

[1]   X.a denotes the value of attribute a of item X.
[2]   X,Y:item of NODES denotes the fact that X and Y are items of the NODES collection that is described below.

several collections of items, such that each item corresponds to one vertex of the directed hypergraph. The different available vertex generators will be described below.

- to all arcs of the directed hypergraph correspond the same n- ary constraint that involves n vertices in a given order[3]. Examples of these constraints, which are mainly unary and binary constraints, were described in the previous section. Since we are interested in regular structures, we describe all the arcs with a set of predefined arc generators that correspond to classical regular structures one can find in the graph literature [16, pages 140-153]. An arc generator takes the different collections of items produced by the vertex generator, a given arity n, and returns the corresponding directed hypergraph.

The available vertex generators are:

- the IDENTITY vertex generator takes one or several collections of items that have the same type and returns the same collections of items.
- the PAIR vertex generator takes one collection of items C where each item has n attributes, and returns a collection C' where each item has $2 \cdot n$ attributes. The items of collection C' are computed in the following way.

Let $|C|$ be the number of items of collection C, $\forall i \in 1..|C|$, $\forall j \in 1..|C|$:

- let $a_1 - v_{i,1} ... a_n - v_{i,n}$ be the ith item of collection C,
- let $a_1 - v_{j,1} ... a_n - v_{j,n}$ be the jth item of collection C.

Then $a_1 - v_{i,1} ... a_n - v_{i,n}, a_1 - v_{j,1} ... a_n - v_{j,n}$ is the $(i-1) \cdot |C| + j^{th}$ item of collection C'.

We now describe the arc generators. Table 2 gives examples of regular structures that we provide, where we apply each arc generator to two collections of items that respectively correspond to items a- 1, a- 2 and to items a- 3, a- 4. We use the following pictogram for the graphical representation of a constraint network. We employ a line for arity 1, an arrow for arity 2, and an ellipse in the other cases. In these last cases, since the vertices of an arc are ordered, a circle at one of the extremity of the ellipse indicates the "direction" of the ellipse. For example, the ellipse that contains vertices 1, 2 and 3 means that a 3-ary constraint is applied on items 1, 2, and 3 in this specific order. For the grid generator we indicate the size of the grid in each dimension. For example, in the case of two dimensions, we indicate the number of vertices in each line and each column.

Finally we mention that one can use more than one arc generator in order to generate the arcs of the directed hypergraph. This is actually the case for the last row of the previous table. The only restriction is that all arcs should have the same arity and correspond to the same elementary constraint. We now give two concrete examples of directed hypergraphs that one would have to create in order to describe some specific constraint.

- the first constraint is about a placement problem where one wants to impose that different rectangles do not overlap each other. The corresponding constraint takes

---

[3] Usually the edges of an hypergraph are not oriented [4, pages 1-2]. However for our purpose we need to define an order on the vertices of an edge since the corresponding n- ary constraint takes their arguments in a given order.

as argument a collection of items that is defined in the following way: RECTANGLES: collection(ori1-dvar, siz1-dvar, end1-dvar, ori2-dvar, siz2-dvar, end2-dvar). We use the arc generator CLIQUE to generate a binary constraint between each pairs of rectangles. Note that CLIQUE will also generate an arc between a vertex and itself.

- the second constraint is about a counting problem where one wants to count how many variables of a given set of variables take their value in a second set of variables. In this case we have two collections of items that are both defined in the following way: VARIABLES: collection(var-dvar). We use the arc generator PRODUCT to generate a binary constraint between each pair (VAR_1, VAR_2) of variables where the first variable VAR_1 belongs to the first collection and the second variable VAR_2 to the second collection.

Table 2. Examples of regular structures produced by the arc generator

ARC GENERATOR	ARC ARITY	EXAMPLE
SELF	1	
LOOP	2	
PATH	2	
PATH	3	
CIRCUIT	2	
CHAIN	2	
CYCLE	2	
GRID 2,2	2	
CLIQUE	2	
CLIQUE (<)	2	
PRODUCT	2	
PRODUCT (=)	2	
LOOP PATH	2	

5   Graph Properties

The purpose of this section is to describe the last basic ingredient that we use in order to define global constraints. This ingredient corresponds to graph characteristics, which we will define now. Lets us first introduce some basic vocabulary on graph.

An *oriented graph* G is a finite set $V(G)$ of vertices together with a set $E(G)$ of ordered pairs of vertices called directed edges or arcs. The *arc*, *path*, *circuit* and *strongly connected component* of a graph G correspond to oriented concepts, while the *edge, chain, cycle* and *connected component* are non-oriented concepts. However as it is reported in [8, page 6] a non-oriented graph can be seen as an oriented graph where to each edge we associate the corresponding two arcs.

We say that e_2 is a *successor* of e_1 if there exist an arc that starts from e_1 and ends at e_2. In the same way, we say that e_2 is a *predecessor* of e_1 if there exist an arc that starts from e_2 and ends at e_1.

A vertex of G that does not have any predecessor is called a *source*. A vertex of G that does not have any successor is called a *sink*.

A sequence $(e_1, e_2, ..., e_k)$ of edges of G such that each edge has a common vertex with the previous edge, and the other vertex common to the next edge is called a *chain* of length k. Each equivalence class of the relation "e_i is equal to e_j or there exist a chain between e_i and e_j" is a *connected component* of the graph G.

A sequence $(e_1, e_2, ..., e_k)$ of arcs of G such that for each arc e_i $(1: i < k)$ the end of e_i is equal to the start of the arc e_{i+1} is called a *path* of length k. Each equivalence class of the relation "e_i is equal to e_j or there exist a path between e_i and e_j" is a *strongly connected component* of the graph G.

A chain $(e_1, e_2, ..., e_k)$ of G is called a *cycle* if the same edge does not occur more than once in the chain and if the two extremities of the chain coincide. A cycle $(e_1, e_2, ..., e_k)$ of G is called a *circuit* if for each edge e_i $(1: i < k)$, the end of e_i is equal to the start of the edge e_{i+1}.

The *rank* function associated to the vertices $V(G)$ of a graph G that does not contain any circuit is defined in the following way:
- the rank of the vertices that do not have any predecessor (*i.e.* the sources) is equal to 0,
- the rank r of a vertex v that is not a source is the length of longest path $(e_1, e_2, ..., e_r)$ such that the start of the arc e_1 is a source and the end of arc e_r is the vertex v.

We list the different characteristics we consider for defining global constraints:
- NVERTEX: cardinality of the set $V(G)$.
- NARC: cardinality of the set $E(G)$.
- NARC_NO_LOOP: cardinality of the set $E(G)$ without considering the arcs that link the same vertices.
- NSOURCE: number of vertices that do not have any predecessor.

- NSINK: number of vertices that do not have any successor.
- NCC: number of connected components of graph G.
- NCC($COMP$, val): number of connected components of graph G such that the number of vertices nv of a connected component verifies the comparison test nv $COMP$ val; val is a non-negative integer and $COMP$ is one of the following tests =, >, $\leqslant$<, $\geq$.
- MIN_NCC: number of vertices of the smallest connected component of graph G.
- MAX_NCC: number of vertices of the largest connected component of graph G.
- RANGE_NCC: difference between the number of vertices of the largest connected component of graph G and the number of vertices of the smallest connected component of graph G.
- NSCC: number of strongly connected components of graph G.
- NSCC($COMP$, val): number of strongly connected components of graph G such that the number of vertices nv of a strongly connected component verifies the comparison test nv $COMP$ val; val is a non-negative integer and $COMP$ is one of the following tests =, >, $\leqslant$<, $\geq$.
- MIN_NSCC: number of vertices of the smallest strongly connected component of graph G.
- MAX_NSCC: number of vertices of the largest strongly connected component of graph G.
- RANGE_NSCC: difference between the number of vertices of the largest strongly connected component of graph G and the number of vertices of the smallest strongly connected component of graph G.
- MAX_IN_DEGREE: number of predecessors of the vertex of G that has the maximum number of predecessors without counting an arc from a vertex to itself.
- NTREE: number of vertices of graph G that do not belong to any circuit and for which at least one successor belongs to a circuit. Such vertices can be interpreted as root nodes of a tree.
- NTREE($ATTR$, $COMP$, val): number of vertices of graph G that do not belong to any circuit, and for which at least one successor belongs to a circuit, and for which value v of attribute $ATTR$ verifies the comparison test v $COMP$ val; $COMP$ is one of the following tests =, $\neq$.
- ORDER(r, d, $ATTR^+$): r and d are integers and $ATTR^+$ designates specific distinct attributes of the items associated to the vertices of graph G. ORDER(r, d, $ATTR^+$) returns the value of attributes $ATTR^+$ associated to the vertices of rank r (if several vertices have the same rank r then returns all corresponding values); ORDER(r, d, $ATTR^+$) returns a specified default value d if no such vertex exists. ORDER ignores the arcs that start and end on the same vertex.
- NSOURCE_EQ_NSINK: 1 if for each connected component the number of sources is equal to the number of sinks, else 0.
- NSOURCE_GREATEREQ_NSINK: 1 if for each connected component the number of sources is greater or equal to the number of sinks, else 0.

A last characteristic is computed on two graphs G_1 and G_2 that have the same set V of vertices and the sets $E(G_1)$ and $E(G_2)$ of arcs. This characteristic corresponds to:

- DISTANCE: cardinality of the set $(E(G_1)-E(G_2))\cup(E(G_2)-E(G_1))$. This is the number of arcs that belong to $E(G_1)$ but not to $E(G_2)$, plus the number of arcs that are in $E(G_2)$ but not in $E(G_1)$.

For directed hypergraphs, we will only consider the NARC characteristic.

6   Description of Simple Global Constraints

A simple global constraint is defined by:

- a term $t(A_1,...,A_m)$ where t corresponds to the name of the constraint and $A_1,...,A_m$ to its arguments, where each argument has a defined type, and where at least one of the arguments is a collection.
- a vertex generator, which takes an argument that is a collection and generates the vertices of the graph.
- an arc generator, which takes two arguments: the first one n is the number of vertices of the arcs (usually $n=2$) and the second argument is an n-ary elementary constraint.
- the graph properties that one wants to be verified on the final primal and dual graphs defined below are associated to an instantiated solution of the constraint.

We now introduce the notion of primal and dual graph according to a given instantiation of all variables that occur in the vertices of an initial graph that is associated to a global constraint. When these variables get instantiated then each n-ary constraint that is associated to an arc becomes either true or false. This creates a primal and a dual graph, which are respectively defined in the following way:

- the primal graph corresponds to the n-ary constraints that hold. A vertex of the initial graph belongs to the primal graph if it is involved in at least one n-ary constraint that holds. An arc belongs to the primal graph if the related constraint holds.
- the dual graph corresponds to the n-ary constraints that fail. A vertex of the initial graph belongs to the dual graph if this vertex is involved in at least one n-ary constraint that fails. An arc belongs to the dual graph if the related constraint fails.

Most of the time a global constraint will be defined by a graph property that has to hold on the primal graph. However certain global constraints require both the primal and the dual graph. Let us now give a small example of how one can define the $\text{nvalue}(D,\{V_1,..,V_n\})$ constraint, where $\{V_1,..,V_n\}$ is a collection of domain variables and D is a domain variable that is equal to the number of distinct values of $\{V_1,..,V_n\}$:

- the vertices of the graph correspond to the variables $V_1,...,V_n$,
- the arity of the constraint that is associated to each arc is 2,
- the constraint that is associated to each arc is the equality constraint,
- the arcs of the initial directed graph are construct with the CLIQUE arcs generator: each vertex is linked to each other vertex,

– the graph properties that one wants to be verified on the final primal graph that is associated to an instantiated solution corresponds to the fact that we want to have exactly D strongly connected components.

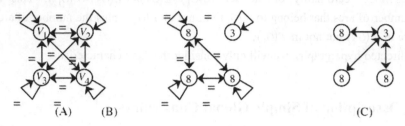

Fig. 1. The different graphs associated to $\text{nvalue}(D = 2, \{V_1 = 8, V_2 = 3, V_3 = 8, V_4 = 8\})$

The figure 1 shows the initial graph (A), the primal (B) and dual (C) graphs that are associated to the instantiation $V_1 = 8$, $V_2 = 3$, $V_3 = 8$ and $V_4 = 8$. For the initial graph we indicate in each vertex the corresponding variable, while we give the value of the variables in the case of the primal and dual graphs. Since the primal graph has two strongly connected components, the constraint $\text{nvalue}(2, \{8, 3, 8, 8\})$ is satisfied.

7   Description of Dynamic Global Constraints

The purpose of a dynamic global constraint is to enforce a condition on different subsets of variables, which are not known in advance. These constraints occur very often in practice and are hard to express since one cannot use a classical constraint for which it is required to provide all variables. One typical example of a dynamic global constraint is the *cumulative* constraint [1] where one wants to impose the sum of some variables to be less or equal than a given limit. In this case, each set of variables is defined by the height of the different tasks that overlap a given instant i. Since the origins of the tasks are not initially fixed, we don't know in advance which task will overlap a given instant and so, we cannot state any inequality constraint initially. A dynamic global constraint is defined in exactly the same way as a simple global constraint, except that we can eventually omit the graph properties, and that we have to provide the two following additional information:

– a generator of sets of vertices, which takes as argument the final primal graph and produces different sets of vertices.
– an elementary or a simple global constraint that one has to apply on each set created by the previous generator.

We now describe the different generators of sets of vertices that we provide:

– PATH(L) generates all paths of L distinct vertices of the primal graph,
– PATH(MAX) generates all maximum paths of distinct vertices of the primal graph,
– CC(MIN) generates all connected components with at least MIN vertices of the primal graph,

- ALL_CC(MIN) generates a set that corresponds to all connected components with at least MIN vertices of the primal graph,
- SCC(MIN) generates all strongly connected components with at least MIN vertices of the primal graph,
- ALL_SCC(MIN) generates a set that corresponds to all strongly connected components with at least MIN vertices of the primal graph,
- CLIQUE(MAX) generates all maximum cliques of the primal graph.

The PATH generator can only be used when the definition of the global constraint implies one of the following conditions:
- discarding the loops, all the vertices of the primal graph have exactly one predecessor.
- discarding the loops, all the vertices of the primal graph have exactly one successor.

The CLIQUE generator can only be applied when the primal graph is a subclass of intersection graphs [12] for which one can compute the maximum cliques in time polynomial in the number of vertices.

Let us now give a small example of how one can define the cumulative(*Tasks, Limit*) constraint, where *Tasks* is a collection of the form collection(*Index - int, Origin - dvar, Duration - dvar, Height - dvar*) and where *Limit* is a non-negative integer. The constraint holds if the following condition is true:

$$\forall i \in \text{IN} \qquad \sum_{j|Origin_j \le i < Origin_j + Duration_j} Height_j \le Limit . \qquad (1)$$

The *cumulative* global constraint is defined by:
- the vertices of the graph correspond to the different tasks of the collection *Tasks* ,
- the arity of the constraint that is associated to each arc is 2.
- the constraint that is associated to each arc is the overlapping constraint that holds if the corresponding two tasks intersect in time.
- the arcs of the initial directed graph are constructed with the CLIQUE(≠) arcs generator: each vertex is linked to each other vertex except itself.
- the sets generator is CLIQUE(MAX). Since the arc constraint is the overlapping constraint, the primal graph will be an interval graph on which one can compute the maximum cliques in a polynomial time according to the number of tasks.
- the dynamic constraint is that the sum of the heights of the tasks that are in a maximum clique should not exceed *Limit* .

The next figure shows the initial graph (A), the primal graph and the maximum cliques (B) that are associated to the following instance:

```
cumulative({Index-1 Origin-1 Duration-3  Height-1,
            Index-2 Origin-2 Duration-9  Height-2,
            Index-3 Origin-3 Duration-10 Height-1,
            Index-4 Origin-6 Duration-6  Height-1,
            Index-5 Origin-7 Duration-2  Height-3}, 8).
```

We indicate in each vertex the index of the corresponding task. On the primal graph an ellipse encloses each maximum clique. The constraint is satisfied, since for the two maximum cliques, the sum of the heights of the involved tasks does not exceed the maximum limit 8.

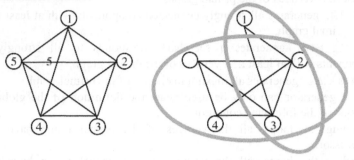

Fig. 2. Initial and primal graphs associated to the *cumulative* instance

8   A Catalogue of Global Constraints

Considering an application point of view, we have regrouped [3] the different global constraints under the following 11 categories:
- order constraints: minimum or maximum value according to some defined ordering relation,
- value constraints: how variables can take values,
- bipartite constraints: constraint involving a bipartite graph,
- value partitioning constraints: partition values according to an equivalence relation,
- sliding sequence constraints: elementary constraint on sliding sequences of variables that partially overlap,
- timetabling constraints: constraints expressing rules how people can work,
- neighborhood constraints: proximity between two series of variables according to a given elementary constraint,
- graph constraints: graph-partitioning constraints,
- scheduling constraints: resource-scheduling constraints,
- geometrical constraints: placement, alignment and crossing constraints,
- miscellaneous constraints: constraints that do not fit in one of the previous categories.

One advantage of the description of global constraints is that one can come with generic programs, which can be applied on any constraint that can be described, in order to perform basic tasks such as parsing and checking the arguments of a constraint, checking an instantiated solution or performing basic propagation. However coming with a general program for handling efficiently all the constraints is beyond our skill. Our approach is rather to create several families of global constraints for which we define one single specific constraint propagation algorithm. Each instance of a family is described by a set of small functions that are provided as parameters to the propagation algorithm associated to the given family. Within an existing family, this allows to define new variants of global constraints. Existing families for which we have provided a propagation algorithm are the *minimum* [5] family, the *number of distinct values* [5] family, the *cardinality-path* [6] family, the *non-overlaping* [4] family and the *maximum resource* [7] family. For instance, the *maximum resource* family regroups the constraints *assign_and_count*, *assign_and_nvalue, interval_and_sum, interval_and_count, bin_packing, cumulative, coloured_cumulative, cumulatives* and *coloured_cumulatives* introduced in [3]. We provide now two examples of new global constraints, which respectively correspond to a graph and to a geometrical constraint. A more complete set of about 70 global constraints examples can be found in [3].

8.1   The *map* Constraint

The *map* constraint is a new global constraint that is useful for covering a graph by a set of disjoint cycles and trees. It has the form map(*NBCYCLE, NBTREE, NODES*), where *NBCYCLE* and *NBTREE* are domain variables, and *NODES* is a collection of graph nodes of the form collection(*index* - int, *succ* - dvar). The *index* attribute gives a unique identifier for each node, while the *succ* attribute designates the successor node that will be used in the covering. *NBTREE* and *NBCYCLE* are respectively equal to the number of trees and the number of cycles of the partition that can be interpreted as a map. For a map, we take the definition from [15, page 459]: "every map decomposes into a set of connected components, also called connected maps. Each component consists of the set of all points that wind up on the same cycle, with each point on the cycle attached to a tree of all points that enter the cycle at that point.". Next figure gives an example of a solution of the *map* constraint.

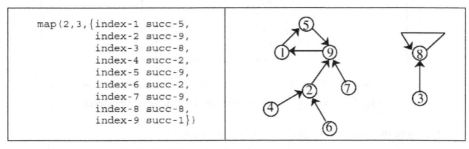

Fig. 3. A *map* constraint and its corresponding interpretation in term of graph

Let us now give the description of the *map* constraint:
- the vertices of the graph correspond to the nodes given in *NODES* ,
- the arity of the constraint that is associated to each arc is 2,
- the constraint that is associated to each arc is NODES.succ[1]=NODES.index[2] where [1] and [2] refers to the two arc extremities,
- the arcs of the initial directed graph are constructed with the CLIQUE arcs generator: each vertex is linked to each other vertex,

– the graph properties that one wants to be verified on the final graph that is associated to an instantiated solution corresponds to NCC=NBCYCLE and to NTREE=NBTREE. The first property enforces NBCYCLE to be equal to the number of connected components of the graph. The second property imposes NBTREE to be equal to the number of trees (*i.e.* number of vertices that do not belong to any circuit and for which at least one successor belongs to a circuit).

8.2   The *crossing* Constraint

The *crossing* constraint is a geometrical global constraint that is useful for controlling the number of line-segments intersections of a given set of line-segments. It has the form crossing(*NCROSS,SEGMENTS*), where *NCROSS* is a domain variable, and *SEGMENTS* is a collection of line-segments of the form collection(*ori_x*- dvar,*ori_y*- dvar,*end_x*- dvar,*end_y*- dvar). Each line-segment is described by the x and y coordinates of its two extremities. The constraint holds if *NCROSS* is equal to the number of line-segments intersections between the different line-segments. Next figure gives an example of a solution of the *crossing* constraint.

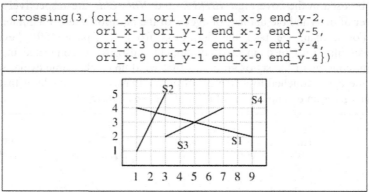

```
crossing(3,{ori_x-1 ori_y-4 end_x-9 end_y-2,
            ori_x-1 ori_y-1 end_x-3 end_y-5,
            ori_x-3 ori_y-2 end_x-7 end_y-4,
            ori_x-9 ori_y-1 end_x-9 end_y-4})
```

Fig. 4. A *crossing* constraint and the corresponding line-segments

Let us give the description of the *crossing* constraint:
– the vertices of the graph correspond to the line-segments given in *SEGMENTS* .
– the arity of the constraint that is associated to each arc is 2.
– the constraint that is associated to each arc is the intersection constraint between two line-segments.
– the arcs of the initial directed graph are construct with the CLIQUE(<) arcs generator. This allows generating one single arc for each pair of segments. Otherwise we would count more than once a given line-segments intersection.
– the graph properties that one wants to be verified on the final graph that is associated to an instantiated solution corresponds to NARC=NCROSS. It enforces NCROSS to be equal to the number of arcs of the final graph.

9   Conclusion

In this paper we have introduced a classification of global constraints that allows to reconstruct and to generalize almost all existing global constraints and to generate new interesting global constraints. A first advantage of this classification scheme is that it is not domain specific: it regroups constraints from different areas such as scheduling, placement, logistics, geometry and timetabling. A second benefit of this classification is that, since it is related to the internal structure of the constraint, it gives also an indication of the algorithms that will be associated to the constraints. It enlights the strong relationship between some global constraints that use a same graph property and binary constraints with the same structural properties. This will allow regrouping apparently differing global constraints in families for which one can hope to come up with similar algorithms. These algorithms will have to reuse and adapt some of the existing work that was done on efficient data structures and on graph algorithms. Finally a last benefit of this unified view is that, it should facilitate to perform in a systematic way such tasks as designing visualization interfaces, generating linear relaxations and expressing heuristics for global constraints.

Acknowledgements

Thanks to Per Kreuger for useful discussions and to Mats Carlsson and anonymous reviewers for comments on an earlier draft of this paper. The work has been founded by the Swedish National Board for Technical and Industrial Development, NUTEK, and by the Swedish Institute of Computer Science, SICS.

References

1.   Aggoun, A., Beldiceanu, N.: Extending CHIP in order to solve complex scheduling and placement problems, *Mathl. Comput. Modelling* 17 (7), 57-73 (1993).
2.   Beldiceanu, N., Contejean, E.: Introducing global constraint in CHIP. *Mathl. Comput. Modelling* Vol. 20, No. 12, 97-123 (1994).
3.   Beldiceanu, N.: Global Constraints as Graph Properties on Structured Network of Elementary Constraints of the Same Type. SICS Technical Report T2000/01, (2000).
4.   Beldiceanu, N.: Sweep as a generic pruning technique. SICS Technical Report T2000/08, (2000).
5.   Beldiceanu, N.: Pruning for the minimum constraint family and for the number of distinct values constraint family. SICS Technical Report T2000/10, (2000).
6.   Beldiceanu, N.: Pruning for the cardinality-path constraint family. SICS Technical Report T2000/11, (2000).
7.   Beldiceanu, N.: A generic sweep algorithm for the maximum resource constraint family. SICS Technical Report T2000/12, (2000).

8.   Berge, C.: *Graphes*. Dunod, 1970; Graphs, Second Revised Edition. North-Holland, New York (1985). In French.
9.   Berge, C.: *Hypergraphes, Combinatoire des ensembles finis*. Dunod, (1987). In French.
10. Graham, R. L., Lawler, E. L., Lenstra, J. K., Rinnooy Kan, A. H. G.: 'Optimization and approximation in deterministic sequencing and scheduling: a survey', *Ann. Discrete Math.*, 5, 287-326 (1979).
11. Herroelen, W., Demeulemeester, E., De Reyck, B.: A Classification Scheme for Project Scheduling Problems. in: Weglarz J. (Ed.), *Handbook on Recent advances in Project Scheduling*, Kluwer Academic Publishers, (1998).
12. McKee, T. A., McMorris, F. R.: *Topics in Intersection Graph Theory*. Siam Monographs on Discrete Mathematics and Applications, (February 1999).
13. Pesant, G., Soriano, P.: An Optimal Strategy for the Constrained Cycle Cover Problem. CRT Pub. no 98-65, (14 pages), (December 1998).
14. Régin, J-C.: Generalized Arc Consistency for Global Cardinality Constraint. In *Proc. of the Fourteenth National Conference on Artificial Intelligence* (AAAI-96), (1996).
15. Sedgewick, R., Flajolet, P.: *An introduction to the analysis of algorithms*. Addison-Wesley, (1996).
16. Skiena, S.: Implementing Discrete Mathematics. *Combinatoric and Graph Theory with Mathematica*. Addison-Wesley, (1990).
17. Zhou, J.: A permutation-based approach for solving the job-shop problem. *Constraints*, 2(2), 185-213, (1997).

Universally Quantified Interval Constraints

Frédéric Benhamou and Frédéric Goualard

Institut de Recherche en Informatique de Nantes
2, rue de la Houssinière, B.P. 92208, F-44322 Nantes Cedex 3
{benhamou,goualard}@irin.univ-nantes.fr

Abstract. Non-linear real constraint systems with universally and/or existentially quantified variables often need be solved in such contexts as control design or sensor planning. To date, these systems are mostly handled by computing a quantifier-free equivalent form by means of Cylindrical Algebraic Decomposition (CAD). However, CAD restricts its input to be conjunctions and disjunctions of polynomial constraints with rational coefficients, while some applications such as camera control involve systems with arbitrary forms where time is the only universally quantified variable. In this paper, the handling of universally quantified variables is first related to the computation of inner-approximation of real relations. Algorithms for solving non-linear real constraint systems with universally quantified variables are then presented along with the theoretical framework on inner-approximation of relations supporting them. These algorithms are based on the computation of outer-approximations of the solution set of the negation of involved constraints. An application to the devising of a declarative modeller for expressing camera motion using a cinematic language is sketched, and results from a prototype are presented.

1 Introduction

Interval constraint-based solvers such as clp(BNR) [8], ILOG Solver [18], and Numerica [24] have been shown to be efficient tools for solving some challenging non-linear constraint systems in various application areas (*e.g.* robotics, chemistry [16], or electronics [19]). Relying on *interval arithmetic* [17], these tools guarantee *completeness* (all solutions in the input are retained), and permit isolating punctual solutions with an "arbitrary" accuracy. Taking as input a constraint system and a Cartesian product of domains (intervals) for the variables occurring in the constraints, their output is a set S_o of boxes approximating each solution contained in the input box.

However, *soundness* is not guaranteed while it is sometimes a strong requirement. Consider, for instance, a civil engineering problem [20] such as floor design where retaining non-solution points may lead to a physically unfeasible structure. As pointed out by Ward *et al.* [25] and Shary [23], one may expect different properties from the boxes composing S_o depending on the problem at hand, namely: every element in any box is a solution, or there exists at least

R. Dechter (Ed.): CP 2000, LNCS 1894, pp. 67–82, 2000.
© Springer-Verlag Berlin Heidelberg 2000

one solution in each box. The foregoing solvers ensure only, at best, the second property.

Furthermore, problems originating from *camera control* [12], *sensor planning* [1], and *control design* [2], not only require the output boxes to contain only solution points, but also that some input variables be universally quantified.

To date, constraint systems with universally/existentially quantified variables have mainly be handled by symbolic methods, among which one may single out Cylindrical Algebraic Decomposition (CAD) by Collins [11]. CAD is quite a powerful method since it permits handling more than one quantified variable for disjunctions/conjunctions of constraints. However, it has strong requirements on the form of the constraints it processes since they are limited to polynomial constraints. As far as camera control is concerned though, only one quantified variable—time—needs to be dealt with for conjunctions of (not necessarily polynomial) constraints. Consequently, there is room for a tailored algorithm to specifically solve temporal constraints.

This paper first presents an algorithm whose output is a set of sound boxes of variable domains for some constraint system. Soundness is achieved by computing *inner approximations* of the underlying real relations, using *box consistency* [7]—a well-known, efficient, *local consistency*—on the negation of the involved constraints. An algorithm is then applied to the solving of constraint systems where one variable is universally quantified. An application to temporal constraints arising from camera motion modelling (*virtual cameraman problem* [14]) is sketched: following the work of Jardillier and Languénou, a prototype for a declarative modeller has been devised, which should eventually allow a non-technician user to control the positioning of a camera by means of cinematic specifications of a *shot* (short "scene").

The outline of the paper is as follows: Section 2 introduces notations and some basic notions related to interval constraint solving: interval representation of real quantities, approximation of relations by supersets, and local consistencies are surveyed. Next, the notion of *inner approximation* of real relations is formally introduced in Section 3, and then related to the solving of constraints containing occurrences of universally quantified variables; the corresponding algorithms are given and compared to a previous approach by Jardillier and Languénou. The prototype of a declarative modeller for camera positioning is presented in Section 4; heuristics for speeding-up computation, along with results on some benchmarks are then given. Finally, Section 5 compares our approach with previous works in the field, and discusses directions for future researches.

2   Interval Constraint Solving

Finite representation of numbers by computers prevents them solving accurately real constraints. *Interval constraint solving* relies on *interval arithmetic* [17] to compute verified approximate solutions of real constraint systems. Underlying real relations may be approximated by considering one of their computer-representable superset or subset. This section presents the basics related to the approximation of real relations the conservative way. Safe approximation by a subset is deferred until the next section.

The organization of the section is as follows: the shift from reals to *bounds* (numbers together with a "bracket") is first described; the notion of open and closed interval relying on bounds is then introduced, followed by a presentation of the way real relations are approximated and interval constraint systems solved.

The reader is referred to the above-mentionned references for a thorough presentation of interval arithmetic. A great part of what is exposed in the following is drawn from [8] and [4]. Proofs not given here may be found in these papers.

2.1   Approximation of a Relation

Solving real constraints requires the ability to represent the underlying relations. The approximate representation by a superset (Cartesian product of intervals) is described in the following.

From Reals to Floating-Point Intervals Let $\mathbb{R}$ be the set of reals and $\mathbb{F} \subset \mathbb{R}$ a finite subset of reals corresponding to *floating-point numbers*. Sets $\mathbb{R}$ and $\mathbb{F}$ are compactified in the usual way by using symbols $-\infty$ and $+\infty$. Let $\mathbb{F}^{\infty} = \mathbb{F} \cup \{-\infty, +\infty\}$. Hereafter, r and s (resp. g and h), possibly subscripted, are assumed to be elements of $\mathbb{R}$ (resp. $\mathbb{F}^{\infty}$).

Four new symbols (*brackets*) are introduced: let $\mathcal{L} = \{(, [\}$ and $\mathcal{U} = \{),]\}$ be respectively the set of left and right brackets. Let $\mathcal{B} = \mathcal{L} \cup \mathcal{U}$ be the *set of brackets* totally ordered by the ordering $\prec$ defined as follows [9]: $) \prec [\prec \prec ($.

The set of *floating-point bounds* $\mathbb{F}^{\diamond}$ is defined from $\mathcal{B}$ and $\mathbb{F}$ as follows:

$$\mathbb{F}^{\diamond} = \mathbb{F}^{\triangleleft} \cup \mathbb{F}^{\triangleright} \quad \text{where} \quad \begin{cases} \mathbb{F}^{\triangleleft} = (\mathbb{F} \times \mathcal{L} \cup \{\langle -\infty, (\rangle, \langle +\infty, (\rangle\}) \\ \mathbb{F}^{\triangleright} = (\mathbb{F} \times \mathcal{U} \cup \{\langle -\infty,)\rangle, \langle +\infty,)\rangle\}) \end{cases}$$

Real bounds set $\mathbb{R}^{\diamond}$ is defined likewise. Given a bound $\beta = \langle x, \alpha \rangle$, let $\beta|_v = x$ and $\beta|_b = \alpha$. Floating-point bounds are totally ordered by the ordering $\triangleleft$: $\forall \beta_1 = \langle g, \alpha_1 \rangle, \beta_2 = \langle h, \alpha_2 \rangle \in \mathbb{F}^{\diamond} \colon \beta_1 \triangleleft \beta_2 \iff (g < h) \vee (g = h \wedge \alpha_1 \prec \alpha_2)$. A similar ordering may be defined over $\mathbb{R}^{\diamond}$.

For each $g \in \mathbb{F}^{\infty}$, let g^{+} be the smallest element in $\mathbb{F}^{\infty}$ greater than g, and g^{-} the greatest element in $\mathbb{F}^{\infty}$ smaller than g (with the IEEE 754 conventions: $(+\infty)^{+} = +\infty$, $(-\infty)^{-} = -\infty$, $(+\infty)^{-} = \max(\mathbb{F})$, $(-\infty)^{+} = \min(\mathbb{F})$).

Bounds are used to construct intervals as follows: let $\mathbb{I}_{o} = \mathbb{F}^{\triangleleft} \times \mathbb{F}^{\triangleright}$ be the set of *closed/open floating-point intervals* (henceforth referred to *intervals*), with the following notations used as shorthands: $(\langle g, [\rangle, \langle h,]\rangle) \equiv [g .. h] \equiv \{r \in \mathbb{R} \mid g \leqslant r \leqslant h\}$, $(\langle g, [\rangle, \langle h,)\rangle) \equiv [g .. h) \equiv \{r \in \mathbb{R} \mid g \leqslant r < h\}$, and so on.

For the sake of simplicity, the empty set $\varnothing$ is uniquely represented in $\mathbb{I}_{o}$ by the interval $(+\infty .. -\infty)$. Let $\mathbb{I}_{\square} \subset \mathbb{I}_{o}$ be the set of *closed intervals*, together with the two special intervals: $(-\infty .. +\infty)$ and $(+\infty .. -\infty)$.

In the rest of the paper, interval quantities are written uppercase, reals or floats are sans-serif lowercase, and vectors are in boldface. A Cartesian product of n intervals $\mathbf{B} = I_1 \times \cdots \times I_n$ is called a *box*. A non-empty interval $I = (\beta_1, \beta_2)$ with $\beta_1 \in \mathbb{F}^{\lhd}$ and $\beta_2 \in \mathbb{F}^{\rhd}$ is said *canonical* whenever $\beta_2|_v \leqslant (\beta_1|_v)^+$. An n-ary box $\mathbf{B}$ is canonical whenever the intervals $I_1, \ldots, I_n$ are canonical. Given an interval $I = (\beta_1, \beta_2)$, let $\inf(I) = \beta_1|_v$ and $\sup(I) = \beta_2|_v$. Given a variable v, an interval I, and boxes $\mathbf{B}$ and $\mathbf{D}$, let $\mathsf{Dom}_{\mathbf{B}}(v) \in \mathbb{I}_\circ$ be the domain of v in box $\mathbf{B}$, $\mathbf{B}|_k = I_k$, the *k-th projection of* $\mathbf{B}$, and $\mathbf{B}|_{v,\mathbf{D}}$ (resp. $\mathbf{B}|_{v,I}$) the box obtained by replacing v's domain in box $\mathbf{B}$ by its domain in box $\mathbf{D}$ (resp. by interval I); given an interval J, let $\mathbf{B}|_{I_k,J}$ be the box $I_1 \times \cdots \times I_{k-1} \times J \times I_{k+1} \times \cdots \times I_n$. Given boxes $\mathbf{B}$ and $\mathbf{D}$, let $\mathbf{B} \setminus \mathbf{D} \subseteq \mathcal{P}(\mathbb{I}_\circ^n)$ be the set of boxes obtained from complementing $\mathbf{B}$ from $\mathbf{D}$.

Approximating a Relation by a Box This section introduces some more notations on constraints, sets, and relations, then presents the notion of *outer approximation, viz.* the approximation of a real relation by a computer-representable superset.

Let $\mathcal{V}_{\mathbb{R}} = \{x_1, x_2, \ldots\}$ (resp. $\mathcal{V}_{\mathbb{I}_\circ} = \{X_1, X_2, \ldots\}$) be a set of variables taking their values over $\mathbb{R}$ (resp. $\mathbb{I}_\circ$). Given $\Sigma_1 = \langle \mathbb{R}, \mathcal{F}_1, \mathcal{R}_1 \rangle$ a structure, a *real constraint* is defined as a first-order formula built from Σ_1 and $\mathcal{V}_{\mathbb{R}}$. An *interval constraint* is defined in the same way over the structure $\Sigma_2 = \langle \mathbb{I}_\circ, \mathcal{F}_2, \mathcal{R}_2 \rangle$ and $\mathcal{V}_{\mathbb{I}_\circ}$.

Without loss of generality, we take n as the default arity of a function, a constraint, or a relation, and k an integer belonging to the set $\{1, \ldots, n\}$. Sets are written in uppercase calligraphic letters. The power set of a set $\mathcal{S}$ is written $\mathcal{P}(\mathcal{S})$. Given a real constraint $c(x_1, \ldots, x_n)$ (resp. an interval constraint $C(X_1, \ldots, X_n)$), ρ_c (resp. ρ_C) denotes the underlying relation—that is, the subspace made of "points" verifying the constraint. For the sake of readability, the relation ρ_{c_i} for some constraint c_i is written ρ_i whenever that notation is non-ambiguous. Given an n-ary constraint c, let $\bar{c}$ be $\neg c$, implying that $\rho_{\bar{c}} = \mathbb{R}^n \setminus \rho_c$.

A real relation ρ may be conservatively approximated by the smallest (w.r.t. set inclusion) union of boxes $\mathsf{Union}_\circ(\rho)$ (resp. the smallest box, $\mathsf{Outer}_\circ(\rho)$) containing it. These operators have closed counterparts $\mathsf{Union}_\square(\rho)$ and $\mathsf{Outer}_\square(\rho)$. $\mathsf{Outer}_\circ(\rho)$ is a coarser approximation than $\mathsf{Union}_\circ(\rho)$ but is far more used, it being computationally easier to obtain.

Given a function f defined over reals, an *interval extension* of f is a function F defined over intervals as follows: $\forall I_1, \ldots, \forall I_n \in \mathbb{I}_\circ : r_1 \in I_1, \ldots, r_n \in I_n \Rightarrow f(r_1, \ldots, r_n) \in F(I_1, \ldots, I_n)$. An *interval extension of a real constraint c* is an interval constraint C defined by: $\forall I_1, \ldots, \forall I_n \in \mathbb{I}_\circ : \exists a_1 \in I_1 \wedge \cdots \wedge \exists a_n \in I_n \wedge c(a_1, \ldots, a_n) \Rightarrow C(I_1, \ldots, I_n)$.

The *projection* of an interval constraint $C(X_1, \ldots, X_n)$ w.r.t. an index $k \in \{1, \ldots, n\}$ and a box $\mathbf{B} = I_1 \times \cdots \times I_n$, written $C|_{k,\mathbf{B}}$, is defined as the univariate interval constraint obtained by replacing all variables X_j but X_k with the corresponding intervals I_j.

2.2   Local Consistencies

Discarding all inconsistent values from a box of variable domains is intractable when the constraints are real ones (consider, for instance, the constraint $\sin(x) = 1, x \in [0 .. 2]$). Consequently, weak consistencies have been devised among which one may cite *hull consistency* [4] and *box consistency* [7]. Both consistencies permit narrowing variable domains to (hopefully) smaller domains, preserving the solution set. Since box consistency alone is used as a basis for the algorithms to be introduced in Section 3, it is the only one to be presented thereunder.

Contracting Operators Depending on the considered consistency, one may define different contracting operators for a constraint. In this section, box consistency is first formally presented. Therefrom, an operator based on it is given. The definition for box consistency given below is an instance of the extended one stated by Benhamou *et al.* [5] that slightly differs from the original definition [7] in that it is parameterized by approximation operators.

Definition 1 (Box consistency [5]) *Let c be a real constraint, C an interval extension for c, and $\mathbf{B} = I_1 \times \cdots \times I_n$ a box. The constraint c is said* box-consistent w.r.t. $\mathbf{B}$ *if and only if:*

$$\forall k \in \{1, \ldots, n\}: \quad I_k = \mathsf{Outer}_\circ(I_k \cap \{\mathsf{r} \in \mathbb{R} \mid \mathsf{Outer}_\circ(\{\mathsf{r}\}) \in \rho_{C|_{k,\mathbf{B}}}\})$$

Intuitively, a constraint c is box-consistent w.r.t. a box $\mathbf{B}$ when each projection $I_j, j \in \{1, \ldots, n\}$, of $\mathbf{B}$ is the smallest interval containing all the elements that cannot be distinguished from solutions of $C|_{k,\mathbf{B}}$ due to the inherently limited precision of the computation with floating-point numbers.

Using box consistency to narrow down the variable domains of a constraint leads to the notion of *outer-box contracting operator*:

Definition 2 (Outer-box contracting operator) *Given an n-ary constraint c and a box $\mathbf{B}$, an outer-box contracting operator $\mathsf{OCb}_c \colon \mathbb{I}_\circ^n \longrightarrow \mathbb{I}_\circ^n$ for c is defined by:*

$$\mathsf{OCb}_c(\mathbf{B}) = \max\{\mathbf{B}' \mid \mathbf{B}' \subseteq \mathbf{B}$$
$$\textit{and } c \textit{ is box-consistent w.r.t. } k \in \{1, \ldots, n\} \textit{ and } \mathbf{B}'\}$$

Proposition 1 (Completeness of OCb) *Given a constraint c, the following relation does hold for any box $\mathbf{B}$: $(\mathbf{B} \cap \rho_c) \subseteq \mathsf{OCb}_c(\mathbf{B})$.*

The consistency and the associated contracting operator considered so far are such that completeness is guaranteed (no solution is lost during the narrowing process). Devising operators ensuring soundness of the results is the topic of the next section.

3 Solving Constraints with Universally Quantified Variables

Constraints arising from the translation of some desired properties for camera control and pathplanning are usually of the form: given I_v, find $x_1, \ldots, x_n$ such that:

$$\forall v \in I_v : c(x_1, \ldots, x_n, v) \qquad (1)$$

From a practical standpoint, Eq. (1) must be translated into a stronger statement in order to allow picking out values from the variable (interval) domains, *viz.* : given I_v, find intervals $I_1, \ldots, I_n$ such that:

$$\forall x_1 \ldots \forall x_n \forall v : v \in I_v \wedge x_1 \in I_1 \wedge \cdots \wedge x_n \in I_n \Rightarrow c(x_1, \ldots, x_n, v)$$

The computed boxes need then be included into the relation ρ_c. More generally, solving constraints with an explicitly universally quantified variable boils down in practice to computing a (subset of) the "inner approximation" of real relations.

Several definitions for the inner-approximation of a real relation exist in the literature, depending on the intended application. Given an n-ary relation ρ, one may single out at least the two following definitions for an inner approximation $\mathsf{Inner}(\rho)$ of ρ:

1. **Def. A.** $\mathsf{Inner}(\rho) = \mathbf{B}_1$, where $\mathbf{B}_1 \in \{\mathbf{B} \in \mathbb{I}_\circ^n \mid \mathbf{B} \subseteq \rho\}$ (an inner-approximation is any box included in the relation) [15,3];
2. **Def. B.** $\mathsf{Inner}(\rho) = \mathbf{B}_1$, where $\mathbf{B}_1 \in \{\mathbf{B} = I_1 \times \cdots \times I_n \mid \mathbf{B} \subseteq \rho \wedge \forall j \in \{1, \ldots, n\}, \forall I_j' \supseteq I_j : \mathbf{B}|_{I_j, I_j'} \subseteq \rho \Rightarrow I_j' = I_j\}$ (an inner-approximation is a box included in the relation that cannot be extended in any direction without containing non-solution points) [23].

In this paper, we consider the following stronger definition for the inner-approximation of a relation :

- **Def. C.** $\mathsf{Inner}(\rho) = \{r \in \mathbb{R}^n \mid \mathsf{Outer}_\circ(\{r\}) \subseteq \rho\}$ (the inner-approximation contains all the elements whose enclosing box is included in the relation).

Definitions **A** and **B** imply that disconnected relations are only very partially represented by only one box, a drawback that is avoided when using Def. **C**.

This section first introduces the notion of inner approximation of a relation ρ (that is the approximation by a computable subset of ρ) based on Def. **C**. Contracting operators to compute this approximation are then defined. Therefrom, an algorithm due to Jardillier and Languénou [14] for solving constraint systems with one universally quantified variable is presented. A new approach based on the use of the complete but unsound operators presented in Section 2.2 for the negation of the involved constraints is then described, and compared to the one of Jardillier and Languénou.

Due to lack of space, the reader is referred to the associated research report [6] for the proofs of the propositions to be stated below.

3.1   Computing Inner Sets

From Def. **C** above, an inner-approximation operator may be defined as follows:

Definition 3 (Inner approximation operator) *Given an n-ary relation* ρ, *an inner-approximation operator* $\mathsf{Inner_o} \colon \mathbb{R}^n \to \mathbb{R}^n$ *is defined by:*

$$\mathsf{Inner_o}(\rho) = \{\mathsf{r} \in \mathbb{R}^n \mid \mathsf{Outer_o}(\{\mathsf{r}\}) \subseteq \rho\}$$

The Inner approximation operator enjoys the following properties:

Proposition 2 (Inner approximation operator properties) *The* Inner *operator is contracting, monotone, idempotent, and distributive w.r.t. the union and intersection of subsets of* $\mathbb{R}^n$.

Inner Contracting Operators   The narrowing of variable domains occurring in a constraint is done in the same way as in the outer-approximation case: an *inner-contracting operator* associated to each constraint discards from the initial box all the inconsistent values along with some consistent values. The result is a set of boxes.

Definition 4 (Inner-contracting operator) *Let c be an n-ary constraint. An* inner-contracting operator *for c is a function* $\mathsf{IC}_c \colon \mathbb{I}_o^n \to \mathcal{P}(\mathbb{I}_o^n)$ *verifying:*

$$\forall \mathbf{B} \colon \mathsf{IC}_c(\mathbf{B}) \subseteq \mathsf{Inner_o}(\mathbf{B} \cap \rho_c)$$

Proposition 3 (Soundness of IC) *Given a constraint c and an inner-contracting operator* IC_c *for c, we have:* $\forall \mathbf{B} \colon \mathsf{IC}_c(\mathbf{B}) \subseteq (\mathbf{B} \cap \rho_c)$.

Inner-contracting operators with stronger properties (computation of the greatest representable set included in a relation) may also be defined. These operators are *optimal* in the sense that $\mathsf{IC}_c(\mathbf{B}) = \mathsf{Inner_o}(\mathbf{B} \cap \rho_c)$ for any box $\mathbf{B}$.

Devising an inner-contracting operator for a constraint is not as easy as devising an outer-contracting operator since interval techniques only permit to enforce some partial consistencies, that is, discarded values are guaranteed to be non-solutions while no information is known about those that are kept. However, it will be shown in Section 3.2 that outer-contracting operators may be used to obtain inner approximations provided they are applied onto the negation of the considered constraints.

The next section addresses the problem of solving constraint systems where each constraint possesses an occurrence of a universally quantified variable v. The first approach to be described, due to Jardillier and Languénou [14], relies on an evaluation/bisection process to compute an inner-approximation of the underlying relations considering v as a given constant domain.

3.2   Universally Quantified Variables

Given an $(n+1)$-ary constraint $c(x_1, \ldots, x_n, x_v)$ and a box $\mathbf{B} = I_1 \times \cdots \times I_n \times I_v$, applying an inner-contracting operator IC_c to $\mathbf{B}$ outputs a set of boxes $U = \{\mathbf{B}'_1, \ldots, \mathbf{B}'_p\}$ where each $\mathbf{B}'_j = D_1 \times \cdots \times D_n \times D_v$ is a sub-box of $\mathbf{B}$ such that: $\forall r_1 \in D_1, \ldots, \forall r_n \in D_n, \forall r_v \in D_v \colon c(r_1, \ldots, r_n, r_v)$ does hold.

Therefore, solving a constraint of the form $\forall v \in I_v \colon c(x_1, \ldots, x_n, v)$ boils down to retaining only boxes $\mathbf{B}' = D_1 \times \cdots \times D_n \times D_v$ of U such that $D_v = I_v$.

In this paper, we address the case of only one explicitly quantified variable. Given a constraint c and a variable v occurring in c, the underlying relation for the constraint $\forall v \in I_v \colon c$ is written $\tilde{\rho}_{c,v,I_v}$. When the names of the variable and its domain are non-ambiguous, the notation is shortened into $\tilde{\rho}_c$.

The Evaluation Approach In order to tighten a box $\mathbf{B}$ of variable domains for a problem of the form $\forall v \in I_v \colon c_1 \wedge \cdots \wedge c_m$, Jardillier and Languénou [14], compute an inner approximation of $\rho_1 \cap \cdots \cap \rho_m$ by decomposing the initial domain I_v of v into canonical intervals $I_v^1, \ldots, I_v^p$, and testing with a function of global satisfaction $\mathsf{GlobSat}$ whether $c_1 \wedge \cdots \wedge c_m$ does hold for the boxes $I_1 \times \cdots \times I_n \times I_v^1, \ldots, I_1 \times \cdots \times I_n \times I_v^p$. These evaluations give results in a three-valued logic (*true*, *false*, *unknown*). Boxes labeled *true* contain only solutions, boxes labeled *false* contain no solution at all, and boxes labeled *unknown* are recursively split and re-tested until they may be asserted true or false, or canonicity is reached. Retained boxes are those verifying:

$$\forall j \in \{1, \ldots, p\} \colon \mathsf{eval}_{\{c_1 \wedge \cdots \wedge c_m\}}(I_1 \times \cdots \times I_n \times I_v^j) = true \qquad (2)$$

In this paper, we will call this algorithm EIA4. This process is, in some way, related to the work of Sam-Haroud and Faltings [21] where true, false, or unknown boxes are organized into 2^k-trees to ease the computation of global consistencies.

Equation (2) implies that each retained box is included in the inner-approximation of ρ_c. Consequently, the property verified by each of them is the strong statement: $\forall x_1 \ldots \forall x_n \forall v \colon v \in I_v \wedge x_1 \in I_1 \wedge \cdots \wedge x_n \in I_n \Rightarrow c_1 \wedge \cdots \wedge c_m$.

Inner Approximation by Negation This section presents algorithms narrowing variable domains and handling one universally quantified variable by reasoning on the negation of the considered constraints. The algorithms described hereafter implement inner-contracting operators for every n-ary constraint c by using $\mathsf{OCb}_{\bar{c}}$. Since values discarded by this operator are guaranteed to be non-solution for $\bar{c}$—by completeness of OCb (see Prop. 1)—, they are guaranteed solutions for c. Formally, a statement of the form $\forall v \in I_v \colon c(x_1, \ldots, x_n, v)$ is replaced by $\neg \exists v \colon v \in I_v \wedge \neg c(x_1, \ldots, x_n, v)$ where Statement $\exists v \colon v \in I_v \wedge \neg c(x_1, \ldots, x_n, v)$ can be handled by the OCb operator. More generally, a constraint system of the form $\forall v \in I_v^1 \colon c_1(x_1, \ldots, x_n, v) \wedge \cdots \wedge \forall v \in I_v^m \colon c_m(x_1, \ldots, x_n, v)$ may be translated into the system $[\neg \exists v \colon v \in I_v^1 \wedge \neg c_1(x_1, \ldots, x_n, v)] \wedge \cdots \wedge [\neg \exists v \colon v \in I_v^m \wedge \neg c_m(x_1, \ldots, x_n, v)]$ where conjunctions at the highest level have been preserved.

Algorithm ICAb3, based on box consistency, to solve one constraint with a universally quantified variable is first presented below (see Alg. 1). Algorithm ICAb5 that handles several constraints is then described.

Proposition 4 (Correctness of ICAb3) *Let c be a constraint, ρ its underlying relation, v a variable, and* **B** *a box. Then, Alg. ICAb3 implements an inner-contracting operator for $\forall v \in \text{Dom}_\mathbf{B}(v)\colon c$.*

Remark 1 *One may note that Line 8 in Alg. 1 may be replaced by "$(\mathbf{D_1}, \mathbf{D_2}) \leftarrow$ $\text{Split}_v(\mathbf{D})$," provided that the initial domain I_v^0 of Variable v is passed as a parameter of ICAb3; Line 6 would then become: "$\mathcal{W} \leftarrow \mathbf{B} \setminus \mathbf{D}|_{v, I_v^0}$."*

Alg. 1. ICAb3_c – Inner contracting algorithm for $\forall v \in \text{Dom}_\mathbf{B}(v)\colon c$

```
1  ICAb3_c(in: B ∈ I_o^n, v ∈ V_ℝ;  out: W ∈ P(I_o^n))
2  begin
3        B' ← OCb_c(B)
4        if (Dom_B'(v) = Dom_B(v)) then
5              D ← OCb_c̄(B')
6              W ← B' \ D|_{v,B'}
7              if (D ≠ ∅ and ¬Canonical_v(D)) then
8                    (D_1, D_2) ← Split_v(D|_{v,B'})
9                    W ← W ∪ ICAb3_c(D_1, v) ∪ ICAb3_c(D_2, v)
10             endif
11             return (W)
12       else
13             return (∅)
14 end
```

Function Split_v splits in two intervals one of the non-canonical domains of **D**. Domain $\text{Dom}_\mathbf{D}(v)$ is never considered for splitting. In the same way, Canonical_v tests canonicity for all domains but the one of variable v.

It is also worthwhile noting that lines 3 and 4 in Alg. ICAb3 are only present to speed up computation: box consistency is first tested for the input box **B***; if the domain of the universally quantified variable is narrowed at this stage, it is no longer necessary to continue further since it implies that there is no solution to the constraint $\forall v \in \text{Dom}_\mathbf{B}(v)\colon c$.*

Handling constraint systems of the form:

$$(\forall v \in I^1 : c_1) \wedge \cdots \wedge (\forall v \in I^m : c_m)$$

is done by Alg. ICAb5 (Alg. 2) as follows: each constraint of the system is considered in turn together with the sets of elements verifying all the considered constraints theretofore; the point concerning Alg. ICAb5 lies in that *each constraint needs only be invoked once*, since after having been considered for the first time, the elements remaining in the variable domains are all solutions of the constraint. As a consequence, narrowing some domain later does not require additional work.

Proposition 5 (Soundness of ICAb5) *Let* $\mathcal{S} = \{(c_1, I^1), \ldots, (c_m, I^m)\}$ *be a set of pairs made of a constraint and a domain. Given* $\mathbf{B}$ *a box and* v *a variable, we have:*

$$\mathsf{ICAb5}(\mathcal{S}, \{\mathbf{B}\}, v) \subseteq \mathsf{Inner}_\circ(\mathbf{B} \cap \tilde{\rho}_1 \cap \cdots \cap \tilde{\rho}_m)$$

Comparison of Evaluation *vs.* Negation Approaches

Proposition 6 (EIA4 *vs.* ICAb5) *Let* v *be a variable,* $\mathbf{B}$ *a box,* I_v, *the domain of* v *in* $\mathbf{B}$, *and* $\mathbf{g} = \inf(I_v)$. *Given* $\mathcal{S} = \{(c_1, I_v), \ldots, (c_m, I_v)\}$, *the following property does hold:*

$$\mathsf{EIA4}(\{c_1, \ldots, c_m\}, \mathbf{B}, v, \mathbf{g}) \subseteq \mathsf{ICAb5}(\mathcal{S}, \{\mathbf{B}\}, v)$$

Alg. 2. ICAb5 – Inner contracting algorithm for $\forall v \in I^1 : c_1 \wedge \cdots \wedge \forall v \in I^m : c_m$

```
1  ICAb5(in: S = {(c₁, I¹),...,(cₘ, Iᵐ)}, A ∈ P(𝕀ₒⁿ), v ∈ 𝒱ℝ; out: 𝒲 ∈ P(𝕀ₒⁿ))
2  begin
3      if (S ≠ ∅) then
4          B ← ∅
5          foreach D ∈ A do
7              B ← B ∪ ICAb3_c₁(D|_{v,I¹}, v,)
9          endforeach
10         if (B = ∅) then
11             return (∅)
12         else
13             return (ICA4(S \ {(c₁, I¹)}, B, v))
14         endif
15     else
16         return (A)
17     endif
18 end
```

Proposition 6 ensures us that decomposing the domain of the universally quantified variable into canonical intervals does not enhance the precision of the computed inner set.

Let ξ_j be the number of floating-point numbers in Interval I_j, and $\xi = \max_j \xi_j$. For a constraint system composed of m n-ary constraints, the number of calls to GlobSat in EIA4 in the worst case is:

$$\Gamma = m^n \prod_{i=1}^n (2\xi_i - 3) = O((m\xi)^n)$$

In the worst case, the number of calls to Alg. OCb in Alg. ICAb5 is also in $O((m\xi)^n)$. However, this evaluation is very pessimistic and does not reflect accurately what happens in practice: as it will be shown in Section 4.3, the filtering induced by Alg. ICAb5 when considering each constraint in turn drastically reduces the number of boxes to consider later, thus speeding up the computation.

Restricting the general framework: correctness In the sequel of this paper, the results presented so far are instantiated for a limited class of constraints, namely inequalities (constraints of the form: $f(x_1, \ldots, x_n) \diamond 0$ with $\diamond \in \{\leqslant, \geqslant\}$. Moreover, only closed intervals are used. Nevertheless, soundness of the algorithms is preserved since computed outer-approximations for the negation of the constraints may only be greater than the one computed on $\mathbb{I}_o$. Operator GlobSat used in Alg. EIA4 is implemented by a straight evaluation over intervals of $f(x_1, \ldots, x_n)$ to determine whether it is greater or equal (resp. lower or equal) to zero.

4   Experimental Results

The algorithms presented in Section 3 have been validated in the context of a high-level declarative modeller for camera motion. In this section, the benchmarks used to test the prototype are first described; Alg. ICAb5 is then compared with Alg. EIA4 both for speed and for the ability to provide as soon as possible the user with a representative sample of all solutions.

4.1   Benchmark Description

In the sequel, every benchmark is parameterized by both the number of variables (not counting time t) and the number of constraints to solve.

School Problem$_{3,1}$ [14] is a benchmark corresponding to finding all parabolas lying above a line:

$$\forall t \in [0 .. 2]: at^2 + bt + c \geqslant 2t + 1 \quad \text{with} \quad a \in [0 .. 1], b \in [0 .. 1], c \in [0 .. 1]$$

Benchmark *School Problem$_{3,2}$* is an inconsistent variant:

$$\forall t \in [0 .. 2]: \begin{cases} at^2 + bt + c \geqslant 2t + 1 \\ at^2 + bt + c \leqslant 2t \end{cases}$$

with same domains for a, b, and c.

Benchmark *Flying Saucer$_{4,1}$* boils down to finding all pairs of points such that the distance between the flying saucer and the line linking both points is above a given value at any time in a given interval:

$$\sqrt{(x_1 + u(x_2 - x_1) - x_3^t)^2 + (y_1 + u(y_2 - y_1) - y_3^t)^2} \geqslant d$$

with $u = (x_3^t - x_1)(x_2 - x_1) + (y_3^t - y_1)(y_2 - y_1)/ \parallel P_2 - P_1 \parallel^2$, where $P_1 = (x_1, y_1)$ and $P_2 = (x_2, y_2)$ are the unknowns, $P_3^t = (x_3^t, y_3^t)$ the coordinates of the flying saucer at time t, and d the minimal distance between the flying saucer and the line (P_1, P_2).

Benchmark *Simple Circle* is also a collision problem: given B a point moving along a circling path, find all points A such that the distance between A and B is always greater than a given value. Benchmarks *Simple Circle$_{2,2}$* and *Simple Circle$_{2,3}$* are instances of the same problems with respectively 2 and 3 points moving round in circles. For only one circling point, we have:

$$\forall t \in [-\pi .. \pi]: \qquad \begin{cases} x \in [-5 .. 5] \\ y \in [-5 .. 5] \\ d_1 = 0.5 \end{cases}$$
$$\sqrt{(r_1 \sin t - x)^2 + (r_1 \cos t - y)^2} \geqslant d_1$$

where d_1 is the minimal required distance between A and B, and $r_1 = 2.5$ is the radius of B's circling path.

Benchmark *Projection$_{3,4}$* checks whether a moving object projects itself into a frame on the screen for a given time. The static camera has three degrees of freedom: x_t^c, y_t^c, and θ_t^c (horizontal orientation). Given x_t^o, y_t^o, and z_t^o the coordinates of the object's path at time t, and x_t^c, y_t^c, z_t^c, ϕ_t^c, θ_t^c, ψ_t^c, γ_t^c the parameters for the camera, we have:

$$x_t' = -(x_t^o - x_t^c) \sin \theta_t^c + (y_t^o - y_t^c) \cos \theta_t^c$$
$$y_t' = -(x_t^o - x_t^c) \cos \theta_t^c \sin \phi_t^c + (y_t^o - y_t^c) \sin \phi_t^c \sin \theta_t^c + (z_t^o - z_t^c) \cos \phi_t^c$$
$$z_t' = -(x_t^o - x_t^c) \cos \theta_t^c \cos \phi_t^c + (y_t^o - y_t^c) \sin \theta_t^c \cos \phi_t^c + (z_t^o - z_t^c) \sin \phi_t^c$$
$$\blacktriangledown x_t^f \leqslant x_t'/(z_t'/\gamma_t^c) \qquad \blacktriangle x_t^f \geqslant x_t'/(z_t'/\gamma_t^c)$$
$$\blacktriangledown y_t^f \leqslant y_t'/(z_t'/\gamma_t^c) \qquad \blacktriangle y_t^f \geqslant y_t'/(z_t'/\gamma_t^c)$$

where $\blacktriangledown x_t^f$ (resp. $\blacktriangle y_t^f$) is the abscissa of the left bound (resp. the ordinate of the right bound) of the frame, $t \in [0 .. 20]$, $x_c \in [-3 .. 3]$, $y_c \in [-3 .. 3]$, $z_c = 2$, $\phi_c \in [-0.5 .. 0.5]$, $\theta_c = 0$, and $\gamma_c^t = 0.8$.

4.2   Improving Computation

Solvers such as Numerica usually isolate solutions with variable domains around 10^{-8} or 10^{-16} in width. By contrast, the applications this paper focuses on are less demanding since the resulting variable domains are used in the context of a display screen, a "low resolution" device. In practice, one can consider that a reasonable threshold ε for the splitting process is some value lower or equal to 10^{-3}.

One of the drawbacks of Alg. EIA4 [14] is that successive output solutions are very similar, while it is of importance to be able to provide the user with a representative sample of solutions as soon as possible.

Tackling this problem using Alg. ICAb5 is done as follows: given a constraint system of the form $\forall v \in I_v : c_1 \wedge \cdots \wedge c_m$ and a Cartesian product of domains $\mathbf{B} = I_1 \times \cdots \times I_n \times I_v$, the solving process has two degrees of freedom, *viz.* the selection of the next constraint to consider, and the selection of the next variable to split. Figure 1 presents the differences with regard to the order of generation of solutions for *Simple Circle$_{2,2}$* for two strategies concerning the variable splitting order: *depth-first*, where each constraint is considered in turn, and each domain is split to the threshold splitting limit; and *semi-depth-first* where each constraint is considered in turn, but each variable is split only once and put at the end of the domain queue.

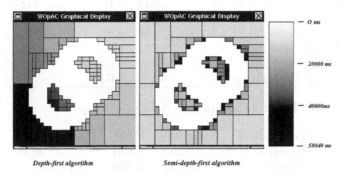

Fig. 1. Depth-first *vs.* semi-depth first

As one may see, the semi-depth-first algorithm computes consecutive solutions spread over all the search space, while the depth-first algorithm computes solutions downwards and from "right" to "left".

4.3 Comparing EIA4 and ICAb5

Algorithms EIA4 and ICAb5 provide different sets of solutions for the same problem. Consequently, a direct comparison of their performances is quite difficult. Moreover, the actual implementation of EIA4 differs from its ideal description since it uses a splitting threshold ω for the domain of the universally quantified variable v instead of checking consistency by eventually reaching canonicity for the samples of the domain I_v.

Tables 1 and 2 compare algorithms EIA4 and ICAb4 from the speed point of view for computing the first solution (*vs.* all solutions). Times are given in seconds on a SUN UltraSparc 166 MHz running Solaris 2.5.

Setting ω and ε to the same value leads to nearly the same solution sets for both algorithms EIA4 and ICAb5.

5 Conclusion

Unlike the methods used to deal with universally quantified variables described in [13], the algorithms presented in this paper are purely numerical ones (except for the negation of constraints). Since they rely on "traditional" techniques used by most of the interval constraint-based solvers, they may benefit from the active researches led to speed up these tools. What is more, they are applicable to

Table 1. EIA4(ω) *vs.* ICAb5 — First solution

Benchmark	EIA4(ω)	ICAb5	EIA4(ω)/ICAb5
Projection$_{3,8}$($\varepsilon = 10^{-1}$)	0.2	0.17	1.18
Projection$_{3,8}$($\varepsilon = 10^{-2}$)	38.59	0.16	241.19
Projection$_{3,8}$($\varepsilon = 10^{-3}$)	> 600	0.16	> 3750.00
Projection$_{3,4}$($\varepsilon = 10^{-2}$)	53.12	0.12	442.67
Projection$_{3,4}$($\varepsilon = 10^{-3}$)	> 600	0.12	> 5000.00
School Problem$_{3,1}$($\varepsilon = 10^{-2}$)	0.02	0.09	0.22
School Problem$_{3,1}$($\varepsilon = 10^{-3}$)	1.58	0.09	17.56
Simple Circle$_{2,2}$($\varepsilon = 10^{-2}$)	0.99	0.05	19.80
Simple Circle$_{2,2}$($\varepsilon = 10^{-3}$)	20.86	0.05	417.20

Table 2. EIA4(ω) *vs.* ICAb5 — All solutions

Benchmark	EIA4	ICAb5	EIA4/ICAb5
Projection$_{3,5}$	783.03	68.83	11.38
Projection$_{3,10}$	>9,000	3,634	> 2476.61
Projection$_{5,5}$	>9,000	3,612	> 2491.69
School Problem$_{3,1}$	156.02	12.72	12.27
Flying Saucer$_{4,1}$	1,459.01	1,078.03	1.35
Simple Circle$_{2,1}$	12,789.03	651.59	19.63
Simple Circle$_{2,2}$	1,579.05	55.95	28.22

the large range of constraints for which an outer-contracting operator may be devised. By contrast, CAD-based methods deal with polynomial constraints only.

However, constraints to be handled by our algorithm need be easily negated, a requirement trivially met with inequalities but not with equalities. The handling of equalities might be done as described by Sam-Haroud and Faltings [21,20] by relaxing the constraint $f = 0$ into $f = \pm\varepsilon$, thus replacing an equality by two inequalities.

Despite the dramatic improvement of the new method described herein over the one given by Jardillier and Languénou, handling of complex scenes with many objects and a camera allowed to move along all its degrees of freedom in a reasonable time is beyond reach for the moment. Nevertheless, a comforting idea is that most of the traditional camera movements involve but few of the degrees of freedom, thenceforth reducing the number of variables to consider.

Collavizza *et al.* [10] devised a scheme for computing inner-approximations of the relation underlying a real constraint system: starting from a "seed" known to be included in the relation, they expand the domain of the variables as much as possible until obtaining a "maximal" subset of the inner-approximation (with maximality to be understood in the sense of Shary [22]). A drawback of their method lies in that they do not provide any means to compute the seed. An interesting direction for research would be to try using our algorithm to quickly isolate such a seed for each connected subset of the inner-approximation, then resorting to their method to obtain maximal inner-approximations.

Acknowledgements

Discussions with Éric Languénou, Marc Christie, and Laurent Granvilliers that helped improving this paper are gratefully acknowledged. The research exposed here was supported in part by a project of the French/Russian A. M. Liapunov Institute.

References

1. S. Abrams and P. K. Alien. Computing camera viewpoints in an active robot work-cell. Technical Report IBM Research Report: RC 20987, IBM Research Division, 1997. 68
2. B. D. O. Anderson, N. K. Bose, and E. I. Jury. Output feedback stabilization and related problems – solution via decision methods. IEEE Trans. on Automatic Control, AC-20(1), 1975. 68
3. J. Armengol, L. Travé-Massuyés, J. Veil, and M. Á. Sainz. Modal interval analysis for error-bounded semiqualitative simulation. In 1r Congrés Català d'lntelligència Artificial, pages 223-231, 1998. 72
4. F. Benhamou. Interval constraint logic programming. In A. Podelski, editor, Constraint programming: basics and trends, volume 910 of LNCS, pages 1-21. Springer-Verlag, 1995. 69, 71
5. F. Benhamou, F. Goualard, L. Granvilliers, and J.-F. Puget. Revising hull and box consistency. InProc. of the 16th Int. Conf. on Logic Programming (ICLP'99), pages 230-244, Las Cruces, USA, 1999. The MIT Press. ISBN 0-262-54104-1. 71
6. F. Benhamou, F. Goualard, É. Languénou, and M. Christie. Universally quantified constraint solving: an application to camera control. Research Report 00.5, Institut de Recherche en Informatique de Nantes, March 2000. Available at http://www.sciences.univ-nantes.fr/irin/Vie/RR/indexGB.html. 72
7. F. Benhamou, D. McAllester, and P. Van Hentenryck. CLP(Intervals) revisited. In Proc. of ILPS'94, pages 124-138. MIT Press, November 1994. 68, 71
8. F. Benhamou and W. J. Older. Applying interval arithmetic to real, integer and boolean constraints. JLP, 32(1): 1-24, 1997. 67, 69
9. J. G. deary. Logical arithmetic. Future Generation Computing Systems, 2(2): 125-149, 1987. 69
10. H. Collavizza, F. Delobel, and M. Rueher. Extending consistent domains of numeric CSP. In Proc. of the 16th IJCAI, volume 1, pages 406-411, July 1999. 80
11. G. E. Collins. Quantifier elimination for real closed fields by cylindrical algebraic decomposition. In Proc. of the 2nd GI Conf. Automata Theory and Formal Languages, volume 33 of LNCS, pages 134-183, Kaiserslauten, 1975. Springer. 68
12. S. M. Drucker. Intelligent Camera Control for Graphical Environments. PhD thesis, MIT Media Lab, 1994. 68
13. H. Hong. Collision problems by an improved CAD-based quantifier elimination algorithm. Technical Report 91-05, RISC-Linz, 1991. 79
14. F. Jardillier and E. Langienou. Screen-space constraints for camera movements: the virtual cameraman. In N. Ferreira and M. Gobel, editors, Eurographics'98 proceedings, volume 17, pages 175-186. Blackwell Publishers, 1998. 68, 72, 73, 74, 77, 78
15. S. M. Markov. On directed interval arithmetic and its applications. JUCS, 1(7):514-526, 1995. 72

16. K. Meintjes and A. P. Morgan. Chemical equilibrium systems as numerical test problems. ACM TOMS, 16(2):143-151, June 1990. 67
17. R. E. Moore. Interval Analysis. Prentice-Hall, Englewood Clis, N. J., 1966. 67, 68
18. J.-F. Puget. A C $^{++}$ implementation of CLP. In Proc. of SPICIS'94, 1994. 67
19. J.-F. Puget and P. Van Hentenryck. A constraint satisfaction approach to a circuit design problem. J. of Global Optimization, 13:75-93, 1998. 67
20. J. Sam. Constraint Consistency Techniques for Continuous Domains. Phd. thesis, École polytechnique fédérale de Lausanne, 1995. 67, 80
21. J. Sam-Haroud and B. V. Fallings. Consistency techniques for continuous constraints. Constraints, 1:85-118, 1996. 74, 80
22. S. P. Shary. Algebraic solutions to interval linear equations and their applications. In G. Alefeld and J. Herzberger, editors, Numerical Methods and Error Bounds, proc. of the IMACS-GAMM Int. Symposium on Numerical Methods and Error Bounds, pages 224-233. Akademie Verlag, July 1995. 80
23. S. P. Shary. Interval Gauss-Seidel method for generalized solution sets to interval linear systems. In Proc. of MISC'99, pages 51-65, February 1999. 67, 72
24. P. Van Hentenryck, L. Michel, and Y. Deville. Numerica: A Modeling Language for Global Optimization. The MIT Press, 1997. 67
25. A. C. Ward, T. Lozano-Bsrez, and W. P. Seering. Extending the constraint propagation of intervals. InProc. of IJCAI'89, pages 1453-1458, 1989. 67

Constraint Propagation for Soft Constraints: Generalization and Termination Conditions

S. Bistarelli[1], R. Gennari[2], and F. Rossi[3]

[1] Università di Pisa, Dipartimento di Informatica
Corso Italia 40, 56125 Pisa
bista@di.unipi.it
[2] ILLC, Institute of Logic, Language and Computation, University of Amsterdam
N. Doelenstraat 15, 1012 CP Amsterdam, The Netherlands gennari@hum.uva.nl
[3] Università di Padova, Dipartimento di Matematica Pura ed Applicata
Via Belzoni 7, 35131 Padova
frossi@math.unipd.it

Abstract. Soft constraints based on semirings are a generalization of classical constraints, where tuples of variables' values in each soft constraint are uniquely associated to elements from an algebraic structure called semiring. This framework is able to express, for example, fuzzy, classical, weighted, valued and over-constrained constraint problems.

Classical constraint propagation has been extended and adapted to soft constraints by defining a schema for *soft local consistency* [BMR97]. On the other hand, in [Apt99a,Apt99b] it has been proved that most of the well known constraint propagation algorithms for classical constraints can be cast within a single schema.

In this paper we combine these two schema and we show how the framework of [Apt99a,Apt99b] can be used for soft constraints. In doing so, we generalize the concept of soft local consistency, and we prove some convenient properties about its termination.

1 Introduction

Soft constraints allow to model faithfully many real-life problems, especially those which possess features like preferences, uncertainties, costs, levels of importance, and absence of solutions. Formally, a soft constraint problem (SCSP) is just like a classical constraint problem (CSP), except that each assignment of values to variables in the constraints is associated to an element taken from a set (usually ordered). These elements will then directly represent the desired features.

There are many formalizations of soft constraint problems. In this paper we consider the one based on semirings [BMR97], where the semiring specifies the partially ordered set and the appropriate operation to use to combine constraints together. This formalism has been shown to have many interesting instances, like classical, fuzzy [DFP93], weighted, valued [SFV95], probabilistic [FL93] and partial [FW92] constraints.

R. Dechter (Ed.): CP 2000, LNCS 1894, pp. 83–97, 2000.

The propagation techniques usually used for classical CSPs have been extended and adapted to deal with soft constraints, provided that certain conditions are met. This has led to a general framework for soft constraint propagation, where at each step a subproblem is solved, as in classical constraint propagation [BMR97]. By studying the properties of this schema, it has been proved that such steps can be seen as applications of functions which are monotonic, inflationary, and idempotent over a certain partial order.

On an orthogonal line of research, the concept of constraint propagation over classical constraints has been studied in depth in [Apt99a,Apt99b], and a general algorithmic schema (called GI) has been developed. In such a schema, constraint propagation is achieved whenever we have a set of functions which are monotonic and inflationary over a partial order with a bottom.

By studying these two frameworks and comparing them, we noticed that the GI schema can be applied to soft constraints (see Section 5.1), since the functions and the order used for soft constraints have all the necessary properties for GI. This is proved in this paper by defining an appropriate partial order over soft constraint problems (see Section 3).

By analyzing the features of the GI algorithm, we also realized (see Section 5.2) that indeed soft constraint propagation can be extended to deal with functions which are not necessarily idempotent. Notice that this is a double generalization: we don't require any longer that each step has to solve a subproblem (it could do some other operation over the problem), nor that it is idempotent. This allows us to model several forms of "approximate" constraint propagation which were instead not modeled in [BMR97]. Example are: bounds-consistency for classical constraints [MS98], and partial soft arc-consistency for soft constraints [BCGR00].

These two results allow us to use the GI algorithm schema for performing a generalized form of soft constraint propagation. What is important to study, at this point, is when the resulting GI schema terminates. In fact, if we work with classical constraints over finite domains, it is easy to see that the GI algorithm always terminates. However, when moving to soft constraints over a semiring, even if the variable domain is finite, we could have an infinite behavior due to an infinite number of elements in the semiring. For example, fuzzy constraints have a semiring containing all reals between 0 and 1, and the semiring of weighted constraints contains all the reals, or all the naturals.

In Section 6 we identify some sufficient conditions for the termination of the GI algorithm over soft constraints. The first, predictable, condition that we consider is the well-foundedness of the partial order over soft constraint problems: if the partial order over which the GI algorithm works has chains of finite length, since constraint propagation never goes from one chain to another one, obviously the whole algorithm terminates.

The second condition is in some sense more precise, although less general: when the propagation steps are defined via the two semiring operations, then we can just consider the sub-order over semiring elements obtained by taking the elements initially appearing in the given problem, and closing it under the two operations. In fact, in this case the GI algorithm cannot reach other elements. Therefore, if such a set (or a superset of it) is well-founded, the GI algorithm terminates.

Each of these two conditions is sufficient for termination. However, they could be difficult to check, unless the partial order has a well-known structure of which we know the well-foundedness. Nevertheless, in a special case we can formally prove that there exists a well-founded set of the shape required by the second condition above, and thus we can automatically deduce termination. This special case is related to the idempotence of the multiplicative operation of the semiring, the one that we use to combine constraints: if this operation is idempotent, then GI terminates. For example, in classical constraints the multiplicative operation is logical and, and in fuzzy constraints it is the minimum, thus we can formally prove that the algorithm GI over *any* classical or fuzzy constraint problem *always* terminates, provided that the functions are defined via the two semiring operations.

We believe that the generalizations and termination conditions that we have developed and proved will make soft constraints more widely applicable, and soft constraint propagation more practically usable.

2   Soft Constraints

In the semiring-based formalism for soft constraints [BMR97], a soft constraint is just a constraint where each instantiation of its variables has an associated value. Combining constraints will then have to take into account such additional values, and thus the formalism has also to provide suitable operations for combination ($\times$) and comparison ($+$) of tuples of values and constraints. This is why the formalization adopted in [BMR97] uses a semiring structure, which is just a set plus two operations.

Semirings and SCSPs. A *semiring* is a tuple $\langle A, +, \times, \mathbf{0}, \mathbf{1} \rangle$ such that: A is a set and $\mathbf{0}, \mathbf{1} \in A$; $+$ is commutative, associative and $\mathbf{0}$ is its unit element; $\times$ is associative, distributes over $+$, $\mathbf{1}$ is its unit element and $\mathbf{0}$ is its absorbing element. Further, we enforce some additional properties, leading to the notion of c-semiring: a *c-semiring* is a semiring $\langle A, +, \times, \mathbf{0}, \mathbf{1} \rangle$ such that $+$ is idempotent with $\mathbf{1}$ as its absorbing element and $\times$ is commutative.

The partial order $\leq_S$ over the set A, defined as $a \leq_S b$ iff $a + b = b$, is used to compare elements in the semiring: $a \leq_S b$ means that b is "better" than a.

A *constraint system* is a tuple $CS = \langle S, D, V \rangle$ where S is a c-semiring, D is a finite set (the domain of the variables) and V is a finite ordered set of variables.

Given a semiring $S = \langle A, +, \times, \mathbf{0}, \mathbf{1} \rangle$ and a constraint system $CS = \langle S, D, V \rangle$, a *constraint* is a pair $\langle def, con \rangle$ where $con \subseteq V$ and $def : D^{|con|} \to A$. Therefore a constraint specifies a set con of variables and assigns each tuple of values of these variables an element of the semiring.

A *Soft Constraint Satisfaction Problem* (SCSP) on a constraint system CS is a pair $P = \langle C, con \rangle$, where $con \subseteq V$ and C is a set of constraints: con represents the set of variables of interest for the constraint set C, which however may contain constraints defined on variables not in con.

Combining and projecting soft constraints. Given two constraints $c_1 = \langle def_1, con_1 \rangle$ and $c_2 = \langle def_2, con_2 \rangle$, their *combination* $c_1 \otimes c_2$ is the constraint $\langle def, con \rangle$ defined by $con = con_1 \cup con_2$ and $def(t) = def_1(t \downarrow_{con_1}^{con}) \times def(t \downarrow_{con_2}^{con})$, where $t \downarrow_Y^X$ denotes the projection of tuple t from X onto Y. In words, combining two constraints means building a new constraint involving all the variables of the original one; the new constraint associates to each tuple of domain values a semiring element obtained by multiplying the elements associated by the original constraints to the appropriate subtuples.

Given a constraint $c = \langle def, con \rangle$ and a subset I of V, the *projection* of c onto I, written $c \Downarrow_I$, is the constraint $\langle def', con' \rangle$ where $con' = con \cap I$ and $def'(t') = \sum_{t \mid t \downarrow_{I \cap con}^{con} = t'} def(t)$. Thus, projecting means eliminating some variables. This is done by associating each tuple t over the remaining variables a semiring element; the last one is the sum of the elements associated by the original constraint to all the extensions of the tuple t over the eliminated variables.

In brief: combination is performed via the multiplicative operation of the semiring, and projection via the additive one.

Examples. Classical CSPs are SCSPs where the chosen c-semiring is $Bool = \langle \{false, true\}, \vee, \wedge, false, true \rangle$. By means of $Bool$ we can associate each tuple of elements in D a Boolean value, $false$ or $true$, then project and combine constraints via the Boolean connectives.

Fuzzy CSPs [DFP93] can instead be modeled by choosing the c-semiring $Fuzzy = \langle [0, 1], max, min, 0, 1 \rangle$. In fact, there each tuple has a value between 0 and 1; constraints are combined via the min operation and compared via the max operation.

Solutions. The *solution* of an SCSP $P = \langle C, con \rangle$ is the constraint $Sol(P) = (\bigotimes C) \Downarrow_{con}$: it is obtained by combining all constraints of P and then projecting over the variables in con. In this way we get the constraint over con that is "induced" by the entire problem P.

Two problems $P_1 = \langle C_1, con \rangle$ and $P_2 = \langle C_2, con \rangle$ (notice that they have the same con) are considered equivalent, and written as $P_1 \equiv_P P_2$, when $Sol(P_1) = Sol(P_2)$.

Soft local consistency. Most of the traditional *local consistency* (also called *propagation*) algorithms can be generalized to SCSPs [BMR97]. In order to define local consistency algorithms for SCSPs, the notion of *local consistency rule* is introduced. The application of one of such rules consists of solving a subproblem of the given problem.

To model this, we use the notion of *typed location*. Informally, a typed location is just a location l (as in ordinary store-based programming languages) which has a set of variables con as type, and thus can only be assigned a constraint

$c = \langle def, con \rangle$ with the same type. In the following we assume to have a location for every set of variables, and thus we identify a location with its type.

Given an SCSP $P = \langle C, con \rangle$, the *value* $[l]_P$ *of the location* l in P is defined as the constraint $\langle def, l \rangle \in C$ if it exists, as $\langle 1, l \rangle$ otherwise. Given n locations $l_1, \ldots, l_n$, the value $[\{l_1, \ldots, l_n\}]_P$ of this set of locations in P is defined as the set of constraints $\{[l_1]_P, \ldots, [l_n]_P\}$.

An *assignment* is a pair $l := c$ where $c = \langle def, l \rangle$. Given an SCSP $P = \langle C, con \rangle$, the result of the assignment $l := c$ is the problem $[l := c](P)$ defined as: $[l := c](P) = \langle \{\langle def', con' \rangle \in C \mid con' \neq l\} \cup c, con \rangle$.

Thus an assignment $l := c$ is seen as a function from constraint problems to constraint problems, that modifies a given problem by changing just one constraint, namely the one with type l. The change consists in substituting such a constraint with c. If there is no constraint of type l, then the constraint c is added to the given problem. In other words, the assignment $l := c$ in P produces a new problem P' which is the same as P, except that it has an additional constraint c over the variables in l, and that the old constraints over l are removed. Note also that when $\mid l \mid = 1$ we are able to modify domains, since a domain can be seen as a unary constraint.

Consider a constraint system $CS = \langle S, D, V \rangle$, a location l and a set of locations L, where $l \in L$; a *local consistency rule* r_l^L is a function r_l^L which, taken any problem P over CS, returns $r_l^L(P) = [l := Sol(\langle [L]_P, l \rangle)](P)$.

Intuitively, the application of r_l^L to P adds the constraint $Sol(\langle [L]_P, l \rangle)$ over the variables in l to P. This constraint, by definition of Sol, is obtained by combining all constraints of P identified by L and then projecting the resulting constraint over l.

Since a local consistency rule is a function from problems to problems, the application of a sequence S of rules to a problem is easily provided by function composition: we write $[r; S](P) = [S]([r_1](P))$ and mean that the problem $[r; S](P)$ is obtained applying *first* the rule r and *then* the rules of the sequence S in the specified order.

An infinite sequence T of rules of a set R is called a *strategy*. A strategy is *fair* if each rule of R occurs in it infinitely often.

We are now ready to define *local consistency algorithms*. Given a problem P, a set of rules R and a fair strategy T for R, a *local consistency algorithm* applies to P the rules in R in the order given by T. The algorithm stops when the current problem is a fixpoint of all functions from R. In that case, we write $lc(P, R, T)$ to denote the resulting problem.

3 Some Useful Orderings over Semiring Constraints

We now review and modify some of the orderings among semiring elements, constraints, and problems, which have been introduced in [BMR97]; moreover, we also define new orderings that will be used in the next sections.

3.1   Semiring Order

All the orderings we will consider in this section are derived from the partial order $\leq_S$ over semiring elements, which, we recall, is defined as follows: $a \leq_S b$ iff $a + b = b$. This intuitively means that b is "better" than a.

Definition 1. *Consider any partial ordering $\langle D, \sqsubseteq \rangle$ and the component-wise ordering $\langle D^n, \sqsubseteq_n \rangle$, with $n \geq 1$, where $\langle d_1, \ldots, d_n \rangle \sqsubseteq_n \langle d'_1, \ldots, d'_n \rangle$ iff $d_i \sqsubseteq d'_i$ for each $i = 1, \ldots, n$. Let f be a function from D^n to D. Then:*

- *f is monotonic iff $\langle d_1, \ldots, d_n \rangle \sqsubseteq_n \langle d'_1, \ldots, d'_n \rangle$ implies $f(\langle d_1, \ldots, d_n \rangle) \sqsubseteq f(\langle d'_1, \ldots, d'_n \rangle)$;*
- *f is inflationary w.r.t. $\sqsubseteq$ iff $d_i \sqsubseteq f(\langle d_1, \ldots, d_n \rangle)$ for every $i = 1, \ldots, n$.*

Given the definition above, it is easy to see that the following results hold when D is the semiring set A and the order considered is $\leq_S$:

- $\leq_S$ is a partial order;
- $\mathbf{0}$ is the minimum;
- $\mathbf{1}$ is the maximum.
- if $\times$ is idempotent, then $\langle A, \leq_S \rangle$ is a distributive lattice where $+$ is the lub and $\times$ is the glb.
- $+$ and $\times$ are monotonic with respect to $\leq_S$;
- $+$ is inflationary with respect to $\leq_S$; instead $\times$ is inflationary with respect to $\geq_S$.

3.2   Constraint Order

From the ordering $\leq_S$ over A, we can also define a corresponding order between constraints. Before introducing the new order we define its domain, namely the set of all possible constraints over a constraint system.

Definition 2. *Given a semiring $S = \langle A, +, \times, \mathbf{0}, \mathbf{1} \rangle$ and a constraint system $CS = \langle S, D, V \rangle$, we define the* Constraint Universe *related to the constraint system CS as follows: $\mathcal{C}_{CS} = \bigcup_{con \subseteq V} \{ \langle def, con \rangle \mid def : D^{|con|} \to A \}$.*

We will write $\mathcal{C}$ (instead of $\mathcal{C}_{CS}$) when the constraint system CS is clear from the context.

Definition 3. *Consider two constraints c_1, c_2 over a constraint system CS; assume that $con_1 \subseteq con_2$ and $\mid con_2 \mid = k$. Then we write $c_1 \sqsubseteq_S c_2$ if and only if, for all k-tuples t of values from D, $def_2(t) \leq_S def_1(t \downarrow^{con_2}_{con_1})$.*

Loosely speaking, a constraint c_1 is smaller than c_2 in the order $\sqsubseteq_S$ iff it constrains possibly less variables and assigns to each tuple a greater value with respect to $\leq_S$ than c_2 does.

Theorem 1 ($\sqsubseteq_S$ is a po). *Given a semiring $S = \langle A, +, \times, \mathbf{0}, \mathbf{1} \rangle$ with $\times$ idempotent and a constraint system $CS = \langle S, D, V \rangle$, we have the following:*

- the relation $\sqsubseteq_S$ is a partial order over the set $\mathcal{C}_{CS}$;
- its bottom is $\langle \mathbf{1}, \emptyset \rangle$, where the 0-arity function $\mathbf{1} : \emptyset \to A$ is the constant $\mathbf{1}$ of the semiring.

Proof. We prove our first claim. We need to demonstrate that $\sqsubseteq_S$ is a reflexive, antisymmetric and transitive relation. Reflexivity holds trivially. To prove anti-symmetry, suppose that $c_1 \sqsubseteq_S c_2$ and $c_2 \sqsubseteq_S c_1$; this yields that $con_1 = con_2$. Now, for all $t \in D^{|con_1|}$, we have both $def_1(t) \leq_S def_2(t)$ and $def_2(t) \leq_S def_1(t)$, hence $def_1(t) = def_2(t)$ and so $c_1 = c_2$. The transitivity of $\sqsubseteq_S$ follows from the transitivity of $\leq_S$. The other claim immediately follows from the definition of $\sqsubseteq_S$. □

3.3   Constraint Set Order

We can easily extend the order $\sqsubseteq_S$ over constraints to a new order over *constraint sets* as follows.

Definition 4. *Consider two sets of constraints C_1, C_2 over a constraint system CS. Suppose furthermore that $C_1 = \{c_i^1 : i \in I\}$, $C_2 = \{c_j^2 : j \in J\}$, $I \subseteq J$ and that, for every $i \in I$, the relation $c_i^1 \sqsubseteq_S c_i^2$ holds. Then we write $C_1 \sqsubseteq_C C_2$.*

The intuitive reading of $C_1 \sqsubseteq_C C_2$ is that C_2 is a problem generally "more constraining" than C_1 is, because C_2 has (possibly) a larger number of "more restrictive" constraints than C_1 has.

Theorem 2 ($\sqsubseteq_C$ is a partial order). *Given a semiring $S = \langle A, +, \times, \mathbf{0}, \mathbf{1} \rangle$, and a constraint system $CS = \langle S, D, V \rangle$, we have that:*

- *the relation $\sqsubseteq_C$ is a partial order over $\wp(\mathcal{C})$;*
- *the bottom of the relation is $\emptyset$.*

Proof. We only prove the first claim, the other one being straightforward. Reflexivity trivially holds. As far as antisymmetry is concerned, suppose that $C_1 = \{c_i^1\}_{i \in I}$, $C_2 = \{c_j^2\}_{j \in J}$ and both $C_1 \sqsubseteq_C C_2$ and $C_2 \sqsubseteq_C C_1$ hold; this means that $I = J$. Moreover, the following relations hold for every $i \in I$: $c_i^1 \sqsubseteq_S c_i^2$ and $c_i^2 \sqsubseteq_S c_i^1$. Hence $c_i^1 = c_i^2$ for every $i \in I$, because $\sqsubseteq_S$ is a partial order relation, cf. Theorem 1. Transitivity follows similarly, by exploiting the transitivity of $\sqsubseteq_S$. □

3.4   Problem Order

So far, we have introduced two partial orders: one between constraints ($\sqsubseteq_S$) and another one between constraint sets ($\sqsubseteq_C$). However, local consistency algorithms take constraint problems as input; therefore we need an ordering relation between problems if we want the GI algorithm to be used for soft local consistency.

First we define the set of all problems that can be built over a constraint system CS.

Definition 5. *Given a semiring* $S = \langle A, +, \times, \mathbf{0}, \mathbf{1} \rangle$ *and a constraint system* $CS = \langle S, D, V \rangle$, *we define the* Problem Set Universe *related to the constraint system* CS *as* $\mathcal{P}_{CS} = \{ \langle C, con \rangle \mid C \subseteq \mathcal{C}_{CS}, con \subseteq var(C) \}$. *When no confusion can arise, we shall simply write* $\mathcal{P}$ *instead of* $\mathcal{P}_{CS}$.

Definition 6. *Given a constraint system* CS, *consider two problems* $P_1 = \langle C_1, con_1 \rangle$ *and* $P_2 = \langle C_2, con_2 \rangle$ *in* $\mathcal{P}_{CS}$. *We write* $P_1 \sqsubseteq_P P_2$ *iff* $C_1 \sqsubseteq_C C_2$ *and* $con_1 \subseteq con_2$.

We now need to define a partially ordered structure that contains all SC-SPs that can be generated by enforcing local consistency, starting from a given problem.

Definition 7. *Consider a constraint system* CS *and an SCSP* P *over it. The* up-closure *of* P, *briefly* $P \uparrow$, *is the class of all problems* P' *on* CS *such that* $P \sqsubseteq_P P'$.

Proposition 1. *Consider a constraint system* CS, *an SCSP* P *over it and its up-closure* $P \uparrow$. *Then the following statements hold:*

1. *if* $P_1 \sqsubseteq_P P_2$ *and* $P_1 \in P \uparrow$, *then* $P_2 \in P \uparrow$;
2. *if* $P_1 \sqsubseteq_P P_2$, *then* $P_2 \uparrow \subseteq P_1 \uparrow$.

The proof of the above proposition is an immediate consequence of the previous definition and of the fact that $\sqsubseteq_C$ is transitive, cf. Theorem 2.

Theorem 3 ($\sqsubseteq_P$ is a po). *Given a constraint system* $CS = \langle S, D, V \rangle$ *and a problem* P *on it, we have:*

- *the relation* $\sqsubseteq_P$ *is a partial order over* $\mathcal{P}_{CS}$;
- *in particular* $\langle P \uparrow, \sqsubseteq_{P|P\uparrow} \rangle$ *is a partial ordering, where* $\sqsubseteq_{P|P\uparrow}$ *is the restriction of* $\sqsubseteq_P$ *to* $P \uparrow$; *when no confusion can arise, we simply write* $\langle P \uparrow, \sqsubseteq_P \rangle$;
- *the bottom* $\perp_{CS}$ *of* $\langle P \uparrow, \sqsubseteq_P \rangle$ *is* P.

Proof. We prove the first claim, the other ones following immediately from the definition of $P \uparrow$ and Proposition 1. As usual, we only prove that the relation is antisymmetric, because transitivity can be proved similarly and reflexivity trivially holds. Hence, suppose that both $P_1 \sqsubseteq_P P_2$ and $P_2 \sqsubseteq_P P_1$ hold. This means that we have the following relations: $con_1 \subseteq con_2$, $C_1 \sqsubseteq_C C_2$, $con_2 \subseteq con_1$, $C_2 \sqsubseteq_C C_1$. From the two previous relations and Theorem 2, it follows that $con_1 = con_2$ and $C_1 = C_2$; hence $P_1 = P_2$. $\square$

3.5   Order-Related Properties of Soft Local Consistency Rules

We recall, from Section 2, that two problems P_1 and P_2, that share the same set of variables, are equivalent if they have the same solution set, and we write $P_1 \equiv_P P_2$.

Now we can list some useful properties of soft local consistency rules, which are related to equivalence and to problem ordering [BMR97]. Here we assume that we are given a constraint system C and a rule r on CS:

- (equivalence) $P \equiv_P r_l^L(P)$ if $\times$ is idempotent.
- (inflationarity) $P \sqsubseteq_P r_l^L(P)$. This means that the new semiring values assigned to tuples by the rule application are always smaller than or equal to the old ones with respect to $\leq_S$.
- (monotonicity) Consider two SCSPs $P_1 = \langle C_1, con_1 \rangle$ and $P_2 = \langle C_2, con_2 \rangle$ over CS. If $P_1 \sqsubseteq_P P_2$, then $r(P_1) \sqsubseteq_P r(P_2)$.

It is easy to prove that all the results about local consistency rules hold also for a whole local consistency algorithm. Moreover, we can prove also that the strategy does not influence the result, if it is fair [BMR97].

4   The Generic Iteration Algorithm

In [Apt99b] the Generic Iteration (GI) algorithm is introduced to find the least fixpoint of a finite set of functions defined on a partial ordering with bottom. This was then used as an algorithmic schema for classical constraint propagation: each step of constraint propagation was seen as the application of one of these functions. Our idea is to compare this schema with the one used for soft constraints, with the aim of obtaining a new schema which is the most general (that is, it can be applied both to classical and to soft constraints) and has the advantages of both of them.

Given a partial ordering with bottom, say $\langle D, \sqsubseteq, \bot \rangle$, consider now a set of functions $F := \{f_1, \ldots, f_k\}$ on D. The following algorithm can compute the least common fix point of the functions in F.

GENERIC ITERATION ALGORITHM (GI)

$d := \bot$;
$G := F$;
while $G \neq \emptyset$ **do**
$\qquad$ choose $g \in G$;
$\qquad$ $G := G - \{g\}$;
$\qquad$ $G := G \cup update(G, g, d)$;
$\qquad$ $d := g(d)$
od

where for all G, g, d the set of functions $update(G, g, d)$ from F is such that:

A. $\{f \in F - G \mid f(d) = d \wedge f(g(d)) \neq g(d)\} \subseteq update(G, g, d)$;
B. $g(d) = d$ implies $update(G, g, d) = \emptyset$;
C. $g(g(d)) \neq g(d)$ implies $g \in update(G, g, d)$.

Assumption **A** states that $update(G, g, d)$ at least contains all the functions from $F - G$ for which d is a fix point but $g(d)$ is not. So at each loop iteration such functions are added to the set G. In turn, assumption **B** states that no functions are added to G in case the value of d did not change. Note that, even though after the assignment $G := G - \{g\}$ we have $g \in F - G$, still $g \notin \{f \in F - G \mid f(d) = d \wedge f(g(d)) \neq g(d)\}$ holds. So assumption **A** does not provide any information when g is to be added back to G. This information is provided in assumption **C**. On the whole, the idea is to keep in G at least all functions f for which the current value of d is not a fix point.

We now recall the results which state the (partial) correctness of the GI algorithm, cf. [Apt99b]:

i. Every terminating execution of the GI algorithm computes in d a common fixpoint of the functions from F.

ii. Suppose that all functions in F are monotonic. Then every terminating execution of the GI algorithm computes in d the least common fixpoint of all the functions from F.

iii. Suppose that all functions in F are inflationary and that D is finite. Then every execution of the GI algorithm terminates.   □

5   Generalized Local Consistency for Soft Constraints via Algorithm GI

In this section we will try to combine the two formalisms described so far (soft constraints and the GI algorithm). Our goal is to exploit the GI algorithm to perform local consistency over soft constraint problems.

5.1   GI for Standard Local Consistency over Soft Constraints

The functions that GI needs in input are defined on a partial ordering with bottom. In the case of local consistency rules for SCSPs, the partial ordering is $\langle P \uparrow, \sqsubseteq_P \rangle$, and the bottom is the problem P itself, cf. Theorem 3. Moreover, the local consistency rules (and also the more general local consistency functions) have all the "good" properties that GI needs. Namely, those functions are monotonic and inflationary. Thus algorithm GI can be used to perform constraint propagation over soft constraint problems. More precisely, we can see that algorithm GI and the local consistency algorithm schema for soft constraints obtain the same result.

Theorem 4 (GI for soft local consistency rules). *Given an SCSP P over a constraint system CS, consider the SCSP $lc(P, R, T)$ obtained by applying to P a local consistency algorithm using the rules in R and with a fair strategy T. Consider also the partial order $\langle P \uparrow, \sqsubseteq_P \rangle$, and the set of functions R, and apply algorithm GI to such input. Then the output of GI coincides with $lc(P, R, T)$.*

5.2   GI for Generalized Local Consistency over Soft Constraints

While all local consistency rules are idempotent (since they solve a subproblem), algorithm GI does not need this property. This means that we can define a generalized notion of local consistency rules for soft constraints, by dropping idempotence.

Definition 8 (local consistency functions). *Consider an SCSP problem P over a semiring S. A* local consistency function *for P is a function* $f : P \uparrow \to P \uparrow$ *which is monotonic and inflationary over* $\sqsubseteq_P$.

With this definition of a local consistency function we relax two conditions about a local consistency step:

- that it must solve a subproblem;
- that it must be idempotent.

The second generalization has been triggered by the results about the GI algorithm, which have shown that idempotence is not needed for the desired results. Moreover, many practical local consistency algorithms do not exactly solve subproblems, but generate an approximation of the solution (see for example the definition of *bounds consistency* in [MS98] or the notion of partial soft arc-consistency in [BCGR00]). Thus the first extension allows one to model many more practical propagation algorithms.

Theorem 5 (GI for soft local consistency functions). *Given a constraint system CS and an SCSP problem P on it, let us apply the* GI *algorithm to the partial order* $\langle P \uparrow, \sqsubseteq_P \rangle$ *and a finite set R of local consistency functions. Then every terminating execution of the* GI *algorithm computes in the output problem P' the least common fixpoint of all the functions from R.*

What is now important to investigate is when the algorithm terminates. This is particularly crucial for soft constraints, since, even when the variable domains are finite, the semiring may contain an infinite number of elements, which is obviously a source of possible non-termination.

6 Termination of the GI Algorithm over Soft Constraints

As noted above, the presence of a possibly infinite semiring may lead to a constraint propagation algorithm which does not terminate. In the following we will give several independent conditions which guarantee termination in some special cases.

The first condition is a predictable extension of the one given in Section 4: instead of requiring the finiteness of the domain of computation, we just require that its chains have finite length, since it is easy to see that constraint propagation moves along a chain in the partial order.

Theorem 6 (termination 1). *Given a constraint system CS and an SCSP problem P on it, let us instantiate the* GI *algorithm with the po* $\langle P \uparrow, \sqsubseteq_P \rangle$ *and a finite set R of local consistency functions. Suppose that the order* $\sqsupseteq_{CS}$ *restricted to P $\uparrow$ is well founded. Then every execution of the* GI *algorithm terminates.*

This theorem can be used to prove termination in many case. For example, classical constraints over finite domains generate a partial order which is finite (an thus trivially well-founded), so the above theorem guarantees termination. Another example occurs when dealing with weighted soft constraints, where we deal with the naturals. Here the semiring is $\langle N, min, +, 0, +\infty \rangle$. Thus we have an infinite order, but well-founded.

However, there are also many interesting cases in which the ordering $\langle P \uparrow, \sqsubseteq_P \rangle$ is not well-founded. Consider for instance the case of fuzzy or probabilistic CSPs. For fuzzy CSPs, the semiring is $\langle [0,1], max, min, 0, 1 \rangle$. Thus the partially ordered structure containing all problems that are smaller than the given one, according to the semiring partial order, is not well-founded, since we have all the reals between 0 and a certain element in [0,1]. Thus the above theorem cannot say anything about termination of GI in this case. However, this does not mean that GI does not terminate, but only that the theorem above cannot be applied. In fact, later we will give another sufficient condition which will guarantee termination in the last two cases as well.

In fact, if we restrict our attention to local consistency functions defined via $+$ and $\times$, we can define another condition on our input problem that guarantees the termination of the GI algorithm; this condition exploits the fact that the local consistency functions are defined by means of the two semiring operations, and the properties of such operations.

Definition 9 (semiring closure). *Consider a constraint system CS with semiring $S = \langle A, +, \times, 0, 1 \rangle$, and an SCSP P on CS. Consider also the set of semiring values appearing in P: $Cl(P) = \bigcup_{\langle def', con' \rangle \in C} \{ def'(d) \mid d \in D^{|con'|} \}$. Then, a semiring closure of P is any set B such that: $Cl(P) \subseteq B \subseteq A$; B is closed with respect to $+$ and $\times$; $<_S$ restricted to B is well founded.*

Theorem 7 (termination 2). *Consider a constraint system CS with semiring $S = \langle A, +, \times, 0, 1 \rangle$, an SCSP P on it and a finite set of local consistency functions R defined via $+$ and $\times$. Assume also there exists a semiring closure of P. Then every execution of the GI algorithm terminates.*

Proof. The proof is similar to the one in [Apt99b] for the termination theorem; just replace the order $\sqsupseteq_{CP}$ with $<_S$ and accordingly the set D with B, where B is a semiring closure of P.   □

Notice that this theorem is similar to the one in [BMR97] about termination; however in [BMR97] they force the set B to be finite in order to guarantee the termination of a local consistency algorithm (cf. Theorem 4.14 of [BMR97]); a hypothesis that is implied by ours.

If we have a fuzzy constraint problem, then we can take B as the set of all semiring values appearing in the initial problem. In fact, this set is closed with respect to min and max, which are the two semiring operations in this case. Moreover, it is well-founded, since it is finite. Another example is constraint optimization over the reals: if the initial problem contains only natural numbers, then the set B can be the set of all naturals, which is is a well-founded subset of the reals and it is closed w.r.t. $+$ (min) and $\times$ (sum).

Therefore, by using Theorem 7 we can prove that also constraint propagation over fuzzy constraint problems always terminates, provided that each step of the algorithm uses a local consistency function which is defined in terms of the two semiring operations only.

However, it is not always easy to find a semiring closure of a given SCSP P, mainly because we should check that the order restricted to a tentative set B, closed and containing $Cl(P)$, is well-founded. Nevertheless, there is a special case in which we don't have to find such a set, because we can prove that it always exists (which is what Theorem 7 requires). This special case occurs when the multiplicative operation of the semiring is idempotent. In fact, we can prove that in this case there exists always a finite (and thus well-founded) semiring closure of any given problem over that semiring. This obviously is very convenient, since it provides us with an easy way to check whether Theorem 7 can be applied.

Theorem 8 (idempotence of × and termination). *Consider a constraint system CS, an SCSP P on it and a finite set of local consistency functions R defined via + and ×. Assume also that × is idempotent. Then there exists a finite semiring closure of P, and thus every execution of the GI algorithm terminates.*

Proof. Consider the set $Cl(P)$ of all semiring elements appearing in P. If we combine any subset of them via the + operation, we generate a set of elements, which contains $Cl(P)$, that we denote by $Cl+$. Notice that this set is finite, because the number of subsets of $Cl(P)$ is finite.

Let us now combine any subset of elements of $Cl+$ via the × operation: in this way we generate a larger set of elements, containing $Cl+$, which we denote by $Cl + \times$. Again, this set is finite. Therefore $Cl + \times$ is a finite semiring closure of P.   □

Consider again the fuzzy constraint example. Here × is min, thus it is idempotent. Therefore, by Theorem 8, GI over such problems always terminates. This is an alternative, and easier, way (to Theorem 7) to guarantee that soft constraint propagation over fuzzy constraints terminates. In fact, we don't have to find a semiring closure of the problem, but just check that the multiplicative operation is idempotent.

Considering all the above results, we can devise the following steps towards proving the termination of algorithm GI on a soft constraint problem P over a semiring S:

- If the local consistency functions are defined via the two operations of S, and the multiplicative operation of S is idempotent, then GI terminates (by Theorems 8).
- If instead × is not idempotent, but we still have local consistency functions defined via the two semiring operations, we can try to find a semiring closure of P. If we find it, then GI terminates (by Theorem 7).
- If we cannot find a semiring closure of P, or the local consistency functions are more general, then we can try to prove that the partial order of problems is well-founded. If it is so, the GI terminates (by Theorem 6).

While Theorem 8 applies in a special case of the hypothesis of Theorem 7, it is interesting to investigate the relationship between the hypothesis of Theorem 6 and 7. What can be proved is that these two conditions, namely, the well-foundedness of the partial order of problems and the existence of a semiring closure, are independent. In other words, there are cases in which one holds and not the other one, and vice versa. To prove this result, we need the following definition.

Definition 10. *Let $S = \langle A, +, \times, \mathbf{0}, \mathbf{1} \rangle$ be a semiring and B a subset of A. The set B is a* down-set *(or an* order ideal*) if, whenever $a \in B$, $a' \in A$ and $a' \leq_S a$, then $a' \in B$. Given any subset B of A, the downward closure of B is*

$$B \downarrow := \{d' \in A \ : \ \exists d \, (d \in B \text{ and } d' \leq_S d)\}.$$

Observe that the class $\mathcal{F}$ of down-sets containing a subset B of A is not empty, since A itself is such a set. Moreover, it is easy to check that the downward closure of B is the smallest down-set of $\mathcal{F}$; hence the downward closure of a set is well defined.

Given a semiring $S = \langle A, +, \times, \mathbf{0}, \mathbf{1} \rangle$, the following result links the upward closure of a problem P with the downward closure of $Cl(P)$, thus allowing us to compare the conditions in Theorem 6 and 7.

Proposition 2. *Given a constraint system CS and a problem P defined on it, consider the set $B := \{def(t) \in A \ : \ \exists P' \in P \uparrow (c := \langle def, con \rangle \in P', \ t \in D^{|con|})\}$. Then $B = Cl(P) \downarrow$.*

Proof. It follows immediately from the definition of $\sqsubseteq_P$, of $P \uparrow$ and $Cl(P) \downarrow$. $\square$

Now we can notice that, given a subset B of a semiring, if $<_S$ restricted to B is well founded, then so is $<_S$ restricted to $\hat{B} := B \cup \{\mathbf{0}, \mathbf{1}\}$. Furthermore, if B is finite, so is $\hat{B}$. In fact it is sufficient to check that the following identities hold because of the fact that $S = \langle A, +, \times, \mathbf{0}, \mathbf{1} \rangle$ is a c-semiring: if $a \in B$ then $a + 0 = a \in B$; if $a \in B$ then $a \times 1 = a \in B$; if $a \in B$ then $a + 1 = 1 \in \hat{B}$; if $a \in B$ then $a \times 0 = 0 \in \hat{B}$. Hence, in Theorem 7, we can replace the hypothesis "$Cl(P) \subseteq B$ and B a semiring closure of $Cl(P)$" with the condition that "Cl(P) is a subset of a well founded sub-c-semiring B of $S = \langle A, +, \times, \mathbf{0}, \mathbf{1} \rangle$".

Moreover, $+$ is the least upper bound operation and, if $\times$ is idempotent, $\times$ is the greatest lower bound operation, cf. Theorem 2.9 and 2.10 of [BMR97]. Hence a sub-c-semiring is also a sub-lattice of $S = \langle A, +, \times, \mathbf{0}, \mathbf{1} \rangle$ and vice versa if $\times$ is idempotent. Thus a subset B of a semiring can be a down-set and yet it may be not closed with respect to $\times$ and $+$. For instance, the set of negative real numbers augmented with $-\infty$ is a down-set in the lattice $\mathbf{R}^\infty$ of reals extended with $\{+\infty, -\infty\}$ and the usual linear ordering; however it is not a sub-lattice itself. Vice versa, there are sub-lattices of $\mathbf{R}^\infty$ - hence sets that are closed with respect to the least upper bound and the greatest lower bound operations - that are not down-sets. For instance, the extended interval $[0, 1] \cup \{+\infty, -\infty\}$. Therefore the two conditions that guarantee the termination of algorithm GI in Theorems 6 and 7 are independent.

7   Conclusions

The results of this paper show that indeed it is possible to treat in a uniform way hard and soft constraints. This was already shown in [BMR97], but restricted to a notion of local consistency where each step solves a subproblem. Here instead we have extended this result also to more general propagation algorithms, which approximate the classical notion in order to be more efficient. Moreover, we have also studied the conditions under which constraint propagation terminates. Some results were already present in [BMR97] and [Apt99b], but here we have generalized and extended them, providing more general, and also more easily checkable, sufficient conditions.

References

Apt99a.   K. R. Apt, The Essence of Constraint Propagation, *Theoretical Computer Science*, 221(1-2), pp. 179-210, 1999. 83, 84

Apt99b.   K. R. Apt, The Rough Guide to Constraint Propagation, *Proc. of the 5th International Conference on Principles and Practice of Constraint Programming (CP'99)*, (invited lecture), Springer-Verlag Lecture Notes in Computer Science 1713, pp. 1-23. 83, 84, 91, 92, 94, 97

B94.   C. Bessière. Arc-consistency and Arc-consistency again. *Artificial Intelligence*, 65(1), 1994.

BCGR00.   S. Bistarelli, P. Codognet, Y. Georget and F. Rossi Labeling and Partial Local Consistency for Soft Constraint Programming *Proc. of the 2nd International Workshop on Practical Aspects of Declarative Languages (PADL'00)*, Springer-Verlag Lecture Notes in Computer Science 1753, 2000. 84, 93

BMR95.   S. Bistarelli, U. Montanari and F. Rossi. Constraint Solving over Semirings. *Proceedings of IJCAI'95*, Morgan Kaufman, 1995.

BMR97.   S. Bistarelli, U. Montanari and F. Rossi. Semiring-based Constraint Solving and Optimization. *Journal of ACM*, vol. 44, no. 2, March 1997. 83, 84, 85, 86, 87, 90, 91, 94, 96, 97

DFP93.   D. Dubois, H. Fargier and H. Prade. The calculus of fuzzy restrictions as a basis for flexible constraint satisfaction. *Proc. IEEE International Conference on Fuzzy Systems*, IEEE, pp. 1131–1136, 1993. 83, 86

FL93.   H. Fargier and J. Lang Uncertainty in Constraint Satisfaction Problems: a Probabilistic Approach *Proc. European Conference on Symbolic and Qualitative Approaches to Reasoning and Uncertainty (ECSQARU)*, Springer-Verlag, LNCS 747, pp. 97–104, 1993. 83

FW92.   E. C. Freuder and R. J. Wallace. Partial Constraint Satisfaction. *AI Journal*, 1992, 58. 83

AC5.   P. Van Hentenryck, Y. Deville and C-M. Teng. A generic arc-consistency algorithm and its specializations. *Artificial Intelligence 57 (1992)*, pp 291-321.

MS98.   K. Marriott and P. Stuckey. Programming with Constraints. MIT Press, 1998. 84, 93

SFV95.   T. Schiex and H. Fargier and G. Verfaille. Valued Constraint Satisfaction Problems: Hard and Easy Problems. *Proc. IJCAI95*, Morgan Kaufmann, pp. 631–637, 1995. 83

Constraints, Inference Channels and Secure Databases

Alexander Brodsky, Csilla Farkas*, Duminda Wijesekera, and X. Sean Wang

Department of Information and Software Engineering,
George Mason University, Fairfax, VA 22030-4444.
{brodsky,cfarkas,duminda,xywang}@gmu.edu

Abstract. This paper investigates the problem of confidentiality violations via illegal data inferences that occur when arithmetic constraints are combined with non-confidential numeric data to infer confidential information. The database is represented as a point in an $(n + k)$-dimensional constraint space, where n is the number of numerical data items stored in the database (extensional database) and k is the number of derivable attributes (intensional database). Database constraints over both extensional and intensional databases form an $(n + k)$-dimensional constraint object. A query answer over a data item x is an interval I of values along the x axis of the database such that I is correct (i.e., the actual data value is within I) and safe (i.e., users cannot infer which point within I is the actual data value). The security requirements are expressed by the accuracy with which users are allowed to disclose data items. More specifically, we develop two classification methods: (1) volume-based classification, where the entire volume of the disclosed constraint object that contains the data item is considered and (2) interval based classification, where the length of the interval that contains the data item is considered. We develop correct and safe inference algorithms for both cases.

1 Introduction

Databases that contain confidential information require that users can access - directly or indirectly - only data for which they have the proper authorization. Direct data accesses are usually controlled by some form of lattice-based (mandatory) access control mechanisms [BL75,Den76]. Each data request is evaluated by comparing the security level of the requested data with the security clearance of the user. If the security requirements are satisfied (i.e., the user's security clearance dominates the security classification of all data) the data access is permitted. It is rejected otherwise. However, lattice-based access control is insufficient to prevent secrecy violations via inferences when non-confidential data is combined with meta-data to derive confidential information. Moreover, the strict security requirements of mandatory access control may unnecessarily

---

* Contact Author: Mail Stop 4A4, George Mason University, Fairfax, VA 22030-4444. Telephone: 703–993–1629, Fax: 703–993-1638, Internet: cfarkas@gmu.edu

R. Dechter (Ed.): CP 2000, LNCS 1894, pp. 98–113, 2000.
© Springer-Verlag Berlin Heidelberg 2000

limit data availability. In a number of applications it is desirable to provide a range of valid answers that would still allow the users to perform their jobs with limited authority while preserving confidentiality. For example, military support services should be able to perform scheduled maintenance work without knowing the mission (e.g., destination) of the serviced equipment. This paper provides a framework to define *flexible security requirements* on data and presents algorithms that compute *correct* and *safe* answers to queries. Intuitively correctness means that the actual data item is contained in the returned interval, and safety means that the user is not able to infer anything beyond what is released.

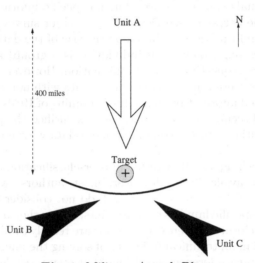

Fig. 1. Military Attack Plan

Most indirect data accesses result from inferences combine non-confidential data with constraints. We illustrate an illegal inference using a military database that contains data about different military units, such as types and specifications of their vehicles, destination distance, fuel and food supply (see Table 1). Assume that the attack strategy is that units **B** and **C** from the south engage in a long-term attack with the main force of the enemy; while, unit **A**, that is equipped with light weapons and thus able to move fast, is summoned from the north to launch a surprise attack on the unprotected northern front of the enemy. Fig. 1 shows the geographical locations of the units and the planned attacks. It is necessary that only authorized officers of the command center and of the units **A**, **B** and **C** know about the surprise attack. However, keeping the military plan secret does not guarantee the secrecy of this information. Consider the situation when an enemy spy is able to gain information about the amount of fuel requested by the different units. Since the number of the vehicles of the units and the mileages of these vehicles are usually known, the amount of available fuel defines the maximal travel distance and, therefore the potential destination of units. In our example, the knowledge of the destination of unit **A** would reveal the attack plan, thus reducing the strategic advantage of surprise.

How can we prevent such inferences? One possible solution is to keep fuel volume secret. However, this would severely limit data availability and require that all users accessing this information must be authorized to access information about the military plan as well. In this paper we present a different approach where users are allowed to access a range of possible data values but not the precise value. This flexible solution allows us to preserve confidentiality and provides improved data availability compared to the previous approaches.

The inference problem in databases first was considered in statistical databases where the security requirement is that aggregate information about groups of individuals can be released but no specific information about an individual should be accessed (see Denning [Den82] for survey). Illegal inferences revealing private information are based on the size of the database used to compute the statistics (e.g., number of individuals is a group) and/or the overlap among the queries requesting related information. However, researchers do not consider inferences raised by combining meta-data with non-confidential data to disclose confidential information. Since the beginning of 1980s, researchers, focusing on multi-level secure relational databases, identified the problem of indirect access to confidential data via combining meta-data with non-confidential data [GM84,Mor88,SO87,Hin88,Smi90,Buc90,Den85,Thu87,MSS88,RJHS95,ST90]. However, these techniques often result in over-classification of data and, therefore reduce data availability. Moreover, most authors, with the exception of [Den85,Hin88,SO91,DdVS99a,DdVS99b], do not consider the problem of actual inference for specific families of constraints; rather they develop a framework assuming that disclosure inference algorithms are readily available. It is our view, however, that the main technical difficulty of solving the inference channel problem lies in developing inference algorithms that guarantee data confidentiality.

Finally, the existing inference prevention techniques, with the exception of [RJHS95], are based on withholding answers from the users. We propose a new approach where confidentiality in numeric databases is achieved by controlling the accuracy of the released data. Our model guarantees that no illegal data access is possible even in the presence of database dependencies while supporting maximal data availability. The work of Rath et. al [RJHS95] is the closest to ours. They consider functional dependencies (FDs) to raise illegal imprecise inferences in databases containing numeric values. While their approach is secure, it is limited in the sense of considering FDs only and does not define security requirements in the context of range values.

In this paper we consider a data model consisting of a set of variables. A database is an instantiation of values to the variables that satisfies the database (arithmetic) constraints. The database is represented as a single point in an $(n + k)$-dimensional space, where n is the number of data items stored in the database (extensional database) and k is the number of values that can be derived from the stored data (intensional database).[1] The arithmetic constraints over extensional and intensional data form an $(n + k)$-dimensional constraint object. When a

---

[1] Note, that the real underlying database may adhere to any existing model, e.g. relational or object-oriented.

user requests a data value a range of possible values, represented as two new constraints, are generated and returned to the user.

The security requirements on the data items are expressed by the accuracy with which users are allowed to know the data values. To the best of our knowledge, this is the first paper that introduces a security model in which the classification of the data items is based on the precision of numeric answers and thus continuous. We propose two methods to assign security classification to the data items: first, the entire *volume* of the constraint object that contains the data item is considered; and second, the length of the *interval* that contains the data item is considered. While volume-based classification is easier to implement than the interval-based one, the second technique is more flexible and it allows higher data availability. For both methods we develop algorithms that generate query answers which are *correct* (i.e., the data item is within the returned interval) and *safe* (i.e., the user is unable to infer which point within the answer is the actual data item).

The organization of the paper is as follows. In Section 2 we give a detailed description of the considered problem and provide intuitive explanations of the concepts involved. In Section 3 we formally define the considered model and the security requirements. Sections 4 and 5 contain the algorithms to generate correct and safe query answers for volume and interval based classification methods, respectively. Finally, in Section 6 we conclude and recommend new directions to extend our research.

2   Problem Formulation

This paper formalizes a security model applicable to numerical databases when a database instance is a vector of numerical values. Users and data items have security classifications. Users (subjects) can access data (objects) through queries. Queries over numeric data return an interval of valid answers, such that the actual data is contained in the interval. The size (length) of the interval (i.e., *precision* of the released data) depends on the security classification of the requested data and the security clearance of the user. Precision of released information can be measured either by the length of the returned data interval or by the volume of the valid constraint space defined by this interval. The system presented in this paper ensures that the interval-based query answers do not allow the users to infer any unauthorized information. The research problem is formulated in terms of the following components: (1) *data model* of which the (numeric) instances consist of objects of discourse, (2) *arithmetic constraints* imposed upon the database, (3) *security classifications* of users and data items, and (4) *queries* requesting numeric values.

The next section provides an example that will be used throughout this paper for illustrative purposes.

2.1   The Running Example

Consider the military database containing information about units **A, B** and **C** mentioned in the Introduction. It contains information about the *number of vehicles, amount of fuel, destination distance, food supply, number of soldiers* etc, as shown in Table 1. Some of these attributes are such as *amount of fuel* are stored, while others such as the *travel range* is derivable. In addition, the database is expected to satisfy the following constraints.

$$\text{number of soldiers} \leq 10,000$$
$$\text{amount of fuel} \leq 20,000(gallon)$$
$$\text{number of vehicles} \geq 45$$
$$3 \times \text{amount of fuel} \geq \text{travel range (miles)}$$

Users of the database are generals, military planners, field commanders, field soldiers, supply supervisors, supply personnel, press and general public. Based on their rank and tasks, users have different access rights to data items. For example, generals are allowed to access all the data in the database while supply personnels are allowed to access information related to supply but can not access information about the field information of the units.

The queries in our model request numerical values, such as *amount of fuel* used by the military unit **A**. Based on the data confidentiality (security classification) the answer is a range of values. In calculating the returned range, we ensure that the user cannot infer other attribute ranges such as the *travel range* of the military unit **A** more precisely than allowed by the security model. Note that we assume that all constraints are known to all users revealing additional information to the users about valid database values.

3   Data Model, Queries and Security Requirements

3.1   Data Model

The data model consists of two sets of attributes of numerical type, and a set of constraints over them.

Database   Each entity of our model consists of a set of n attributes that are directly stored in the data base. Furthermore, there is a set of k derivable attributes, not stored in the database. Consequently, every entity is viewed as a $(n+k)$-dimensional vector $(a_1, \ldots, a_n, a_{n+1} \ldots a_{n+k})$ of numerical type. We say that $(n + k)$ is the dimension of the data model. The set $x_1, \ldots, x_n, x_{n+1} \ldots x_{n+k}$ of variables represents attributes, and $x_1 \mid a_1, \ldots, x_n \mid a_n, x_{n+1} \mid a_{n+1}, \ldots, x_{n+k} \mid a_{n+k}$ represent instantiations of values $a_1, \ldots, a_{n+k}$ to the variables. In the running example the attributes (variables) are unit name, soldiers, food supply, fuel, number of vehicles, destination, fuel/vehicle, and travel range. The database is given in Table 1. As stated, the derivable attributes are not stored explicitly in the database, but can be computed from publically available statistics, and the values stored in the database. We use both derivable and explicitly stored attributes without distinction.

Table 1. A Database of Military Operations

Stored Attributes						Derived Attributes	
Unit Name	Soldiers	Food Suppl. (days)	Fuel (gals)	Number Vehicl.	Destination (miles)	Fuel/Vehicl. (gals)	Travel Rng. (miles)
A	1000	10	15,000	75	400	200	600
B	500	18	7,000	140	85	50	150
C	100	25	3,000	45	67	60	180

Arithmetic Constraints We consider conjunctions of arithmetic constraints of the following forms:

$$f(x_1, x_2, \ldots, x_n, x_{n+1}, \ldots, x_{n+k}) \geq b$$

$$f(x_1, x_2, \ldots, x_n, x_{n+1}, \ldots, x_{n+k}) > b$$

where f is a function, $x_1, \ldots, x_{n+k}$ are variables, and b is a real number.[2]

Let C be the conjunction of constraints of the above forms over variables $x_1, \ldots, x_n, x_{n+1}, \ldots, x_{n+k}$. C defines an $(n + k)$-dimensional *constraint object*, that is all possible instances of database entities that satisfy C.

Consider our military example again. Fig. 2 shows the valid constraint space (possible instances) of the database over attributes amount of fuel (per vehicle) and the destination. The point $A(400, 200)$ correspond to the instance of unit **A**, where the available fuel is 200 gallons for each vehicle and the destination distance is 400 miles. Clearly, $A(400, 200)$ satisfies the constraints.

Queries and Answers We consider *queries* where a user requests a particular data value of x_i, i.e., the coordinate (a_i) of the database along the x_i axis. The *answer* to the query is an interval $I = [a_{i_1}, a_{i_2}]$ of data values, such that $a_{i_1} \leq a_i \leq a_{i_2}$. The query answer can be viewed as two new constraints of the form $a_{i_1} \leq x_i$ and $x_i \leq a_{i_2}$. The *data revealed* by the answer of the query is the new constraint object C' defined by $C \wedge (a_{i_1} \leq x_i) \wedge (x_i \leq a_{i_2})$. C' is a restriction of the original constraint object C.

3.2 Security Model

Multi-level secure relational database systems contain data classified at difference security levels. Users of the database have security clearances assigned.

---

[2] Note that the conjunction of a finite number of arithmetic constraints of the above form can express equalities as well.

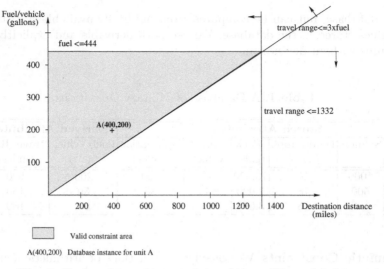

Fig. 2. Fuel and travel range data of the military database

Security classifications and clearances are expressed by security labels that contain two components:(1) a hierarchical component (e.g., top-secret < secret < unclassified) and (2) a non-hierarchical categories (e.g., { supply, press, field-info }). Security labels form a lattice structure with the *dominance* ($\leq$) among the labels. A data access is permitted if the security clearance label of the user dominates the security classification label of the requested data items. For example, in our model, the attribute *destination distance* of unit **A** could be classified as *(top-secret, field-info)* and only officers with security clearances that dominates *(top-secret, field-info)* are allowed to access this data, e.g., generals, with security clearance *(top-secret,{press,supply,field-info})*. However, supply officers with security clearance *(top-secret, supply)* are not allowed to access this data.

For simplicity, we assume that the subjects of our security model are the users.[3] To define the security objects of our model, it is necessary to understand what information a user gains if a query is answered. Let us give an intuitive explanations before formally defining the objects and their security classifications of our model.

Originally a user knows:
– The (n+k) -dimensional constraint object C.
– The data instances satisfy C.
– If C is bounded for a data value of x_i, then the value of x_i must be in the interval $[min(a_i), max(a_i)]$, where $min(a_i)$ and $max(a_i)$ are the smallest and largest possible values of x_i defined by C.

After Answering a Query that is an interval $[a_{i_1}, a_{i_2}]$ containing a_i, the value of x_i the user knows:

---

[3] Usually in security, a distinction is made between the users and the principals (subjects) acting on behalf of them.

- C', the restriction of C by the two new constraints $a_{i_1} \leq x_i$ and $x_i \leq a_{i_2}$.
- The database is a point within C'.
- If C' is bounded for a data item x', than the value of x' must be in the interval $[a', a'']$, where a' and a'' are the smallest and largest possible values of x' defined by C'.

Intuitively, the size of the constraint object (or its projection) known by the user to contain the database represents how accurately the user knows the actual data value. The smaller the volume (projection), the more accurate the user's knowledge about the actual data values. We assume that all possible instances of an entity within a constraint space have the same probability to be the actual database, i.e., the database is *uniformly distributed* within the constraint object. We use the properties of the constraint object, such as volume, projection, to define the security requirements on the data items.

Definition 1. *(Volume and Projection of a constraint Object)*
Let C be an $(n + k)$-dimensional constraint object. The volume *of C is defined as the volume of the $(n + k)$-dimensional geometrical shape. The* projection *of C on axis x (data item x) is an interval $[a_1, a_2]$, where a_1 and a_2 are the minimal and maximal values along the x axis defined by C.*

In this papers we present two approaches to define the *security* of objects in our database. First, we use the *volume* of C as the security object. While this method is simple and can be easily implemented, it does not allow to assign different sensitivity levels to the different data items. [4] Second, we propose a security classification based on *projections* of C to represent the security restrictions on the individual data items. This method is enhanced by a probability measurement that incorporates the shape of the constraint object, which is not reflected in the projection. The second approach allows not only the assignment of different security classifications to the individual data items but also, to represent partial disclosure. The following sections contain the detailed descriptions of the two methods and algorithms that generate safe query answers according to the security restrictions.

4   Security by Volume

In this section we present a security model in which the absolute volumes of the disclosed (known by the user to contain the database) constraint objects are used to represent the sensitivity of the database.

Definition 2. *(Volume Objects)*
Let $l_1, \ldots, l_k$ be a set of security labels and C a constraint object with volume V. For each security label l_i, $i = 1, \ldots, k$ we create a volume object, denoted by V_{l_i}, as follows:

---

[4] Same as database level of security granularity in relational databases.

1. $V_{l_i} \leq V$, *i.e., the volume object must be smaller than the volume of the constraint object.*
2. *If $l_i \leq l_j$ then $V_{l_i} \geq V_{l_j}$, i.e., volume objects at lower security levels can not be smaller than volume objects at higher security level.*

The secrecy of the database is violated if a user with security clearance l_i is able to disclose a constraint object with volume less than V_{l_i}. We propose a security mechanism based on controlling the *volume* of the constraint object disclosed by the user. For this approach it is necessary that the original constraint object C is bounded from every direction.

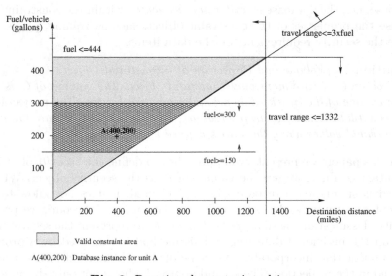

Fig. 3. Restricted constraint object

To visualize the security classifications, consider Fig. 2. The shaded area defines the valid data values. Since knowing that the database must satisfy the constraints, the user knows that the available fuel per vehicle cannot exceed 444 gallons (maximum 20,000 gallons fuel available for each unit divided by the minimum number of vehicles 45 for each unit) and, therefore, the maximal travel distance (3 times the available gallons of fuel per vehicle) is less than or equal to 1332 miles. The actual value of available fuel for each vehicle of unit **A** is 200 gallons, and the destination distance is 400 miles. The total volume of the valid constraint space is 295,704.

Assume, that in addition to the constraints of the database, the user knows that the amount of fuel available per vehicle is between 150 and 300 gallons. Clearly, the user's knowledge about the fuel is more accurate now than before. The darkly shaded area of Fig. 3 shows the new constraint object C' after the addition of $150 \leq fuel/vehicle \leq 300$. The volume of C' is 101,250. The increase of the user's knowledge about the data value is reflected by the decrease of the size (volume) of constraint object. Observation of the reduced constraint object indicates that the user also gained information about travel distance. The maximal travel distance cannot exceed 900 miles.

Definition 3. *(Correct, Safe and Efficient Query Answer by Volume)*
Let DB be the database, x the data item in DB requested by the user, l the user's security clearance, C the constraint object known by the user to contain the database, and V_l the volume object at security level l. A query answer $[a_1, a_2]$ is

1. Correct *if $a \in [a_1, a_2]$, i.e., the actual data value a of x is within the returned interval.*
2. Safe *if the query answer does not violate the security requirements, i.e., if C' is the new constraint object $C \wedge (a_1 \le x) \wedge (x \le a_2)$ with volume V' then:*
   (a) $V' \ge V_l$ *and*
   (b) *DB is uniformly distributed in C', i.e., the user knows only that the data item satisfies C'.*
3. Efficient *if given $l_i < l$ and V_{l_i} the volume object at security level l_i $V' \le V_{l_i}$, i.e., released information is more accurate at higher security level.*

The algorithm given in Fig. 4 generates a correct, safe and efficient query answer. It uses a random number generator based on the uniform distribution. To ensure that the algorithm terminates, we use a threshold value 100,000 to limit the number of trials to generate correct, safe, and efficient query answer. If no such answer is found, the algorithm returns a default answer, that is the minimal and maximal valid values defined by the constraint object.

Theorem 1. *Algorithm 1 (1) terminates and returns a (2) correct, (3) safe and (4) efficient answer according to Definition 3.*

Proof. 1. *Termination:* straightforward by Step 3.
2. *Correctness:* By the construction of points a_1 and a_2 in Steps 3.b and 3.c, respectively, Algorithm 1 ensures that the data value a is within the generated interval.
3. *Safety:* (a) By comparing the volume of the restricted constraint object V' with the volume object V_l in Step 6, Algorithm 1 ensures that V' is not smaller than V_l. (b) By using a random number generator based on uniform distribution, any point within the restricted constraint structure C' has the same probability to be the database, i.e., the database is uniformly distributed within C'. Also, since any new information about a data item is fully contained in the previous answers thus no possibly hazardous overlap can occur.
4. *Efficiency:* Follows from step 7.II.a.

Returning back to our running example, assume that the answer given as a result of a query made by a user with clearance *(secret,press)* for the amount of fuel used by unit **A** is $[150, 300]$, as given by Fig. 3. Furthermore assume that the volume objet associated with this security level is $V_{(secret,press)} = 150,000$. Since the volume of the restricted constraint object as given is 101,250, the answer is correct, safe, and efficient (but not optimal).

Algorithm 1: Query Answer by Volume
INPUT   • User's query Q requesting data item x • User's previous query answers $q_1, \ldots, q_m$ • User's security clearance l • Constraints object C known by the user to contain the DB • Database point DB • Volume objects $V_{l_1}, \ldots, V_{l_h}$
OUTPUT   • Answer to Q • Restricted constraint object C'

METHOD
    1. **If** $q_1, \ldots, q_m$ contains an answer $[a_1', a_2']$ for data item x, **then**
      (a) Return $[a_1', a_2']$ as the answer.
      (b) *Generate* C' as $C' = C$.
    2. Initialization:
      (a) Let a' be the smallest and a'' the largest possible value of x defined by C.
      (b) $r = 0$
    3. **If** $r > 100,000$ **then** Return $[a', a'']$ as default answer.
      Else *Generate* two points a_1 and a_2 as follows:
      (a) Let a be the actual value of data item x
      (b) *Randomly* pick a_1 from the interval $[a', a]$
      (c) *Randomly* pick a_2 from the interval $[a, a'']$
    4. *Generate* two linear constraints:
      (a) $a_1 \leq x$
      (b) $x \leq a_2$
    5. *Generate* the new constraint object $C' = C \wedge (a_1 \leq x) \wedge (x \leq a_2)$
    6. *Calculate* volume V' of C'
    7. *Verify* security requirements:
      I. **If** V' smaller than V_l (security requirement is violated) **then**
      (a) $r = r + 1$ and return to 3
      II. **Else** (security is not violated) **then**
      (a) **If** $V_{l'} \leq V'$, where $V_{l'}$ is the volume object at security level l' such that $l' \leq l$ **then** (more accurate answer is possible)
        $r = r + 1$ and return to 3
      (b) **Else**
        i. *Return* $[a_1, a_2]$ as the answer to the query
        ii. *Store* C' as the new constraint object known by the user.

Fig. 4. Query Answer by Volume

5   Security by Interval

Similarly to the previous section, the information disclosed by a user is reflected in the *constraint object* by this users. However, in this section we explore a flexible security classification that is based on the projection of the constraint object on the data items. The proposed method allows the security officer to individually classify each data item.

First, let us give an intuitive example. Consider the military database we presented earlier and assume that the travel range is more sensitive than the amount of fuel, e.g., the enemy (public) is not allowed to deduce the travel range with accuracy of 200 miles, while fuel information is allowed for release within 50 gallons range, e.g., each vehicle has fuel between 180 and 230 gallons. However, by releasing this fuel information, the travel range is reduced to $690 - 540 = 150$ miles. While the security requirement is satisfied for fuel, it is clearly violated for travel range.

Moreover, it is possible, that the security officer would like to consider disclosures, where the data item is not fully disclosed within a given interval size but has high probability. Note, that we assumed that originally the database is uniformly distributed within the constraint object C. Because of this uniform distribution, the probability that the database is within a sub-object C' of C is proportion to the volumes of C' and C. For example, if the the volume of C is V and the volume of C' is V', the probability that the database is contained in C' is V'/V. This observation allows the security officer to protect data from partial disclosures. For example, we can assign that users with unclassified security clearances are not allowed to know the travel distance within 100 miles with probability 85%.

Definition 4. *(Interval objects)*
Let $x_1, \ldots, x_{n+k}$ be a database, $l_1, \ldots, l_h$ a set of security labels and C a constraint object with volume V. For each data item x_i $i = 1, \ldots, n+k$ and for each security label l_j, $j = 1, \ldots, h$ we create an interval object, *denoted by (I_{i_j}, p_{i_j}), as follows:*

1. *I_{i_j} defines the smallest interval length (accuracy) with which users with security clearances l_j are allowed to know the value of x_i with probability p_{i_j}.*
2. *If $l_s \leq l_r$ and $p_{i_s} = p_{i_r}$ then $I_{i_s} \geq I_{i_r}$, i.e., interval size of an object at a low security level can not be smaller than the interval size of the same object at high security level.*
3. *If $l_s \leq l_r$ and $I_{i_s} = I_{i_r}$ then $p_{i_s} \leq p_{i_r}$, i.e., if two interval sizes of a data item are the same at different security levels, then the high security level can not have lower probability assigned to than the low security level.*

Intuitively, given a data item x and its interval object (I, p) at security level l, the secrecy of x is violated if a user with security clearance l is able to disclose a constraint object C such that C contains a sub-object C', with projection size on x smaller than or equal to I, that contains the database with probability higher than p.

Definition 5. *(Correct and Safe Query Answer - Interval)*
Let $x_1, \ldots, x_{n+k}$ be the database, x_i the data item in DB requested by the user, l the user's security clearance, C the constraint object known by the user to contain the database, and $(I_{1_l}, p_{1_l}), \ldots, (I_{n+k_l}, p_{n+k_l})$ the interval objects of data items $x_1, \ldots, x_i, \ldots, x_{n+k}$ at security level l. A query answer $[a_1, a_2]$ is correct and safe if

1. Correct: $a \in [a_1, a_2]$, where a is the actual data value of x_i.
2. Safe: the query answer does not violate the security requirements, i.e., if C'
   is the new constraint object $C \wedge (a_1 \leq x_i) \wedge (x_i \leq a_2)$ with volume V' then
   (a) C' does not contain a sub-object C'_j with projection size I'_{j_l} on data
       item x_j such that $I'_{j_l} \leq I_{j_l}$ $j = 1, \ldots, n + k$ and volume V'_j, such that
       V'_j / V' greater than p_{j_l} and
   (b) DB is uniformly distributed in C', i.e., the user knows only that the
       database is any point within C'.

We propose a security mechanism to control the *length of the answer interval*
returned to the user ensure that the security requirements are satisfied. This
approach does not require that the original constraint object is bounded.

Theorem 2. *Algorithm 2 (1) terminates and returns a (2) correct and (3) safe
query answer according to Definition 5.*

Proof. 1. *Termination:* straightforward by Step 3 and 6.
2. *Correctness:* By the construction of lengths l (Step 3), l' (Step 6) and the
   points a_1 (Steps 4,5) and a_2 (Steps 7,8), Algorithm 2 ensures that the data
   value a is within the generated interval.
3. *Safety:* (a) By verifying for every data item that no disallowed *interval object*
   is disclosed (Step 12), Algorithm 2 ensures that the security requirements are
   not violated. Further, (b) by using a random number generator based on the
   uniform distribution, any point within the restricted constraint structure C'
   has the same probability to be the database, i.e., the database is uniformly
   distributed within C'. Similarly to the security classifications via volume
   objects, note that any new information about a data item is fully contained
   in the previous answers thus no possibly hazardous overlap can occur.

Note, that since we do not enforce any restriction on the correlation of interval
size and probability we can't define efficient answer similarly to the volume based
model. However, if one of these measurements are fixed, e.g., all interval objects
given with 0.8 probability, we can define effective answer similarly to the volume
based method.

6   Conclusions

We have presented a model to specify the accuracy with which users are allowed to access numeric values. As shown, restrictions can be enforced either on
the volume of the disclosed constraint object that surrounds the protected data
items, or on the interval of a specific data value. While volume based accuracy
is easier to enforce than the interval based one, the later provides more flexibility, therefore improved data availability. We developed algorithms to compute
correct and safe answers to queries for both measures of accuracy.

Finally, we conclude by recommending further research directions. Currently
our algorithms provide an effectively accurate answer that is not optimal, i.e.,

Algorithm 2: Query Answer by Interval	
INPUT	1. User's query requesting data item x
	2. User's previous query answers $q_1, \ldots, q_m$
	3. User's security clearance l
	4. Constraints object C known by the user
	5. Database point DB
	6. Set S of Interval objects of the form (I_l, p_l)
OUTPUT	1. Answer to Q
	2. Restricted constraint object C'
METHOD	

1. **If** $q_1, \ldots, q_m$ contains an answer $[a_1', a_2']$ for x **then**
   (a) Return $[a_1', a_2']$ as the answer
   (b) Generate C' as $C' = C$
2. Initialization:
   (a) Let a' be the smallest and a'' the largest possible value of x defined by C.
   (b) $r = 0$
3. **If** $r > 100,000$ **then** Return $[a', a'']$ as default answer.
   Else *Generate* a random length l
4. Randomly *pick a point* a_1 in the interval $[a - l, a]$ (starting point of the answer), where a is the actual value of x in the database.
5. **If** $a_1 < a'$ **then** (security is violated) **then**
   $r = r + 1$ and return to Point 3.
6. **If** $r > 100,000$ **then** Return $[a', a'']$ as default answer.
   Else *Generate* a random length l'
7. **If** $l' \leq l$ (incorrect answer) or $l' < I_l$ (security is violated) **then**
   $r = r + 1$ and return to Point 6
   Else generate $a_2 = a_1 + l'$ (end point of the answer)
8. **If** $a_2 > a''$ **then** (security is violated) **then**
   $r = r + 1$ and return to Point 6.
9. *Generate* two linear constraints:
   (a) $a_1 \leq x$
   (b) $x \leq a_2$
10. *Generate* the new constraint object $C' = C \wedge (a_1 \leq x) \wedge (x \leq a_2)$
11. *Calculate* volume V' of C'
12. *Verify* security requirements for every data item y in the DB
    If there exist a sub-object C_i' of C' such that
    (a) $\mid C_i' \mid_y \leq I_{y_l}$, where $\mid C_i' \mid_y$ is the projection of C_i' on y and I_{y_l} is from (I_{y_l}, p_{y_l}), and
    (b) $V_i'/V' > p_{y_l}$
    then (security is violated) $r = r + 1$ and return to Point 3
13. **Else** (security is not violated)
    (a) *Return* $[a_1, a_2]$ as the answer to the query
    (b) *Store* C' as the new constraint object known by the user.

Fig. 5. Query Answer by Interval

the most accurate value allowed to the user. While we believe it is impossible to provide a general algorithm that generates safe, correct, and optimal query answer such a method may exist for restricted families of arithmetic constraints. Also, in this paper we considered queries that request the value of a single data item. Our work could be extended to incorporate queries requesting several data items simultaneously and incorporating selection conditions. Finally, the interval based accuracy can handle sets of sensitive intervals and probabilities for each data item. For example, a data item x may be accessed by a user only if none of the classifications $(I_{x_1}, p_{x_1}), \ldots, (I_{x_k}, p_{x_k})$ is violated.

References

BL75.   D. E. Bell and L. J. LaPadula. Secure computer systems: Mathematical foundation and model. Technical report, Mitre Corp. Report No. M74-244, Bedford, Mass., 1975. 98

Buc90.   L. J. Buczkowski. Database inference controller. In D. L. Spooner and C. Landwehr, editors, *Database Security III: Status and Prospects*, pages 311–322. North-Holland, Amsterdam, 1990. 100

DdVS99a.   S. Dawson, S. De Capitani di Vimercati, and P. Samarati. Minimal data upgrating to prevent inference and association attacks. In *Proc. of the 18th ACM SIGMOD-SIGACT-SIGART Symposium on Principles of Database Systems*, pages 114–125, 1999. 100

DdVS99b.   S. Dawson, S. De Capitani di Vimercati, and P. Samarati. Specification and enforcement of classification and inference constraints. In *Proc. IEEE Symp. on Security and Privacy*, 1999. 100

Den76.   D. E. Denning. A lattice model of secure information flow. *Comm. ACM*, 19(5):236–243, May 1976. 98

Den82.   D. E. Denning. *Cryptography and Data Security*. Addison-Wesley, Mass., 1982. 100

Den85.   D. E. Denning. Commutative filters for reducing inference threats in multilevel database systems. In *Proc. IEEE Symp. on Security and Privacy*, pages 134–146, 1985. 100

GM84.   J. A. Goguen and J. Meseguer. Unwinding and inference control. In *Proc. IEEE Symp. on Security and Privacy*, pages 75–86, 1984. 100

Hin88.   T. H. Hinke. Inference aggregation detection in database management systems. In *Proc. IEEE Symp. on Security and Privacy*, pages 96–106, 1988. 100

Mor88.   M. Morgenstern. Controlling logical inference in multilevel database systems. In *Proc. IEEE Symp. on Security and Privacy*, pages 245–255, 1988. 100

MSS88.   S. Mazumdar, D. Stemple, and T. Sheard. Resolving the tension between integrity and security using a theorem prover. In *Proc. ACM Int'l Conf. Management of Data*, pages 233–242, 1988. 100

RJHS95.   S. Rath, D. Jones, J. Hale, and S. Shenoi. A tool for inference detection and knowledge discovery in databases. In *Proc. of the 9th IFIP WG11.3 Workshop on Database Security*, pages 317–332, 1995. 100

Smi90.   G. W. Smith. Modeling security-relevant data semantics. In *Proc. IEEE Symp. Research in Security and Privacy*, pages 384–391, 1990. 100

SO87.   T. Su and G. Ozsoyoglu. Data dependencies and inference control in mul-
           tilevel relational database systems. In *Proc. IEEE Symp. Security and
           Privacy*, pages 202–211, 1987. 100
SO91.   T. Su and G. Ozsoyoglu. Inference in MLS database systems. *IEEE Trans.
           Knowledge and Data Eng.*, 3(4):474–485, December 1991. 100
ST90.   P. D. Stachour and B. Thuraisingham. Design of LDV: A multilevel secure
           relational database management system. *IEEE Trans. Knowledge and Data
           Eng.*, 2(2):190–209, June 1990. 100
Thu87.   B. M. Thuraisingham. Security checking in relational database management
           systems augmented with inference engines. *Computers and Security*, 6:479–
           492, 1987. 100

Refinements and Independence: A Simple Method for Identifying Tractable Disjunctive Constraints

Mathias Broxvall*, Peter Jonsson**, and Jochen Renz***.

Department of Computer and Information Science
Linköpings Universitet
S-581 83 Linköping, Sweden
{matbr,petej,g-jocre}@ida.liu.se

Abstract. The constraint satisfaction problem provides a natural framework for expressing many combinatorial problems. Since the general problem is NP-hard, an important question is how to restrict the problem to ensure tractability. The concept of independence has proven to be a useful method for constructing tractable constraint classes from existing classes. Since checking the independence property may be a difficult task, we provide a simple method for checking this property. Our method builds on a somewhat surprising connection between independence and refinements which is a recently established way of reducing one constraint satisfaction problem to another. Refinements have two interesting properties: (1) they preserve consistency; and (2) their correctness can be easily checked by a computer-assisted analysis. We show that all previous independence results of the point algebra for totally ordered and partially ordered time can be derived using this method. We also employ the method for deriving new tractable classes.

1 Introduction

The constraint satisfaction problem provides a framework for expressing combinatorial problems in computer science and elsewhere. The basic computational problem is NP-hard [12] so an important question is how to restrict the problem to ensure tractability. This research has mainly followed two different paths: restricting the scope of the constraints [8, 7], *i.e.*, which variables may be constrained with other variables, or restricting the constraints [6, 10, 17], *i.e.*, the allowed values for mutually constrained variables. In this paper, we will only consider problems where the constraints are restricted.

* This research has been supported by the ECSEL graduate student program.
** This research has been supported by the Swedish Research Council for the Engineering Sciences (TFR) under grant 97-301.
*** This research has been supported by the Deutsche Forschungsgemeinschaft under grant Ne 623/1-2 which is part of the DFG priority program "Spatial Cognition"

R. Dechter (Ed.): CP 2000, LNCS 1894, pp. 114-127, 2000.

As we already have noted, quite a large number of tractable subclasses of the CSP problem has been identified in the literature. Thus, it is of considerable interest to investigate how tractable constraint types may be combined in order to yield more general problems which are still tractable. Cohen *et al.* [5] have studied so-called "disjunctive constraints", *i.e.*, constraints which are disjunctions of constraints of specified types. They identified a certain property, *independence*, which allows for new tractable constraint classes to be constructed from existing classes. Several important classes of tractable constraints can be obtained by their method such as the Horn fragment of propositional logic, the ORD-Horn fragment [13] of Allen's Interval Algebra, and the class of max-closed constraints [10].

It is hardly surprising that deciding the independence property may be a highly non-trivial task in many cases. The main goal of this paper is to present a simple method for checking the independence property. Our method builds on a connection between the independence property and *refinements* [15]. Loosely speaking, a refinement is a way of reducing one CSP problem to another and it has the property that if the second problem can be decided by path-consistency, then path-consistency decides the first problem, too. Refinements were successful in proving tractability of large subsets of the Region Connection Calculus as well as Allen's Interval Algebra [15]. One important aspect of refinements is that their correctness can be easily checked by a computer-assisted analysis which implies that the independence property can be automatically checked in many cases.

Using our method, we show that all previous independence results on the time point algebra for partially ordered time [4, 3, 1] and the point algebra for linear time [4, 5] can be derived using refinements and that this is sufficient to identify *all* tractable sets of disjunctions of relations for the partially ordered time-point algebra as well as for the point algebra for linear time. We also use this method for deriving new tractable subclasses of the Region Connection Calculus [14].

The paper is organized as follows: In Section 2 we introduce the basic concepts that are needed in the rest of the paper. In Section 3 we relate refinements and independence and prove the main result that refinements imply independence. In Section 4 we apply this result to various tractable sets of relations and derive independent relations which form large tractable sets of disjunctions of relations. Finally, the last section contains some concluding remarks.

2   Preliminaries

2.1   CSPs, Disjunctions, and Independence

Let $\mathcal{A}$ be a finite set of jointly exhaustive and pairwise disjoint binary relations, also called *basic* relations. We denote the standard operations composition, intersection and converse by $\circ$, $\cap$ and $^{-1}$, respectively. Furthermore, we define the unary operation $\neg$ such that $\neg \mathcal{S} = \mathcal{A} \backslash \mathcal{S}$ for all $\mathcal{S} \subseteq \mathcal{A}$.

The consistency problem $\text{CSPSAT}(\mathcal{S})$ for sets $\mathcal{S} \subseteq 2^{\mathcal{A}}$ over a domain $\mathcal{D}$ is defined as follows [16]:

Instance: A set V of variables over a domain D and a finite set Θ of binary constraints xRy, where $R \in S$ and $x, y \in V$.

Question: Is there an instantiation of all variables in Θ such that all constraints are satisfied?

Naturally, a set of basic relations is to be interpreted as a disjunction of its member relations. Given an instance Θ of CSPSAT(R), let Mods(Θ) denote the class of models of Θ (*i.e.* the satisfying instantiations) and Vars(Θ) the variables appearing in Θ.

Next, we introduce operators for combining relations.

Definition 1 Let R_1, R_2 be relations of arity i, j and define the disjunction $R_1 \vee R_2$ of arity $i + j$ as follows:

$$R_1 \vee R_2 = \{(x_1, \ldots, x_{i+j}) \in D^{i+j} | (x_1, \ldots, x_i) \in R_1 \vee \\ (x_{i+1}, \ldots, x_{i+j}) \in R_2\}$$

Thus, the disjunction of two relations with arity i, j is the relation with arity $i+j$ satisfying either of the two relations. Note that the CSPSAT problem trivially can be extended to handle disjunctive and non-binary constraints.

To give a concrete example, let $D = \{0, 1\}$ and let the relations And $= \{\langle 1, 1 \rangle\}$ and Xor $= \{\langle 0, 1 \rangle, \langle 1, 0 \rangle\}$ be given. The disjunction of And and Xor is given by:

$$\text{And} \vee \text{Xor} = \left\{ \begin{array}{l} \langle 0,0,0,1 \rangle, \langle 0,1,0,1 \rangle, \langle 1,0,0,1 \rangle, \langle 1,1,0,1 \rangle, \\ \langle 0,0,1,0 \rangle, \langle 0,1,1,0 \rangle, \langle 1,0,1,0 \rangle, \langle 1,1,1,0 \rangle, \\ \langle 1,1,0,0 \rangle, \langle 1,1,0,1 \rangle, \langle 1,1,1,0 \rangle, \langle 1,1,1,1 \rangle \end{array} \right\}$$

We see that the constraint x And $y \vee x$ Xor z is satisfiable when x, y and z has, for instance, been instantiated to $1, 0, 0$, respectively.

The definition of disjunction can easily be extended to sets of relations.

Definition 2 Let Γ_1, Γ_2 be sets of relations and define the disjunction $\Gamma_1 \overset{\times}{\vee} \Gamma_2$ as follows:

$$\Gamma_1 \overset{\times}{\vee} \Gamma_2 = \Gamma_1 \cup \Gamma_2 \cup \{R_1 \vee R_2 \mid R_1 \in \Gamma_1, R_2 \in \Gamma_2\}$$

The disjunction of two sets of relation $\Gamma_1 \overset{\times}{\vee} \Gamma_2$ is the set of disjunctions of each pair of relations in Γ_1, Γ_2 plus the sets Γ_1, Γ_2. It is sensible to include Γ_1 and Γ_2 since one wants to have the choice of using the disjunction or not. In many cases we shall be concerned with constraints that are specified by disjunctions of an arbitrary number of relations. Thus, we make the following definition: for any set of relations, Δ, define $\Delta^* = \bigcup_{i=0}^{\infty} \Delta^{\vee i}$ where $\Delta^{\vee 0} = \{\bot\}$ and $\Delta^{\vee i+1} = \Delta^{\vee i} \overset{\times}{\vee} \Delta$.

We continue by defining the independence property.

Definition 3 For any sets of relations Γ and Δ, we say that Δ is independent with respect to Γ if for any set of constraints C in CSPSAT($\Gamma \cup \Delta$), C has a solution whenever every $C' \subseteq C$, which contains at most one constraint whose constraint relation belongs to Δ, has a solution.

Theorem 4 For any sets of relations Γ and Δ, if $\mathsf{CSPSAT}(\Gamma \cup \Delta)$ is tractable and Δ is independent with respect to Γ, then $\mathsf{CSPSAT}(\Gamma_\vee^\times \Delta^*)$ is tractable.

The notion of independence can alternatively (but equivalently) be defined as follows: Let $C = \{c_1, \ldots, c_k\}$ and $D = \{d_1, \ldots, d_n\}$ be arbitrary finite sets of constraints over Γ and Δ, respectively. Then, Δ is independent of Γ iff for every possible choice of C and D, the following holds: if $C \cup \{d_i\}$, $1 \leq i \leq n$, is satisfiable, then $C \cup D$ is satisfiable.

2.2   Refinements

We review the basics of *refinements* in this subsection. For proofs and additional results, see Renz [15]. A *refinement* of a constraint xRy is a constraint $xR'y$ such that $R' \subseteq R$. A refinement of a set of constraints Θ is a set of constraints Θ' such that every constraint of Θ' is a refinement of a constraint of Θ. We assume that a set of constraints Θ contains n ordered variables $x_1, \ldots, x_n$. The following definition is central.

Definition 5 Let $\mathcal{S}, \mathcal{T} \subseteq 2^{\mathcal{A}}$. $\mathcal{S}$ can be *reduced by refinement* to $\mathcal{T}$, if for every relation $S \in \mathcal{S}$ there is a relation $T_S \in \mathcal{T}$ with $T_S \subseteq S$ and every path-consistent set Θ of constraints over $\mathcal{S}$ can be refined to a set Θ' by replacing $x_i S x_j \in \Theta$ with $x_i T_S x_j \in \Theta'$ for $i < j$, such that enforcing path-consistency to Θ' does not result in an inconsistency.

Lemma 6 If path-consistency decides $\mathsf{CSPSAT}(\mathcal{T})$ for a set $\mathcal{T} \subseteq 2^{\mathcal{A}}$, and $\mathcal{S}$ can be reduced by refinement to $\mathcal{T}$, then path-consistency decides $\mathsf{CSPSAT}(\mathcal{S})$.

In order to handle different refinements, we introduce a *refinement matrix* that contains for every relation $S \in \mathcal{S}$ all specified refinements.

Definition 7 A *refinement matrix* M of $\mathcal{S}$ has $|\mathcal{S}| \times 2^{|\mathcal{A}|}$ Boolean entries such that for $S \in \mathcal{S}$, $R \in 2^{\mathcal{A}}$, $M[S][R] = true$ only if $R \subseteq S$.

M is called the *basic refinement matrix* if $M[S][R] = true$ if and only if $S = R$.

The algorithm CHECK-REFINEMENTS (see Figure 1) takes as input a set of relations $\mathcal{S}$ and a refinement matrix M of $\mathcal{S}$ and either succeeds or fails. A similar algorithm, GET-REFINEMENTS, returns the revised refinement matrix if CHECK-REFINEMENTS returns `succeed` and the basic refinement matrix if CHECK-REFINEMENTS returns `fail`. Since $\mathcal{A}$ is a finite set of relations, M can be changed only a finite number of times, so both algorithms always terminate.

If CHECK-REFINEMENTS returns `succeed` and GET-REFINEMENTS returns M', we have pre-computed all possible refinements of every path-consistent triple of variables as given in the refinement matrix M'. Thus, applying these refinements to a path-consistent set of constraints can never result in an inconsistency when enforcing path-consistency.

Theorem 8 Let $\mathcal{S}, \mathcal{T} \subseteq 2^{\mathcal{A}}$, and let M be a refinement matrix of $\mathcal{S}$. GET-REFINEMENTS$(\mathcal{S}, M)$ returns the refinement matrix M'. If for every $S \in \mathcal{S}$ there is a $T_S \in \mathcal{T}$ with $M'[S][T_S] = true$, then $\mathcal{S}$ can be reduced by refinement to $\mathcal{T}$.

Algorithm: CHECK-REFINEMENTS
Input: A set $\mathcal{S}$ and a refinement matrix M of $\mathcal{S}$.
Output: `fail` if the refinements specified in M can make
a path-consistent triple of constraints over $\mathcal{S}$ inconsistent;
`succeed` otherwise.

1. changes $\leftarrow$ true
2. *while* changes *do*
3. $oldM \leftarrow M$
4.   *for every* path-consistent triple
       $T = (R_{12}, R_{23}, R_{13})$ of relations over $\mathcal{S}$ *do*
5.   *for every* refinement $T' = (R'_{12}, R'_{23}, R'_{13})$ of T
           with $oldM[R_{12}][R'_{12}] = oldM[R_{23}][R'_{23}] =$
           $oldM[R_{13}][R'_{13}]$ =true *do*
6. $T'' \leftarrow$ PATH-CONSISTENCY(T')
7.   *if* $T'' = (R''_{12}, R''_{23}, R''_{13})$ contains the empty
               relation *then return* `fail`
8.   *else do* $M[R_{12}][R''_{12}] \leftarrow$ true,
                       $M[R_{23}][R''_{23}] \leftarrow$ true,
                       $M[R_{13}][R''_{13}] \leftarrow$ true
9.   *if* $M = oldM$ *then* changes $\leftarrow$ false
10. *return* `succeed`

Fig. 1. Algorithm CHECK-REFINEMENTS

Now, the procedures CHECK-REFINEMENTS and GET-REFINEMENTS can be used to prove tractability for sets of relations.

Theorem 9 Let $\mathcal{S}, \mathcal{T} \subseteq 2^{\mathcal{A}}$ be two sets such that path-consistency decides CSPSAT$(\mathcal{T})$, and let M be a refinement matrix of $\mathcal{S}$. GET-REFINEMENTS$(\mathcal{S}, M)$ returns M'. If for every $S \in \mathcal{S}$ there is a $T_S \in \mathcal{T}$ with $M'[S][T_S] = true$, then path-consistency decides CSPSAT$(\mathcal{S})$.

Given this theorem, what is needed for proving a set $\mathcal{S}$ to be tractable is a set $\mathcal{T}$ for which path-consistency is known to decide consistency and a refinement matrix M. Although it might be difficult to find a suitable refinement matrix, the simple heuristic of eliminating all identity relations from disjunctive relations led to a suitable refinement matrix for many interesting sets of relations (cf. [15]). For the scope of this paper we are interested in a particular type of refinement matrices which we define as follows:

Definition 10 Let $R \in \mathcal{A}$. M^R is the *R-refinement matrix* of a set $S \subseteq 2^{\mathcal{A}}$ if for every $S \in \mathcal{S}$, $M^R[S][S'] = true$ iff $S' = S \cap R$ and $S' \neq \emptyset$ or $S' = S$.

Definition 11 Let $\mathcal{S} \subseteq 2^{\mathcal{A}}$ such that path-consistency decides CSPSAT$(\mathcal{S})$ and $R \in 2^{\mathcal{A}}$. We say that R is a *refinement* of $\mathcal{S}$ if CHECK-REFINEMENTS$(\mathcal{S}, M^R)$ returns `succeed`.

Since the refinement matrix we are interested in, namely M^R for a particular relation R is given, we do not face the difficulty of the refinement method of finding a suitable refinement matrix.

3   Relating Refinements and Independence

The independence property has been proven for many different relations [5, 4], but there is no general proof schema for proving this property, so it is usually a matter of luck or intuition if a proof of independence can be found. In contrast to this, it is possible to verify refinements automatically [15] by merely running the algorithm given in Figure 1. It would, hence, be a large improvement if the same could be done for proving independence. In this section, we study the relationship between the notion of refinements and independence. It turns out that the two notions are very similar and that the algorithm for verifying refinements can also be used for proving independence.

When looking at the definitions of refinements and independence one notes that refinements eliminate labels from given constraints without changing consistency while by the independence property it is possible to add additional constraints without changing consistency. Eliminating a label R from a given constraint xTy, however, is equivalent to adding the constraint $x\neg Ry$. The correspondence between the two notions is formulated in the following theorem.

Theorem 12 Given a set of relations $\mathcal{S} \subseteq 2^{\mathcal{A}}$ for which path-consistency decides consistency and a refinement matrix M^R. If CHECK-REFINEMENTS$(\mathcal{S}, M^R)$ returns succeed, then R is independent of S.

Proof. Given a path-consistent set Θ of constraints over $\mathcal{S}$. Θ' is obtained from Θ by refining all constraints $x_i T_i y_i \in \Theta$ with $T_i \not\subseteq \neg R$ to $x_i T_i \cap R y_i$. Since CHECK-REFINEMENTS$(\mathcal{S}, M^R)$ returns succeed, all these refinements can be made without making Θ' inconsistent. Instead of refining a constraint $x_i T_i y_i$ to $x_i T_i \cap R y_i$ it is equivalent to add the constraint $h_i \equiv x_i R y_i$ to Θ. Unless the constraint $x_i S y_i$ with $S \subseteq \neg R$ is contained in Θ, $\Theta \cup \{h_i\}$ is consistent. Thus, $\Theta \cup H$ ($H = \{h_1, \ldots, h_n\}$) is consistent if and only if $\Theta \cup \{h_i\}$ is consistent for all i, and, therefore, R is independent of $\mathcal{S}$.   □

This theorem gives us the possibility to prove independence of a relation R with respect to a set $\mathcal{S}$ automatically by simply running CHECK-REFINEMENTS $(\mathcal{S}, M^R)$. If the algorithm returns succeed, we know that R is independent of $\mathcal{S}$. In order to make use of a negative answer of the algorithm, we also have to prove the opposite direction, *i.e.*, independence of a relation R with respect to a set $\mathcal{S}$ implies that CHECK-REFINEMENTS$(\mathcal{S}, M^R)$ returns succeed. Proving this is equivalent to saying that $\Theta \cup H$ is consistent if and only if $\Theta \cup \{h_i\}$ is consistent for all i implies that $\Theta \cup \{h_i\}$ is always consistent for all i unless $\neg h_i \in \Theta$. Although this is a highly desirable property, we have not been able to prove this nor did we find a counterexample. There are, however, many examples for which this conjecture holds. As we will see in Section 4, this includes all independence results for the point algebra for partially ordered time given by Broxvall and Jonsson [4] as well as those given for the point algebra for linear time. We give a proof of a slightly limited version of this conjecture.

Definition 13 Let $\mathcal{S} \subseteq 2^{\mathcal{A}}$ and $R \in \mathcal{S}$. We say that *path-consistency makes R explicit* iff for every path-consistent instance Θ of $\mathsf{CSPSAT}(\mathcal{S})$, the following holds: if $M(x)RM(y)$ for every $M \in \mathrm{Mods}(\Theta)$, then $xSy \in \Theta$ and $S \subseteq R$.

Theorem 14 Let $\mathcal{S} \subseteq 2^{\mathcal{A}}$ and assume that $R \in \mathcal{S}$ is independent of $\mathcal{S}$. Then, CHECK-REFINEMENTS$(\mathcal{S}, M^R)$ returns succeed if and only if path-consistency makes $\neg R$ explicit.

Proof. only-if: Assume to the contrary that there exists a path-consistent instance Θ of $\mathsf{CSPSAT}(\mathcal{S})$ and there exists $x, y \in \mathrm{Vars}(\Theta)$ such that for all $M \in \mathrm{Mods}(\Theta)$, $M(x)\neg RM(y)$ but $xSy \in \Theta$ and $S \cap R \neq \emptyset$. Since CHECK-REFINEMENTS$(\mathcal{S}, M^R)$ returns succeed, the instance

$$\Theta' = \Theta \cup \{uRv \mid uTv \in \Theta \text{ and } T \cap R \neq \emptyset\}$$

is consistent. However, $S \cap R \neq \emptyset$ so $xRy \in \Theta'$. We know that all models M of Θ have the property $M(x)\neg RM(y)$ so every model M' of Θ' must also have this property. This contradicts the fact that Θ' has a model and, consequently, $S \cap R = \emptyset$ and $S \subseteq \neg R$. We have thus shown that path-consistency makes $\neg R$ explicit.

if: Let Θ be a path-consistent instance of $\mathsf{CSPSAT}(\mathcal{S})$ and arbitrarily choose a constraint $xSy \in \Theta$ such that $S \cap R \neq \emptyset$. The fact that path-consistency makes $\neg R$ explicit gives that $\Theta \cup \{xRy\}$ is consistent and, by independence, $\Theta' = \Theta \cup \{uRv \mid uTv \in \Theta \text{ and } T \cap R \neq \emptyset\}$ is consistent. However, Θ' is equivalent to Θ refined by the matrix M^R so CHECK-REFINEMENTS$(\mathcal{S}, M^R)$ returns succeed by Theorem 8 $\square$

Corollary 15 Given a set of relations $\mathcal{S} \subseteq 2^{\mathcal{A}}$ for which path-consistency computes minimal labels and a refinement matrix M^R. Then, CHECK-REFINEMENTS-$(\mathcal{S}, M^R)$ returns succeed if and only if R is independent of S.

Proof. Simply note that if path-consistency computes minimal labels, then it makes $\neg R$ explicit. $\square$

Examples of when path-consistency computes minimal labels can, for instance, be found in Bessière *et al.* [2].

4   Applications

We will now demonstrate that many known independence results can be obtained using refinements. We will also employ the method on constraint satisfaction problems where no independence results has yet been derived. In the following, we will not discuss the empty relation and the top relation (*i.e.* the relation containing all basic relations) since they are always independent of any set of relations.

4.1   The Region Connection Calculus

A well-known framework for qualitative spatial reasoning is the so-called Region Connection Calculus (RCC) [14] which models topological relations between spatial regions using first-order logic. Of particular interest is the RCC-8 calculus which is based on eight basic relations definable in the RCC theory. The eight basic relations are denoted as DC, EC, PO, EQ, TPP, NTPP, TPP^{-1}, and $NTPP^{-1}$, with the meaning of *DisConnected, Externally Connected, Partial Overlap, EQual, Tangential Proper Part, Non-Tangential Proper Part*, and their converses. RCC-5 is a subclass of RCC-8 where the boundary of spatial regions is not taken into account. Hence, it is not distinguished between DC and EC and between TPP and NTPP. These relations are combined to the RCC-5 relations DR for *DiscRete* and PP for *Proper Part*, respectively. Thus, RCC-5 contains the five basic relations DR, PO, PP, PP^{-1} and EQ. The consistency problem of both RCC-8 and RCC-5 is NP-complete [16], but large maximal tractable subsets have been identified [16, 11, 15]. In the following we demonstrate the usefulness of our method by identifying tractable disjunctive constraint classes of RCC-8 and RCC-5.

We begin with RCC-5 which contains four maximal tractable subsets, R_{28} (the only maximal tractable subset which contains all basic relations [16]), R_{20}, R_{17} (which consists of all relations containing the equality relation) and R_{14} [11]. We have applied the algorithm CHECK-REFINEMENTS on these sets using all different R-refinement matrices and found the following refinements (where Δ_{28}, Δ_{20}, Δ_{17} and Δ_{14} contain all refinements of R_{28}, R_{20}, R_{17} and R_{14}, respectively).

The sets Δ_{28}, Δ_{20} and Δ_{14} are defined by the following graphs where a relation R is present in Δ_X iff there exists a path from the initial node $\emptyset$ in the given graph to some other node such that exactly those relations present in R are visited, or if such a path exists for R's converse. Δ_{17} is given by $\Delta_{17} = R^{17}$.

$$\Delta_{28}: \quad \emptyset \rightarrow \{DR\} \rightarrow \{PO\} \rightarrow \{PP\} \rightarrow \{PP^{-1}\}$$

$$\Delta_{20}: \quad \emptyset \rightarrow \{DR\} \rightarrow \{PO\} \rightarrow \{PP\} \rightarrow \{PP^{-1}\}$$

with branches to $\{EQ\}$, $\{EQ\}$ above and $\{PO\}$, $\{PP\} \rightarrow \{PPI\}$ below

$$\Delta_{14}: \quad \emptyset \rightarrow \{PP, PP^{-1}\} \rightarrow \{DR\} \rightarrow \{PO\}$$

with branch to $\{PO\}$ above

In order to apply Theorem 12 and use these refinement results as independence results we must show that R_{28}, R_{20}, R_{17} and R_{14} are decidable by path-consistency. As shown in [16], R_{28} is decidable by path-consistency. From the refinements given above, it can be shown that R_{20} can be reduced by refinement to R_{28} and hence R_{20} is also decidable by path-consistency by Theorem 9. Sets of constraints over R_{17} are trivially consistent, thus R_{17} also is decidable by path-consistency. In order to show that R_{14} is decided by path-consistency we define R_{Tot} as the following:

$$R_{\mathrm{Tot}} = \{\, \{\mathsf{PP}\}, \{\mathsf{PP}\}^{-1}, \{\mathsf{PP}, \mathsf{PP}^{-1}\}, \{\mathsf{EQ}\}, \{\mathsf{PP}, \mathsf{EQ}\}, \{\mathsf{PP}^{-1}, \mathsf{EQ}\} \,\}$$

From the previous refinements it follows that R_{14} can be reduced by refinement to R_{Tot}. It is easy to show that R_{Tot} is equivalent to the point algebra for linear time [18] by making a straightforward translation of the basic relations $\mathsf{PP}, \mathsf{PP}^{-1}, \mathsf{EQ}$ into $<, >, =$, respectively. Since the point algebra for linear time is decidable by path consistency, Theorem 9 gives that R_{14} is also decidable by path-consistency.

Having proven that R_{28}, R_{20}, R_{17} and R_{14} are decidable by path-consistency, Theorem 12 gives that $\Delta_{28}, \Delta_{20}, \Delta_{17}$, and Δ_{14} are independent of R_{28}, R_{20}, R_{17}, and R_{14}, respectively. Thus, $\mathsf{CSPSAT}(R_i \stackrel{\times}{\triangledown} \Delta_i)$ is tractable for $i \in \{28, 20, 17, 14\}$.

RCC-8 contains three maximal tractable subsets $\widehat{\mathcal{H}}_8, \mathcal{C}_8$ and $\mathcal{Q}_8$ which all contain the basic relations and which are all decidable by path-consistency [16, 15]. By using our method we can easily identify all relations which are refinements of the three sets. We let $\Delta_{\widehat{\mathcal{H}}_8}$, $\Delta_{\mathcal{C}_8}$, and $\Delta_{\mathcal{Q}_8}$ contain all refinements of the maximal tractable subsets which implies that $\mathsf{CSPSAT}(\Gamma \stackrel{\times}{\triangledown} \Delta_\Gamma)$ is tractable for $\Gamma \in \{\widehat{\mathcal{H}}_8, \mathcal{C}_8, \mathcal{Q}_8\}$.

The sets $\Delta_{\widehat{\mathcal{H}}_8}, \Delta_{\mathcal{Q}_8}$ and $\Delta_{\mathcal{C}_8}$ are defined by the following graphs which are to be interpreted in the same way as the previous graphs for RCC-5.

$$\Delta_{\widehat{\mathcal{H}}_8}:\ \emptyset \to \{\mathsf{DC}\} \to \{\mathsf{EC}\} \to \{\mathsf{PO}\} \to \{\mathsf{TPP}\} \xrightarrow{\{\mathsf{NTPP}\}} \{\mathsf{TPP}^{-1}\} \xrightarrow{\{\mathsf{EQ}\}} \{\mathsf{NTPP}\} \xrightarrow{\{\mathsf{EQ}\}} \{\mathsf{NTPP}^{-1}\}$$

$$\Delta_{\mathcal{Q}_8}:\ \emptyset \to \{\mathsf{DC}\} \to \{\mathsf{EC}\} \to \{\mathsf{PO}\} \xrightarrow{\{\mathsf{EQ}\}} \{\mathsf{TPP}\} \xrightarrow{\{\mathsf{EQ}\}} \{\mathsf{TPP}^{-1}\} \xrightarrow{\{\mathsf{EQ}\}} \{\mathsf{NTPP}\} \xrightarrow{\{\mathsf{EQ}\}} \{\mathsf{NTPP}^{-1}\}$$
$$\{\mathsf{NTPP}\} \longrightarrow \{\mathsf{EQ}\}$$

$$\Delta_{\mathcal{C}_8}:\ \emptyset \to \{\mathsf{DC}\} \to \{\mathsf{PO}\} \to \{\mathsf{NTPP}\} \xrightarrow{\{\mathsf{NTPP}^{-1}\}} \{\mathsf{TPP}\} \longrightarrow \{\mathsf{NTPP}^{-1}\} \to \{\mathsf{TPP}^{-1}\} \xrightarrow{\{\mathsf{EQ}\}} \{\mathsf{EC}\}$$
$$\{\mathsf{EC}\} \longrightarrow \{\mathsf{NTPP}\} \longrightarrow \{\mathsf{TPP}\} \to \{\mathsf{NTPP}^{-1}\}$$
$$\{\mathsf{NTPP}^{-1}\}$$

	Γ'_A	Δ'_A	Γ_A	Δ_A	Γ'_B	Δ'_B	Γ_B	Δ_B	Γ'_C	Δ'_C	Γ_C	Δ_C	Δ_D
$\{<\}$			•				•		•		•		
$\{<,=\}$	•		•		•		•						•
$\{<,>\}$							•	•					
$\{<,>,=\}$					•	•	•	•					•
$\{\|\|\}$	•	•	•	•			•		•	•			
$\{\|\|,=\}$	•		•								•	•	•
$\{=\}$			•				•				•		•
$\{<,>,\|\|\}$	•	•	•	•	•	•	•	•	•	•	•	•	
$\{<,\|\|\}$			•	•							•	•	
$\{<,\|\|,=\}$			•						•	•	•	•	•

Table 1. Tractable classes of the point algebra for partially ordered time.

4.2 The point algebra for partially ordered time

After having demonstrated that new independence results can be derived using refinements we will now show that many previously presented independence results can also be derived using refinements. We begin by showing that all independence results for the point algebra for partially ordered time can be derived using refinements and, moreover, that *every* maximal tractable set of disjunctions of relations for partially ordered time can be derived using refinements. This, of course, requires a definition of a maximal tractable set of disjunctions of relations.

Let Γ be a set of disjunctive relations constructed from a set $\mathcal{B}$ of binary relations by applying the $\breve{\times}$ operator. We say that Γ is a *maximal tractable subclass* iff Γ is tractable and for every set $X \not\subseteq \Gamma$ of relations which can be constructed by the relations in $\mathcal{B}$ and $\breve{\times}$, $\Gamma \cup X$ is intractable.

The point algebra for partially ordered time is based on the notion of *relations* between pairs of variables interpreted over a partially-ordered set. We consider four basic relations which we denote by $<, >, =$ and $\|$. If x, y are points in a partial order $\langle T, \leq \rangle$ then we define these relations in terms of the partial ordering $\leq$ as follows:

1. $x\{<\}y$ iff $x \leq y$ and not $y \leq x$
2. $x\{>\}y$ iff $y \leq x$ and not $x \leq y$
3. $x\{=\}y$ iff $x \leq y$ and $y \leq x$
4. $x\{\|\}y$ iff neither $x \leq y$ nor $y \leq x$

The point algebra for partially ordered time has been throughly investigated earlier and a total classification with respect to tractability has been given in Broxvall and Jonsson [3]. In Broxvall and Jonsson [4] the sets of relations in Table 1 are defined and it is proven that $\Gamma_A \breve{\times} \Delta_A^*, \Gamma_B \breve{\times} \Delta_B^*, \Gamma_C \breve{\times} \Delta_C^*$ and Δ_D^* are the unique maximal tractable disjunctive classes of relations for partially ordered time. The proofs of tractability for those sets rely on several handmade independence proofs. We will now derive these independence results using refinements.

To do so, we need to show that the classes $\Gamma_A, \Gamma_B, \Gamma_C$ and Δ_D are decidable by path-consistency. We begin by proving a useful connection between RCC-5 and the point algebra for partially ordered time which in turn will be needed to prove that path-consistency decides Γ_A.

Lemma 16 Let Γ be a set of relations in the point algebra for partially ordered time and define the function σ such that

1. $\sigma(<) = \{\mathsf{PP}\}$;
2. $\sigma(>) = \{\mathsf{PP}^{-1}\}$;
3. $\sigma(=) = \{\mathsf{EQ}\}$; and
4. $\sigma(\|) = \{\mathsf{DR}, \mathsf{PO}\}$.

Then, Γ can be decided by path-consistency if the set

$$\Gamma' = \{\bigcup_{r \in R} \sigma(r) \mid R \in \Gamma\}$$

of RCC-5 relations can be decided by path-consistency.

Proof. Let Π be an arbitrary CSP instance over the relations in Γ. Define the set Σ of RCC-5 formulae as follows: for each $x_i \, R \, x_j \in \Pi$, add the formula $x_i \bigcup_{r \in R} \sigma(r) x_j$. Note that Σ is a CSP instance over Γ' that can be decided by path-consistency by our initial assumptions.

We begin by comparing the composition tables for partially-ordered time and the RCC-5 relations $\{\mathsf{PP}\}, \{\mathsf{PP}^{-1}\}, \{\mathsf{EQ}\}, \{\mathsf{DR}, \mathsf{PO}\}$:

	$\{<\}$	$\{>\}$	$\{=\}$	$\{\|\}$
$\{<\}$	$\{<\}$	$\top$	$\{<\}$	$\{<, \|\}$
$\{>\}$	$\top$	$\{>\}$	$\{>\}$	$\{>, \|\}$
$\{=\}$	$\{<\}$	$\{>\}$	$\{=\}$	$\{\|\}$
$\{\|\}$	$\{<, \|\}$	$\{>, \|\}$	$\{\|\}$	$\top$

	$\{\mathsf{PP}\}$	$\{\mathsf{PP}^{-1}\}$	$\{\mathsf{EQ}\}$	$\{\mathsf{DR}, \mathsf{PO}\}$
$\{\mathsf{PP}\}$	$\{\mathsf{PP}\}$	$\top$	$\{\mathsf{PP}\}$	$\{\mathsf{PP}, \mathsf{DR}, \mathsf{PO}\}$
$\{\mathsf{PP}^{-1}\}$	$\top$	$\{\mathsf{PP}^{-1}\}$	$\{\mathsf{PP}^{-1}\}$	$\{\mathsf{PP}^{-1}, \mathsf{DR}, \mathsf{PO}\}$
$\{\mathsf{EQ}\}$	$\{\mathsf{PP}\}$	$\{\mathsf{PP}^{-1}\}$	$\{\mathsf{EQ}\}$	$\{\mathsf{DR}, \mathsf{PO}\}$
$\{\mathsf{DR}, \mathsf{PO}\}$	$\{\mathsf{PP}, \mathsf{DR}, \mathsf{PO}\}$	$\{\mathsf{PP}^{-1}, \mathsf{DR}, \mathsf{PO}\}$	$\{\mathsf{DR}, \mathsf{PO}\}$	$\top$

After having made this comparison, it should be fairly obvious that the empty relation can be derived from Π by enforcing path-consistency if and only if it can be derived from Σ. Thus, we only have to show that whenever Σ has a model, Π also has a model.

Let M be a model that assigns sets to the variables $x_1, \ldots, x_n$ that appear in Σ. We define an interpretation N from the variables in Π to the partial order

$\langle\{M(x_i) \mid 1 \leq i \leq n\}, \subseteq\rangle$ as follows: $N(x_i) = M(x_i)$ for $1 \leq i \leq n$. To conclude the proof, we pick an arbitrary constraint $x_i R x_j$ in Σ and show that it is satisfied by the interpretation N. Assume now, for instance, that $M(x_i) \{\mathsf{PP}\} M(x_j)$. By the definition of σ, we know that $\{<\} \subseteq R$ and it follows immediately that $N(x_i) < N(x_j)$ and the constraint $x_i R x_j$ is satisfied. The remaining cases can easily be proved analogously.

Theorem 17 Path-consistency decides consistency for Γ_A, Γ_B, Γ_C and Δ_D.

Proof. Let $\Gamma' = \{\bigcup_{r \in R} \sigma(r) \mid R \in \Gamma_A\}$ (where σ is defined as in Lemma 16) and note that $\Gamma' \subseteq R_{28}$. Since R_{28} can be decided by path-consistency [16], Lemma 16 implies that path-consistency decides Γ_A.

By using CHECK-REFINEMENTS, it can be verified that Γ_B can be reduced by refinements to Γ_A which by Theorem 9 gives that Γ_B is decided by path-consistency. For Γ_C the result follows from the fact that it is a subset of Γ_A. Finally, Δ_D is trivially decided by path-consistency. $\qquad\square$

Using the algorithm CHECK-REFINEMENTS, we can automatically verify that $\Delta_A, \Delta_B, \Delta_C$ and Δ_D are valid refinements of $\Gamma_A, \Gamma_B, \Gamma_C$ and Δ_D, respectively. Theorems 17 now gives that $\Delta_A, \Delta_B, \Delta_C$ and Δ_D are independent of $\Gamma_A, \Gamma_B, \Gamma_C$ and Δ_D, respectively and we have proven tractability of *all* maximal tractable sets of disjunctions of relations for the point algebra for partially ordered time.

4.3 The point algebra for linear time

In Broxvall and Jonsson [4] the time-point algebra for linear time is also investigated and the following two classes are defined:

$$\mathcal{X}_1 = \{\{<\}, \{<, =\}, \{<, >\}, \{=\}\}^{\check{\vee}}\{\{<, >\}\}$$

$$\mathcal{X}_2 = \{\{<, =\}, \{=\}\}^*$$

Furthermore, proof is also given that these two classes are the only two maximal tractable sets of disjunctions of relations. Both independence results needed for that classification can be derived using refinements. In Renz [15] it is noted that disequality is a refinement in the point algebra for linear time. The other independence result consisting of all relations containing equality can easily be verified using the refinement algorithm, and decidability by path consistency is trivial.

It should thus be noted that both in the case of the point algebra for partially ordered time and for the point algebra for linear time it is sufficient only to look at the refinements in order to derive *all* tractable sets of disjunctions. However, we have no guarantee that this holds in the general case.

5 Discussion and Conclusions

Independence of relations with respect to tractable sets of relations is a very useful tool for generating expressive tractable disjunctive constraint classes. However, proving independence is often a highly non-trivial task. In this paper we proposed a method for proving independence which we obtained by relating the notion of refinement to the notion of independence. We found that if a relation R is a refinement of a set of relations $\mathcal{S}$, then R is also independent of $\mathcal{S}$. Since refinements can be checked by running a simple algorithm, this allows us to automatically generate independence results. The only requirement for applying this method is the sufficiency of path-consistency for deciding consistency in $\mathcal{S}$. In many cases this can, however, also be shown by using refinement techniques.

In order to demonstrate the usefulness of our method, we applied it to the Region Connection Calculi RCC-5 and RCC-8 and derived many previously unknown independence results. Furthermore, using our method we were able to obtain all previously known independence results of the point algebra for partially ordered time as well as for linear time. This is particularly interesting since in this case refinements are sufficient for identifying all maximal tractable sets of disjunctions, *i.e.*, in this case independence seems to imply refinement. We have not been able so far to prove this implication in the general case and instead specified a certain condition of when independence implies refinements. It would be very interesting to know whether the correspondence between refinements and independence holds in the general case or alternatively which restrictions must be made in order to have this correspondence. Then, refinements can be used to derive all independence results in a simple way.

So far we have only used a restricted form of refinement matrices, namely, an R-refinement matrix M^R for some relation R. We did this because previously tractable disjunctive constraint classes formed by two sets Γ and Δ required that all relations of Δ are independent of all relations of Γ. Using the refinement method it is possible to verify more complex refinement matrices. These refinement matrices can be used for proving an advanced notion of independence such as "Δ is *subset independent* of Γ iff there are (non-disjoint) subsets $\Delta = \Delta_1 \cup \ldots \cup \Delta_n$ and $\Gamma = \Gamma_1 \cup \ldots \cup \Gamma_n$ such that Δ_i is independent of Γ_i". It might well be possible that this advanced notion of independence allows to generate new types of tractable disjunctive constraint classes whose tractability can, again, be proven using refinements techniques.

Another piece of further work which seems to be worthwhile is to analyze the relationship between the refinement method and a method for proving tractability which was developed by Jeavons *et al.* [9].

References

1. F. Anger, D. Mitra, and R. Rodriguez. Temporal constraint networks in nonlinear time. Technical report, ECAI Workshop on Temporal and Spatial Reasoning, 1998.
2. C. Bessière, A. Isli, and G. Ligozat. Global consistency in interval algebra networks: tractable subclasses. In W. Wahlster, editor, *Proceedings of the 12th European*

Conference on Artificial Intelligence (ECAI-96), pages 3–7, Budapest, Hungary, Aug. 1996. Wiley.

3. M. Broxvall and P. Jonsson. Towards a complete classification of tractability in point algebras for nonlinear time. In *Proceedings of the 5th International Conference on Principles and Practice of Constraint Programming (CP-99)*, pages 448–454, Alexandria, VA, USA, Oct. 1999.

4. M. Broxvall and P. Jonsson. Disjunctive temporal reasoning in partially ordered time structures. In *Proceedings of the Seventeenth National Conference on Artificial Intelligence (AAAI-2000)*. AAAI Press, 2000. To appear.

5. D. Cohen, P. Jeavons, and M. Koubarakis. Tractable disjunctive constraints. In *Proceedings of the 3rd International Conference on Principles and Practice for Constraint Programming*, pages 478–490, 1997.

6. Y. Deville, O. Barette, and P. van Hentenryck. Constraint satisfaction over connected row convex constraints. *Artificial Intelligence*, 109(1–2):243–271, 1999.

7. E. C. Freuder. A sufficient condition for backtrack-bounded search. *Journal of the ACM*, 32:755–761, 1985.

8. G. Gottlob, N. Leone, and F. Scarcello. A comparison of structural CSP decomposition methods. In *Proceedings of the 16th International Joint Conference on Artificial Intelligence (IJCAI-99)*, pages 394–399, Stockholm, Sweden, 1999.

9. P. G. Jeavons, D. Cohen and M. Gyssens. A test for tractability. In *Proceedings of the 2nd International Conference on Principles and Practice for Constraint Programming*, pages 267–281, 1996.

10. P. G. Jeavons and M. C. Cooper. Tractable constraints on ordered domains. *Artificial Intelligence*, 79:327–339, 1996.

11. P. Jonsson and T. Drakengren. A complete classification of tractability in RCC-5. *Journal of Artificial Intelligence Research*, 6:211–221, 1997.

12. A. K. Mackworth. Consistency in networks of relations. *Artificial Intelligence*, 8:99–118, 1977.

13. B. Nebel and H.-J. Bürckert. Reasoning about temporal relations: A maximal tractable subclass of Allen's interval algebra. *Journal of the ACM*, 42(1):43–66, 1995.

14. David A. Randell, Zhan Cui, and Anthony G. Cohn. A spatial logic based on regions and connection. In B. Nebel, W. Swartout, and C. Rich, editors, *Principles of Knowledge Representation and Reasoning: Proceedings of the 3rd International Conference*, pages 165–176, Cambridge, MA, October 1992. Morgan Kaufmann.

15. J. Renz. Maximal tractable fragments of the Region Connection Calculus: A complete analysis. In *Proceedings of the 16th International Joint Conference on Artificial Intelligence (IJCAI-99)*, pages 129–143, Stockholm, Sweden, 1999.

16. J. Renz and B. Nebel. On the complexity of qualitative spatial reasoning: A maximal tractable fragment of the Region Connection Calculus. *Artificial Intelligence*, 108(1–2):69–123, 1999.

17. P. van Beek and R. Dechter. On the minimality and decomposability of row-convex constraint networks. *Journal of the ACM*, 42:543–561, 1995.

18. M. B. Vilain, H. Kautz and P. van Beek. Constraint propagation algorithms for temporal reasoning: A revised report. In *Readings in Qualitative Reasoning about Physical Systems*, pages 373–381. Morgan Kaufmann, San Mateo, CA, 1989.

A Language for Audiovisual Template Specification and Recognition

Jean Carrive[1], Pierre Roy[2], François Pachet[3], Rémi Ronfard[1]

[1] INA, 4 avenue de l'Europe
94 366 Bry-sur-Marne, France
{jcarrive, rronfard}@ina.fr
[2] INRIA, Domaine de Voluceau, Rocquencourt
78 153 Le Chesnay Cedex, France
Pierre.Roy@lip6.fr
[3] SONY CSL Paris, 6 rue Amyot
75 005 Paris, France
pachet@csl.sony.fr

Abstract. We address the issue of detecting automatically occurrences of high level patterns in audiovisual documents. These patterns correspond to recurring sequences of shots, which are considered as first class entities by documentalists, and used for annotation and retrieval. We introduce a language for specifying these patterns, based on an extension of Allen's algebra with the regular expression operator +, which denotes an iteration of arbitrary length. We propose a formulation of this pattern language using the constraint satisfaction framework, in which templates are represented as constraint problems. We propose an efficient representation of domains (all subsequences of a given graph) and filtering methods for the Allen constraints. We illustrate the resulting system on a corpus of real world news broadcast examples.

1   Introduction

Indexing and retrieving the contents of temporal media such as audio or video can be made more effective by associating manual annotations (metadata) at various temporal scales in the media. This process is known as *analytic indexing* and is notoriously time consuming, for two reasons. First, it is often difficult to state the rules to be followed in segmenting the media: how many segments ? How many levels of details ? Second, even when such rules can be set, the segmentation remains repetitive and time-consuming. In this paper, we present a framework designed to facilitate the two tasks of *defining* and *recognizing* temporal structures in video. An application of this framework is presented in the context of the DiVAN project, a prototype audiovisual digital library management system funded by ESPRIT.

In recent years, great effort has been made on automatically extracting low-level features from the video and audio streams [1], such as *shots, gradual transitions*

R. Dechter (Ed.): CP 2000, LNCS 1894, pp. 128-142, 2000.

between shots, regions of the screen corresponding to *captions* or *faces*, *logos*, or occurrences of a given *jingle* in the audio track. Unfortunately, the resulting segments and features are not directly exploitable by documentalists, for two reasons. First, the segments extracted are of short duration. Even if a shot provides more synthetic information than a frame, it is still too "low-level" to be used as a reference for annotation. Second, extracted features usually bear too little semantic to be directly annotated. For instance, a face region detected in a shot makes no sense to the documentalist as such, and will be useful only if more contextual information is provided, to infer, e.g. that the face is indeed the reporter's face, and that the text region on the bottom left of the screen is the reporter's name. The aim of *macro-segmentation* is precisely to extract higher level features and sequences from low level descriptors.

Macro-segmentation methods have been proposed for grouping together shots into longer and more meaningful segments, such as sequences or scenes. For example, [2] proposes an unsupervised algorithm which clusters shots into classes according to an image similarity measure; [3] presents a rule-based approach to detect scene boundaries, founded on empirically observed regularities such as alternations of gradual transitions and cuts in traditional movies. At the opposite of these general methods, specific methods have been designed for specific types of documents, especially news broadcasts [4].

In this paper, we are interested in *collections* of documents which share common characteristics, such as anchor persons, sets, graphics, and which follow a common general scenario. Such collections can be for instance the 6:30 p.m. news broadcast on a given channel during 1998. These documents generally present typical regularities which can be used for macro-segmentation. For instance, the temporal structure of short news broadcasts is often a succession of reports, a characteristic audio jingle indicating the beginning of a new report, as illustrated by Fig.1. Reports can be detected provided that the document has been segmented into shots and that occurrences of the jingle have been detected.

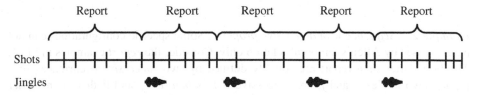

Fig. 1. Reports in a simple news broadcast

In this paper, we are interested in describing such sequences and in detecting occurrences of these sequences automatically in the video.

1.1 Requirements and examples

In our context of automatic video indexing, a video sequence is made up of segments coming from automatic analysis tools. Those tools produce classified segments which are the primitive terms of our language. The primitive classes – or *analysis classes* – are for instance *Shot, Jingle, Text Region* or *Face Region*, for which there exist robust extraction algorithms [5, 6]. We further organize analysis classes hierarchically. For instance, the face region detection algorithm produces regions of screen containing a human face. Depending on the relative size of the region, shots can be classified into so-called *shot values*, which range from close-up (CU) where the face occupies approximately half of the screen, to the long shot (LS) where the human body is seen entirely. Intermediate shot values are medium close-up (MCU), medium shot (MS) and medium long-shot (MLS). In our case, primitive segments and their classes are represented in a Description Logic formalism, using the CLASSIC system [7, 8].

Classes of *sequences* can be defined by giving information on the temporal arrangement of primitive segments. Let us give three typical examples of such sequences.

Example 1: a simple one shot sequence. Fig.2 illustrates a simple sequence made up of only one medium close-up shot *during which* some text is displayed at the bottom left of the screen. In the "France 2" evening newscast from which the example is extracted, the text usually contains the name of the person on-screen, so this shot can be classified as *NamedPersonShot.*

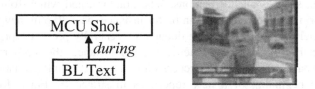

Fig. 2. *Named Person Shot* in a "France 2" evening newscast

Example 2: a sequence with a negative property. Some specific configurations can not be expressed by Allen's temporal relation only. Consider the *report* examples in Fig.1. The boundaries of a report are roughly defined by two *successive* occurrences of a jingle. Two jingles j_1 and j_2 are successive if j_1 is *before*[1] j_2, and if there is no other jingle j_3 such that j_3 is *before* j_2 and j_1 is *before* j_3. To express this relationship, we need to introduce negation in our description language, with expressions such as: "there must be no instance of class C between some components n_1 and n_2 of the sequence".

Example 3: an iterated sequence. The broadcast news illustrated by Fig.1 is made up of a set of contiguous reports (themselves made up of a set of contiguous shots bounded by two jingles). This example illustrates the need for specifying contiguous

---

[1] *before* is one of the 13 Allen's basic relations, which are presented below.

sequences of segments of arbitrary length. We define the notion of an *iterated sequence* of class *C* as a sequence of contiguous segments of class *C*. Two segments are contiguous if they are related by Allen's *meet* relation. By definition, an iterated sequence contains at least one element, and its temporal extension is the temporal union of the temporal extensions of its elements.

1.2   Related works

Temporal information holding between the components of a sequence are given by Allen's temporal relations [9]. A temporal relation is defined from 13 basic relations which represent all the possible topological arrangements of two intervals placed on an oriented axis: *before* [b], *meets* [m], *overlaps* [o], *during* [d], *starts* [s], *finishes* [f] and their symmetric relations, *after* [a], *is-met* [mi], *is-overlapped* [oi], *is-during* [di], *is-started* [si], *is-finished* [fi], plus *equals* [e] which is its own symmetric relation. Common intuitions on relative temporal arrangement of two temporal objects can be expressed by temporal disjunctions of these basic relations. For instance, temporal inclusion may be expressed as {*starts* ∨ *during* ∨ *finishes* ∨ *equals*}. In the current implementation we use the complete Allen's interval algebra. This algebra was shown to be too general for our purpose. Furthermore, it does not allow numerical constraint. We thus may choose in a second step a more appropriate formalism, such as [10].

As we have already mentioned, primitive segments and classes are represented in a Description Logic (DL) formalism. In such a formalism, classes are described by *concepts* which are automatically organized into a taxonomy by way of *subsumption* – *is-a* – links. Segments are represented by *individuals* which are automatically classified by computing their most specific parents in the taxonomy. Some propositions have been made to extend a DL language with temporal operators [11]. These works are mostly theoretical and no effective methods are designed for classifying temporal objects. In [12], Weida proposes in the context of plan recognition a Constraint Satisfaction Problem (CSP) approach in which plans to be recognized are represented as constraint networks whose vertices are associated with concepts in a DL language and whose edges are temporal relations. Weida, however, concentrates on the plan subsumption problem and the recognition is realized by a straightforward node-to node matching process. Moreover, Weida's language can accommodate only example 1, and does not address negation nor iterative sequences.

The paper is organized as follows. In this section we proceed with an introduction to our language. In section 2, we describe the template matching problem as a constraint satisfaction problem, we introduce a representation of domains which allows to represent arbitrary subsequences of the observation graph and we present filtering methods for temporal and domain-specific constraints. Finally in Section 3, we report on the use of our system on real world examples.

1.3   A Language for describing templates

Following the CSP approach pioneered by Weida we propose a language for describing classes of audio visual sequences, called *templates*. The goal of this language is to be flexible enough to accommodate at least the three categories of examples given above. We therefore propose to extend Weida's formalism with specific constraints and with iterated sequences. As we will see, this flexibility forces us to give up template subsumption, at least as a first approximation. For instance, a *NamedPersonShot* in Fig.2 is defined by the following template expression:

```
NamedPersonShot        constraints
    s1[BLText]             s1 d s2
    s2[MCUShot]
```

This example is written in Weida's formalism, since it uses only Allen relations. The following expression is the template definition for the broadcast news reports shown in Fig.1:

```
Report                 constraints
    s1[Shot]               s1 m s2
    s2[Shot+]              s2 m s3
    s3[Shot]               s1 {o s si di} s4
    s4[Jingle]             s3 {o s si di} s5
    s5[Jingle]             s1 s this
                           s2 f this
                           no Jingle between s4 s5
```

This template is illustrated by Fig.3. The '+' symbol in the definition of s_2 indicates an iterated sequence of shots; temporal relations between braces indicate a disjunction of Allen's basic relation; the "this" keyword is used to set constraints between the instances of the Report template and their components. Thus, the temporal extension of a report includes the first jingle, during which important information such as titles may be given, but not the last one, which is part of the next report. The last constraint in the definition indicates that no instance of the Jingle analysis class should appear between the jingles matched with the s_4 and s_5 vertices. The temporal relation between s_1 and s_4 (or between s_3 and s_5) states that the shot matched by s_1 must be the earliest shot having a non empty temporal intersection with the jingle matched by s_4. Note that this template does not describe the first and last reports of the broadcast, which have to be dealt with separately.

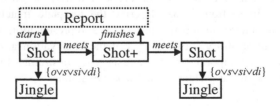

Fig. 3. Graphical representation of a "Report" template

1.4   Definition and notation of templates

A template is a graph whose vertices are associated to classes or, recursively, other templates. Additionally, a vertex can represent an iterated sequence of an analysis class or template. Such vertices are called *iterated vertices*. Schematically, vertices of a template represent elements or sub-sets of the set of observations. The edges of a template represent the temporal relations to be satisfied between the observations matched by the vertices. Some additional constraints may be set between the vertices of a template, such as a constraint forbidding that an instance of some class C appears between the observations matched by two vertices (see example 2). Finally, the temporal extension of a template may be defined by setting temporal constraints in the template definition between the instance itself and its components. We use the following notation:

- n : a vertex in a template definition
- n_C : a non iterated vertex associated with an analysis class C
- n_C^+: an iterated vertex associated with an analysis class C
- n_T: a non iterated vertex associated with a template T
- n_T^+ : an iterated vertex associated with a template T
- OG (*observation graph*) is the set of observations

Let t' be a set of observations, $t' \subset OG$. t' is an *instance* of template T', noted $t' \prec T'$, if and only if:

- every n_C of T' is matched with some observation o, $o \in t'$, $o \prec C$
- every n_C^+ of T' is matched with some iterated sequence $o = \{o_1,...,o_m\}$, $o \subset t'$, $o_i \prec C$, $\forall i \in [1;m]$
- every n_T of T' is matched with some set of observations t, $t \subset t'$, $t \prec T$
- every n_T^+ of T' is matched with some iterated sequence $t = \{t_1,..., t_m\}$, $t \subset t'$, $t_i \prec T$, $\forall i \in [1;m]$
- temporal constraints defined by the edges of T, and specific constraints defined in T, are satisfied.

The goal of our study is therefore the following: given 1) an observation graph and 2) a template definition, find all the instances of the template in the observation graph.

1.5   Embedded templates

As we have seen, a template vertex may be associated with an analysis class or with another template. In the latter case, temporal constraints set on the vertex have to be propagated on other vertices. The templates illustrated by Fig.4 define *SimpleReport* as two contiguous shots with a jingle being heard during the first shot, and *TwoReports* as two contiguous simple reports.

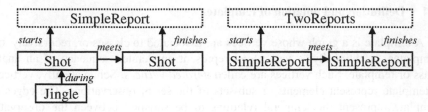

Fig. 4. Embedded templates in a template definition

Since the initial observation graph contains only instances of analysis classes, the *TwoReports* template cannot be recognized directly. A possible solution would consist in first recognizing instances of the *SimpleReport* template, then to add them into the observation graph, and finally to recognize instances of the *TwoReports* template. But this supposes that the temporal extension of instance of *SimpleReport* can be precisely computed from the temporal constraints set on "this" in the template definition, which is not necessarily the case. We thus choose to expand the components of the *SimpleReport* template into the *TwoReports* template. As a result, temporal constraints have to be propagated so that the definition of the whole constraint graph is complete. For reasons of simplicity, we choose to propagate all constraints using the 3-consistency algorithm proposed by Allen to minimize the temporal constraint network [9]. The resulting definition of the *TwoReports* template is illustrated by Fig.5.

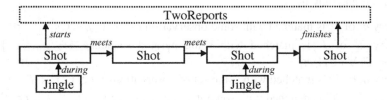

Fig. 5. Expansion of embedded templates

In the case of iterated vertices associated with a template, sub-templates cannot be expanded in the same way. We must revert in that case to the first solution mentioned above, which consists in first recognizing instances of embedded templates and to add them in the observation graph. This limits the templates that can be iterated to so-called *bounded* templates, *i.e.* templates for which the temporal extension of instances can always be computed. Bounded templates are roughly templates which are in one of the Allen's basic relation *equals*, *starts*, *meets*, *finishes* – or their symmetric relations – with some of their components.

2   Template matching as a Constraint Satisfaction Problem

We represent the template matching problem as a constraint satisfaction problem. In this section, we focus on the representation of domains, which is of key importance for the filtering of constraints. The filtering methods as well as the general constraint satisfaction algorithm are implemented in the BackJava system [13]. For reasons of clarity, we will concentrate in this section on templates whose iterated vertices are not associated with sub-templates but only with analysis classes. As mentioned, recognition of iterated components n_T^+ is done by recognizing all instances of sub-template T and by adding them to the observation graph.

2.1   Representation of domains

Each template is represented by a set of constrained variables. Variables representing non iterated vertices have a straightforward domain: all the nodes of the observation graph which are instances of the class associated with the vertex. For each non iterated vertex n_C of a template T, we create a variable v_C associated with n_C, whose domain is $dom(v_C) = \{x \in OG \mid x \prec C\}$.

The problem is to represent the domains of iterated variables v_C^+ which are associated with iterated vertices n_C^+ of the template. In principle, the domain of an iterated variable v_C^+ is the set of all possible iterated sequences made up of instances of C. This set is very large, and grows exponentially with the number of observations. However, one can observe that some of these iterated sequences are subsequences of others. For a given iterated sequence made of N observations associated with class C, the number of possible iterated subsequences is: N subsequences of length 1, $(N-1)$ subsequences of length 2, ..., $N - p + 1$ subsequences of length p, ..., and 1 subsequence of length N. The total number of subsequences is therefore:

$$\sum_{i=1}^{N}(N-i+1)=\frac{N(N+1)}{2} \tag{1}$$

This observation may be exploited to yield an efficient representation of the set of all possible iterated sequences. We call a *maximal sequence* an iterated sequence which is not a subsequence of another iterated sequence. For a given class C, we first compute the set of maximal sequences. We then represent implicitly each possible iterated sequence as a subsequence of one of the maximal sequences.

The computation of the complete set of maximal sequences is performed by a standard graph search algorithm: starting with the set of all edges between two contiguous instances of C, the algorithm walks through all possible paths from one edge until it finds the extremum vertices and records the corresponding maximal sequence. It then repeats the process until exhaustion of the set. The algorithm is of high worst-case complexity but is in practice very efficient. Furthermore, it is computed only once, for each class C appearing in an iterated variable.

2.2   An indexing scheme for subsequences of maximal sequences.

The representation of domains is critical for the efficiency of the resolution. In the CSP, each iterated vertex is represented by a constrained variable whose domain is the set of all iterated sequences, which is potentially huge. Handling and storing all the iterated sequences explicitly would be extremely costly, both in space and time.

Fortunately, each subsequence S can be fairly represented by three integers, namely 1) the index of a maximal sequence S_M of S, 2) the index of the first element of S in S_M and 3) the length of S (see Fig.6). This makes up an implicit and more characterization of iterated sequences.

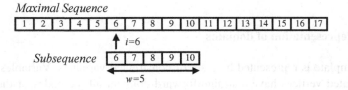

Fig. 6. Subsequences of maximal sequences

In BackJava, integer domains are stored as lists of integer ranges. To efficiently represent iterated domains, we have to design a one-to-one mapping of the three-dimensional implicit representation of subsequences onto integers. We want this mapping to be fast to compute, and to create as dense an integer domain as possible.

For a given maximal sequence S of length N, the idea is to sort subsequences of S by their length. We then number the sequences starting from 0 as follows:
- from 0 to N-1 : subsequences of length 1.
- from N to $2N$-2 : subsequences of length 2.
- etc.
- $\dfrac{N(N+1)}{2}-1$: subsequence of length N.

Let F be the indexing function of subsequences. $F(w,i,N)$ is the index of the subsequence of length w, whose first element is at position i in a maximal sequence of length N. The index of the first subsequence of length w, with $w \geq 2$, is the number of subsequences of length less than w:

$$F(w,0,N)=\sum_{j=1}^{w-1}(N-j+1)=N(w-1)-\frac{(w-1)(w-2)}{2} \qquad (2)$$

Finally, the indexes of subsequences are therefore obtained by:

$$F(w,i,N) = F(w,0,N)+i \qquad (3)$$

In the case of several maximal sequences, the maximal sequences are themselves ordered in a table *Shift*. The indexes of subsequences are systematically shifted by the total number of subsequences of preceding maximal sequences.

Finally, a procedure is applied to remove possible – though unlikely – duplications of subsequences. Indeed, the subsequence representation scheme is redundant, since a given sequence may appear in several maximal sequences. We solve this problem by computing all sequences having multiple definitions, and removing the redundant ones.

This mapping F is at the same time easy to compute and very economic (*i.e.* it maps sequences onto a quasi-minimal range). When needed, an explicit representation of sequence s is easily computed from its index k. The maximal sequence S of length N to which s belongs is determined by scanning the *Shift* table. The length w of s is given by equation (4) which gives the integer part of the first root of function F. The index i of the first element of s in S is given by: $i = k - F(w, 0, N)$.

$$w = E\left(\frac{2N - 3 - \sqrt{(2N - 3)^2 - 8(N + k + 1)}}{2} \right) \tag{4}$$

2.3   Filtering procedures for temporal constraints

To solve the CSP, we use a complete resolution scheme based on an exhaustive enumeration loop and on constraint-specific filtering procedures. Implementing constraint filtering procedures allows to speed up domain reductions, which is critical for the overall efficiency of the resolution [13]. The implementation of our filtering scheme is based on specific objects, called *demons*. A demon is a link between a constraint and a variable, which reacts to modifications of the state of the variable, such as instantiation, and in turn triggers the corresponding filtering procedure for the associated constraint.

Temporal constraints $\mathrm{AllenCt}_R$ (v_1, v_2) are all binary, and parameterized by an arbitrary Allen relation R. We distinguish between two cases, depending on the nature of the variable which is *not* instantiated. For the sake of conciseness, we assume that v_1 is the variable that is instantiated – so v_2 is *not* instantiated.

V₂ is non iterated. All values which do not satisfy relation R with the temporal extension of the value of v_1 are simply removed from $dom(v_2)$. Note that we do not have to consider whether v_1 is iterated or not, for only the temporal extension of the value of v_1 is taken into account.

V₂ is iterated. The problem here is to remove from $dom(v_2)$ all the values which do not satisfy relation R with (the value of) v_1, without enumerating $dom(v_2)$. This method is designed as follows.

First, we define one main basic access protocol for the domain of an iterated variable: $remove(D, s, w, b, e)$ removes from domain D all subsequences of the sth maximal sequence, of length w, whose first element is between b and e in the maximal sequences. This methods removes from D the interval $[f_1, f_2]$, with:

$f_1 = F(w, b, N_s) + Shift[s]$
$f_2 = F(w, e, N_s) + Shift[s].$

Second, we define 13 domain reduction methods, one for each basic Allen relation r_i. These methods remove from the domain of v_2 all values which do satisfy r_i with the value of v_1. For instance, the method for the *after* relation is:

```
basicRemove_after(v₁, v₂)
    for s=0 to number of maximal sequences - 1
        Mₛ = sᵗʰ maximal sequence
        i = index of 1ˢᵗ element in Mₛ just after val(v₁)
        for w=1 to length(Mₛ) - i
            remove(dom(v₂), w, i, length(Mₛ)-w))
```

For each r_i which is *not* an element of R, execute $basicRemove_{r_i}(v_1, v_2)$, *i.e.* the method which removes from $dom(v_2)$ all the values which are in the r_i relation with the value of v_1.

For specific cases, however, we can define more efficient methods, thus avoiding the execution of up to 12 of the basic domain reduction methods. For instance, in Fig.7, v_1 is associated with the *Jingle* vertex of the template, and v_2 is associated with *Shot+*. if $v1$ is instantiated with $jingle_1$, it is possible to remove from $dom(v_2)$ all the iterated sequences which do *not* start with S_6.

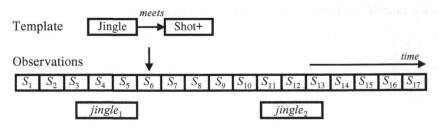

Fig. 7. Domain reduction method for the *meets* relation

Specific methods have been implemented for some of Allen's basic relations, namely *equals*, *before*, *after*, *meets* and *is-met*. The method for the *meets* relation is given below.

```
keep_meets (v_1, v_2)
    for s=0 to number of maximal sequences - 1
        M_s = s^th maximal sequence
        i = index of 1^st element in M_s which meets val(v_1)
        for w=1 to length(M_s)
            ind_1 = 0
            ind_2 = min(i-1, length(M_s)-w)
            ind_3 = i+1
            ind_4 = length(M_s)-w
            if ind_2 ≥ ind_1 then remove(D, s, w, ind_1, ind_2)
            if ind_4 ≥ ind_3 then remove(D, s, w, ind_3, ind_4)
```

This particular filtering method actually achieves arc consistency for the constraint when one of the variables is instantiated. The complexity of the general method to achieve arc consistency, as presented in [14] for instance, is linear in the size of the domain of the non-instantiated variable. More precisely, for each maximal sequence of length N, it is linear in the number of subsequences, namely $N.(N+1)/2$. By contrast, the complexity of our method is linear in the length of the maximal sequences.

2.4   Filtering specific constraints

The specific constraints described above as "no instance of class C between vertices n_1 and n_2," are filtered in a straightforward way. When one of the variable associated with n_1 or n_2 is instantiated – say v_1 –, we remove from $dom(v_2)$ all values v such that there exists an instance of C *after* the value of v_1 and *before* v.

3   Experimentations

In this section, we present two sets of experiments. The first one was made on a corpus of six different evening news broadcasts recorded in 1996, which have been entirely segmented and labeled by hand as a reference. In this experiment, the task was to design the templates suitable for each newscast. The other experiment was made in the context of the DiVAN project, and used five different exemplars of the same evening news collection (Soir3). In this second experiment, the task was to verify that results obtained on one exemplar could be applied to the whole collection.

3.1   Reports from the "M6" broadcast news

The first experiment concerns the recognition of the temporal structure of the evening broadcast news of the "M6" French channel which is illustrated by Fig.1. The template of a report has been described above. As mentioned, specific templates must be defined for the first and the last reports. Provided that the first shot has been classified as *FirstShot*, the template of the first report is given by the following template:

```
FirstReport                constraints
  s1[FirstShot]              s1 m s2
  s2[Shot+]                  s2 m s3
  s3[Shot]                   s3 {o s si di} s4
  s4[Jingle]                 s1 s this
                             s2 f this
                             no Jingle between s1 s3
```

The *LastReport* template is defined in a similar manner. The temporal structure of the whole newscast is simply a succession of a *FirstReport*, an iterated sequence of *Reports* and an *LastReport*:

```
NewsCast                   constraints
  s1[FirstReport]            s1 m s2
  s2[Report+]                s2 m s3
  s3[LastReport]             s1 s this
                             s3 f this
```

We applied the newscast template to a "M6" newscast containing 174 shots and 10 jingles. The recognition process gives exactly 1 matching for the newscast, which is made of 1 first report, a sequence of 9 reports, and 1 last report, which means that all reports have been recognized and that each report was recognized only once. Note that in a first attempt, we defined a report as a sequence of shots "between" two successive templates with the following template:

```
NaiveReport                constraints
  s1[Shot+]                  s1 {si oi} s2
  s2[Jingle]                 s1 {m o} s3
  s3[Jingle]                 s1 e this
                             no Jingle between s2 s3
```

Given this template, a report can start or end with any shot which has a non empty temporal intersection with a jingle. In the newscast we mentioned above, there are 485 distinct occurrences of this template – all of them recognized by the system in less than 3.5 seconds in a 266 Mhz PC. Considering that shots appearing "during" a jingle are not of much importance for documentation, each one of the recognized reports constituted a "good" solution, but most of them were redundant. We then refined the definition of the template by isolating bounds of the shot sequence and by adding convenient temporal constraints. As mentioned, this new definition gave exactly one solution for each expected report.

3.2   Reports from the "France 3" broadcast news

In this experiment, we are interested in comparing two ways of recognizing reports from the evening broadcast news of the "France 3" French channel. The first method which serves as a reference, directly defines a report as the sequence of shots appearing between two successive shots of the anchor person. The second method   defines a report as the sequence of shots appearing between two successive gradual transitions (wipe or dissolve). The second method can be used as an approximation when shots of the anchor person cannot be recognized, based on the observation that shots of the anchor person generally starts or finishes with a wipe or a dissolve. Gradual transitions which appear in the course of a report lead to an over-segmentation of reports; shots or sequences of shots of the anchor person neither started nor finished by a gradual transition lead to unrecognized reports. Shots or sequences of shots of the anchor person both started and finished by gradual transitions lead to misclassified reports. Results obtained in five different editions of the "France 3" broadcast news are summarized in Table 1.

Reports from anchor person	Reports from gradual transitions	Misclassified reports	Missed reports
12	15	3	1
11	24	11	0
10	17	6	1
13	26	4	1
10	31	6	0

Table 1. Recognition of reports using shots of the anchor person, and using gradual transitions

Templates for the Soir3 and other collections are currently being investigated in the prototype DiVAN system, with real implementations of all segmentation and classification tools. Segments corresponding to a recognized template are presented to the documentalists as candidate database entries, for confirmation and manual annotation. In effect, this gives the documentalists control of the system at both ends of the indexing process – template definition and validation.

4   Conclusion

We have described a CSP formulation of a template matching problem in the context of audiovisual document indexing. The formulation yields a language for expressing templates which is flexible enough to accommodate most of the regularities occurring in high level audiovisual structures. The implementation of the language using the CSP formalism yields an efficient and sound solving procedure and the resulting system improves on existing macrosegmentation approaches, by providing an efficient yet general framework to the issue.

Various aspects of the system may benefit from improvements. For instance, the template completion could be avoided and a graph analysis could allow to propagate only   necessary   temporal   constraints,   thereby   limiting   the   number   of   redundant constraints.

Finally, the experiments showed that templates specified even with very simple primitives could produce useful macrosegmentations. Current work focuses on the definition of templates for other classes of audiovisual documents such as sport events, the implementation of more elaborate and specific primitives, and the validation of the approach on a much larger scale.

5   References

1. Brunelli, R., Mich, O., Modena, C.M.: A Survey on the Automatic Indexing of Video Data. Journal of Visual and Image Representation **10** (1999) 78-112
2. Yeung, M., Liu, B.: Efficient matching and clustering of video shots. In: 1995 IEEE International Conference on Image Processing (1995) 338-341
3. Aigrain, P., Joly, P., Longueville, V.: Medium Knowledge-Based Macro-Segmentation of Video into Sequences. In: Maybury, M. (eds): Intelligent Multimedia Information Retrieval. AAAI Press, MIT Press (1997) 159-173
4. Watclar, H.D., Kanade, T., Smith, M.A., Stevens, S.M.: Intelligent Access to Digital Videos: Informedia Project. IEEE Computer **29**(5) (1996) 46-52
5. Garcia, C., Tziritas, G.: Face Detection Using Quantized Skin Color Regions Merging and Wavelet Packet Analysis. IEEE Transactions on Multimedia **1**(3) (1999) 264-277
6. Garcia, C., Apostolidis, X.: Text Detection and Segmentation in Complex Color Images. In: IEEE International Conference on Acoustics, Speech, and Signal Processing (ICASSP'2000). Istambul, Turkey, June 5-9 (2000)
7. Carrive, J., Pachet, F., Ronfard, R.: Using Description Logics for Indexing Audiovisual Documents. In: 1998 Workshop on Description Logics (DL'98). Trento, Italy, June 2-5 (1998)
8. Borgida, A., Brachman, R.J., McGuiness, D.L., Resnick, L.A.: CLASSIC: A Structural Data Model for Objects. In: 1989 ACM SIGMOD International Conference on Management of Data. Porland, Oregon, USA, May 31 - June 2 (1989) 59-67
9. Allen, J.F.: Maintaining knowledge about temporal intervals. Communications of the ACM **26** (1983) 832-843
10. Kautz, H.A., Ladkin, P.B.: Integrating Metric and Qualitative Temporal Reasoning. In: 9th National Conference on Artificial Intelligence (AAAI'91). Anaheim, Californi (1991) 241-246
11. Artale, A., Franconi, E.: Temporal Description Logics. In: Vila, L., *et al.* (eds): Handbook of Time and Temporal Reasoning in Artificial Intelligence (to appear). MIT Press (1999)
12. Weida, R., Litman, D.: Terminological Reasoning with Constraint Networks and an Application to Plan Recognition. In: 3rd International Conference on Principles of Knowledge Representation and Reasoning (KR'92). Cambridge, Massachussetts, USA (1992) 282-293
13. Roy, P., Liret, A., Pachet, F.: A Framework for Objected-Oriented Constraint Satisfaction Problem. In: Fayad, M., Schmidt, D., Johnson, R. (eds): Implementing Application Frameworks: Object-Oriented Frameworks at work. Wiley & Sons (1999) 359-401
14. Mackworth, A.: Consistency in Networks of Relations. Artificial Intelligence **8**(1) (1977) 99-118

Random 3-SAT: The Plot Thickens

Cristian Coarfa, Demetrios D. Demopoulos*, Alfonso San Miguel Aguirre**,
Devika Subramanian***, and Moshe Y. Vardi†

Department of Computer Science, Rice University
6100 S. Main St MS 132, Houston TX 77005-1892

Abstract. This paper presents an experimental investigation of the following questions: how does the average-case complexity of random 3-SAT, understood as a function of the order (number of variables) for fixed density (ratio of number of clauses to order) instances, depend on the density? Is there a phase transition in which the complexity shifts from polynomial to exponential? Is the transition dependent or independent of the solver? To study these questions, we gather median and mean running times for a large collection of random 3-SAT problems while systematically varying both densities and the order of the instances. We use three different complete SAT solvers, embodying very different underlying algorithms: GRASP, CPLEX, and CUDD. We observe new phase transitions for all three solvers, where the median running time shifts from polynomial in the order to exponential. The location of the phase transition appears to be solver-dependent. While GRASP and CUDD shift from polynomial to exponential complexity at a density of about 3.8, CUDD exhibits this transition between densities of 0.1 and 0.5. We believe these experimental observations are important for understanding the computational complexity of random 3-SAT, and can be used as a justification for developing density-aware solvers for 3-SAT.

1 Introduction

The last decade has seen an intense focus on the complexity of randomly generated combinatorial problems. This interest was stimulated by the discovery of a fascinating connection between the *density* of combinatorial problems and their computational complexity, see [9,29]. A problem that has received a lot of attention in this area is the *3-satisfiability problem* (3-SAT), a paradigmatic

---

* Supported in part by NSF grant CCR-9700061, and by a grant from the Intel Corporation.

** The author's address is: Dept. of Computer Science, Instituto Tecnologico Autonomo de Mexico, Rio Hondo 1, 01000 Mexico City. This work was done while the author was on sabbatical at Rice University, supported in part by CONACyT grant 145502.

*** Supported in part by NSF grant IRI-9796046.

† Supported in part by NSF grant CCR-9700061, and by a grant from the Intel Corporation.

R. Dechter (Ed.): CP 2000, LNCS 1894, pp. 143–159, 2000.

combinatorial problem which is also important for its own sake. An instance of 3-SAT consists of a conjunction of clauses, each one a disjunction of three literals. The goal is to find a truth assignment that satisfies all clauses. The density of a 3-SAT instance is the ratio of the number of clauses to the number of Boolean variables (we refer to the latter number as the *order* of the instance). Clearly, a low density suggests that the instance is under-constrained, and therefore is likely to be satisfiable, while a high density suggests that the instance is over-constrained and is unlikely to be satisfiable. Experimental research [12,29] has shown that for ratio below (roughly) 4.26, the probability of satisfiability goes to 1 as the order increases, while for ratio above 4.26 the probability goes to 0. At 4.26, the probability of satisfiability is 0.5. We call this density the *crossover point*. Formally establishing the density at the crossover point is difficult, and is the subject of continuing research, cf. [15,14,1].

The experiments in [12,29], which applied algorithms based on the so-called *Davis-Longemann-Loveland method* (abbr., DLL method) (a depth-first search with unit propagation [13]), also show that the density of a 3-SAT instance is intimately related to its computational complexity. Intuitively, under-constrained instances are easy to solve, as a satisfying assignment can be found fast, and over-constrained instances are also easy to solve, as all branches of the search terminate quickly. Indeed, the data displayed in [12,29] demonstrate a peak in running time essentially at the crossover point. Using finite-size scaling techniques, [22] demonstrated a *phase transition* at the crossover point, viz., a marked qualitative change in the structural properties of the problem. This pattern of behavior with a peak at the crossover point is called the *easy-hard-easy* pattern and is the subject of much research, cf. [28].

This picture, however, is quite simplistic for various reasons. First, it is not clear where the boundaries between the "easy", "hard", and "easy" regions are. Second, the terms "easy" and "hard" do not carry any rigorous meaning. The computational complexity of a problem is typically studied on an infinite collection of instances, and is specified as a function of problem size or order. The easy-hard-easy pattern, however, is observed when the order is fixed while the density varies, but once the order is fixed, there are only finitely many possible instances. For that reason, theoretical analyses of the random 3-SAT problem focus on collections of fixed-density instances, rather than on collections of fixed-order instances, cf. [2]. Third, in the context of a concrete application, e.g., bounded model checking [3], it is typically the order that tends to grow while the density stays fixed, for example, as we search for longer and longer counterexamples in bounded model checking. Thus, the easy-hard-easy pattern tells us little about the complexity of 3-SAT in such settings. There is, however, almost no experimental work that studies how the running time of a SAT solver varies as a function of the order for fixed-density instances (a few results of this nature, though not a systematic study, are reported in [11,12,28]). Finally, the experiments reported in [29,12] are based solely on DLL algorithms. While these are indeed the most popular algorithms for the satisfiability problem, one cannot jump to conclusions about the inherent and practical complexity of random 3-SAT based solely on experiments using these algorithms. We may observe different phenomena by experimenting with SAT solvers that embody different algorithms.

The goal of our experimental algorithmic research is to determine how the average-case complexity of random 3-SAT, understood as a function of the order for fixed density instances, depends on the density. Is there a phase transition in which the complexity shifts from polynomial to exponential? Is such a transition dependent or independent of the solver?

To explore these questions, we set out to obtain a good coverage of an initial quadrangle of the two-dimensional $d \times n$ quadrant, where d is the density and n is the order. We explored the range $0 \leq d \leq 15$. We attempted to maximize the order of the sampled instances, given our resource constraints. We used three different SAT solvers, embodying different underlying algorithms. GRASP (`vinci.inesc.pt/~jpms/grasp/`) is based on the DLL method, but it augments the search with a conflict-analysis procedure that enables it to backtrack non-chronologically and record the causes of conflict. Experimental results [24] show that GRASP is very efficient for a large number of realistic SAT instances, and it has proven to be a very effective SAT solver in the context of automated hardware design [27]. The CPLEX MIP Solver is a commercial optimizer for linear-programming problems with integer variables (`www.cplex.com`). It employs a branch-and-bound technique using linear-programming relaxations that can be complemented with the dynamic generation of cutting planes. While branch-and-bound is related to depth-first-search, the cutting-planes technique is more powerful than resolution [21]. CUDD (`bessie.colorado.edu/~fabio/CUDD`) implements functions to manipulate Reduced Ordered Binary Decision Diagrams (ROBDDs), which provides an efficient representation for Boolean functions [7]. Unlike GRASP and CPLEX, CUDD does not search for a single satisfying truth assignment. Rather, it constructs a compact symbolic representation of the set of satisfying truth assignments and then checks whether this set is nonempty. Uribe and Stickel [34] compared ROBDDs with the David-Putnam method for SAT solving, concluding that the methods are incomparable, and that ROBDDs dominate the DLL method on many examples. Recent work by Groote and Zantema proved the incomparability of ROBDDs and resolution [19].

Our aim was not to directly compare the performance of the different solvers in order to see which one has the "best" performance, but rather to understand their behavior in the $d \times n$ quadrant in order to make qualitative observations on how the complexity of random 3-SAT is viewed from different algorithmic perspectives. It is important to note that the algorithms used in GRASP, CPLEX, and CUDD do not explicitly refer to the density of the input instances. Thus, a qualitative change in the behavior of the algorithm, as a result of changing the density, indicates a genuine structural change in the SAT instances from the perspective of the algorithm.

In analyzing our experimental results we focus on measuring the *median* running time as a function of the order for a set of instances of fixed density.[1] This gives us a measure of the running time of the algorithm for that density. Our findings show that for GRASP and CPLEX the easy-hard-easy pattern is better described as an *easy-hard-less-hard* pattern, where, as is the standard usage in computational complexity theory, "easy" means *polynomial time* and "hard" means *exponential time*. When we start with low-density instances and then increase the density, we go from a region of polynomial running time, to a region of exponential running time, where the exponent first increases and then decreases as a function of the density. Thus, we observe at least *two* phase transitions as the density is increased: a transition at around density 3.8 from polynomial to exponential running time and a transition at around density 4.26 (the crossover point) from an increasing exponent to a decreasing exponent. The region between 3.8 and 4.26 is also characterized by the prevalence of very hard instances, the so called "heavy-tail phenomenon", cf. [20,25,28]. Our results indicate one or more phase transitions in this region, where the ratio of the mean to median running time peaks. For CPLEX we also observe another phase transition at around density 1.7 from linear running time to quadratic running time.

A very different picture emerges for CUDD. Here the algorithm is exponential (in both time and space) for densities between 0.5 and 15. There is, however, no peak around the crossover point and no heavy-tail phenomenon was observed. We observed, however, a peak in the size of the final BDDs constructed by the algorithm at around density 2, indicating a phase transition at around this density. At a very low density (0.1) we did observe polynomial (cubic) behavior, which suggests that another phase transition is "lurking" between densities 0.1 and 0.5. Thus, unlike earlier predictions (cf. [23]), phase transition phenomena related to random 3-SAT are not solver-independent.

2   Related Work

The fact that the "easy-hard-easy" pattern is quite simplistic is known, though rather under-emphasized, cf. [30]. For example, in the high-density region (above density 5.2), an exponential lower bound on the length of resolution proofs is proved in [10]. This entails an exponential lower bound on the running time of DLL algorithms, implying that the high-density region can, at best, be described as "less hard". (Note that this lower bound does not apply to algorithms that are based on cutting planes or ROBDDs [21,19].) It is also known that the probability crossover is not the only phase transition involving random 3-SAT and that phase transitions can be solver dependent. In [6,26], the authors proved linear median

---

[1] It is easy to see that 3-SAT is NP-complete for instances of each fixed density, as the generic reduction of NP to 3-SAT produces instances of fixed density and each density above 1.0 can be obtained by adding redundant variables or redundant clauses. Thus, we'd expect the worst-cases running time to be exponential for all densities. The issue of median vs. mean running time is discussed later.

running time of the pure-literal algorithm at the low-density region (below 1.63) and showed a phase transition at 1.63 for this algorithm. In [16], the authors proved a linear median running time for another heuristic algorithm for low-density instances and showed a phase transition near density 3 for this algorithm. In [32], the authors demonstrated experimentally a change from exponentially fast to power law relaxation at around density 3.

These latter results indicate that the low-density region is indeed in some sense "easy", but they do not establish that complete SAT solvers have polynomial median running time in this region. The analytical results of Franco and his collaborators suggest that in this region we might expect a polynomial median running time for certain heuristic algorithms, cf. [8], but they do not prove it definitively. In [11], the authors reported linear median running time of Tableau, their SAT solver, for densities 1, 2, and 3, and an exponential median running time for densities 4.26 and 10. In [28], the authors reported linear median running time of their DLL SAT solver for density 3, and an exponential median running time for density 4.26. Neither of these papers, however, systematically explores the dependence on the density of the running time as a function of the order.

The performance of integer-programming algorithms on random SAT instances is studied in [21], but the author did not systematically study how the running time depends on the density of the instances. Similarly, in [5,18] the authors studied the behavior of ROBDDs on random SAT instances, but did not study how this behavior varies as a function of the density.

While we focused in this paper on the study of collections of fixed-density instances, it would also be interesting to study the behavior of SAT solvers on instances where the order and the density vary simultaneously; for example, the density may increase together with the order. For DLL solvers, the results in [2] show that unless the density increases linearly with the order we should still expect to see exponential running time. Indeed, if one considers a logarithmic increase of the density as a function of the order, then our data (e.g., using Figure 1) shows that the median running time for GRASP is still exponential.

While the finite-size scaling studies in [17,28] do aim to explore how both the density and the order affect the running time of SAT solvers, they do not reveal the same detailed picture that emerges from our experiments on the density-order quadrant. First, the finite-size scaling studies for SAT are limited to DLL solvers. Second, finite-size scaling studies show a very good fit only around the scale value 0 (i.e., at the crossover point), but the fit gets worse as the scale value gets further from 0. This makes it very difficult to draw conclusions on the dependence on the order for fixed-density instance. For example, it is not at all clear how one can obtain the linear-time behavior at density 3 reported in [28] from their normalized and rescaled results. Finally, the fact that the running time of DLL is exponential in the high-density region and polynomial in the low-density region makes it rather unlikely that the scaling observed in [28] applies anywhere but very near the crossover point.

3   Experimental Setup

Our experimental setup is identical to that of [12,29]. We generate dn clauses, each by picking three distinct variables (out of n) at random and choosing their polarity uniformly. For each studied point in the $d \times n$ quadrant we generate at least 100 random instances and apply our solvers. Our experiments were run on Sun Ultra 1 machines. As in [29], we chose to focus on median running time rather than mean running time. The difficulty of completing the runs on very hard instances makes it less practical to measure the mean. Furthermore, the median and the mean are typically quite close to each other, except for the regions that display heavy-tail phenomena, where the median and the mean diverge dramatically[28]. It would be interesting to analyze our data at percentiles other than the 50th percentile (the median) (cf. [28]), though a meaningful analysis for high percentiles would require many more sample points than we have in our experiments.

For the statistical analysis and plotting of data, we used MATLAB, which is an integrated technical computing environment that combines numeric computation, advanced graphics and visualization, and a high-level programming language. The MATLAB (www.mathworks.com) functions we used for statistical analysis were:

- *polyfit*, for computing the best linear, quadratic, or cubic fit to the data (or the logarithm of the data) using polynomial regression, and
- *corrcoef*, for computing r^2, the square of correlation (r^2 is the fraction of the variance of one variable that is explained by regression on the other variable).

Unless stated otherwise, for the results reported in this paper, r^2 exceeded 0.98. This establishes high confidence in the validity of the fit of the curve to the data points.

4   Random 3-SAT and GRASP

GRASP [24] is a SAT solver that augments the basic backtracking search with a conflict-analysis procedure. In order to cut down on the search space, a dynamic-learning mechanism based on diagnosing the causes of the conflicts is used. By analyzing conflicts and discovering their causes, GRASP can backtrack non-chronologically to earlier levels in the search tree, potentially pruning large portions of the search space. Moreover, by recording the causes of conflicts, GRASP can avoid running into similar conflicts later during the search.

The experiments described in this section were run on a Sun Ultra 1 with a 167MHz UltraSPARC processor and 128MB RAM. Some changes were made to the default GRASP configuration; we increased the maximum number of back-tracks allowed to 1,000,000 and the maximum number of conflicts allowed to 2,000,000. CPU time limit was set to 10,800 seconds. These changes were necessary in order to limit the portion of SAT instances on which GRASP aborted.

This artificially lowers our measurements of mean running time, but does not affect our measurements of median running time.

The goal of the experiments was to evaluate GRASP's performance on an initial quadrangle of the $d \times n$ quadrant. We explored densities from 0.9 to 15. The order of the instances explored depends on the density:

- Density 0.9: 2000 variables (25 variables per step)
- Densities 1, 2 and 3: 1000 variables (10 variables per step)
- Density 3.8: 450 variables (10 variables per step)
- Density: 4.26: 170 variables (10 variables per step)
- Density 5: 210 variables (10 variables per step)
- Densities 4, 6-15: 250 variables (10 variables per step)

In Figure 1 the median running time is shown on a logarithmic (base 2) scale. (For densities 4.26 and 5 we extrapolated the data up to 250 variables).

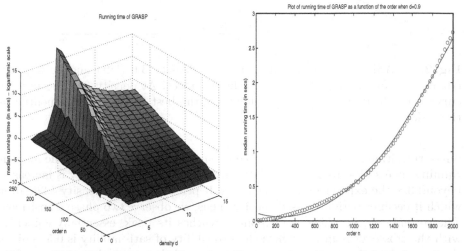

Fig. 1. GRASP – (left) 3-D Plot of median running time, and (right) median running time for density 0.9 as a function of the order of the instances. A quadratic function fits these points better (with an $r^2 > 0.98$) than an exponential function

We analyzed the median running time as a function of the order for fixed density instances. For low densities (at or below 3.6), our data indicate a quadratic running time. See Figures 1 and 2, where we plot the median running time as a function of the order for instances of density 0.9 and 3.6, respectively. The quadratic behavior of GRASP at low densities should be contrasted with the linear running time at low densities that was reported in [11,28]. It seems that GRASP's conflict-analysis component has a quadratic overhead.

At densities 3.8 and above, the median running time is exponential in the order, i.e., it behaves as $2^{\alpha n}$, where the exponent α depends on d (see discussion

below). See Figure 2 where we plot the median running time as a function of
the order for instances of density 3.8 (the r^2 for this plot is 0.95). Thus, a

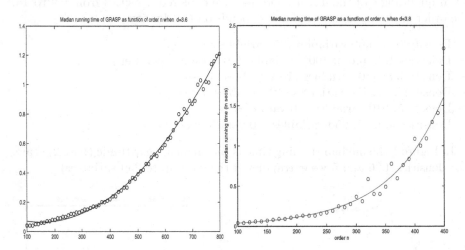

Fig. 2. GRASP – median running time for density 3.6 (left) and density 3.8
(right) as a function of the order of the instances. At density 3.6, the best fit
curve is quadratic in the order, while at 3.8, the best fit curve is exponential in
the order

phase transition seems to occur between densities 3.6 and 3.8, where the median
running time shifts from polynomial to exponential. As the density is increased
beyond 3.8, the exponent α also increases. It peaks at around density 4.26, after
which it declines with increased density. Thus, we observe two phase transitions.
The second one, in which the exponent reaches its peak, essentially coincides
with the crossover point, at which the probability of satisfiability is 0.5. This is
the phase transition that was reported at [29] and then studied extensively. This
transition, however, is preceded by another one, in some sense a more significant
one, at around density 3.8, where we observe a qualitative shift in the behavior of
GRASP. A transition from polynomial to exponential behavior in graph coloring
was predicted in [20]. Such a transition in random 3-SAT near the crossover point
is claimed in [11]; this claim, however, was removed in a later paper [12]. We
believe that we are the first to demonstrate such a transition in random 3-SAT,
and to show that it occurs significantly below the crossover point.

The phase transition at around 3.8 is accompanied by a "heavy-tail phenomenon", which is a prevalence of *outliers*, i.e., instances on which the actual
running time is at least an order of magnitude (10) larger than the median running time, as well as a divergence of the mean and the median. See Figure 3,
where we plot the mean to median ratio and the proportion of outliers as a function of the density. The plots show a drastic change in the region between density
3.7 and density 4.3. Both plots show a quick rise and decline. The mean to me-

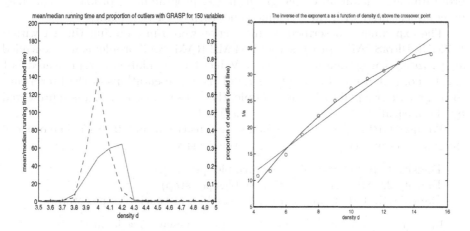

Fig. 3. GRASP – (left) Ratio of mean to median running time and the proportion of outliers, and (right) the exponent $1/\alpha$ of median running time as a function of density

dian ratio peaks at around density 4.0 and the proportion of outliers peaks at around density 4.2. For densities between 3.7 and 4.0 we found it quite difficult to analyze the median running time as a polynomial (of low degree) or exponential function of the order (note the lower r^2 reported above for density 3.8).

Our data suggest that as the density increases from 3.7 to 4.3, random 3-SAT formulas go through a series of changes and perhaps more than one phase transition. The heavy-tail phenomenon for random 3-SAT deserves further study (with many more samples per point in the $d \times n$ quadrant) to confirm our findings. In particular, the divergence of the two peaks in Figure 3 needs to be reconfirmed or refuted.

As noted above, beyond density 4.26 the exponent α declines. A theoretical analysis suggests that for DLL solvers α may decline inversely linearly, i.e., as $\frac{c}{d}$, for some constant c, see [2]. Our data, however, suggest a slower decline, even though one may expect GRASP to be faster than DLL solvers. See Figure 3, where we plot $\frac{1}{\alpha}$ as a function of d. Thus, GRASP is not as efficient in the high-density region as it could be. (We should caution, however, that we only have 11 data points, and these data points themselves have been obtained by fitting a linear curve to the logarithm of the median running time. Thus, the finding of a slower decline should be viewed as quite preliminary.)

5   Random 3-SAT and CPLEX

The CPLEX MIP Solver is a commercial linear-programming solver for integer variables. It employs a branch-and-bound technique starting from a linear-programming relaxation of the given integer-programming problem. This may be complemented with the dynamic generation of cutting planes

The experiments described in this section were run on a Sun Ultra 1 with a 167MHz UltraSPARC processor and 64 MB RAM. SAT problems were encoded as 0-1 integer-programming problems. Values true and false are represented as 1 and 0. For a clause to be true the sum of the representations of the literals has to be greater or equal to 1. For example, the clause $\neg x_1 \vee x_2 \vee \neg x_3$ is represented by the inequality $(1 - x_1) + x_2 + (1 - x_3) \geq 1$.

We used CPLEX to solve problems for densities from 0.9 to 15. The order of the instances was chosen according to the density:

- Density 1: 10000 variables (50 variables per step)
- Density 2: 1800 variables (25 variables per step)
- Densities 3, 4, 4.26, and 5-15: 120 variables (10 variables per step)

In Figure 4, the median running time is shown on a logarithmic (base 2) scale. Note that the peak at the crossover point is much less pronounced than the one in Figure 1.

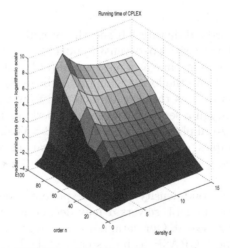

Fig. 4. CPLEX – 3-D Plot of median running time

The median running time was analyzed as a function of the order for fixed density-instances. For low densities (below 1.7) our data indicate a linear running time. See Figure 5 for median running times for instances of density 1 with up to 10000 variables. For densities 2, 3, and up to 3.5, the median running time is quadratic. See Figure 5 for median running time for instances of density 2, where for order above 400 the behavior is quadratic. Thus we seem to have a phase transition, corresponding to a shift from linear to quadratic behavior, between densities 1 and 2. This may coincide with the phase transition proved in [6,26] around density 1.63, as described in Section 2.

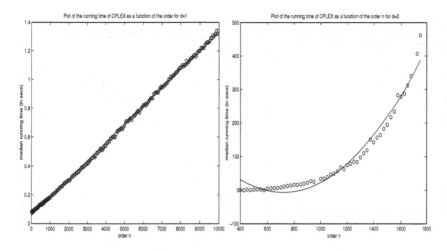

Fig. 5. CPLEX – median running time for density 1 (left) and density 2 (right) as a function of the order of the instances

At densities 4.0 and above, the median running time is exponential in the order, i.e., it behaves as $2^{\alpha n}$, where the exponent α depends on d. As with GRASP, a phase transition seems to occur between densities 3.6 and 4.0. It corresponds to the shift from polynomial to exponential behavior, and is accompanied by heavy-tail phenomena. See Figure 6, where we plot the mean to median ratio and the proportion of outliers as a function of the density. Note that the heavy-tail phenomenon for CPLEX is not as marked as with GRASP; both peak mean-to-median ratio and peak proportion of outliers are lower for CPLEX than for GRASP. Intriguingly, the peak for CPLEX occurs at lower densities (around 3.6) then for GRASP (around 4.0).

As with GRASP, the exponent α peaks at density 4.26 and then declines. Again, our data show a slower decline than $\frac{c}{d}$, as suggested in [2] (though the analysis there is for resolution-based procedures, which are weaker than the cutting-planes method used in CPLEX.) See Figure 6, where we plot $\frac{1}{\alpha}$ as a function of d.

6   Random 3-SAT and CUDD

CUDD [31] is a package that provides functions for the manipulation of Boolean functions, based on the reduced, ordered, binary decision diagram (ROBDD) representation [7]. A binary decision diagram (BDD) is a rooted directed acyclic graph that has only two terminal nodes labeled 0 and 1. Every non-terminal node is labeled with a Boolean variable and has two outgoing edges labeled 0 and 1. An ordered binary decision diagram (OBDD) is a BDD with the constraint that the input variables are ordered and every path in the OBDD visits the variables

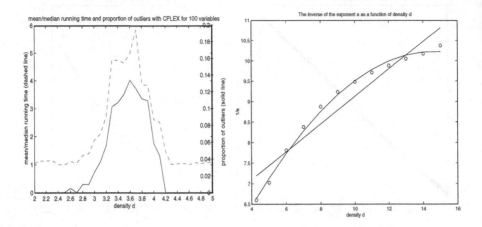

Fig. 6. CPLEX – (left) Ratio of mean to median running time and proportion of outliers, and (right) the exponent $1/\alpha$ of median running time as a function of density

in ascending order. An ROBDD is an OBDD where every node represents a distinct logic function.

Unlike GRASP and CPLEX, CUDD does not search for a satisfying truth assignment. Rather, it constructs a compact symbolic representation of the set of all satisfying truth assignments. Then, the resulting ROBDD is compared against the predefined constant 0 in order to find if an instance is (un)satisfiable.

The experiments described in this section were run on a Sun Ultra 1 with a 167MHZ UltraSPARC processor and 64MB RAM. The CUDD package has been used through the GLU C–interface [33], a set of low-level utilities to access BDD packages. It is well known that the size of the ROBDD for a given function depends on the variable order chosen for that function. We have used automatic dynamic reordering during the tests with the default method for automatic re-ordering of CUDD.

As in the preceding two sections, the goal of the experiments was to evaluate CUDD's performance on an initial quadrangle of the $d \times n$ quadrant. We explored densities 0.1, 0.5, and 1 to 15. The order of the instances explored depends on the density:

- Density 0.1: 1470 variables (10 variables per step)
- Density 0.5: 136 variables (2 variables per step)
- Density 1: 68 variables (2 variables per step)
- Densities 1.5, 2-4, 4.26, 5-15: 46 variables (2 variables per step)

In Figure 7 the median running time is shown on a logarithmic (base 2) scale. Note the absence of a peak (contrast with Figures 1 and 4).

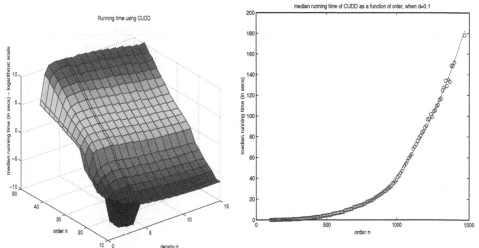

Fig. 7. CUDD – (left) 3-D Plot of median running time and (right) median running time for density 0.1

We analyzed the median running time as a function of the order for fixed-density instances. At densities 0.5 and above, the median running time is exponential in the order, i.e., it behaves as $2^{\alpha n}$. At density 2 and above the exponent α is independent of the density. In particular, there seems to be nothing special about the crossover point at density 4.26. The explanation for this behavior is that the running time of ROBDD-based algorithms is determined mostly by the size of the manipulated ROBDDs. Our algorithm involves dn product operations between a possibly large ROBDD (representing all truth assignments of the clauses processed so far) and a small ROBDD (representing seven truth assignments of the currently processed clause). Thus, the running time of our algorithm is determined by the largest intermediate ROBDD constructed. As is shown in Figure 8, the peak in ROBDD size is attained after processing about $2n$ clauses, which explains the flattening of the running-time plot at density 2, and suggests that a phase transition in terms of ROBDD size occurs at round this density.

As ROBDDs are symmetrical with respect to the set they represent and its complement, both very small sets and very large sets can be represented by small ROBDDs [7]. This suggests that we may see polynomial behavior for very low density instances, which have a large number of satisfying truth assignments. To check this conjecture we measured the median running time of CUDD for instances of density 0.1. Our results indicate a cubic-time behavior, see Figure 7. This suggests the existence of another phase transition between densities 0.1 and 0.5. This result should be contrasted with that of [30], in which the running time for explicitly enumerating all solutions of random constraint-satisfaction instances increases as the density decreases.

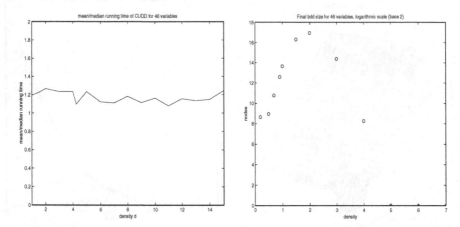

Fig. 8. CUDD – (left) Ratio of mean to median running time and (right) median ROBDD size as a function of density

Unlike with GRASP and CUDD, we did not observe a heavy-tail phenomenon with CUDD: there are no outliers and the mean to median ratio is independent of the density (see Figure 8).

7   Discussion

We provide experimental evidence for the following two hypotheses. First, not only does the peak-hardness density vary with the choice of solver as noted in [25], but the very shape of the surface of the median running time (an experimental surrogate for average-time complexity), as a function of the density d and the order n, changes with the solver. Second, the density-order quadrant contains several phase transitions; in fact, the region between density 0 and density 4.26 seems to be rife with phase transitions, which are also solver dependent. In essence, each solver provides us with a different tool with which to study the complexity of random 3-SAT. This is analogous to astronomers observing the sky using telescopes that operate at different wave lengths. We thus hope to alleviate the "fixation" with DLL solvers and the crossover point at 4.26. While our results are purely empirical, as the lack of success with formally proving a sharp threshold at the crossover point indicates (cf. [15,14,1]), providing rigorous proof for our qualitative observations may be a very difficult task, especially for sophisticated solvers like the ones studied in this paper.

Our experiments reveal a marked difference between solvers like GRASP and CPLEX, which are search based and display interesting similarities in the shapes of the median running time surface despite their different underlying algorithmic techniques, and ROBDD-based solvers, like CUDD, which are based on compactly representing all satisfying truth assignments. While the interesting region for GRASP and CPLEX is between 3.7 and 4.3, the interesting region for CUDD occurs below density 2. This refutes earlier conjectures (cf. [23]) that the peak in median running time around the crossover point is essentially solver independent. For both GRASP and CPLEX, we observed a new phase transition at around density 3.8 where the median running time shifts from being polynomial in the order to being exponential in the order. From the perspective of average-time complexity this is a significant phase transition because it corresponds to a qualitative shift in the behavior of the solver. We also observed several other phase transitions for CPLEX and for CUDD. This suggests that it would be interesting to explore the behavior of other SAT solvers, such as Tableau or RELSAT, on the $d \times n$ quadrant.

With fine grained sampling of the density parameter, and by exploring a greater range in the number of variables, we can start to document for each solver, phase transitions that correspond to significant shifts in the shape of the running time of the solver. These phase transitions are important to our understanding of the computational complexity of random 3-SAT, and can be used as a justification to develop density-based solvers for 3-SAT, i.e., solvers which use information about the density of an instance, to choose the most appropriate algorithmic technique.

Acknowledgement

The last author is grateful to Phokion G. Kolaitis for stimulating discussions.

References

1. D. Achlioptas. Setting two variables at a time yields a new lower bound for random 3-SAT. In *Proc. 32th ACM Symp. on Theory of Computing*, pages 28–37, 2000. 144, 156
2. P. Beame, R. M. Karp, T. Pitassi, and M. E. Saks. On the complexity of unsatisfiability proofs for random k-CNF formulas. In *Proc. 30th ACM Symp. on Theory of Computing*, pages 561–571, 1998. 144, 147, 151, 153
3. A. Biere, A. Cimatti, E. M. Clarke, M. Fujita, and Y. Zhu. Symbolic model checking using SAT procedures instead of BDDs. In *Proc. 36th Conf. on Design Automation*, pages 317–320, 1999. 144
4. R. E. Bixby. Implementing the Simplex method: The initial basis. *ORSA J. on Computing*, 4(3):267–284, 1992.
5. F. Bouquet. *Gestion de la dynamicité et énumération d'implicants premiers: une approche fondée sur les Diagrammes de Décision Binaire*. PhD thesis, Université de Provence, France, 1999. 147
6. A. Z. Broder, A. M. Frieze, and E. Upfal. On the satisfiability and maximum satisfiability of random 3-CNF formulas. In *Proc. 4th Annual ACM-SIAM Symp. on Discrete Algorithms*, pages 322–330, 1993. 146, 152
7. R. E. Bryant. Graph-based algorithms for Boolean function manipulation. *IEEE Trans. on Computers*, 35(8):677–691, 1986. 145, 153, 155
8. M. Chao and J. V. Franco. Probabilistic analysis of a generalization of the unit-clause literal selection heuristics for the k satisfiability problem. *Information Sciences*, 51:289–314, 1990. 147

9. P. Cheeseman, B. Kanefsky, and W. M. Taylor. Where the really hard problems are. In *Proc. 12th Int'l Joint Conf. on Artificial Intelligence (IJCAI '91)*, pages 331–337, 1991. 143

10. V. Chvátal and E. Szemerédi. Many hard examples for resolution. *J. of the ACM*, 35(4):759–768, 1988. 146

11. J. M. Crawford and L. D. Auton. Experimental results on the crossover point in satisfiability problems. *AAAI*, pages 21–27, 1993. 144, 147, 149, 150

12. J. M. Crawford and L. D. Auton. Experimental results on the crossover point in random 3-SAT. *Artificial Intelligence*, 81(1-2):31–57, 1996. 144, 148, 150

13. M. Davis, G. Longemann, and D. Loveland. A machine program for theorem proving. *Comm. of the ACM*, 5:394–397, 1962. 144

14. O. Dubois, Y. Boufkhad, and J. Mandler. Typical random 3-SAT formulae and the satisfiability theshold. In *Proc. 11th Annual ACM-SIAM Symp. on Discrete Algorithms*, pages 126–127, 2000. 144, 156

15. E. Friedgut. Necessary and sufficient conditions for sharp threshold of graph properties and the k-SAT problem. *J. Amer. Math. Soc.*, 12:1917–1054, 1999. 144, 156

16. A. Frieze and S. Suen. Analysis of two simple heuristics for random instances of *k*-SAT. *J. of Algorithms*, 20(2):312–355, 1996. 147

17. I. P. Gent and T. Walsh. The SAT phase transition. In *Proc. European Conf. on Artificial Intelligence*, pages 105–109, 1994. 147

18. J. F. Groote. Hiding propositional constants in BDDs. *Formal Methods in System Design*, 8:91–96, 1996. 147

19. J. F. Groote and H. Zantema. Resolution and binary decision diagrams cannot simulate each other polynomially. Technical report, Department of Computer Science, Utrecht University, 2000. Technical Report UU-CS-2000-14. 145, 146

20. T. Hogg and C. P. Williams. The hardest constraint problems: A double phase transition. *Artificial Intelligence*, 69(1-2):359–377, 1994. 146, 150

21. J. N. Hooker. Resolution vs. cutting plane solution of inference problems: Some computational experience. *Operations Research Letters*, 7:1–7, 1988. 145, 146, 147

22. S. Kirkpatrick and B. Selman. Critical behavior in the satisfiability of random formulas. *Science*, 264:1297–1301, 1994. 144

23. T. Larrabee and Y. Tsuji. Evidence for a satisfiability threshold for random 3CNF formulas. Technical report, University of California, Santa Cruz, 1992. Technical report USCS-CRL-92042. 146, 157

24. J. P. Marques Silva and K. A. Sakallah. GRASP–A search algorithm for propositional satisfiability. *IEEE Trans. on Computers*, 48(5):506–521, 1999. 145, 148

25. D. G. Mitchell and H. J. Levesque. Some pitfalls for experimenters with random SAT. *Artificial Intelligence*, 81(1-2):111–125, 1996. 146, 156

26. M. Mitzenmacher. Tight thresholds for the pure literal rule. Technical report, Digital System Research Center, Palo Alto, California, 1997. SRC Technical Note 1997 - 011. 146, 152

27. G. J. Nam, K. A. Sakallah, and R. A. Rutenbar. Satisfiability-based layout revisited: Detailed routing of complex fpgas via search-based boolean sat. In *Proc. ACM Int'l Symp. on Field-Programmable Gate Arrays (FPGA'99)*, pages 167–175, 1999. 145

28. B. Selman and S. Kirkpatrick. Critical behavior in the computational cost of satisfiability testing. *Artificial Intelligence*, 81(1-2):273–295, 1996. 144, 146, 147, 148, 149

29. B. Selman, D. G. Mitchell, and H. J. Levesque. Generating hard satisfiability problems. *Artificial Intelligence*, 81(1-2):17–29, 1996. 143, 144, 148, 150

30. B. M. Smith and M. E. Dyer. Locating the phase transition in binary constraint satisfaction problems. *Artificial Intelligence Journal*, 8(1–2):155–181, 1996. 146, 155

31. F. Somenzi. CUDD: CU Decision Diagram package. release 2.3.0., 1998. Dept. of Electrical and Computer Engineering. University of Colorado at Boulder. 153

32. P. Svenson and M. G. Nordahl. Relaxation in graph coloring and satisfiability problems. *Phys. Rev. E*, 59(4):3983–3999, 1999. 147

33. The VIS Group. VIS: A system for verification and synthesis. In *Proc. 8th Int'l Conf. on Computer Aided Verification (CAV '96)*, pages 428–432, 1996. LNCS 1102. Ed. by R. Alur and T. Henziger. 154

34. T. E. Uribe and M. E. Stickel. Ordered binary decision diagrams and the Davis-Putnam procedure. In *First Int'l Conf. on Constraints in Computational Logics*, volume 845 of *Lecture Notes in Computer Science*, pages 34–49, Munich, September 1994. Springer-Verlag. 145

New Tractable Classes from Old

David Cohen[1], Peter Jeavons[2], and Richard Gault[2,*]

[1] Department of Computer Science
Royal Holloway, University of London, UK
[2] Oxford University Computing Laboratory
Wolfson Building, Parks Road, Oxford, UK

Abstract. Many combinatorial problems can be naturally expressed as "constraint satisfaction problems". This class of problems is known to be NP-hard in general, but a number of restrictions of the general problem have been identified which ensure tractability. This paper introduces a method of combining two or more tractable classes over disjoint domains, in order to synthesise larger, more expressive tractable classes. We demonstrate that the classes so obtained are genuinely novel, and have not been previously identified. In addition, we use algebraic techniques to extend the tractable classes which we identify, and to show that the algorithms for solving these extended classes can be less than obvious.

1 Introduction

Many combinatorial problems can be naturally expressed as "constraint satisfaction problems" (CSPs) [12], in which the aim is to find an assignment to a given set of variables which satisfies one or more constraints.

The constraint satisfaction problem is known to be NP-hard in general [20]. However, by imposing conditions on the forms of constraints allowed (see, amongst others, [6,9,10,16,17,18,23,25]) it is possible to obtain restricted versions of the problem which are tractable (that is, solvable in polynomial time).

This considerable body of research is at least partially motivated by the long-term goal of classifying *all* subproblems of the constraint satisfaction problem with respect to their tractability. This classification was completed by Schaefer [24] in the case of CSPs over a two-valued domain. Recently, the classification of problems over a three-valued domain was completed by Bulatov, Krokhin, and Jeavons [3]. The present paper provides a stepping stone towards extending these classifications to domains of greater sizes. In particular, we ask how currently known tractable classes may be combined, to yield new, larger constraint classes which are still tractable.

This question has been posed before [4], but whereas the authors of that paper considered the effect of combining tractable classes over some fixed domain, in the present paper we generally consider the effect of combining two tractable classes from *disjoint* domains.

---

* Supported by an EPSRC grant, number GR/M12926.

R. Dechter (Ed.): CP 2000, LNCS 1894, pp. 160–171, 2000.

We focus in particular on the "multiple relational union" of two sets of constraint relations, which is defined in Section 3. We show that whenever both sets of relations are tractable, then their multiple relation union is a tractable set also. In addition, we show that its tractability cannot in general be deduced from previously known results about tractability. Using the results of [12] we then show that the multiple relational union is itself just one small subset of a much larger set of tractable relations, whose proof of tractability is much less obvious than that of the multiple relational union itself. We round off the paper with our conclusions, and suggest directions for future work in this area.

2   Definitions

2.1   The Constraint Satisfaction Problem

In this paper, we treat relations as subsets of D^n, where D is some domain, and n is the *arity* of the relation. The length of a tuple t is denoted $|t|$, and its ith element $t[i]$.

Definition 1. [20,22,19] *An instance of a* constraint satisfaction problem *consists of a finite set of variables, V; a finite domain of values, D; and a finite set of constraints $\{C_1, C_2, \ldots, C_q\}$. Each constraint C_i is a pair (s_i, R_i), where s_i is a tuple of variables of length m_i (called the 'constraint scope'); and R_i is an m_i-ary relation over D, (called the 'constraint relation').*

For each constraint, (s_i, R_i), the tuples in R_i indicate the allowed combinations of simultaneous values for the variables in s_i. A *solution* to a constraint satisfaction problem instance is a function from the variables to the domain such that the image of each constraint scope is an element of the corresponding constraint relation.

Deciding whether or not a given problem instance has a solution is NP-complete in general [20]. In this paper we shall consider how restricting the allowed constraint relations to some fixed subset of all the possible relations affects the complexity of this decision problem. We therefore make the following definition.

Definition 2. *For any set of relations Γ, $\mathbf{C}_\Gamma$ is the class of decision problems in which all constraint relations are elements of Γ.*

If there is a deterministic algorithm which solves every problem instance in $\mathbf{C}_\Gamma$ in polynomial time, then we shall say that Γ is a *tractable* set of relations. If $\Gamma = \{R\}$ is a singleton set, then we shall usually refer to the relation R as being tractable itself.

Example 1. The binary disequality relation over a set D is defined as follows.

$$\neq_D \equiv \{\langle d_1, d_2 \rangle \in D^2 \mid d_1 \neq d_2\}$$

For any finite set D, the class of constraint satisfaction problem instances $\mathbf{C}_{\{\neq_D\}}$ corresponds to the GRAPH $|D|$-COLOURABILITY problem [11]. This problem is tractable when $|D| \leq 2$ and NP-complete when $|D| \geq 3$. Consequently, when $|D| \leq 2$, $\{\neq_D\}$ is a tractable set of relations.

Not every set of relations has its tractability or otherwise known however (even up to the question of whether P = NP).

Example 2. The relation R defined by

$$R \equiv \{\langle 2, 3, 2, 2, 2 \rangle,$$
$$\langle 0, 1, 2, 0, 0 \rangle,$$
$$\langle 0, 0, 2, 0, 1 \rangle,$$
$$\langle 1, 0, 2, 0, 0 \rangle,$$
$$\langle 2, 2, 2, 3, 3 \rangle,$$
$$\langle 1, 1, 2, 0, 1 \rangle\}$$

cannot be shown to be tractable using previously known methods. Nevertheless, it *is* tractable, as we will discover below.

2.2   Operations on Tuples

A k-ary operation φ on a set D is just a function from D^k to D. We call k the *arity* of the operation. Except where stated otherwise, φ is permitted to be *partial*, that is, to be undefined at one or more places. The domain, $dom(\varphi)$, and range, $range(\varphi)$, of φ are defined by:

$$dom(\varphi) \equiv \bigcup \{x_1, x_2, \ldots, x_k \in D : \varphi(x_1, x_2, \ldots, x_k) \text{ is defined}\}$$
$$range(\varphi) \equiv \{x \in D : \exists x_1, x_2, \ldots, x_k \in D \text{ s.t. } \varphi(x_1, x_2, \ldots, x_k) = x\}.$$

Any operation defined on the domain of a relation can be used to define an operation on tuples from that relation, as follows:

Definition 3. *Let R be an n-ary relation over a domain D, and let $\varphi : D^k \to D$ be a k-ary operation on D. For any collection of tuples, $t_1, t_2, \ldots, t_k \in R$, (not necessarily all distinct) define the tuple $\varphi(t_1, t_2, \ldots, t_k)$ as follows:*

$$\varphi(t_1, t_2, \ldots, t_k) = \langle \varphi(t_1[1], t_2[1], \ldots, t_k[1]),$$
$$\varphi(t_1[2], t_2[2], \ldots, t_k[2]), \ldots, \varphi(t_1[n], t_2[n], \ldots, t_k[n]) \rangle$$

Note that in this definition, and indeed throughout this paper, we allow the possibility that $k = 0$; that is, that φ is a nullary operation. Such an operation takes no arguments, but always returns some (constant) domain element, d.

Definition 4. *Let R be a relation over a domain D, and let $\varphi : D^k \to D$ be a k-ary (possibly partial) operation on D.*

R is said to be closed *under φ if, for all $t_1, t_2, \ldots, t_k \in R$ such that $\varphi(t_1, t_2, \ldots, t_k)$ is defined, it happens that $\varphi(t_1, t_2, \ldots, t_k) \in R$. A set of relations is closed under φ if all relations in the set are closed under φ.*

The set of all *total* (*i.e.*, not partial) operations under which Γ remains closed is called the set of *polymorphisms* of Γ, and is denoted by $Pol(\Gamma)$. Similarly, if Φ is a set of operations over D, then the set of all relations which are closed under every operation of Φ is called the set of *invariants* of Φ, and denoted by $Inv(\Phi)$. Note that $Inv(\Phi)$ always contains the relations $=_D\equiv \{\langle d,d\rangle : d \in D\}$ and $\otimes_D \equiv D \times D$, since these are closed under all operations. Between them, the mappings $Pol()$ and $Inv()$ establish a *Galois connection* between sets of relations and sets of operations [5,21].

The following theorem was proved in [12].

Theorem 1. *A set of relations Γ over some domain is tractable if, and only if, $Inv(Pol(\Gamma))$ is tractable.*

A set of relations of the form $Inv(Pol(\Gamma))$, for some Γ, is known as a *relational clone*.

We will sometimes need to refer to operations with various special properties. *Constant* operations, for example, are those which always return a constant value, regardless of the values taken by their arguments. *Projections* simply return the value of their i^{th} argument (for some fixed i). A *binary ACI* operation is an arity-2 operation which is associative, commutative, and idempotent. A *majority* operation is a ternary operation φ with the property that for all $a,b \in dom(\varphi)$, $\varphi(a,a,b) = \varphi(a,b,a) = \varphi(b,a,a) = a$. Finally, an *affine* operation is a ternary operation φ with the property that for all $a,b,c \in dom(\varphi)$, $\varphi(a,b,c) = a - b + c$, where $(dom(\varphi),+)$ is an Abelian group.

Jeavons, Cohen, and Gyssens [14] were able to identify four distinct classes of tractable sets of relations. These were characterised as those sets of relations which were closed under a constant operation, a majority operation, a binary ACI operation, or an affine operation respectively. At the time, these four classes together captured all known tractable sets of relations. Subsequently however, other researchers have discovered some more tractable sets [1,2,3,7,8,17]. These too may be characterised as those sets closed under certain operations. In this paper we shall refer explicitly only to the four classes from [14]. Most of what we shall say however, will also apply to the novel sets of relations.

3   Combining Sets of Relations

3.1   Multiple Relational Unions

Definition 5. *Let Γ_1 and Γ_2 be sets of relations over the non-empty sets D_1 and D_2 respectively. Then the* multiple relational union *of Γ_1 and Γ_2, denoted $\Gamma_1 \bowtie \Gamma_2$, is defined to be the following set of relations over $D_1 \cup D_2$:*

$$\Gamma_1 \bowtie \Gamma_2 \equiv \{R_1 \cup R_2 : R_1 \in \Gamma_1, R_2 \in \Gamma_2 \wedge arity(R_1) = arity(R_2)\}$$

In this paper, we shall generally consider the case when D_1 and D_2 are disjoint sets. In particular, we shall show how this allows us to combine well-studied tractable sets of relations in order to generate previously unknown tractable sets. The following theorem is our main tool in this regard.

Theorem 2. *Let Γ_1 and Γ_2 be two tractable sets of relations over the disjoint domains D_1 and D_2 respectively. Then $\Gamma_1 \bowtie \Gamma_2$ is also a tractable set of relations.*

Proof. Let $\mathcal{P}$ be an instance of $\mathbf{C}_{\Gamma_1 \bowtie \Gamma_2}$. The following algorithm assumes that the hypergraph of constraint scopes is connected; if it is not then we may apply the algorithm over each connected component in turn.

First, determine whether or not there is an assignment to the variables of $\mathcal{P}$ in which every variable takes a value from D_1. This test is tractable since every relation $R \in \Gamma_1 \bowtie \Gamma_2$ can be decomposed into the union of two relations R_1 and R_2 over the domains D_1 and D_2 respectively, and the R_2 part "thrown away". The tractability of the test then follows from the tractability of Γ_1. If there is such an assignment, then return True.

If there is no such assignment, then determine whether or not there is an assignment to the variables of $\mathcal{P}$ in which every variable takes a value from D_2. If there is, then return True. Otherwise, return False.

It is easy to see that this algorithm runs in polynomial time, and that if it returns True then $\mathcal{P}$ is a yes-instance of $\mathbf{C}_{\Gamma_1 \bowtie \Gamma_2}$. To show the converse, we must observe that in *any* satisfying assignment to the variables of $\mathcal{P}$, if some variable v is assigned a value from D_1 (say), then all the variables from $\mathcal{P}$ must be assigned values from D_1. This follows immediately from the definition of the $\bowtie$ operator, and the connectivity of the constraint hypergraph.

Technically, the above proof relies on the implicit assumption that it is tractable to decompose a relation $R \in \Gamma_1 \bowtie \Gamma_2$ into its two component parts. The assumption is valid provided that we represent relations in such a way that every relation is the same size (to within a polynomial factor) as it would have been if it had been encoded in the natural way as a set of tuples.

For Theorem 2 to be of any interest, it had better not be the case that $\Gamma_1 \bowtie \Gamma_2$ is tractable for previously known reasons. The remainder of this section is devoted to developing a theoretical framework which will allow us to prove that in many cases one does indeed end up with a genuinely new tractable class. Since every known tractable class of relations can be characterised by its polymorphisms, we must therefore calculate $Pol(\Gamma_1 \bowtie \Gamma_2)$.

Definition 6. *Let D be a set, and fix $k \in \mathbb{N}$ (note that k may be 0). A k-ary pattern on D is just a k-tuple of subsets of D.*

Definition 7. *Let D be a set, and let p be a k-ary pattern on D. For any k-ary total operation φ on D, the restriction of φ to p, written φ_p, is the partial operation defined so that*

$$\varphi_p(x_1, x_2, \ldots, x_k) = \varphi(x_1, x_2, \ldots, x_k)$$

whenever each $x_i \in p[i]$, and which is undefined everywhere else. We say that the arguments of φ_p must all be of pattern p. Similarly, if Φ is a set of operations over D, then

$$\Phi_p \equiv \{\varphi_p : \varphi \in \Phi \land \varphi \text{ has arity } k\}$$

Clearly, a k-ary operation is completely defined by giving its restriction to all possible k-ary patterns. The next lemma goes further, and says that if we consider just patterns from $\{D_1, D_2\}^k$ (where D_1 and D_2 are disjoint) then we can build all polymorphisms of $\Gamma_1 \bowtie \Gamma_2$ by putting together arbitrary partial closure operations: one for each possible pattern.

Lemma 1. *Let Γ_1 and Γ_2 be sets of relations over disjoint domains D_1 and D_2 respectively. Let $\varphi : (D_1 \cup D_2)^k \to (D_1 \cup D_2)$ be some operation. Then $\varphi \in Pol(\Gamma_1 \bowtie \Gamma_2)$ if, and only if, for every $p \in \{D_1, D_2\}^k$, $\Gamma_1 \bowtie \Gamma_2$ is closed under φ_p.*

Proof. We begin by proving the "if" direction. If $\Gamma_1 \bowtie \Gamma_2 = \emptyset$ then the result is trivially true. Otherwise, pick an arbitrary relation $R = (R_1 \cup R_2) \in \Gamma_1 \bowtie \Gamma_2$, where $R_1 \in \Gamma_1$ and $R_2 \in \Gamma_2$. We shall show that R is closed under φ. Consider an arbitrary k-tuple $\langle t_1, t_2, \ldots, t_k \rangle$ of tuples from R. Define the pattern $p \in \{D_1, D_2\}^k$ by:

$$p[i] \equiv \begin{cases} D_1 \text{ if } t_i \in R_1; \\ D_2 \text{ if } t_i \in R_2. \end{cases}$$

By assumption, $\varphi_p(t_1, t_2, \ldots, t_k)$ is defined and equal to some tuple $t \in R$. Thus $\varphi(t_1, t_2, \ldots, t_k) = t$, and we are done. The proof of the converse is trivial: *any* set Γ of relations is closed under all partial versions of each of its polymorphisms.

Now, $Pol(\Gamma_1 \bowtie \Gamma_2)$ always contains at least one function of every arity (for example, it contains every projection). By Lemma 1 therefore, if $p \in \{D_1, D_2\}^k$, and φ_p is a partial closure operation on $\Gamma_1 \bowtie \Gamma_2$ which is defined for all tuples of pattern p, then φ_p can be extended to a total closure operation on $D_1 \cup D_2$. Thus, $Pol(\Gamma_1 \bowtie \Gamma_2)$ is precisely characterised by the set $\{Pol(\Gamma_1 \bowtie \Gamma_2)_p : p \in \{D_1, D_2\}^*\}$ of restrictions of $Pol(\Gamma_1 \bowtie \Gamma_2)$ to each possible "natural" pattern of each possible arity. It is therefore reasonable to ask how each set $Pol(\Gamma_1 \bowtie \Gamma_2)_p$ depends upon $Pol(\Gamma_1)$ and $Pol(\Gamma_2)$. To answer this question, we first need the following definition.

Definition 8. *Let D be a set, and let Ψ be a set of operations over D, where each operation $\psi \in \Psi$ is a total operation $\psi : D_\psi^i \to D_\psi$ for some i and $D_\psi \subseteq D$.*

We say that a total operation $\varphi : D^k \to D$ is synthesisable *from Ψ if the following conditions both hold.*

- *There is some $\Psi' \subseteq \Psi$ such that $\bigcup \{D_\psi : \psi \in \Psi'\} = D$; and*
- *For every $p = \langle D_{\psi_1}, D_{\psi_2}, \ldots, D_{\psi_k} \rangle$, with each $\psi_i \in \Psi'$ (not necessarily all distinct), there is some set D_ψ, which occurs at positions $u_1, u_2, \ldots, u_r$ of p, and some r-ary operation $\psi \in \Psi'$, such that $\psi : D_\psi^r \to D_\psi$ and the following identity holds:*

$$\varphi_p(x_1, x_2, \ldots, x_k) = \psi(x_{u_1}, x_{u_2}, \ldots, x_{u_r})$$

That is, φ_p ignores all of its arguments, except for some subset which all lie in D_ψ, and on these it behaves exactly like ψ.

The set of all operations which are synthesisable from Ψ will be denoted $Syn(\Psi)$.

Note that any total operation φ is synthesisable from $\{\varphi\}$. In addition, if $\varphi \in Syn(\Phi)$ for some Φ, then $\varphi \in Syn(\Phi')$ for each $\Phi' \supseteq \Phi$.

Example 3. Suppose that $D = \{0,1,2,3\}$, that Ψ_1 consists precisely of the projections of every arity > 0 on the domain $\{0,1\}$, and that Ψ_2 consists precisely of the negations of the projections of every arity > 0 on the domain $\{2,3\}$. That is, Ψ_1 contains operations such as $\psi(x,y,z) = y$, where $x,y,z \in \{0,1\}$; and Ψ_2 contains operations such as $\psi(x,y,z) = 5 - z$, where $x,y,z \in \{2,3\}$.

If $\Psi = \Psi_1 \cup \Psi_2$ then the restriction of any k-ary operation $\varphi \in Syn(\Psi)$ to a pattern p from $\{\{0,1\},\{2,3\}\}^k$ will be such that φ_p will depend on exactly one of its arguments: x_i, say, and furthermore:

$$\varphi_p(x_1,x_2,\ldots,x_k) = \begin{cases} x_i & \text{if } p[i] = \{0,1\} \\ 5 - x_i & \text{if } p[i] = \{2,3\}. \end{cases}$$

Proposition 1. *Let Γ_1 and Γ_2 be sets of relations over the disjoint domains D_1 and D_2 respectively. Then*

$$Syn(Pol(\Gamma_1) \cup Pol(\Gamma_2)) \subseteq Pol(\Gamma_1 \bowtie \Gamma_2).$$

Proof. Fix any $\varphi \in Syn(Pol(\Gamma_1) \cup Pol(\Gamma_2))$, of arity k, and let $p \in \{D_1, D_2\}^k$. By Lemma 1, it is enough to show that $\Gamma_1 \bowtie \Gamma_2$ is closed under φ_p. Take any $R \in \Gamma_1 \bowtie \Gamma_2$, where R is the union of some $R_1 \in \Gamma_1$ and $R_2 \in \Gamma_2$. Without loss of generality, there exists some $\psi \in Pol(\Gamma_1)$ of arity r such that

$$\varphi_p(x_1,x_2,\ldots,x_k) = \psi(x_{u_1}, x_{u_2}, \ldots, x_{u_r})$$

where the u_i are those values, in ascending order, for which $p[u_i] = D_\psi = D_1$.

Consider an arbitrary k-tuple $\langle t_1, t_2, \ldots, t_k \rangle$ of tuples from R with the property that for each i, t_i comes from relation R_1 if $p[i] = D_1$, and from R_2 otherwise. (By the definition of closure, these are the only tuples which we need to consider.) Then

$$\varphi_p(t_1,t_2,\ldots,t_k) = \psi(t_{u_1}, t_{u_2}, \ldots, t_{u_r}) = t$$

for some t where, since R_1 is closed under ψ, $t \in R_1$. But $R_1 \subseteq R$, so $t \in R$, and hence R is closed under φ_p.

Example 4. To continue Example 3, observe that the domains $\{0,1\}$ and $\{2,3\}$ of Ψ_1 and Ψ_2 respectively are disjoint. So all the operations described in that example are contained within $Pol(\Gamma_1 \bowtie \Gamma_2)$.

3.2   Restricting the Possible Polymorphisms

Proposition 1 is a positive result: it tells us that no matter which sets Γ_1 and Γ_2 of relations we begin with, we can always guarantee the existence of certain operations in $Pol(\Gamma_1 \bowtie \Gamma_2)$. We now turn our attention in the other direction, and examine how placing restrictions on the allowable Γ_i restricts the polymorphisms of their multiple relational union. The motivation for doing this is provided by the fact that the containment demonstrated in Proposition 1 is not, in general, an equality. By restricting the Γ_i however, we will be able to give a sufficient condition to ensure that equality does hold in many important cases.

Proposition 2. *Let Γ_1 and Γ_2 be relational clones over disjoint domains D_1 and D_2 respectively. Then for every $\varphi_p \in Pol(\Gamma_1 \bowtie \Gamma_2)_p$ of arity k (with $p \in \{D_1, D_2\}^k$) it is the case that either $range(\varphi_p) \subseteq D_1$ or $range(\varphi_p) \subseteq D_2$.*

Proof. Fix k, let $p \in \{D_1, D_2\}^k$ be a pattern, and choose any $\varphi_p \in Pol(\Gamma_1 \bowtie \Gamma_2)$. Define $R = \otimes_{D_1} \cup \otimes_{D_2}$ (recall that $\otimes_D$ is defined to be $D \times D$). Since each Γ_i is a relational clone, $R \in \Gamma_1 \bowtie \Gamma_2$, and is therefore closed under φ_p. Let t and t' be two k-tuples of pattern p. We shall show that $\varphi_p(t)$ and $\varphi_p(t')$ lie in the same domain.

Consider the sequence $s_1, s_2, \ldots, s_k$ of tuples from R defined by $s_i = \langle t[i], t'[i] \rangle$ for every i. Then $\varphi_p(s_1, s_2, \ldots, s_k)$ is well-defined (since t and t' are both of pattern p), and equal to some pair $r \in R$. Both elements of r lie in the same domain. But $r[1] = \varphi_p(t)$ and $r[2] = \varphi_p(t')$, so in particular, $\varphi_p(t)$ lies in the same domain as $\varphi_p(t')$.

Lemma 2. *Let Γ_1 and Γ_2 be relational clones over disjoint domains D_1 and D_2 respectively, and let $p \in \{D_1, D_2\}^k$ be a pattern. For every $\varphi \in Pol(\Gamma_1 \bowtie \Gamma_2)$, it is the case that φ_p depends solely on those of its arguments which come from the same domain as does $range(\varphi_p)$.*

Proof. By Proposition 2 we may assume without loss of generality that $range(\varphi_p) \subseteq D_1$. Define $R \in \Gamma_1 \bowtie \Gamma_2$ by $R \equiv (\otimes_{D_2}) \cup (=_{D_1})$. By definition, R is closed under φ_p.

Let $t, t' \in (D_1 \cup D_2)^k$ be tuples of pattern p with the property that whenever $p[i] = D_1$, it is the case that $t[i] = t'[i]$. It is enough to show that $\varphi_p(t) = \varphi_p(t')$. So define the sequence $s_1, s_2, \ldots, s_k$ of tuples from R by setting $s_i = \langle t[i], t'[i] \rangle$ for every i. Then φ_P is well-defined and, by assumption equal to some $r \in (=_{D_1})$. But then $\varphi_p(t) = r[1] = r[2] = \varphi_p(t')$.

Theorem 3. *Let Γ_1 and Γ_2 be relational clones over the disjoint domains D_1 and D_2 respectively. Then*

$$Pol(\Gamma_1 \bowtie \Gamma_2) = Syn(Pol(\Gamma_1) \cup Pol(\Gamma_2)).$$

Proof. The inclusion $Syn(Pol(\Gamma_1) \cup Pol(\Gamma_2)) \subseteq Pol(\Gamma_1 \bowtie \Gamma_2)$ was proved in Proposition 1. Here, we prove the inclusion in the other direction.

Take Ψ' in the definition of synthesis to be the whole of $Pol(\Gamma_1) \cup Pol(\Gamma_2)$. Every operation from Ψ' is total (on its own domain), and the union of all the domains of the operations in Ψ' is $D_1 \cup D_2$, as required.

Now, $\{D_\psi : \psi \in \Psi'\}^k = \{D_1, D_2\}^k$. So choose an arbitrary $\varphi \in Pol(\Gamma_1 \bowtie \Gamma_2)$ of arity k, and take some $p \in \{D_1, D_2\}^k$. Assume without loss of generality that $range(\varphi_p) \subseteq D_1$, and consider any r-ary operation φ' over D_1, which has been obtained from φ_p by arbitrarily fixing those of its arguments which come from D_2. Since every relation in $\Gamma_1 \bowtie \Gamma_2$ is closed under φ_p, it is clear that every relation in Γ_1 is closed under φ'; that is, that $\varphi' \in Pol(\Gamma_1) \subseteq \Psi'$. Now, by Lemma 2, the same operation φ' results regardless of how the arguments from D_2 are fixed. Thus, $\varphi_p(x_1, x_2, \ldots, x_k) = \varphi'(x_{u_1}, x_{u_2}, \ldots, x_{u_r})$, where $u_1, u_2, \ldots, u_r$ are those values for which $p[u_i] = D_i$. Since this holds for any pattern p, it follows that $\varphi \in Syn(Pol(\Gamma_1) \cup Pol(\Gamma_2))$.

4 Generating Novel Tractable Classes

We are now in a position to determine whether combining tractable relations using the multiple relational union operator gives rise to tractable classes which are genuinely novel. The following result shows that in some cases it does not.

Proposition 3. *Let Γ_1 and Γ_2 be sets of relations over the disjoint domains D_1 and D_2 respectively. Then the following statements all hold.*

1. *If Γ_1 is closed under a constant function φ, then $\Gamma_1 \bowtie \Gamma_2$ is closed under that constant function.*
2. *If Γ_1 and Γ_2 are closed under ACI operations φ_1 and φ_2 respectively, then $\Gamma_1 \bowtie \Gamma_2$ is closed under an ACI operation.*
3. *If Γ_1 and Γ_2 are closed under majority operations φ_1 and φ_2 respectively, then $\Gamma_1 \bowtie \Gamma_2$ is closed under a majority operation.*

Proof. The proof is a routine exercise involving the use of Proposition 1 to construct polymorphisms out of partial closure operations.

Note that the analogous result to Proposition 3 fails to hold when we turn our attention to affine operations. That is, if Γ_1 and Γ_2 are both closed under an affine operation then the same is not in general true of $\Gamma_1 \bowtie \Gamma_2$. This is because any relation R which is closed under an affine operation defined via some Abelian group G, must be such that $|G|$ is an exact multiple of $|R|$. But $|R_1 \cup R_2|$ is not, in general, a divisor of $|G|$.

Proposition 3 is not the end of the story however, as the following result demonstrates.

Proposition 4. *Suppose that Γ_1 and Γ_2 are relational clones over the disjoint domains D_1 and D_2 respectively. Let Φ be some property of operations which can be defined by identities, and suppose that there is no $\varphi \in Pol(\Gamma_1)$ which has the property Φ. Then there is no non-constant $\varphi \in Pol(\Gamma_1 \bowtie \Gamma_2)$ which has property Φ.*

Proof. Let $\varphi \in Pol(\Gamma_1 \bowtie \Gamma_2)$ be a non-constant operation. By Theorem 3, $\varphi \in Syn(Pol(\Gamma_1) \cup Pol(\Gamma_2))$. Now, φ has a strictly positive arity, and so the restriction of φ to the domain D_1 is a member of $Pol(\Gamma_1)$, and thus does not have property Φ. Since Φ is defined by identities, it follows that φ itself does not have property Φ.

Since all known tractable sets of relations can be defined by closure under some operation defined by identities, it follows that the $\bowtie$ operation is capable of generating genuinely new tractable sets of relations.

The question now arises as to whether there are any other relations, apart from those in $\Gamma_1 \bowtie \Gamma_2$, whose tractability we can deduce. Theorem 1 says that in fact the whole of $Inv(Pol(\Gamma_1 \bowtie \Gamma_2))$ is tractable, so our question reduces to the following: Are there any relations which are present in $Inv(Pol(\Gamma_1 \bowtie \Gamma_2))$, but which are not present in $\Gamma_1 \bowtie \Gamma_2$?

Consider the Cartesian product operator, $\times$, defined on pairs of relations by:

$$R^1 \times R^2 \equiv \{r_1 r_2 : r_1 \in R^1 \wedge r_2 \in R^2\}$$

(where $r_1 r_2$ denotes the concatenation of the two tuples).

The following lemma comes essentially from [12].

Lemma 3. *Let Γ_1 and Γ_2 be sets of relations over the disjoint domains D_1 and D_2 respectively, and let $R^1, R^2 \in Inv(Pol(\Gamma_1 \bowtie \Gamma_2))$ be two relations. Then $R^1 \times R^2 \in Inv(Pol(\Gamma_1 \bowtie \Gamma_2))$.*

Example 5. Suppose that

$$\begin{aligned}
R_1 = \{ & \langle 0,0,1,0\rangle, \text{ and } R_2 = \{\langle 3,2,2,3\rangle, \\
& \langle 0,1,0,0\rangle, \qquad\qquad\quad \langle 2,3,2,2\rangle\}. \\
& \langle 1,0,0,0\rangle, \\
& \langle 1,1,1,0\rangle\}
\end{aligned}$$

Let $\Gamma_1 = Inv(Pol(R_1))$ and $\Gamma_2 = Inv(Pol(R_2))$. It is easy to check that R_1 is closed under an affine operation, but not under any other operation known to yield tractability. Similarly, R_2 is closed under both majority and affine operations, but not under anything else significant. We may verify by hand that $\Gamma_1 \bowtie \Gamma_2$ is not closed under any affine operations. By Proposition 4 therefore, $\Gamma_1 \bowtie \Gamma_2$ is a tractable set of relations which does not fall into any previously known tractable class. Moreover, $Inv(Pol(\Gamma_1 \bowtie \Gamma_2))$ contains further relations whose tractability could not have been previously deduced. Amongst these is not only the relation $R_1 \times R_2$ itself, but also the relation R of Example 2. For R is a permutation of $(R_1 \cup R_2) \times \{\langle 2\rangle\}$, where $\{\langle 2\rangle\}$, being a projection of R_2, is a member of $\Gamma_1 \bowtie \Gamma_2$.

The point of this example is to demonstrate that although the algorithm given in Theorem 2 is a straightforward one, the algebraic techniques presented above and in [12,13,15] can be used to establish the existence of a collection of more complicated tractable algorithms, each of which can be used in more general situations than can the original algorithm itself.

5   Conclusions

In this paper we have shown how combining tractable sets of constraint relations on disjoint domains can yield hitherto unknown, tractable sets of relations. The algorithm which establishes the tractability of this combination is particularly simple, yet we have been able to exploit algebraic properties of the new sets of tractable relations to show that even more sets of relations are tractable than those which can be directly solved by the algorithm. This result demonstrates once again the power of the algebraic approach to analysing constraint satisfaction problems.

This work is related to that of [4]. In that paper, the authors considered the effect of combining tractable sets of relations on a *single* domain. One question which naturally arises is to ask what happens when there are two domains which are partially disjoint, but which overlap in one or more places. This is a question we intend to address in the future.

Finally, the results presented in this paper take us one step closer to the ultimate goal of classifying the complexity of all possible sets of relations over domains of arbitrary finite size.

References

1. M. Bjäreland and P. Jonsson. Exploiting bipartiteness to identify yet another tractable subclass of CSP. In J. Jaffar, editor, *Principles and Practice of Constraint Programming — CP'99*, number 1713 in Lecture Notes in Computer Science, pages 118–128. Springer, 1999. 163
2. A. A. Bulatov, A. A. Krokhin, and P. Jeavons. Constraint satisfaction problems and finite algebras. Technical Report TR-4-99, Oxford University Computing Laboratory, 1999. 163
3. A. A. Bulatov, A. A. Krokhin, and P. Jeavons. Constraints over a three-element domain: tractable maximal relational clones. Unpublished Manuscript, 1999. 160, 163
4. D. Cohen, P. Jeavons, and M. Koubarakis. Tractable disjunctive constraints. In *Proceedings 3rd International Conference on Constraint Programming — CP'96 (Linz, October 1997)*, volume 1330 of *Lecture Notes in Computer Science*, pages 478–490. Springer-Verlag, 1996. 160, 170
5. P. Cohn. *Universal Algebra*. Harper & Row, 1965. 163
6. M. Cooper, D. Cohen, and P. Jeavons. Characterising tractable constraints. *Artificial Intelligence*, 65:347–361, 1994. 160
7. V. Dalmau. A new tractable class of constraint satisfaction problems. In *6th International Symposium on Mathematics and Artificial Intelligence*, 2000. 163
8. V. Dalmau and J. Pearson. Closure functions and width 1 problmes. In J. Jaffar, editor, *Principles and Practice of Constraint Programming — CP'99*, number 1713 in Lecture Notes in Computer Science, pages 159–173. Springer, 1999. 163
9. R. Dechter and J. Pearl. Tree clustering for constraint networks. *Artificial Intelligence*, 38:353–366, 1989. 160
10. E. Freuder. A sufficient condition for backtrack-bounded search. *Journal of the ACM*, 32:755–761, 1985. 160
11. M. Garey and D. Johnson. *Computers and Intractability: A Guide to the Theory of NP-Completeness*. Freeman, San Francisco, CA., 1979. 161
12. P. Jeavons. On the algebraic structure of combinatorial problems. *Theoretical Computer Science*, 200:185–204, 1998.

13. P. Jeavons and D. Cohen. An algebraic characterization of tractable constraints. In *Computing and Combinatorics. First International Conference COCOON'95 (Xi'an,China,August 1995)*, volume 959 of *Lecture Notes in Computer Science*, pages 633–642. Springer-Verlag, 1995. 160, 161, 163, 169 169

14. P. Jeavons, D. Cohen, and M. Gyssens. A unifying framework for tractable constraints. In *Proceedings 1st International Conference on Constraint Programming — CP'95 (Cassis, France, September 1995)*, volume 976 of *Lecture Notes in Computer Science*, pages 276–291. Springer-Verlag, 1995. 163

15. P. Jeavons, D. Cohen, and M. Gyssens. A test for tractability. In *Proceedings 2nd International Conference on Constraint Programming — CP'96 (Boston, August 1996)*, volume 1118 of *Lecture Notes in Computer Science*, pages 267–281. Springer-Verlag, 1996. 169

16. P. Jeavons, D. Cohen, and M. Gyssens. Closure properties of constraints. *Journal of the ACM*, 44:527–548, 1997. 160

17. P. Jeavons and M. Cooper. Tractable constraints on ordered domains. *Artificial Intelligence*, 79(2):327–339, 1995. 160, 163

18. L. Kirousis. Fast parallel constraint satisfaction. *Artificial Intelligence*, 64:147–160, 1993. 160

19. P. Ladkin and R. Maddux. On binary constraint problems. *Journal of the ACM*, 41:435–469, 1994. 161

20. A. Mackworth. Consistency in networks of relations. *Artificial Intelligence*, 8:99–118, 1977. 160, 161

21. R. McKenzie, G. McNulty, and W. Taylor. *Algebras, Lattices and Varieties*, volume I. Wadsworth and Brooks, California, 1987. 163

22. U. Montanari. Networks of constraints: Fundamental properties and applications to picture processing. *Information Sciences*, 7:95–132, 1974. 161

23. B. Nebel and H.-J. Burckert. Reasoning about temporal relations: a maximal tractable subclass of Allen's interval algebra. *Journal of the ACM*, 42:43–66, 1995. 160

24. T. Schaefer. The complexity of satisfiability problems. In *Proceedings 10th ACM Symposium on Theory of Computing (STOC)*, pages 216–226, 1978. 160

25. P. van Beek and R. Dechter. On the minimality and decomposability of row-convex constraint networks. *Journal of the ACM*, 42:543–561, 1995. 160

Expressiveness of Full First Order Constraints in the Algebra of Finite or Infinite Trees

Alain Colmerauer and Thi-Bich-Hanh Dao

Laboratoire d'Informatique de Marseille, CNRS,
Universités de la Méditerranée et de Provence

Abstract. We are interested in the expressiveness of constraints represented by general first order formulae, with equality as unique relational symbol and functional symbols taken from an infinite set F. The chosen domain is the set of trees whose nodes, in possibly infinite number, are labeled by elements of F. The operation linked to each element f of F is the mapping $(a_1, \ldots, a_n) \mapsto b$, where b is the tree whose initial node is labeled f and whose sequence of daughters is $a_1, \ldots, a_n$.

We first consider constraints involving long alternated sequences of quantifiers $\exists \forall \exists \forall \ldots$. We show how to express winning positions of two-person games with such constraints and apply our results to two examples.

We then construct a family of strongly expressive constraints, inspired by a constructive proof of a complexity result by Pawel Mielniczuk. This family involves the huge number $\alpha(k)$, obtained by evaluating top down a power tower of 2's, of height k. With elements of this family, of sizes at most proportional to k, we define a finite tree having $\alpha(k)$ nodes, and we express the result of a Prolog machine executing at most $\alpha(k)$ instructions.

By replacing the Prolog machine by a Turing machine we rediscover the following result of Sergei Vorobyov: the complexity of an algorithm, deciding whether a constraint without free variables is true, cannot be bounded above by a function obtained by finite composition of elementary functions including exponentiation.

Finally, taking advantage of the fact that we have at our disposal an algorithm for solving such constraints in all their generality, we produce a set of benchmarks for separating feasible examples from purely speculative ones. Among others we solve constraints involving alternated sequences of more than 160 quantifiers.

1 Introduction

The algebra of (possibly) infinite trees plays a fundamental role in computer science: it is a model for data structures, program schemes and program executions. As early as 1976, Gérard Huet proposed an algorithm for unifying infinite terms, that is solving equations in that algebra [11]. Bruno Courcelle has studied the properties of infinite trees in the scope of recursive program schemes [8,9]. Alain Colmerauer has described the execution of Prolog II, III and IV programs in terms of solving equations and disequations in that algebra [4,5,6,1]. Michael

R. Dechter (Ed.): CP 2000, LNCS 1894, pp. 172–186, 2000.

Maher has introduced and justified a complete theory of the algebra of infinite trees [12]. Among others, he has shown that in this theory, and thus in the algebra of infinite trees, any first order formula is equivalent to a Boolean combination of conjunctions of equations (partially or totally) existentially quantified. Sergei Vorobyov has shown that the complexity of an algorithm, deciding whether a formula without free variables is true in that theory, cannot be bounded above, by a function obtained by finite composition of elementary functions, including exponentiation [14]. Pawel Mielniczuk has shown a similar result in the theory of feature trees, but with a more constructive method, which has inspired some of our examples [13].

We have recently developed an algorithm for solving general first order constraints in the algebra of infinite trees [10]. The purpose of this paper is not the presentation of this algorithm, but of examples, first imagined as tests, then extended to show the expressiveness of such general constrains. The paper is organized as follows.

(1) We end this first section by making clear the notions of tree algebra and first order constraints in that algebra.

(2) In the second section we consider constraints involving long alternated sequences of quantifiers $\exists \forall \exists \forall \dots$. We show how to express winning positions of two-person games with such constraints and apply our results to two examples.

(3) In the third section, we investigate the most expressive family of constraints we know. It involves the truly huge number $\alpha(k)$, obtained by evaluating top down a tower of powers of 2's, of height k. With elements of this family, of sizes at most proportional to k, we define a finite tree having $\alpha(k)$ nodes, and we express the result of a Prolog machine executing at most $\alpha(k)$. By replacing the Prolog machine by a Turing machine we rediscover the complexity result of Sergei Vorobyov mentioned at the beginning of this section. This part has been strongly influenced by the work of Pawel Mielniczuk [13].

(4) We conclude by discussions and benchmarks separating the feasible examples from the purely speculative ones.

1.1   The Algebra of Infinite Trees

Trees are well known objects in the computer science world. Here are some of them:

Their nodes are labeled by the symbols $0, 1, s, f$, of respective arities $0, 0, 1, 2$, taken from a set F of functional symbols, which we assume to be infinite. Note that the first tree is the only one having a finite set of nodes, but that the second one has still a finite set of (patterns of) subtrees. We denote by $\mathbf{A}$ the set of all trees[1] constructed on F.

We introduce in $\mathbf{A}$ a set of construction operations[2], one for each element $f \in F$ which is the mappings $(a_1, \ldots, a_n) \mapsto b$, where n is the arity of f and b the tree whose initial node is labeled f and the sequence of daughters is $(a_1, \ldots, a_n)$ and which be schematized as

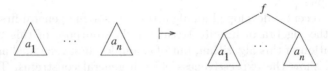

We thus obtain the *algebra of infinite trees* constructed on F, which we denote by $(\mathbf{A}, F)$.

1.2 Tree Constraints

We are interested in the expressiveness of constraints represented by general first order formulae, with equality as unique relational symbol and functional symbols taken from an infinite set F. These *tree constraints* are of one of the 9 forms:

$$s = t, \; true, \; false, \; \neg(p), \; (p \wedge q), \; (p \vee q), \; (p \rightarrow q), \; \exists x\, p, \; \forall x\, p,$$

where p and q are shorter tree constraints, x a variable taken from an infinite set and s, t terms, that are expressions of one of the forms

$$x, \; f t_1 \ldots t_n$$

where $n \geq 0$, $f \in F$, with arity n, and the t_i's are shorter terms.

The variables represent elements of the set $\mathbf{A}$ of trees constructed on F and the functional symbols f are interpreted as construction operations in the algebra of infinite trees $(\mathbf{A}, F)$. Thus a constraint without free variables is either true or false and a constraint $p(x_1, \ldots, x_n)$ with n free variables x_i establish an n-ary relation in the set of trees.

---

[1] More precisely we define first a *node* to be a word constructed on the set of strictly positive integers. A *tree* a, constructed on F, is then a mapping of type $E \rightarrow F$, where E is a non-empty set of nodes, each one $i_1 \ldots i_k$ (with $k \geq 0$) satisfying the two conditions: (1) if $k > 0$ then $i_1 \ldots i_{k-1} \in E$, (2) if the arity of $a(i_1 \ldots i_k)$ is n, then the set of nodes of E of the form $i_1 \ldots i_k i_{k+1}$ is obtained by giving to i_{k+1} the values $1, \ldots, n$.

[2] In fact, the *construction* operation linked to the n-ary symbol f of F is the mapping $(a_1, \ldots, a_n) \mapsto b$, where the a_i's are any trees and b is the tree defined as follows from the a_i's and their set of nodes E_i's: the set E of nodes of a is $\{\varepsilon\} \cup \{ix \,|\, x \in E_i \text{ and } i \in 1..n\}$ and, for each $x \in E$, if $x = \varepsilon$, then $a(x) = f$ and if x is of the form iy, with i being an integer, $a(x) = a_i(y)$.

2   Long Nesting of Alternated Quantifiers

We first introduce the notions of k-winning and k-losing position in any two-person games and in two examples. We show how to express, in any domain, the set of k-winning positions by a constraint. We end the section by expressing the k-winning positions of the two examples by tree constraints involving an alternated embedding of $2k$ quantifiers.

2.1   Winning Positions in a Two-Person Game

Let (V, E) be a directed graph, with V a set of vertices and $E \subseteq V \times V$ a set of edges. The sets V and E may be empty and the elements of V are also called *positions*. We consider a two-person game which, given an initial position x_0, consists, one after another, in choosing a position x_1 such that $(x_0, x_1) \in E$, then a position x_2 such that $(x_1, x_2) \in E$, then a position x_3 such that $(x_2, x_3) \in E$ and so on... The first one who cannot play any more has lost and the other one has won. For example the two following infinite graphs correspond to the two following games:

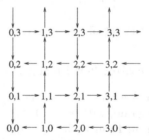

Game 1 A non-negative integer i is given and, one after another, each partner subtracts 1 or 2 from i, but keeping i non-negative. The first person who cannot play any more has lost.

Game 2 An ordered pair (i, j) of non-negative integers is given and, one after another, each partner chooses one of the integers i, j. Depending on the fact that the chosen integer u is odd or even, he then increases or decreases the other integer v by 1, but keeping v non-negative. The first person who cannot play any more has lost.

Let $x \in V$ be any vertex of the directed graph (V, E) and suppose that it is the turn of person A to play. The position x is said to be *k-winning* if, no matter the way the other person B plays, it is always possible for A to win in making at most k moves. The position x is said to be *k-losing* if, no matter the way A plays, B can always force A to lose and to play at most k moves.

Consider the two preceding graphs and mark with $+k$ the positions which are k-winning and with $-k$ the positions which are k-losing, with each time k being as small as possible. Vertex 0 of the first graph and vertex $(0, 0)$ of the second one being the only 0-losing positions, are marked with -0. Starting from the vertices marked with -0 and following the arrows in reverse direction, we find successively the set of vertices to be marked by $+1$, then -1, then $+2$, then -2, then $+3$, then -3, and so on. We get

and convince ourselves that the set of k-winning positions of game 1 is

$$\{i \in \mathbf{N} \mid i < 3k \text{ and } i \bmod 3 \neq 0\}$$

and of game 2

$$\{(i,j)) \in \mathbf{N}^2 \mid i+j < 2k \text{ and } (i+j) \bmod 2 = 1\}.$$

where $\mathbf{N}$ is the set of non-negative integers.

2.2   Expressing k-Winning Positions by a Constraint

Let $\mathbf{D}$ be a *domain*, that is a non-empty set and let $G = (V, E)$ the graph of a two-person game, with $V \subseteq \mathbf{D}$. We will express the k-winning positions of G by a constraint in $\mathbf{D}$ involving an embedding $\exists \forall \exists \ldots$ of $2k$ alternated quantifiers.

Let us introduce in $\mathbf{D}$ the properties *move*, *winning$_k$* et *losing$_k$*, defined by

$$
\begin{aligned}
&move(x,y) \;&&\leftrightarrow (x,y) \in E,\\
&winning_k(x) &&\leftrightarrow x \text{ is a } k\text{-winning position of } G,\\
&losing_k(x) &&\leftrightarrow x \text{ is a } k\text{-losing position of } G.
\end{aligned}
\tag{1}
$$

In $\mathbf{D}$ we then have the equivalences, for all $k \geq 0$:

$$
\begin{aligned}
&winning_0(x) \;&&\leftrightarrow false,\\
&winning_{k+1}(x) &&\leftrightarrow \exists y \; move(x,y) \wedge losing_k(y),\\
&losing_k(x) &&\leftrightarrow \forall y \; move(x,y) \rightarrow winning_k(y).
\end{aligned}
\tag{2}
$$

Contrary to what we may believe, it follows that we have:

$$winning_k(x) \rightarrow winning_{k+1}(x), \qquad losing_k(x) \rightarrow losing_{k+1}(x).$$

Indeed, from the first and the last equivalence of (2) we conclude that these implications hold for $k = 0$ and, if we assume that they hold for a certain $k \geq 0$, from the last two equivalences in (2) we conclude that they also hold for $k+1$.

From (3) we deduce an explicit formulation of $winning_k$, for all $k \geq 0$:

$$winning_k(x) \leftrightarrow \begin{bmatrix} \exists y \, move(x,y) \wedge \neg(\\ \exists x \, move(y,x) \wedge \neg(\\ \exists y \, move(x,y) \wedge \neg(\\ \exists x \, move(y,x) \wedge \neg(\\ \dots \\ \exists y \, move(x,y) \wedge \neg(\\ \exists x \, move(y,x) \wedge \neg(\\ false \qquad)\dots) \\ \underbrace{\qquad\qquad}_{2k} \end{bmatrix} \qquad (3)$$

where of course all the quantifiers apply on elements of $\mathbf{D}$. By moving down the negations, we thus get an embedding of $2k$ alternated quantifiers.

In equivalence (3) it is possible to use a more general definition of $move$ than the one given in (1). We first remark, that for any non-negative k, the following property holds:

Property 1 Let three directed graphs be of the form $G_1 = (V_1, E_1)$, $G_2 = (V_2, E_2)$ and $G = (V_1 \cup V_2, E_1 \cup E_2)$. The graphs G_1 and G have the same set of k-winning positions, if both:

1. the sets of vertices V_1 and V_2 are disjoint,
2. for all $x \in V_2$, there exists $y \in V_2$ with $(x, y) \in E_2$.

Indeed, from the first condition it follows that E_1 and E_2 are disjoint and thus that the set of k-winning positions of G is the union of the set of k-winning positions of G_1 with the set of k-winning positions of G_2. This last set is empty because of the second condition.

It follows that:

Property 2 (Generalized move relation) *Equivalence (3) holds also for any* move *relation obeying to the two conditions:*

1. *for all $x \in V$ and $y \in V$, $move(x, y) \leftrightarrow (x, y) \in E$,*
2. *for all $x \in \mathbf{D}-V$ there exists $y \in \mathbf{D}-V$ such that $move(x, y)$.*

2.3   Formalizing Game 1 in the Algebra of Infinite Trees

We now reconsider game 1 introduced in section 2.1. As domain $\mathbf{D}$ we take the set $\mathbf{A}$ of trees constructed on a set F of functional symbols including among others the symbols $0, s$, of respective arities $0, 1$. We code the vertices i of the game graph by the trees[3] $s^i(0)$. Let $G = (V, E)$ be the graph obtained this way.

As generalized relation $move$ we then can take in the algebra of infinite trees:

$$move(x, y) \stackrel{\text{def}}{=} x = s(y) \vee x = s(s(y)) \vee (\neg(x = 0) \wedge \neg(\exists u \, x = s(u)) \wedge x = y)$$

---

[3] Of course, $s^0(0) = 0$ and $s^{i+1}(0) = s(s^i(0))$.

and according to property 2 the set of k-winning positions of game 1 is the set
of solutions in x of the constraint $winning_k(x)$ defined in (3).

For example, with $k = 1$ the constraint $winning_k(x)$ is equivalent to

$$x = s(0) \lor x = s(s(0))$$

and with $k = 2$ to

$$x = s(0) \lor x = s(s(0)) \lor x = s(s(s(s(0)))) \lor x = s(s(s(s(s(0)))))$$

2.4   Formalizing Game 2 in the Algebra of Infinite Trees

We also reconsider game 2 introduced in section 2.1. As domain $\mathbf{D}$ we take the
set $\mathbf{A}$ of trees constructed on a set F of functional symbols including among
others the symbols $0, f, g, c$, of respective arities $0, 1, 1, 2$. We code the vertices
(i, j) of the game graph by the trees $c(\bar{i}, \bar{j})$ with $\bar{i} = (fg)^{\frac{i}{2}}(0)$ if i is even, and
$\bar{i} = g(\overline{i-1})$ if i is odd[4]. Let $G = (V, E)$ be the graph obtained this way.

The perspicacious reader will convince himself that, as generalized relation
$move$, we can take in the algebra of infinite trees:

$$move(x, y) \overset{\text{def}}{=} transition(x, y) \lor (\neg(\exists u \, \exists v \, x = c(u, v)) \land x = y)$$

with

$$transition(x, y) \overset{\text{def}}{=} \begin{bmatrix} \exists u \, \exists v \, \exists w \\ \begin{bmatrix} (x = c(u, v) \land y = c(u, w)) \lor \\ (x = c(v, u) \land y = c(w, u)) \end{bmatrix} \\ \land \\ \begin{bmatrix} (\exists i \, u = g(i) \land succ(v, w)) \lor \\ (\neg(\exists i \, u = g(i)) \land pred(v, w)) \end{bmatrix} \end{bmatrix}$$

$$succ(v, w) \overset{\text{def}}{=} \begin{bmatrix} ((\exists j \, v = g(j)) \land w = f(v)) \lor \\ (\neg(\exists j \, v = g(j)) \land w = g(v)) \end{bmatrix}$$

$$pred(v, w) \overset{\text{def}}{=} \begin{bmatrix} (\exists j \, v = f(j) \land \begin{bmatrix} (\exists k \, j = g(k) \land w = j) \lor \\ (\neg(\exists k \, j = g(k)) \land w = v) \end{bmatrix}) \lor \\ (\exists j \, v = g(j) \land \begin{bmatrix} (\exists k \, j = g(k) \land w = v) \lor \\ (\neg(\exists k \, j = g(k)) \land w = j) \end{bmatrix}) \lor \\ (\neg(\exists j \, v = f(j)) \land \neg(\exists j \, v = g(j)) \land \neg(v = 0) \land w = v) \end{bmatrix}$$

According to property 2, the set of k-winning positions of game 2 is the set of
solutions in x of the constraint $winning_k(x)$ defined in (3).

For example, with $k = 1$ the constraint $winning_k(x)$ is equivalent to

$$x = c(g(0), 0) \lor x = c(0, g(0))$$

and with $k = 2$ to

$$\begin{bmatrix} x = c(0, g(0)) \lor x = c(g(0), 0) \lor x = c(0, g(f(g(0)))) \lor \\ x = c(g(0), f(g(0))) \lor x = c(f(g(0)), g(0)) \lor x = c(g(f(g(0))), 0) \end{bmatrix}$$

---

[4]   Of course, $(fg)^0(x) = x$ and $(fg)^{i+1}(x) = (fg)^i(f(g(x)))$.

3   Quasi-universality of Tree Constraints

After all these quantifiers, we move to constraints, which are so expressive that their solving becomes quasi-undecidable.

3.1   Defining a Huge Finite Tree by a Constraint

We set $\alpha(k) = 2^{2^{\cdot^{\cdot^2}}}$, with k occurrences of 2. More precisely we take

$$\alpha(0) = 1, \qquad \alpha(k+1) = 2^{\alpha(k)},$$

with $k \geq 0$. The function α increases in a stunning way, since $\alpha(0) = 1$, $\alpha(1) = 2$, $\alpha(2) = 4$, $\alpha(3) = 16$, $\alpha(4) = 65536$ and $\alpha(5) = 2^{65536}$. Thus $\alpha(5)$ is greater than 10^{20000}, a number probably much greater than the number of atoms of the universe or the number of nanoseconds which elapsed since its creation!

We suppose that the set **A** of trees is constructed on a set F of functional symbols including among others the symbols $0, 1, 2, 3, s, f$, of respective arities $0, 0, 0, 0, 1, 4$. For $k \geq 0$ let us introduce the constraint:

$$huge_k(x) \overset{\text{def}}{=} \exists z \; triangle_k(3, x, z, 0)$$

with still for $k \geq 0$,

$$triangle_0(t, x, z, y) \overset{\text{def}}{=} z = x \wedge z = y$$

$$triangle_{k+1}(t, x, z, y) \overset{\text{def}}{=} \left[\begin{array}{l} [\exists u_1 \, \exists u_2 \; z = f(x, u_1, u_2, y)] \\ \wedge \\ \left[\begin{array}{l} \forall t' \, \forall y' \, \forall z' \\ \left[\begin{array}{l} (t' = 1 \vee t' = 2) \wedge \\ triangle_k(t', z, z', y') \end{array}\right] \rightarrow \\ \left[\begin{array}{l} (t' = 1 \wedge form1\,(y')) \vee \\ \left[(t' = 2 \wedge \begin{array}{l} \exists u \, \exists v \; form2\,(u, y', v) \wedge \\ (t = 1 \rightarrow trans1\,(u, v)) \wedge \\ (t = 2 \rightarrow trans2\,(u, v)) \wedge \\ (t = 3 \rightarrow trans3\,(u, v)) \end{array} \right] \end{array}\right] \end{array}\right] \end{array}\right] \tag{4}$$

and

$$form1\,(x) \overset{\text{def}}{=} \exists u_1 \ldots \exists u_4 \; x = f(u_1, f(u_2, u_2, u_2, u_2), f(u_3, u_3, u_3, u_3), u_4)$$

$$form2\,(x, z, y) \overset{\text{def}}{=} \exists u_1 \ldots \exists u_6 \; z = f(u_1, f(u_1, u_2, u_3, x), f(y, u_4, u_5, u_6), u_6)$$

$$trans1\,(x, y) \overset{\text{def}}{=} \exists u_1 \ldots \exists u_4 \; x = f(u_1, u_2, u_3, u_4) \wedge (y = u_2 \vee y = u_3)$$

$$trans2\,(x, y) \overset{\text{def}}{=} trans1\,(x, y) \vee x = y$$

$$trans3\,(x, y) \overset{\text{def}}{=} x = s(y)$$

To give a feeling of what $triangle_k(t, x, z, y)$ means, here are three trees x, z, y such that $triangle_2(t, x, z, y)$, with $t = 1$, $t = 2$ and $t = 3$, from left to right:

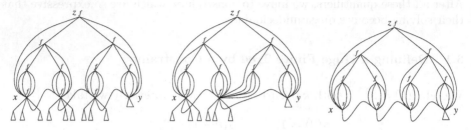

Let us agree that the size $|p|$ of a constraint p, is the number of occurrences of all symbols except parentheses and commas. (Constraints could be written in infix notation.) We then have the double property:

Property 3 (small constraint, big tree)

$$|huge_k(x)| = 9 + 158k \qquad \text{and} \qquad huge_k(x) \leftrightarrow x = s^{\alpha(k)-1}(0).$$

To prove the equality, it is sufficient to count:

$$
\begin{aligned}
|huge_k(x)| &= |triangle_k(t, x, z, y)| + 2, \\
|triangle_0(t, x, z, y)| &= 7, \\
|triangle_{k+1}(t, x, z, y)| &= |triangle_k(t, x, z, y)| + (54 + 27 + 23 + 27 + 23 + 4)
\end{aligned}
$$

and to conclude. The proof of the equivalence (in the algebra of infinite trees) is the subject of next subsection.

3.2   Proof of the Second Part of Property 3

We write $x\{f, k_1, ..., k_m\}y$ for expressing that x is a tree whose initial node is labeled f and that there exists $i \in \{k_1, ..., k_m\}$ such that tree y is the ith daughter of x. We also agree that:

$$
\begin{aligned}
x\{f, k_1, ..., k_m\}^0 y &\leftrightarrow x = y, \\
x\{f, k_1, ..., k_m\}^{n+1} y &\leftrightarrow \exists u \; x\{f, k_1, ..., k_m\}u \wedge u\{f, k_1, ..., k_m\}^n y
\end{aligned}
$$

with $n \geq 0$.

Given the definition of $huge_k(x)$, to show the second part of property 3 it is sufficient to show that, in the algebra of infinite trees, the last of the three following equivalences holds:

$$
\begin{aligned}
(\exists z \; triangle_k(1, x, z, y)) &\leftrightarrow x\{f, 2, 3\}^{\alpha(k)-1} y \\
(\exists z \; triangle_k(2, x, z, y)) &\leftrightarrow \bigvee_{i=0}^{\alpha(k)-1} x\{f, 2, 3\}^i y \\
(\exists z \; triangle_k(3, x, z, y)) &\leftrightarrow x\{s, 1\}^{\alpha(k)-1} y
\end{aligned}
\qquad (5)
$$

Let us show by induction on k that the three equivalences hold. They hold for $k = 0$. Let us assume that they hold for a certain $k \geq 0$ and let us proof that they hold for $k+1$. Definition (4) can be reformulated as

$$triangle_{k+1}(t, x, z, y) \;\leftrightarrow$$

$$\left[\begin{array}{l} [\exists u_1 \, \exists u_2 \; z = f(x, u_1, u_2, y)] \\ \wedge \\ \left[\begin{array}{l} \forall y' \\ (\exists z' \; triangle_k(1, z, z', y')) \rightarrow \\ form1\,(y') \end{array}\right] \end{array}\right] \;\wedge\; \left[\begin{array}{l} \forall y' \\ (\exists z' \; triangle_k(2, z, z', y')) \rightarrow \\ \left[\begin{array}{l} \exists u \, \exists v \; form2\,(u, y', v) \wedge \\ (t = 1 \rightarrow trans1\,(u, v)) \wedge \\ (t = 2 \rightarrow trans2\,(u, v)) \wedge \\ (t = 3 \rightarrow trans3\,(u, v)) \end{array}\right] \end{array}\right]$$

Taking into account our assumptions and using our new notations, we get

$$triangle_{k+1}(t, x, z, y) \;\leftrightarrow$$

$$\left[\begin{array}{l} [z\{f, 1\}x \wedge z\{f, 4\}y] \\ \wedge \\ \left[\begin{array}{l} \forall y' \\ z\{f, 2, 3\}^{\alpha(k)-1}y' \rightarrow \\ form1\,(y') \end{array}\right] \end{array}\right] \;\wedge\; \left[\begin{array}{l} \forall y' \\ [\bigvee_{i=0}^{\alpha(k)-1} z\{f, 2, 3\}^i y'] \rightarrow \\ \left[\begin{array}{l} \exists u \, \exists v \; form2\,(u, y', v) \wedge \\ (t = 1 \rightarrow u\{f, 2, 3\}v) \wedge \\ (t = 2 \rightarrow u\{f, 2, 3\}v \vee u = v) \wedge \\ (t = 3 \rightarrow u\{s, 1\}v) \end{array}\right] \end{array}\right]$$

Since the top of a tree x satisfying $form1\,(x)$ and the top of a tree z satisfying $form2\,(x, z, y)$ are respectively of the form

the top of a tree z satisfying $triangle_{k+1}(t, x, z, y)$ is of the form

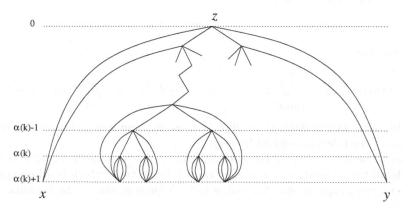

It follows that

$\exists z\ triangle_{k+1}(t,x,z,y) \leftrightarrow$

$$\exists z \left[\begin{array}{l} \left[z\{f,2\}^{\alpha(k)+1}x \wedge z\{f,3\}^{\alpha(k)+1}y\right] \\ \wedge \\ \exists z \left[\begin{array}{l} \left[\bigwedge_{i=0}^{\alpha(k)} \left[\begin{array}{l}\forall y'\ z\{f,2,3\}^i y' \rightarrow \\ \left[\begin{array}{l}\exists u\,\exists v \\ y'\{f,2\}u \wedge y'\{f,3\}v\end{array}\right]\end{array}\right]\right] \\ \wedge \\ \left[\begin{array}{l}\forall y'\,\forall u\,\forall v \\ \left[\begin{array}{l}z\{f,2,3\}^{\alpha(k)}y' \wedge \\ y'\{f,2\}u \wedge y'\{f,3\}v\end{array}\right] \rightarrow \\ u=v\end{array}\right] \end{array}\right] \end{array} \wedge \left[\begin{array}{l}\bigwedge_{i=0}^{\alpha(k)-1} \\ \left[\begin{array}{l}\forall y'\,\forall u\,\forall v\,\forall u'\,\forall v' \\ \left[\begin{array}{l}z\{f,2,3\}^i y' \wedge \\ y'\{f,2\}u' \wedge u'\{f,3\}^{\alpha(k)-i}u \wedge \\ y'\{f,3\}v' \wedge v'\{f,2\}^{\alpha(k)-i}v \wedge\end{array}\right] \rightarrow \\ \left[\begin{array}{l}(t=1 \rightarrow u\{f,2,3\}v) \wedge \\ (t=2 \rightarrow u\{f,2,3\}v \vee u=v) \wedge \\ (t=3 \rightarrow u\{s,1\}v)\end{array}\right]\end{array}\right] \end{array}\right] \right]$$

Since, in a binary tree the number of nodes of depth n is equal to 2^n,

$\exists z\ triangle_{k+1}(t,x,y,z) \leftrightarrow$

$$\exists u_1 \ldots \exists u_{\alpha(k+1)} \left[\begin{array}{l} x=u_1 \wedge u_{\alpha(k+1)}=y \wedge \\ \left[\bigwedge_{i=1}^{\alpha(k+1)-1}\left[\begin{array}{l}(t=1 \rightarrow u_i\{f,2,3\}u_{i+1}) \wedge \\ (t=2 \rightarrow u_i\{f,2,3\}u_{i+1} \vee u_i=u_{i+1}) \wedge \\ (t=3 \rightarrow u_i\{s,1\}u_{i+1})\end{array}\right]\right]\end{array}\right]$$

We conclude that the equivalences (5) hold for $k+1$, which ends the proof.

3.3 Expressing a Logic Program Performing a Multiplication

Let $step\,(x,y)$ be a formula involving two free variables x and y. If we modify formula $triangle_k(t,x,z,y)$ by setting

$$trans3\,(x,y) \overset{\text{def}}{=} x=y \vee step\,(x,y)$$

and if we introduce the formula

$$iteration_k(x,y) \overset{\text{def}}{=} \exists z\,\exists u\ triangle_k(3,x,z,u) \wedge trans3\,(u,y)$$

we then have

$$iteration_k(x,y) \leftrightarrow \bigvee_{n=0}^{\alpha(k)} (\exists u_0 \ldots \exists u_n\ x=u_0 \wedge u_n=y \wedge \bigwedge_{i=1}^{n} step\,(u_{i-1},u_i)) \quad (6)$$

The binary relation defined by $iteration$ is in some way a *bounded* transitive closure of the relation defined by $step$.

Let T be the theory of trees, that is a set of first order propositions which entails all the properties of the algebra of infinite trees which can be expressed as first order propositions. According to logic programming, the formula

$$times\,(s^i(0), s^j(0), x),$$

in the theory

$$T \cup \begin{cases} \forall i\, \forall j\, \forall k\, \forall k' \\ (times\,(0,j,0) \leftarrow true) & \wedge \\ (times\,(s(i),j,k') \leftarrow times\,(i,j,k) \wedge plus\,(j,k,k')) \wedge \\ (plus\,(0,j,j) \leftarrow true) & \wedge \\ (plus\,(s(i),j,s(k)) \leftarrow plus\,(i,j,k)) & \wedge \end{cases}$$

is equivalent to

$$x = s^{i \times j}(0).$$

Given the way a Prolog interpreter works and given equivalence (6), the constraint

$$iteration_k(c(f(s^i(0), s^j(0), x), 0), 0)$$

with

$$step\,(x,y) \stackrel{\text{def}}{=} \begin{bmatrix} \exists i\, \exists j\, \exists k\, \exists k'\, \exists l \\ (x\!=\!c(f(0,j,0),l) \wedge y\!=\!l) & \vee \\ (x\!=\!c(f(s(i),j,k'),l) \wedge y\!=\!c(f(i,j,k),c(p(j,k,k'),l))) \vee \\ (x\!=\!c(p(0,j,j),l) \wedge y\!=\!l) & \vee \\ (x\!=\!c(p(s(i),j,s(k)),l) \wedge y\!=\!c(p(i,j,k),l)) & \vee \end{bmatrix}$$

is equivalent in the algebra of infinite trees to

$$x = s^{i \times j}(0)$$

provided that $i(j+2)+1 \leq \alpha(k)$. For $k = 5$ we could consider that this restriction is quasi-satisfied. Thus we would have a systematic way to replace a logic Horn clauses program by a tree constraint.

3.4   Universality versus Complexity

Instead of a Prolog machine we can take a Turing machine M, and express by $step\,(x,y)$ the fact that M may move from configuration x to configuration y by executing one instruction. We then conclude that:

Property 4 *The result produced by a Turing machine, executing at most $\alpha(k)$ instructions, can be expressed by a tree constraint of size less or equal to a number proportional to k.*

Here also, by taking $k = 5$ it is possible to express any result that the most powerful computer could compute. Thus the tree constraints have a quasi-universal expressiveness and the complexity of the algorithms for solving them must be very high. Let us examine this point in more details and in the case of constraints without free variables.

Let us consider an algorithm as a Turing machine M whose execution terminates for all word $x \in V^*$ given as input. The complexity of M is the mapping of type $\mathbf{N} \to \mathbf{N}$:

$$n \mapsto \max\left\{ i \in \mathbf{N} \,\middle|\, \begin{array}{l} \text{there exists } x \in V^*, \text{ with } |x| = n, \text{ such that } M \\ \text{executes } i \text{ instructions, with } x \text{ as input.} \end{array} \right\}$$

Let Φ_α be a set of non-decreasing functions of type $\mathbf{N} \to \mathbf{N}$ such that

1. the functions of the form $n \mapsto an + f(bn)$, with $a \in \mathbf{N}$, $b \in \mathbf{N}$ and $f \in \Phi_\alpha$, belong also to Φ_α,
2. there exists a language L, recognizable by a Turing machine of complexity bounded above by α, but by no Turing machine of complexity bounded above by an element of Φ_α, where α is still the function defined at the beginning of section 3.1.

Property 5 *Let T be a Turing machine deciding whether a tree constraint without free variables holds. The complexity of T can not be bounded above by an element of Φ_α.*

Proof. Let us suppose that there exists such a machine T with a complexity bounded above by an element f of Φ_α and let us show that this leads us to a contradiction. Since Φ_α is not empty, the language $L \subseteq V^*$ in part 2 of the definition of Φ_α, exists. According to property 4, to each word $x \in V^*$, corresponds a tree constraints p_x, without free variables, such that

1. $x \in L$ if and only if p_x holds,
2. $|p_x| \leq b|x|$, for some constant $b \in \mathbf{N}$,
3. the transformation $x \mapsto p_x$ can be performed by a Turing machine S with a complexity bounded above by $n \mapsto an$, for some constant $a \in \mathbf{N}$. (This point could be more detailed.)

By linking together the executions of machines S and T, we then build a machine M' which recognizes L and whose complexity is bounded above by $n \mapsto an + f(bn)$, a function which by definition belongs to Φ_α. Thus there is a contradiction about the properties of L, which ends the proof.

Under the condition of having shown that, as set Φ_α, we can take the set of functions, of type $\mathbf{N} \to \mathbf{N}$, obtained by finite composition of the elementary functions: $n \mapsto \mathrm{cst}$, $+$, $\times$, $n \mapsto 2^n$, we rediscover the result of Sergei Vorobyov [14], but in the spirit of Pawel Mielniczuk [13]:

Property 6 *The complexity of an algorithm, which decides whether a tree constraint, without free variables, holds, can not be bounded above by a function obtained by finite composition of elementary functions mentioned above.*

4   Discussions and Conclusion

The presented examples show the contribution of embedded quantifiers and operators $\neg, \wedge, \vee, \to$ in the expressiveness of tree constraints. They do not really use the fact that the trees may be infinite and are also valid in the algebra of finite trees. It would be interesting to give examples involving infinite trees for coding cyclic structures like finite states automata, context-free grammars or λ-expressions, as it has been done in [3,7] in the frame of logic programming.

At subsection 3.4 we have provided a glimpse of the huge theoretical complexity of an algorithm for solving tree constraints. However, we have succeeded in producing benchmarks on all our examples [10]. The results are summarized in the following table, with CPU times given in milliseconds:

k	$winning_k$ game 1	$winning_k$ game 2	$huge_k$	$iteration_k$ 1×1
0	0	0	0	-
1	0	150	0	-
2	10	360	10	70
3	10	610	230	-
4	20	840	-	-
5	30	1180	-	-
10	300	5 970	-	-
20	4 270	236 350	-	-
40	89 870	-	-	-
80	3 841 220	-	-	-

The algorithm is programmed in C++ and the benchmarks are performed on a 350Mhz Pentium II processor, with 512Mb of RAM.

It must be noted that we were able to compute the k-winning positions of game 1 with $k = 80$, which corresponds to a formula involving an alternated embedding of more than 160 quantifiers. We were prepared to experience difficulties in computing the tree of $\alpha(k)$ nodes, beyond $k = 3$, since $\alpha(4)$ is already 65536. With respect to multiplication by $iteration_k$, we were unable to succeed beyond $k = 2$ and had to satisfy ourselves with the computation of 1×1!

These test have also removed some of our doubts about the correctness of the complicated formulae of our examples, even if, for readability, we have introduced predicates for naming sub-formulae. Of course the definitions of theses predicates are supposed not to be circular and the solver unfold and eliminates them in a first step.

If circular definitions are accepted then our constraints look like generalized completions of logic programs [2]. Our solver can also take into account such possibly circular definitions by delaying their unfoldings as much as possible. With bad luck the solver does not terminate, with luck it terminates and generates obligatory a simplified constraint without intermediary predicates.

References

1. Benhamou F., P. Bouvier, A. Colmerauer, H. Garetta, B. Giletta, J. L. Massat, G. A. Narboni, S. N'Dong, R. Pasero, J. F. Pique, Touraïvane, M. Van Caneghem and E. Vétillard, *Le manuel de Prolog IV*. PrologIA, Marseille, June 1996. 172
2. Clark K. L., Negation as failure, in *Logic and Databases*, edited by H. Gallaire and J. Minker, Plenum Press, New York, pp. 293–322, 1978. 185
3. Colmerauer A., Prolog and Infinite Trees, in *Logic Programming*, K. L. Clark and S. A.. Tarnlund editors, Academic Press, New York, pp. 231–251, 1982. 184

4. Colmerauer A., Henry Kanoui and Michel Van Caneghem, Prolog, theoretical principles and current trends, in *Technology and Science of Informatics*, North Oxford Academic, vol. 2, no 4, August 1983. English version of the journal *TSI*, AFCET-Bordas, where the paper appears under the title: Prolog, bases théoriques et développements actuels. 172

5. Colmerauer A., Equations and Inequations on Finite and Infinite Trees, in *Proceeding of the International Conference on Fifth Generation Computer Systems (FCGS-84)*, ICOT, Tokyo, pp. 85–99, 1984. 172

6. Colmerauer A., An Introduction to Prolog III, *Communications of the ACM*, 33(7) : 68–90, 1990. 172

7. Coupet-Grimal S. and O. Ridoux, On the use of advanced logic programming features in computational linguistics. *The Journal of Logic Programming*, 24(1-2), pages 121–159. 184

8. Courcelle B., Fundamental Properties of Infinite Trees, *Theoretical Computer Science*, 25(2), pp. 95–169, March 1983. 172

9. Courcelle B., Equivalences and Transformations of Regular Systems - Applications to Program Schemes and Grammars, *Theoretical Computer Science*, 42, pp. 1–122, 1986. 172

10. Dao T. B. H., Résolution de contraintes du premier ordre dans la théorie des arbres fini ou infinis, *Neuvièmes Journées Francophones de Programmation Logique et Programmation par Contraintes* (JFPLC'2000), Marseille, June 2000, proceedings to be published by Hermes Science Publications. 173, 185

11. Huet G., *Résolution d'équations dans les langages d'ordre* $1, 2, \ldots, \omega$., Thèse d'Etat, Université Paris 7, 1976. 172

12. Maher M. J., *Complete Axiomatization of the Algebra of Finite, Rational and Infinite Trees*, Technical report, IBM - T. J.Watson Research Center, 1988. 173

13. Mielniczuk P., Basic Theory of Feature Trees, submitted to *Journal of Symbolic Computation*, also available at http://www.tcs.uni.wroc.pl/~mielni. 173, 184

14. Vorobyov S., An Improved Lower Bound for the Elementary Theories of Trees, *Proceeding of the 13th International Conference on Automated Deduction (CADE'96)*. Springer Lecture Notes in Artificial Intelligence, vol 1104, pp. 275–287, New Brunswick, NJ, July/August, 1996. 173, 184

Cutting Planes in Constraint Programming: An Hybrid Approach

Filippo Focacci[1], Andrea Lodi[2], and Michela Milano[2]

[1] Dipartimento di Ingegneria, Università di Ferrara - Italy
focacci@ilog.fr
[2] D.E.I.S., Università di Bologna - Italy
{alodi,mmilano}@deis.unibo.it

Abstract. In recent years, a growing number of attempts have been performed in order to integrate well known Operations Research (OR) techniques in Constraint Programming (CP) tools. The aim of the integration is to maintain the modelling facilities of the CP paradigm, while improving its performances by exploiting effective OR techniques. In our previous work, we proposed the use of *optimization constraints* [9], embedding a linear relaxation of the constraint itself and performing pruning on the basis of costs. In particular, domain values can be removed whenever it can be shown that their assignment will necessarily lead to solutions worse than the best solution found. In this setting, the use of cutting planes in global constraints allows to tighten the relaxation so as to infer more accurate bounds on the problem. We propose different ways of using cutting-planes in optimization constraints achieving different levels of tightness of the integration and pruning power. Even if the proposed technique is general, we use as testing application the Travelling Salesman Problem (TSPs) and its time constrained variant. Computational results compare different relaxations in terms of pruning achieved and computational complexity.

1 Introduction

The idea of solving integer (or mixed integer) linear programs by strengthening the initial formulation through the iterative addition of valid inequalities, called *cutting planes*, is known in mathematical programming since the seminal work of Gomory [12] in 1958. Roughly speaking, at each step of the algorithm, the addition of a cutting plane cuts off the fractional solution of the current continuous relaxation, thus producing a stronger formulation of the original problem. However, this idea became computationally effective only in the late eighties, due to a couple of important advances: the improvement of Linear Programming (LP) solvers and the integration of cutting planes into a tree search framework leading to the solving method called *branch-and-cut*. Starting from the original branch-and-cut algorithm of Padberg and Rinaldi [18] for the Travelling Salesman Problem (TSP), the method has been applied to a wide variety of combinatorial optimization problems, often obtaining the state-of-the-art results. In

R. Dechter (Ed.): CP 2000, LNCS 1894, pp. 187–201, 2000.

these more than ten years, branch-and-cut became very sophisticated but, quite surprisingly, the advances mainly concerned the LP solution and the cut generation, whereas other important features of the original framework, e.g., branching strategies and problem reductions, did not receive the same attention.

Completely independently, the exploitation of Constraint Satisfaction techniques has lead to the development of effective *Constraint Programming* (CP) tools [16] used in the last decade to solve also optimization problems. These tools have obtained remarkable results through the extensive use of problem dependent heuristics for branching and problem reductions obtained by constraint propagation.

The aim of this paper is to investigate hybridization methods for the integration of cutting planes generation into CP tools which represent, in the light of the above discussion, a flexible and well-structured environment particularly suitable to exploit these techniques. Interesting results in this direction have been obtained by Hooker et al. [14] [17], Refalo [21], Barth and Bockmayr [3].

In this paper, we study hybrid approaches in order to integrate cutting planes in global constraints for solving optimization problems, called *optimization constraints*. Beside a filtering algorithm that removes infeasible values from variable domains, optimization constraints [9] embed an *optimization component* representing a linear relaxation of the constraint itself. This component provides the optimal solution of the relaxation and a gradient function that estimates each variable-value assignment cost. These pieces of information can be exploited both for propagation, and for guiding the search. This technique has been successfully applied to Travelling Salesman Problems [10], its time constrained variant [8], Matching Problems [11] and Scheduling Problems with Sequence Dependent Setup Times [7], and will be discussed in Section 2.2.

In this setting, we embed in optimization constraints one or more *cut generators* producing a set of valid inequalities given the optimal solution of the relaxation of the constraint itself. We exploit cutting planes in order to tighten the formulation of the relaxation of the constraint (say P_{Rel}). Cuts are computed and added to P_{Rel}, in order to obtain a modified problem P_{Rel}^{cut}. This modified problem can be solved (and possibly updated) in the optimization component during the search in order to compute bounds and reduced costs on the basis of the current problem configuration. We have tested the addition of cuts at the root node and at each node during search.

An interesting point concerns the structure of P_{Rel}^{cut}. The optimization component can be a general Linear Programming solver accepting any linear problem. In this case, if P_{Rel} is a linear problem, computed cuts can be simply added to P_{Rel} since the resulting problem, i.e., P_{Rel}^{cut}, is again a linear problem. Alternatively, the optimization component can be a special purpose algorithm that is able to solve structured problems since the constraint relaxation P_{Rel} presents a special structure. In this case, cuts cannot just be added to the linear formulation of the problem since the structure would be lost, i.e., P_{Rel}^{cut} in general has a different structure with respect to P_{Rel}. We choose to relax cuts in a Lagrangian way and we obtain a problem with the same structure of P_{Rel}, but different coefficients. We will discuss these alternatives, and the use of *purging* techniques in order to remove no longer needed cuts. A tighter integration is achieved by generating cuts at each node of the search tree. In fact, the addition of cuts only at the root node has the main drawback of generating cuts that during the search can be no longer tight. Moreover, information derived during the search due to branching choices and constraint propagation can be exploited in order to generate other valid cuts which can help the calculation of better bounds and reduced costs at each node. We provide computational results that show when it is worth exploiting cutting planes techniques.

The proposed integration is general and can be applied to a wide variety of constraints and problems. However, in order to prove its effectiveness, we have performed computational tests on TSPs and TSPs with Time Windows. Again, we can use any kind of valid cuts for the problem represented by the constraint. In this case, cuts used are subtour elimination and sequential ordering inequalities which have been generated and embedded in a path constraint.

In Section 2 we provide some basic notions on cutting planes generation and on cost-based filtering. Section 3 is devoted to explain different integrations of cutting planes in global constraints. Section 4 is devoted to computational results on TSP and TSPTW instances. Section 5 presents some related approaches. A discussion and future work description concludes the paper.

2   Preliminaries

2.1   Cutting Planes

In this section, we provide some preliminary notions on the use of cutting planes.

Intuitively, given an Integer Linear Problem P, the cutting planes method is based on the solution of a continuous relaxation of P, called P_{Lin}, which typically does not involve all the constraints of P. The optimal solution of P_{Lin} provides a lower bound (for minimization problems) on the optimal solution of P where, in general, some constraints of the original problem are violated. The aim of the cutting planes generation is to determine some *linear inequalities* corresponding to violated constraints that remove the optimal solution of P_{Lin}, say x^*, infeasible for P, and do not prune any integral solution of the original problem P.

In principle, one can iteratively add all such inequalities up to the definition of the convex hull of the set of solutions of P. However, there is no efficient way of generating the convex hull of a problem. Therefore, the general method used in branch-and-cut algorithms is to iteratively add a subset S_{cut} of all inequalities so as to increase the optimal solution value of P_{Lin}, and still having a linear problem formulation. When the addition of cuts becomes ineffective (the bound does not increase any longer), a branching step is performed. We call the resulting (final) problem P_{Lin}^{cut}.

In this paper, we consider, as examples, the TSP and the TSPTW. The TSP is the problem of finding the least-cost Hamiltonian cycle visiting a set of cities, whereas the TSPTW is its time constrained variant in which the visit of each city must be performed within a fixed *time window*. We model these problems by using a path constraint which ensures that, given a set of nodes V, there exists one path visiting all nodes in V once. Each node will have only one predecessor and only one successor node.

We consider a graph theory model based on a directed graph $G = (V, A)$ in which there is a variable x_{ij} and a cost c_{ij} associated to each $(i, j) \in A$. Given any set of nodes $S \subset V$, the path constraint has a corresponding Integer Linear Programming (ILP) formulation, as follows[1]:

$$\min c^T x \tag{1}$$
$$\text{s.t.} \quad x(\delta^+(i)) = 1 \quad \forall\, i \in V \tag{2}$$
$$x(\delta^-(i)) = 1 \quad \forall\, i \in V \tag{3}$$
$$x(A(S)) \leq |S| - 1 \,\forall\, S \subset V, S \neq \emptyset \tag{4}$$
$$x_{ij} \in \{0, 1\} \quad \forall\, (i, j) \in A \tag{5}$$

where $A(S)$ is the set of arcs connecting nodes in S, $\delta^+(i)$ (resp. $\delta^-(i)$) represents the set of arcs whose starting (resp. ending) node is i. Being A a set of arcs, $x(A)$ identifies the sum of all x_{ij} with arc $(i, j) \in A$.

Constraints (2)-(3) are degree constraints assuring each node (city) be visited exactly once, whereas constraints (4) are the *Subtour Elimination Constraints* (SECs).

A relaxation of this model can be obtained by eliminating constraints (4) and relaxing the integrality constraint (5). The resulting linear problem is known as Assignment Problem (AP). The AP is the graph theory problem of finding a set of *disjoint* subtours such that all the nodes are visited and the overall cost is a minimum. AP provides an optimal integer solution, and, if such a solution is composed by a single tour, is then optimal for TSP. The addition of cutting planes is aimed at improve (i.e., increase) the lower bound provided by the AP. Many different kinds of valid inequalities can be defined for TSP and its variants. Different classes of inequalities can be used simultaneously.

Being x^* the optimal solution of the linear problem, the problem of finding an inequality $\alpha x \leq \alpha_0$ valid for each feasible solution of P, and such that $\alpha x^* > \alpha_0$, is called *separation problem*. Although the separation problem is in general NP-hard, several polynomial time algorithms have been defined for particular classes of cuts.

In this paper, we consider subtour elimination (SECs) and sequential ordering (SOPs) cutting planes. The separation problem for SECs can be solved in polynomial time by computing the *minimum capacity cut* in the graph induced by x^*, and the same holds for each following LP obtained by the iterative addition of cuts. For the separation problem we use an implementation [15] of the Padberg and Rinaldi *micut* algorithm [19] to compute a set of subtour elimination cuts.

---

[1] This is the ILP model of the Asymmetric version of TSP (ATSP) to which we refer for a more general discussion.

At each iteration, the separation procedure returns a set of nodes involved in a subtour S. The corresponding generated cut has the form $x(A(S)) \leq |S| - 1$. At the end of the iterative process, these inequalities define the subtour polytope of the TSP, i.e., a problem where no subtour is violated, but the solution is possibly fractional. Obviously, the optimal solution of the problem generated by the AP plus the SECs is still a valid lower bound for the original problem, and, in general, it is much better than the AP solution value.

We have also tested specific valid inequalities studied by Balas, Fischetti and Pulleyblank [2] for the TSPTW relaxation called *precedence constrained* TSP or *Sequential Ordering Problem* (SOP). All the inequalities for SOP are also valid for TSPTW, provided the information on precedences among nodes. In this paper we consider: (*i*) *Predecessor inequalities* (π inequalities). Let $S \subseteq V$, $\bar{S} := V \setminus S$, then

$$x((S \setminus \pi(S)), (\bar{S} \setminus \pi(S))) \geq 1 \qquad (6)$$

where $\pi(S)$ indicates the set of nodes which *preceed* the nodes in S^2; (*ii*) *Successor inequalities* (σ inequalities). Let $S \subseteq V$, $\bar{S} := V \setminus S$, then

$$x((\bar{S} \setminus \sigma(S)), (S \setminus \sigma(S))) \geq 1 \qquad (7)$$

where $\sigma(S)$ indicates the set of nodes which *follow* the nodes in S.

In the following, these inequalities are referred to as SOP inequalities, and we use the heuristic separation procedure proposed in [2] and the corresponding computer code by Ascheuer, Fischetti and Grötschel [1].

2.2   Cost-Based Domain Filtering

In this section, we recall the technique, based on reduced cost fixing, proposed in [9] which allows to perform domain filtering on the basis of costs. In particular, we are able to prune domain values when their contribution in terms of costs on the objective function is too high with respect to the best solution found.

For this purpose, we embed in global constraints an *optimization component* (see Figure 1) which is able to optimally and efficiently solve a relaxation of the constraint itself and provides three pieces of information: the optimal solution LB of the relaxed problem, its value x^* and a gradient function $grad(X, v)$ which computes the costs of variable-value assignments, e.g., in terms of reduced costs. We create a mapping between CP entities (variables and domains) and variables in the relaxation so as to allow the two parts to exchange information. In particular, the assignment of the CP variable X_i to the value j corresponds to the linear variable fixing $x_{ij} = 1$.

On the basis of this information, we perform the following filtering. The lower bound value LB is trivially linked to the variable representing the objective function Z through the constraint $LB \leq Z$. More interesting is the propagation based on gradient function. Given the gradient function $grad(X, val)$,

---

2   With the notation $x(U, W)$, where $U, W \subset V$, we indicate the sum of all arcs in A with starting node in U and ending node in W.

Global constraint

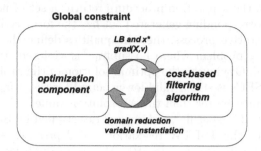

Fig. 1. Structure of optimization constraints

$LB_{X=val} = LB + grad(X, val)$ is a valid lower bound for the problem where X is assigned to val. Therefore, we can impose: $X \neq val$ if $LB_{X=val} > Z_{max}$. Reduced costs can be used to calculate the gradient function as proposed in [9].

As optimization component, we can use any *solver* able to compute the optimal solution of the relaxation of the constraint. The solver of the relaxation can be a simplex algorithm, or a special purpose algorithm. For instance, in [10] we have run experiments on ATSPs using either a solver for the Minimum Spanning Arborescence (MSA) or one for the Assignment Problem (AP). The main feature of the solver is that it should be incremental since the re-computation of the optimal solution of the relaxed problem should be triggered each time a value in the optimal solution of the relaxation is deleted from the corresponding (through the mapping) CP variable domain. For example, for the AP we can use the Hungarian Algorithm, the *primal-dual* algorithm described in [5]. In this case, the AP relaxation at the root node requires in the worst case $O(n^3)$ where n is the number of variables, whereas each following AP re-computation due to domain reduction can be efficiently computed in $O(n^2)$ time through a single augmenting path step (see [5] for details). The reduced cost matrix is obtained without extra computational effort during the AP solution.

The events triggering this propagation are changes in the upper bound of the objective function variable Z and each change in the problem variable domains. Note that the AP solution is re-computed only if the removed value j belongs to the solution of the AP. In fact, only in this case the bound can increase.

3   Integration of Cutting Planes in Global Constraints

The main idea of this paper is to embed in global constraints, beside an optimization component, one or more cut generators that provide valid linear inequalities, given the global constraint declarative semantics and the optimal solution of the corresponding linear relaxation. These cuts can be added to the linear formulation which in turns produces better bounds that enable to perform more powerful domain filtering. Thus, we have embedded cutting plane generators in the optimization component of a path constraint.

Depending on the semantics of the global constraint and its relaxation, we can use different sets of cuts. For the path constraint we have used Subtour Elimination and Sequential Ordering cuts. We have followed two different approaches: in the first, cuts are generated and added when the constraint is posted for the first time, but no longer updated during the search; in the second, instead, cuts are generated and added at each node.

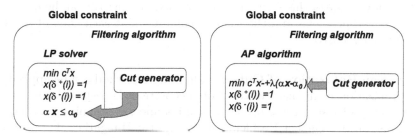

Fig. 2. Addition of cuts in optimization constraints

3.1   Adding Cuts at the Root Node

When cuts are added only at the root node, we have experimented three alternative approaches: (i) cuts can be simply added to the initial LP if the optimization component considered in the global constraint is a general Linear Programming solver able to handle any kind of Linear Problems, with no special structure; (ii) cuts can be relaxed in a Lagrangian way in order to obtain a structured problem if the optimization component is a special purpose algorithm aimed at solving a problem with a special structure, say the Assignment Problem; (iii) purging techniques are applied to the second approach in order to remove no longer needed cuts.

Adding Cuts to the Problem Formulation This first integration can be performed when the optimization component in the global constraint is a general purpose Linear Programming solver which can handle and solve any kind of linear problem with no special structure. Thus, the computed cuts can be directly added to the problem formulation as shown in the left hand side of Figure 2. The resulting linear problem is solved at each node during the whole search space. A linear solver (ILOG Planner in our case) is used to compute the optimal solution of the LP at each node.

In the case of the path constraint, the starting problem considered in the optimization component, called P_{Lin} is the problem composed by constraints (2)-(3) described in Section 2.1 (which is the constraint set of an Assignment Problem). A set of subtour inequalities S^{cut} are generated by the cut generator at each iteration, and the subtour polytope is finally derived. The resulting problem P_{Lin}^{cut} is a Linear Problem composed by P_{Lin} together with S^{cut}. Note that the structure of P_{Lin}^{cut} is no longer an AP, but a general LP.

Clearly, during the search the added cuts may be no longer effective when they are trivially satisfied by the current partial solution of the problem. The satisfied cuts in principle can be removed in order to reduce the linear formulation of the problem. However, leaving these cuts in the formulation does not affect the accuracy of the bound.

During the search, the resulting LP, P_{Lin}^{cut}, is changed at each node when variables are fixed and constraint propagation removes values from variable domains, but not with the addition of new cuts.

A disadvantage of this technique is that the resulting LP can be quite heavy for non-trivial problems and the LP re-computation at each node of the search tree can be expensive.

Lagrangian Relaxation of Cuts An alternative method can be applied when the optimization component in the global constraint is a special purpose algorithm able to solve structured problems. For instance, as optimization component we can use an Assignment Problem solver, e.g., the Hungarian algorithm [5]. It has a polynomial time complexity and an incremental behavior, thus is more suitable in CP framework w.r.t. general LP solvers.

In this case, we generate cuts (set S^{cut}) as described in the previous approach. Then, at the end of the cut generation phase, we have the Linear Problem P_{Lin}^{cut} composed by the initial Assignment Problem P_{Lin} and the set of cuts S^{cut}. The solution at the end of the root node can be transformed into an integer one with exactly the same objective function value, say LB_{Root}, by relaxing in Lagragian way the linear inequalities of set S^{cut}. In particular, the optimal Lagrangian multipliers for the cuts are the dual values (associated to the cuts) computed by the linear solver. The problem obtained, say AP_{Lagr}, is again an AP with a different cost matrix, and, as mentioned, by solving AP_{Lagr} (through the Hungarian algorithm) we have an integer solution whose value is LB_{Root}.

More formally, consider the Lagrangian relaxation of the cut $\alpha x \leq \alpha_0$ in the objective function $\min c^T x$. We call λ ($\lambda \geq 0$) the optimal Lagrangian multiplier of the cut, i.e., the dual value associated to the cut in the LP solution[3]. The objective function of the Lagrangian relaxation becomes: $\min c^T x + \lambda(\alpha x - \alpha_0)$, i.e., $-\lambda\alpha_0 + \min(c^T + \lambda\alpha)x$. In the objective function, we have a constant factor and we can change each value in the cost matrix c by adding the coefficient corresponding to x (see the right hand side of Figure 2).

The AP_{Lagr} solution can be seen as an advanced starting point for the CP algorithm which is now applied exactly as in [8] to complete the search. AP_{Lagr} is considered at each node as relaxation and modified through variable fixing derived at each step, but no more cuts nor Lagrangian multipliers are re-computed.

The addition in Lagrangian way of the generated cuts to the objective function can have some drawback for the remaining nodes of the search tree. In fact, the Lagrangian multipliers associated to these cuts are fixed to values which are optimal at the root node, but could be "far" from the optimal ones during

---

[3] Since the cuts are in ≤ 0 form, the corresponding dual variables are non-positive, thus they must be inverted to be used as Lagrangian multipliers.

the search, and no re-optimization (subgradient optimization) is performed. In particular, if during the search, a cut $\alpha x \leq \alpha_0$, which was tight at the root node (i.e., $\alpha x = \alpha_0$), becomes trivially satisfied with respect to the current partial instantiation of CP variables, i.e., $\alpha x < \alpha_0$, its contribution to the objective function represents a penalty with respect to the same solution where the cut is removed. In fact, the term $\alpha x - \alpha_0 < 0$ added to the objective function of the original AP, i.e., $\min c^T x$, leads to produce a worse bound (since $\lambda \geq 0$). Thus, while at the root node, the bound produced by the Lagrangian relaxation is in general better (higher) than the bound produced by the AP solution (without cuts), during the search if cuts become no longer tight, it decreases and at some point it may becomes worse than the AP bound. In Figure 3 we depict the qualitative trend of the lower bound produced by the Lagrangian relaxation LB_{Lagr} and the bound produced by the AP, LB_{AP}.

However, the optimization over AP_{Lagr} is always a valid lower bound for the problem, and the above limitation can be reduced by performing some kind of *purging* in order to disable during the search those cuts which are no longer necessary, i.e., both not tight and trivially satisfied.

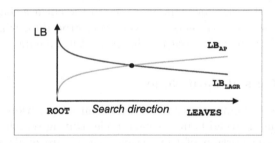

Fig. 3. Trend of lower bounds in different relaxations

Purging During the search, the current instantiation of CP variables and the reduction of their domains can lead the corresponding linear variables to assume values that trivially satisfy some of the cuts. Suppose, for example, that a generated cut has the form: $x_{12} + x_{21} + x_{13} + x_{31} + x_{23} + x_{32} \leq 2$ and removes the subtour visiting nodes 1, 2 and 3. Moreover, suppose that during the search the CP variable X_1 is instantiated to the value 2 (thus, $x_{12} = 1$ and $x_{13} = 0$), values 1 and 3 are removed from the domain of variable X_2 (thus, $x_{23} = 0$ and $x_{21} = 0$) and values 1 and 3 are removed from the domain of variable X_3 (thus, $x_{31} = 0$ and $x_{32} = 0$). The cut is satisfied and can be removed in order to reduce the linear formulation of the problem. Moreover, in case of Lagrangian relaxation, the added and satisfied cut can produce a penalty in the objective function and it is preferable to remove it. Note that the concept of purging is standard for branch-and-cut (cuts which are no longer "effective" are removed and included in the *Cut Pool*). However, in case of Lagrangian relaxation the performed operation is even more crucial since it affects the value of the bound.

Thus, during the search, each time a linear variable x_{ij} is fixed, all added cuts are taken into account and removed if they are trivially satisfied. In particular, in the Lagrangian relaxation the contribution of the cut in the objective function $-\lambda\alpha_0 + \min(c^T + \lambda\alpha)x$ should be removed, by restoring the cost matrix to its original values and removing $\lambda\alpha_0$ from the objective function.

A drawback of the purging technique is that each time the cost matrix is changed, i.e., one or more cuts are removed, the AP plus the remaining cuts (always relaxed in a Lagrangian way) should be re-computed from scratch and it takes $O(n^3)$ instead of $O(n^2)$.

An interesting point concerns the exploitation of the problem specific knowledge on cuts. Consider the above cut involving nodes in the set $S = \{1, 2, 3\}$. We know that as soon as an arc starting (resp. ending) from (resp. in) one of the nodes 1, 2 or 3 and ending (resp. starting) in a node not contained in S belongs to the current solution, the subtour is not violated. This conclusion can be drawn despite the values of the other variables are still unbound. Thus, it is much more powerful to exploit information on the special structure of cuts since we can remove trivially satisfied cuts earlier. In this paper, the cuts have been removed when variable values lead the constraint to be trivially satisfied. An interesting extension is currently investigated: we can associate to the cut generator an event that is raised each time some variables in the cut are changed (due to CP propagation). The event triggers an evaluation procedure which determines if the cut should be removed or not on the basis of its semantics.

3.2   Adding Cuts at Each Node

An alternative use of cuts, closer to the traditional Operations Research branch and cut technique, is to add cuts at each node. During search, we acquire more information on the portion of the search tree we are exploring, thus we can generate more *informed* cuts. We have experimented the addition of cuts at each node after the computation of the optimal solution of the LP corresponding to that node.

An important point concerns the use of local or global cuts. Considering the TSP and TSPTW, the SECs are globally valid cuts, while SOPs are locally valid. Thus, while SECs could be left in the problem formulation when backtracking is performed, the SOPs must be removed. In our current implementation, however, both SECs and SOPs are removed upon backtracking.

4   Computational Results

In this section, we provide computational results on TSP and TSPTW instances. The overall approach has been implemented using the ILOG Optimization Suite [23], and runs on a Pentium II 200 MHz with 64MB of RAM. A time limit of 30 minutes has been imposed for each instance of both problems.

The purpose of this section is to try to compare different pruning abilities achieved by different relaxations:

- the AP without cuts, referred to as **AP**;
- the AP generated by adding cuts at the root node and relaxing them in a Lagrangian way before branching, referred to as **LAGR**;
- the same relaxation as **LAGR** where purging techniques have been exploited in order to remove no longer necessary cuts, referred to as **LAGR-Pg**;
- the LP generated by the AP plus the addition of cuts directly to the problem only at the root node, referred to as **LP**.
- the LP generated by the AP plus the addition of cuts at every node, referred to as **LP-CN**.

The different techniques used are ordered in the above mentioned list by increasing complexity. In fact, the AP has an initial complexity of $O(n^3)$ whereas each following re-computation is performed in $O(n^2)$. The second method also has the same complexity, but the initial complexity is increased by the fact that a Linear Problem should be solved through the simplex algorithm which provides the optimal Lagrangian multipliers. The third method has the same complexity of the second, but each time a cut is removed, the AP cost matrix is changed and it implies a whole AP re-computation which is again $O(n^3)$. Finally, the last two approaches use the LP solver within each node which has an exponential worst case complexity (using the simplex algorithm).

The first group of results reported in Table 1 concerns symmetric TSPs from TSPLIB. The size of the problems is self evident from the name of the instance; the lower bound at root node, the run time (in seconds) and the number of backtracks are reported. The search strategy used is very simple; it chooses the variable with the smallest domain first and it assign the value corresponding to the optimal assignment in the relaxed problem.

Table 1. Results on small symmetric TSP instances

Inst.	OPT	AP			LAGR			LAGR-Pg			LP			LP-CN		
		LB	Time	Fail	LB	Time	Fail	LB	Time	Fail	LB	Time	Fail	LB	Time	Fail
gr17	2085	1652	1.31	1926	2085	1.38	59	2085	0.5	59	2085	0.84	15	2085	0.82	15
gr21	2707	2420	0.22	165	2707	0.3	62	2707	0.32	62	2707	0.47	19	2707	0.53	19
gr24	1272	1052	0.39	300	1272	0.86	133	1272	0.86	133	1272	36.4	1793	1272	44.0	1294
fri26	937	833	2.36	2863	937	2.46	1191	937	2.44	1191	937	180.1	8342	937	102	2969
bays29	2020	1764	2.87	2803	2014	1.67	601	2014	1.67	601	2014	82.6	3320	2014	138	2892
dantzig42	699	532	*	*	697	6.19	1277	697	8.13	1006	697	181.9	3810	697	106	700

From the results we can see that for small problems, it is not worth adding cutting planes either in the Lagrangian relaxation or in the LP. Although the AP is not a good lower bound for symmetric TSPs, it is nevertheless good enough to quickly solve small problems. On the other hand, it is known that pure OR Branch and Cut is the best exact method to solve large TSPs. For medium size problems the AP with Lagrangian relaxation performs better than the AP since the increased complexity of adding cuts is balanced by a great reduction in the number of fails. Dantzig42 could not be solved by the AP (indeed the optimal solution can be found but the proof of optimality falls outside the time limit), whereas it is solved in few seconds with the Lagrangian relaxation both with and without purging techniques. An important point here is that the AP does not provide in general a good lower bound for symmetric TSPs. In fact, small cycles are created. Thus, the addition of SECs in general improves the bound significantly.

Concerning the LP approach, it performs always worse than all the other approaches. This is mainly due to the fact that the simplex algorithm in general does not behave as efficiently as a special purpose (incremental) algorithm. In addition, the chosen branching strategy is certainly not the most effective for the LP. An alternative, more effective strategy considers the optimal solution of the linear relaxation and branches on fractional variables.

The second set of problems is derived from the RC instances of Solomon [22] for the Vehicle Routing Problem with Time Windows (VRPTW). In particular, the TSPTW instances are obtained by considering the single-vehicle decomposition deriving from VRPTW solutions. This decomposition generates instances with up to 40 cities and has been solved by Pesant et al. [20]. The results for these instances are reported in Table 2 in terms of lower bound at root node, computing times (in seconds) and number of failures. The model of the problem combines a scheduling model in order to treat time windows and a TSP model that takes into account the routing part. The model has been extensively described in [8] where other results using different search strategies are reported and comparison with related literature is presented. In this paper, the purpose is to compare the "pruning ability" of different relaxation with the same search strategy, i.e., the chronological strategy, typically used for scheduling problems [8]. In Table 2 we do not report the results obtained using a generic LP solver since when the cuts are generated only at root node the results are always dominated by the Lagrangian approach, and when the cuts are generated at every node, we experienced memory problems. Further investigation will concern ad hoc branching strategy for the LP formulation. Also the application of the purging technique on the Lagrangian relaxation did not improve the quality of the results of the Lagrangian approach.

The effectiveness of the LAGR w.r.t. the AP is not always clear; in fact, despite the good increase of the lower bound, this did not always translated into an improvement in performances. The reasons for this behaviour is due to the fact that the LAGR approach has to solve several LP at root node in order to generate the cuts.

As mentioned, the purpose of this computational section is *not* to find the best method to solve a specific problem (TSP or TSPTW). For this purpose we should have used search strategies tailored to the specific bound used. Nevertheless is interesting to compare the different lower bounds obtained and to see that the chosen method should be carefully evaluated considering the size of the problem, the lower bound, and the complexity of the bound calculation. We believe that a constraint should separate its semantic from the actual algorithm used which should be chosen by the user even during the execution of a search strategy.

Table 2. Results on rc2 instances from Solomon et al. [22]

Inst.	N	OPT	No Bound			AP			LAGR		
			LB	Time	Fail	LB	Time	Fail	LB	Time	Fail
rc201.0	25	378.62	257.38	3.1	1.9k	367.67	0.15	20	378.62	1.24	16
rc201.1	28	374.7	201.92	270.4	106k	256.16	48.22	15.4k	346.74	37.3	9.89k
rc201.3	19	232.55	183.89	0.8	543	216.79	0.16	51	217.82	0.24	51
rc202.0	25	246.23	160.57	242.9	175k	180.38	4.11	1.62k	241.92	5.05	1.28k
rc202.1	22	206.52	127.91	46.7	27.6k	146.77	3.50	1.23k	177.87	9.98	2.37k
rc202.2	27	341.76	211.75	198.9	102k	282.05	5.07	1.71k	334.06	51.2	17.3k
rc202.3	26	367.85	217.09	*	*	282.41	345.2	148.6k	330.06	314.2	98.8k
rc205.0	26	251.66	128.21	1.3k	967k	196.99	4.91	1.98k	230.68	1.22	131
rc205.1	22	271.2	174.23	37.9	25.8k	240.54	0.28	98	270.44	0.48	86
rc205.2	28	434.69	212.73	*	*	294.67	1.09k	460k	320.5	*	*
rc205.3	24	361.24	218.57	27.5	13.9k	261.49	6.0	2.43k	329.95	10.3	2.14k
rc207.0	37	436.67	270.15	*	*	331.62	698.2	118k	397.58	1.62k	203k
rc207.1	33	396.39	248.34	*	*	288.24	1.78k	406k	374.38	361	56.2k
rc207.2	30	246.43	145.70	*	*	200.31	210	60.3k	238.17	66.1	11.9k

5   Related Literature

The idea of integrating cutting planes in Constraint Programming is not new. The first attempt is probably due to Barth and Bockmayr [3] who integrate cutting planes in CLP on Pseudo Boolean where variables range on a finite domain of integers containing only two values, i.e., 0 and 1, and constraints are linear equations and inequalities between integer polynomials in 0-1 variables. In this setting, local consistency techniques are rather weak since they do not detect the infeasibility of a set of constraints. The use of a LP solver for finding the optimal solution of the linear relaxation of the problem and the addition of cutting planes enable the earlier detection of infeasibility, easier decision of entailment and the computation of lower/upper bounds on the objective function. In [3] the authors follow the more general research field called *logic-based methods for optimization*, that was not precisely developed in the Constraint Programming setting. Hooker [13] points out the correspondence between logical inference and cutting plane generation. In fact, cuts are nothing else than constraints that are logically entailed by a given constraint set.

An interesting perspective on cutting planes is provided by Bockmayr and Kasper [4] in the Branch and Infer framework. Cutting planes are considered as primitive constraint for IP solvers. Thus, authors argue that there is a similarity between inference due to constraint propagation in Constraint Programming and cutting planes generation in IP solvers. This similarity gives rise to different forms of integration.

More recently, the use of cutting planes in Constraint Programming has been investigated for piecewise-linear functions $y = f(x)$. Ottosson, Thorsteinsson and Hooker [17] and Refalo [21] have shown how to embed the piecewise structure as a global constraint that enables to maintain a tight formulation during the search. In [17] the constraint is given a linear convex hull formulation in the original space, i.e., the two dimensional space (x, y), and thus no new variables need to be introduced. Besides an improved relaxation, which is dynamically updated and tightened during the search as part of the constraint propagation, the global piecewise constraint also provides information for better search strategies.

In [21] the tight cooperation scheme between constraint propagation and linear formulation is investigated. For each constraint $y = f(x)$ the convex hull of the formulation is maintained, taking into account the domain reduction performed during the search. To maintain this convex hull, cutting planes are added in the two dimensional space (x, y). On some problems, cutting plane generation can outperform standard IP approaches. Note that these cuts are only locally valid since they depend on domain reductions performed on x and y at a particular node of the search tree. Consequently, they must be removed upon backtracking, similarly to standard constraint propagation.

6   Concluding Remarks

We have proposed different integrations of cutting planes in Constraint Programming. The idea is to embed in global constraints, beside an optimization component that represents a relaxation of the constraint, one or more cut generators which provides a set of valid inequalities for the problem represented by the constraint itself. Generated cuts have been exploited in two ways: only at the root node and never changed during search, and at each node.

Acknowledgments

We warmly thank Norbert Ascheuer, Matteo Fischetti and Philippe Refalo for many interesting discussions on the topic.

References

1. N. Ascheuer, M. Fischetti, and M. Grötschel. "Solving atsp with time windows by branch-and-cut", Tech. Report ZIB Berlin, 1999. 191
2. E. Balas, M. Fischetti and W. Pulleyblank. "The precedence constrained asymmetric travelling salesman problem", *Mathematical Programming* 68, 241–265, 1995. 191
3. P.Barth and A. Bockmayr, "Finite Domain and Cutting Plane Techniques in CLP($\mathcal{PB}$)", in Proceedings of the 14th International Conference on Logic Programming - ICLP'95, MIT Press, 1995. 188, 199
4. A. Bockmayr and T. Kasper, "Branch-and-Infer: A Unifying Framework for Integer and Finite Domain Constraint Programming", INFORMS J. Computing, 10(3), p.287-300, 1998. 199
5. G. Carpaneto, S. Martello and P. Toth. "Algorithms and codes for the assignment problem", in *Annals of Operations Research*, 13, pp.193-223, 1988. 192, 194

6. M. Fischetti and P. Toth, "A Polyhedral Approach to the Asymmetric Traveling Salesman Problem", *Management Science*, 43, pp.1520-1536, 1997.

7. F. Focacci, P. Laborie and W. Nuijten, "Solving Scheduling Problems with Setup Times and Alternative Resources", *Proceedings of the Fifth International Conference on Artificial Intelligence Planning and Scheduling (AIPS2000)*, pp. 92–101, April 2000. 188

8. F. Focacci, A. Lodi and M. Milano, "Solving TSP with Time Windows with Constraints", in De Schreye, D., Ed., *Proceedings of the 16th International Conference on Logic Programming - ICLP'99*, pp. 515-529, MIT Press, 1999. 188, 194, 198

9. F. Focacci, A. Lodi and M. Milano, "Cost-based domain filtering", in *Proceedings of the International Conference on Principles and Practice of Constraint Programming CP'99*, LNCS 1713, Springer Verlag, pp. 189-203, 1999. 187, 188, 191, 192

10. F. Focacci, A. Lodi, M. Milano and D. Vigo, "Solving TSPs through the integration of CP and OR techniques", in *Proceedings of Workshop on Hybrid Approaches to Large Scale Combinatorial Optimization Problems*, in Electronic Notes of Discrete Mathematics, 1, 1999. 188, 192

11. F. Focacci, A. Lodi and M. Milano, "Integration of CP and OR methods for Matching Problems", in *Proceedings of Workshop on Integration of AI and OR techniques in Constraint Programming for Combinatorial Optimization Problems*, Ferrara, 1999. 188

12. R. E. Gomory, "Outline of an Algorithm for Integer Solution to Linear Programs", *Bulletin Amer. Math. Soc.* 64, 5, 1958. 187

13. J. N. Hooker, "Generalized Resolution and Cutting Planes", *Annals of Operations Research*, 12, pp. 217-239, 1988. 199

14. J. N. Hooker, "Constraint Satisfaction Methods for Generating Valid Cuts", in *Advances in Computational and Stochastic Optimization, Logic Programming and Heuristic Search*, Kluwer, pp. 1-30, 1997. 188

15. M. Jünger, G. Rinaldi and S. Thienel, "MINCUT, software package", Universität zu Köln, 1996. 190

16. K. Marriott and P. J. Stuckey, *Programming with Constraints*, MIT Press, 1998. 188

17. G. Ottoson, E. S. Thorsteinsson and J. N. Hooker, *Mixed Global constraints and inference in hybrid CLP-IP solvers*, in Proc. CP99 Post Conference Workshop on LSCO and Constraints, Electronic Notes in Discrete Mathematics, Elsevier Science, 1999. 188, 199, 200

18. M. Padberg and G. Rinaldi, "Optimization of a 532-city symmetric traveling salesman problem by branch-and-cut", *Oper. Res. Lett.*, 6, pp. 1-7, 1987. 187

19. M. Padberg and G. Rinaldi, "An Efficient Algorithm for the Minimum Capacity Cut Problem", *Mathematical Programming*, 47, pp. 19-36, 1990. 190

20. G. Pesant, M. Gendreau, J. Y. Potvin and J. M. Rousseau, "An Exact Constraint logic programming algorithm for the travelling salesman problem with time windows, Transportation Science, 32(1), pp. 12-29, 1998. 198

21. P. Refalo, "Tight cooperation and its application in piecewise linear optimization", *Proceedings of the International Conference on Principles and Practice of Constraint Programming CP'99*, Springer Verlag, 1999. 188, 199, 200

22. M. M. Solomon, Algorithms for the Vehicle Routing and scheduling problem with time window constraints,Operations Research, 35, pp. 254-265, 1987. 198, 199

23. ILOG Solver 4.4 User's Manual, ILOG Planner 3.2 User's Manual, ILOG Scheduler 4.4 User's Manual, 1999. 196

A Constraint-Based Framework for Prototyping Distributed Virtual Applications

Vineet Gupta[1], Lalita Jategaonkar Jagadeesan[2], Radha Jagadeesan[3],
Xiaowei Jiang[1], and Konstantin Läufer[3]*

[1] PurpleYogi.com
201 Ravendale, Mountain View, CA 94043
{vineet,xjiang}@purpleyogi.com
[2] Software Production Research Dept., Bell Laboratories, Lucent Technologies
263 Shuman Blvd., Naperville, IL 60566
lalita@research.bell-labs.com
[3] Dept. of Mathematical and Computer Sciences, Loyola University Chicago
6525 N. Sheridan Road, Chicago, IL 60626
{radha,laufer}@cs.luc.edu

Abstract. This paper describes the architecture and implementation
of a constraint-based framework for rapid prototyping of distributed applications such as virtual simulations, collaborations and games. Our
framework integrates three components based on (concurrent) constraint
programming ideas: (1) **Hybrid cc**, a (concurrent) constraint modeling
language for hybrid systems, (2) **Sisl**, a (discrete) timed constraint language for describing interactive services with flexible user interfaces and
(3) **Triveni**, a process-algebraic language for concurrent programming.
The framework is realized as a collection of tools implemented in Java.
The utility of the ideas are illustrated by sketching the implementations
of simple distributed applications.

1 Introduction

The focus of this paper is rapid prototyping in the domain of systems that
include hybrid components, concurrency and reactivity, (virtual/code) mobility
and distribution. The following systems exemplify the applications of interest:

- Consider the computer simulation aspects of NASA's Airport Surface
  Development and Test Facility (see http://sdtf.arc.nasa.gov/sdtf), an airport operations simulator. A typical virtual simulation in such a context
  involves large numbers of planes in large sections of airspace around an airport.
- Consider the emerging area of distributed collaborative applications. In their
  simplest forms (Instant Messaging, MSN Messenger Service, ICQ etc.), this
  consists of contact/buddy lists and automatic notification of presence of

---

* R. Jagadeesan, X. Jiang and K. Läufer were supported in part by a grant from NSF.

R. Dechter (Ed.): CP 2000, LNCS 1894, pp. 202–218, 2000.
© Springer-Verlag Berlin Heidelberg 2000

contacts and so on. In more sophisticated virtual world scenarios, e.g., Gelernter's vision of cyberbodies and lifestreams [19], this idea is generalized to mobile and distributed repositories of information called cyberbodies. Chronological streams are the most common kind of cyberbody, since time and causality are natural ways to organize information. The most common computational task is the exchange of information between different such streams, e.g., exchange credit card information between a shopper cyberbody and a bank cyberbody.

Both of these examples have the four conceptual components: (1) hybrid systems, (2) concurrency, (3) interaction via flexible user interfaces and (4) mobility and distribution.

Hybrid systems: Reactive systems react with their environment at a rate controlled by the environment. In each phase, the environment stimulates the system with an input and obtains a response within a bounded amount of time. Continuous systems, such as mechanical and physical systems, are those in which the system has the potential of evolving autonomously and continuously. The description of this behavior is usually in the form of differential equations that arise naturally in the description and modeling of the behavior of physical systems. In contrast to the discrete notion of time in reactive systems, the appropriate notion of time in continuous systems is dense, i.e. the rationals or the reals. Complex applications are *hybrid systems* that combine both of these ideas. Consider for example the model of the dynamics of the airplanes. It is a reactive system responding to inputs from the sensors, the pilot program etc. Each plane is modeled as an object with dynamics given by differential equations based on the physics of flight. There are discrete changes in the motion of the plane based on inputs from the pilots. Thus, the execution of the plane simulation alternates between open intervals in which the state of the plane (e.g., the position or velocity) changes continuously in a manner prescribed by the laws of flight, and points at which discontinuous change can occur, such as when the pilots take an action. Similarly, the evolution of a lifestream is naturally modeled as a hybrid system. In general, precise virtual simulation of physical artifacts in collaborative spaces naturally leads to hybrid systems.

Concurrency: Concurrency is omnipresent in the above collection of examples. Concurrency arises in two ways. Firstly, it arises in an intrinsic way because of the modeling of several independent activities, e.g., several aspects of the model of an airplane, several virtual participants in a collaborative discussion. Secondly, it arises as an abstraction mechanism useful in the implementation of responsive user interfaces.

Interaction via flexible user interfaces: Modern interactive services are becoming increasingly more flexible in the user interfaces they support. These interfaces incorporate automatic speech recognition (ASR) and natural language understanding, and include graphical user interfaces on the desktop and web-based interfaces using applets and HTML forms. The key role of flexible and varied user interfaces in our target application area is evident.

Mobility and distribution: In the collaboration and lifestreams examples, distribution and mobility issues arise naturally in the context of geographically spread-out groups of participants. In the airplane simulation, the potential for large number of airplanes in large sections of airspace mandates the modular organization of the objects of the simulation into "logical locations", also termed "ambients" [8,18]. For example, there are ambients for each airplane object and for each section of the physical airspace. The computations of each ambient are performed by (a collection of) computing nodes, and the physical motion of the airplanes naturally leads to considerations of mobility in the simulation.

1.1 Current Programming Practice and Shortcomings

The class of applications in which we are interested is implemented using concurrency, say in the form of threads, and some form of distributed programming. For concreteness, we phrase the following discussion about current programming practice in terms of the Java language; however, we note that the Java language largely reflects current popular practice. Monitors guard shared memory between threads, and these monitors cause additional indirect communication between threads; threads can wait for access to a monitored region, yield control of the monitor, and notify other threads waiting on the monitor. Threads are equipped with priorities that facilitate scheduling of threads. Finally, the thread groups of Java provide rudimentary structuring facilities for building collections of threads that are controlled in unison. Java supports two different mechanisms for distribution: RMI (remote method invocation) is Java's RPC (remote procedure call) mechanism, integrated with Java's object-oriented approach; the Servlet API provides infrastructure for the special case of client-server programming, especially when the communication (between client and server) is handled via web-based infrastructure such as the hypertext transfer protocol (HTTP). These approaches suffer from the following shortcomings.

- The model lacks support for a modularity notion of abstract *behavior*, which in the systems of interest is essentially the interaction of the system with its environment. For example, suppose one is given a computer model A of an airplane that emits position readings, Pos(t) events, from time to time (perhaps among others), and accepts Turn(dir) requests (perhaps among others). Consider the task of implementing a controller for the plane, e.g., to accept Pos(t) events and emit Turn(dir) events when appropriate. Furthermore, we would like to *compose* our controller with A to yield an activity *ControlledA* that internalizes the Turn(dir) event.
  For modularity reasons, we would like to design and implement the controller knowing only the interface of A described above, without access to the implementation fact that a behavior could be realized by one or more threads, potentially based at several processors. The operations in Java, as briefly described above, do not *directly* support this kind of software design.

- The model fails to provide coherence between the concurrent and distributed aspects. For instance, a user of a system cannot reason about system properties (such as safety specifications and deadlock behavior) independently of the nature of distribution of the system (such as the location and communication of the individual planes A and the other components of the system). We are not demanding uniformity of performance across different kinds of distribution; we are merely demanding a uniform view of distribution that does not violate the semantics of the concurrent aspects of the programming language.

  However, the operations in Java expose the programmer to the *details* of the distribution of the program components. For instance, it is possible that a Java program involving threads and RMI will be deadlock-free if the processors reside on the same file system, but will deadlock if the processors reside on different file systems.
- Finally, the two different mechanisms for distribution in Java, namely RMI and Servlets, are not presented in a unifying distributed programming model. There is no direct support for parameterizing the basic program logic over the mode of distribution. This in turn leads to duplication of effort/code and serious problems in software maintenance.

1.2   Our Approach

In our prior work, we have explored declarative programming languages, inspired by the constraint programming paradigm, targeted at some of these application areas.

- `Hybrid cc` [26,25,24] is an executable specification/programming language for hybrid systems in the concurrent constraint programming framework [41]. `Hybrid cc` can be viewed as a declarative high-level programming notation for the appropriate operational model for this context, namely hybrid automata [2].
- `Triveni` [12,13,14] is a programming methodology for concurrent programming with threads and events. `Triveni` has its operational basis in formalisms from concurrency theory, such as process algebras [37,31] and synchronous programming languages [6,30,23,29,42]. The logical semantics of `Triveni` permits viewing `Triveni` programs as formulas in a fragment of linear-time temporal logic.
- `Sisl` (Several interfaces, single logic) [3] is a deterministic constraint language [32] for the description of interactive services with multiple user interfaces. `Sisl` utilizes its constraint programming foundations to allow users considerable flexibility in the way they input their requests to such services.

In this paper, we present an architecture that combines these components smoothly in a coherent framework for prototyping distributed applications of the kind described earlier. This integration yields the following advantages with respect to the current (pragmatic) state of the art.

Concurrent composition as a first class primitive. Our approach takes the point of view of formalisms from concurrency theory, such as process algebras and concurrent constraint programming – these formalisms are designed from the start around behaviors, termed *processes.* These paradigms then describe a algebra of processes in which, for instance, the concurrent composition of two processes yields a process. Extending the viewpoint of `Triveni` to distributed situations, combinators in our framework operate on behaviors and the result of the combinators are behaviors: the implementation yields the correct combination of behaviors. Thus, our framework enables concurrent composition to be used freely for the modular decomposition of designs. The concurrent composition of programs yields programs that are indistinguishable from simple ones (in much the same way that a complex function in functional programming has the same status as a simple function). The correct dispatch of events sent by concurrent components is done automatically by our framework, and thus, the implementation of a program can closely reflect its design.

Parameterization over distribution. With regard to distribution issues, our architecture provides a framework to describe the essential features of the program logic without specifying the distribution mechanism. Thus, in our framework, we can informally think of a program P as the concurrent composition of its logic P_{logic} and its distribution mode P_{dist}. Thus, the distribution becomes a "pluggable" parameter to the program and enables the sharing of the program logic across different distribution mechanisms. We re-emphasize that our aim is not to ensure identical performance or even behavior across different distribution mechanisms. Rather, our approach enables us to achieve:

– Reuse of the extensive work done in the protocols and frameworks for distributed communication, such as Ensemble [40], which provide the ability to combine modularly basic protocol layers that implement simple properties.
– Parametric, with respect to distribution mode, reasoning about program logic by providing a clear "slot" for assumptions about the guarantees (e.g., total order or causal broadcast) provided by the distribution model.

Enlarging domain of applicability of `Hybrid cc`. `Hybrid cc` is a synchronous programming language that operates on a "global clock" assumption. This tunes it for modeling systems of tightly coupled hybrid components where subcomponents evolve at approximately similar rates. Thus, the following desiderata remain.

– There is tremendous overhead in using the models constructed by `Hybrid cc` as subcomponents in a general asynchronous environment. For example, in our work on the model of the Sprint AERCam [1], the model is interfaced with an animation interface to allow a user to interact with the model as it evolves. This interaction was achieved by traditional concurrent programming, and the synchronization code consumed almost half the total time spent in implementation.

– Secondly, we have observed (e.g., [1]) that the synchronous hypothesis of Hybrid cc leads to inefficiencies when the model has several loosely coupled hybrid sub-components. For instance, in the airport simulations, each airplane mainly interacts with nearby airplanes, thus any discrete actions it takes affect only nearby planes. However the synchronicity assumption underlying Hybrid cc forces each such discrete action to cause a *global* synchronization point involving all the objects in the simulation, including those that are not affected by the action.

The framework of this paper provides a structured methodology to arrange the interaction of Hybrid cc components in a general context of asynchrony and distribution.

1.3   Rest of the Paper

The rest of the paper is organized as follows. In Section 2, we review our earlier work on Hybrid cc, Triveni and Sisl, and we present a comparison with related work. In the following section, we describe the architecture and give an overview of its current implementation. We illustrate the ideas in the context of some concrete examples that have been realized using the framework: an n-player variation of the board game Battleship (using two different distribution mechanisms), as well as a multi-user instant messaging application.

2   Background

2.1   Hybrid cc

Hybrid cc is an executable specification/programming language for hybrid Systems [26] in the concurrent constraint programming framework [41]. Hybrid cc can be viewed as a high-level programming notation for hybrid automata [2], much as synchronous programming languages are high level notation for discrete automata[1].

Hybrid cc incorporates two key ideas – (1) Continuous constraint systems (ccs) and (2) extending (concurrent) constraint programming over (real) time. We sketch these ideas here, referring the reader to [26] for a precise foundational description. Intuitively, continuous constraint systems express the information content of initial value problems in integration. Continuous constraint systems support an integration operation, $\int^r \text{init}(a) \wedge \text{cont}(b)$ which determines the effect of b holding continuously in the interval $(0, r)$, if a held at time 0. For example, $\int^7 \text{init}(x = 3) \wedge \text{cont}(x' = 4) \vdash x = 31$. [26] describes a set of axioms for continuous constraint systems – these include intuitive properties of integration such as the monotonicity and continuity of integration, and some computability axioms to enable finite description and implementation. We add

---

[1] Functional **R**eactive **AN**imation [17], built on functional programming, has similar goals.

a single temporal control to the untimed (concurrent) constraint programming: hence A. Declaratively, hence A imposes the constraints of A at every time instant after the current one. [26] shows how hence can be combined in very powerful ways with ask operations to yield rich patterns of temporal evolution, e.g., do A watching P – execute A at every time point beyond the current one until the first time instant at which P is true, assuming that there is, in fact, a first time instant at which P is true.

While conceptually simple to understand, hence A requires the execution of A at every subsequent real time instant. Hybrid cc is made computationally realizable by exploiting the basic intuition we exploit is that, in general, physical systems change slowly, with points of discontinuous change, followed by periods of continuous evolution. Computation at a time point establishes the constraint in effect at that instant, and sets up the program to execute subsequently. Computation in the succeeding open interval determines the length of the interval r and the constraint whose continuous evolution over $(0, r)$ describes the state of the system over $(0, r)$. We recall:

- Hybrid cc is declarative [26] – programs can be understood as formulas that place constraints on the (temporal) evolution of the system, with concurrent composition regarded as conjunction.
- Hybrid cc is amenable to the tools developed for the verification of hybrid systems [24] – for any Hybrid cc program, there is a hybrid automaton whose valid runs are precisely execution traces of the program; and for any given safety property expressed in (real-time) temporal logic, there is a Hybrid cc program that "detects" if the property is violated.
- We have implemented Hybrid cc [9,25] and used this implementation for several examples, e.g., an (executable) model of the paper path of a photocopier [27], an (executable) model and controller for a robotic camera of the Space Shuttle [1].

2.2 Triveni

Triveni [12,13,14] is a programming methodology for concurrent programming with threads and events. Triveni has its basis in formalisms from concurrency theory, such as process algebras [37,31,38] and synchronous programming languages [6,28,30,42]. Communication is via broadcast of (labeled) events that are abstractions of names of communication channels. In addition to the usual process-algebraic combinators of event emission, concurrent composition and waiting for events, Triveni supports exceptions via preemption combinators in the style of synchronous programming languages.

The semantic study of Triveni [14] includes an operational semantics that includes a precise formalization of the fairness assumptions of the current implementation, and a denotational semantics based on (fair) traces. Furthermore, the logical semantics of Triveni proceeds via a compilation of the Triveni control combinators as constructions on Buchi automata. In the light of the automata-theoretic approach to temporal logic [44], this shows that Triveni programs constitute a carefully chosen fragment of linear time (temporal) logic [35].

The current implementation of `Triveni` (in Java) makes `Triveni` compatible with existing threads standards such as P-threads and Java threads, and includes an integrated specification-based testing environment that automates the testing of safety properties. We have used this implementation to perform a case study from telecommunication [13], to prototype a domain specific language for writing flexible interactive services [3], and in the classroom as an environment and tool for teaching the rudiments of designing, implementing, and reasoning about concurrent programs [15].

2.3 Sisl

The context of `Sisl` is modern interactive services. It is now common for such services to have more than one interface for accessing the same data, e.g., personal banking services from an automated teller machine, a bank-by-phone interface, or a web-based interface. Furthermore, telephone-based services are starting to support automatic speech recognition and natural language understanding. In this context, it is desirable for the programming methodology to provide the following capabilities:

 - allowing requests to be phrased in various ways (e.g., needed information can be provided in any order),
 - prompting for missing information,
 - lookahead (to allow the user to speak several commands at once), and
 - backtracking to earlier points in the service logic.

In `Sisl`, the service logic (i.e., the code that defines the essence of the service) of an application is specified as a *reactive constraint graph*, which is a directed acyclic graph with an enriched structure on the nodes. The traversal of reactive constraint graphs is driven by the reception of events from the environment: these events have an associated label (the event name) and may carry associated data. In response, the graph traverses its nodes and executes actions; the reaction of the graph ends when it needs to wait for the next event to be sent by the environment.

The key kind of node is $\texttt{constraint}(P_{\texttt{next}}, \langle (\phi_i, \sigma_{\phi_i}, P^i_{\texttt{viol}}) \rangle i = 1 \ldots n)$, where the ϕ_i are predicates on events. Intuitively a constraint node is awaiting *all* the events in $\cup_i \sigma(\phi_i)$. These events can be sent to the constraint node in any order. When control reaches the constraint node, the `Sisl` service logic automatically sends out a prompt event for every event that is still needed in order to evaluate some constraint. In addition, it automatically sends out a optional prompt for all other events mentioned in the constraints – these correspond to information that can still be corrected by the user. In every round of interaction, the constraint node waits for the user to send any event that is mentioned in its associated predicates. Each predicate associated with a constraint node is evaluated as soon as all of its events have arrived. If an event is re-sent by the user interfaces (i.e, information is corrected), all predicates with that event in their signature are re-evaluated.

Sisl is implemented as a library in Java and supports the development of services that are shared by multiple user interfaces including automatic speech recognition-based or text-based natural language understanding, telephone voice access, web, and graphics-based interfaces. Sisl has been integrated with VeriSoft [20], a systematic state-space exploration tool, and hence supports automated and efficient testing of Sisl applications [21]. Sisl is currently being used to prototype a new generation of call-processing services for a Lucent Technologies switching product.

2.4   Related Work

We have already referred to several pieces of work that have inspired and influenced this paper. [43] is an eminently readable survey of concurrent logic programming languages. This line of work has now developed into extensive work on temporal logic programming languages with perhaps some notions of distribution (e.g., [7,4,5,39,36,22]). Our work differs from this literature in that our approach has tended to emphasize the reuse of the extensive existing work in the design, implementation and analysis of (concurrent) programming languages. For example, the compatibility of our work with existing threads standards and event models, such as P-threads and JavaBeans, has enabled us to easily use our languages and framework in the context of concrete applications. More substantially, our methodology is significantly influenced by ideas from process algebras and synchronous programming languages. This is revealed in the explicit treatment of operational notions such as fairness in our framework, and has permitted our study to be compatible with the extensive analysis methodologies/tools developed for testing and verifying concurrent systems in this context, such as computer-aided verification via model checking (e.g., [20,11,34,10] to name but a few) and specification-based testing of temporal properties (e.g., [16]). Indeed, both Triveni and Sisl support a systematic and efficient testing architecture based on these methods.

3   Examples

In this section, we discuss two examples with respect to their hybrid, reactive, and distributed characteristics. MyMessaging is an multi-user instant messaging application. This system has has rich multi-modal reactive and distributed behavior. Battle, an n-player variation of the 2-player board game Battleship, is a modified version of an example from [13]. This game has a significant hybrid component to model the motion of the ships, in addition to the evident reactive and distributed behavior. We have used both examples as projects in courses.

4   Architecture

This section describes the architecture of our framework and its use of multiple interacting constraint-based paradigms. The framework exploits the capa-

Contact List. Each user has a contact list ("buddy list") of people with whom he or she usually communicates. The contact list can be managed by adding or removing users and organizing them by category. The contact list can be viewed in different ways, including by current online status.

Online Status. Each user can change between different online statuses: online, do-not-disturb, offline, etc.

Messaging. A user can send different types of messages to one or more users. Message types include text messages, files or URLs, and chat invitations.

Fig. 1. Features of `MyMessaging`

bilities of each paradigm and decouples application-specific from application-independent aspects.

Building upon existing implementations of `Hybrid cc` (21,000 lines of C code and 1000 lines of Yacc code; used from within Java through the Java Native Interface (JNI)), `Triveni` (7,000 lines of Java code), and `Sisl` (5,000 lines of Java code), the framework consists of about 1,900 lines of application-independent Java code; this includes support for both RMI-based and servlet-based physical distribution. The prototype implementation of `Battle` contains about 2,200 lines of application-specific new code: 700 lines of `Triveni` code for the control logic, 1500 lines of Java code for user interface and animation, 100 lines of `Hybrid cc` code for the physical model, and 400 lines of Java code for hooking the application together with the servlet-based distribution architecture. The prototype implementation of `MyMessaging` contains about 400 lines of application-specific new Java code: 300 lines for the control logic and support classes, and 100 lines for the user interface.

In the remainder of this section, the figures depicting the various aspects of the architecture use shaded shapes for application-specific components and unfilled shapes for application-independent components.

4.1 Logical Architecture

We first consider the logical architecture of a virtual simulation. A simulation consists of zero or more scenes, zero or more dialogs, and a control logic. These components coexist using `Triveni`'s concurrent composition combinator (| |) and communicate through logical events; the simulation system constitutes the environment in which these events are visible.

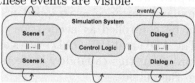

– A scene models a collection of closely interacting physical objects. A scene occasionally emits events that describe the scene by providing information such as the position, speed, direction, or other attributes of certain objects. A scene responds to incoming events that control the objects in the scene.

Loss. A player loses when all his/her ships are destroyed.

Oceans. Each player has a collection of ships on an individual ocean grid. The n ocean grids are disjoint. Each player's screen displays all n oceans, but a player can see only his/her own ships. A player's ships are confined to the player's ocean. Each ocean has a surface current that causes its ships to drift in the direction of the current.

Ships. Each ship occupies a rectangular sub-grid of the player's ocean and sinks after each point in its grid area has been hit. Ships can move on the surface of the player's ocean. Once set in motion, a ship moves along a straight line that factors in the surface current. If a ship hits an edge of the ocean, it bounces back. If it collides with another ship, the usual conservation of energy and momentum laws apply.

Moves. A player can move as fast as the user-interface/reflexes allow. Player i can make 3 kinds of moves:

1. Fire a round of ammunition on a square of another player j's ocean by clicking on it. The ammunition may hit a previously unmarked point on one of player j's ships, in which case a mark is displayed at that point in player j's ocean on all players' screens. No information is reported in case of a miss.
2. Impart a velocity to a battleship that lasts until it receives another velocity command or until it collides with an edge or another battleship.
3. Raise a shield over his/her entire ocean for a game-specific interval of time, during which player i's ships are invulnerable. When a player raises an ocean-wide shield, his/her ocean becomes dim on the screens of all players. Each player has a limited supply of shields.

Fig. 2. Features of `Battle`

- A dialog provides interaction with outside systems such as users. A dialog receives input from outside systems and emits corresponding events into the simulation. A dialog receives response events from the simulation and transmits the corresponding information back to the outside system.
- The control logic specifies how the scenes and dialogs of the simulation interact.

Scene. A simulation scene has three interacting components. Concurrency and communication between these components is again managed through `Triveni`:

- The application-independent *simulator* simulates a `Hybrid cc` program and communicates with the other components via events and methods. The `Hybrid cc` program provides the physical model for the objects in this scene. The `Hybrid cc` simulator instance is wrapped inside a suitable `Triveni` component and can be controlled as needed via the START, INTR, and REWIND events. The ADD and UPLOAD events are used to make changes to the `Hybrid cc` program; this capability is necessary for controlling the physical model from the outside.
  The simulator occasionally emits events that inform the other components about the state of the simulation. SAMPLE is emitted whenever a data sample from the simulation is available. STOPPED is emitted in response to an incoming INTR event to indicate that the simulator has in fact stopped.

- The *controller* is responsible for converting logical events to pieces of Hybrid cc code that are uploaded to the simulator for controlling the scene.
- The *animator* is responsible for converting data samples into logically meaningful events that describe the status of the scene.

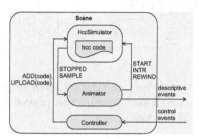

Example 1. In Battle, the Hybrid cc program provides physical modeling of the ships in a single ocean using Newtonian laws of motion in the form of differential equations. For instance, the fragment that governs collisions between ships and edges looks as follows:

```
Edges = () {
    always forall Battleship(X) do {
        if (X.px = hw || X.px = xMax - hw) then {
            XEdgeCollision,
            X.ChangeX, X.vx = - prev(X.vx)
        },
        if (X.py = hh || X.py = yMax - hh) then {
            YEdgeCollision,
            X.ChangeY, X.vy = - prev(X.vy)
        }}}
```

The controller converts move events coming from the player to the corresponding changes in the Hybrid cc program. The animator simply renders ships on the screen using the Java 2d package.

Dialog. A dialog has two components:

- The application-independent *pluggable* external user interfaces that convert back and forth between concrete input and output events and the corresponding abstract dialog events. In a model-view-controller architecture [33], these components can be viewed as the view/controller pairs of the interaction.
- The application-specific Sisl code that describes the logical interaction with an outside system. In a model-view-controller architecture, this component can be viewed as the model of the interaction. The Sisl code is responsible for mediating between abstract dialog events and logical simulation events.

Sisl provides the ability to switch between or combine multiple concrete user interfaces without changing the abstract dialog. Examples of such interfaces include graphical user interfaces, speech recognition and synthesis, web browsers using applets or HTML, voice browsers using VoiceXML, and other XML-based interfaces.

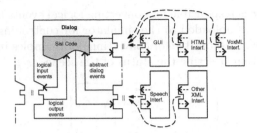

Example 2. In `Battle`, the player can interact with ships by clicking on or dragging them with the mouse. Alternatively, the player can use speech to cause ships to move or to shield his/her ocean.

Control Logic. The control logic mediates between the scenes and the dialogs via events and is provided as a `Triveni` component.

Example 3. In `Battle`, the control logic is responsible for a number of tasks, including enforcement of the rules of the game. The following code defines the top-level logic for one player.

```
ReadyAbortButton
|| await Ready -> Shield(container, numOfShields, shieldDuration)
|| await Ready -> suspend Shield [playerOcean] resume Unshield
|| await Ready_0 -> OpponentOcean(0)
   ... (except this player's ocean)
|| await Ready_n -> OpponentOcean(n = maxNumOfPlayers-1)
```

The following code fragment ensures that a player can use a shield only as long as shields are still available.

```
Shield(numOfShields, shieldDuration) =
    local OutOfShields in
        do shieldBtn Watching OutOfShields
    || loop
            await Shield -> if (--numOfShields == 0) emit OutOfShields
    || rename Start, Finish to Shield, Unshield in Act(Timer(duration))
```

4.2 Distribution – Logical and Physical

As stated above, the components of a simulation system communicate through logical events. There are two conceptually different degrees of communication coupling between components. Communication between components on a single node is *synchronizing*, that is, components can wait until an emitted event has been received by all other components in the sub-system – all communication inside `Hybrid cc` and a significant portion of the communication inside `Triveni` is of this kind. On the other hand, communication between components on two distinct nodes is is better carried out asynchronously. Components that require synchronizing communication logically belong to the same subsystem, whereas components that do not require tight coupling logically belong to distinct subsystems. The logical distribution is a partitioning of scenes, dialogs, and control logic into logical nodes and involves breaking the control logic up into suitable pieces – this process is facilitated by the explicit concurrent/parallel composition combinator supported in our framework.

Consider now the physical architecture of a virtual simulation, which allows distribution over (possibly) multiple physical nodes. In our architecture, communication between nodes is provided in a way that is completely transparent to the local simulations. This allows us to decouple the logical architecture of the simulation system from its physical distribution architecture and topology. Concretely, on each node, the local simulation system is paired with a communication component that is responsible for transmitting nonlocal events between the local simulation and other nodes. The remote client hides the details of the specific distribution mechanism used. The pairing between the simulation and communication components occurs as concurrent composition at the `Triveni` level. Thus, the physical distribution architecture becomes a *pluggable* parameter of the former in the following two senses.

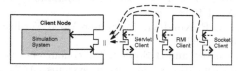

- Firstly, it is possible to switch between distribution mechanisms without making changes to the simulation system. For example, we support the following distribution architectures: applet/servlet, remote method invocation (RMI), and sockets.
- Secondly, mechanisms that guarantee reliable communication over asynchronous networks, particularly those based on protocol stacks such as Ensemble [40], are naturally incorporated in this architecture as layers around the communication components.

Example 4. In `Battle`, each logical node consists of a single scene for modeling the player's ocean, a single dialog for interaction with this player, and the control logic. In the RMI-based implementation, the physical nodes use RMI for communication and are arranged in a clique topology with a central server for initial client registration. In the servlet-based implementation, the physical nodes use HTTP and sockets for communication and are arranged in a star topology around a central server for client registration and routing.

References

1. L. Alenius and V. Gupta. Modeling an AERCam: A case study in modeling with concurrent constraint languages. In *CP'98 Workshop on Modeling and Computation in the Concurrent Constraint Languages*, October 1998. 206, 207, 208
2. R. Alur, C. Coucoubetis, N. Halbwachs, T.A. Henzinger, P.-H. Ho, X. Nicollin, A. Olivero, J. Sifakis, and S. Yovine. The algorithmic analysis of hybrid systems. *Theoretical Computer Science*, 138:3–34, 1995. 205, 207
3. T. Ball, C. Colby, P. Danielsen, L. J. Jagadeesan, R. Jagadeesan, K. Läufer, P. Mataga, and K. Rehor. Sisl: Several interfaces, single logic. *Intl. J. of Speech Technology*, 2000. Kluwer Academic Publishers, to appear. 205, 209

4. H. Barringer, M. Fisher, D. Gabbay, G. Gough, and R. Owens. Metatem: A framework for programming in temporal logic. In J. W. de Bakker, W. P. de Roevere, and G. Rozenberg, editors, *Stepwise Refinement of Distributed Systems– Models, Formalisms, Correctness.* Springer- Verlag, 1990. LNCS 430. 210

5. M. Baudinet. Temporal logic programming is complete and expressive. In *Proc. ACM Symp. on Principles of Programming Languages*, 1989. 210

6. A. Benveniste and G. Berry. The synchronous approach to reactive and real-time systems. In *Special Issue on Another Look at Real-time Systems*, Proc. IEEE, September 1991. 205, 208

7. C. Brzoska. Temporal logic programming and its relation to constraint logic programming. In V. A. Saraswat and K. Ueda, editors, *Logic Programming: Proc. 1991 Intl. Symp.*, pages 661 – 677, 1991. 210

8. L. Cardelli and A. D. Gordon. Mobile ambients. In *Foundations of Software Science and Computational Structures*, LNCS 1378, 1998. 204

9. B. Carlson and V. Gupta. Hybrid CC and interval constraints. In T. A. Henzinger and S. Sastry, editors, *Hybrid Systems 98: Computation and Control*, LNCS 1386. Springer Verlag, April 1998. 208

10. E. M. Clarke and R. P. Kurshan. Computer-Aided Verification. *IEEE Spectrum* **33***(6)*, pages 61–67, (1996). 210

11. R. Cleaveland, J. Parrow, and B. Steffen. The concurrency workbench: A semantics based tool for the verification of concurrent systems. *ACM Transactions on Prog. Lang. and Systems*, 15(1), 1993. 210

12. C. Colby, L. J. Jagadeesan, R. Jagadeesan, K. Läufer, and C. Puchol. Design and implementation of Triveni: A process-algebraic API for threads + events. In *Proc. IEEE Intl. Conf. on Computer Languages.* IEEE Computer Press, 1998. 205, 208

13. C. Colby, L. J. Jagadeesan, R. Jagadeesan, K. Läufer, and C. Puchol. Objects and concurrency in Triveni: A telecommunication case study in Java. In *Proc. Fourth USENIX Conf. on Object Oriented Technologies and Systems*, 1998. 205, 208, 209, 210

14. C. Colby, L. J. Jagadeesan, R. Jagadeesan, K. Läufer, and C. Puchol. Semantics of Triveni: A process-algebraic API for threads + events. *Electronic Notes in Theoretical Computer Science*, 14, 1999. 205, 208

15. C. Colby, R. Jagadeesan, K. Läufer, and C. Sekharan. Interaction, concurrency, and oop in the curriculum: a sophomore course. In *Proc. 1998 OOPSLA Educators Workshop*, 1998. 209

16. L. K. Dillon and Q. Yu. Oracles for checking temporal properties of concurrent systems. *Software Engineering Notes*, 19(5):140–153, December 1994. Proc. 2nd ACM SIGSOFT Symp. on Foundations of Software Engineering. 210

17. C. Elliott and P. Hudak. Functional reactive animation. In *ACM SIGPLAN Intl. Conf. on Functional Programming*, 1997. 207

18. C. Fournet, G. Gonthier, J.-J. Lévy, L. Maranget, and D. Rémy. A calculus of mobile agents. In *7th Intl. Conf. on Concurrency Theory (CONCUR'96)*, pages 406–421, Pisa, Italy, August 26-29 1996. Springer-Verlag. LNCS 1119. 204

19. D. Gelernter. Now that the PC is dead. *Wall Street Journal*, Jan 1 2000. http://www.mirrorworlds.com/. 203

20. P. Godefroid. Model checking for programming languages using VeriSoft. In *Proc. 24th ACM Symp. on Principles of Programming Languages*, pages 174–186, 1997. 210

21. P. Godefroid, L. J. Jagadeesan, R. Jagadeesan, and K. Läufer. Automated systematic testing for constraint-based interactive services. In *Proc. 8th Intl. Symp. on the Foundations of Software Engineering*, November 2000. To appear. 210

22. S. Gregory. A declarative approach to concurrent programming. In *Proc. 9th Intl. Symp. on Programming Languages, Implementations, Logics, and Programs*, 1997. 210

23. P. Le Guernic, M. Le Borgne, T. Gauthier, and C. Le Maire. Programming real time applications with SIGNAL. In *Special Issue on Another Look at Real-time Systems*, Proc. IEEE, September 1991. 205

24. V. Gupta, R. Jagadeesan, and V. Saraswat. Hybrid cc, hybrid automata, and program verification. *LNCS 1066*, 1996. 205, 208

25. V. Gupta, R. Jagadeesan, V. Saraswat, and D. G. Bobrow. Programming in hybrid constraint languages. *LNCS 999*, 1995. 205, 208

26. V. Gupta, R. Jagadeesan, and V. A. Saraswat. Computing with continuous change. *Science of Computer Programming*, 30((1,2)):3–49, 1998. 205, 207, 208

27. Vineet Gupta, Vijay Saraswat, and Peter Struss. A model of a photocopier paper path. In *Proc. 2nd IJCAI Workshop on Engineering Problems for Qualitative Reasoning*, August 1995. 208

28. N. Halbwachs. *Synchronous programming of reactive systems*. The Kluwer International Series in Engineering and Computer Science. Kluwer Academic Publishers, 1993. 208

29. N. Halbwachs, P. Caspi, and D. Pilaud. The synchronous programming language LUSTRE. In *Special Issue on Another Look at Real-time Systems*, Proc. IEEE, September 1991. 205

30. D. Harel. Statecharts: A visual approach to complex systems. *Science of Computer Programming*, 8:231 – 274, 1987. 205, 208

31. C. A. R. Hoare. *Communicating Sequential Processes*. Prentice-Hall, 1985. 205, 208

32. J. Jaffar and J. L. Lassez. Constraint logic programming. In *Proc. 14th Annual ACM Symp. on Principles of Programming Languages*, 1987. 205

33. G. Krasner and S. Pope. A cookbook for using the model-view-controller user interface. *J. Object-Oriented Programming*, 1(3):26–49, August/September 1988. 213

34. R. P. Kurshan. *Computer-aided Verification of Coordinating Processes: the automata-theoretic approach*. Princeton U. Press, 1994. 210

35. Z. Manna and A. Pnueli. *The Temporal Logic of Reactive and Concurrent Systems*. Springer-Verlag, 1991. 427 pp. 208

36. R. Merz. Efficiently executing temporal logic programs. In M. Fisher and R. Owens, editors, *Proc. of IJCAI*, 1993. 210

37. R. Milner. *Communication and Concurrency*. Prentice-Hall, 1989. 205, 208

38. R. Milner, J. Parrow, and D. Walker. Mobile processes. Technical report, U. Edinburgh, 1989. 208

39. B. Moszkowski. *Executing Temporal Logic Programs*. Cambridge Univ. Press, 1986. 210

40. R. V. Renesse, K. P. Birman, and S. Maffeis. Horus, a flexible group communication system. *Communications of the ACM*, April 1996. 206, 215

41. V. A. Saraswat. *Concurrent Constraint Programming*. Logic Programming and Doctoral Dissertation Award Series. MIT Press, March 1993. 205, 207

42. V. A. Saraswat, R. Jagadeesan, and V. Gupta. Timed Default Concurrent Constraint Programming. *J. Symbolic Computation*, 22:475–520, 1996. Extended abstract appeared in the *Proc. 22nd ACM Symp. on Principles of Programming Languages*, San Francisco, January 1995. 205, 208

43. E. Shapiro. The family of concurrent logic programming languages. *ACM Computing Surveys*, 21(3):413–510, September 1989. 210

44. M. Y. Vardi and P. Wolper. An automata-theoretic approach to automatic program verification. In *Proc. IEEE Symp. on Logic in Computer Science*, pages 322–331, 1986.   208

A Scalable Linear Constraint Solver for User Interface Construction

Hiroshi Hosobe

National Institute of Informatics
2-1-2 Hitotsubashi, Chiyoda-ku, Tokyo 101-8430, Japan
hosobe@nii.ac.jp

Abstract. This paper proposes an algorithm for satisfying systems of linear equality and inequality constraints with hierarchical strengths or preferences. Basically, it is a numerical method that incrementally obtains the LU decompositions of linear constraint systems. To realize this, it introduces a novel technique for analyzing hierarchical systems of linear constraints. In addition, it improves performance by adopting techniques that utilize the sparsity and disjointness of constraint systems. Based on this algorithm, the HiRise constraint solver has been designed and implemented for the use of constructing interactive graphical user interfaces. This paper shows that HiRise is scalable up to thousands of simultaneous constraints in real-time execution.

1 Introduction

Constraints have been widely recognized to be powerful in the construction of *graphical user interfaces* (GUIs). The main usage of constraints in GUIs is to lay out graphical objects. Once a programmer defines the geometric relationship of objects with constraints, a constraint solver will automatically maintain the relationship afterward. Therefore, the programmer will be freed from the burden of writing the code to manage the layout. It is effective especially when the layout is too complex for the programmer to specify with a simple loop or recursion. Apart from geometric layouts, constraints can be used, for example, to adjust the sizes of graphical objects to internal data, and also to manage the relationships between internal data.

A major subject of the research on constraints for GUIs is how to model and solve various over-constrained real-world problems. For this purpose, *constraint hierarchies* [3] are often used as a theoretical framework. By definition, a constraint hierarchy is a constraint system that consists of constraints with hierarchical *strengths*, which can be regarded as the preferences or priorities of the constraints. Intuitively, (optimal) solutions of constraint hierarchies are determined so that they will satisfy as many strong constraints as possible, leaving weaker inconsistent constraints unsatisfied.

Another issue of the study on constraints for GUIs is how to improve the *scalability* of constraint satisfaction. For this purpose, incremental local propagation algorithms have been extensively explored [6, 9, 14, 15]. However, since

R. Dechter (Ed.): CP 2000, LNCS 1894, pp. 218–233, 2000.

local propagation is basically limited to dataflow (or functional) equality constraints, the resulting algorithms inevitably impose restrictions on the kinds of possible constraint problems. A typical hurdle is to solve arbitrary hierarchies of linear equality and inequality constraints, although such constraint hierarchies arise naturally in actual GUI applications.

To address these issues, this paper proposes an algorithm for satisfying hierarchies of linear equality and inequality constraints. Its main contributions are summarized as follows:

- By introducing a novel technique called *hierarchical independence analysis*, it efficiently realizes the incremental satisfaction of hierarchies of linear equality constraints based on LU decomposition.
- It provides a way of handling linear inequality constraints in combination with quasi-linear optimization.
- It presents techniques for improving performance by utilizing the *sparsity* and *disjointness* of constraint hierarchies.

Based on this algorithm, the HiRise[1] constraint solver has been designed and implemented for the use of constructing interactive GUIs. Particularly, it is fitted to large-scale diagrams defined with numerous constraints. This paper shows that HiRise is scalable up to thousands of simultaneous constraints in real-time execution.

2   Related Work

There have been various algorithms proposed for solving constraint hierarchies. Particularly, in the area of GUIs, local propagation algorithms for dataflow equality constraints have been extensively studied. DeltaBlue [6] is the first efficient incremental algorithm in this category. SkyBlue [14], the successor of DeltaBlue, copes with the multiple outputs and cyclic dependencies of constraints. Quick-Plan [15] ensures that it can solve a constraint hierarchy by local propagation if the hierarchy has at least one acyclic solution. The author proposed the *DE-TAIL* algorithm [9], which accommodated local propagation to the least-squares method as well as cyclic dependencies.

For the purpose of GUIs, there have been algorithms that deal with constraint hierarchies including inequalities in limited ways. Indigo [2] efficiently handles hierarchies with nonlinear inequality constraints by interval propagation, although it does not cope with the cyclic dependencies of constraints. The algorithm using projection [7] statically compiles constraint hierarchies with inequalities into program code.

The recent algorithms for solving constraint hierarchies with inequalities are Cassowary [1, 4] and QOCA [4, 10]. Both of the algorithms solve hierarchies of linear constraints by converting them into optimization problems. Cassowary uses the simplex method to obtain solutions based on the weighted sums of

---

[1] HiRise stands for 'HieRarchical linear system engine.'

constraint errors, while QOCA exploits linear complementary pivoting to find least-squares solutions.[2] Later, Section 8 provides further discussions about these algorithms.

Linear constraint satisfaction has also been studied in the community of constraint logic programming [13]. Its main issue is how to enhance the incremental satisfaction of ordinary (non-hierarchical) systems of linear equality and inequality constraints. By contrast, this paper primarily focuses on the incremental maintenance of hierarchical systems of linear constraints.

3   The Basic Algorithm

This section presents the basic algorithm for HiRise to satisfy hierarchical systems of linear equality constraints.

3.1   Problem Formulation

The basic algorithm focuses on linear equality constraints only. Instead of ordinary constraint hierarchies, it internally treats constraint systems formulated as follows:

Definition 1 (constraint system). A constraint system is an ordered set of m linear equations on n variables $x_1, x_2, \ldots, x_n$, where the i-th equation is represented as $a_{i1}x_1 + a_{i2}x_2 + \cdots + a_{in}x_n = c_i$. The *coefficient vector* of the i-th equation is $a_i = (a_{i1}\ a_{i2}\ \cdots\ a_{in})$, and the *coefficient matrix* A, *variable vector* x, and *constant vector* c of the system are defined as follows:

$$
A = \begin{pmatrix} a_1 \\ a_2 \\ \vdots \\ a_m \end{pmatrix} = \begin{pmatrix} a_{11} & a_{12} & \cdots & a_{1n} \\ a_{21} & a_{22} & \cdots & a_{2n} \\ \vdots & \vdots & & \vdots \\ a_{m1} & a_{m2} & \cdots & a_{mn} \end{pmatrix}, \quad x = \begin{pmatrix} x_1 \\ x_2 \\ \vdots \\ x_m \end{pmatrix}, \quad c = \begin{pmatrix} c_1 \\ c_2 \\ \vdots \\ c_m \end{pmatrix}.
$$

Intuitively, the first equation is the strongest, and the latter an equation, the weaker it is. The notion of strength is similar to that of constraint hierarchies; that is, an equation has absolute priority over latter ones in determining solutions, which is strictly defined later.

For simplicity, the rest of this paper writes a constraint system as $A\,x = c$. Also, for brevity, it obeys the following notation rules: it assumes that the numbers of constraints and variables are m and n respectively; writing i and j, it intends indices that range over 1 to m and over 1 to n respectively. It sometimes attaches primes or subscripts to these symbols.

Solutions of constraint systems are defined using an ordering:

---

[2] Precisely, the QOCA constraint solving toolkit also provides the Cassowary solver to handle linear inequality constraints [10]. However, for convenience, this paper refers to the algorithm based on linear complementary pivoting as QOCA.

Definition 2 (solution). Given a constraint system $A\,\boldsymbol{x} = \boldsymbol{c}$, its solution set is

$$S(A\,\boldsymbol{x} = \boldsymbol{c}) \equiv \{\, \boldsymbol{v} \in \boldsymbol{R}^n \mid \forall\, \boldsymbol{v}' \in \boldsymbol{R}^n.\, |A\,\boldsymbol{v} - \boldsymbol{c}| \leq_{\text{lex}} |A\,\boldsymbol{v}' - \boldsymbol{c}| \,\}$$

where $\leq_{\text{lex}}$ is the lexicographic ordering, i.e., $|A\,\boldsymbol{v} - \boldsymbol{c}| \leq_{\text{lex}} |A\,\boldsymbol{v}' - \boldsymbol{c}|$ is

$$|A\,\boldsymbol{v} - \boldsymbol{c}| =_{\text{lex}} |A\,\boldsymbol{v}' - \boldsymbol{c}| \equiv \forall i.\, |\,\boldsymbol{a}_i\,\boldsymbol{v} - c_i| = |\,\boldsymbol{a}_i\,\boldsymbol{v}' - c_i|$$

$$\text{or} \quad |A\,\boldsymbol{v} - \boldsymbol{c}| <_{\text{lex}} |A\,\boldsymbol{v}' - \boldsymbol{c}| \equiv \exists i.\, \forall i' < i.\, |\,\boldsymbol{a}_{i'}\,\boldsymbol{v} - c_{i'}| = |\,\boldsymbol{a}_{i'}\,\boldsymbol{v}' - c_{i'}|$$
$$\land\, |\,\boldsymbol{a}_i\,\boldsymbol{v} - c_i| < |\,\boldsymbol{a}_i\,\boldsymbol{v}' - c_i| \ .$$

A solution set $S(A\,\boldsymbol{x} = \boldsymbol{c})$ means that a solution of $A\,\boldsymbol{x} = \boldsymbol{c}$ is $x_1 = v_1, x_2 = v_2,$ $\ldots, x_n = v_n$ for $\boldsymbol{v} = (v_1, v_2, \ldots, v_n)^{\text{T}} \in S(A\,\boldsymbol{x} = \boldsymbol{c})$. This paper simply refers to such a vector $\boldsymbol{v}$ as a solution.

Intuitively, $\leq_{\text{lex}}$ 'hierarchically' compares two error vectors, and the solution set of the given constraint system is the set of all the variable value vectors that result in the minimum error vectors in the sense of $\leq_{\text{lex}}$. Therefore, constraint systems may be regarded as holding preferential constraints in the total order.

Unlike constraint hierarchies, constraint systems by these definitions have no levels that contain constraints with equal preferences. However, the author has proved a theorem [8] that they have a close relationship with constraint hierarchies consisting of linear equations and solved with the locally-error-better (LEB, also known as locally-metric-better) comparator [3]. Informally, LEB determines the appropriateness of potential solutions based on how much each constraint is satisfied (see Section 8 for the discussion on comparators). The proved theorem means that the system obtained by 'serializing' (or putting in the total order) the constraints in each level of a hierarchy will always yield a subset of the LEB solution set of the original hierarchy. Thus, if all solutions are not necessary, Definitions 1 and 2 substitute for constraint hierarchies. Such a situation is common in various applications including GUIs that usually need only one solution. Therefore, the author believes that the notion of such constraint systems is useful as an alternative method to handle constraint hierarchies.

3.2   Hierarchical Independence

This subsection presents the notion of *hierarchical independence*, a foundation for analyzing hierarchical systems of linear constraints. It is the key technology for the basic algorithm to achieve efficiency.

A row of a coefficient matrix is said to be hierarchically independent if and only if it is linearly independent of all the upper (or stronger) ones:

Definition 3 (hierarchical independence). Given a constraint system $A\,\boldsymbol{x} = \boldsymbol{c}$, the condition that the i-th row of A is hierarchically independent, denoted as $\text{hindep}(A, i)$, is defined as follows:

$$\text{hindep}(A, i) \equiv \neg\, \exists \alpha_1 \exists \alpha_2 \cdots \exists \alpha_{i-1}.\ \boldsymbol{a}_i = \alpha_1\,\boldsymbol{a}_1 + \alpha_2\,\boldsymbol{a}_2 + \cdots + \alpha_{i-1}\,\boldsymbol{a}_{i-1} \ .$$

Also, a row that is not hierarchically independent is said to be hierarchically dependent.

The following theorem shows that solutions of constraint systems can be obtained by collecting and satisfying all the constraints corresponding to hierarchically independent rows:

Theorem 4. *For any constraint system $A\,\boldsymbol{x} = \boldsymbol{c}$, $\boldsymbol{v}$ is its solution if and only if*

$$\forall i.\,\mathrm{hindep}(A,i) \Rightarrow \boldsymbol{a}_i\,\boldsymbol{v} = c_i \ .$$

Proof. See [8]   □

Conversely, if an equation has a dependent coefficient vector, it exhibits either inconsistency that must be discarded, or redundancy that may be ignored.

The rest of this paper says, for conciseness, that a constraint is *active* if and only if its coefficient vector is hierarchically independent, and refers to nonactive constraints as *inactive* constraints. Also, for a constraint system $A\,\boldsymbol{x} = \boldsymbol{c}$, it considers an ordinary linear system $B\,\boldsymbol{x} = \boldsymbol{d}$ that contains all the active constraints of $A\,\boldsymbol{x} = \boldsymbol{c}$ in some arbitrary order. Obviously, the solution set of $A\,\boldsymbol{x} = \boldsymbol{c}$ is equal to that of $B\,\boldsymbol{x} = \boldsymbol{d}$. It calls such B and $\boldsymbol{d}$ an *active coefficient matrix* and an *active constant vector* respectively.

3.3   Solving a Constraint System from Scratch

This subsection presents how the basic algorithm solves a constraint system from scratch. For simplicity, the following description assumes that the given constraint system has n active constraints; for any system, it can be realized simply by adding to each variable a very weak default stay constraint that tries to preserve its current value.

Generally, given a constraint system $A\,\boldsymbol{x} = \boldsymbol{c}$, the basic algorithm obtains an LU decomposition in the following form:

$$BT_1 T_2 \cdots T_t = L \tag{1}$$

where B is an active coefficient matrix, each T_k is a transformation matrix described later, and L is a lower triangular matrix:

$$B = \begin{pmatrix} \boldsymbol{b}_1 \\ \boldsymbol{b}_2 \\ \vdots \\ \boldsymbol{b}_n \end{pmatrix}, \qquad L = \begin{pmatrix} 1 & & & \\ l_{21} & 1 & & \\ \vdots & & \ddots & \\ l_{n1} & l_{n2} & & 1 \end{pmatrix}.$$

Intuitively, (1) means that a sequence $T_1 T_2 \cdots T_t$ transforms B into L.

Once the algorithm computes (1), it can solve $B\,\boldsymbol{x} = \boldsymbol{d}$ for $\boldsymbol{x}$ efficiently. First, it resolves $L\,\boldsymbol{y} = \boldsymbol{d}$ by computing $y_j \leftarrow d_j - \sum_{j'=1}^{j-1} l_{jj'} y_{j'}$, which is known as forward substitution [12]. Then it obtains $\boldsymbol{x}$ by calculating $\boldsymbol{x} = T_1 T_2 \cdots T_t\,\boldsymbol{y}$.

When the basic algorithm solves $A\,\boldsymbol{x} = \boldsymbol{c}$ from scratch, it obtains an LU decomposition in the form:

$$BP_1 U_1 P_2 U_2 \cdots P_n U_n = L$$

where each P_j and U_j is a permutation matrix and an upper triangular eta matrix respectively:[3]

$$P_j = \left(\begin{array}{c|c|c} E_{j-1} & & \\ \hline 0 & & 1 \\ \hline & E_{j'-j-1} & \\ \hline 1 & & 0 \\ \hline & & E_{n-j'} \end{array} \right), \quad U_j = \left(\begin{array}{c|c|ccc} E_{j-1} & & & & \\ \hline & \frac{1}{b'_{jj}} & -\frac{b'_{j,j+1}}{b'_{jj}} & \cdots & -\frac{b'_{jn}}{b'_{jj}} \\ \hline & & & E_{n-j} & \end{array} \right). \quad (2)$$

To determine which row to select as b_j, the algorithm performs hierarchical independence analysis: until the j-th step, it has obtained a 'partial' LU decomposition as

$$\left(\begin{array}{c} b_1 \\ b_2 \\ \vdots \\ b_{j-1} \end{array} \right) P_1 U_1 P_2 U_2 \cdots P_{j-1} U_{j-1} = \left(\begin{array}{ccccccc} 1 & & & & & & \\ l_{21} & 1 & & & & & \\ \vdots & & \ddots & & \ddots & & \\ l_{j-1,1} & \cdots & l_{j-1,j-2} & 1 & 0 & \cdots & 0 \end{array} \right).$$

Then it picks up the uppermost unprocessed row a_i from A, and multiplies it by $P_1 U_1 P_2 U_2 \cdots P_{j-1} U_{j-1}$:

$$a_i P_1 U_1 P_2 U_2 \cdots P_{j-1} U_{j-1} = (a'_{i1} \ a'_{i2} \ \cdots \ a'_{i,j-1} \ a'_{ij} \ \cdots \ a'_{in}).$$

If $a'_{ij'}$ is not a zero for some $j' \geq j$, a_i is a hierarchically independent row of A; then the algorithm assigns a_i to b_j, and determines P_j and U_j with (2). Otherwise, it moves to the next uppermost unprocessed row since a_i is hierarchically dependent. Intuitively, P_j swaps the j-th column for the j'-th so that the resulting (j, j)-entry is not a zero. Then U_j changes the (j, j)-entry into one, and also 'eliminates' all the (j, j'')-entries for $j'' > j$.

The algorithm may be easily understood when compared with Gaussian elimination [12]: it transforms a matrix B into a lower triangular matrix L, while Gaussian elimination transforms a matrix into an upper triangular matrix. Unlike Gaussian elimination, it records its transformation process as a sequence of P_j's and U_j's.

In addition to ordinary linear equality constraints, the algorithm can handle *edit* and *stay* constraints, which usually arise in GUI applications: an edit constraint for a variable attempts to change its value, while a stay constraint tries to fix the value of the designated variable. The algorithm realizes an edit constraint by expressing it as $x = c$ and calculating the necessary parts of $L\,y = d$ and $x = T_1 T_2 \cdots T_t\, y$ whenever it tries to alter the value of x. By contrast, the algorithm implements a stay constraint simply by representing it as $x = c$ where c indicates the value of x immediately before it becomes active.

The time complexity for constructing an LU decomposition from scratch is $O(mn^2)$. Also, the time complexity for calculating variable values using the LU decomposition is $O(n^2)$.

---

[3] In this paper, E_k represents the $k \times k$ identity matrix.

3.4   Inserting a Constraint Incrementally

When a new constraint is inserted between constraints in the current system, the basic algorithm takes one of the following actions:

- If it needs to activate the new constraint, it updates the current LU decomposition. To do this, it first finds an appropriate 'victim' constraint that should be deactivated instead. After eliminating the row for the victim and appending the row for the new one, it revises the LU decomposition.
- Otherwise, it keeps the present LU decomposition unchanged.

The criterion for activating or deactivating a constraint is its hierarchical independence in the new system. The victim is the constraint that has been active in the previous system but becomes inactive in the new system because of the stronger, inserted constraint. When a constraint is inserted, there will be at most one victim because all the constraints are linear equations.

The technique for updating LU decompositions is inspired by Forrest-Tomlin method [5], which was originally devised for linear programming. The technique is as follows: assume that the new constraint $a\,x = c$ should be activated, and that the row for the victim is found to be the j-th one of the active coefficient matrix B, which has been decomposed into (1). Let

$$
B' = \begin{pmatrix} b_1 \\ \vdots \\ b_{j-1} \\ b_{j+1} \\ \vdots \\ b_n \end{pmatrix}, \qquad
Q_j = \left(\begin{array}{c|c} E_{j-1} & \\ \hline & 1 \\ \hline E_{n-j} & \end{array} \right)
$$

and then the following holds:

$$
B'T_1 T_2 \cdots T_t Q_j = \begin{pmatrix}
1 & & & & & & \\
\vdots & \ddots & & & & & \\
l_{j-1,1} & & 1 & & & & \\
l_{j+1,1} & \cdots & l_{j+1,j-1} & 1 & & & l_{j+1,j} \\
\vdots & & \vdots & & \ddots & & \vdots \\
l_{n1} & \cdots & l_{n,j-1} & l_{n,j+1} & & 1 & l_{nj}
\end{pmatrix}.
$$

Thus, all the entries at the rightmost column can be eliminated with appropriate matrices $U'_j, U'_{j+1}, \ldots, U'_{n-1}$ in the form (2). Then, with U'_n such that

$$
aT_1 T_2 \cdots T_t Q_j U'_j U'_{j+1} \cdots U'_{n-1} U'_n = (l_1\ l_2\ \cdots\ l_{n-1}\ 1)
$$

the following new LU decomposition is obtained:

$$
\begin{pmatrix} b_1 \\ \vdots \\ b_{j-1} \\ b_{j+1} \\ \vdots \\ b_n \\ a \end{pmatrix} T_1 \cdots T_t Q_j U'_j \cdots U'_{n-1} U'_n = \begin{pmatrix}
1 & & & & & \\
\vdots & \ddots & & & & \\
l_{j-1,1} & & 1 & & & \\
l_{j+1,1} & \cdots & l_{j+1,j-1} & 1 & & \\
\vdots & & \vdots & & \ddots & \\
l_{n1} & \cdots & l_{n,j-1} & l_{n,j+1} & 1 & \\
l_1 & \cdots & l_{j-1} & l_j & l_{n-1} & 1
\end{pmatrix}.
$$

To judge whether to activate the new constraint and (if necessary) which active constraint to victimize, the algorithm carries out hierarchical independence analysis: it finds the row index j for the first active constraint, in the descending order of the index (or preference) i of the constraint, such that

$$\boldsymbol{a}T_1T_2\cdots T_tQ_jU_j'U_{j+1}'\cdots U_{n-1}' = (a_1'\ a_2'\ \cdots\ a_{n-1}'\ a_n')$$

where $a_n' \neq 0$ and U_j', U_{j+1}', ..., U_{n-1}' are the ones obtained with the above technique. If such i is no smaller than the index where the new constraint is inserted, the algorithm needs to revise the LU decomposition, and the i-th constraint is the victim. Otherwise, it should not change the current decomposition.

The time complexity for inserting a constraint into a system is $O(m'n^2)$, where m' indicates the number of the constraints tested for a victim. Usually $m' = 1$ holds since the weakest active constraint tends to be the victim.

3.5 Deleting a Constraint Incrementally

When an existing constraint is deleted from the current constraint system, the basic algorithm applies one of the following processes:

- If the deleted constraint is active in the present LU decomposition, it updates the decomposition. To do this, it first eliminates the row for the deleted one by the method described in the previous subsection. Then it detects a proper alternative constraint that should be activated instead, and updates the decomposition by attaching the row for the alternative.
- Otherwise, it preserves the current LU decomposition.

To decide which inactive constraint $\boldsymbol{a}_i\ \boldsymbol{x} = c_i$ to activate alternatively, the algorithm employs hierarchical independence analysis: assume that j is the row index in B of the deleted constraint, and that U_j', U_{j+1}', ..., U_{n-1}' are obtained with the elimination of the j-th row; then it searches for the index (or preference) i of the first inactive constraint, in the ascending order of i, such that

$$\boldsymbol{a}_iT_1T_2\cdots T_tQ_jU_j'U_{j+1}'\cdots U_{n-1}' = (a_{i1}'\ a_{i2}'\ \cdots\ a_{i,n-1}'\ a_{in}')$$

where $a_{in}' \neq 0$. With such an alternative constraint, the algorithm obtains the new LU decomposition.

The time complexity for deleting a constraint from a system is $O(m'n^2)$, where m' represents the number of the constraints tried for an alternative. If the system does not have many conflicting (or possibly redundant) constraints, m' will be bounded by a small number.

4 Handling Inequalities

This section provides a functionally enhanced algorithm for handling inequality constraints. First, it solves a given constraint system in the same way as the basic algorithm. Then it collects all the inactive constraints and resolves them with quasi-linear optimization, which is similar to the Cassowary constraint solver [1, 4]. Quasi-linear optimization finds a vector that satisfies a set of linear equality and inequality constraints and also that minimizes an objective function composed as a sum of absolute values of linear expressions.

The enhanced algorithm treats both equality constraints $a\,x = c$ and inequality ones $a\,x \geq c$. However, in the first step, it assumes that all the constraints were equations, and obtains an LU decomposition (1) in the same way as the basic algorithm.

In the second step, it correctly adjusts the constraints by introducing what are called 'slack variables' in the area of linear programming. It rewrites each constraint into $a\,x = c + \sigma s$ where $s \geq 0$, and $\sigma = 0$ if the constraint is an equation, or $\sigma = 1$ if not. With the rewriting, the constraint system can be expressed as $A\,x = c + F\,s$ where $s = (s_1, s_2, \ldots, s_m)^{\mathrm{T}} \geq 0$ and F is the $m \times m$ diagonal matrix whose (i,i)-th entry is $\sigma_i\ (= 0 \text{ or } 1)$.

Next, the algorithm represents each inactive constraint $a_i\,x = c + \sigma_i s_i$ with only s. To do this, it expresses x with s (more precisely, s_i's for the active constraints) by introducing an $n \times m$ matrix G that consists of the rows of F corresponding to the active constraints. Then, solving $L\,y = d + G\,s$ and $x = T_1 T_2 \cdots T_t\,y$, it obtains $x = v + H\,s$. Thus it rewrites the inactive constraint into $a_i H\,s - \sigma_i s_i = c_i - a_i\,v$.

Finally, to obtain the values of s, the algorithm creates a quasi-linear optimization problem and resolves it with the simplex method [12]. For the indices $i_1, i_2, \ldots, i_{m'}$ of the inactive constraints, it constructs the following problem by introducing new non-negative variables $\delta_{i_k}^+$ and $\delta_{i_k}^-$ for $1 \leq k \leq m'$:

$$\text{minimize } \sum_{k=1}^{m'} \left\{ w_{i_k} (\delta_{i_k}^+ + \delta_{i_k}^-) \right\} \tag{3}$$
$$\text{subject to } a_{i_k} H\,s - \sigma_{i_k} s_{i_k} = c_{i_k} - a_{i_k}\,v + \delta_{i_k}^+ - \delta_{i_k}^- \quad (1 \leq k \leq m')$$

where w_{i_k} indicates the weight corresponding to the preference of the i_k-th constraint (e.g. 10^6, 10^3, and 1 for strong, medium, and weak constraints respectively).[4] Intuitively, each $(\delta_{i_k}^+ + \delta_{i_k}^-)$ indicates the error $| a_{i_k} H\,s - \sigma_{i_k} s_{i_k} - c_{i_k} + a_{i_k}\,v |$ of the k-th inactive constraint, and the problem minimizes the sum of the weighted errors of the inactive constraints.

To understand the enhanced algorithm, consider the constraint system consisting of $x_1 \geq 0$, $x_2 \geq 0$, $-x_1 \geq -2$, $-x_2 \geq -2$, and $x_1 + x_2 = 5$ in this order, and also assume that their weights are 10^6, 10^6, 10^3, 10^3, and 1 respectively. First, the algorithm selects $x_1 \geq 0$ and $x_2 \geq 0$ as the active constraints, and constructs an LU decomposition for $x_1 = 0$ and $x_2 = 0$. Second, it introduces non-negative variables s_1, s_2, s_3, s_4, and s_5, and rewrites all the constraints into $x_1 = 0 + s_1$, $x_2 = 0 + s_2$, $-x_1 = -2 + s_3$, $-x_2 = -2 + s_4$, and $x_1 + x_2 = 5 + 0 \cdot s_5$ respectively. Next, using the LU decomposition, it expresses x_1 and x_2 as $x_1 = s_1$ and $x_2 = s_2$.

---

[4] It should be noted that such real-valued weights might lead to incorrect solutions. In fact, Cassowary avoids this problem by introducing 'symbolic' weights [1]. However, HiRise is optimistic about the problem since it is assumed to handle a relatively small number of inequality conflicting constraints (see Section 8).

Then it rewrites the remaining inactive constraints into $-s_1-s_3 = -2$, $-s_2-s_4 = -2$, and $s_1+s_2-0 \cdot s_5 = 5$. Finally, it resolves the optimization problem that minimizes $10^3(\delta_3^+ + \delta_3^-) + 10^3(\delta_4^+ + \delta_4^-) + (\delta_5^+ + \delta_5^-)$ subject to $-s_1-s_3 = -2 + \delta_3^+ - \delta_3^-$, $-s_2 - s_4 = -2 + \delta_4^+ - \delta_4^-$, and $s_1 + s_2 - 0 \cdot s_5 = 5 + \delta_5^+ - \delta_5^-$. Any solution to this problem must satisfy $s_1 = s_2 = 2$, $s_3 = s_4 = \delta_3^+ = \delta_3^- = \delta_4^+ = \delta_4^- = \delta_5^+ = 0$, and $\delta_5^- = 1$ (s_5 may be arbitrary). Thus the solution to the original system is $x_1 = 2$ and $x_2 = 2$. Note that the weakest constraint $x_1 + x_2 = 5$ is maximally satisfied.

Similar to the basic algorithm, the enhanced algorithm as a whole can be regarded as handling the locally-error-better (LEB) comparator. It is because the objective function (3) implements weighted-sum-better (WSB), which is more strictly restrictive than LEB; that is, any WSB solution is also an LEB one [3].

If edit constraints try to change variable values, the algorithm updates $c_{i_k} - a_{i_k} v$ for each k (which also reflects stay constraints), and then incrementally re-optimizes the problem in the same way as Cassowary. If inserted or deleted constraints update the LU decomposition, it reconstructs a problem.

Usually, the algorithm can considerably reduce the sizes of optimization problems as follows:

– If the i-th constraint is equality ($\sigma_i = 0$), it may eliminate s_i. In the above example, s_5 could be deleted.
– If the k-th inactive constraint is inequality ($\sigma_{i_k} = 1$), it can omit $\delta_{i_k}^+$. The above example could remove δ_3^+ and δ_4^+.

With these reductions, the numbers of variables and constraints in an optimization problem become $(m_1 + m_2 + m - n)$ and $(m - n)$ respectively, where m_1 and m_2 indicate the numbers of the inequality constraints and inactive equality ones respectively.[5] Therefore, if the given system contains only small numbers of inequality constraints and conflicting (or possibly redundant) constraints, the algorithm can efficiently solve the optimization problem.

5   Performance Techniques

This section provides two techniques for improving the performance of the basic algorithm. Both of them can be used together with the technique for handling inequality constraints.

5.1   Utilizing Sparsity

In usual GUI applications, constraint systems are *sparse*, that is, most individual constraints refer to only small numbers of variables even if entire systems are large. Therefore, resulting coefficient matrices are also sparse ones where most entries are zeros. From the viewpoint of efficiency, it is desirable for the algorithm

---

[5] Note that the simplex method needs not to introduce artificial variables. For each rewritten inactive constraint, it can always select one of $\delta_{i_k}^+$, $\delta_{i_k}^-$, and s_{i_k} as a basic variable.

to preserve the sparsity of the matrices. However, in transforming them into lower triangular ones, it sometimes yields nonzero entries called 'fill-ins' [11] at the positions where nonzero entries have been lain. Thus it may degrade the sparsity of the original matrices.

This subsection describes a performance technique using the sparsity of constraint systems. It restrains the occurrences of fill-ins by adopting an ordering method for sparse matrices [11]. Generally, ordering methods exchange rows and columns of matrices to minimize the numbers of fill-ins.

To realize this, the proposed technique separates constraints in a system into required and preferential ones, and applies an ordering method to the partial matrix corresponding to required constraints. This process is possible because there are no differences among the preferences of required constraints.

The technique performs kernel generation and Tewarson's method [11] below while the basic algorithm is computing an LU decomposition from scratch.

1. Generate a kernel in the following two steps:
   (a) Seek a required constraint with only one variable. If such a constraint is found, move its nonzero entry to the pivot position, transform it into one, and repeat this operation (ignore the processed variable afterward).
   (b) Search for a required constraint with a variable referred by no other required ones. If such a constraint is detected, move the corresponding entry to the pivot, alter it into one, eliminate the remaining entries, and iterate this operation (disregard this constraint afterward).
2. Perform LU decomposition successively for the rest of the required constraints. Use Tewarson's method in selecting variables and constraints for pivoting; that is, by examining the partial lower triangular matrix obtained by the current LU decomposition, minimize the product {(the number of the unprocessed nonzero entries in the row corresponding to the constraint) − 1} × {(the number of the unprocessed nonzero entries in the column corresponding to the variable) − 1}.

For some situations, handling the sparsity of preferential constraints might be promising. The above technique is also applicable to the inside of each preferential level of constraint hierarchies, although it has not been implemented.

5.2 Exploiting Disjointness

In many GUI applications, constraint systems have *disjointness*; that is, large systems may be divided into multiple smaller independent components. For efficiency, it is preferable for the algorithm to solve such disjoint components separately.

This subsection explains a performance technique adopting the disjointness of constraint systems. Basically, for each disjoint component of a system, it maintains and solves a distinct subsystem.

It is necessary to integrate LU decompositions when added constraints merge multiple components. For simplicity, suppose that two components need to be merged. Since they are disjoint, they do not share any variables. Therefore, even if they are merged, the hierarchical independence of each constraint will not change. Thus, with the active constraint sets $B\,x = c$ and $B'\,x' = c'$ for these components, the merged set can be expressed as follows:

$$\begin{pmatrix} B & 0 \\ 0 & B' \end{pmatrix} \begin{pmatrix} x \\ x' \end{pmatrix} = \begin{pmatrix} c \\ c' \end{pmatrix}. \tag{4}$$

Now, let the LU decompositions of B and B' be $BT_1T_2 \cdots T_t = L$ and $B'T_1'T_2' \cdots T_{t'}' = L'$ respectively. Then the following holds:

$$\begin{pmatrix} B & 0 \\ 0 & B' \end{pmatrix} \begin{pmatrix} T_1 & 0 \\ 0 & E \end{pmatrix} \begin{pmatrix} T_2 & 0 \\ 0 & E \end{pmatrix} \cdots \begin{pmatrix} T_t & 0 \\ 0 & E \end{pmatrix} \begin{pmatrix} E & 0 \\ 0 & T_1' \end{pmatrix} \begin{pmatrix} E & 0 \\ 0 & T_2' \end{pmatrix} \cdots \begin{pmatrix} E & 0 \\ 0 & T_{t'}' \end{pmatrix} = \begin{pmatrix} L & 0 \\ 0 & L' \end{pmatrix}.$$

It can be regarded as an LU decomposition of the active coefficient matrix of (4) in the form of (1). Thus multiple separately solved components can be efficiently integrated.

It might be more fruitful to utilize the 'partial' disjointness of constraint systems that consist of almost disjoint components. The current (perhaps unsatisfactory) solution to this issue is to recursively apply the above disjointness technique, which actually depends on the way of the construction of constraint systems. Another more aggressive solution is an open problem.

6   The HiRise Constraint Solver

Based on the proposed algorithm, Java and C++ versions of the HiRise constraint solver have been developed. Mainly, HiRise was designed for the construction of interactive GUIs. It allows programmers to create variables and constraints as Java or C++ objects, and to insert/delete constraints into/from the solver object. The supported kinds of constraints are linear equality, linear inequality, stay, and edit. Currently, the Java version provides the full functionality of HiRise, whereas the C++ version implements only the basic algorithm. The present Java implementation consists of approximately ten thousand lines of code. Fig. 1 illustrates the screen snapshots of sample applications developed in C++ for Microsoft Windows.

7   Experiments

This section provides the results of two experiments on the performance of the HiRise constraint solver. Both of the experiments used an actual application for editing a tree depicted in Fig. 2. In the application, the layout of a tree is defined with constraints as follows: subtrees sharing the same parent nodes are adjacent, and the intervals of neighboring leaves are equal. Also, it adds six inequality constraints to a tree: four inequalities confine the tree in the window, and the other two prevent it from getting reversed. The application automatically generates a tree with an irregular structure using random numbers.

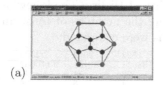   (a)   (b)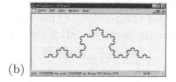

Fig. 1. Sample applications of HiRise: (a) one that allows a user to edit a graph by adding, moving, and staying nodes, and fixing edge directions, where each inner node is constrained at the barycenter of its adjacent nodes; (b) another that enables a user to operate a picture that approximates the fractal diagram known as the Koch curve, which is realized with a finite number of vertices constrained by linear equations

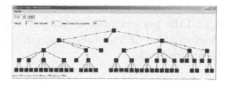

Fig. 2. An application for editing a tree

First, Experiment 1 compared the performance of HiRise with Cassowary [1, 4] and QOCA [4, 10] using medium-scale constraint systems. The used implementations of Cassowary and QOCA were version 0.55 in Java and version 1.0 beta 2 of LinIneqSolver in Java respectively, both of which were distributed by the authors of the original papers. These programs were compiled and executed with Java Development Kit 1.2.1 from Sun Microsystems. The execution environment was a Sun Ultra 60 workstation with a single 296 MHz UltraSPARC-II processor running Solaris 7.

The table below shows the results of Experiment 1. It gives the numbers of inserted and deleted constraints, the total numbers of constraints, and the times in milliseconds required for executing operations of editing a tree. In the experiment, each solver was given a tree of the same shape generated with a certain seed of random numbers.

	Numbers of constraints			Times for execution		
	Insert	Delete	Total	HiRise	Cassowary	QOCA
Initial layout	512	4	508	1771	2289	4953
Start move	2	0	510	8	1316	34
Repeat move	0	0	510	1	2	3
Finish move	0	2	508	8	1485	1
Add node	6	2	512	28	117	741
Remove node	2	6	508	26	103	122

Overall, HiRise exhibited higher performance than Cassowary and QOCA. In particular, its incremental constraint satisfaction is usually much faster than them, which impresses the power of hierarchical independence analysis.

Next, Experiment 2 measured the scalability of HiRise. The following table illustrates the results of this experiment, where the numbers of constraints are the ones immediately after the initial solutions were computed:

Numbers of constraints	508	1024	1524	2012	2536
Initial layout	1771	12777	38634	87161	170062
Start move	8	15	23	31	40
Repeat move	1	3	4	5	6
Finish move	8	13	21	28	35
Add node	28	148	265	452	694
Remove node	26	114	189	245	380

The results indicate that HiRise is sufficiently rapid even for a system of more than two thousand constraints. The only problem is that it costs much times to obtain initial solutions, which is $O(mn^2)$ in time complexity. However, the author is attempting to alleviate this problem since the current implementation for utilizing the sparsity of constraint systems is rather naive.

It should be noted that the performance of HiRise actually depends on various aspects of its algorithm, that is, hierarchical independence analysis, the way of inequality handling, and the performance techniques for sparsity and disjointness. A more thorough evaluation of how much each of them works for different situations is one of the future work.

8 Discussion

As shown in the experimental results, HiRise is usually faster than Cassowary [1, 4] and QOCA [4, 10] for hundreds of constraints, and is further scalable up to thousands of constraints. It is because HiRise performs hierarchical independence analysis for fast handling preferential constraints, and also because it adopts the performance techniques using the sparsity and disjointness of constraint systems. Only, it may slow down as the number of inequalities grows, since it must reconstructs an internal simplex tableau after updating the corresponding LU decomposition.

To solve constraint hierarchies, HiRise uses the locally-error-better (LEB) comparator, which is the same as Indigo [2]. By contrast, Cassowary adopts weighted-sum-better, which is a little more restrictive than LEB, and QOCA exploits least-squares-better (LSB), which is further more discriminative than LEB. It is known that LSB is useful to applications with many conflicting preferential constraints, because it relaxes the constraints by uniformly distributing their errors and thus exhibits the 'least-surprise' behavior to users. Therefore, QOCA is sometimes the most functionally advantageous among these solvers.

In summary, HiRise is suitable for massive constraint systems including relatively small numbers of inequalities and not necessitating the uniform relaxation of conflicts. Particularly, it is fitted to properly designed large-scale diagrams, as proved in the previous section.

9 Conclusions and Future Work

This paper proposed an algorithm for satisfying systems of linear equality and inequality constraints with hierarchical preferences. It also presented the HiRise constraint solver, which is based on the algorithm and is designed for user interface construction, and it showed that HiRise is scalable up to thousands of simultaneous constraints in real-time execution.

Using HiRise, the author is developing a Java-based constraint programming language that allows programmers to specify constraints more easily. Also, the author is planning to revise the C++ version of HiRise so that it will provide the full functionality and also a further scalability.

Acknowledgments

The author would like to thank the anonymous referees for their insightful reviews. This research was supported in part by the Japan Society for the Promotion of Science, Grant-in-Aid for Encouragement of Young Scientists, 12780252, 2000.

References

[1] Badros, G. J., Borning, A.: The Cassowary linear arithmetic constraint solving algorithm: Interface and implementation. Tech. Rep. 98-06-04, Dept. of Computer Science and Engineering, Univ. of Washington, 1998. 219, 226, 230, 231

[2] Borning, A., Anderson, R., Freeman-Benson, B.: Indigo: A local propagation algorithm for inequality constraints. In *Proc. ACM UIST*, pp. 129–136, 1996. 219, 231

[3] Borning, A., Freeman-Benson, B., Wilson, M.: Constraint hierarchies. *Lisp and Symbolic Computation*, 5(3):223–270, 1992. 218, 221, 227

[4] Borning, A., Marriott, K., Stuckey, P., Xiao, Y.: Solving linear arithmetic constraints for user interface applications. In *Proc. ACM UIST*, pp. 87–96, 1997. 219, 226, 230, 231

[5] Chvátal, V.: *Linear Programming*. Freeman, 1983. 224

[6] Freeman-Benson, B. N., Maloney, J., Borning, A.: An incremental constraint solver. *Comm. ACM*, 33(1):54–63, 1990. 218, 219

[7] Harvey, W., Stuckey, P., Borning, A.: Compiling constraint solving using projection. In *Principles and Practice of Constraint Programming—CP97*, vol. 1330 of *LNCS*, pp. 491–505. Springer, 1997. 219

[8] Hosobe, H.: *Theoretical Properties and Efficient Satisfaction of Hierarchical Constraint Systems*. PhD thesis, Dept. of Information Science, Univ. of Tokyo, 1998. 221, 222

[9] Hosobe, H., Miyashita, K., Takahashi, S., Matsuoka, S., Yonezawa, A.: Locally simultaneous constraint satisfaction. In *Principles and Practice of Constraint Programming—PPCP'94*, vol. 874 of *LNCS*, pp. 51–62. Springer, 1994. 218, 219

[10] Marriott, K., Chok, S. C., Finlay, A.: A tableau based constraint solving toolkit for interactive graphical applications. In *Principles and Practice of Constraint Programming—CP98*, vol. 1520 of *LNCS*, pp. 340–354. Springer, 1998. 219, 220, 230, 231

[11] Oguni, C., Murata, K., Miyoshi, T., Dongarra, J. J., Hasegawa, H.: *Matrix Computing Software*. Maruzen, 1991. In Japanese. 228

[12] Press, W. H., Flannery, B. P., Teukolsky, S. A., Vetterling, W. T.: *NUMERICAL RECIPES in C: The Art of Scientific Computing.* Cambridge University Press, 1988. 222, 223, 226

[13] Refalo, P., Hentenryck, P. V.: CLP(R_{lin}) revised. In *Proc. JICSLP*, pp. 22–36. MIT Press, 1996. 220

[14] Sannella, M.: SkyBlue: A multi-way local propagation constraint solver for user interface construction. In *Proc. ACM UIST*, pp. 137–146, 1994. 218, 219

[15] Vander Zanden, B.: An incremental algorithm for satisfying hierarchies of multi-way dataflow constraints. *ACM Trans. Prog. Lang. Syst.*, 18(1):30–72, 1996. 218, 219

A Constraint Programming Approach for Solving Rigid Geometric Systems

Christophe Jermann[1,*], Gilles Trombettoni[1],
Bertrand Neveu[2], and Michel Rueher[1]

[1] Université de Nice–Sophia Antipolis, I3S, ESSI
930 route des Colles, B.P. 145, 06903 Sophia Antipolis Cedex, France
{jermann,rueher,trombe}@essi.fr
[2] CERMICS
2004 route des lucioles, 06902 Sophia.Antipolis cedex, B.P. 93, France
neveu@sophia.inria.fr

Abstract. This paper introduces a new rigidification method -using interval constraint programming techniques- to solve geometric constraint systems. Standard rigidification techniques are graph-constructive methods exploiting the degrees of freedom of geometric objects. They work in two steps: a planning phase which identifies rigid clusters, and a solving phase which computes the coordinates of the geometric objects in every cluster. We propose here a new heuristic for the planning algorithm that yields in general small systems of equations. We also show that interval constraint techniques can be used not only to efficiently implement the solving phase, but also generalize former ad-hoc solving techniques. First experimental results show that this approach is more efficient than systems based on equational decomposition techniques.

1 Introduction

Modeling by geometric constraints is a promising method in the CAD field. It allows a user to build a shape by stating geometric constraints in a declarative way. In practice, geometric systems contain numerous rigid subparts. Recursive rigidification techniques [HLS97] allow a bottom-up computation of a rigid system by discovering and aggregating rigid subsystems. We introduce a new rigidification algorithm which is general enough to tackle systems in 2D or 3D. This algorithm yields a decomposition of a rigid system into several subsystems to be solved one by one. The paper aims at showing that this semantic-guided approach proves to be efficient when every subsystem is solved by interval techniques. Moreover, when the subsystems are small, the system may be tractable by symbolic tools.

The paper is organized as follows. The next subsections introduce the problem and recursive rigidification. Section 2 describes the new planning phase we have designed. Section 3 presents a solving phase based on interval techniques. Section 4 provides first experimental results.

---

* Supported by CNRS and region Provence Alpes Côte d'Azur

R. Dechter (Ed.): CP 2000, LNCS 1894, pp. 233–248, 2000.
© Springer-Verlag Berlin Heidelberg 2000

1.1   Problem Description

The problem considered in this paper is the computation of all possible positions and orientations of *geometric objects* satisfying *constraints* that make them rigid relative to each other [FH97].

Definition 1 *A **geometric constraint problem** is defined by a set of geometric objects and a set of geometric constraints.*

*A **geometric object** is defined by a set of generalized coordinates in a reference system of given dimension such as the Euclidean plane or 3D-space.* **Generalized coordinates** *are parameters defining the position and the orientation of an object.*

*A **geometric constraint** is a relation between geometric objects.*

Examples of geometric objects are points, lines, circles in 2D, or points, lines, spheres, cylinders in 3D space. Geometric constraints can state properties like incidence, tangency, orthogonality, parallelism, distance or angle.

Although the algorithms described in the paper works in 3D space, our implementation is restricted to the following entities in the Euclidean plane:

- Geometric objects: points, lines and circles,
- Geometric constraints: incidence, orthogonality, parallelism, distance and angle.

We will also assume that:

- *The geometric constraints are binary.* This is not a strong limitation since most of geometric constraints are binary. Moreover, no restriction holds on the arity of the corresponding algebraic equations. For instance, a distance constraint involves only two points but the corresponding equation involves four generalized coordinates: the points coordinates.
- *All objects are non-deformable*, that is, the involved generalized coordinates cannot be independent from the reference system. For example, a circle is defined by the two coordinates of the center, but the radius must be constant. Moreover, constraints can only define relations which involve coordinates of objects. For instance, a distance constraint for which the distance parameter is variable cannot be handled.

The second limitation is intrinsic to recursive rigidification which performs rigid-body transformations [JASR99].

1.2   Recursive Rigidification

Recursive rigidification is based on a degree of freedom analysis performed on a weighted geometric constraint graph [HLS97].

Definition 2 *A **weighted geometric constraint graph** $G = (O, C)$ is defined as follows:*

- *A vertex $o \in O$ represents a geometric object. Its weight $w(o)$ characterizes the number of its **degrees of freedom**, i.e., the number of generalized coordinates that must be determined to fix it. For example, a point and a line* [1] *have two degrees of freedom in the Euclidean plane.*
- *An edge $c \in C$ represents a geometric constraint. Its weight $w(c)$ gives the number of parameters that are fixed by the constraint; usually the number of corresponding equations. For example, a distance constraint fixes 1 parameter, and then has weight 1.*

So, the degree of freedom analysis exploits a structural property of the geometric constraint graph, called *structural rigidity*[2].

Definition 3 *Let S be a geometric constraint problem, and let $G = (O, C)$ be the corresponding weighted geometric constraint graph. Let W be the function which computes the difference between the sum of object weights and the sum of constraint weights: $W(G) = \sum_{o \in O}(w(o)) - \sum_{c \in C}(w(c))$.*
*In dimension d, the system S is **structurally rigid** (in short **s-rigid**) iff:*

- $W(G) = d(d+1)/2$
- *For every sub-graph G' of G, $W(G') \geq d(d+1)/2$*

*An s-rigid sub-graph of a geometric constraint graph will be called a **cluster** in this paper. Intuitively, in 2D, a cluster has 3 degrees of freedom since it can be translated and rotated.*

The structural rigidity is similar to the property P defined in [LM98] and to the *density* notion introduced in [HLS97].

Recursive rigidification creates iteratively a new cluster in the graph: a single node replaces the objects in the created cluster, and arcs connecting several objects in this cluster to one object outside the cluster are condensed into a single arc labeled by the sum of the weights of the synthesized arcs. Figure 1 illustrates the above notions.

The planning phase aims at decomposing the whole system into a sequence of small blocks of equations. It interleaves two steps called *merge* and *extension* steps which produce clusters recursively:

- The **merge step** finds how to form a bigger cluster based on several clusters or geometric objects.
- The **extension step** extends the obtained cluster by adding to it connected objects one by one.

---

[1] Roughly, the a and b of the corresponding equation: $y = ax + b$
[2] The s-rigidity is a necessary condition to prove rigidity. However, it is not a sufficient condition, except for distance constraints between points in 2D [Hen92]. Hence it should only be considered as a heuristic to detect rigid subparts in a geometric constraint system. Several counterexamples in 2D and 3D show that redundant constraints are the main cause of failure of the guess given by the s-rigidity [LM98].

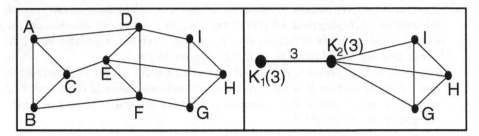

Fig. 1. Graphs associated to a geometric constraint problem.
(Left) All objects are points and distance constraints are posted between points.
All edges have weight 1 and all vertices have weight 2 (they are not labeled).
Every pair of connected points forms a cluster. Every triangle is also a cluster.
Points C, D, E do not form an s-rigid sub-graph since it has 4 degrees of freedom.
(Right) Another graph where triangles (A, B, C) and (D, E, F) have been condensed in two clusters K_1 and K_2. The arc of weight 3 condenses the arcs (A, D), (C, E) and (B, F)

Merge steps would be sufficient to perform a plan. However, a merge step can traverse the whole constraint graph. So, an extension is more or less a heuristic to perform an efficient merge step: one checks incrementally whether the s-rigidity is maintained when only one object is added to the current cluster.

The solving phase, also called construction phase, follows the plan given by the previous phase and computes the coordinates of the geometric objects in every cluster.

1.3   Existing Work

Recursive rigidification techniques have been developed [VSR92,BFH+95,FH93] [FH97,DMS98] to assemble points and lines in 2D systems constrained by distances and angles. [HV95] and [Kra92] describe first attempts to work in 3D. In all these systems, a specific algorithm is used to merge two or three predefined clusters. The possible construction "patterns" appear in a library.

Hoffmann et al. [HLS97,HLS98] have introduced a flow-based algorithm to perform the merge step. This algorithm finds a *minimal dense sub-graph* in a weighted geometric constraint graph, that is, it computes an s-rigid cluster of minimal size (i.e. which has no proper s-rigid sub-graph). Ad-hoc solving methods are used to achieve the actual construction. The algorithm works in any dimension, including 2D and 3D, and can be applied on any type of geometric objects.

The main limitation of Hoffmann's approach comes from the fact that no general method is proposed to perform the solving phase. Symbolic tools could also be considered but are generally not efficient enough to handle these problems. Of course, ad-hoc solving methods can be used, but they must be defined for every cluster the flow-based algorithm can generate.

1.4   Contribution

In this paper, we propose:

1. A new extension step's heuristic for Hoffmann's planning algorithm [HLS97]. The aim is to generate smaller subsystems of equations.
2. A new and general solving framework which is based on interval techniques. Interval narrowing algorithms [Lho93,HMD97] manage floating intervals and can solve a system of numeric equations by using filtering and domain splitting methods. They are used to compute solutions in every subsystem.
   Using interval techniques to carry out a construction step of recursive rigidification has two advantages: the approach is general and can replace ad-hoc methods related to specific patterns, and, no solutions are lost.

2   The Planning Phase

The goal of the planning phase is to find an ordering which can solve the constraints in an incremental way. More precisely, the aim is to identify rigid subparts, that can be solved independently (and then assembled).

Hoffmann et al. [HLS97] have introduced an algorithm which achieves such a planning. The main limit of their algorithm comes from the fact that large blocks of constraints have to be added in some cases. Thus the solving process may become very costly. We introduce here a heuristic to limit the number of constraints that are added at each step.

Next sub-section illustrates the principle and the limits of Hoffmann's algorithm on a short example. Afterwards, we detail the proposed heuristic.

2.1   Hoffmann's Algorithm

Hoffmann's planning algorithm builds a reverse tree of clusters called *cluster tree*: the root is the final cluster covering the whole system; the leaves are the geometric objects; there is an arc between a cluster K and all the clusters that have been merged to yield K.

Roughly speaking, the algorithm builds clusters in sequence by interleaving merge and extension steps. It stops as soon as the whole system has been rigidified or when the system cannot be rigidified further. The algorithm updates a geometric weighted graph G_m while achieving merge and extensions steps. For instance, consider an example in 2D made of 15 points and 27 distance constraints between them (see Figure 2 - G_m^0).

The first merge step finds the sub-graph $G = < A, B >$ of G_m. This cluster is extended until a fix-point is reached. The set of adjacent points of this cluster is $\{C, H, I\}$. Since $< A, B, I >$ is s-rigid, I is added to G. The same

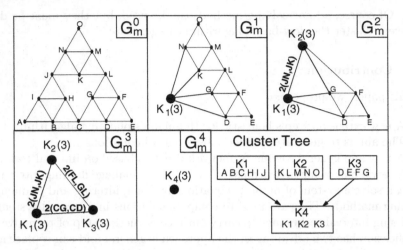

Fig. 2. Snapshots of the graph G_m during the execution of Hoffmann's planning method, and resulting cluster tree

process is performed to add H, C and J to G. Now the set of adjacent points is $\{D, G, N, K\}$. None of these points can be added by extension, so we have reached the fix-point $G =< A, B, I, H, C, J >$. A new vertex K_1 of weight 3 is added and A, B, I, H, C, J are removed from G_m as well as all constraints among them (see Figure 2 - G_m^1). K_1 is placed into the cluster tree and the next merge step is performed. It identifies $< M, N >$ as minimal s-rigid sub-graph of G_m. This cluster is extended to $K_2 =< M, N, O, K, L >$ (see Figure 2 - G_m^2). Note that K_2 could have been extended onto J if $< M, N >$ were identified at the beginning. Finally, G, F, D and E are merged into K_3 (note again that C and L could have been included in K_3) (see Figure 2 - G_m^3).

Since clusters do not share points, inter-cluster constraints (i.e., the distance constraints $dist(J, K)$, $dist(J, N)$, $dist(G, C)$, $dist(G, L)$, $dist(F, L)$ and $dist(C, D)$) are handled by the last merge step (see Figure 2 - G_m^4), for which the solving step can hence be expensive.

Therefore, we propose a new heuristic where clusters can share objects, the aim being to maximize the extension capabilities, and thus, to reduce the number of constraints which have to be handled during the merging steps. This heuristic generalizes previous ad-hoc techniques [BFH⁺95].

2.2   The Proposed Heuristic

Like Hoffmann's algorithm, Algorithm `Rigidification` interleaves merge and extension steps. To facilitate object sharing it uses the following two graphs:

– The merge graph G_m which corresponds to the graph of clusters used in Hoffmann's algorithm. However, in our algorithm, G_m is used only for the merge step.

– The extension graph G_e which is specially maintained for the extension step. It contains the shared objects as well as the objects which have not yet been included in a cluster.

The algorithm performs three main steps iteratively (within the `while` loop): a *merge step*, an *extension step* and an *update step*.

One merge step is achieved by the `MinimalSRigid`(G_m, d, G_e) function. This function first computes G_1, a minimal dense sub-graph of G_m, with the flow-based algorithm described in [HLS97]. The dense sub-graph is then converted into a sub-graph of G_e and returned. The empty set is returned if G_m contains a single node or if no s-rigid sub-graph can be found.

One extension step extends the cluster G_1 found by the merge step. The `repeat` loop incrementally adds one object to G_1. Objects are added as long as the obtained graph remains s-rigid.

The last step updates the two graphs G_m and G_e.

Updating the Graph G_m

A new cluster K is created in G_m and replaces the included clusters and objects (sub-graph G_2). This is performed by the function `Condense`(G_2, K, G_m) as follows: (a) replace all vertices in G_2, the sub-graph of G_m corresponding to G_1, by a single node K in G_m; (b) combine all arcs from one vertex v of $G_m - G_2$ to vertices of G_2 into one arc from v to K with a weight equal to the sum of the combined arcs.

The newly created cluster K may contain shared variables which have been previously included in other clusters. Coincidence constraints are thus added in G_m to take them into account. Intuitively, coincidence constraints are added to preserve the right number of degrees of freedom in G_m. They state that the different occurrences of a shared object correspond in fact to a single object (function `AddCoincidences`(K, G_m)).

Updating the Graph G_e

The nodes in the newly created cluster K are partitioned into two sets: the *interface objects* that are connected to other objects in G_e and the *internal objects*. Function `RemoveVertices` removes the internal objects since they are s-rigid relative to each other (that results from the fact that they are included in the same cluster K). In the opposite, interface objects remain in G_e since they may potentially be shared by other clusters in further steps.

To maintain the right number of degrees of freedom, the interface objects in G_e must be rigidified. The function `Rigidify` adds *interface constraints* between them in G_e as follows: if the cluster K contains two interface objects o_1 and o_2, a weighted arc (o_1, o_2) is added to make them s-rigid; if there are more than two interface objects, every other object o_i in K is rigidified by adding arcs (o_i, o_1) and (o_i, o_2) (see for coming [JTNR00]).

Algorithm `Rigidification` terminates since the number of objects in G_m decreases at each step. The correction is ensured by the fact that the s-rigidity property is preserved in G_m and G_e as long as the algorithm runs.

Algorithm 1 Rigidification (in G: Graph; **in** d: Integer; **out** CT: ClusterTree)

> {G is the initial weighted geometric graph; d is the dimension of the problem (2D, 3D); CT is the plan (cluster tree) that is produced by the algorithm.}
> $CT \leftarrow \emptyset$; $G_m \leftarrow G$; $G_e \leftarrow G$
> $G_1 \leftarrow$ `MinimalSRigid`(G_m, d, G_e) {First merge step}
> **while** $G_1 \neq \emptyset$ **do**
>   {Extension step}
>   **repeat**
>   **for all** $o \in G_e | \exists o_1 \in G_1$ and edge $(o, o_1) \in \text{Edges}(G_e)$ **do**
>   **if** $G_1 \cup \{o\}$ is s-rigid **then**
>   {Add o and corresponding edges to G_1}
>   `AddVertex`(G_1, o, G_e)
>   **end if**
>   **end for**
>   **until** FixPoint {G_1 is no more modified}
> $G_2 \leftarrow$ `Convert`(G_1, G_m) {G_2 is a sub-graph of G_m corresponding to G_1}
>   `Condense`(G_2, K, G_m) {Replace G_2 by a new vertex K in G_m}
>   `AddCoincidences`(K, G_m)
>   `InsertCluster`(K, CT) {Insert K in the cluster tree}
>   `Rigidify`(`InterfaceObjects`(G_1))   {Add interface constraints of G_1 in G_e}
>   `RemoveVertices`(`InternalObjects`(G_1), G_e)   {Remove from G_e internal objects and connected arcs}
> $G_1 \leftarrow$ `MinimalSRigid`(G_m, d, G_e) {Merge step}
> **end while**

2.3   Example

Figure 3 illustrates the behavior of Algorithm `Rigidification` on the example introduced in Figure 2.

The first merge and extension steps are similar to Hoffmann's one and yield a sub-graph G_1 containing the points A, B, I, H, C, J. A new vertex K_1 of weight 3 replaces these points in G_m. The internal points A, B, H, I are removed from G_e, along with the internal constraints, but an interface constraint is added between J and C.

The cluster K_2 is then created in the same way. It is condensed into G_m. Since K_2 includes the point J which also belongs to K_1, a coincidence constraint of weight 2 is added in G_m between K_1 and K_2.

The cluster K_3 is finally created. It includes all the remaining points in G_e, and in particular, the interface constraints. Then, the planning phase is finished.

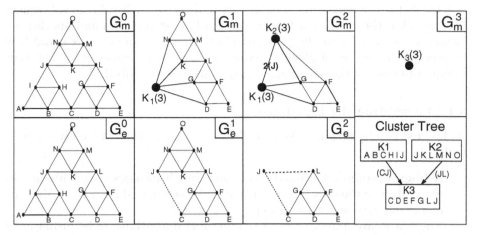

Fig. 3. Snapshots of the graphs G_m and G_e during the run of the algorithm, and obtained cluster tree. Interface constraints are drawn in dotted lines

2.4   Comparing with Hoffmann's Approach

Hoffmann's algorithm uses a single graph to achieve merging steps and extension steps whereas Algorithm `Rigidification` performs the extensions on a specific graph that contains shared objects. Thus, Algorithm `Rigidification` may be able to achieve more extensions. It is important to understand that one extension implies the creation of a system of equations the size of which is not greater than 3 in 2D (6 in 3D), that is, the number of degrees of freedom of the added object. Since this heuristic maximizes the number of extensions steps, it should reduce the solving cost of the merge steps.

For instance, on the previous example, Hoffmann's algorithm builds clusters K_1, K_2 and K_3 before merging them into K_4 (see Figure 2). This corresponds to 9 extension steps and 4 merge steps; the last one will have to merge 3 clusters with 6 distance constraints between them. On the same example, Algorithm `Rigidification` achieves 13 extensions and only 3 merges. None of these steps involve more than 2 distance constraints.

3   The Solving Phase

This section shows how to use interval constraint techniques for solving the tree of clusters built in the planning phase.

Atomic steps of the planning phase generate subsystems of equations, called *blocks* in the paper, that can be solved in sequence. Interval constraint techniques solve every block and yield numeric solutions[3]. When a solution is found

---

[3] A superset of the solutions is in fact obtained: eliminated parts of the search space never contain any solution, but the remaining non-empty intervals might contain no solution.

in a block, the corresponding variables are replaced by their value in subsequent blocks. When the resolution fails, a backtracking step occurs and another solution is searched for in the previous block. The next subsections detail how to generate the blocks of algebraic equations based on a cluster tree. Different solving processes of the decomposed system are also described.

3.1   Generating the Equations

A directed acyclic graph (DAG) of blocks is created while the cluster tree is built.

- A **block** contains a (sub)system of equations. It includes the equations corresponding to the arcs (geometric constraints) removed from G_e during one merge step or one extension step;
- There is an arc from a block A to a block B if a variable to be instantiated in A also occurs in an equation of B.

Note that interface constraints are considered in the same way as others in this process. Figure 4 provides an example of such a DAG of blocks.

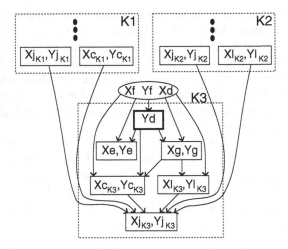

Fig. 4. DAG of blocks associated to the cluster tree of the example in Fig. 3. Blocks are represented by small rectangles showing the computed variables. All the blocks in K_3 are shown. The block at the top of K_3 is created by the merge step (merging D and F). Descendant blocks are created by extension. The last block contains the two interface constraints added during the process

Now, let us detail how interface constraints are handled. Each block computes its own set of variables. The variables corresponding to an interface object are replicated in each cluster where the object occurs. Object J shared by clusters K_1, K_2 and K_3 leads to define variables $x_{J_{K_1}}$, $y_{J_{K_1}}$, $x_{J_{K_2}}$, $y_{J_{K_2}}$, $x_{J_{K_3}}$, $y_{J_{K_3}}$.

Variables $x_{J_{K_1}}$, $y_{J_{K_1}}$ (resp. $x_{J_{K_2}}$, $y_{J_{K_2}}$) are computed when solving clusters K_1 (resp. K_2). When solving cluster K_3, the block computing $x_{J_{K_3}}$, $y_{J_{K_3}}$ is made of the 2 interface constraints $dist(J_3, L_3) = dist(J_2, L_2)$ and $dist(J_3, C_3) = dist(J_1, C_1)$. In this block, the last one in cluster K_3, all the variables except $x_{J_{K_3}}$, $y_{J_{K_3}}$ have already been computed in previous blocks.

Now we will describe the different solving processes based upon interval narrowing techniques.

3.2   Domain Splitting and Filtering per Block

A first approach to solve a DAG of blocks has been described at the beginning of this section. Standard filtering and domain splitting can compute a set of solutions in every block and an inter-block backtracking process is performed when an inconsistent combination of block solutions occurs.

Performing interval narrowing on a block is straightforward, the variables of the entire block being subject to domain splitting and filtering. However, one should pay attention to the inter-block process: the computed values, which will be replaced in a subsequent block, are not floating numbers, but an interval of floating points (even very small, e.g., 10^{-8} large). We could handle such constant intervals by slightly modifying the LNAR function of Numerica [IMD97] [4]. We have chosen another process: the middle point of the reduced constant interval replaces the variable in equations included in subsequent blocks. This middle point heuristic is easy and general. It is correct if the set of intervals obtained at the end is checked, by a filtering process, against all the equations in the entire system. In practice, this final check is very fast since the intervals are really small. Of course, this process does not guarantee to find all solutions but we did never lose any solution in practice on the tested examples.

This approach is very efficient because replacing a variable by a constant simplifies the system of equations.

3.3   Performing Propagation on the Whole System

Another algorithm could be applied that limits domain splitting in one block at a time, but performs filtering by propagation on the whole system. There are two different ways to implement propagation:

1. All the blocks are managed by a standard inter-block backtracking process, just like the pure backtracking algorithm described in the previous subsection. Two systems of equations are thus handled by the interval constraint solver: one system corresponding to the current block to be solved by filtering and domain splitting, and another one which includes the equations in the blocks not yet solved. The second system can be filtered by propagation when an interval is reduced in the first one. This approach will be called *block solving with propagation* in the rest of the paper.

---

[4] The LNAR function, applied to a variable in an equation, replaces all the other variables by a constant interval and searches for the left most zero.

2. Another approach, where all the system is in a single block, is called *global solving* in the following. It considers the given plan as a heuristic to select the next variables for domain splitting with respect to the decomposition. Their domains are split until the desired precision is reached. Filtering is applied on the full system after each split.

The global solving algorithm is simpler to design than block solving with propagation. However, global solving is less efficient for two reasons. First, all blocks are checked for filtering anyway. Second, it cannot benefit from the middle point heuristic.

Conceptually, it is possible to bring the inter-block backtracking process together with any solving algorithm that can yield several solutions for one block. Symbolic algorithms can be used when no trigonometric equations are required to model the system. Plugging such an algorithm in our inter-block process ensures completeness and could be considered for solving small blocks. On the contrary, classical numerical algorithms should not be used in this decomposition scheme since they provide only one solution per block and those partial solutions may not be combinable.

3.4   Unifying Reference Systems

Once the solving phase is finished, every object in the root cluster has been placed in the final reference system. Only internal objects of clusters have not yet been placed in this system. To do so, rigid-body transformations must be done on the cluster tree. The cluster tree is traversed from the root to the leaves. At each node, one performs a rigid body transformation, in the final reference system, of the coordinates belonging to the internal objects of the cluster. More precisely:

1. The coordinates of the interface objects are known in the final system, as the tree is followed from the root to the leaves, and are used them to compute the transformation coefficients.
2. The internal coordinates of the cluster are then recomputed in the final reference system, based on the obtained transformation matrix.

By traversing the tree in reverse order of its construction, a coordinate of an object is computed only once as an objects becomes internal only once.

4   Experimental Results

This section provides preliminary results on three examples (see Figure 5). Their constraint systems contain points and distance constraints. Since we wanted to compare the time spent for computing all solutions, we have adjusted the distance values in order to obtain a limited number of solutions per problem (128 for Ex1, 64 for Ex2 and 256 for Ex3).

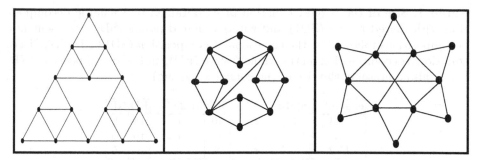

Fig. 5. From left to right, the three 2D examples we consider, made of points and distance constraints: Triangles (Ex1), Diamonds (Ex2) and Hexagon (Ex3)

First, we compare the decomposition obtained by recursive rigidification with a more general equational decomposition which works at the equation and variable level and does not take into account the s-rigidity property of the geometric system [AAJM93,BNT98]. This approach is based upon a structural analysis of the graph of variables and equations, using a maximum matching algorithm and a Dulmage and Mendelsohn decomposition. We also apply our solving techniques on this equational decomposition. For the sake of simplicity, we will use the following abbreviations:

- ED stands for the equational decomposition based on a maximum matching;
- SD1 denotes the decomposition based on shared objets we have introduced in Section 2 (Algorithm `Rigidification`);
- SD2 denotes Hoffmann's rigidification algorithm.

4.1 Maximal Block Size

We can see in Table 1 that the SD1 decomposition leads to smaller blocks than SD2.

The first two examples are decomposed by SD1 into blocks made of 2 equations. With the SD2 decomposition, the maximum block size is 10 or 12. In fact, these blocks of size 10 or 12 can further be decomposed by the equational decomposition technique and the blocks finally solved have a maximum size of 6 in both cases (SD2+ED). For SD1, ED cannot further decompose the obtained blocks. In the third example, a block of size 8 remains in both decompositions and cannot be decomposed by ED anymore.

4.2 Solving with Interval Narrowing Techniques

We provide here the time spent to solve the examples for different decompositions: SD1+ED, SD2+ED, ED and ND. Times for solving with SD1 decomposition are exactly the same as SD1+ED since the plan remains the same with or without applying ED. Times for solving SD2+ED are necessarily better than

Table 1. Size of the biggest equation block obtained by semantic decomposition with shared points (SD1) and without shared points (SD2), the semantic decompositions followed by the equational decomposition (SD1+ED, SD2+ED), equational decomposition on the whole system (ED), and no decomposition (ND, which also represents the size of the complete system)

examples	SD1	SD1+ED	SD2	SD2+ED	ED	ND
Ex1	2	2	10	6	14	26
Ex2	2	2	12	6	10	20
Ex3	8	8	8	8	8	20

times for SD2 alone since SD2+ED provides a better decomposition. For the decomposed systems, we run the 3 methods presented in Sections 3.2 and 3.3: the inter-block backtracking (M1), the inter-block backtracking with propagation (M2), and the global solving which uses the decomposition as a heuristic for choosing the next domain to split (M3).

All experiments were performed on a Pentium III 500, using Ilog Solver [ILO98], with the IlcNumerica library which implements domain filtering by Box-Consistency [BAH94].

Table 2. Results in CPU time (in seconds) for the decompositions SD1+ED, SD2+ED and ED with the solving methods M1, M2 et M3 and for a solving without decomposition (ND)

Examples	SD1+ED			SD2+ED			ED			ND
	M1	M2	M3	M1	M2	M3	M1	M2	M3	-
Ex1	17	9	455	43	28	1322	58	29	385	5795
Ex2	1.4	11	77	9	13	178	56	117	467	6640
Ex3	0.9	3.4	289	2.6	12.2	1646	1.5	3.7	533	2744

4.3   Analysis

These results show that:

- Any decomposition is always fruitful: without decomposition, the solving times may be 2 orders of magnitude higher.
- The semantic decomposition (SD1) based on rigidification yields in general smaller blocks than equational decomposition (ED). The performances are better when the maximal block size is smaller.
- Methods M1 and M2 give even better results than M3, which shows the interest of the middle point heuristic.

- The effect of the propagation depends on the problem itself: when many inter-block backtracks occur, like in Ex1, the inter-block constraint propagation (M2) does pay off.

5 Conclusion

This paper has introduced a complete framework for handling geometric constraints. It is composed of:

- A new heuristic for the planning algorithm which allows us to build small subsystems of equations. This semantic-guided phase yields a better decomposition of a rigid system than a syntactic one.
- A solving phase based on interval techniques. This approach is general and does not lose any solution. It is a promising alternative to ad-hoc or classical numeric approaches.

To validate this framework, further experiments have to be performed.

References

AAJM93. Samy Ait-Aoudia, Roland Jegou, and Dominique Michelucci. Reduction of constraint systems. In *Compugraphic*, 1993. 245

BAH94.   F. Benhamou, D. Mc Allester, and P. Van Hentenryck. Clp(intervals) revisited. In *Proc. Logic Programming, MIT Press*, 1994. 246

BFH+95. William Bouma, Ioannis Fudos, Christoph Hoffmann, Jiazhen Cai, and Robert Paige. Geometric constraint solver. *Computer Aided Design*, 27(6):487–501, 1995. 236, 238

BNT98.   Christian Bliek, Bertrand Neveu, and Gilles Trombettoni. Using graph decomposition for solving continuous csps. In *Principles and Practice of Constraint Programming, CP'98*, volume 1520 of *LNCS*, pages 102–116. Springer, 1998. 245

DMS98.   Jean-François Dufourd, Pascal Mathis, and Pascal Schreck. Geometric construction by assembling subfigures. *Artificial Intelligence*, 99:73–119, 1998. 236

FH93.   Iaonnis Fudos and Christoph Hoffmann. Correctness proof of a geometric constraint solver. Technical Report TR-CSD-93-076, Purdue University, West Lafayette, Indiana, 1993. 236

FH97.   Iaonnis Fudos and Christoph Hoffmann. A graph-constructive approach to solving systems of geometric constraints. *ACM Transactions on Graphics*, 16(2):179–216, 1997. 234, 236

Hen92.   Bruce Hendrickson. Conditions for unique realizations. *SIAM J Computing*, 21(1):65–84, 1992. 235

HLS97.   Christoph Hoffmann, Andrew Lomonosov, and Meera Sitharam. Finding solvable subsets of constraint graphs. In *Proc. Constraint Programming CP'97*, pages 463–477, 1997. 233, 234, 235, 236, 237, 239

HLS98.   Christoph Hoffmann, Andrew Lomonosov, and Meera Sitharam. Geometric constraint decomposition. In B. Brüderlin and D. Roller, editors, *Geometric Constraint Solving and Applications*, pages 170–195. Springer, 1998. 236

HMD97.   Pascal Van Hentenryck, Laurent Michel, and Yves Deville. *Numerica : A Modeling Language for Global Optimization.* MIT Press, 1997. 237, 243

HV95.   C. M. Hoffmann and P. J. Vermeer. A spatial constraint problem. In J.-P. Merlet and B. Ravani, editors, *Computational Kinematics'95*, pages 83–92. Kluwer Academic Publishers, 1995. 236

ILO98.   ILOG. Ilog solver reference manual. Technical report, ILOG, 1998. 246

JASR99. R. Joan-Arinyo and A. Soto-Riera. Combining constructive and equational constraint solving techniques. *ACM Transactions on Graphics*, 18(3):35–55, 1999. 234

JTNR00. Christophe Jermann, Gilles Trombettoni, Bertrand Neveu, and Michel Rueher. A constraint programming approach for solving rigid geometric systems. Technical Report 00-43, University of Nice, France, 2000. 239

Kra92.   G. Kramer. *Solving Geometric Constraint Systems.* MIT Press, 1992. 236

Lho93.   O. Lhomme. Consistency techniques for numeric csps. In *Proc. IJCAI*, Chambery, France, 1993. 237

LM98.   Hervé Lamure and Dominique Michelucci. Qualitative study of geometric constraints. In Beat Bruderlin and Dieter Roller, editors, *Geometric Constraint Solving and Applications*, pages 234–258. Springer, 1998. 235

VSR92.   A. Verroust, F. Schonek, and D. Roller. Rule oriented method for parametrized computer aided design. *Computer Aided Design*, 24(6):531–540, 1992. 236

Maintaining Arc-Consistency within Dynamic Backtracking

Narendra Jussien, Romuald Debruyne, and Patrice Boizumault

École des Mines de Nantes
4 rue Alfred Kastler – BP 20722, F-44307 Nantes Cedex 3
{jussien,rdebruyn,boizu}@emn.fr

Abstract. Most of complete search algorithms over Constraint Satisfaction Problems (CSP) are based on *Standard Backtracking*. Two main enhancements of this basic scheme have been studied: first, to integrate constraint propagation as mac which maintains arc consistency during search; second, intelligent backtrackers which avoid repeatedly falling in the same dead-ends by recording nogoods as *Conflict-directed BackJumping* (cbj) or *Dynamic Backtracking* (dbt). Integrations of constraint propagation within intelligent backtrackers have been done as mac-cbj which maintains arc consistency in cbj. However, Bessière and Régin have shown that mac-cbj was very rarely better than mac. However, the inadequacy of mac-cbj is more related to the fact that cbj does not avoid thrashing than to the cost of the management of nogoods.
This paper describes and evaluates mac-dbt which maintains arc-consistency in dbt. Experiments show that mac-dbt is able to solve very large problems and that it remains very stable as the size of the problems increases. Moreover, mac-dbt outperforms mac on the structured problems we have randomly generated.

1 Introduction

Most of complete search algorithms over Constraint Satisfaction Problems (CSP) are based on *Standard Backtracking* (sb): a depth-first search is performed using chronological backtracking. Various *intelligent* backtrackers have been proposed: *Conflict-directed BackJumping* (cbj) [16], *Dynamic Backtracking* (dbt) [10], *Partial order Dynamic Backtracking* (pdb) [11], *Generalized Dynamic Backtracking* (gpb) [6], etc. In those algorithms, information (namely nogoods) is kept when encountering inconsistencies so that the forthcoming search will not get back to already known traps in the search space.

Constraint propagation has been included in sb leading to forward checking fc and more recently to the *Maintaining Arc-Consistency* algorithm (mac) [18]. mac is nowadays considered as one of the best algorithms for solving CSP [5].

Several attempts to integrate constraint propagation within intelligent backtrackers have been done: for example, Prosser has proposed mac-cbj which maintains arc consistency in cbj [16]. But, Bessière and Régin [5] have stopped further research in that field by showing that mac-cbj was very rarely better than mac.

R. Dechter (Ed.): CP 2000, LNCS 1894, pp. 249–261, 2000.
© Springer-Verlag Berlin Heidelberg 2000

They concluded that there was no need to spend time nor space for intelligent backtracking because the brute force of mac simply does it more quickly.

From our point of view, the inadequacy of mac-cbj is more related to the fact that cbj does not avoid thrashing[1] than to the cost of the management of no-goods. When backtracking occurs, cbj comes back to a relevant assignment, and then forgets all the search space developed since this assignment has been performed: as sb, cbj has a **multiplicative** behavior on independent sub-problems. dbt does not only use nogoods to perform *intelligent* backtracking but also to avoid thrashing and so becomes **additive** on independent sub-problems [10].

[5] had another point preventing the use of nogoods: it is always possible to find an intelligent labeling heuristic so that a *standard backtracking*-based algorithm will perform a search as efficiently as an intelligent backtracker. In our experience, using a good heuristic reduces the number of problems on which the algorithm thrashes but does not make it additive on independent subproblems: there are still problems on which the heuristic cannot prevent thrashing.

Although many works have been done about dbt, nothing, as far as we know, has ever been published on maintaining arc consistency in dbt. Even *Forward Checking* and *Dynamic Backtracking* (fc+dbt) has never been fully described [21].

The aim of this paper is to describe and evaluate mac-dbt which maintains arc-consistency in dbt. We first recall the principles of dbt and then describe how to integrate constraint propagation. Then we experiment mac-dbt and compare it to dbt, fc-dbt and mac. These experiments show that mac-dbt is able to solve very large problems and that it remains very stable as the size of the problems arise. Furthermore, mac-dbt outperfoms mac on the structured problems we have randomly generated.

2   Improving Standard Backtracking

To increase the search efficiency, intelligent backtrackers store for each dead-end a **nogood**, namely a subset of assignments responsible of the dead-end. Record-ing this information avoids falling repeatedly in the same dead-ends. *Dependency Directed Backtracking* (ddb) [20] was the first algorithm to use this enhancement, however it has an important drawback: its space complexity is exponential since the number of nogoods it stores increases monotically.

To address this problem, algorithms such as cbj and dbt eliminate nogoods that are no longer relevant to the current variable assignment. By doing so, the space complexity remains polynomial.

---

[1] A thrashing behavior consists in repeatedly performing the same search work due to the backtrack mechanism.

2.1 Nogoods and Eliminating Explanations

Let consider a CSP (V, D, C). A **nogood** is a globally inconsistent partial assignment of values a_i to variables v_i (no solution can contain a nogood)[2]:

$$C \vdash \neg (v_1 = a_1 \wedge \ldots \wedge v_k = a_k) \tag{1}$$

For every nogood, a variable v_j can be selected and the previous formula rewritten as:

$$C \vdash \bigwedge_{i \in [1..k] \backslash j} (v_i = a_i) \rightarrow v_j \neq a_j \tag{2}$$

The left hand side of the implication constitutes an **eliminating explanation** for the removal of value a_j from the domain of variable v_j (noted $\texttt{expl}(v_j \neq a_j)$).

When the domain of variable v_j becomes empty during filtering, a new nogood is deduced from the eliminating explanations of all its removed values:

$$C \vdash \neg \left(\bigwedge_{a \in d(v_j)} \texttt{expl}(v_j \neq a) \right) \tag{3}$$

There generally exist several eliminating explanations for a value removal. One may want to record all of them as in ddb but as we saw this leads to an exponential space complexity. Another way relies in *forgetting* (erasing) nogoods that are no longer relevant[3] to the current variable assignment. By doing so, the space complexity remains polynomial. dbt (and its extensions pdb, gpb) therefore records only **one** explanation at a time for a value removal. In the worst case, the space required to manage nogoods is $O(n^2 d)$ where n is the number of variables and d the maximum size of the domains in the CSP. Indeed, the size of each eliminating explanation is at most $(n - 1)$ and there are at most $n \times d$ eliminating explanations: one for each value of each domain.

2.2 From Standard to Dynamic Backtracking

When a failure occurs, sb, cbj and dbt have to identify the assignment to be reconsidered (suspected to be a **culprit** for the failure).

sb always considers the most recent assignment to be a culprit. This selection may be completely irrelevant for the current failure leading to unuseful exploration of parts of the search tree already known to be dead-ends.

cbj stores the nogoods but not like in dbt. In cbj a conflict set is associated to each variable: CS_{v_i} (for the variable v_i) contains the set of the assigned variables whose value is in conflict with the value of v_i. When identifying a dead-end while assigning v_i, cbj considers the most recent variable in CS_{v_i} to be a culprit. But

---

[2] The *nogood* is a logical consequence of the set of constraints C.

[3] A nogood is said to be relevant if all the assignments in it are still valid in the current search state [3].

as opposed to dbt, with cbj a backtrack occurs: the conflict sets and domains of the future variables are reset to their original value. By doing so, cbj forgets a lot of information that could have been useful. This leads to thrashing.

dbt, similarly to cbj, selects the most recent variable in the computed nogood (the conflict set of cbj) in order to undo the assignment. However, thanks to the eliminating explanations, dbt only removes related information that depends on it and so avoids thrashing: useful information is kept. Indeed, there is no real backtracking in dbt and like in a repair method, only the assignments that caused the contradiction are undone.

Consequently, sb and cbj have both a multiplicative behavior on independent sub-problems while dbt is additive.

Note that sb can also be considered as selecting the most recent assignment of a nogood, namely the nogood that contains all the current variable assignments (which fails to give really relevant information).

2.3   Dynamic Backtracking

In the remaining, dom_i is the initial domain of the variable i and D_i is the current domain of this variable. The algorithm Dynamic Backtracking is presented in fig. 1.

Function dbt performs the main loop which tries to assign values to variables as long as a complete consistent assignment has not been found. $\mathcal{V}$ will denote the set of variables to be assigned and I is the current instantiation. Function dbt-giveValueAndCheck(I, $\mathcal{V}$, i, a) determines if the new partial assignment (including the new assignment $i = a$) is consistent; if not, this function returns a nogood explaining the failure. In order to restore a coherent state of computation, the function dbt-handleContradiction jumps to another consistent partial assignment. Domains and nogoods are restored thanks to the eliminating explanations (see function dbt-updateDomains).

dbt-checkConstraintsBackwards checks backwards whether the constraints are verified for the new current partial assignment. If not, this function returns such a failing constraint. From that constraint, dbt-giveValueAndCheck computes a nogood (line 8). This nogood contains only the assignments involved in the failure.

Function dbt-handleContradiction is the contradiction handling mechanism. The assignment to be undone is determined on line 2 and *backtracking* (or more exactly *jumping*) is achieved by removing irrelevant nogoods which is performed by the dbt-updateDomains function.

In fact, dbt does not perform real backtracks. When a dead-end occurs, it reconsiders only the most recent assignment that caused the contradiction. Especially, all the assignments that not caused the dead-end remain unchanged. This is why dbt has an additive behavior on independent sub-problems.

```
function dbt()
1   I ← ∅;
2   while V ≠ ∅ do
3       (i, a) ← chooseAssignment(V, D);
4       E ← dbt-giveValueAndCheck(I, V, i, a);
5       if E is not a success then dbt-handleContradiction(E, I, V)
6   return I;

function dbt-giveValueAndCheck(I, V, i, a)
1   C_i = constraint(i = a); C ← C ∪ {C_i} ;
2   D_i ← {a} ;
3   foreach b ∈ D_i s.t.  b ≠ a do
4       expl(i ≠ b) ← {C_i};
5   I ← I ∪ {(i, a)} ; V ← V\{i} ;
6   c ← dbt-checkConstraintsBackwards(I);
7   if c is a success then return success
8   else return {C_i} ∪ {C_k|k ∈ vars(c)}

function dbt-checkConstraintsBackwards(I)
1   foreach c ∈ C s.t.(vars(c) ∩ V = ∅) do
2       if c is not verified then return c ;
3   return success;

function dbt-handleContradiction(E, I, V)
1   if E = ∅ then fail
2   C_j ← mostRecentCulprit(E); b ← I[j];
3   dbt-updateDomains({(k, c)|C_j ∈ expl(k ≠ c)});
4   I ← I\(j, b)}; V ← V ∪ {j};
5   D_j ← D_j\{b}; expl(j ≠ b) ← E\{C_j};
6   if D_j = ∅ then dbt-handleContradiction(⋃_{a∈dom_j} expl(j ≠ a), I, V);

function dbt-updateDomains(Back)
1   foreach (i, a) ∈ back do
2       expl(i ≠ a) ← ∅;  D_i ← D_i ∪ {a};
```

Fig. 1. Dynamic Backtracking

3   Integrating Constraint Propagation

Integrating constraint propagation in dbt is more complex than integrating forward checking [19].

First, when a failure occurs, computing nogoods as before (the variable assignments in the failing constraint) will not even provide a nogood. Effects of propagation (value removals) have to be taken into account: eliminating explanations produced by the filtering algorithm need to be kept.

Second, another problem arises when undoing a variable assignment. Putting back in the domains values with irrelevant explanations will not be sufficient since there may exist another relevant explanation for the deleted value. Indeed, there may exist several ways of removing a value through propagation and since only one way is retained as an explanation, any value restoration need to be confirmed by the propagation algorithm. This is similar to what is done for maintaining arc-consistency in dynamic CSPs [4]. A proof of termination can be found in [12].

```
function mac-dbt()
1   if (AC4() = false) then return ∅;
2   I ← ∅ ; Q ← ∅ ;
3   while V ≠ ∅ do
4       (i, a) ← chooseAssignment(V, D);
5       E ← mac-dbt-giveValueAndCheck(I, V, i, a, Q);
6       if E is not a success then mac-dbt-handleContradiction(E, I, V, Q)
7   return I;
```

```
function mac-dbt-handleContradiction(E, I, V, Q)
1   if E = ∅ then fail
2   Cj ← mostRecentCulprit(E); b ← I[j];
3   E' ← mac-dbt-updateDomains({(k, c)|Cj ∈ expl(k ≠ c)}, Q);
4   I ← I\{(j, b)}; V ← V ∪ {j};
5   if E' is not a success then mac-dbt-handleContradiction(E', I, V, Q);
6   if (E\{Cj}) ⊆ C then
7       expl(j ≠ b) ← E\{Cj}; Dj ← Dj\{b};
8       Q ← Q ∪ {(j, b)};
9       E' ← mac-dbt-propagSuppress(Q);
10      if E' is not a success then mac-dbt-handleContradiction(E', I, V, Q);
```

```
function mac-dbt-propagSuppress(Q)
1   while (Q ≠ ∅) do
2       (i, a) ← dequeue(Q) ;
3       if expl(i ≠ a) ⊆ C then
4           foreach Cij ∈ C do
5               E ← mac-dbt-localArcConsExpl(Cij, i, a, Q) ;
6               if E is not a success then return E;
7   return success;
```

```
function mac-dbt-localArcConsExpl(Cij, i, a, Q)
1   foreach b ∈ Dj  s.t.  b ∈ supports(Cij, a) do
2       nbSupports(j, b)- -;
3       if nbSupports(j, b) = 0 then
4           Dj ← Dj\{b} ;  expl(j ≠ b) ← ⋃_{a' ∈ supports(Cji, b)} expl(i ≠ a');
5           Q ← Q ∪ {(j, b)};
6           if Dj = ∅ then return ⋃_{a' ∈ domj} expl(j ≠ a');
7   return success
```

```
function mac-dbt-giveValueAndCheck(I, V, i, a, Q)
1   Ci = constraint(i = a); C ← C ∪ {Ci} ;
2   Di ← {a} ;
3   foreach b ∈ Di  s.t.  b ≠ a do
4       expl(i ≠ b) ← {Ci};
5       Q ← Q ∪ {(i, b)};
6   E ← mac-dbt-propagSuppress(Q);
7   if E is a success then
8       I ← I ∪ {(i, a)}; V ← V\{i};
9 return E;
```

```
function mac-dbt-updateDomains(Back, Q)
1   foreach (i, a) ∈ back do
2       expl(i ≠ a) ← ∅; Di ← Di ∪ {a};
3   foreach (i, a) ∈ back do
4       if ∃Cij ∈ C s.t. (i, a) has no support on Cij then Q ← Q ∪ {(i, a)};
5   return mac-dbt-propagSuppress(Q);
```

Fig. 2. mac-dbt

3.1 Implementing `mac-dbt`

First, we describe our proposal in the sight of the two previous problems. Then we address an implementation issue and finally discuss complexity results.

Computing Nogoods during Filtering The main loop of the algorithm remains unchanged (see function `mac-dbt` in fig. 2 compared to function `dbt` in fig. 1) except for the call to the `dbt-giveValueAndCheck` and `dbt-handle-Contradiction` functions which are replaced by a call to the `mac-dbt-give-ValueAndCheck` and `mac-dbt-handleContradiction` functions. `mac-dbt-give-ValueAndCheck(`I`, `$\mathcal{V}$`, `i`, `a`, `Q`)` merely assigns the value a to the variable i by removing all the other values from its domain and propagating those removals thanks to the `mac-dbt-propagSuppress` function.

`mac-dbt-propagSuppress` constantly takes a value removal from the propagation queue in order to propagate it on the related constraints. The key point is that the propagation scheme for any constraint needs to *explain* (to give an eliminating explanation for) each of its value removal. Function `mac-dbt-localArc-ConsExpl` shows how to do it for an `ac4`-like constraint propagation handling. When the number of supports for a given value of a variable reaches zero, that value needs to be removed. An explanation for that can be derived from the explanation for the removal of each of the supports (line 4 of the function).

Undoing Past Computations without Real Backtracking The `dbt-update-` Domains function needs to be modified to take into account the complete arc-consistent state restoration after undoing a variable assignment. This leads to the `mac-dbt-updateDomains` function.

The modifications (from `dbt-updateDomains`) starts at line 3 where value restorations are tested against each constraint of the system in order to get back to an arc-consistent state. If a value has been unduly reinserted, it is removed and all those removals are then propagated thanks to `mac-dbt-propagSuppress`.

Handling New Contradiction Cases First of all undoing a variable assignment as in lines 3–4 of `mac-dbt-handleContradiction` may not be as straightforward as in the original algorithm since that undoing may not be sufficient to come back to a consistent state due to constraint propagation. That is why it may be needed to handle a new contradiction: Henceforth the recursive call to `mac-dbt-handleContradiction` at line 5.

Moreover, that contradiction handling may lead to variable unassignment making irrelevant the would-be explanation for removing the original unassigned value to the first-place failing variable. Hence, the test in line 6 before actually removing the value which conversely may lead to a new contradiction that must be handled.

3.2 Complexity Issues

As stated above, the total space complexity needed to manage nogoods is in the worst case $O(n^2 d)$. Using local consistency algorithms provides very short explanations since the assignments appearing in the explanations are more relevant than in the explanations of dbt. In practice, the space required to store the explanations is less important than the space needed to represent the problem $O(ed^2)$. Furthermore, mac-dbt does not store information to backtrack to a previous state on a stack, which leads to lower space requirements compared to traditional approaches. Finally, space requirement had never been a limitation for our experiments, even on very large instances.

The time complexity involves a slight overhead comparing to the mac algorithm to compute explanations but obviously this does not change the worst case time complexity. This is a quite inexpensive additional task that allows avoiding some thrashing and provides explanations for failures.

4 Discussion

4.1 Dynamic Arc-Consistency

There are similarities between mac-dbt and the techniques used to maintain arc-consistency in dynamic CSPs [4,7] since they both use a deduction maintenance system. However, there are real differences between the system of **justifications** used by DnAC-4 (and DnAC-6) and the system of explanations used by mac-dbt. Furthermore, the aim of the algorithms DnAC-* is to maintain arc consistency in dynamic CSPs and not to solve static CSPs. Even if we consider an assignment as a constraint restricting a domain, the ideas of DnAC-* cannot be used to solve a static CSP without an important work (explain how to build the succession of constraint additions/relaxations that have to be performed to solve the problem, specify how to deduce the set of constraints responsible of a dead-end, tell which of the assignments has to be reconsidered when a dead-end occurs, etc.).

4.2 Extensions

The key feature of mac-dbt relies on eliminating explanations which are associated to value removals. This could be extended to set of values: a first work on using explanations for intervals has been done for numerical CSP [14].

Any constraint solver able to provide explanations can be integrated in dbt in the same way we previously described it for arc-consistency. It would be the case for high level of *stronger* consistencies in binary CSP (see [9,8] for high-level consistencies) or for non-binary constraints.

mac-dbt can also be used for different kinds of problems, for example to drastically improve the resolution of scheduling problems [13].

5   Experiments

Our experiments have been performed with an implementation of `mac-dbt` where constraints are handled *à la* `ac6`. `dbt` and `fc-dbt` were implemented using the eliminating explanations developed for `mac-dbt` leading to comparable versions of those algorithms.

5.1   `dbt` and `fc-dbt` versus `mac-dbt`

In our first set of experiments, we compare the three *dynamic backtracking* based algorithms: `dbt`, `fc-dbt` and `mac-dbt`.

Figure 3 shows results obtained on randomly generated[4] problems of 15 variables whose domain size is 10 with 45 constraints (a 43% density). The varying parameter is the tightness of the considered constraints: from 10% to 90%.

The figure shows that the more constraint propagation is provided into the `dbt`, the less time is required to get an answer. On those problems, the advantage of `mac-dbt` is obvious.

5.2   `mac-dbt` versus `mac`

We compare now `mac-dbt` with the `mac7ps` [17] version of `mac`. Following [2] experiments, we generated problems which have an inherent structure[5]: the phase transition characteristics of regular problems is exploited to conveniently generate under-constrained instances containing a well-concealed small sub-problem chosen closed to the phase transition. That structure cannot be identified using a preprocessing phase and the problems need to be actually solved in order to discover that particularity.

Our first experiments were conducted on large instances: a series of problems consisting in 200 variables with domains of size 10 with 2500 constraints containing a small hard to solve instance of 15 variables and 43 constraints. Although `mac-dbt` solved each of that instances in a matter of seconds, it appeared that, for some of the instances, `mac` was unable to give any answer within several days of computation.

We therefore tried to find problems for which `mac` and `mac-dbt` performances were more similar. Figure 4 reports results obtained on a specific set of problems: the structured CSPs we have generated involve from 20 to 26 variables, each having 15 values in its domain. Each CSP contains two subproblems of 8 variables at .57 density and .76 tightness. Additional constraints of .05 tightness have been added in order to connect any couple of variables that are not in the same subproblem. Note that despite the artificial construction of those problems, they are more likely to be encountered in real life than pure random problems.

---

[4] D. Frost, C. Bessiere, R. Dechter, and J.C. Regin. Random uniform CSP Generators, 1996, http://www.ics.uci.edu/~dfrost/csp/generator.html

[5] As expected, average results on pure random CSP present a slight overhead for `mac-dbt` due to the explanations management that is of no benefit on that kind of problems.

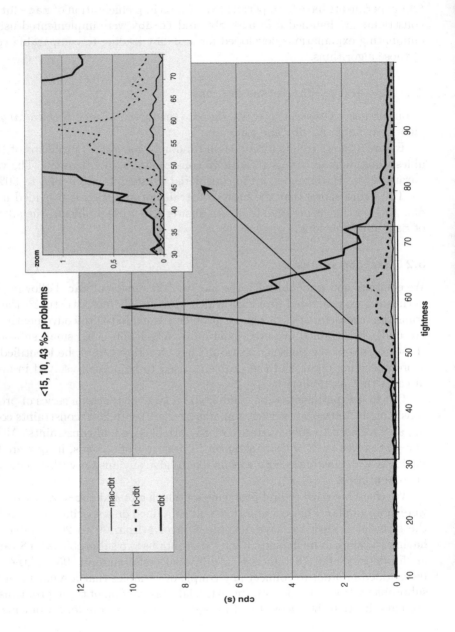

Fig. 3. Comparing dbt, fc-dbt and mac-dbt

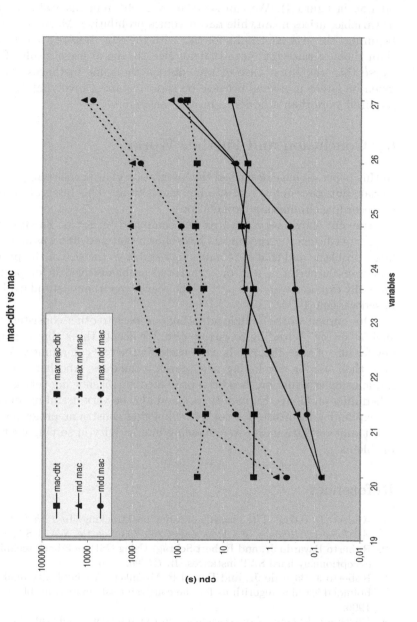

Fig. 4. Comparing mac-dbt and mac

We report in figure 4 the average and maximum cpu time in seconds to solve series of 500 problems in each point for both mac-dbt and mac using the min dom/deg and mindom variable dynamic ordering heuristic (resp. mdd mac and md mac in figure 4). We can see that mac-dbt remains stable as the number of variables arises meanwhile mac becomes prohibitive. Moreover, even if at the beginning the average results for mac with the min dom/deg heuristic are better than those of mac-dbt, note that for size 26, the average result of mac is even worse than the worst case of mac-dbt on the same instances. No results are given on larger problems because on some instances involving 27 variables mac required more than 4 hours to provide answers.

6   Conclusion and Further Works

In this paper we have described the integration of arc-consistency in dbt, leading to mac-dbt. mac-dbt is to dbt what mac is to sb. This integration relies mainly on recording eliminating explanations.

mac-dbt shows very good results compared to dbt or fc-dbt: propagation improves efficiency. Experiments have shown that mac-dbt was able to solve very large problems and that it remains very stable as the size of the problems arises and even outperforms mac on structured problems even if for particular cases mac-dbt explores a greater part of the search tree than a standard backtracking based version [1].

Our current works include adapting our ideas to other consistency techniques such as quick [8] leading to quick-dbt. We deeply think that explanations, the key feature of mac-dbt, can be very useful in the CSP community. We have shown here their use for developing new search techniques. Another new search technique using explanations has been presented in [15] showing very good results on scheduling problems. Explanations could also be very useful in other fields such as explaining inconsistencies when debugging constraint programs or enabling constraint relaxation and so enhancing interactivity in solving over constrained problems.

References

1. Andrew B. Baker. The hazards of fancy backtracking. In *12th National Conf. on Artificial Intelligence, AAAI94*, pages 288–293, Seattle, WA, USA, 1994.
2. Roberto Bayardo Jr. and Robert Schrag. Using CSP look-back techniques to solve exceptionnaly hard SAT instances. In *CP'96*, 1996.
3. Roberto J. Bayardo Jr. and Daniel P. Miranker. A complexity analysis of space-bounded learning algorithms for the constraint satisfaction problem. In *AAAI'96*, 1996.
4. Christian Bessière. Arc consistency in dynamic constraint satisfaction problems. In *Proceedings AAAI'91*, 1991.
5. Christian Bessière and Jean-Charles Régin. MAC and combined heuristics: Two reasons to forsake FC (and CBJ?) on hard problem. In *CP'96*, Cambridge, MA, 1996.

6. C. Bliek. Generalizing partial order and dynamic backtracking. In *Proceedings of AAAI*, 1998.
7. Romuald Debruyne. Arc-consistency in dynamic CSPs is no more prohibitive. In 8th *Conference on Tools with Artificial Intelligence (TAI'96)*, pages 299–306, Toulouse, France, 1996.
8. Romuald Debruyne. *Local consistencies for large CSPs*. PhD thesis, Université de Montpellier II, December18 1998. In French.
9. Romuald Debruyne and Christian Bessière. From restricted path consistency to max-restricted path consistency. In *CP'97*, pages 312–326, Linz, Austria, October 1997.
10. Matthew L. Ginsberg. Dynamic backtracking. *Journal of Artificial Intelligence Research*, 1:25–46, 1993.
11. Matthew L. Ginsberg and David A McAllester. Gsat and dynamic backtracking. In *International Conference on the Principles of Knowledge Representation (KR94)*, pages 226–237, 1994.
12. Narendra Jussien. *Relaxation de contraintes pour les CSP dynamiques*. PhD thesis, Université de Rennes I, October24 1997. In French.
13. Narendra Jussien and Christelle Guéret. Improving branch and bound algorithms for open shop problems. In *Conference of the International Federation of Operational Research Societies (IFORS'99)*, Beijing, China, August 1999.
14. Narendra Jussien and Olivier Lhomme. Dynamic domain splitting for numeric csp. In *European Conference on Artificial Intelligence*, pages 224–228, Brighton, United Kingdom, August 1998.
15. Narendra Jussien and Olivier Lhomme. The path-repair algorithm. In *CP99 Postconference workshop on Large scale combinatorial optimisation and constraints*, Alexandria, VA, USA, October 1999.
16. Patrick Prosser. MAC-CBJ: maintaining arc-consistency with conflict-directed backjumping. Research Report 95/177, Department of Computer Science – University of Strathclyde, 1995.
17. Jean-Charles Régin. *Développement d'outils algorithmiques pour l'Intelligence Artificielle. Application à la chimie organique*. Thèse de doctorat, Université de Montpellier II, 21 December 1995. In French.
18. Daniel Sabin and Eugene Freuder. Contradicting conventional wisdom in constraint satisfaction. In Alan Borning, editor, *Principles and Practice of Constraint Programming*, volume 874 of *Lecture Notes in Computer Science*. Springer, May 1994. (PPCP'94: Second International Workshop, Orcas Island, Seattle, USA).
19. Thomas Schiex and Gérard Verfaillie. Nogood Recording fot Static and Dynamic Constraint Satisfaction Problems. *International Journal of Artificial Intelligence Tools*, 3(2):187–207, 1994.
20. R. M. Stallman and G. J. Sussman. Forward reasoning and dependency directed backtracking in a system for computer-aided circuit analysis. *Artificial Intelligence*, 9:135–196, 1977.
21. Gérard Verfaillie and Thomas Schiex. Dynamic backtracking for dynamic csps. In Thomas Schiex and Christian Bessière, editors, *Proceedings ECAI'94 Workshop on Constraint Satisfaction Issues raised by Practical Applications*, Amsterdam, August 1994.

New Search Heuristics for Max-CSP*

Kalev Kask

Department of Information and Computer Science
University of California, Irvine, CA 92697-3425
kkask@ics.uci.edu

Abstract. This paper evaluates the power of a new scheme that generates search heuristics mechanically. This approach was presented and evaluated first in the context of optimization in belief networks. In this paper we extend this work to Max-CSP. The approach involves extracting heuristics from a parameterized approximation scheme called Mini-Bucket elimination that allows controlled trade-off between computation and accuracy. The heuristics are used to guide Branch-and-Bound and Best-First search, whose performance are compared on a number of constraint problems. Our results demonstrate that both search schemes exploit the heuristics effectively, permitting controlled trade-off between preprocessing (for heuristic generation) and search. These algorithms are compared with a state of the art complete algorithm as well as with the stochastic local search anytime approach, demonstrating superiority in some problem cases.

1 Introduction

In this paper we will present a general scheme of mechanically generating search heuristics for solving combinatorial optimization problems, using either Branch and Bound or Best First search. This heuristic generation scheme is based on the Mini-Bucket technique; a class of parameterized approximation algorithms for optimization tasks based on the bucket-elimination framework [1]. The mini-bucket approximation uses a controlling parameter which allows adjustable levels of accuracy and efficiency [3]. It was presented and analyzed for deterministic and probabilistic tasks such as finding the most probable explanation (MPE), belief updating, and finding the maximum a posteriori hypothesis. Encouraging empirical results were reported on a variety of classes of optimization domains, including medical-diagnosis networks and coding problems [5]. However, as evident by the error bound produced by these algorithms, in some cases the approximation is seriously suboptimal even when using the highest feasible accuracy level. In such cases, augmenting the Mini-Bucket approximation with search could be cost-effective.

Recently, we demonstrated how the mini-bucket scheme can be extended and used for mechanically generating heuristic search algorithms that solve optimization tasks, using the task of finding the Most Probable Explanation in a Bayesian

---

* This work was supported by NSF grant IIS-9610015 and by Rockwell Micro grant #99-030.

network. We showed that the functions produced by the Mini-Bucket method can serve as heuristic evaluation functions for search [7], [6]. These heuristics provide an upper bound on the cost of the best extension of a given partial assignment. Since the Mini-Bucket's accuracy is controlled by a bounding parameter, it allows heuristics having varying degrees of accuracy and results in a spectrum of search algorithms that can trade-off heuristic computation and search, all controlled by an input parameter.

In this paper we extend this approach to Max-CSP; an optimization version of Constraint Satisfaction. Instead of finding an assignment that satisfies all constraints, a Max-CSP solution satisfies a maximum number of constraints. We will use the Mini-Bucket approximation to generate a heuristic function that computes a lower bound on the minimum number of constraints that are violated in the best extension of any partial assignment. We evaluate the power of the generated heuristic within both *Branch-and-Bound* and *Best-First* search on a variety of randomly generated constraint problems. Specifically, we evaluate a Best-First algorithm with Mini-Bucket heuristics (BFMB) and a Branch-and-Bound algorithm with Mini-Bucket heuristics (BBMB), and compared empirically against the full bucket elimination and its Mini-Bucket approximation over randomly generated constraint satisfaction problems for solving the Max-CSP problem. We also compare the algorithms to two state of the art algorithms - PFC-MPRDAC [10] and a variant of Stochastic Local Search.

We show that both BBMB and BFMB exploit heuristics' strength in a similar manner: on all problem classes, the optimal trade-off point between heuristic generation and search lies in an intermediate range of the heuristics' strength. As problems become larger and harder, this optimal point gradually increases towards the more computationally demanding heuristics. We show that BBMB/BFMB outperform both SLS and PFC-MRDAC on some of the problems, while on others SLS and PFC-MRDAC are better. Unlike our results in [6], [7] here Branch-and-Bound clearly dominates Best-First search.

Section 2 provides preliminaries and background on the Mini-Bucket algorithms. Section 3 describes the main idea of the heuristic function generation which is built on top of the Mini-Bucket algorithm, proves its properties, and embeds the heuristic within Best-First and Branch-and-Bound search. Sections 4-6 present empirical evaluations, while Section 7 provides conclusions.

2   Background

2.1   Notation and Definitions

Constraint Satisfaction is a framework for formulating real-world problems as a set of constraints between variables. They are graphically represented by nodes corresponding to variables and edges corresponding to constraints between variables.

Definition 1 (Graph Concepts). *An* undirected graph *is a pair,* $G = \{V, E\}$, *where* $V = \{X_1, ..., X_n\}$ *is a set of variables, and* $E = \{(X_i, X_j)|X_i, X_j \in V\}$ *is the set of edges. The degree of a variable is the number of edges incident to it.*

Definition 2 (Constraint Satisfaction Problem (CSP)). *A Constraint Satisfaction Problem (CSP) is defined by a set of variables $X = \{X_1, ..., X_n\}$, associated with a set of discrete-valued domains, $D = \{D_1, ..., D_n\}$, and a set of constraints $C = \{C_1, ..., C_m\}$. Each constraint C_i is a pair (S_i, R_i), where R_i is a relation $R_i \subseteq D_{i1} \times ... \times D_{ik}$ defined on a subset of variables $S_i = \{X_{i1}, ..., X_{ik}\}$ called the scope of C_i, consisting of all tuples of values for $\{X_{i1}, ..., X_{ik}\}$ which are compatible with each other. For the max-CSP problem, we express the relation as a cost function $C_i(X_{i1} = x_{i1}, ..., X_{ik} = x_{ik}) = 0$ if $(x_{i1}, ..., x_{ik}) \in R_i$, and 1 otherwise. A constraint network can be represented by a constraint graph that contains a node for each variable, and an arc between two nodes iff the corresponding variables participate in the same constraint. A solution is an assignment of values to variables $x = (x_1, ..., x_n)$, $x_i \in D_i$, such that each constraint is satisfied. A problem that has a solution is termed* satisfiable *or* consistent*. A binary CSP is a one where each constraint involves at most two variables.*

Many real-world problems are often over-constrained and don't have a solution. In such cases, it is desirable to find an assignment that satisfies a maximum number of constraints.

Definition 3 (Max-CSP). *Given a CSP, the Max-CSP task is to find an assignment that satisfies the most constraints.*

Although a Max-CSP problem is defined as a maximization problem, it can be implemented as a minimization problem. Instead of maximizing the number of constraints that are satisfied, we minimize the number of constraints that are violated.

Definition 4 (Induced-width). *An ordered graph is a pair (G, d) where G is an undirected graph, and $d = X_1, ..., X_n$ is an ordering of the nodes. The width of a node in an ordered graph is the number of its earlier neighbors. The width of an ordering d, $w(d)$, is the maximum width over all nodes. The induced width of an ordered graph, $w^*(d)$, is the width of the induced ordered graph obtained by processing the nodes recursively, from last to first; when node X is processed, all its earlier neighbors are connected.*

Example 1. A graph coloring problem is a typical example of a CSP problem. It is defined as a set of nodes and arcs between the nodes. The task is to assign a color to each node such that adjacent nodes have different colors. An example of a constraint graph of a graph coloring problem containing variables A, B, C, D, and E, with each variable having 2 values (colors) is in Figure 1. The fact that adjacent variables must have different colors is represented by an inequality constraint. The problem in Figure 1 is inconsistent. When formulated as a Max-CSP problem, its solution satisfies all but one constraint. Given the ordering $d = A, E, D, C, B$ of the graph, the width and induced-width of the ordered graph is 3.

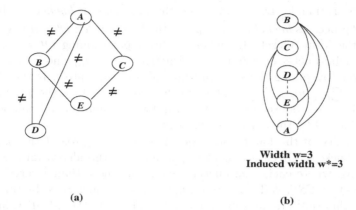

(a)   (b)

Fig. 1. a) Constraint graph of a graph coloring problem, b) an ordered graph
along $d = (A, E, D, C, B)$

2.2   Bucket and Mini-Bucket Elimination Algorithms

Bucket elimination is a unifying algorithmic framework for dynamic-
programming algorithms applicable to probabilistic and deterministic reasoning [1]. In the following we will present its adaptation to solving the Max-CSP
problem.

The input to a bucket-elimination algorithm consists of a collection of functions or relations (e.g., clauses for propositional satisfiability, constraints, or
conditional probability matrices for belief networks). Given a variable ordering,
the algorithm partitions the functions into buckets, each associated with a single variable. A function is placed in the bucket of its argument that appears
latest in the ordering. The algorithm has two phases. During the first, top-down
phase, it processes each bucket, from the last variable to the first. Each bucket
is processed by a variable elimination procedure that computes a new function
which is placed in a lower bucket. For Max-CSP, this procedure computes the
sum of all constraint matrices and minimizes over the bucket's variable. During
the second, bottom-up phase, the algorithm constructs a solution by assigning a
value to each variable along the ordering, consulting the functions created during
the top-down phase (for more details see [8]). It can be shown that

Theorem 1. *[1] The time and space complexity of Elim-Max-CSP applied along
order d, are exponential in the induced width $w^*(d)$ of the network's ordered
moral graph along the ordering d.* □

The main drawback of bucket elimination algorithms is that they require too
much time and, especially, too much space for storing intermediate functions.
Mini-Bucket elimination is an approximation scheme designed to avoid this space
and time complexity of full bucket elimination [3] by partitioning large buckets into smaller subsets called mini-buckets which are processed independently.

Here is the rationale. Let $h_1, ..., h_j$ be the functions in $bucket_p$. When *Elim-Max-CSP* processes $bucket_p$, it computes the function h^p: $h^p = min_{X_p} \sum_{i=1}^{j} h_i$. Instead, the Mini-Bucket algorithm creates a partitioning $Q\prime = \{Q_1, ..., Q_r\}$ where the mini-bucket Q_l contains the functions $h_{l_1}, ..., h_{l_k}$ and it processes each mini-bucket (by taking the sum and minimizing) separately. It therefore computes $g^p = \sum_{l=1}^{r} min_{X_p} \sum_{l_i} h_{l_i}$. Clearly, $h^p \geq g^p$. Therefore, the lower bound g^p computed in each bucket yields an overall lower bound on the number of constraints violated by the output assignment.

The quality of the lower bound depends on the degree of the partitioning into mini-buckets. Given a bounding parameter i, the algorithm creates an i-partitioning, where each mini-bucket includes no more than i variables. Algorithm *MB-Max-CSP(i)*, described in Figure 2, is parameterized by this i-bound. The algorithm outputs not only a lower bound on the Max-CSP value and an assignment whose number of violated constraints is an upper bound, but also the collection of augmented buckets. By comparing the lower bound to the upper bound, we can always have a bound on the error for the given instance.

Algorithm MB-Max-CSP(i)
Input: A constraint network $P(X, D, C)$; an ordering of the variables d. Each constraint is represented as a function $C_i(X_{i1} = x_{i1}, ..., X_{ik} = x_{ik}) = 0$ if $(x_{i1}, ..., x_{ik}) \in R_i$, and 1 otherwise.
Output: An upper bound on the Max-CSP, an assignment, and the set of ordered augmented buckets.
1. **Initialize:** Partition constraints into buckets. Let $S_1, ..., S_j$ be the scopes of constraints in $bucket_p$.
2. **Backward** For $p \leftarrow n$ down-to 1, do
• **If** $bucket_p$ contains an instantiation $X_p = x_p$, assign $X_p = x_p$ to each h_i and put each in appropriate bucket.
• **Else,** for $h_1, h_2, ..., h_j$ in $bucket_p$, generate an (i)-partitioning, $Q\prime = \{Q_1, ..., Q_r\}$. For each $Q_l \in Q\prime$ containing $h_{l_1}, ...h_{l_t}$ generate function h^l, $h^l = min_{X_p} \sum_{i=1}^{t} h_{l_i}$. Add h^l to the bucket of the largest-index variable in $U_l \leftarrow \bigcup_{i=1}^{j} S(h_{l_i}) - \{X_p\}$.
3. **Forward** For $p = 1$ to n do, given $x_1, ..., x_{p-1}$ choose a value x_p of X_p that minimizes the sum of all the cost functions in X_p's bucket.
4. Output the ordered set of augmented buckets, an upper bound and a lower bound assignment.

Fig. 2. Algorithm *MB-Max-CSP(i)*

The algorithm's complexity is time and space $O(exp(i))$ where $i \leq n$. When the bound, i, is large enough (i.e. when $i \geq w^*$), the Mini-Bucket algorithm coincides with the full bucket elimination. In summary,

Theorem 2. *Algorithm MB-Max-CSP(i) generates a lower bound on the exact Max-CSP value, and its time and space complexity is exponential in i.* □

Example 2. Figure 3 illustrates how algorithms *Elim-Max-CSP* and *MB-Max-CSP(i)* for $i = 3$ process the network in Figure 1a along the ordering (A, E, D, C, B). Algorithm *Elim-Max-CSP* records new functions $h^B(a, d, e)$, $h^C(a, e)$, $h^D(a, e)$, and $h^E(a)$. Then, in the bucket of A, $min_a h^E(a)$ equals the minimum number of constraints that are violated. Subsequently, an assignment is computed for each variable from A to B by selecting a value that minimizes the sum of functions in the corresponding bucket, conditioned on the previously assigned values. On the other hand, the approximation *MB-Max-CSP(3)* splits bucket B into two mini-buckets, each containing no more than 3 variables, and generates $h^B(e)$ and $h^B(d, a)$. A lower bound on the Max-CSP value is computed by $L = min_a(h^E(a) + h^D(a))$. Then, a suboptimal tuple is computed similarly to the Max-CSP tuple by assigning a value to each variable that minimizes the sum of functions in the corresponding bucket.

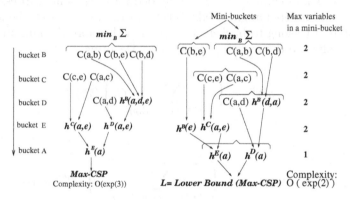

(a) A trace of *Elim-Max-CSP*   (b) A trace of *MB-Max-CSP(2)*

Fig. 3. Execution of *Elim-Max-CSP* and *MB-Max-CSP(i)*

3   Heuristic Search with Mini-Bucket Heuristics

3.1   The Heuristic Function

In the following, we will assume that a Mini-Bucket algorithm was applied to a constraint network using a given variable ordering $d = X_1, ..., X_n$, and that the algorithm outputs an ordered set of augmented buckets $bucket_1, ..., bucket_p, ..., bucket_n$, containing both the input constraints and the newly generated functions. Relative to such an ordered set of augmented buckets, we use the following convention:

- h_j^k stands for a function created by processing the j-th mini-bucket in $bucket_k$.

- $buckets(1..p)$ the union of all functions in the bucket of X_1 through the bucket of X_p.

We will now show that the functions recorded by the Mini-Bucket algorithm can be used to lower bound the number of constraints violated by the best extension of any partial assignment, and therefore can serve as heuristic evaluation functions in a *Best-First* or *Branch-and-Bound* search.

Definition 5 (Exact Evaluation Function). *Given a variable ordering $d = X_1, ..., X_n$, let $\bar{x}^p = (x_1, ..., x_p)$ be an assignment to the first p variables in d. The number of constraints violated by the best extension of $\bar{x}^p$, denoted $f^*(\bar{x}^p)$ is defined by*

$$f^*(\bar{x}^p) = min_{x_{p+1}, ..., x_n} \sum_{k=1}^{n} C_k$$

The above sum defining f^* can be divided into two sums expressed by the functions in the ordered augmented buckets. In the first sum all the arguments are instantiated (belong to buckets $1, ..., p$), and therefore the minimization operation is applied to the second product only. Denoting

$$g(\bar{x}^p) = \left(\sum_{C_i \in \ buckets(1..p)} C_i \right)(\bar{x}^p)$$

and

$$h^*(\bar{x}^p) = min_{(x_{p+1}, ..., x_n)} \left(\sum_{C_i \in buckets(p+1..n)} C_i \right)(\bar{x}^p, x_{p+1}, ..., x_n)$$

we get

$$f^*(\bar{x}^p) = g(\bar{x}^p) + h^*(\bar{x}^p).$$

During search, the g function can be evaluated over the partial assignment $\bar{x}^p$, while h^* can be estimated by a heuristic function h, derived from the functions recorded by the Mini-Bucket algorithm, as defined next:

Definition 6. *Given an ordered set of augmented buckets generated by the Mini-Bucket algorithm, the heuristic function $h(\bar{x}^p)$ is defined as the sum of all the h_j^k functions that satisfy the following two properties: 1) They are generated in buckets $p + 1$ through n, and 2) They reside in buckets 1 through p. Namely, $h(\bar{x}^p) = \sum_{i=1}^{p} \sum_{h_j^k \in bucket_i} h_j^k$, where $k > p$.*

Theorem 3 (Mini-Bucket Heuristic). *For every partial assignment $\bar{x}^p = (x_1, ..., x_p)$, of the first p variables, the evaluation function $f(\bar{x}^p) = g(\bar{x}^p) + h(\bar{x}^p)$ is: 1) Admissible - it never overestimates the number of constraints violated by the best extension of $\bar{x}^p$, and 2) Monotonic - namely $f(\bar{x}^{p+1})/f(\bar{x}^p) \geq 1$.*

Notice that monotonicity means better accuracy at deeper nodes in the search tree. In the extreme case when each bucket p contains exactly one mini-bucket, the heuristic function h equals h^*, and the full evaluation function f computes the exact number of constraints violated by the best extension of the current partial assignment.

3.2 Search with Mini-Bucket Heuristics

The tightness of the lower bound generated by the Mini-Bucket approximation depends on its i-bound. Larger values of i generally yield better lower-bounds, but require more computation. Since the Mini-Bucket algorithm is parameterized by i, we get an entire class of Branch-and-Bound search and Best-First search algorithms that are parameterized by i and which allow a controllable trade-off between preprocessing and search, or between heuristic strength and its overhead.

Both algorithms (BBMB(i) and BFMB(i)) are initialized by running the Mini-Bucket algorithm that produces a set of ordered augmented buckets. Branch-and-Bound with Mini-Bucket heuristics (BBMB(i)) traverses the space of partial assignments in a depth-first manner, instantiating variables from first to last, along ordering d. Throughout the search, the algorithm maintains an upper bound on the value of the Max-CSP assignment, which corresponds to the number of constraints violated by the best full variable instantiation found thus far. When the algorithm processes variable X_p, all the variables preceding X_p in the ordering are already instantiated, so it can compute $f(\bar{x}^{p-1}, X_p = v) = g(\bar{x}^{p-1}, v) + h(\bar{x}^p, v)$ for each extension $X_p = v$. The algorithm prunes all values v whose heuristic estimate (lower bound) $f(\bar{x}^p, X_p = v)$ is greater than or equal to the current best upper bound, because such a partial assignment $(x_1, \ldots x_{p-1}, v)$ cannot be extended to an improved full assignment. The algorithm assigns the best value v to variable X_p and proceeds to variable X_{p+1}, and when variable X_p has no values left, it backtracks to variable X_{p-1}. Search terminates when it reaches a time-bound or when the first variable has no values left. In the latter case, the algorithm has found an optimal solution. The virtue of Branch-and-Bound is that it requires a limited amount of memory and can be used as an anytime scheme; whenever interrupted, Branch-and-Bound outputs the best solution found so far.

Algorithm Best-First with Mini-Bucket heuristics (BFMB(i)) starts by adding a dummy node x_0 to the list of open nodes. Each node in the search space corresponds to a partial assignment $\bar{x}^p$ and has an associated heuristic value $f(\bar{x}^p)$. Initially $f(x_0) = 0$. The basic step of the algorithm consists of selecting an assignment $\bar{x}^p$ from the list of open nodes having the smallest heuristic value $f(\bar{x}^p)$, expanding it by computing all partial assignments $(\bar{x}^p, v)$ for all values v of X_{p+1}, and adding them to the list of open nodes.

Since, as shown, the generated heuristics are admissible and monotonic, their use within Best-First search yields A* type algorithms whose properties are well understood. The algorithm is guaranteed to terminate with an optimal solution. When provided with more powerful heuristics it explores a smaller search space, but otherwise it requires substantial space. It is known that Best-First algorithms are optimal. Namely, when given the same heuristic information, Best-First search is the most efficient algorithm in terms of the size of the search space it explores [2]. In particular, Branch-and-Bound will expand any node that is expanded by Best-First (up to tie breaking conditions), and in many cases it explores a larger space. Still, Best-First may occasionally fail because of its memory requirements, because it has to maintain a large subset of open nodes during search, and because of tie breaking rules at the last frontier of nodes having evaluation function value that equals the optimal solution. As we will indeed observe in our experiments, Branch-and-Bound and Best-First search have complementary properties, and both can be strengthen by the Mini-Bucket heuristics.

4   Experimental Methodology

We tested the performance of BBMB(i) and BFMB(i) on set of random binary CSPs. Each problem in this class is characterized by four parameters: $< N, K, C, T >$, where N is the number of variables, K is the domain size, C is the number of constraints, and T is the tightness of each constraint, defined as the number of tuples not allowed. Each problem is generated by randomly picking C constraints out of $\binom{N}{2}$ total possible constraints, and picking T nogoods out of K^2 maximum possible for each constraint.

We used the min-degree heuristic for computing the ordering of variables. It places a variable with the smallest degree at the end of the ordering, connects all of its neighbors, removes the variable from the graph and repeats the whole procedure.

In addition to MB(i), BBMB(i) and BFMB(i), we ran, for comparison, two state of the art algorithms for solving Max-CSP : PFC-MPRDAC as defined in [10] and a Stochastic Local Search (SLS) algorithm we developed for CSPs [9].

PFC-MPRDAC [10] is a Branch-and-Bound search algorithm. It uses a forward checking step based on a partitioning of unassigned variables into disjoint subsets of variables. This partitioning is used for computing a heuristic evaluation function that is used for determining variable and value ordering.

As a measure of performance we used the accuracy ratio $opt = F_{alg}/F_{Max-CSP}$ between the value of the solution found by the test algorithm (F_{alg}) and the value of the optimal solution ($F_{Max-CSP}$), whenever $F_{Max-CSP}$ is available. We also record the running time of each algorithm.

We recorded the distribution of the accuracy measure opt over five predefined ranges : $opt \geq 0.95$, $opt \geq 0.5$, $opt \geq 0.2$, $opt \geq 0.01$ and $opt < 0.01$. However, we only report the number of problems that fall in the range 0.95. Problems in this range were solved optimally.

In addition, during the execution of both BBMB and BFMB we also stored the current upper bound U at regular time intervals. This allows reporting the accuracy of each algorithm as a function of time.

Table 1. Search completion times for problems with 10 values. 100 instances

T	MB BBMB BFMB i=2 #/time	MB BBMB BFMB i=3 #/time	MB BBMB BFMB i=4 #/time	MB BBMB BFMB i=5 #/time	MB BBMB BFMB i=6 #/time	PFC-MRDAC #/time
N=10, K=10, C=45. Time bound 180 sec. dense network.						
84	2/0.02	4/0.11	6/0.87	10/7.25	16/56.7	100/4.00
	26/180	98/90.7	100/11.7	**100/10.0**	100/57.6	
	2/189	4/184	78/65.7	**98/17.9**	100/59.3	
85	0/-	3/0.11	2/0.89	8/7.45	10/57.3	100/3.95
	20/180	100/80.1	100/11.6	**100/9.62**	100/57.3	
	0/-	5/124	82/54.4	**100/18.7**	100/58.9	
N=15, K=10, C=50. Time bound 180 sec. medium density.						
84	0/-	0/-	3/0.96	6/8.77	14/78.3	100/13.5
	10/180	60/161	90/50.1	**100/26.2**	100/86.2	
	0/-	0/-	21/70.5	65/49.8	97/89.7	
85	1/0.02	2/0.13	3/0.95	7/8.12	17/71.0	100/13.2
	20/180	68/164	98/79.0	**100/28.7**	100/74.9	
	1/190	5/184	16/82.0	63/59.6	97/82.8	
N=25, K=10, C=37. Time bound 180 sec. sparse network.						
84	0/-	7/0.10	30/0.60	84/3.41	99/9.74	100/4.16
	36/114	99/4.42	**100/0.77**	100/3.70	100/9.93	
	3/56.9	94/8.67	**100/1.28**	100/3.77	100/9.93	
85	0/-	10/0.10	34/0.60	79/3.20	99/9.36	100/7.51
	31/88.6	100/7.55	**100/0.75**	100/3.31	100/9.58	
	9/51.1	89/17.1	**100/1.34**	100/3.34	100/9.59	

5 Results

Here we evaluate performance of algorithms as complete ones. Tables 1-3 report results of experiments with three classes of over-constrained binary CSPs with domain sizes : K=10, K=5 and K=3. Tables 1 and 2 contain three blocks, each corresponding to a set of CSPs with a fixed number of variables and constraints. Within each block, there are two small blocks each corresponding to a different constraint tightness, given in the first column. In columns 2 through 6 (Tables 1 and 3), and columns 2 through 7 (Table 2), we have results for MB, BBMB and BFMB (in different rows) for different values of i-bound. In the last column we have results for PFC-MRDAC. Each entry in the table gives a percentage of the problems that were solved exactly within our time bound (fall in the 0.95 range), and the average CPU time for these problems.

For example, looking at the second block of the middle large block in Table 1 (corresponding to binary CSPs with N=15, K=10, C=70 and T=85) we see that MB with i=2 (column 2) solved only only 1% of the problems exactly in 0.02

Table 2. Search completion times for problems with 5 values. 100 instances

T	MB BBMB BFMB i=2 #/time	MB BBMB BFMB i=3 #/time	MB BBMB BFMB i=4 #/time	MB BBMB BFMB i=5 #/time	MB BBMB BFMB i=6 #/time	MB BBMB BFMB i=7 #/time	MB BBMB BFMB i=8 #/time	PFC-MRDAC #/time
N=15, K=5, C=105. Time bound 180 sec. dense network.								
18	0/-	0/-	0/-	12/0.56	13/2.27	31/11.7	34/49.7	
	10/180	32/180	64/148	96/81.4	100/33.4	**100/21.9**	100/52.5	100/9.61
	0/-	0/-	0/-	13/111	59/64.5	88/47.4	100/58.1	
19	0/-	0/-	0/-	0/-	5/2.78	12/14.6	40/60.3	
	16/180	40/180	77/155	100/76.8	100/29.7	**100/22.8**	100/60.9	100/7.69
	0/-	0/-	2/188	3/182	42/54.0	88/39.2	100/61.9	
N=20, K=5, C=100. Time bound 180 sec. medium density.								
18	0/-	0/-	7/0.17	10/0.71	11/3.12	23/14.4	29/68.7	
	5/180	15/180	38/170	71/132	86/82.3	95/57.4	96/90.6	100/18.7
	0/-	0/-	1/183	2/60.0	9/76.9	33/81.5	59/98.9	
19	0/-	0/-	0/-	4/0.70	4/3.21	4/14.9	4/70.7	
	4/180	24/180	56/160	64/121	84/97.5	96/85.4	92/90.0	100/17.4
	0/-	0/-	0/-	12/89.5	12/76.5	32/77.3	52/96.8	
N=40, K=5, C=55. Time bound 180 sec. sparse network.								
18	0/-	12/0.02	36/0.07	54/0.19	88/0.53	100/1.03	100/1.14	
	44/87.7	100/4.41	**100/0.21**	100/0.23	100/0.56	100/1.04	100/1.15	100/4.94
	3/4.56	92/14.9	100/0.45	**100/0.27**	100/0.57	100/1.04	100/1.16	
19	0/-	7/0.03	25/0.07	55/0.20	79/0.56	96/1.29	100/1.89	
	38/104	99/8.35	100/0.34	**100/0.25**	100/0.61	100/1.35	100/1.90	100/8.04
	1/25.4	83/14.4	100/1.28	**100/0.30**	100/0.63	100/1.36	100/1.90	

seconds of CPU time. On the same set of problems BBMB, using Mini-Bucket heuristics, solved 20% of the problems optimally using 180 seconds of CPU time, while BFMB solved 1% of the problems exactly in 190 seconds. When moving to columns 3 through 6 in rows corresponding to the same set of problems, we see a gradual change caused by a higher level of Mini-Bucket heuristic (higher values of the i-bound). As expected, Mini-Bucket solves more problems, while using more time. Focusing on BBMB, we see that it solved all problems when the i-bound is 5 or 6, and its total running time as a function of time forms a U-shaped curve. At first (i=2) it is high (180), then as i-bound increases the total time decreases (when i=5 the total time is 28.7), but then as i-bound increases further the total time starts to increase again. The same behavior is shown for BFMB as well.

This demonstrates a trade-off between the amount of preprocessing performed by MB and the amount of subsequent search using the heuristic cost function generated by MB. The optimal balance between preprocessing and search corresponds to the value of i-bound at the bottom of the U-shaped curve. The

Table 3. Search completion times for problems with 3 values. 10 instances

T	MB BBMB BFMB i=2 #/time	MB BBMB BFMB i=4 #/time	MB BBMB BFMB i=6 #/time	MB BBMB BFMB i=8 #/time	MB BBMB BFMB i=10 #/time	PFC-MRDAC #/time
	N=100, K=3, C=200. Time bound 180 sec. sparse network.					
1	70/0.03 90/12.5 80/0.03	90/0.06 **100/0.07** **100/0.07**	100/0.32 100/0.33 100/0.33	100/2.15 100/2.16 100/2.15	100/15.1 100/15.1 100/15.1	100/0.08
2	0/- 0/- 0/-	0/- 0/- 0/-	10/0.34 40/38.0 20/0.76	10/2.03 80/19.6 70/19.8	40/15.7 **100/22.6** 100/33.2	100/757
3	0/- 0/- 0/-	0/- 0/- 0/-	0/- 60/72.4 30/39.2	0/- 70/27.7 60/28.7	10/16.2 **100/24.5** 90/28.9	100/2879
	N=100, K=3, C=200. Time bound 600 sec. sparse network.					
4	0/- 0/- 0/-	0/- 0/- 0/-	0/- 60/431 0/-	0/- 80/236 20/243	0/- **100/165** 20/165	100/7320

added amount of search on top of MB can be estimated by $t_{search} = t_{total} - t_{MB}$. As i increases, the average search time t_{search} decreases, and the overall accuracy of the search algorithm increases (more problems fall within higher ranges of *opt*). However, as i increases, the time of MB preprocessing increases as well.

One crucial difference between BBMB and BFMB is that BBMB is an anytime algorithm - it always outputs an assignment, and as time increases, the solution improves. BFMB on the other hand only outputs a solution when it finds an optimal solution. In our experiments, if BFMB did not finish within the preset time bound, it returned the MB assignment.

From the data in the Tables we can see that the performance of BFMB is consistently worse than that of BBMB. BFMB(i) solves fewer problems than BBMB(i) and, on the average, takes longer on each problem. This is more pronounced when non-trivial amount of search is required (lower i-bound values) - when the heuristic is weaker. These results are in contrast to the behavior we observed when using this scheme for optimization in belief networks [7]. We speculate that this is because, for Max-CSP, there are large numbers of frontier nodes with the same heuristic value.

Tables 1-3 also report results of PFC-MRDAC. When the constraint graph is dense PFC-MRDAC is up to 2-3 times faster than the best performing BBMB. When the constraint graph is sparse the best BBMB is up to two orders of magnitude faster than PFC-MRDAC. The superiority of our approach is most notable for larger problems (Table 3).

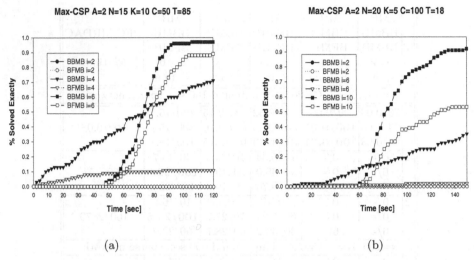

Fig. 4. Distribution of search completion

In Figure 4 we provide an alternative view of the performance of BBMB(i) and BFMB(i). Let $F_{BBMB(i)}(t)$ and $F_{BFMB(i)}(t)$ be the fraction of the problems solved completely by BBMB(i) and BFMB(i), respectively, by time t. Each graph in Figure 4 plots $F_{BBMB(i)}(t)$ and $F_{BFMB(i)}(t)$ for several values of i. These figures display trade-off between preprocessing and search in a clear manner. Clearly, if $F_{BBMB(i)}(t) > F_{BBMB(j)}(t)$ for all t, then BBMB(i) completely dominates BBMB(j). For example, in Figure 4a BBMB(4) completely dominates BBMB(2) (here BBMB(2) and BFMB(2) overlap). When $F_{BBMB(i)}(t)$ and $F_{BBMB(j)}(t)$ intersect, they display a trade-off as a function of time. For example, if we have less than 70 seconds, BBMB(4) is better than BBMB(6). However, when sufficient time is allowed, BBMB(6) is superior.

6   Anytime Algorithms

Next we evaluate anytime performance of relevant algorithms - SLS, that is inherently incomplete and can never guarantee an optimal solution for Max-CSP, and BBMB, that returns a (suboptimal) solution any time during search.

A Stochastic Local Search (SLS) algorithm, such as GSAT [12], [15], starts from a randomly chosen complete instantiation of all the variables, and moves from one complete instantiation to the next. It is guided by a cost function that is the number of unsatisfied constraints in the current assignment. At each step, the value of the variable that leads to the greatest reduction of the cost function is changed. The algorithm stops when either the cost is zero (a *global minimum*), in which case the problem is solved, or when there is no way to improve the current assignment by changing just one variable (a *local minimum*).

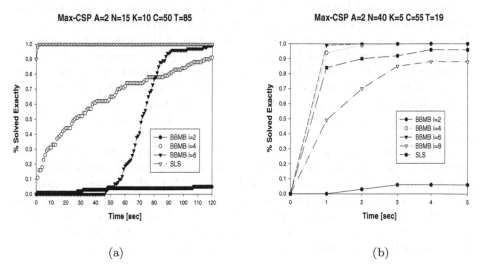

Fig. 5. Distribution of anytime performance

A number of heuristics have been designed to overcome the problem of local minima [11], [14], [13], [4]. In our implementation of SLS we use the basic greedy scheme combined with the constraint re-weighting as introduced in [11]. In this algorithm, each constraint has a weight and the cost function is the weighted sum of unsatisfied constraints. Whenever the algorithm reaches a local minimum, it increases the weights of unsatisfied constraints.

An SLS algorithm for CSPs can immediately be applied to a Max-CSP problem. When measuring the performance of SLS we treat it as an anytime algorithm - we report the fraction of problems solved exactly by time t as a function of t. To do that, we use the optimal cost found by BBMB.

In Figure 5 we present results comparing BBMB and SLS as anytime algorithms. Figure 5a (5b) corresponds to one row in Table 1 (2). When the constraint graph is dense (Figure 5a), SLS is substantially faster than BBMB. However, when the constraint graph is sparse (Figure 5b), BBMB(4) and BBMB(6) are faster than SLS. We should note that for most of the problem instances we ran where the graph exceeds a certain sparseness threshold, SLS exhibits impressive performance, arriving at an optimal solution within a few seconds.

7   Summary and Conclusion

The paper evaluates the power of a new scheme that generates search heuristics mechanically for solving a variety of optimization tasks. The approach was presented and evaluated for optimization queries over belief networks [7]. In this paper we extend the approach to the Max-CSP task and evaluate its potential on a variety of randomly generated constraint satisfaction problems. The basic idea is to extract heuristics for search from the Mini-Bucket approximation method which allows controlled trade-off between computation and accuracy. Our experiments demonstrate again the potential of this scheme in improving general search, showing that the Mini-Bucket heuristic's accuracy can be controlled to yield a trade-off between preprocessing and search. We demonstrate this property in the context of both Branch-and-Bound and Best-First search. Although the best threshold point cannot be predicted a priori, a preliminary empirical analysis can be informative when given a class of problems that is not too heterogeneous.

We show that this approach can be competitive with state of the art algorithms for solving the Max-CSP problem. In particular, it outperformed a complete algorithm developed specifically for MAX-CSP on sparse constraint problems and is even competitive as anytime scheme against an SLS algorithm when the problems are sparse. Although, overall SLS performance was impressive on the classes of problems we experimented with, an SLS approach cannot prove optimality and therefore its termination time is speculative.

References

1. R. Dechter. Bucket elimination: A unifying framework for reasoning. *Artificial Intelligence*, 113:41–85, 1999. 262, 265
2. R. Dechter and J. Pearl. Generalized best-first search strategies and the optimality of a*. *Journal of the ACM*, 32:506–536, 1985. 270
3. R. Dechter and I. Rish. A scheme for approximating probabilistic inference. In *Proceedings of Uncertainty in Artificial Intelligence (UAI97)*, pages 132–141, 1997. 262, 265
4. I. P. Gent and T. Walsh. Towards an understanding of hill-climbing procedures for sat. In *Proceedings of the Eleventh National Conference on Artificial Intelligence (AAAI-93)*, pages 28–33, 1993. 275
5. K. Kask I. Rish and R. Dechter. Approximation algorithms for probabilistic decoding. In *Uncertainty in Artificial Intelligence (UAI-98)*, 1998. 262
6. K. Kask and R. Dechter. Branch and bound with mini-bucket heuristics. In *Proc. IJCAI*, pages 426–433, 1999. 263
7. K. Kask and R. Dechter. Mini-bucket heuristics for improved search. In *Proc. UAI*, 1999. 263, 273, 275
8. K. Kask and R. Dechter. Using mini-bucket heuristics for max-csp. *UCI Technical report*, 2000. 265
9. K. Kask and R. Dechter. Gsat and local consistency. In *International Joint Conference on Artificial Intelligence (IJCAI95)*, pages 616–622, Montreal, Canada, August 1995. 270
10. J. Larossa and P. Meseguer. Partition-based lower bound for max-csp. *Proc. CP99*, 1999. 263, 270
11. P. Morris. The breakout method for escaping from local minima. In *Proceedings of the Eleventh National Conference on Artificial Intelligence (AAAI-93)*, pages 40–45, 1993. 275
12. A. B. Philips, S. Minton, M. D. Johnston and P. Laired. Solving large scale constraint satisfaction and scheduling problems using heuristic repair methods. In

National Conference on Artificial Intelligence (AAAI-90), pages 17–24, Anaheim, CA, 1990. 274

13. B. Selman and H. Kautz. An empirical study of greedy local search for satisfiability testing. In *Proceedings of the Eleventh National Conference on Artificial Intelligence*, pages 46–51, 1993. 275

14. B. Selman, H. Kautz, and B. Cohen. Noise strategies for local search. In *Proceedings of the Eleventh National Conference on Artificial Intelligence*, pages 337–343, 1994. 275

15. B. Selman, H. Levesque, and D. Mitchell. A new method for solving hard satisfiability problems. *National Conference on Artificial Intelligence (AAAI-92)*, 1992. 274

Analysis of Random Noise and Random Walk Algorithms for Satisfiability Testing

Bhaskar Krishnamachari[1], Xi Xie[1], Bart Selman[2], and Stephen Wicker[1]

[1] School of Electrical Engineering
Cornell University, Ithaca, NY 14853
{bhaskar,xie,wicker}@ee.cornell.edu
[2] Department of Computer Science
Cornell University, Ithaca, NY 14853
selman@cs.cornell.edu

Abstract. Random Noise and Random Walk algorithms are local search strategies that have been used for the problem of satisfiability testing (SAT). We present a Markov-chain based analysis of the performance of these algorithms. The performance measures we consider are the probability of finding a satisfying assignment and the distribution of the best solution observed on a given SAT instance. The analysis provides exact statistics, but is restricted to small problems as it requires the storage and use of knowledge about the entire search space. We examine the effect of p, the probability of making non-greedy moves, on these algorithms and provide a justification for the practice of choosing this value empirically.

1 Introduction

Local search algorithms such as GSAT, Random Walk and Random Noise search have been shown to be good at solving CNF satisfiability (SAT) problems [4,13]. Such methods perform better than systematic search algorithms on large satisfiability problems involving thousands of variables. They may be used for the problem of maximum satisfiability (finding a truth assignment that satisfies as many clauses as possible) as well as complete satisfiability (satisfying all clauses).

However, due to the complex interactions between the problem instance and algorithm implementation details, it is hard to predict the performance of these algorithms. Researchers have, therefore, mainly relied upon empirical studies for this purpose [5,14]. Although this approach provides very useful results, it is still desirable to have some theoretical understanding of algorithm performance.

A large portion of the literature on theoretical analysis of local search algorithms for other problems has been devoted to determining the convergence of search algorithms to the global optimum using Markov models [2,3,7,8,9,11]. The rates of convergence to the optimum have also been discussed assuming various properties of cost functions and search spaces [15,16]. Some work in the area of complexity theory has been focused on studying PLS (polynomial local search) problems regarding the time required to locate local optima [6,10].

R. Dechter (Ed.): CP 2000, LNCS 1894, pp. 278–290, 2000.
© Springer-Verlag Berlin Heidelberg 2000

In this paper, we show how the Random Walk and Random Noise algorithms can be modeled using discrete Markov chains. We present a procedure to determine the probability of finding the global optimum as well as complete statistics of the best solution observed in a given number of iterations. The former measure of algorithm performance is most relevant to maximum satisfiability problems, while the latter is the statistic of interest when considering complete satisfiability. These measures are relevant because they tell us quantitatively how the algorithm will perform on a given problem in limited computational time. This in turn will help us to determine the best parameters for these search algorithms to use.

The procedure presented requires the storage and use of complete knowledge about the search space. Hence, it can only be carried out for small-scale satisfiability problems. Still, this analysis provides some insights regarding the performance of these algorithms on real world problems. Real world problems are characterized by the existence of local minima which hinder the performance of greedy local search. Both Random Noise and Random Walk algorithms provide ways of escaping local minima, using the parameter p, the probability of making random non-greedy moves. The value of p that provides optimum algorithm performance is of great interest. We find theoretical support for the practice of empirically choosing an optimal value for this parameter.

The rest of the paper is organized as follows: section 2 reviews the definitions of the Random Noise and Random Walk algorithms. Section 3 shows how these algorithms can be modeled as discrete Markov chains and presents a procedure for determining the performance statistics for these algorithms. The method of determining the one-step state transition matrix for these algorithms is described in section 4. Section 5 presents and discusses results obtained using this procedure. Concluding comments are presented in section 6.

2 Random Noise and Random Walk Algorithms for Satisfiability

The Random Noise and Random Walk algorithms are both based on GSAT, a greedy local search procedure for satisfiability which works as follows [12]:

Procedure GSAT

```
for i:= 1 to MAX-TRIES
    T:= a randomly generated truth assignment
    for j := 1 to MAX-FLIPS
        if T satisfies expression then return T
        Flip any variable in T that results in greatest decrease
                (could even be 0) in the number of unsatisfied clauses
    end for
end for
return "No satisfying assignment found"
```

The success of GSAT depends on its ability to make either strictly improving or "sideways" moves (moves to assignments with an equal number of unsatisfied clauses). When the algorithm finds itself at a non-optimal point in the search space where no further improvements are possible, it is essentially trapped in a region which is a local minimum and needs to be restarted with a random new assignment. Another mechanism for escaping such local minima that is widely used is to permit the search to make uphill moves occasionally. Random Noise and Random Walk algorithm are both closely related in the way they allow for the possibility of uphill moves [13]:

Random Noise

```
With probability p, pick any variable at random
     and flip its truth assignment.
With probability 1-p, follow the standard GSAT scheme,
          i.e., make the best possible local move
```

Random Walk

```
With probability p, pick a variable occurring in some
          unsatisfied clause and flip its truth assignment.
With probability 1-p, follow the standard GSAT scheme,
          i.e., make the best possible local move
```

Experimental results comparing the basic GSAT algorithm, Simulated Annealing, Random Walk and Random Noise strategies on a test suite including randomly-generated CNF problems and Boolean encodings of circuit synthesis, planning and circuit diagnosis problems can be found in [13]. The authors of this paper found that the Random Walk strategy significantly out-performed the other algorithms on these problems.

3   Modeling and Analysis

If we look at the search process as a sequence of decisions for moving from point to point in the search space, most local search algorithms can be called "memoryless" in the sense that the process of selecting the next point depends iteratively only on the current point. Therefore, the search process is a Markov process with finite *states* (e.g. the points in the search space). Furthermore, the search algorithms are performed at discrete steps/iterations and this allows us to model them as Markov chains. Such models for two widely used local search algorithms – Simulated Annealing and Genetic Algorithms, can be found in [1] and [9] respectively. In the context of satisfiability problems, each point in the search space corresponds to a unique truth assignment.

Theorem 1: The sequence of points visited by the Random Noise (also Random Walk) algorithm forms a Homogeneous Markov Chain.

Proof: To prove that this sequence forms a Markov chain, it suffices to show that the point visited at the $(k + 1)^{st}$ iteration depends only upon which point was visited at the kth iteration. This can be seen as follows: by the definition of both these algorithms, the truth assignment at the $(k + 1)^{st}$ iteration differs from the truth assignment at the kth iteration at exactly one variable. The set of variables that may be flipped at the kth iteration depends only upon whether we are considering the Random Noise or Random Walk algorithm and not the points visited at any previous iteration. Finally, the probability of flipping each variable in this set also depends only on the value of p and not the points visited in the first $(k - 1)$ iterations. The Markov chain will be homogeneous because the state transition probabilities will only be a function of p which is assumed to be constant for the duration of the search. **Q.E.D.**

In a SAT problem, if N is the number of variables, the search space X consists of a total of $|X| = 2^N$ possible truth assignments. Let $x^{[j]}$, $1 \leq j \leq |X|$ be a point in the search space. The cost $f(x^{[j]})$ is the number of unsatisfied clauses in the corresponding truth assignment. For simplicity of analysis and description, we assume that the points in the search space are sorted in non-decreasing order of costs, i.e. $j < k \Rightarrow f(x^{[j]}) \leq f(x^{[k]})$. The search space may contain two points with the exact same cost function value. We represent the sorted list of costs using a row vector $\overrightarrow{f}$ of size $|X|$ such that the jth element $\overrightarrow{f}_{[j]} = f(x^{[j]})$.

Let x_i be the random variable describing which point the search is at during iteration i. The *probability mass function* (pmf) of x_i is represented by a row vector $\overrightarrow{\pi}_i$ of size $|X|$ such that the mth element $\overrightarrow{\pi}_{i,[m]} = P\{x_i = x^{[m]}\}$. A homogeneous Markov chain based local search algorithm can then be described by a one-step state transition matrix $\mathbf{P}$ such that:

$$\overrightarrow{\pi}_i = \overrightarrow{\pi}_{i-1}\mathbf{P} \tag{1}$$

The performance statistics of interest (probability of finding the global optimum within a given number of iterations, best solution observed to date) require us to incorporate the search history as well. For this purpose, it is necessary to fully describe the state that the search algorithm is in at a given iteration. This description should include a) the pmf describing the probability that the search algorithm is at any given point in the search space, and b) the conditional pmf's of the best (lowest) cost seen up to the current iteration given that the search is currently at a certain point in the search space. Both these pmf's can be iteratively calculated at each step as they depend on only the pmf's of the previous iteration and on the search algorithm being analyzed.

Let x_i^* denote the point with the lowest cost function seen up to iteration i. We can use a matrix $\mathbf{D}_i^*$ to represent the conditional probability of the lowest cost seen to date given the current search point, i.e. $D_{i,[jk]}^* = P\{x_i^* = j | x_i = k\}$. Note that $\mathbf{D}_0^* = \mathbf{I}$. For entries representing equal value points, it does not matter how the weight is distributed among them as long as the total probability remains the same.

For the ith iteration, the distribution $\vec{\pi}_i$ can be calculated from $\vec{\pi}_{i-1}$ using equation (1). The following formulae[1] can be used in sequence to calculate $\mathbf{D_i^*}$ from $\vec{\pi}_{i-1}$ and $\mathbf{D_{i-1}^*}$:

$$\mathbf{B_i^*} = \mathbf{D_{i-1}^*} \mathbf{diag}(\vec{\pi}_{i-1})\mathbf{P} \tag{2}$$

$$C_{i,[jk]}^* = \begin{cases} B_{i,[jk]}^* & j < k \\ \sum_{l=j}^{|X|} B_{i,[lk]}^* & j = k \\ 0 & j > k \end{cases} \tag{3}$$

$\mathbf{B_i^*}$ and $\mathbf{C_i^*}$ are temporary matrices. The best-to-date point cannot be worse than the current point at any time. An entry $B_{i,[jk]}^*$ in $\mathbf{B_i^*}$ represents the probability of having j as the best observed point and k as the current search point without this consideration. $\mathbf{C_i^*}$ contains the corresponding probabilities after considering this fact. Equation (4) normalizes $\mathbf{C_i^*}$ to the desired conditional pmf matrix [2]:

$$\mathbf{D_i^*} = \mathbf{C_i^*}(\mathbf{diag}(\vec{\pi}_i))^{-1} \tag{4}$$

Thus, given the initial state distribution $\vec{\pi}_0$ and the state transition matrix $\mathbf{P}$, we can derive $\mathbf{D_n^*}$ – the conditional pmf's of the lowest cost function value seen to date, and $\vec{\pi}_n$ – the distribution of costs at the nth iteration. It is typically assumed that each point in the search space is equally likely to be picked as the starting point (uniform initial distribution). Once $\mathbf{D_n^*}$ and $\vec{\pi}_n$ are known, the expectation and variance of the best-to-date cost can then be readily calculated by definition:

$$E[f(x_n^*)] = \vec{f}\mathbf{D_n^*}\vec{\pi}_n^T \tag{5}$$

$$VAR[f(x_n^*)] = \vec{f}\,\mathbf{diag}(\vec{f})\mathbf{D_n^*}\vec{\pi}_n^T - (\vec{f}\mathbf{D_n^*}\vec{\pi}_n^T)^2 \tag{6}$$

The expectation and variance of best-to-date cost are useful measures if we are interested in the problem of maximum satisfiability. For complete satisfiability, we would like to know the probability $P[f(x_n^*) = f^*]$ of achieving the global optimum f^* within n iterations. This can be calculated as follows:

$$P[f(x_n^*) = f^*] = \vec{e}\mathbf{D_n^*}\vec{\pi}_n^T \tag{7}$$

where $\vec{e} = [1\ 0\ 0\ 0\ \dots\ 0]$, consisting of a 1 followed by $(|X| - 1)$ zeros.

We note here that the above procedure for calculating these statistics up to iteration n, as outlined in equations (1) through (7), has a computational

---

[1] In these formulae, $\mathbf{diag}(\vec{v})$ represents the diagonal matrix derived from a vector $\vec{v}$; $\mathbf{B_i^*}$ and $\mathbf{C_i^*}$ are temporary matrices used during this updating process.

[2] Rigorously, the inverse of $\mathbf{diag}(\vec{\pi}_i)$ does not exist if any of the elements of $\vec{\pi}_i$ are 0 – although this only happens when using purely greedy search. However the notation used in equation 4 is convenient and the difficulty can be overcome by treating these 0 elements as arbitrarily small values ϵ.

complexity of $O(|X|^3 n)$, where $|X| = 2^N$ is the size of the search space. The exponential dependence on the number of variables renders this exact analysis infeasible for larger problems.

4 Determining the State Transition Matrix

Table 1. Sample 3-SAT instance with 3 variables, 15 clauses

{ 3, 1, −2}	{−1, 2, −3}	{−3, 2, 1}	{ 2, 1, −3}	{ 1, 2, 3}
{ 3, −2, −1}	{−2, 1, −3}	{ 1, −3, −2}	{ 3, 1, 2}	{ 1, 3, 2}
{−3, 2, −1}	{ 1, 3, 2}	{ 3, 1, 2}	{ 1, 3, −2}	{ 1, −2, 3}

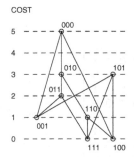

Fig. 1. Neighborhood definition and cost values for a randomly generated 3SAT instance with 3 variables and 15 clauses; 111 and 100 are satisfying assignments

We have shown how the performance statistics of interest may be obtained once the state transition matrix **P** is known. This matrix depends upon both the specific problem instance, as well as the algorithm used. We discuss here via an example how the matrix can be obtained for Random Noise algorithms if the satisfiability instance is known.

Table 1 shows a randomly generated 3-SAT instance with 3 variables and 15 clauses[3]. The cost for each truth assignment, i.e. the number of unsatisfied clauses as well as the neighboring truth assignments are shown in figure 1. From the figure, it is easy to see that the assignment 001 is a local minimum and that the global minima 111 and 100 are satisfying assignments.

Given a problem instance, the one-step transition matrix **P** can be determined for the Random Noise algorithm as follows:

---

[3] It may be seen that a number of these clauses are identical in this example, but this is to due to the small number of variables used for illustration.

- Determine the transition matrix $\mathbf{P_{greedy}}$ for the GSAT algorithm ($p = 0$).
- Determine the transition matrix $\mathbf{P_{random}}$ for the random noise algorithm with $p = 1$.
- $\mathbf{P} = (1-p)\,\mathbf{P_{greedy}} + p\,\mathbf{P_{random}}$

For the SAT instance presented in figure 1, the corresponding transition matrices for the Random Noise algorithm: $\mathbf{P_{greedy}}$ and $\mathbf{P_{random}}$ are shown in figure 2. The $\mathbf{P_{random}}$ matrix is constructed by assigning equal transition probabilities to each neighbor of a given truth assignment (elements corresponding to non-Neighboring points are 0). The $\mathbf{P_{greedy}}$ is constructed by assigning equal transition probabilities from any given truth assignment to the neighbor(s) which have the greatest decrease in cost (0 or more). The procedure is nearly identical for obtaining the $\mathbf{P}$ for the Random Walk algorithm, with the only difference being in the construction of $\mathbf{P_{random}}$. To construct $\mathbf{P_{random}}$ for the Random Walk algorithm, assign equal state transition probabilities to each neighbor of a given truth assignment that can be obtained by flipping a variable involved in unsatisfied clauses.

$$
P_{random} = \frac{1}{3}
\begin{bmatrix}
0 & 0 & 0 & 1 & 0 & 0 & 1 & 1 \\
0 & 0 & 0 & 1 & 1 & 0 & 1 & 0 \\
0 & 0 & 0 & 0 & 1 & 0 & 1 & 1 \\
1 & 1 & 0 & 0 & 0 & 1 & 0 & 0 \\
0 & 1 & 1 & 0 & 0 & 1 & 0 & 0 \\
0 & 0 & 0 & 1 & 1 & 0 & 0 & 1 \\
1 & 1 & 1 & 0 & 0 & 0 & 0 & 0 \\
1 & 0 & 1 & 0 & 0 & 1 & 0 & 0
\end{bmatrix}
\qquad
P_{greedy} = \frac{1}{2}
\begin{bmatrix}
2 & 0 & 0 & 0 & 0 & 0 & 0 & 0 \\
0 & 2 & 0 & 0 & 0 & 0 & 0 & 0 \\
0 & 0 & 2 & 0 & 0 & 0 & 0 & 0 \\
1 & 1 & 0 & 0 & 0 & 0 & 0 & 0 \\
0 & 2 & 0 & 0 & 0 & 0 & 0 & 0 \\
0 & 0 & 2 & 0 & 0 & 0 & 0 & 0 \\
1 & 1 & 0 & 0 & 0 & 0 & 0 & 0 \\
2 & 0 & 0 & 0 & 0 & 0 & 0 & 0
\end{bmatrix}
$$

Fig. 2. Constructing State Transition Probability Matrices

5   Results

Using the method of analysis presented in this paper, it is possible to investigate the effect of p, the non-greedy move probability, on the performance of random noise algorithms. One significant result is the following:

Theorem 2: $E[f(x_n^*)]$, the expected best cost seen by a random noise or random walk algorithm after n iterations, is a polynomial in p of order at most n.

Proof: See appendix A.

Corollary 1: The variance of the best cost $VAR[f(x_n^*)]$ is a polynomial in p of order at most $2n$.

Corollary 2: $P[f(x_n^*) = f*]$, the probability of having found the global best assignment after n iterations, is a polynomial in p of order at most n.

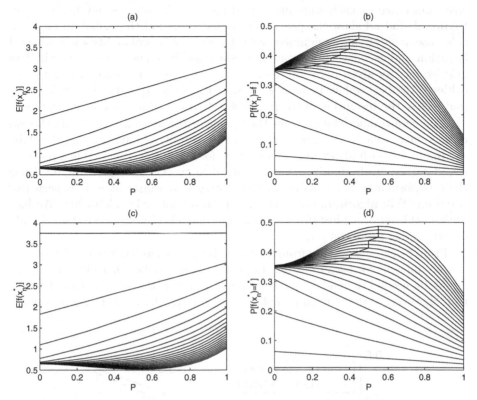

Fig. 3. Performance for Random Noise and Random Walk algorithms with respect to p for a randomly generated 3-SAT instance with 7 variables. Figures (a) and (c) show the curves for expectation of best-to-date costs for Random Noise and Random Walk algorithms respectively. Figures (b) and (d) show the curves for the probability of finding a satisfiable solution for Random Noise and Random Walk algorithms respectively. In (b) and (d), the locus connecting the peaks of the curves of the various iterations indicate the value of p for which this probability is maximized. For the expectation figures (a) and (c), each successively lower curve represents an increasing iteration number, while the opposite is true for the probability figures (b) and (d)

We applied the procedure described in equations (1) through (7) on randomly generated 3-SAT instances to determine the performance of Random Walk and Random Noise algorithms. Table 2, in appendix B, shows a typical instance with 7 variables and 30 clauses. Figure 3 shows the effect of p on Random Noise (3a,3b) and Random Walk (3c,3d) algorithms for this instance.

The data in figure 3 is for 21 values of p ranging from 0 to 1, with 0.05 increment, for the first 20 iterations of the algorithms. Figures 3a and 3c show the expected best cost. The first line on top corresponds to iteration 0, the starting point of the search. As the iteration number increases, the expected cost goes down at each step and is indicated by the successively lower curves. Figure 3b and 3d show the probability of having found the global optimum (in this case, a satisfying assignment with 0 cost). This probability increases with iteration and is hence represented by successively higher curves. In all these graphs, for any given iteration, there is some $p = p_{best}$ for which the algorithm achieves the best value. In figures 3b and 3d, the p_{best} points for each iteration (subject to the resolution of the p values tested) are connected, forming a locus.

The performance statistics for the two algorithms are different, and this can be seen more clearly in figure 4, where the probability of having found the global minimum for both algorithms is compared for $p = 0, 0.5, and$ 1. When $p = 0$, as noted earlier, both algorithms are identical to the GSAT algorithm and hence their performance is the same. For the other two values of p, it is seen that Random Walk algorithm out-performs the Random Noise algorithm. We have noticed this on other instances as well. This has also been observed empirically on large-scale problems [13,14].

From figure 3, especially from the loci in figure 3b and 3d, we can see that p_{best} can be different for each iteration. In practice, this implies that different p value might be needed depending on how many iterations the search algorithm is to run. However, as the iteration number increases, the change in p_{best} gets smaller.

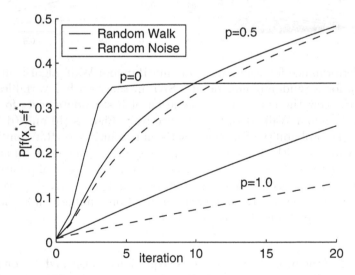

Fig. 4. Comparison of Random Noise and Random Walk algorithms

6   Conclusion

Local search algorithms can be modeled as Markov chains. We have shown how the Random Noise and Random Walk algorithms for satisfiability testing can also be described using such a model. Based on this modeling, we are able to derive the probability of finding a satisfying assignment, and the statistics of the best solution observed within a given number of iterations. The former measure of algorithm performance is useful when considering problems of complete satisfiability, while the latter is more relevant to the problem of maximum satisfiability and related optimization problems.

For real world problems, it is almost always the case that a value of $p = p_{best} \in (0,1)$ offers the best performance on a given problem. The results obtained for randomly generated 3-SAT instances using our analysis also show this behavior. The value of p_{best} depends upon the specific problem instance, as well as the iteration number. We observed that the performance measures vary slowly with respect to p. Further, we have proved that these performance measures are polynomial (hence continuous) functions of p, the probability of making non-greedy moves. Therefore, for real world problems, if the value of p chosen via experiments is close to p_{best}, it will result in near-optimal performance. In nearly all the 3-SAT instances we tested, the Random Walk algorithm out-performed the Random Noise algorithm. This merits further study.

The characteristics of a search space have a big impact on the algorithm performance. Only a limited number of SAT problem instances are tested in the experiments. Future research may include the study of effects of changes in parameters such as the ratio of constraints to variables. This may reveal more insights on how the structure of a problem and the search algorithms interact.

References

1. E. H. L. Aarts and J. H. M. Korst, *Simulated Annealing and Boltzmann Machines*, Wiley, 1989. 280
2. J. R. Cruz and C. C. Y. Dorea, "Simple conditions for the convergence of simulated annealing type algorithms," *Journal of Applied Probability*, vol. 35, no. 4, p. 885-92, December 1998. 278
3. A. E. Eiben, E. H. L. Aarts, and K. M. Van Hee, "Global convergence of genetic algorithms: a markov chain analysis," *Parallel Problem Solving from Nature, PPSN 1*, p. 4-12, October 1990. 278
4. J. Gu, "Efficient Local Search for Very Large Scale Satisfiability Problems," *Sigart Bulletin*, vol. 3, no. 1, p. 8-12, 1992. 278
5. J. Hansen and B. Jaumard, "Algorithms for the maximum satisfiability problem," *Computing*, vol. 44, pp. 279-303, 1990. 278
6. D. S. Johnson, C. H. Papadimitriou, and M. Yannakakis, "How easy is local search?," *Journal of Computer and System Sciences*, vol. 37, no. 1, p. 79-100, August 1998. 278
7. C. Y. Mao and Y. H. Hu, "Analysis of Convergence Properties of a Stochastic Evolution Algorithm," *IEEE Transactions on Computer-Aided Design of integrated circuits and systems*, vol. 15, no. 7, July 1996. 278
8. D. Mitra, F. Romeo, and A. Sangiovanni-Vincentelli, "Convergence and finite-time behavior of simulated annealing," *Proceedings of the 24th IEEE Conference on Decision and Control*, vol. 2, p. 761-7, December 1985. 278

9. A. E. Nix and M. D. Vose, "Modeling genetic algorithms with Markov Chains," *Annals of Mathematics and Artificial Intelligence*, vol. 5, no. 1, p. 79-88. 278, 280
10. C. H. Papadimitriou, A. A. Schaffer, M. Yannakis, "On the complexity of local search," *Proceedings of the Twenty Second Annual ACM Symposium on Theory of Computing*, p. 438-45, May 1990. 278
11. G. Rudolph, "Convergence Analysis of Canonical Genetic Algorithms," *IEEE Transactions on Neural Networks*, vol. 5, no. 1, January 1994. 278
12. B. Selman, H. J. Levesque and D. G. Mitchell, "A new Method for Solving Hard Satisfiability Problems, *Proceedings AAAI-92*, San Jose, CA, pp. 440-446, 1992. 279
13. B. Selman, H. A. Kautz, and B. Cohen, "Local Search Strategies for Satisfiability Testing," *Second DIMACS Challenge on Cliques, Coloring, and Satisfiability*, October 1993. 278, 280, 286
14. B. Selman, H. A. Kautz, and B. Cohen, "Noise Strategies for Improving Local Search," *Proceedings of Twelfth National Conference on Artificial Intelligence, AAAI-94*, vol.1, pp. 337-43, July 1994. 278, 286
15. G. B. Sorkin, "Efficient simulated annealing on fractal energy landscapes," *Algorithmica*, vol. 6, no. 3, p. 367-418, 1991. 278
16. J. C. Spall, S. D. Hill, D. R. Stark, "Theoretical Comparisons of Evolutionary Computation and Other Optimization Approaches," *Congress on Evolutionary Computation*, vol. 2, p. 1398-405, July 1999. 278

Appendix A

Remark – Properties of the Transition Matrix: Since the sum of any row of the transition matrix $\mathbf{P}$ is 1, $\mathbf{P}\,\vec{1}^T = \vec{1}^T$, where $\vec{1}$ is a 1×2^N vector of 1's. The elements of $\mathbf{P}$ are polynomials in p of degree either 0 or 1.

Definition: If a matrix $\mathbf{A}$ has elements that are polynomials in p, $\overline{O}(\mathbf{A})$ is defined as the highest possible degree of these polynomials.

Theorem 2: For a given neighborhood, $E[f(x_n^*)]$, the expected best cost seen by a random noise algorithm after n iterations, is a polynomial in p of order at most n.

Proof: By substituting equation (4) into (5), we have:

$$E[f(x_i^*)] = \vec{f}\,\mathbf{C_i^*}(\mathbf{diag}(\vec{\pi}_i))^{-1}\vec{\pi}_i^T = \vec{f}\,\mathbf{C_i^*}\,\vec{1}^T \tag{8}$$

If the elements of $\mathbf{C_i^*}$ be polynomials in p, then $E[f(x_i^*)]$ is also a polynomial in p, and

$$\overline{O}(E[f(x_i^*)]) = \overline{O}(\mathbf{C_i^*}\,\vec{1}^T) \tag{9}$$

Hence it suffices to show that the elements of $\mathbf{C_i^*}$ are polynomials in p, and that $\overline{O}(\mathbf{C_i^*}) = i$. This can be done inductively:

Base Case (n = 1)

From the fact that $\mathbf{D_0^*} = \mathbf{I}$ and equation (2), we get $\mathbf{B_1^*} = \mathbf{diag}(\vec{\pi}_0)\mathbf{P}$. Hence the elements of $\mathbf{B_1^*}$ are polynomials in p and $\overline{O}(\mathbf{B_1^*}) = 1$. All the rows of $\mathbf{B_1^*}$ add up to one:

$$\overline{O}(\mathbf{B_1^*}\,\vec{1}^T) = \overline{O}(\mathbf{diag}(\vec{\pi}_0)\mathbf{P}\,\vec{1}^T) = \overline{O}(\mathbf{diag}(\vec{\pi}_0)\,\vec{1}^T) = 0 \tag{10}$$

The operations in equation (3) consist of adding all elements of $\mathbf{B}_1^*$ that are below the diagonal to the diagonal element in each column and then setting these below-diagonal elements to 0. Thus $\mathbf{C}_1^*$ is an upper-triangular matrix such that all its elements are also polynomials in p and $\overline{O}(\mathbf{C}_1^*) = \overline{O}(\mathbf{B}_1^*) = 1$. When each row of $\mathbf{C}_1^*$ is summed, the order 1 terms will not necessarily cancel out, and hence $\overline{O}(\mathbf{C}_1^* \overrightarrow{1}^T) = 1$.

Inductive Hypothesis

For any $k > 1$, the elements of $\mathbf{B}_{k-1}^*$ and $\mathbf{C}_{k-1}^*$ are polynomials in p. Further, $\overline{O}(\mathbf{C}_{k-1}^*) = \overline{O}(\mathbf{B}_{k-1}^*) = k - 1$, $\overline{O}(\mathbf{B}_{k-1}^* \overrightarrow{1}^T) = k - 2$, and $\overline{O}(\mathbf{C}_{k-1}^* \overrightarrow{1}^T) = k - 1$.

Inductive Step

This is similar to the verification of the base case. From equations (2) and (4), we get:

$$\mathbf{B}_i^* = \mathbf{C}_{i-1}^*(\text{diag}(\overrightarrow{\pi}_{i-1}))^{-1}\text{diag}(\overrightarrow{\pi}_{i-1})\mathbf{P} = \mathbf{C}_{i-1}^*\mathbf{P} \tag{11}$$

By this equation, the elements of $\mathbf{B}_k^*$ are polynomial in p, and $\overline{O}(\mathbf{B}_k^*) = \overline{O}(\mathbf{C}_{k-1}^*)$ $+ \overline{O}(\mathbf{P}) = k$. The operations in equation (3) ensure that $\mathbf{C}_k^*$ is an upper-triangular matrix and that all its elements are polynomials in p with $\overline{O}(\mathbf{C}_k^*) = \overline{O}(\mathbf{B}_k^*) = k$. Also from equation (11),

$$\overline{O}(\mathbf{B}_k^* \overrightarrow{1}^T) = \overline{O}(\mathbf{C}_{k-1}^*\mathbf{P} \overrightarrow{1}^T) = \overline{O}(\mathbf{C}_{k-1}^* \overrightarrow{1}^T) = k - 1 \tag{12}$$

This means that when each row of $\mathbf{B}_k^*$ is summed, any terms of degree k all cancel out. After the below-diagonal elements of $\mathbf{B}_k^*$ are moved to the diagonal terms in equation 3, when the rows of $\mathbf{C}_k^*$ are summed, the terms of degree k will not necessarily cancel. Hence $\overline{O}(\mathbf{C}_k^* \overrightarrow{1}^T) = k$.

Therefore by induction, we have that the elements of $\mathbf{C}_n^*$ are polynomials in p and that $\overline{O}(\mathbf{C}_n^* \overrightarrow{1}^T) = n$, $\forall n \geq 1$. **Q. E. D.**

Corollary 1: The variance of the best cost $VAR[f(x_n^*)]$ is a polynomial in p of order at most $2n$.

This follows immediately from the result of Theorem 1 and equation 6.

Corollary 2: $P[f(x_n^*) = f^*]$, the probability of having found the global best assignment after n iterations, is a polynomial in p of order at most n.

To see this, compare equations (5) and (7). The properties of $E[f(x_n^*)]$ with respect to p hold for $P[f(x_n^*) = f^*]$ as well.

Appendix B

Table 2. sample 3-SAT instance with 7 variables, 30 clauses

{−4, 7, 2}	{−3, −6, −4}	{−6, 4, −2}	{−4, −1, 7}	{ 5, 6, −7}	{−6, −7, 4}
{−3, 7, 2}	{−5, 2, −1}	{−6, −5, 4}	{−2, −1, 3}	{−7, 1, −3}	{ 4, 6, 3}
{−7, −4, 5}	{−7, −5, −3}	{−1, −7, −5}	{3, 5, 4}	{ 7, −6, −5}	{−1, 4, −6}
{ 1, 3, −2}	{ 2, −4, 5}	{ 4, −5, −3}	{−3, −2, −5}	{−1, 5, 2}	{−6, −1, 3}
{ 5, −2, −7}	{ 1, −5,6}	{ 6, −1, −4}	{ 1, 6, −3}	{−3, −6, 1}	{ 5, 6, −2}

Boosting Search with Variable Elimination*

Javier Larrosa

Dep. Llenguatges i Sistemes Informàtics
Universitat Politècnica de Catalunya, Barcelona, Spain
larrosa@lsi.upc.es

Abstract. *Variable elimination* is the basic step of *Adaptive Consistency*[4]. It transforms the problem into an equivalent one, having one less variable. Unfortunately, there are many classes of problems for which it is infeasible, due to its exponential space and time complexity. However, by restricting variable elimination so that only low arity constraints are processed and recorded, it can be effectively combined with search, because the elimination of variables, reduces the search tree size.
In this paper we introduce $VarElimSearch(\mathcal{S}, k)$, a hybrid meta-algorithm that combines search and variable elimination. The parameter $\mathcal{S}$ names the particular search procedure and k controls the tradeoff between the two strategies. The algorithm is space exponential in k. Regarding time, we show that its complexity is bounded by k and a structural parameter from the constraint graph. We also provide experimental evidence that the hybrid algorithm can outperform state-of-the-art algorithms in binary sparse problems. Experiments cover the tasks of finding *one solution* and the *best solution* (Max-CSP). Specially in the Max-CSP case, the advantage of our approach can be overwhelming.

1 Introduction

Many problems arising in a variety of domains such as scheduling, design, diagnosis, temporal reasoning and default reasoning, can be naturally modeled as constraint satisfaction problems. A *constraint satisfaction problem* (CSP) consists of a finite set of *variables*, each associated with a finite *domain* of values, and a set of *constraints*. A *solution* is an assignment of a value to every variable such that all constraints are satisfied.

Typical tasks of interest are to determine if there exists a solution, to find one or all solutions and to find the best solution relative to a preference criterion. All these tasks are NP-*hard*. Therefore, general algorithms are likely to require exponential time in the worst-case.

Most algorithms for constraint satisfaction belong to one of the two following schemes: *search* and *consistency inference*. Search algorithms can be complete

---

* This work was carried out while the author was visiting the *University of California at Irvine* with grant from *Generalitat de Catalunya*. The author is thankful to Rina Dechter for many useful comments and suggestions on previous versions of this paper. This research is partially funded by the Spanish CICYT under the project TAP1999-1086-C03-03 and by the NSF under grant IIS-9610015.

R. Dechter (Ed.): CP 2000, LNCS 1894, pp. 291–305, 2000.
© Springer-Verlag Berlin Heidelberg 2000

or incomplete. In this paper we are concerned with complete ones. These algorithms transform a problem into a set of subproblems by selecting a variable and considering the assignment of each of its domain values. The subproblems are solved in sequence applying recursively the same transformation rule, often referred to as *branching* or *conditioning*. Each time a search algorithm assigns a value to a variable it is, in a way, making a *guess* about the right value for that variable. If the guess is not correct, the algorithm will eventually *backtrack* to that point and a new guess for the same variable will have to be made. Incorrect guesses at early levels of the search tree cause the algorithm to *thrash*. This is the main drawback of these kind of algorithms. On the other hand, they have the good property of having linear space complexity.

Consistency inference algorithms transform the original problem into an equivalent one (i.e. having the same set of solutions) by *inferring* constraints that are implicit in the original problem and adding them explicitly. Each time a new constraint is added, there is more knowledge available about the relations among variables and the problem becomes presumably simpler. Consistency inference algorithms include incomplete methods which only enforce some form of *local consistency* (such as arc-consistency) as well as complete methods which enforce *global consistency*. In a globally consistent problem, a solution can be computed in a *backtrack-free* manner.

Adaptive Consistency (*AdCons*) [4] is a complete consistency inference algorithm which relies on the general schema of *variable elimination*[5]. This algorithm proceeds by selecting one variable at a time and replacing it by a new constraint which summarizes the effect of the chosen variable. The main drawback of *AdCons* is that constraints (either from the original problem, or added by the algorithm) can have large arities (i.e. scopes). These constraints are exponentially hard to process and require exponential space to store. The exponential space complexity in particular limits severely the algorithm usefulness. However, a nice property of adaptive consistency is that it never needs to make a guess. Once a variable is replaced by the corresponding constraint, the process never has to be reconsidered.

In this paper we propose a general solving scheme, *VarElimSearch*, which combines search and variable elimination in an attempt to exploit the best of each. The meta-algorithm selects a variable and attempts its elimination, but this is only done when the elimination generates a small arity constraint. Otherwise, it switches to search. Namely, branches on the variable and transforms the problem into a set of smaller subproblems where the process is recursively repeated. *VarElimSearch* has two parameters, S and k, where S names a specific search algorithm and k controls the trade-off between variable elimination and search.

The idea of combining inference and search was presented earlier by Rish and Dechter [12] within the *satisfiability* domain. They combined Directional Resolution, a variable elimination scheme for SAT, with the Davis-Putnam search procedure. Different hybrids were considered. One of them, DCDR(i), has a direct correspondence to *VarElimSearch*. The contributions of this paper beyond this earlier work are: *a*) in extending this approach to general constraint satisfaction *decision* and *optimization* tasks, *b*) in providing a new worst-case time bound based on refined graph parameters and *c*) in the empirical demonstration that this can speed-up *state-of-the-art* algorithms.

Our approach is applicable to many search strategies and a variety of tasks. In this paper, we report results of *VarElimSearch* with three search strategies: *forward checking* FC [7], *really full look-ahead* RFLA [10] and *partial forward checking* PFC [8]. We provide experimental results for the tasks of finding *one solution* and *the best solution* (namely, violating the least number of constraints, known as Max-CSP) in binary problems and fixed $k = 2$. In all cases, we show empirically that the hybrid algorithms improve the performance of plain search for *sparse* problems and has no worsening effect on dense problems. Higher levels of k should be explored in the context of non-binary solvers, and are likely to yield a tradeoff between inference and search that will be tied to the problem's structure, as was shown in [12]. This, however, is outside the scope of our current investigation.

This paper is organized as follows: The next Section introduces notation and necessary background. In Section 3 we describe the hybrid meta-algorithm *VarElimSearch*. In Section 4 we discuss the algorithm complexity both in terms of time and space. In Section 5 we provide experimental results supporting the practical usefulness of our approach. Finally, Section 6 contains some conclusions and directions of further research.

2   Preliminaries

A *constraint satisfaction problem* consists of a set of variables $\mathcal{X} = \{X_1, \ldots, X_n\}$, domains $\mathcal{D} = \{D_1, \ldots, D_n\}$ and constraints $\mathcal{C} = \{R_{S_1}, \ldots, R_{S_t}\}$. A constraint is a pair (R, S) where $S \subseteq \mathcal{X}$ is its *scope* and R is a relation defined over S. Tuples of R denote the legal combination of values. The pair (R, S) is also denoted R_S. We denote by n and d the number of variables and the size of the largest domain, respectively. A *solution* for a CSP is a complete assignment that satisfies every constraint. If the problem is over-constrained, it may be of interest to find a complete assignment that satisfies the maximum number of constraints. This problem is denoted Max-CSP [6].

A *constraint graph* associates each variable with a node and connects any two nodes whose variables appear in the same scope. The *degree* of a variable, $degree(X_i)$, is its degree in the graph. The *induced graph* of G relative to the ordering o, denoted $G^*(o)$, is obtained by processing the nodes in reverse order from last to first. For each node all its earlier neighbors are connected, while taking into account old and new edges created during the process. Given a graph and an ordering of its nodes, the *width* of a node is the number of edges connecting it to nodes lower in the ordering. The *induced width of a graph*, denoted $w^*(o)$, is the maximum width of nodes in the induced graph.

Join and *projection* are two operations over relations. The join of two relations R_A and R_B denoted $R_A \bowtie R_B$ is the set of tuples over $A \cup B$ satisfying the two constraints R_A and R_B. Projecting a relation R_A over a set B ($B \subset A$),

---

Algorithm 1: Adaptive Consistency

AdCons$((\mathcal{X}, \mathcal{D}, \mathcal{C}), o = X_1, ..., X_n)$
Input: a CSP and a variable ordering.
Output: a solution, if there is any.
for $i = n$ downto 1 **do**

> Let $\{(R_{i_1}, S_{i_1}), ..., (R_{i_q}, S_{i_q})\}$ be the set of constraints in $\mathcal{C}$ which contain X_i
> in their scope and do not contain any higher indexed variable
> $A \leftarrow \bigcup_{j=1}^{q}(S_{i_j} - \{X_i\})$
> $R_A \leftarrow R_A \cap \Pi_A(\bowtie_{j=1}^{q} R_{i_j})$
> $\mathcal{C} \leftarrow \mathcal{C} \cup R_A$
> **if** $R_A = \emptyset$ **then**
>
>> | the problem does not have solution

for $i = 1$ to n **do**

> | assign a value to X_i consistent with previous assignments and all constraints
> | in $\mathcal{C}$ whose scope is totally assigned

return the assignment to $X_1, \ldots, X_n$

---

written as $\Pi_B(R_A)$ removes from R_A the columns associated with variables not included in B and eliminates duplicate rows from the resulting relation.

Adaptive consistency (AdCons) [4] is a complete algorithm for solving constraint satisfaction problems (Algorithm 1). Given a variable ordering o, variables are processed (or, eliminated) one by one from last to first. For each variable, the algorithm *infers* a new constraint that summarizes the effect of the variable on the rest of the problem. The variable is then replaced by the constraint. Let R_A be the constraint generated by the elimination of variable X_i. The scope A is the set of neighbors of X_i in the remaining set of variables. The relation R, is the join of all constraints involving X_i in the current subproblem, projected on A and possibly intersected with any other existing constraint on A. If this process produces an empty constraint the problem does not have any solution. Otherwise, after all variables have been processed, a solution is generated in a backtrack-free manner. Variables are assigned from first to last. Variable X_i is assigned a value consistent with previous assignments and with all constraints whose scope is totally assigned. Note that the elimination of a variable X_i generates a new constraint of arity $degree(X_i)$ in the constraint graph of the remaining variables.

The complexity of *AdCons* along o is time $O(n\ d^{w^*(o)+1})$ and space $O(n\ d^{w^*(o)})$. Finding the ordering o with minimum $w^*(o)$ is an NP-*complete* problem [2].

Example:
Consider a binary CSP with the constraint graph depicted in Figure 1.*a* (each edge corresponds to a binary constraint) and the lexicographical ordering of its variables. *AdCons* starts by eliminating X_9 which causes the addition of a new ternary constraint $R_{\{1,4,5\}} = \Pi_{\{1,4,5\}}(R_{\{1,9\}} \bowtie R_{\{4,9\}} \bowtie R_{\{5,9\}})$. Next, the elimination of X_8 causes a new ternary constraint $R_{\{1,2,3\}} = \Pi_{\{1,2,3\}}(R_{\{1,8\}} \bowtie R_{\{2,8\}} \bowtie R_{\{3,8\}})$. The process continues until every variable is eliminated.

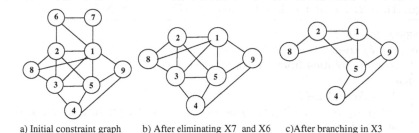

a) Initial constraint graph   b) After eliminating X7 and X6   c)After branching in X3

Fig. 1.

The induced graph $G^*(o)$, whose width gives a bound for the space and time complexity of *AdCons*, is obtained by adding two new edges $(1, 4)$ and $(2, 4)$. Its width $w^*(o)$ is 4. It indicates that *AdCons* computes and stores constraints of arity up to 4.

3   Combining Search and Variable Elimination

In this section we introduce *VarElimSearch(S, k)*, a meta-algorithm that combines search and variable elimination. Let's suppose that we have a problem that we cannot solve with *AdCons* due to our limited space resources. We can still use *AdCons* as an approximation algorithm and eliminate some variables. It will transform the problem into an equivalent one having fewer variables. Subsequently, we can solve the reduced problem with a search algorithm. The recursive application of this idea is the basis of *VarElimSearch*. It is illustrated in the following example.

Example:
Consider the *binary* CSP of Figure 1.*a*. We want to choose a variable for its elimination. If our search algorithms are geared for binary CSPs, a natural criterion is to choose those variables whose elimination adds unary or binary constraints. That is, variables connected to at most two variables. In our example, variable X_7 is the only one that can be eliminated while maintaining the problem binary. Its elimination modifies a constraint $R_{\{1,6\}}$ (it becomes $R_{\{1,6\}} \cap \Pi_{\{1,6\}}(R_{\{1,7\}} \bowtie R_{\{6,7\}})$). After the elimination, X_6 has its degree decreased to two, so it can also be eliminated. The constraint graph of the current subproblem is depicted in Figure 1.*b*. At this point, every variable has degree greater than two, so we switch to a search schema which selects a variable, say X_3, branches over its values and produces a set of subproblems, one for each value of X_3. All of them have the same constraint graph, depicted in Figure 1.*c*. Now, it is possible to eliminate variable X_8 and X_4. After their elimination it is possible to eliminate X_2 and X_9, and subsequently X_5 and X_1. At this point, a solution can be computed in a back-track free manner. Only one branching has been made. The elimination of variables has reduced the search space size from d^9 to d, where d is the size of the domains.

Algorithm 2: Recursive description of $VarElimSearch(\mathcal{S}, k)$

$\mathrm{VES}(\mathcal{S}, k, (t, F, E, \mathcal{C}))$
if $(F = \emptyset)$ then
 | compute solution from t, E and $\mathcal{C}$ then stop
else
 | $X_i \leftarrow SelectVar(F)$
 | Let $\{(R_{i_1}, S_{i_1}), ..., (R_{i_q}, S_{i_q})\}$ be the set of constraints in $\mathcal{C}$ whose scope is
 | in F and includes X_i
 | if $q \leq k$ then
 | | $\mathrm{VarElim}(\mathcal{S}, k, X_i, t, F, E, \mathcal{C})$
 | else
 | | $\mathrm{VarBranch}(\mathcal{S}, k, X_i, t, F, E, \mathcal{C})$

Procedure $\mathrm{VarElim}(\mathcal{S}, k, X_i, t, F, E, \mathcal{C})$
$A \leftarrow \bigcup_{j=1}^{q}(S_{i_j} - \{X_i\})$
$R_A \leftarrow R_A \cap \Pi_A(\bowtie_{j=1}^{q} R_{i_j})$
if $R_A \neq \emptyset$ then
 | $\mathrm{VES}(\mathcal{S}, k, P, F - \{X_i\}, E \cup \{X_i\}, \mathcal{C} \cup R_A)$

Procedure $\mathrm{VarBranch}(\mathcal{S}, k, X_i, t, F, E, \mathcal{C})$
foreach $a \in D_i$ do
 | $\mathrm{LookAhead}(\mathcal{S}, X_i, a, F, \mathcal{C})$
 | if *(no empty domain)* then
 | | $\mathrm{VES}(\mathcal{S}, k, t \bowtie (i, a), F - \{X_i\}, E, \mathcal{C})$

Observe that we have not made any assumption about the branching strategy. The only condition is that after the assignment of a variable, the variable stops being relevant in the corresponding subproblem. Most look-ahead algorithm satisfy this condition, because they prune all future values that are inconsistent with the assignment. Look-back search strategies may also be used but they may require some more elaborate integration. Therefore, $VarElimSearch(\mathcal{S}, k)$ has a parameter $\mathcal{S}$ which instantiates the search strategy of choice.

In the example, we limited the arity of the new constraints to two. However, in general $VarElimSearch(\mathcal{S}, k)$ bounds the arity of the new constraints to k. This parameter ranges from -1 to $n - 1$ and controls the tradeoff between variable elimination and branching. Low values of k allow recording small arity constraints which are efficiently computed and stored. However, they may allow substantial search. On the other hand, high values of k allow recording high arity constraints. It leads to substantial reduction of the search space, at the cost of processing and recording high arity constraints.

In the extreme case that k is set to -1, the algorithm never eliminates any variable and therefore performs plain search according to $\mathcal{S}$. When k is set to 0, only variables disconnected from the problem are eliminated. If k is set to its maximum value, $n - 1$, every variable elimination is permitted, so the algorithm becomes *AdCons*.

Algorithm VES (Algorithm 2) is a recursive description of *VarElimSearch(S, k)*, where context restoration and domain updating is omitted for the sake of clarity. Each recursive call receives the search algorithm S, the control parameter k and the current subproblem. The current subproblem is defined by the current assignment t, the set of future F and eliminated E variables, and the current set of constraints C. In the initial call $t = \emptyset$, $F = X$, $E = \emptyset$.

If VES is called with an empty set of future variables, the problem has a solution. It can be generated by processing variables in the opposite order in which they were selected. Eliminated variables are assigned as they would with *AdCons*, branched variables are assigned the obvious value.

If there are future variables, VES starts selecting one. This selection can be done using any heuristic, either static or dynamic. Then, if the variable has less than k neighbors in F, it is eliminated (VarElim). Else, the algorithm branches on its values (VarBranch).

If VarElim receives a variable connected to zero neighbors, the scope of the new constraint is empty, so there is no constraint to add and the variable is just discarded. If the variable is connected to one neighbor, a unary constraint is added which in practice means a domain pruning. Therefore, only when the variable is connected to more than one variable there is a real addition of a new constraint (or a tightening of a previously existing one). If the elimination causes an empty constraint, the current subproblem does not have solution and the algorithm backtracks. Otherwise, the eliminated variables is shifted from F to E, the new constraint is added to C and a recursive call to VES is made.

VarBranch iterates over the set of feasible values of the current variable. For each value, a call to LookAhead is made. The precise effect of LookAhead depends on the actual search method S. In general, it prunes future values that are inconsistent with the current assignment. If LookAhead causes an empty domain, the next value is attempted. Otherwise, a recursive call is made in which the current variable is removed from F and the current assignment is extended to (i, a).

4   Complexity Analysis

VarElimSearch(S, k) stores constraints of arity at most k which require $O(d^k)$ space. It only keeps constraints added in the current search path, so there are at most n simultaneously stored constraints. Therefore, *VarElimSearch(S, k)* has $O(n\, d^k)$ space complexity. Regarding time, the algorithm visits at most $O(d^n)$ nodes, because in the worst-case it performs plain search on a tree of depth n and branching factor d. The actual time complexity depends on the effort per node of the search algorithm S and it is the product of the search tree size and the computation per node. Clearly, this worst-case bound is loose since it ignores the search space reduction caused by variable eliminations.

It is possible to obtain a more refined upper bound for the number of visited nodes and the time complexity, if we assumed that *VarElimSearch(S, k)* is

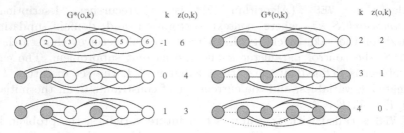

Fig. 2. An ordered constraint graph G and its k-*restricted induced graphs* $G^*(o, k)$ for $-1 \leq k \leq 4$. Note that $G = G^*(o, -1)$. Ordering o is lexicographic

executed with a static variable ordering. The bound is based on the following definition:

Definition:
Given a constraint graph G and an ordering o of its nodes, the k-*restricted induced graph* of G relative to o, denoted $G^*(o, k)$, is obtained by processing the nodes in reverse order from last to first. For each node, if it has k *or less* earlier neighbors (taking into account old and new edges), they are all connected, else the node is ignored. The number of nodes in $G^*(o, k)$ with width higher than k is denoted $z(o, k)$. The number of nodes in $G^*(o, k)$ with width lower than or equal to k is denoted $e(o, k)$. Clearly, $z(o, k) + e(o, k) = n$. Note also that $z(o, k) < n - k$ because the first k nodes cannot have width higher than k.

In what follows, and for the sake of analysis, we assume that *VarElimSearch*$(\mathcal{S}, k)$ is executed with a static variable ordering and that it selects the variables *from last to first*. The k-*restricted induced graph* $G^*(o, k)$ can be used to synthesize the search space traversed by the algorithm. The nodes in $G^*(o, k)$ having width lower than or equal to k are exactly the variables that *VarElimSearch*$(\mathcal{S}, k)$ eliminates. The edges added during the computation of $G^*(o, k)$ coincide with the constraints that the algorithm adds when it performs variable elimination. The nodes that are ignored during the computation of $G^*(o, k)$ have width higher than k and thus correspond to the variables in which *VarElimSearch*$(\mathcal{S}, k)$ branches.

Proposition:
VarElimSearch$(\mathcal{S}, k)$ with a static variable ordering o runs in time $O(d^{z(o,k)} \times (L(\mathcal{S}) + e(o, k)d^{k+1}))$ where $L(\mathcal{S})$ is the cost of the look-ahead in $\mathcal{S}$.

Proof:
The algorithm branches in $z(o, k)$ variables with a branching factor of d, so the search space size is bounded by $d^{z(o,k)}$. At each node, the algorithm performs the look-ahead, with cost $L(\mathcal{S})$, and at most $e(o, k)$ variable eliminations. Eliminating a variable with up to k neighbors has cost d^{k+1}. Therefore, the total cost is $O(L(\mathcal{S}) + e(o, k) \, d^{k+1})$. Multiplying this by the total number of nodes, $d^{z(o,k)}$, we obtain the total time complexity. □

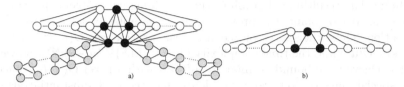

Fig. 3. A constraint graph and a subgraph after the elimination of grey variables and branching on two black variables

This proposition shows that *VarElimSearch(S, k)* is exponential in $k + z(o, k)$. Increasing k, is likely to decrease $z(o, k)$, which means that less search takes place at the cost of having more expensive (in time and space) variable elimination. Figure 2 illustrates this fact. Given an ordered constraint graph G (Figure 2 top left), we can see how $G^*(o, k)$ changes as k varies from -1 to 4 (note that $G = G^*(o, -1)$ because no edge can be possibly be added). The value of k appears at the right side of each graph, along with the corresponding $z(o, k)$. Grey nodes are those with width lower than or equal to k and correspond to the variables that *VarElimSearch(S, k)* eliminates. Dotted edges are those added during the computation of $G^*(o, k)$. White nodes are those with width higher than k and correspond to branching variables. For example, when $k = 1$, variable 6 is branched first, next variable 5 is branched, then variable 4 is eliminated, and so on. The space requirements, search space size and effort per node as k varies is depicted in the following table.

k	$z(o, k)$	space	search space size	effort per node
-1	6	0	d^6	$L(S)$
0	4	$6\ d^0$	d^4	$L(S) + 2\ d^1$
1	3	$6\ d^1$	d^3	$L(S) + 3\ d^2$
2	2	$6\ d^2$	d^2	$L(S) + 4\ d^3$
3	1	$6\ d^3$	d^1	$L(S) + 5\ d^4$
4	0	$6\ d^4$	d^0	$6\ d^5$

The time complexity of the algorithm suggests a class of problems for which *VarElimSearch(S, k)* is likely to be effective. Namely, problems having a subset of the variables highly connected while the rest have low connectivity. The highly connected part renders *AdCons* infeasible. Similarly, a search procedure may branch on the low connectivity variables causing the algorithm to thrash. *VarElimSearch(S, k)* with a low k may efficiently eliminate the low-connectivity variables and search on the dense subproblems.

Example:
Consider a problem having the constraint graphs of Figure 3.*a*. There is a clique of size 5 (black nodes), which means that the complexity of *AdCons* is at least $O(nd^4)$ and $O(nd^5)$ space and time, respectively. Search algorithms have, in general, time complexity $O(d^n L(S))$. However, *VarElimSearch(S, k)*, with $k = 2$ if provided with the appropriate variable ordering eliminates all grey nodes before any branching. Subsequently, it may branch on the two bottom nodes of

the clique. The resulting subgraph of the remaining subproblems is depicted in Figure 3.*b*. At this point, the problems can be completely solved with variable elimination. Thus, the space complexity of the process was $O(n\ d^2)$, the search space size $O(d^2)$ and the time complexity $O(d^2 \times (L(\mathcal{S}) + (n-2)d^3))$. So we were able to achieve time bounds similar to *AdCons* with a lower $O(n\ d^2)$ space.

A special class of constraint problems that received substantial attention in the past two decades are binary CSPs. Many efficient algorithms that were developed were geared particularly to this class of problems. Two well known algorithms for binary problems are *forward checking* FC [7] and *really full look-ahead* RFLA [10]. Both algorithms are worst-case exponential in n, but in practice demonstrate better performance. The following proposition provides the time complexity of *VarElimSearch*(FC,2) and *VarElimSearch*(RFLA,2) (note that parameter k cannot be set to values higher than 2 because it would add non-binary constraints).

Proposition:
1. *VarElimSearch*(FC,2) has time complexity $O(n\ d^{z(o,2)+3})$.
2. *VarElimSearch*(RFLA,2) has time complexity $O(n^2\ d^{z(o,2)+3})$.

The proposition shows that the complexity of the algorithms depends on the constraint graph topology. Since $z(o,2) < n - 2$, both algorithms are, at most, exponential in n.

5   Empirical Results

In this section we provide some empirical evaluation of the potential of our approach. We restrict the experiments to binary constraint problems and we use search algorithms geared for binary problems with parameter k equal to two. The main reason for this restriction is that search algorithms are well defined, well understood and widely available for the binary case. Clearly, the extention of this empirical work to the general case and the evaluation of the effect of larger values of k is a necessary future work.

The experiments were performed on Sun WorkStations. Although different machines were used, competing algorithms were always executed on the same machine. All implementations have been coded in C, and algorithms share code and data structures whenever possible. In all the experiments *VarElimSearch* algorithms select first variables that can be eliminated. If there are none that qualify, the current domain size divided by the number of future constrained variables is computed for each future variable and the variable with the lowest ratio is selected for branching. Algorithms that do not eliminate variables, select always the variable with the lowest ratio.

In our experiments we have used binary *random* CSPs as defined in [11] [1] . A binary random CSP class is characterized by $\langle n, d, p_1, p_2 \rangle$ where n is the number of variables, d the number of values per variable, p_1 the graph *connectivity*

---

[1] Our benchmarks are not affected by the result of [1] because, as we will show, problem instances cannot be trivially solved with algorithms that enforce arc-consistency. Therefore, they cannot have flawed variables.

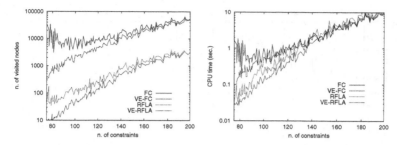

Fig. 4. Average search effort of four algorithms on the classes $\langle 50, 10, \frac{75}{1225} : \frac{200}{1225}, p_2^* \rangle$. Mean number of visited nodes and CPU time is reported. Note that plot curves come in the same top-to-bottom order than legend keys

defined as the ratio of existing constraints to maximum number of constraints, and p_2 is the constraint *tightness* defined as the ratio of forbidden value pairs. The constrained variables and the forbidden value pairs are randomly selected. Instances with a disconnected constraint graph are discarded. The *average degree* in a random problem is $\overline{dg} = p_1 \times (n - 1)$.

We denote $\langle n, d, p_1 : p_1', p_2 \rangle$ the consecutive classes of problems ranging from $\langle n, d, p_1, p_2 \rangle$ to $\langle n, d, p_1', p_2 \rangle$ and making the smallest possible increments (that is, each class has problems with one more constraint than the previous class). A similar notation is used to denote sequences of problem classes with respect n, d and p_2. In all the experiments, samples have 50 instances.

5.1 Finding one Solution (CSP)

In our first set of experiments we consider the task of finding one solution (CSP). We compare FC and RFLA versus *VarElimSearch*(FC,2) and *VarElimSearch*(RFLA,2) (VE-FC and VE-RFLA, for short). Our implementation of RFLA is based on AC6 [3]. Since the overhead of AC6 cannot be fairly evaluated in terms of consistency checks, we consider the CPU time as the main computational effort measure. We also report the number of visited nodes.

In our first experiment we ran the four algorithms on $\langle 50, 10, \frac{75}{1225} : \frac{200}{1225}, p_2^* \rangle$, where p_2^* denotes the *cross-over* tightness (tightness that produces 50% satisfiable problems and 50% unsatisfiable) or the closest approximation. In these set of problems $\overline{dg}$ increases with the connectivity. It ranges from 3 to 8. Figure 4 reports the average number of visited nodes and average CPU time for each algorithm (note the *log* scale). We observe that VE-FC (resp. VE-RFLA) clearly outperforms FC (resp. RFLA) both in terms of nodes and CPU time. The maximum gain is observed in the most sparse problems where VE-FC (resp. VE-RFLA) can be 2 or 3 times faster than FC (resp. RFLA). As a matter of fact, in the most sparse problems variable elimination usually does most of the work and search only takes place in a few variables. As problems become more connected, the gain decreases. However, typical gains in problems with $\overline{dg}$ around

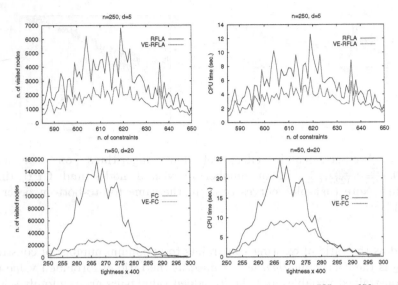

Fig. 5. Experimental results on the classes $\langle 250, 5, \frac{585}{31125} : \frac{650}{31125}, p_2^* \rangle$ and $\langle 50, 20, 125, \frac{250}{400} : \frac{300}{400} \rangle$. Mean number of visited nodes and CPU time is reported

5 (i.e. 125 constraints) are still significant (20% to 40%). As problems approach $\overline{dg} = 8$, it becomes less and less probable to find variables with degree lower than or equal to 2. Therefore, the gain of VE-FC and VE-RFLA gracefully vanishes. Interestingly, detecting that no variable elimination is possible can be done while searching for the variable with the smallest domain, so in those problems where no variables are eliminated, the overhead of variable elimination is negligible.

Next, we investigate how the algorithms scale up, while keeping the average degree around 5. The four algorithms were executed in the classes $\langle 250, 5, \frac{585}{31125} : \frac{650}{31125}, p_2^* \rangle$ and $\langle 50, 20, 125, \frac{250}{400} : \frac{300}{400} \rangle$. In the first set of problems, FC performed very poorly compared to RFLA, in the second it was RFLA who performed poorly compared to FC, so we report the results with the better algorithm for each class only. Figure 5(top) reports the average results of executing RFLA and VE-RFLA in the 250 variables problems. The superiority of VE-RFLA is again apparent in this class of problems. VE-RFLA is always faster than RFLA and the gain ratio varies from 1.2 to 3. Figure 5(bottom) reports the average results of executing FC and VE-FC in the $\langle 50, 20, 125, \frac{250}{400} : \frac{300}{400} \rangle$ problems. VE-FC is also clearly faster than FC. At the complexity peak, VE-FC is 2.5 times faster than FC.

5.2 Finding the Best Solution (Max-CSP)

In our second set of experiments we consider the task of finding a solution that violates the least number of constraints in over-constrained problem instances. This task is known as Max-CSP [6]. We experiment with *Partial Forward Check-*

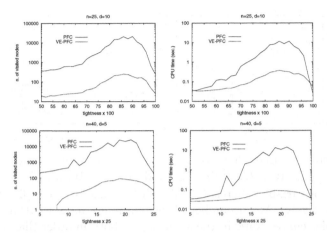

Fig. 6. Average search effort of PFC and VE-PFC on $\langle 25, 10, \frac{37}{300}, p_2 \rangle$ and $\langle 40, 5, \frac{55}{780}, p_2 \rangle$. Mean number of visited nodes and CPU time is reported

ing algorithms, which are the extension of forward checking to *branch & bound*. Specifically, we consider PFC-MRDAC [8], a state-of-the-art algorithm that uses arc-inconsistencies to improve the algorithm pruning capabilities. We compare PFC-MRDAC with *VarElimSearch*(PFC-MRDAC,2) (PFC and VE-PFC, for short).

The implementation of VE-PFC requires the adaptation of *VarElimSearch* to optimization tasks. This requires to modify the search schema to *branch and bound* and the variable elimination schema to Max-CSP. We interested reader can find a precise description of it in a full version of this paper ([9]).

In our first experiment on Max-CSP we select the same class of sparse random problems that was used in [8] to prove the superiority of PFC over other competing algorithms. Namely, the classes $\langle 25, 10, \frac{37}{300}, p_2 \rangle$ and $\langle 40, 5, \frac{55}{780}, p_2 \rangle$. Figure 6 reports the average results. As can be seen, the superiority of VE-PFC over PFC is impressive both in terms of nodes and CPU time (note the *log* scale). VE-PFC is sometimes 30 times faster than PFC and can visit 100 times fewer nodes in the 25 variable problems. In the 45 variable problems, the gain is even greater. VE-PFC is up to 130 times faster and visits nearly 300 times fewer nodes than PFC in the hardest instances. As a matter of fact, VE-PFC can solve the instances with lowest tightness without any search at all.

The problem classes of the previous experiment are very sparse (the average degree is bellow 3). So the next experiment considers denser problems. The two algorithms are executed in the three following sequences of classes: $\langle 10 : 39, 10, 1.5n, \frac{85}{100} \rangle$, $\langle 10 : 27, 10, 2n, \frac{85}{100} \rangle$ and $\langle 10 : 17, 10, 3n, \frac{85}{100} \rangle$. In these problem sets, we increase the number of variables and constraints proportionally, so the average degree remains fixed ($\overline{dg}$ is 3, 4 and 6, respectively). Figure 7 reports the search measures obtained in this experiment. Again, the superiority of VE-PFC is crystal clear. However, as could be expected, the gain decreses as $\overline{dg}$

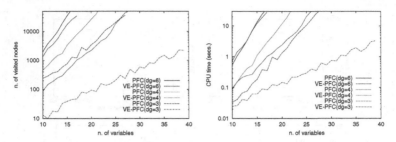

Fig. 7. Average search effort of PFC and VE-PFC on three classes $\langle 10 : 39, 10, 1.5n, \frac{85}{100} \rangle$, $\langle 10 : 27, 10, 2n, \frac{85}{100} \rangle$ and $\langle 10 : 17, 10, 3n, \frac{85}{100} \rangle$. In each class, the number of variables increases while the average degree is fixed ($\overline{dg}$ is 3, 4 and 6, respectively). Mean number of visited nodes and CPU time is reported. Note that plot curves come in the same top-to-bottom order than legend keys

increases. In the problems with $\overline{dg} = 3$, VE-PFC is up to 70 times faster and visits up to 300 fewer nodes. In the problems with $\overline{dg} = 4$, the gain ratio of the hybrid algorithm is of about 9 times in terms of time and 18 times in terms of visited nodes. In the problems with $\overline{dg} = 6$, both algorithms are very close. PFC is slightly faster in the smallest instances and VE-PFC is 30% faster in the largest instances. Regarding visited nodes, the gain of VE-PFC ranges from 40% in the smallest instances, to 250% in the largest. The plots also indicate that the advantage of VE-PFC over PFC seems to increase with the size of the problems if the average degree remains fixed.

6 Conclusions and Future Work

Variable elimination is the basic step of *Adaptive Consistency*. It transforms the problem into an equivalent one, having one less variable. Unfortunately, there are many classes of problems for which it is infeasible, due to its exponential space and time complexity. However, by restricting variable elimination so that only low arity constraints are processed and recorded, it can be effectively combined with search to reduce the search tree size.

In this paper, we have extended a previous work of [12] in the satisfiability domain. We have introduced *VarElimSearch*, a hybrid meta-algorithm for constraint satisfaction that combines variable elimination and search. The tradeoff between the two solving strategies is controlled by a parameter.

We have introduced a worst-case bound for the algorithm's time complexity that depends on the control parameter and on the constraint graph topology. The bound can be used to find the best balance between search and variable elimination for particular problem instances. So far, our analysis is restricted to static variable orderings. However it can effectively bound also dynamic orderings, since those tend to always be superior. Further analysis on dynamic ordering remains in our future research agenda.

We have provided empirical evaluation on sparse binary random problems for a fixed value of $k = 2$. The results show that augmenting search with variable elimination is very effective for both decision and optimization constraint satisfaction. In fact, they demonstrate a general method for boosting the behavior of search procedures. The gains are very impressive (sometimes up to two orders of magnitude). This results are even more encouraging than those reported in [12], where the hybrid approach was sometimes counter-productive. Clearly, we need to extend our evaluation to the non-binary case, since its practical importance is more and more recognized in the constraints community.

Finally, we want to note that the idea behind our algorithm can be applied to a variety of constraint satisfaction and automatic reasoning tasks, because variable elimination and search are widely used in a variety of domains [5]. We have demonstrated its usefulnes in decision and optimization constraint satisfaction tasks. An ultimate goal of our research is to understand the synergy between these two schemes within a general framework of automated reasoning.

References

1. D. Achlioptas, L. M. Kirousis, E. Kranakis, D. Krizanc, M. S. O. Molloy and C. Stamatious. Random constraint satisfaction: A more accurate picture. *CP'97*, 1997. 300
2. S. A. Arnborg. Efficient algorithms for combinatorial problems on graphs with bounded decomposability - A survey. *BIT*, 25:2–23, 1985. 294
3. C. Bessiere. Arc-Consistency and Arc-Consistency Again. *Artificial Intelligence*, 65(1):179–190, 1994. 301
4. R. Dechter and J. Pearl. Tree Clustering for Constraint Networks. *Artificial Intelligence*, 38:353–366, 1989. 291, 292, 294
5. R. Dechter. Bucket elimination: A unifying framework for reasoning. *Artificial Intelligence*, 113:41–85, 1999. 292, 305
6. E. C. Freuder and R. J. Wallace. Partial Constraint Satisfaction *Artificial Intelligence*, 58:21–70, 1992. 293, 302
7. R. M. Haralick and G. L. Elliot. Increasing tree seach efficiency for constraint satisfaction problems. *Artificial Intelligence*, 14:263–313, 1980. 293, 300
8. J. Larrosa, P. Meseguer and T. Schiex. Maintaining Reversible DAC for Max-CSP. *Artificial Intelligence*, 107:149–163, 1998. 293, 303
9. J. Larrosa and R. Dechter Dynamic Combination of Search and Variable Elimination in CSP and Max-CSP. available at http://www.ics.uci.edu/~dechter. 303
10. B. Nudel. Tree search and arc consistency in constraint satisfaction algorithms. L. N. Kanal and V. Kumar, editors, *Search in Artifical Intelligence*, 287–342, Springer-Verlag, 1988. 293, 300
11. B. M. Smith. Phase transition and mushy region in constraint satisfaction problems. In *Proceedings of ECAI'94*. pg. 100–104. 1994. 300
12. I. Rish and R. Dechter. Resolution vs. SAT: two approaches to SAT To appear in *Journal of Approximate Reasoning. Special issue on SAT.* 292, 293, 304, 305

Faster Algorithms for Bound-Consistency of the Sortedness and the Alldifferent Constraint

Kurt Mehlhorn and Sven Thiel

Max-Planck-Institut für Informatik, Saarbrücken, Germany
{mehlhorn,sthiel}@mpi-sb.mpg.de

Abstract. We present narrowing algorithms for the sortedness and the alldifferent constraint which achieve bound-consistency. The algorithm for the sortedness constraint takes as input $2n$ intervals $X_1, \ldots, X_n$, $Y_1, \ldots, Y_n$ from a linearly ordered set D. Let $\mathcal{S}$ denote the set of all tuples $t \in X_1 \times \cdots \times X_n \times Y_1 \times \cdots \times Y_n$ such that the last n components of t are obtained by sorting the first n components. Our algorithm determines whether $\mathcal{S}$ is non-empty and if so reduces the intervals to bound-consistency. The running time of the algorithm is asymptotically the same as for sorting the interval endpoints. In problems where this is faster than $O(n \log n)$, this improves upon previous results.
The algorithm for the alldifferent constraint takes as input n integer intervals $Z_1, \ldots, Z_n$. Let $\mathcal{T}$ denote all tuples $t \in Z_1 \times \cdots \times Z_n$ where all components are pairwise different. The algorithm checks whether $\mathcal{T}$ is non-empty and if so reduces the ranges to bound-consistency. The running time is also asymptotically the same as for sorting the interval endpoints. When the constraint is for example a permutation constraint, i.e. $Z_i \subseteq [1; n]$ for all i, the running time is linear. This also improves upon previous results.

1 The Sortedness Constraint

1.1 Introduction

Let D be a non-empty linearly ordered set. An interval X in D consists of all elements of D which lie between two given elements a and b of D, i.e., $X = \{d \in D ; a \le d \le b\}$. For a non-empty interval X we use $\underline{X}$ and $\overline{X}$ to denote the smallest and largest element in X, respectively. The function *sort* maps any n-tuple over D to its sorted version, i.e., if $(d_1, \ldots, d_n) \in D^n$ then $sort(d_1, \ldots, d_n) = (e_1, \ldots, e_n)$ with $e_1 \le e_2 \le \ldots \le e_n$ and $e_i = d_{f(i)}$ for all i, $1 \le i \le n$, for some permutation f of $[1; n]$.
Let $X_1, \ldots, X_n, Y_1, \ldots, Y_n$ be $2n$ non-empty intervals in D which we consider fixed in this section. We use $\mathcal{S}$ to denote all $2n$-tuples $(d_1, \ldots, d_n, e_1, \ldots, e_n)$ with $d_i \in X_i$ and $e_i \in Y_i$ for all i and $(e_1, \ldots, e_n) = sort(d_1, \ldots, d_n)$. The *task of narrowing the sortedness constraint* is to decide whether $\mathcal{S}$ is non-empty and, if so, to compute the minimal and maximal element in each of its $2n$ components. Bleuzen-Guernalec and Colmerauer [BGC97,BGC00] gave an $O(n \log n)$

R. Dechter (Ed.): CP 2000, LNCS 1894, pp. 306–319, 2000.

algorithm for narrowing the sortedness constraint. We relate the problem to matching theory and derive an alternative algorithm. The new algorithm has two advantages over the previous algorithms: it is simpler and its running time is $O(n)$ plus the time required to sort the interval endpoints of the x-ranges. In particular, if the interval endpoints are from a integer range of size $O(n^k)$ for some constant k the algorithm runs in linear time.

The last n components of any $2n$-tuple in $\mathcal{S}$ are sorted in increasing order and hence we may restrict our attention to *normalized* $2n$-tuples $(X_1, \ldots, X_n, Y_1, \ldots, Y_n)$ with $\underline{Y}_i \le \underline{Y}_{i+1}$ and $\overline{Y}_i \le \overline{Y}_{i+1}$ for all i with $1 \le i < n$. Normalization can be achieved algorithmically by setting $\underline{Y}_{i+1}$ to $\max(\underline{Y}_i, \underline{Y}_{i+1})$ for i from 1 to $n-1$ and $\overline{Y}_{i-1}$ to $\min(\overline{Y}_i, \overline{Y}_{i-1})$ for i from n to 2. We assume from now on (assumption of normality) that our $2n$-tuple $(X_1, \ldots, X_n, Y_1, \ldots, Y_n)$ is normalized.

Example. We use the following running example in this section:

$$X_1 = [1; 16] \; X_2 = [5; 10] \; X_3 = [7; 9] \quad X_4 = [12; 15] \; X_5 = [1; 13]$$
$$Y_1 = [2; 3] \;\; Y_2 = [6; 7] \;\; Y_3 = [8; 11] \; Y_4 = [13; 16] \; Y_5 = [14; 18]$$

1.2   A Connection to Matchings

We define a bipartite graph G which we call the *intersection graph*. The nodes of G are $\{x_i \; ; \; 1 \le i \le n\}$ and $\{y_j \; ; \; 1 \le j \le n\}$ and there is an edge $\{x_i, y_j\}$ if $X_i \cap Y_j \ne \emptyset$. Clearly, if $(d_1, \ldots, d_n, e_1, \ldots, e_n) \in \mathcal{S}$ and f is a permutation such that $d_{f(j)} = e_j$ for all j then the set $\{\{x_{f(j)}, y_j\} \; ; \; 1 \le j \le n\}$ is a perfect matching in G. The following lemma provides a partial converse and gives a first indication of the relevance of the intersection graph. The lemma was stated as property (4) in [BGC00].

Lemma 1 (Characterization of input ranges). *Fix a perfect matching* $M = \{\{x_i, y_{g(i)}\} \; ; \; 1 \le i \le n\}$ *in the intersection graph. For each i let d_i be an arbitrary element in $X_i \cap Y_{g(i)}$. Then there is a tuple in $\mathcal{S}$ whose i-th component is equal to d_i for all i with $1 \le i \le n$.*

Proof. Consider a tuple $t = (d_1, \ldots, d_n, e_1, \ldots, e_n)$ with $d_i \in X_i \cap Y_{g(i)}$ and $e_{g(i)} = d_i$ for all i. Thus $e_j \in Y_j$ for all j. If $e_1 \le \ldots \le e_n$ we have $t \in \mathcal{S}$ and we are done. So assume that there is a j with $e_j > e_{j+1}$. We know $e_j \in Y_j$ and $e_{j+1} \in Y_{j+1}$ and, by the assumption of normality, $\underline{Y}_j \le \underline{Y}_{j+1}$ and $\overline{Y}_j \le \overline{Y}_{j+1}$. Thus $e_j \in Y_{j+1}$ and $e_{j+1} \in Y_j$ and hence we may swap e_j and e_{j+1} to obtain the tuple $(d_1, \ldots, d_n, e'_1, \ldots, e'_n)$ with $e_i = e'_i$ for $i \notin \{j, j+1\}$, $e'_j = e_{j+1}$ and $e'_{j+1} = e_j$. We have again $e'_j \in Y_j$ for all j. Continuing in this way we can construct a tuple in $\mathcal{S}$. □

For a node v (either an x or a y) we use $N(v)$ to denote its set of neighbors in G and for a set V of nodes we use $N(V) = \cup_{v \in V} N(v)$ to denote the set of all neighbors of nodes in V. We use $I(v)$ to denote the set of indices of the nodes in $N(v)$. The set of neighbors $N(x_i)$ of each x_i forms an interval

$I(x_i) = [\min\{j \; ; \; X_i \cap Y_j \neq \emptyset\} ; \max\{j \; ; \; X_i \cap Y_j \neq \emptyset\}]$ or simply I_i in the y's. Glover (see [Glo67] and [Law76, Section 6.6.6]) called graphs with this property convex and gave a simple matching algorithm for them: $f(1), f(2), \ldots, f(n)$ are defined in this order. Assume that $f(1), \ldots, f(j-1)$ are already defined. Let $I = I(y_j) \setminus \{f(1), \ldots, f(j-1)\}$ and set $f(j)$ to i where $i \in I$ is such that $\overline{I}_i$ is minimal.

Example. In the following table we show how the algorithm would compute the function f for our example (in the second column the x's are sorted such that the interval endpoints of their ranges are increasing):

y_j	$N(y_j)$	$I(y_j) \setminus \{f(1),\ldots,f(j-1)\}$	$f(j)$
y_1	x_5, x_1	$5, 1$	5
y_2	x_3, x_2, x_5, x_1	$3, 2, 1$	3
y_3	x_3, x_2, x_5, x_1	$2, 1$	2
y_4	x_5, x_4, x_1	$4, 1$	4
y_5	x_4, x_1	1	1

Lemma 2 (Glover). *If the intersection graph has a perfect matching, the algorithm above constructs one.*

Proof. Assume that the intersection graph has a perfect matching π. We use induction on k to show that there is a perfect matching π_k which matches y_j with $x_{f(j)}$ for all $j \leq k$. The claim holds for $k = 0$ with $\pi_0 = \pi$. So assume $k > 0$. If π_{k-1} matches y_k with $x_{f(k)}$ we take $\pi_k = \pi_{k-1}$. Otherwise π_{k-1} matches y_k with x_i and $x_{f(k)}$ with y_l for some i and l. Then $l > k$ and by definition of $f(k)$ we have $\overline{X}_i \geq \overline{X}_{f(k)}$ and hence $y_l \in N(x_i)$. Thus we can switch the roles of $x_{f(k)}$ and x_i in π_{k-1} to obtain π_k, i.e. we match y_k with $x_{f(k)}$ and y_l with x_i. □

We are interested in the edges that belong to some perfect matching of the intersection graph. These edges form the *reduced* intersection graph. They are easy to characterize; this characterization was already used by Regin in his arc-consistency algorithm for the alldifferent constraint [Reg94].

Lemma 3. *Assume that M is a perfect matching in G. Let us construct the oriented intersection graph $\mathbf{G}$ by orienting all edges in G from their x-endpoint to their y-endpoint and adding the reverse edge for all edges in M. An edge (x_i, y_j) belongs to some perfect matching iff it belongs to a strongly connected component of $\mathbf{G}$.*

Proof. standard matching theory (see for example Section 7.6 in [MN99]) □

We next show how a perfect matching and the strongly connected components of the intersection graph can be computed. We start by sorting the x_i according to both their lower interval endpoints $\underline{X}_i$ and their upper interval endpoints $\overline{X}_i$, i.e. we compute the sorting permutations.

The probably most suggesting implementation of Glover's algorithm maintains a priority queue P. After iteration $j - 1$, the queue P contains all

$i \in I(\{y_1, \ldots, y_{j-1}\}) \setminus \{f(1), \ldots, f(j-1)\}$ ordered according to their upper interval endpoint $\overline{X}_i$. In iteration j we first add all i to P with $\overline{Y}_{j-1} < \underline{X}_i \leq \overline{Y}_j$. We then select the i with smallest $\overline{X}_i$ from P. If P is empty or $\overline{X}_i < \underline{Y}_j$, we detect that there is no perfect matching. Otherwise we set $f(j) = i$. This implementation has complexity $O(n \log n)$.

But as we have the sorting of the x's according to both bounds of their ranges, we can implement the algorithm in linear time. We reduce the problem to an instance of the offline-min problem [AHU74, Chapter 4.8], which can be solved in linear time using the union-find data structure of Gabow and Tarjan [GT83]. We show that we can construct the sequence of *insert* and *extractmin* operations performed on the priority queue whithout knowing the results of the extract operations. The construction is iterative. We start with an empty sequence, in iteration j we append the following operations: *insert*(i) for all i with $\overline{Y}_{j-1} < \underline{X}_i \leq \overline{Y}_j$ and then *extractmin*$_j$. The offline-min data structure determines, if possible, for every insertion the corresponding extraction. If there is a matching in the intersection graph, the algorithm will run to completion and find the same matching as before. If there is no matching there are two ways to get stuck: The result of *extractmin*$_j$ is a value i with $\overline{X}_i < \underline{Y}_j$. Or the offline-min data structure detects an insert operation for which there is no corresponding extract operation. Since we have n insertions and n extractions in our sequence, this means that there is an extraction which is performed on an empty priority queue.

We next show how to compute the strongly connected components of the intersection graph. By construction, we have that for every j the edges $(x_{f(j)}, y_j)$ and the reverse edge $(y_j, x_{f(j)})$ belong to $\boldsymbol{G}$. Thus the two nodes always belong to the same strongly connected component and we can imagine that the nodes have been merged into a single node xy_j. The incoming edges are the edges of y_j and the outgoing edges are the edges of $x_{f(j)}$. It helps to visualize the graph with the nodes $xy_1, \ldots, xy_n$ drawn from left to right in that order. There are many algorithms for computing strongly connected components, all based on depth-first search. We use the algorithm of [CM96] as a basis and adapt it to the special structure of our graph. We will show how to compute the components in time $O(n)$. This is not trivial since the intersection graph may have $\Omega(n^2)$ edges.

The algorithm is based on DFS. It maintains the strongly connected components of $\boldsymbol{G}_{\mathrm{cur}}$, the graph consisting of all nodes and edges visited by DFS. A component is completed if the call to DFS is completed for all nodes in the component and uncompleted otherwise. The root of a component is the node in the component with the smallest DFS-number. We maintain two stacks. The stack S_1 contains the nodes in uncompleted components in order of increasing DFS-number. It was shown in [CM96] that each uncompleted component forms a contiguous segment in S_1 and that the roots of all uncompleted components lie on a single tree path. The second stack S_2 contains an item $\langle root, rightmost, maxX \rangle$ for every uncompleted component. The fields *root* and *rightmost* denote the indices of the root (also leftmost) node and the rightmost node of the component. The field *maxX* is the maximum upper interval endpoint of an x-node in the component, this determines the rightmost xy_j that can be reached from within the component. We still need to say how we scan the edges out of a node. We scan from left to right, i.e., the edge (xy_i, xy_j) is scanned before (xy_i, xy_k) iff $j < k$. We maintain the invariant that for a node xy in a component $\langle root, rightmost, maxX \rangle$ all edges (xy, xy_i) with $i \leq rightmost$ have been scanned. Since the outgoing edges of a node xy form an interval and we scan them from left to right, we have that DFS visits the nodes in the order $xy_1, \ldots, xy_n$, provided that top-level calls to DFS are always performed on the unreached node xy with the smallest index. Thus tree edges are easy to recognize if we maintain the index $next$ of the unreached node with minimal index.

The algorithm proceeds like this. If the stack S_2 of uncompleted components is empty, we start a new component by pushing a corresponding item on the stack. We also push xy_{next} on the stack S_1. This amounts to a top-level call of DFS. Otherwise we consider the topmost uncompleted component $\langle root, rightmost, maxX \rangle$ and determine whether it can reach xy_{next}. This is the case iff $maxX \geq \underline{Y}_{next}$. Assume first that it can reach xy_{next}. Then xy_{next} forms a new uncompleted component which extends the path of uncompleted components. In the algorithm of [CM96] we would push xy_{next} onto S_1 and the item $C = \langle xy_{next}, xy_{next}, \overline{X}_{f(next)} \rangle$ onto S_2. Then we would scan the outgoing edges from left to right. The leftward edges out of xy_{next} could cause merging of components: Consider the components $C_1, \ldots, C_k$ on S_2, where $C_k = C$ is the topmost component. Let j be minimal such that xy_{next} can reach a node in C_j, i.e. $\overline{Y}_{rightmost_j} \geq \underline{X}_{f(next)}$. Then the components $C_j, \ldots, C_k$ would be merged into a single component, which is represented by the item $C' = \langle root_j, next, \max(maxX_j, \ldots, maxX_k) \rangle$. In order to avoid unnecessary push and pop operations, our algorithm checks first whether components can be merged before pushing C onto S_2. If this is the case, it pops $C_{k-1}, \ldots, C_j$, computes C' and pushes it onto S_2. Otherwise it pushes C onto S_2. In either case we push xy_{next} onto S_1.

We come to the case where the topmost component cannot reach xy_{next}. Then we have explored all edges out of that component and hence can declare it completed. We pop all nodes between the root and the rightmost node from the stack S_1 of unfinished nodes and label them with their scc-number.

Example. We show a table of the states of our algorithm when it computes the strongly connected components for our example:

$next$	S_1	S_2	completed SCCs	action
1	1	$\langle 1,1,13 \rangle$	-	start component
2	1,2	$\langle 1,1,13 \rangle, \langle 2,2,9 \rangle$	-	start component
3	1,2,3	$\langle 1,1,13 \rangle, \langle 2,3,10 \rangle$	-	merge
4	1	$\langle 1,1,13 \rangle$	$\{xy_2, xy_3\}$	complete component
4	1,4	$\langle 1,1,13 \rangle, \langle 4,4,15 \rangle$	$\{xy_2, xy_3\}$	start component
5	1,4,5	$\langle 1,5,16 \rangle$	$\{xy_2, xy_3\}$	merge
-	-	-	$\{xy_2, xy_3\}, \{xy_1, xy_4, xy_5\}$	complete component

Theorem 1. *The asymptotic time complexity of constructing a matching M and the strongly connected components of the intersection graph is $O(n)$ plus the time for sorting the endpoints of the x-ranges.*

Proof. by the discussion above. □

1.3 Output Ranges

For j, $1 \leq j \leq n$, we use T_j to denote the projection of S onto the y_j-coordinate. We show how to compute $\overline{T}_j$ for all j. Assume that the intersection graph has a perfect matching and that our algorithm computed the function f. For $j = 1, \ldots, n$ let $\tau_j = \max X_{f(j)} \cap Y_j$. We claim that $\overline{T}_j = \tau_j$ for all j. First we show that $\tau_1 \leq \ldots \leq \tau_n$ which implies $(\tau_{f^{-1}(1)}, \ldots, \tau_{f^{-1}(n)}, \tau_1, \ldots, \tau_n) \in S$ and hence $\tau_j \leq \overline{T}_j$. Assume $\tau_j < \tau_{j-1}$ for some j; then $\overline{X}_{f(j)} < \tau_{j-1} = \min(\overline{X}_{f(j-1)}, \overline{Y}_{j-1})$. Since $\overline{X}_{f(j)} < \overline{X}_{f(j-1)}$ the value $f(j)$ must have entered the priority queue in iteration j and not earlier. Thus $\overline{Y}_{j-1} < \underline{X}_{f(j)} \leq \overline{X}_{f(j)} < \tau_{j-1} \leq \overline{Y}_{j-1}$, a contradiction.

Now we prove by induction that $\overline{T}_j$ cannot be larger than τ_j. Assume we have already established $\tau_h = \overline{T}_h$ for all $h < j$. Imagine that we restrict Y_j to a single value $e \in [\tau_j; \overline{Y}_j]$ and set $\overline{Y}_h$ to $\min(e, \overline{Y}_h)$ for $h < j$ and $\underline{Y}_h$ to $\max(e, \underline{Y}_h)$ for $h > j$. Note that this change preserves normality and does not restrict $\overline{Y}_h$ below $\overline{T}_h$ for $h < j$. If we rerun our matching algorithm, it will construct the same matching as before, until it tries to match y_j. It will also extract $f(j)$ from the priority queue, but in case $e > \tau_j$ the algorithm will get stuck. Thus $\tau_j = \overline{T}_j$.

Example. In our example we get $(\overline{T}_1, \ldots, \overline{T}_5) = (3, 7, 10, 15, 16)$.

The symmetric procedure computes the lower bounds. We start with a function f' which is obtained in the following way: $f'(n), \ldots, f'(1)$ are defined in that order. When $f'(n), \ldots, f'(j+1)$ are already determined, we let $I = I(y_j) \setminus \{f'(n), \ldots, f'(j+1)\}$ and set $f'(j)$ to $i \in I$ such that $\underline{I}_i$ is maximal. Then $\underline{T}_j = \min X_{f'(j)} \cap Y_j$.

Note that we can compute the output ranges from any graph whose edge-set is a superset of the reduced intersection graph and a subset of the intersection graph. We can do it in linear time, provided that we have the sortings of the x's.

1.4 Input Ranges

Given Lemmas 1 and 3, the narrowing of the input intervals becomes easy. For i, $1 \leq i \leq n$, we use S_i to denote the projection of S onto the x_i-coordinate.

Lemma 4. *We have $S_i = X_i \cap \bigcup_{y_j \in N'(x_i)} Y_j$, where $N'(x_i)$ denote the set of neighbors of x_i in the reduced intersection graph. In particular, $\underline{S}_i = \min X_i \cap Y_{j_l}$ and $\overline{S}_i = \max X_i \cap Y_{j_h}$ where y_{j_l} and y_{j_h} are the minimal and maximal elelements in $N'(x_i)$, respectively.*

Proof. immediate. □

We now show how to compute the minimal neighbors of the x's, a symmetric procedure can find the maximal neighbors. Recall that each node xy in an scc C stands for a pair $\{x_{f(j)}, y_j\}$ of matched nodes. Assume that an scc C consists of the nodes $(x_{i_1}, \ldots, x_{i_k})$ and $(y_{j_1}, \ldots, y_{j_k})$ with $\underline{X}_{i_1}, \leq \ldots \leq \underline{X}_{i_k}$ and $j_1 < \ldots < j_k$. Because of the normalization of the y's we have $\overline{Y}_{j_1} \leq \ldots \leq \overline{Y}_{j_k}$. We can determine the minimal neighbor of every x in C by merging the sequences; observe that the minimal neighbor of x_{i_s} is y_{j_t} iff $\overline{Y}_{j_{t-1}} < \underline{X}_{i_s} \leq \overline{Y}_{j_t}$. The two sortings of the nodes can be computed as follows. The sorting of the y's is already determined by the scc-algorithm. The sorting of the x's is obtained by going through the sorted list of all x's and partitioning it according to scc-number. This bucket-sort step requires linear time and gives us the sorting of the x-nodes for all components. This proves that we can narrow the input ranges in time $O(n)$.

Example. If we split up the xy-nodes in our example, we get the two components $C_1 = \{y_2, x_3, y_3, x_2\}$ and $C_2 = \{y_1, x_5, y_4, x_4, y_5, x_5\}$. By merging the sequences $(\underline{X}_2, \underline{X}_3) = (5, 7)$ and $(\overline{Y}_2, \overline{Y}_3) = (7, 11)$, the algorithm discovers that the minimal neighbor of x_2 and x_3 in the reduced intersection graph is y_2 and hence $(\underline{S}_2, \underline{S}_3) = (6, 7)$. When the algorithm processes C_2, it finds out that y_1 is the minimal neighbor of x_5 and x_1 and that y_4 is the minimal neighbor of x_4. Thus it can compute $(\underline{S}_5, \underline{S}_1, \underline{S}_4) = (2, 2, 13)$.

1.5   Summary of the Full Algorithm

The full algorithm is as follows:

1. Sort the x-ranges according to their lower and their upper endpoints.
2. Normalize the y-ranges.
3. Perform a down sweep to compute the matching M_0 and the upper bounds of the y-ranges and an up sweep to compute a matching M_1 and the lower bounds of the y-ranges.
4. Compute the strongly connected components.
5. Reduce the x-ranges.

Except for the first step, all steps take linear time. Thus the complexity of the whole algorithm is asymptotically the same as for sorting the lower and upper endpoints of the x-ranges. This is $O(n \log n)$ in general, but is $O(n)$ if the interval endpoints are drawn from a range of size $O(n^k)$ for some constant k. As Bleuzen-Guernalec and Colmerauer have stated in [BGC00], every narrowing algorithm for the sortedness constraint which achieves bound-consistency can be used for sorting n elements of the set D in time $O(n)$ plus the running time of the algorithm. Thus the complexity of our algorithm is asymptotically optimal in all models of sorting.

1.6   Implementation

We have a stand-alone implementation of the algorithm and we have also incorporated it in the constraint programming system MOZ [Moz]. The implementation can be obtained from the second author.

2 Alldifferent Constraint

2.1 Introduction

Let $X_1, \ldots, X_n$ be n non-empty intervals in the integers. We use S to denote the set of all n-tuples $(d_1, \ldots, d_n)$ in $X_1 \times \cdots \times X_n$ such that $d_i \neq d_j$ for all $i < j$. The *task of narrowing the alldifferent constraint* is to decide whether S is non-empty and, if so, to compute the minimal and maximal element in each of its n components. Puget [Pug98] gave an $O(n \log n)$ algorithm for this task. The running time of our algorithm is $O(n)$ plus the time required for sorting the interval endpoints. In particular, if the endpoints are from a range of size $O(n^k)$ for some constant k, the algorithm runs in linear time. This is for example the case when $X_1, \ldots, X_n$ encode a permutation, i.e. $X_i \subseteq [1; n]$ for all i, or in the alldifferent constraints used in [Pug98] to model the n-queens problem.

Example. In this section we use the following running example:

$$X_1 = [3; 4], X_2 = [7; 7], X_3 = [2; 5], X_4 = [2; 7], X_5 = [1; 3], X_6 = [3; 4]$$

2.2 A Connection to Matchings

As before we reduce the problem to determining the matchings in a bipartite graph G. Let $l = \min_{1 \leq i \leq n} \underline{X}_i$ and $h = \max_{1 \leq i \leq n} \overline{X}_i$. We assume that $m = h - l + 1 \geq n$, otherwise we know that S is empty. The nodes of G are $\{x_i \; ; \; 1 \leq i \leq n\}$ and $\{y_j \; ; \; l \leq j \leq h\}$ and there is an edge $\{x_i, y_j\}$ if $j \in X_i$. We have the following one-to-one correspondence:

Lemma 5. *Every Matching* $M = \{\{x_i, y_{g(i)}\} \; ; \; 1 \leq i \leq n\}$ *in G corresponds to the tuple* $(g(1), \ldots, g(n))$ *in S and vice versa.*

Proof. by the definition of a matching. □

It is clear that G is convex. We use a slightly modified version of the algorithm in section 1.2 to compute a matching M in G. We encode the matching by a function $f : [l; h] \rightarrow [1; n] \cup \{\textit{free}\}$ which maps every y-node to its mate on the x-side or indicates that that the node has no mate. We compute $f(l), f(l + 1), \ldots, f(h)$ in that order. Assume that $f(l), \ldots, f(j - 1)$ are already defined. Let $I = I(y_j) \setminus \{f(l), \ldots, f(j-1)\}$ denote the set of all unmatched neighbors of y_j. If I is empty we set $f(j)$ to *free*, otherwise we set $f(j)$ to i such that $\overline{X}_i$ is minimal.

Example. In our example we get the following function f:

j	1	2	3	4	5	6	7
$f(j)$	5	3	1	6	4	*free*	2

Lemma 6. *If there is a matching of cardinality n in G, the algorithm above constructs one.*

Proof. Consider the graph G' which is obtained from G by adding the nodes $x_{n+1}, \ldots, x_m$ to the x-side and connecting them to all nodes on the y-side. Clearly G' has a perfect matching. Thus the algorithm in section 1.2 will construct a mapping f' encoding it. Assume that we have modified both algorithms such that in case of multiple choices for $f(j)$ or $f'(j)$ the smallest index i (with maximal $\overline{X}_i$) is chosen. Then $f(j) = f'(j)$ if $f'(j) \leq n$, and $f(j) = \textit{free}$ otherwise. □

The matching constructed by this algorithm has an interesting property which we will use later:

Lemma 7. *Let $\{x_i, y_j\}$ be an edge in the matching M constructed by the algorithm above. Then any $y_{j'}$ with $j' < j$ and $j' \in X_i$ is matched in M.*

Proof. Assume $y_{j'}$ is free. At the time when the algorithm determined $f(j')$, the node x_i was not matched since y_j had not been processed. This contradicts $f(j') = \textit{free}$. □

How do we implement the algorithm? We have to take care of the fact that we do not have a bound on m, i.e. the number of nodes on the y-side. We want an algorithm whose time complexity does not depend on m. Let us first look at a priority queue implementation: We sort the x-ranges according to their lower interval endpoints. After iteration $j - 1$, our priority queue P contains all $i \in I(\{y_1, \ldots, y_{j-1}\} \setminus \{f(1), \ldots, f(j-1)\}$ ordered according to their upper interval endpoint $\overline{X}_i$. In iteration j we first add all i to P with $\overline{Y}_{j-1} < \underline{X}_i \leq \overline{Y}_j$. If P is empty, the node y_j becomes a free node. And so will all his successors until the next insertion into P. Since we know the index i_0 of the unmatched x-node with the smallest interval endpoint, we can advance directly to iteration $j' = \underline{X}_{i_0}$. If P is non-empty, we select the i with the smallest $\overline{X}_i$ from P and check whether $\overline{X}_i < \underline{Y}_j$. If so, we detect that there is no matching of cardinality n, otherwise we set $f(j)$ to i.

The sequence of *insert* and *extractmin* operations can be computed in advance. When we construct that sequence we can also determine the free nodes. By counting the number of insertions and extractions, we know when the priority queue would become empty. This means that if we know the sorting of the x-ranges according to lower and upper endpoint, we can compute the matching M and the intervals of free nodes in time $O(n)$ using an offline-min data structure.

We are interested in the edges that belong to some matching in G where all x-nodes are matched. Therefore we construct the oriented graph $\mathbf{G}$. We orient all edges in G from their x-endpoint to their y-endpoint and add the reverse edge for all edges in M. The following lemma was already used by Regin in [Reg94], it characterizes the edges we are looking for:

Lemma 8. *An edge (x_i, y_j) belongs to some matching of cardinality n in G iff it belongs to a strongly connected component of $\mathbf{G}$ or lies on a path to a free node.*

Proof. standard matching theory (see for example Section 7.6 in [MN99])   □

The computation of the strongly connected components can be carried out as earlier because every single free node forms a component of its own. Thus we only have to consider the n matched nodes on the y-side.

Now we show how to mark all matched y-nodes that can reach a free node in time $O(n)$. First we want to put down a few facts about the strongly connected components of the graph $\boldsymbol{G}$. Let C be a component of $\boldsymbol{G}$ and let *root* and *rightmost* denote the minimal and maximal index of a y-node in C. We define $I(C)$ to be the interval $[root; rightmost]$.

1. Let $j \in I(C)$. Then there is a path from y_{root} to y_j. If $y_j \in C$ there is nothing to show. Otherwise consider a path $y_{root} = y_{j_1}, x_{i_1}, y_{j_2}, x_{i_2}, \ldots, y_{j_k} = y_{rightmost}$ in C from the root to the rightmost node. Since $j_1 < j < j_k$ there must be a κ with $1 \leq \kappa < k$ such that $j_\kappa < j < j_{\kappa+1}$. We have $X_{i_\kappa} \supseteq [j_\kappa; j_{\kappa+1}] \ni j$.

2. Let C be a non-trivial component, i.e. C does not consist of a single free node. Then any y_j with $j \in I(C)$ is a matched node. Assume that y_j is free. Considering a path from $y_{rightmost}$ to y_{root}, one can show similarly as in fact 1) that there is a node $y_{j'} \in C$ matched to some node $x_{i'}$ with $j' > j$ and $j \in X_{i'}$. This is a contradiction to Lemma 7.

3. For two different strongly connected components C and C' exactly one of the following 3 statements holds:

$$\text{i)} \quad I(C) \cap I(C') = \emptyset \qquad \text{ii)} \quad I(C) \subset I(C') \qquad \text{iii)} \quad I(C') \subset I(C)$$

This follows directly from the fact 1). If statement iii) holds, we say that C' is *nested* in C. And we say that C' is *directly nested* in C, if there is no strongly connected component C'' different from C and C' such that $I(C') \subset I(C'') \subset I(C)$.

4. Let C and C' be two components such that C' is nested in C. Let x_i be a node in C' and let (x_i, y_j) be an edge in $\boldsymbol{G}$. We claim that y_j lies in a component nested in C. Assume otherwise. By fact 1) there is a path from the root of C to x_i. Thus if $y_j \in C$ then $C = C'$, a contradiction. If $j \notin I(C)$, i.e. y_j lies to the left or to the right of C, then there is also an edge from x_i to the root or to the rightmost node of C since the set of neighbors of x_i forms an interval. Again we can conclude $C = C'$ and derive a contradiction. We say that the edges of C' cannot escape from C. They can only lie within C' or between C' and an other component C'' nested in C.

Consider the top-level components $C_1, \ldots, C_k$ of $\boldsymbol{G}$, i.e. all components which are not nested in an other component. This also includes free nodes, which form top-level components of their own by fact 2). We know that the intervals $I(C_1), \ldots I(C_k)$ are a partition of the set of indices of the y-nodes. Thus we can assume that the components are numbered such that $\overline{I}(C_i) < \underline{I}(C_j)$ for all $i < j$.

Imagine that we shrink each top-level component and its nested components to a single node keeping only the edges between different top-level components.

Then we get an acyclic graph G_s. To be precise, the nodes of G_s are $C_1, \ldots, C_k$ and there is an edge (C_i, C_j) iff there are $u \in C_i$ and $v \in C_j$ such that the edge (u, v) is in G and $i \neq j$. We call a node F of G_s *free* iff F consists of a single free node of G. Let us consider a path in G from a node y_j in a top-level component C to a free node y_f. This path cannot visit a node in a nested component, because edges from nested components cannot escape from their enclosing top-level component by fact 4). Thus the path corresponds to a path in G_s from C to the free node $F = \{y_f\}$.

Clearly, the converse is also true. If we have a path in G_s from a node C to a free node $F = \{y_f\}$, we can find a path in G from any node $u \in C$ to y_f. In order to find all nodes of G_s that can reach a free node we exploit the following property of G_s:

Lemma 9. *Assume that the nodes of G_s are numbered as described above and that there is a path from C to C' in G_s. Then there is also a monotone path from C to C', which means a path $C = C_{i_1}, C_{i_2}, \ldots, C_{i_k} = C'$ with $i_1 < \ldots < i_k$ or $i_1 > \ldots > i_k$.*

Proof. Consider any path $C = C_{l_1}, C_{l_2}, \ldots, C_{l_k} = C'$ from C to C' in G_s and assume w.l.o.g. that $l_1 < l_2$. If the path is not monotone then there is a κ with $1 < \kappa < k$ such that $l_{\kappa-1} < l_\kappa > l_{\kappa+1}$. We distinguish two cases:

- $l_{\kappa-1} < l_{\kappa+1} < l_\kappa$:
  Since G_s contains the edge $(C_{l_{\kappa-1}}, C_{l_\kappa})$ there must be an edge $(x_{i_{\kappa-1}}, y_{j_\kappa})$ in G with $x_{i_{\kappa-1}} \in C_{l_{\kappa-1}}$ and $y_{j_\kappa} \in C_{l_\kappa}$. As $x_{i_{\kappa-1}}$ can reach a node in $C_{l_{\kappa-1}}$ (its mate) and a node in C_{l_κ}, we have that $I(x_{i_{\kappa-1}}) \supset I(C_{l_{\kappa+1}})$. Thus the edge $(C_{l_{\kappa-1}}, C_{l_{\kappa+1}})$ is in G_s and we can shorten the path.
- $l_{\kappa+1} \leq l_{\kappa-1} < l_\kappa$:
  Since G_s contains the edge $(C_{l_\kappa}, C_{l_{\kappa+1}})$ there must be an edge $(x_{i_\kappa}, y_{j_{\kappa+1}})$ in G with $x_{i_\kappa} \in C_{l_\kappa}$ and $y_{j_{\kappa+1}} \in C_{l_{\kappa+1}}$. As the neighbors of x_{i_κ} form an interval in the y-nodes, we have that there is an edge from x_{i_κ} to the rightmost node of $C_{l_{\kappa-1}}$, and hence the edge $(C_{l_\kappa}, C_{l_{\kappa-1}})$ is in G_s. This contradicts the fact that this graph is acyclic.

This proves that we can shorten the path until it becomes monotone.   □

The statement of Lemma 7 implies that no free node (either in G or G_s) has an incoming edge from the right. And hence, we only have to consider monotone paths from left to right in our search for nodes that can reach free nodes. Now it is easy to design an algorithm that marks all matched y-nodes of G which can reach a free y. We know by the facts 2) and 4) that these nodes can only reside in non-trivial top-level components. We can easily modify the algorithm which computes the strongly connected components such that it generates a list L of these components, for the stack of uncompleted components represents the nesting relation. Whenever a top-level component becomes completed, we append the corresponding item $\langle root, rightmost, maxX, nodes \rangle$ to L, where *nodes* is a list of the indices of all y-nodes in the component. The overhead of this is only a constant factor.

After we have finished the computation of the components we perform a sweep over the non-trivial top-level components from right to left. We maintain the index $j^\star$ of the leftmost node that we have seen so far and that is either free or marked. We know that all y-nodes outside the non-trivial components (and their nested components) are free. So when the sweep moves from a non-trivial component C' to its immediate non-trivial successor C to the left, we advance $j^\star$ to $\overline{I}(C)+1$ if there is a gap between the rightmost node of C and the root of C', i.e. $\overline{I}(C) < \underline{I}(C')-1$. With the aid of the value $maxX$, we can determine whether the node $y_{j^\star}$ can be reached from C. If so, we mark all y-nodes in the component and advance $j^\star$ to the index of the root of C. The complexity of the sweep is linear in the number of matched y-nodes in top-level components. Thus the marking can be done in $O(n)$ time.

Example. In our example, we have one nested component $\{y_3, x_1, y_4, x_6\}$ and three top-level components $\{y_1, x_5\}$, $\{y_2, x_3, y_5, x_4\}$ and $\{y_7, x_2\}$. The sweep from right to left will first mark y_2 and y_5 because the $maxX$-value for their component is 7 and hence it can reach the free node y_6. Then it will also mark y_1 since its component can reach y_2.

2.3   Narrowing of the Ranges

Let S_i denote the projection of $\mathcal{S}$ onto the x_i-coodinate for $i = 1, \ldots, n$. Because of Lemma 7, we do not have to consider free nodes when we determine the lower bounds $\underline{S}_1, \ldots, \underline{S}_n$, and hence we can do it in the same way as the input ranges for the sortedness-constraint (cf. section 1.4). Since no x-node in a nested component can reach a free node, the computation of the upper bounds does not change for these nodes either.

In order to compute $\overline{S}_i$ for a node x_i in a top-level component we must determine two things:

1. We must compute the maximal neighbor y_{s_i} of x_i which belongs to the same strongly connected component as x_i.
2. We have to find the maximal neighbor y_{t_i} of x_i that is either free or marked. (If x_i has no such neighbor, we make sure that $t_i \leq s_i$.)

We have $\overline{S}_i = \max(s_i, t_i)$ by the Lemmas 5 and 8. The neighbor y_{s_i} can be found as in section 1.4. The computation of y_{t_i} is similar. First we generate the sequence $(U_1, \ldots, U_k)$ where $U_1, \ldots, U_k$ are non-empty intervals that form a partition of the set of unmarked matched y-nodes with the property $\overline{U}_{j-1} < \underline{U}_j - 1$ for $1 < j \leq k$. Since every interval contains a matched node, we have $k < n$. The sequence is easily constructed. Assume that our matching algorithm has computed the sequence of matched nodes sorted by ascending index. We step through this sequence, sort out the marked nodes and generate the intervals. In linear time we can generate a sorting $(i_1, \ldots, i_l)$ of the ranges of the x-nodes in top-level components such that $\overline{X}_{i_1}, \leq \ldots \leq \overline{X}_{i_l}$.

We determine $t_{i_1}, \ldots, t_{i_l}$ by merging the sequence $(\overline{X}_{i_1}, \ldots \overline{X}_{i_l})$ and the sequence $(\underline{U}_1, \overline{U}_1, \ldots, \underline{U}_k, \overline{U}_k)$. When an $\overline{X}_i$ does not lie within a U-interval, we set $t_i = \overline{X}_i$, because then the maximal neighbor of x_i is free or marked. Otherwise $\overline{X}_i \in U_j$ for some j, and we set $t_i = \underline{U}_j - 1$. Note that y_{t_i} is either the maximal free or marked neighbor of x_i or we have $t_i < \underline{X}_i \le s_i$.

Example. We want to look now at the x-nodes which belong to top-level components. The sorted sequence of the upper interval endpoints of their ranges is $(\overline{X}_5, \overline{X}_3, \overline{X}_4, \overline{X}_2) = (3, 5, 7, 7)$. In our example the unmarked matched y-nodes are partitioned in two intervals $(U_1, U_2) = ([3; 4], [7; 7])$. Thus the merging step produces $(t_5, t_3, t_4, t_2) = (2, 5, 6, 6)$. The indices of the maximal neighbors of the x-nodes in their component are $(s_5, s_3, s_4, s_2) = (1, 5, 5, 7)$. And hence the narrowed upper bounds are $(\overline{S}_5, \overline{S}_3, \overline{S}_4, \overline{S}_2) = (2, 5, 6, 7)$.

2.4 Summary of the Full Algorithm

The full algorithm looks like this:

1. Sort the ranges according to their upper and lower endpoints.
2. Perform a sweep to compute the initial matching M.
3. Compute the strongly connected components of $\boldsymbol{G}$.
4. Mark all matched y-nodes that can reach a free node.
5. Narrow the ranges

Except for the first step, all steps take linear time, and hence the complexity of the algorithm is asymptotically the same as for sorting endpoints of the ranges. If we have a permutation constraint, the narrowing can be done in linear time. In this case there are no free nodes and the forth step can be left out.

2.5 Implementation

We have not implemented the algorithm yet, but we expect that it will also show good performance in pratice.

3 Conclusion

We have presented narrowing algorithms for the alldifferent and the sortedness constraint which achieve bound-consistency. Our algorithms are competitive with the best previously known algorithms. Under some circumstances our algorithm have a better asymptotic running time. For example, we can narrow instances of the alldifferent constraint in linear time when the variables encode a permutation.

Bleuzen-Guernalec and Colmerauer [BGC97] have already noticed that a bound-consistency narrowing algorithm for the sortedness constraint can be used for narrowing permutation constraints. We feel that translating both constraints to matching problems in bipartite graphs has made the relationship more obvious, because the matching problems for both constraints are the same. The matching problems originating from general instances of the alldifferent constraint are more difficult, because one has to cope with free nodes. Thus we think that matching theory has not only provided some efficient algorithms but also some deeper insight into the structure of the sortedness and the alldifferent constraint.

References

AHU74.   Alfred V. Aho, John E. Hopcroft, and Jeffrey D. Ullman. *The Design and Analysis of Computer Algorithms.* Addison-Wesley, Reading, MA, 1974. 309
BGC97.   N. Bleuzen-Guernalec and A. Colmerauer. Narrowing a 2n-block of sortings in $O(n \log n)$. *Lecture Notes in Computer Science,* 1330:2-16, 1997. 306, 318
BGC00.   N. Bleuzen-Guernalec and A. Colmerauer. Optimal narrowing of a block of sortings in optimal time. *Constraints : An international Journal,* 5(1-2):85-118, 2000. 306, 307, 312
CM96.   Joseph Cheriyan and Kurt Mehlhorn. Algorithms for dense graphs and networks on the random access computer. *Algorithmica,* 15(5):521-549, 1996. 309, 310
Glo67.   F. Glover. Maximum matchings in a convex bipartite graph. *Naval Res. Logist. Quart.,* 14:313-316, 1967. 308
GT83.   H. N. Gabow and R. E. Tarjan. A linear-time algorithm for a special case of disjoint set union. In *ACM Symposium on Theory of Computing (STOC '83),* pages 246-251. ACM Press, 1983. 309
Law76.   Eugene L. Lawler. *Combinatorial Optimization: Networks and Matroids.* Holt, New York;Chicago;San Francisco, 1976. 308
MN99.   Kurt Mehlhorn and Stefan Naher. *LED A: a platform for combinatorial and geometric computing.* Cambridge University Press, Cambridge, November 1999. 308, 315
Moz.   The Mozart Programming System, *http://www.MOZ-oz.org.* 312
Pug98.   Jean-Fran\c{c}ois Puget. A fast algorithm for the bound consistency of alldiff constraints. In *Proceedings of the 15th National Conference on Artificial Intelligence (AAAI-98) and of the 10th Conference on Innovative Applications of Artificial Intelligence (IAAI-98),* pages 359-366, Menio Park, July 26-30 1998. AAAI Press. 313
Reg94.   J.-C. Regin. A filtering algorithm for constraints of difference in CSPs. In *Proc. 12th Conf. American Assoc. Artificial Intelligence,* volume 1, pages 362-367. Amer. Assoc. Artificial Intelligence, 1994. 308, 314

Practical Investigation of Constraints with Graph Views

Tobias Müller

Programming Systems Lab, Universität des Saarlandes
Postfach 15 11 50, D-66041 Saarbrücken, Germany
tmueller@ps.uni-sb.de

Abstract. Combinatorial problems can be efficiently tackled with constraint programming systems. The main tasks of the development of a constraint-based application are modeling the problem at hand and subsequently implementing that model. Typically, erroneous behavior of a constraint-based application is caused by either the model or the implementation (or both of them). Current constraint programming systems provide limited debugging support for modeling and implementing a problem.

This paper proposes the Constraint Investigator, an interactive tool for debugging the model and the implementation of a constraint-based application. In particular, the Investigator is targeted at problems like wrong, void, or partial solutions. A graph metaphor is used to reflect the constraints in the solver and to present them to the user. The paper shows that this metaphor is intuitive and proposes appraoches to deal with real-life problem sizes.

The Investigator has been implemented in Mozart Oz and complements other constraint programming tools as an interactive visual search engine, forming the base for an integrated constraint debugging environment.

1 Introduction

The state of the art of solvers based on constraint propagation has made tremendous progress [5,16,19,15], to the point where large combinatorial problems can be tackled successfully. But developing such applications has only limited support by debugging tools. This deficiency has been identified and dedicated projects (as DiSCiPl [6]) have been set up.

The first step to be taken when solving a combinatorial problem is to design a constraint model of the respective problem, i.e., to find a problem formulation in terms of constraints. Next this model is implemented by some constraint solver. Testing the implementation reveals quite frequently that no solution can be found, the solution found is not correct, or the solution found still contains undetermined variables. These situations suggest that the constraint model or its implementation do not reflect the combinatorial problem to be solved. To support the development process at this stage, the programmer needs adequate interactive debugging tools which are currently not available.

R. Dechter (Ed.): CP 2000, LNCS 1894, pp. 320–336, 2000.
© Springer-Verlag Berlin Heidelberg 2000

Current constraint debugging tools focus on improving search behavior [17,1,9], i.e., on finding search heuristics[1] for exploring the search tree most efficiently. There is a lack of intuitive interactive tools for debugging the correctness of constraint models and/or their implementations. In particular, large problems need tools with a sophisticated presentation to handle the overwhelming amount of information. Hence, providing an appropriate metaphor to present the data is crucial. The model of data presentation proposed in this paper [2] is derived from graph-based visualization, as proposed by Carro and Hermengildo in [2]. The graph metaphor was first formally introduced in constraint programming by Montanari and Rossi [10].

The contribution of this work is the development of different graph-based views for correctness debugging constraint programs and the proposal of debugging methodologies based on these views for frequently occurring incorrect behavior of constraint programs. Furthermore, we propose techniques for handling large problems.

To prove the viability of our approach, we have designed and implemented an interactive tool, the Constraint Investigator, that allows the user to investigate the state of constraints and variables in a constraint solver by analyzing the corresponding graph views. The Investigator is characterized by the following points:

- It is not restricted to any specific constraint system.
- It relies on a propagation-based constraint solver (see Section 3).
- It provides intuitive data presentation and interaction, while affording detailed insights about the solver.
- It is fully configurable by the user and requires no changes to the actual constraint program.
- It is suitable for users at different levels of expertise.
- It reveals operational aspects of the solver by displaying the events that trigger constraints.

The Constraint Investigator is implemented in Mozart Oz [11] and the visualization of the graph views relies on *daVinci* [18]. The Investigator complements the Oz Explorer [17], an interactive visual search engine, which does not take into account the aspect of constraint propagation. Both tools form the base of an integrated constraint debugging environment.

The Constraint Investigator can be also useful for performance debugging. For example, its graph views can be aumented with execution costs of constraints such that the program code causing these costs can be identified. Furthermore, operational aspects of constraint execution (see Section 3 about events) are revealed and can be used to improve execution performance.

Plan of the Paper Section 2 discusses issues of debugging constraint programs. Section 3 introduces notions and concepts of propagation-based constraint solving. The model of the Constraint Investigator is discussed in Section 4. The

---

[1] A search heuristics determines the policy of traversing the search space of a problem.
[2] Note that [12] is a previous version of this paper.

Investigator itself is explained by means of a prototypical debugging session in Section 5. Section 5 proposes also techniques for handling large problems. The paper closes with related work (Section 6) and concluding remarks (Section 7).

2   Debugging Constraints

Debugging an application focuses first on correctness and then on performance. Approaches to debugging can be identified as *experimental* and *analytic* [9]. Experimental debugging, i.e., modifying the program text until it seems to work, requires a large set of methods to experiment with. In contrast, analytic debugging needs to obtain a detailed description of the state of the constraint solver. Such a description has to be presented to the programmer by a debugging tool in a way that supports program analysis in the best possible fashion.

After designing and implementing the constraint model of a given problem, testing the implementation typically produces erroneous situations as:

- The solver fails immediately, i.e., the constraints are inconsistent. Either the implementation of the constraint model is incorrect or the model itself is. It is often the case that by accident the constraint model is over-constrained though the combinatorial problem is not. For example, the model states an equivalence where an implication is required. In such a case, if a solution is available (perhaps manually derived), it is a promising strategy to debug this situation by adding this solution to the constraint statements. The propagator which is observed to fail is not necessarily the culprit for the bug in the implementation but it helps to track down the problem in the constraint model.
- Propagation is incomplete in the sense that some solution variables remain undetermined. This is an indicator that the implementation or the model is incomplete.
- The solution found is wrong. Either the constraint model is incorrect or if this is not the case, the implementation of the model is incorrect.

The proposed debugging approach and the corresponding tool are aimed at analytic correctness debugging, i.e., to spot bugs in the constraint model and its implementation.

Analytic debugging requires an interactive tool that enables the programmer to analyze the actual constraints in the solver. The amount of information, i.e., typically the number of variables and constraints, is huge. The way these data are presented in analytic debugging is important since constraint programs are data-driven and an appropriate presentation helps the programmer to draw the right conclusions. Hence, data representation has to match the programmer's intuition of constraints in a constraint solver. Consequently, we choose a graph-based metaphor for representation since it makes possible to emphasize different aspects of the state of a constraint solver appropriately (see the different views presented in Section 4) and to relate the program structure to the representation (see Section 5.2).

3   A Model for Propagation-Based Constraint Inference

Propagation-based constraint inference involves a *constraint store*, holding so-called *basic* and *non-basic* constraints. A basic constraint is of the form $x = v$ (x is bound to a value v), $x = y$ (x is equated to another variable y), or $x \in B$ (x takes its value in B).

Non-basic constraints, as for example "$\neq$", are more expressive than basic constraints and hence, require more computational effort. A non-basic constraint is implemented by a *propagator* which is a concurrent computational agent observing the basic constraints of its *parameters* (which are variables in the constraint store). The purpose of a propagator is to infer new basic constraints for its parameters and add them to the store. A propagator terminates if it is inconsistent with the constraint store (`failed`) or if it is explicitly represented by the basic constraints in the store (`entailed`). A non-terminated propagator is either `sleeping` or `running`. A so-called *event* triggers the transition from `sleeping` to `running`. An event occurs when a basic constraint is added to the store. For example, a propagator might wait for a parameter to be bound to a value, while a different propagator has to be rerun as soon as an element is removed from a basic constraint connected to one of its parameters.

The constraints of a problem instance can be regarded as a network of propagators P, variables V, and events E. The variables in V are the parameters of the propagators in P. The events in E denote the changes to the basic constraints that trigger propagator transitions from `sleeping` to `running`. A propagator $p(v_1^{e_1 \in E_p}, \ldots, v_n^{e_n \in E_p})$ has a set of parameters $V_p = \{v_1, \ldots, v_n\} \subseteq V$ and is triggered by the events $E_p \subseteq E$. The notation $v_i^{e_i \in E_p}$ means that the propagator p is rerun as soon as event e_i occurs at parameter v_i. A variable $v(p_1^{e_1 \in E_v}, \ldots, p_m^{e_m \in E_v})$ is a parameter of the propagators $P_v = \{p_1, \ldots, p_m\} \subseteq P$ and changes to the basic constraint at v can cause the events $E_v \subseteq E$. The notation $p_i^{e_i \in E_v}$ means that the propagator p_i is rerun as soon as event e_i occurs at the variable v.

4   Graph-Based Visualization of Constraints

In this section, we illustrate different graph views using a trivial scheduling application. The problem is to serialize two tasks, such that they do not overlap. The first (second) task starts at starting time *T1* (*T2*) and has a fixed duration of *D1* (*D2*). The corresponding constraint model is the disjunction $T1 + D1 \leq T2 \vee T2 + D2 \leq T1$. The concrete implementation uses reified constraints to implement the disjunction. A reified constraint has an extra boolean parameter that reflects the validity of the constraint, i.e., whether it is `entailed` or `failed`. For example, $B1 = (T1 + D1 \leq T2)$ is the reified version of $T1 + D1 \leq T2$ and if this constraint is `entailed` (`failed`) $B1$ is bound to 1 (0). Conversely, in case $B1$ is bound to 1 (0) the constraint $T1 + D1 \leq T2$ ($T1 + D1 > T2$) is stated. The (exclusive) disjunction of the constraints can be implemented by stating that the sum of the boolean variables associated with the reified constraints is 1. The following Oz code implements the serialization constraint for two tasks [3]:

```
B1 =: (T1 + D1 =<: T2)    % implemented by FD.reified.sumC
B2 =: (T2 + D2 =<: T1)    % implemented by FD.reified.sumC
B1 + B2 =: 1              % implemented by FD.sumC
```

We present four different views of the above constraint program. The shape of a node represents its kind: a propagator node is a rectangle, a variable node is an ellipse, and an event node is a rhombus. A propagator node is annotated with the name of the respective propagator and the location of the propagator invocation in the source program, i.e., the file name and the line number. A variable node is annotated with the name of the respective variable and if the variable is constrained, the basic constraint connected to the variable is also shown. Note that there are no variable nodes for D1 and D2 since they denote integers.

The Propagator Graph View A propagator graph is the graphical representation of a propagator net, i.e., the propagators are the nodes. Note that the
edges are not directed since data flow
between propagators is bidirectional.

This, for example, is different for a constraint solver using indexicals [3] because an indexical is a function rather than a relation. For instance, the leftmost node corresponds to the propagator FD.sumC which happens to occur at line 260 of file opi.oz (the location of FD.sumC when we did the example graph views). This annotation depends on the concrete location of a propagator in a source file. An edge between two nodes means that the propagators share at least one variable parameter.

Using the sets P, V, and E defined in Section 3, a propagator graph $pg(P_{pg})$ consists of nodes $N_{pg} = P_{pg}$ and edges $E_{pg} = \{(p_i, p_j) | V_i \cap V_j \neq \emptyset \wedge i < j\}$.

The Single Propagator Graph View A single propagator view presents a single propagator and its parameters as a
tree. The parameters are grouped
by the events. Note a variable may
occur several times as parameter.
The single propagator graph view
of FD.reified.sumC shows that
the propagator waits for two events,

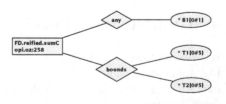

namely the **bounds**-event, i.e., the bounds of the domain are narrowed, and the **any**-event, i.e., an arbitrary element is removed from the domain. Furthermore, the view shows that a **bounds** event at the parameters T1 resp. T2 and an **any** event at B1 cause a rerun of the propagator. A variable node is annotated, as for example the node for T1: *T1{0#5}. This means that T1 takes a value from $\{0, 1, 2, 3, 4, 5\}$. The asterisk ('*') denotes a variable passed directly by the

---

[3] Note that D1 and D2 refer to integers and all other variables are finite domains. The
=-constraint is implemented by Oz's finite domain operator =: (and $\leq$ by =<:).

user to the Investigator in contrast to variables collected while traversing the constraint network.

More formally, a single propagator graph $spg(p)$ for a propagator p is a tree with a root node $R_{spg} = p$, connected to the root node are event nodes $E_{spg} = E_p$ and connected to the event nodes variable nodes $V_{spg} = V_p$. An edge between an event node and a variable node is established if the events of the event node and variable node are the same.

The Variable Graph View   A variable graph view is dual to the propagator graph view. The nodes represent the variables. An edge between two vari- 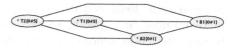 able nodes indicates that the variables are simultaneously constrained by one or more propagators. The information of what propagators are concerned is available by a menu associated with the edge. The variable graph view shows that in our example, all variables are connected with each other.

The formal description of a variable graph makes the duality to a propagator graph obvious: a variable graph $vg(V_{vg})$ is composed by the nodes $N_{vg} = V_{vg}$ and the edges $E_{vg} = \{(v_i, v_j)|P_i \cap P_j \neq \emptyset \wedge i < j\}$. An edge between two variable nodes is present if the respective variables share at least one propagator.

The Single Variable Graph View   A single variable graph view represents a constrained variable, events it can cause and the propagators waiting for these events to happen. One can see 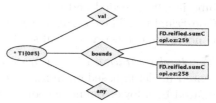 that the two reified propagators wait for the **bounds** event and no propagator waits either for the **any** event nor for the **val** event.

A single variable graph $svg(v)$ of a variable v is a tree with a root node $R_{svg} = v$. Event nodes $E_{svg} = E_v$ are connected to the root node. Furthermore, each event node of an event e is connected to the propagator nodes $P^e_{svg} = \{p^e|p^e \in P_v\}$, i.e., an edge between an event node and a propagator node is established if the propagator waits for this event to happen to this variable.

5   Correctness Debugging with the Constraint Investigator

This section introduces the *Constraint Investigator* as an interactive tool for debugging practical constraint problems. Using the Investigator does not require any changes to the constraint program. The program has to be recompiled with appropriate compiler switches.

5.1   An Example Session with the Investigator

We start off with a deliberately buggy constraint model and program and demonstrate how to track down two hidden bugs. Of course, the bugs are trivial to fix for experienced programmers but the approaches demonstrated are suitable for handling real-life situations.

The Problem   Consider the following bin-packing problem: a given set of weighted items I has to be assigned to three bins $b_{1,2,3}$, without exceeding the maximum capacity of each bin. All bins have the same maximum capacity c. Furthermore, as soon as at least two items are put into a bin one extra unit of packaging material must be added as protection. Moreover, the bins must be color-coded to indicate the presence of a fragile item.

The Constraint Model   The given problem is a set partitioning problem of three sets with extra constraints. Each bin b_n is modeled as set s_n and each item $i \in I$ has a weight w_i.

$$I = \uplus s_n \quad (1) \qquad |s_n| \geq 2 \leftrightarrow \text{packaging material} \in s_n \quad (2)$$
$$\Sigma_{\forall i \in s_n} w_i \leq c \quad (3) \qquad i_{fragile} \in s_n \rightarrow color(s_n) = red \quad (4)$$
$$\text{where} \quad n = 1, 2, 3.$$

Constraint (1) states a set partitioning and Constraint (2) adds extra packaging if necessary. Furthermore, Constraint (3) enforces that the capacity of the bins is not exceeded and takes also into account packaging material added by Constraint (2). The coloring of the bins is modeled by Constraint (4). The model is not quite correct as we will see later on.

The Implementation of the Constraint Model   The implementation of the presented model is based on finite set constraints [8,14], i.e., a set value is approximated by a lower bound set and a upper bound set. The constraint solver has been implemented by the procedure `BinPacking`:

```
proc {BinPacking Weights Capacity Sol}
```

The argument `Weights` is a list of pairs `Id#Weight`. The variable `Capacity` determines the maximum capacity of the bins. The solution is returned in `Sol` and contains the colored bins with the assigned items.

The procedure starts with variable definitions: it declares the variables `Red` and `Green` for the bin-coloring constraint for the fragile item defined by `Fragile`. Next, it adds for the packaging material an extra item (`Packaging=100`) with weight 1 to the list of all weighted items `AllWeights`. The list of `Items` is extracted from the weight list (`AllWeights`).

```
   Red = 0   Green = 1   Fragile = 1   Packaging = 100
   WeightedPackaging = [Packaging#1]
   AllWeights = {Append WeightedPackaging Weights}
   Items = {Map AllWeights fun {$ E} E.1 end}
in
```

The body of the procedure starts by creating the solution list `Sol` of length 3. Each list element represents a bin as a record `bin(items:S color:C)` where `S` is the set of items and `C` is the color of the bin. The application of `{FS.var.upperBound Items}` constrains `S` to the set constraint $\emptyset \subseteq S \subseteq setof(\text{Items})$.

```
Sol = {List.make 3}
{ForAll Sol
 fun {$}
   S = {FS.var.upperBound Items}  C = {FD.int [Red Green]}
 in bin(items: S color: C) end}
```

Next the partitioning constraint is stated (`FS.partition`). The `Map` function extracts the sets that form the partition from the bin records. The variable `Items` is converted to a set value by `FS.value.make` representing the set to be partitioned.

```
% constraint (1): partitioning
{FS.partition
 {Map Sol fun {$ S} S.items end} {FS.value.make Items}}
```

The weight restriction constraint maps the presence of elements to the list of boolean variables `BL` by `FS.reified.areIn`. The constraint `{FD.sumC ... ˆ=<:ˆ ...}` enforces that the scalar product of the list of boolean variables `BL` and the corresponding list of weights (produced by `Map`) does not exceed `Capacity`.

```
% constraint (3): enforce weight restriction in bins
{ForAll Sol proc {$ S} BL in
               {FS.reified.areIn Items S.items BL}
               {FD.sumC {Map AllWeights fun {$ E} E.2 end}
               BL ˆ=<:ˆ Capacity}
            end}
```

The constraints for adding packaging material and assigning the bin color close the procedure and use reified constraints. Reified propagators are used to conditionally state constraints according to constraint (2) in the constraint model. As soon as the cardinality of `S.items` is at least 2 the item `Packaging` is added to `S.items`. This is caused by the connection through the boolean variables of the reified constraints.

```
% constraint (2): add extra packaging material
{ForAll Sol proc {$ S}
               ({FS.card S.items} >=: 2) =:
               {FS.reified.include Packaging S.items} end}
```

The constraint for coloring the bins also uses reified constraints and implements the "→"–operator of constraint (4) by the implication constraint `FD.impl`[4].

---

[4] This is a reified constraint such that the last parameter 1 is required.

```
% constraint (4): assign colors to bins
{ForAll Sol proc {$ B} {FD.impl
                             {FS.reified.include Fragile
B.items}
                             (Red =: B.color) 1}
          end}
end % BinPacking
```

The code for controlling search is omitted since it is not of interest here and we assume an adequate search strategy. Now we submit our bin-packing solver to a search engine, like the Oz Explorer (see Figure 8 in Section 5.3):

```
{ExploreOne {BinPacking [1#3 2#2 3#2 4#6 5#2 6#4 7#3 8#5] 10}}
```

This results in an immediately failed search tree. The Investigator is now demonstrated in a prototypical debugging session.

The Implementation is not Faithful to the Constraint Model Invoking the Investigator from the failed node switches the Investigator to the single propagator graph view (see Figure 1). The node representing the failed propagator is colored red throughout the session.

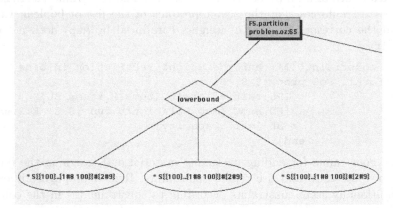

Fig. 1. Single propagator view of the failed propagator FS.partition

The single propagator graph view in Figure 1 shows the partition propagator with its parameters connected via the lowerbound event. The parameters are set constraint variables and are represented by S{{100}..{1#8 100}}#{2#9}[5]. This corresponds to the basic constraint $\{100\} \subseteq S \subseteq \{1,\ldots,8,100\} \wedge 2 \leq |S| \leq 9$. We notice that all three parameters contain at least element 100. Hence, the partitioning propagator must fail. This reveals an incorrectness but this is not

---

[5] That all variables have the same name S does not mean that they are equal. The name is derived from the source code of constraint (1), cf. {FS.partition {Map Sol **fun** {$ S} S.items **end**} ...}.

necessarily the actual bug. A single click on the propagator node highlights the
line of source code where the partitioning propagator is stated (see Figure 2).

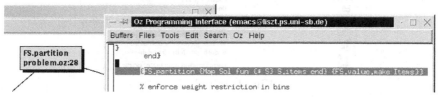

Fig. 2. Associating the failed propagator to the source program

We see that the parameters concerned are the sets of items for each of the
bins in the solution Sol. Checking the program text suggests that only the implementation of the packaging constraint (3) adds to all item fields of Sol the
element Packaging (which is 100). Verifying the code for adding extra packaging material reveals the bug in the implementation: instead of using different
packaging material for each bin, the same material is used for all bins. This is
not the intention of the constraint model and hence an implementation bug. The
bug fix simply consists of using different packaging material items for each bin
and modifies the ForAll – loop to select for different bins different packaging
material.

```
% packaging material for every bin
WeightedPackaging =
  [(Packaging+1)#1 (Packaging+2)#1 (Packaging+3)#1]
...
{List.forAllInd Sol
 proc {$ I S} % 'I' counts from 1 to length of 'Sol'
    % select different packaging material by the index I
    ({FS.card S.items} >=: 2) =:
       {FS.reified.include 100+I S.items} end}
```

After fixing the implementation bug, we obtain as solution

```
Sol = [bin(color:0        items:{1#3 5 101}#5)
       bin(color:_{0#1} items:{4 7 102}#3)
       bin(color:_{0#1} items:{6 8 103}#3)]
```

and we notice that not all variables are bound to a single value (observe the
color fields). The next section demonstrates how to track down the reason for
this problem.

Identification of Remaining Propagators   A solution with unbound variables
suggests that there is a lack of propagation. The variable graph view shown in
Figure 3 is produced when starting the Investigator from the solution node of
the Explorer.

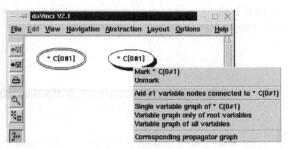

Fig. 3. Initial view

The variable Sol is not displayed because it is bound to the solution list and hence no variable anymore. We try to find remaining propagators starting from one of the variable nodes. We decide to switch to the variable graph view of all reachable variables (Figure 4(a)), to get an overview over all variables left unbound. The menu associated with an edge between two variable nodes (Figure 4(b)) offers to switch to a single propagator graph view of a propagator being imposed upon two variables.

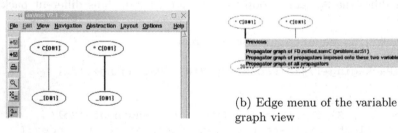

(a) Variable graph view of all reachable variables

(b) Edge menu of the variable graph view

Fig. 4. Variable graph view

Since we try to find remaining propagators, we switch to the offered single variable graph view of a reified sum propagator (Figure 5).

A click on the propagator node immediately reveals the suspicious program text: the assignment of the bin colors seems to be too weak whenever a fragile item is not contained in a bin (implementation of constraint (4)). The problem can be fixed by replacing the implication by an equivalence (FD.equi). The correct constraint (4) in the constraint model is $\forall n : i_{fragile} \in s_n \leftrightarrow color(s_n) = red$. That means that the implementation was correct but the constraint model had a flaw. After applying the fix the solver produces a proper solution.

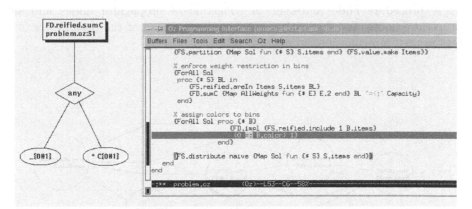

Fig. 5. Single propagator graph view

5.2   Approaches for Dealing with Realistic Applications

Realistic problems may have thousands of propagators and variables. It is impossible and without any practical use to represent all at once. This section proposes techniques for selecting problem-relevant fractions of propagators or variables. This scheme allows for a user-controlled incremental exploration of the graphs which is essential for the investigation of large problems.

A common approach of designing a constraint model is to decompose the problem into subproblems and to decompose these subproblems until predefined propagators can be used. Since procedures implement subproblems, it seems reasonable to structure propagators, sub-procedures, and variables according to the procedures which stated them. This requires the introduction of procedure nodes to the graph views. A procedure node is depicted as circle.

Selection via the Tree of Execution Traces   The tree representation of a constraint program's execution trace (see Figure) is used to select propagators and variables. By clicking on a node, a possible action is to select the propagators created by the corresponding procedure invocation. Incremental expansion of the tree makes possible to handle large collections of propagators and variables. Different selection schemes, e.g., all propagators stated by a procedure with respectively without their sub-procedures, extend the functionality.

Collapsing and Expanding Propagator and Procedure Nodes   A common technique for handling large collections of data represented by graphs is to collapse and expand appropriate subsets of nodes to single nodes. We propose for the propagator graph view to determine subsets of nodes according to the procedures which created them. That means a collapsed node represents a collection of propagators and sub-procedures. This is very close to the model the programmer has in mind when structuring the problem and hence, is very intuitive.

A procedure node represents a collection of propagator nodes and sub-procedure nodes. It takes as its parameters the union of the parameters of all represented propagators and sub-procedures.

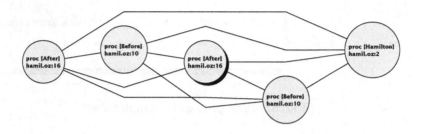

(a) Fully collapsed procedure graph, i.e., all propagator nodes are collapsed

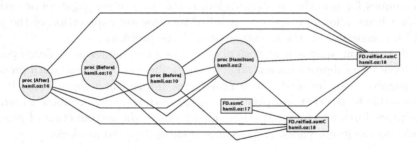

(b) Partially collapsed propagator graph, i.e., a procedure's node is expanded to its propagator nodes

Fig. 6. Transition of a graph view by expanding a procedure node

Figure 6 shows the expansion of the marked procedure node to a collection of propagator nodes. Expansion can be undone by collapsing propagator and procedure nodes to a single procedure node.

Filtering Propagators and Variables   Another interesting feature is the option of displaying only those propagators resp. variables which meet a criterion specified by the user. For example, it might be interesting to limit the investigation to those propagators that are connected to boolean variables when symptoms of a bug suggest that.

5.3 Additional Features

This section discusses features of the Investigator not covered before but important for effective use of the tool.

Navigating Through Graphs Navigation through the different graph views is done by menus associated with nodes and edges of the respective views. Figure 7 shows possible transitions from one view to another one. A history mechanism is also available, allowing to recall previous views by moving in the chain of views produced so far.

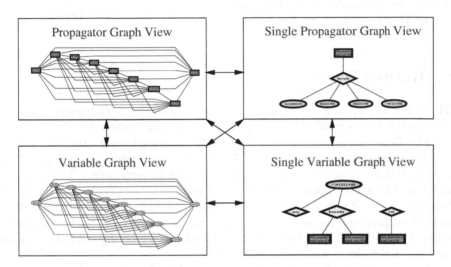

Fig. 7. Navigation overview

To further improve navigation and to keep track of a certain node in different views, the Investigator is able to mark nodes in graph views which then remain marked throughout all views.[6] Additionally, the Investigator automatically marks nodes of variables with which the session was initiated (Figure 3) and in case there is a failed propagator, the node of this propagator (Figure 1).

Changing the Representation of Nodes The Investigator provides a plug-in mechanism for changing the representation of variables and propagators. This enables the user to produce a more obvious and intuitive representation. For example, a propagator for a constraint in a scheduling application might be represented as Gantt-chart, reflecting its role in the concrete application.

Interaction with the Oz Explorer The Oz Explorer [17] is a graphical search

---

[6] For the purpose of this paper, a marked node is drawn with double lines. Other schemes, for example using colors, might be more suitable in connection with color displays.

engine where the user can control search. It visualizes the search tree as search proceeds. The shape of a node tells the user whether a node denotes either a failure (square resp. a triangle for a failed subtree), a solution (rhombus), or a choice (circle). By default, clicking an Explorer node displays the basic constraints of the corresponding constraint store. This action can be modified by plugs-ins as the Investigator is one (as demonstrated in Section 5.1).

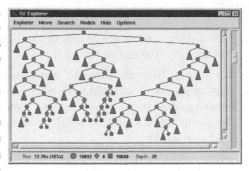

Fig. 8: The Oz Explorer

6   Related Work

The tools discussed in this section focus on improving performance. Since our approach is orthogonal, it can be used to supplement existing tools.

The Grace constraint debugger by Meier [9] supplements the Prolog-based constraint programming system ECL^iPS^e [7] and is intended to support performance debugging of finite domain constraint programming. The constraint program has to be appropriately instrumented to be run under Grace. The debugging model of Grace is based upon the Prolog-box-model. It is able to follow individual propagation steps in the trace and to inspect the backtrack stack of finite domain variables. Furthermore, Grace is highly configurable by assigning user-written code to each propagation step.

The search tree debugger of Chip [1,4] is largely influenced by the Oz Explorer[7]. Its focus is performance debugging. It provides different types of views, mostly in a compact matrix-like fashion, to provide the user with more detailed information about search and constraint propagation. A nice feature is to analyze the evolution of constraints and variables along a search path. This is certainly most valuable for optimizing search heuristics.

7   Conclusion

We have presented a novel approach for correctness debugging constraint programs based on graph views. Based on this approach, we have implemented an interactive tool, the Constraint Investigator. The use of the Investigator has been demonstrated with an example derived from a realistic constraint programming application. The Investigator has been tested with problems of medium size (500 propagators and 600 variables) and has helped to understand and to debug the constraint-based implementation of a natural language parser. To our knowledge,

---

[7] See in [1] Section 3 on related work.

no other interactive constraint debugging tool uses a graph metaphor in the way presented in this paper and that makes the Constraint Investigator unique.

Implementation The implementation of the Investigator is straightforward. It traverses the network of constraints in the solver starting from the solution variables to collect all propagators and variables. Thereby the implementation takes advantage of propagators being first-class values [13]. Every variable and propagator is assigned a unique integer. That makes it possible to store relations between variables and propagators in sets of integers. The computation of the different graph views follows closely the definitions of the graph views in Section 4. The complexity of the graph-generation algorithm is worst-case quadratic and depends in practice on the degree of connectivity of the constraint network, i.e., if the propagators can be stated in reasonable time then the corresponding graph can be computed in reasonable time too.

Acknowledgements

I would like to thank the *daVinci* team for making this brilliant tool available. I am grateful to Leif Kornstaedt for helping me with the implementation. I am also grateful to Christian Schulte for many fruitful discussions. Denys Duchier exercised the Investigator in the development of linguistic applications and helped with invaluable comments and suggestions. The aforementioned, Katrin Erk and the anonymous referees gave invaluable comments on earlier versions of this paper.

References

1. A. Agoun and H. Simonis.   Search tree visualization.   Technical Report D.WP1.1.M1.1-2, COSYTEC SA, June 1997. In the ESPRIT LTR Project 22352 DiSCiPl. 321, 334
2. Manuel Carro and Manuel Hermenegildo. Some design issues in the visualization of constraint logic program execution. In *AGP'98*, A Coruña, Spain, 1998. 321
3. Philippe Codognet and Daniel Diaz. Compiling constraints in clp(FD). *Journal of Logic Programming*, 27(3):185–226, June 1996. 324
4. M. Dincbas, P. Van Hentenryck, H. Simonis, A. Aggoun, T. Graf, and F. Berthier. The constraint logic programming language CHIP. In *Proceedings of the International Conference on Fifth Generation Computer Systems FGCS-88*, pages 693–702, Tokyo, Japan, December 1988. Institute for New Generation Computer Technology (ICOT),Tokyo, Japan. 334
5. Mehmet Dincbas, Helmut Simonis, and Pascal Van Hentenryck. Solving large combinatorial problems in logic programming. *Journal of Logic Programming*, 8:75–93, 1990. 320
6. DiSCiPl.   Debugging   systems   for   constraint   programming. http://discipl.inria.fr/. 320
7. ECRC and International Computers Limited and IC-Parc. *ECL^{i}PS^e*, *User Manual Version 3.7*, February 1998. 334

8. Carmen Gervet. Interval propagation to reason about sets: Definition and implementation of a practical language. *Constraints*, 1(3):191–244, 1997. 326
9. Micha Meier. Debugging constraint programs. In Ugo Montanari and Francesca Rossi, editors, *Proceedings of the First International Conference on Principles and Practice of Constraint Programming*, volume 976 of *Lecture Notes in Computer Science, Springer*, pages 204–221, Cassis, France, September 1995. 321, 322, 334
10. Ugo Montanari and Francesca Rossi. True concurrency in concurrent constraint programming. In Vijay Saraswat and Kazunori Ueda, editors, *Proceedings of the 1991 International Symposium on Logic Programming*, pages 694–713, San Diego, USA, June 1991. The MIT Press. 321
11. The Mozart Consortium. *The Mozart Programming System*. http://www.mozart-oz.org/. 321
12. Tobias Müller. Practical investigation of constraints with graph views. In Konstantinos Sagonas and Paul Tarau, editors, *Proceedings of the International Workshop on Implementation of Declarative Languages (IDL'99)*, September 1999. 321
13. Tobias Müller. Promoting constraints to first-class status. In *Proceedings of the First International Conference on Computational Logic*, London, July 2000. To appear. 335
14. Tobias Müller and Martin Müller. Finite set constraints in Oz. In François Bry, Burkhard Freitag, and Dietmar Seipel, editors, *13. Workshop Logische Programmierung*, pages 104–115, Technische Universität München, 17–19 September 1997. 326
15. Tobias Müller and Jörg Würtz. Extending a concurrent constraint language by propagators. In Jan Małuszyński, editor, *Proceedings of the International Logic Programming Symposium*, pages 149–163. The MIT Press, Cambridge, 1997. 320
16. Jean-François Puget and Michel Leconte. Beyond the glass box: Constraints as objects. In John Lloyd, editor, *Logic Programming – Proceedings of the 1995 International Symposium*, pages 513–527. The MIT Press, Cambridge, December 1995. 320
17. Christian Schulte. Oz Explorer: A visual constraint programming tool. In Lee Naish, editor, *Proceedings of the Fourteenth International Conference on Logic Programming*, pages 286–300, Leuven, Belgium, 8-11 July 1997. The MIT Press, Cambridge. 321, 333
18. Universität Bremen, Group of Prof. Dr. Bernd Krieg-Brückner. *The Graph Visualization System daVinci*. http://www.informatik.uni-bremen.de/~davinci/. 321
19. Mark Wallace, Stefano Novello, and Joachim Schimpf. ECL^{i}PS^e: A platform for constraint logic programming. *ICL Systems Journal*, 12(1), May 1997. 320

A Hybrid Search Architecture Applied to Hard Random 3-SAT and Low-Autocorrelation Binary Sequences

Steven Prestwich

Department of Computer Science
National University of Ireland at Cork
s.prestwich@cs.ucc.ie

Abstract. The hybridisation of systematic and stochastic search is an active research area with potential benefits for real-world combinatorial problems. This paper shows that randomising the backtracking component of a systematic backtracker can improve its scalability to equal that of stochastic local search. The hybrid may be viewed as stochastic local search in a constrained space, cleanly combining local search with constraint programming techniques. The approach is applied to two very different problems. Firstly a hybrid of local search and constraint propagation is applied to hard random 3-SAT problems, and is the first constructive search algorithm to solve very large instances. Secondly a hybrid of local search and branch-and-bound is applied to low-autocorrelation binary sequences (a notoriously difficult communications engineering problem), and is the first stochastic search algorithm to find optimal solutions. These results show that the approach is a promising one for both constraint satisfaction and optimisation problems.

1 Introduction

The *low-autocorrelation binary sequence* (LABS) problem has many applications to communications and electrical engineering, and a long history. The problem is as follows. Consider a binary sequence $S = (s_1, \ldots, s_N)$ where each $s_i \in \{1, -1\}$. The *off-peak autocorrelations* of S are defined as:

$$C_k(S) = \sum_{i=1}^{N-k} s_i s_{i+k} \quad (k = 1 \ldots N - 1)$$

and the *energy* of S is defined as:

$$E(S) = \sum_{k=1}^{N-1} C_k^2(S)$$

The LABS problem is to assign values to the s_i such that $E(S)$ is minimised. A standard measure of sequence quality is the *merit factor* $F = N^2/2E$. Theoretical considerations [13] give an upper bound of $F \approx 12.32$ for $N \gg 1$, and

R. Dechter (Ed.): CP 2000, LNCS 1894, pp. 337–352, 2000.

empirical curve fitting on known optimal sequences [23] yields an estimate of $F \approx 9.3$. LABS is of interest to the Constraints community because of its difficulty; it is problem number 5 in the CSPLIB benchmark library [8], a web-based collection of constraint problems. Since the 1970s researchers, many from the Physics community, have applied various methods to the problem. Analytical methods have been used to construct optimal sequences for certain values of N using *periodic boundary conditions* (see [24] for example), but for the general *aperiodic* case search is necessary. Two possibilities are *systematic* and *stochastic* search. LABS is particularly challenging because it poses difficulties for both search paradigms.

Systematic search often involves the enumeration of possibilities by backtracking, using whatever constraint programming techniques are available to eliminate redundant parts of the search space. Golay [13] used exhaustive enumeration to find optimal sequences for $N \leq 32$. Mertens [23] enumerated optimal sequences for $N \leq 48$ using systematic search augmented with two techniques to reduce the size of the search space: *branch-and-bound* and *symmetry breaking*. Branch-and-bound improves performance significantly: a systematic search for sequences of length 44 took approximately 2 days, as opposed to an extrapolated 68 days for exhaustive enumeration. [1] Symmetry breaking exploits the fact that sequences occur in equivalence classes of size 8. Gent & Smith [10] have also successfully applied *generic* symmetry breaking techniques to LABS. However, even with these enhancements, systematic search is unlikely to scale up to large sequences. LABS provides little scope for constraint propagation, and it is conjectured [23] that for $N > 100$ progress will be made through mathematical insight rather than computer power.

When systematic search breaks down, a standard approach for solving combinatorial problems is to resort to stochastic search: simulated annealing, evolutionary algorithms, neural networks, ant colonies or hill climbers. Such algorithms are often able to solve much larger instances. Unfortunately, they perform quite poorly on some problems, and finding optimal LABS solutions seems to be an example. This is despite decades of research effort using simulated annealing [3,13], evolutionary algorithms [6], analogies with molecular evolution [38] and several other heuristic search algorithms [2]. The cause is considered to be the search space normally used for LABS (the space of all sequences of a given length) whose cost function E has a very irregular structure with isolated minima [3].

A technique that may be used with both systematic and stochastic search is *sieves* to restrict the search to a promising subspace. The most common sieve is *skew-symmetry*: only sequences of length $N = 2n - 1$ satisfying $s_{n+i} = (-1)^i s_{n-i}$ ($i = 1 \ldots n - 1$) are considered, roughly halving the number of independent variables in the problem and greatly reducing the search space size. Skew-symmetric sequences have been enumerated for $N \leq 71$ [6] and often have rather good merit factors because $C_k = 0$ for all odd k. However, stochastic search finds large skew-symmetric sequences with only $F \approx 6$.

---

[1] On a Sun UltraSparc I 170 workstation.

Thus neither systematic nor stochastic search seems suitable for finding large optimal sequences. This situation is mirrored in some other combinatorial problems, and though both systematic and stochastic search are highly successful, neither is seen as adequate for all problems. Hence a recent trend in Artificial Intelligence toward *hybrid* search, with the aim of combining advantages of both. A variety of approaches have been described (see Section 5) but most allow constraint violations. The hybrid approach described in this paper is inspired by the observation that systematic search is able to exploit constraint programming techniques but sometimes scales poorly; perhaps by sacrificing systematicity, scalability might be improved. Because a randomised backtracker can be viewed as a stochastic local search algorithm, we call this hybrid approach Constrained Local Search (CLS).

This paper is an expanded version of a technical report [28]. Previous papers on CLS have dealt with graph colouring [29] and satisfiability [30]. The paper is organised as follows. Section 2 briefly describes the CLS approach to constraint problems. Section 3 cites previous work on CLS for SAT problems, and gives new scaling results for hard random 3-SAT. Section 4 applies CLS to LABS. Section 5 discusses related work. Finally, Section 6 draws conclusions.

2 Constrained Local Search

CLS hybrid algorithms are constructed by randomising the backtracking component of a systematic algorithm; that is, allowing backtracking to occur on *arbitrarily-chosen* variables. The CLS schema is shown in Figure 1. A is the current set of assigned variables, initialised to $\{\}$. U is the current set of unassigned variables, initialised to the full set of variables $\{v_1, \ldots, v_N\}$. $B \geq 1$ is an integer parameter called the *noise level*. The condition "assigning x to u is consistent" means that assigning the value x to the variable u does not violate any constraints after propagation, if constraint propagation is used. The algorithm proceeds by selecting unassigned variables using a selection rule VAR, and assigns values to them using a selection rule VAL. On reaching a dead-end ($D = \{\}$) it backtracks on B variables selected by a rule BACK, which selects variables either randomly or heuristically; in either case, no attempt is made to maintain completeness. Termination is not guaranteed but occurs if all variables are assigned ($U = \{\}$). The constraint propagation, the variable domains, the value of B, and the VAL, VAR and BACK rules are problem-dependent. The *unpropagation* of constraints is the hardest part of implementing a new CLS algorithm: the effects of an arbitrary variable on the constraint store must be undone. For details on the graph colouring and SAT implementations see [29,30] respectively. Unpropagation is easy for LABS, where the only constraint reasoning used is branch-and-bound (see Section 4).

Why should randomised backtracking be expected to perform well? Intuitively, it appears inferior to intelligent backtracking schemes, and it has the disadvantage that completeness is lost. The rationale is that randomised backtracking can be viewed as a *stochastic local search* algorithm. Local search ex-

```
function CLS(B):
    A = {}
    U = {v₁, ..., vₙ}
    while U ≠ {}
        u = VAR(U)
        D = {x ∈ domain(u) | assigning x to u is consistent}
        if D = {}
            for i=1 to min(B,|A|)
                a = BACK(A)
                unassign a and unpropagate
                A = A - {a}
                U = U ∪ {a}
        else
            assign VAL(D) to u and propagate
            A = A ∪ {u}
            U = U - {u}
    return current assignments
```

Fig. 1. The CLS randomised backtracking schema

plores the *neighbourhood* of a point σ in a space by making *local moves*. The neighbourhood consists of the set of points σ' that can be reached by a single local move. The aim is to minimise (or equivalently to maximise) some *objective function* $f(\sigma)$ on the space. A local move $\sigma \rightarrow \sigma'$ can be classified as *backward*, *forward* or *sideways*, depending on whether $f(\sigma') - f(\sigma)$ is positive, negative or zero. Local search may converge on a *local minimum*: a point that has lower value than all its neighbours but is not a global minimum. The aim of backward moves is to escape from local minima by providing *noise*, while sideways moves are used to traverse function plateaus.

Local search is usually applied to optimisation problems (such as LABS) by defining the search space as the total assignments (LABS sequences of a given length), a local move as a change in the value of a single variable, and using the given objective function (the LABS sequence energy). It is often applied to constraint satisfaction problems (such as SAT) by searching the same space with the same local moves, but using a measure of constraint violation as the objective function. CLS can be viewed as a local search algorithm whose search space is the consistent partial assignments; variable assignments are forward local moves, backtracks are backward local moves, and the number of unassigned variables is the objective function to be minimised. The crucial difference between CLS and most other local search algorithms is that, like systematic backtracking, it is *constructive*: it violates no constraints and can therefore exploit techniques such as forward checking (for SAT [30]), branch-and-bound (for LABS) or both (for graph colouring [29]).

It might be objected that *all* backtracking algorithms are local search algorithms in the same sense as CLS: they search the same space and try to minimise the same function. However, systematic backtracking has so far failed to achieve the scalability of local search. There seems to be a missing ingredient, though there is currently no consensus on what the ingredient is. An obvious candidate is randomness, but research has shown that randomness is not a necessary property for scalability [9,25]. Likely candidates are hill-climbing and freedom of movement in the search space; see [7] for a debate on this issue. Whatever the ingredient is, we aim to show that CLS has it.

3   CLS for SAT

The SAT problem is to determine whether a Boolean expression has a satisfying set of truth assignments. The problems are usually expressed in conjunctive normal form: a conjunction of clauses $C_1 \wedge \ldots \wedge C_m$ where each clause C is a disjunction of literals $l_1 \vee \ldots \vee l_n$ and each literal l is either a Boolean variable v or its negation $\neg v$. A Boolean variable can be labeled *true* or *false*. The CLS implementation for the SAT problem described in [30] will be used, which maintains consistency by forward checking. The noise level B is set to 1 for all problems. CLS has previously been applied to several SAT benchmarks. Here we evaluate it on a standard benchmark: hard random 3-SAT. The random 3-SAT problem is the SAT problem where each clause contains three literals, each literal being negated with probability $\frac{1}{2}$. The *hard* problems are in the *crossover* region where 50% of problems are satisfiable, which occurs when the ratio of clauses c to variables v is approximately $c/v = 4.258 + 58.26v^{-5/3}$ [5].

A note on experimental details. Throughout this paper, CLS is executed on a 300 MHz DEC Alphaserver 1000A 5/300 under Unix. Times are in seconds, and those from other papers are normalised to the Alphaserver using benchmark timings from [18]. For readers wishing to normalise our execution times to other platforms, the DIMACS [2] benchmark program dfmax r500.5 takes 46.2 seconds on the Alphaserver.

First we consider published results by Parkes & Walser [26], who apply the WSAT local search algorithm to these problems. They use a statistical technique called *retrospective parameter variation* to optimise a WSAT parameter. Using between 10^3 and 10^4 runs they find the median number of *flips* (changes to the truth value of a variable) necessary to find solutions to problems of various sizes. Solvable problems were generated using a systematic SAT algorithm (TABLEAU [5]) then passed to WSAT. Results for CLS were generated differently: it was applied to 10^3 problems of each size, and the 25th percentile taken of the execution time to find a solution. Because 50% of problems from the crossover region are satisfiable, the 25th percentile for all problems is the median for the solvable problems. This is faster than using exhaustive search to generate solvable problems. Figure 2 shows median results for CLS and WSAT, counting WSAT flips and CLS backtracks required to find a solution. The results for CLS and WSAT are remarkably similar. Moreover, both curves show

---

[2] ftp://dimacs.rutgers.edu/pub/challenge/

a *less-than-exponential* increase, in contrast to chronological backtrackers. However, the relationship is not a simple monomial because a log-log plot shows a distinct upward curve. This property has also been noted by Gent & Walsh [9] for variants of GSAT (an ancestor of WSAT).

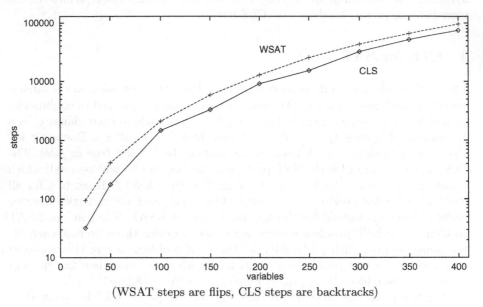

(WSAT steps are flips, CLS steps are backtracks)

Fig. 2. Median steps on hard random 3-SAT problems

Next we consider published results by Selman, Kautz & Cohen [34] for GSAT with random walk, and by Shang & Wah [35] for DLM [35] (a recent local search algorithm based on Lagrange multipliers). Figure 3 compares mean times for the three algorithms on instances with 600, 1000 and 2000 variables. It is unclear whether these are precisely the same problem instances but the results are nevertheless comparable. The times for CLS are averaged over 10 runs. CLS is several times slower than both DLM and GSAT but it clearly has the scalability of a local search algorithm. In contrast to local search, systematic algorithms scale exponentially and cannot solve problems with more than approximately 400 variables [5]. An interesting experiment would be compare the scalability of intelligent backtracking algorithms (such as RELSAT [1]). However, it has not been claimed that intelligent backtracking can solve such large 3-SAT instances, so we believe that such algorithms will also scale exponentially.

CLS backtracks are more expensive than WSAT, GSAT or DLM flips, as shown in the second experiment. Parkes and Walser found that WSAT performed approximately 70,000 down to 60,000 flips per second. CLS performed 31,716 down to 26,315 backtracks per second: a similarly small degradation but a slower rate, especially given the different platforms. CLS backtracks are also

problem	GSAT+w	DLM	CLS
f600	7.0	3.6	8.4
f1000	219	27.2	96.1
f2000	651	389	2145

Fig. 3. Mean times on hard random 3-SAT problems

more expensive than systematic backtracks, because of the book-keeping necessary to maintain consistency during randomised backtracking (though the cost of
sophisticated variable ordering heuristics may outweigh this expense). In spite of
this, on some large, structured SAT problems CLS out-performs both systematic
and pure local search [30].

4   CLS for LABS

The starting point for the hybrid LABS algorithm is a simplified variant of
Mertens' systematic algorithm, retaining branch-and-bound but not symmetry
breaking (for reasons given below). Variables are initially *unassigned*: they have
no assigned values. The simplified systematic algorithm proceeds by assigning
either the value 1 or −1 to each variable in turn. A record E_{best} is maintained,
which is the energy of the best solution found so far. E_{best} may be initialised
to ∞ or some finite value above the known optimal energy, and on finding a
better solution it is updated. Whenever an assignment causes the constraint $E <
E_{best}$ to be violated (where E is the energy of the sequence under construction),
backtracking occurs. Selecting a value for a variable s_i is the *branch* part of
the algorithm, while the use of the constraint $E < E_{best}$ is the *bound* part. As
the search proceeds E_{best} is refined, and more solutions are excluded from the
search. Branch-and-bound's gain in efficiency comes from the fact that constraint
violation can sometimes be detected before all variables have been assigned.

Constraint violation is detected as follows. Call a product $s_i s_j$ *computable*
if s_i and s_j are both assigned. Then a lower bound E_L for the energy E is:

$$E_L = \sum_{k=1}^{N-1} L_k$$

where $L_k = \max(b_k, |T_k| - U_k)^2$, $b_k = (N - k) \bmod 2$, T_k is the sum of its
computable products and U_k is the number of its non-computable products. [3]
Constraint violation occurs if $E_L \geq E_{best}$. The lower bound E_L is incrementally computed. On assigning a variable v the algorithm does the following for
each occurrence $s_v s_w$ in some C_k where s_w is assigned: subtract L_k from E_L,
decrement U_k, add $s_v s_w$ to T_k, recalculate L_k and add it to E_L. Conversely,

---

[3] This is a slightly different lower bound to that used in [23] but is based on similar
reasoning.

on unassigning a variable v, it does the following for each occurrence $s_v s_w$ in some C_k where s_w is assigned: subtract L_k from E_L, increment U_k, subtract $s_v s_w$ from T_k, recalculate L_k and add it to E_L. The occurrences of each variable v are stored in a table, together with the numbers w and k.

To obtain a hybrid LABS algorithm CLS is used in place of chronological backtracking, with the following heuristics:

- The noise level B is set to 1.
- The backtracking heuristic BACK selects random assigned variables.
- The dynamic variable ordering heuristic VAR usually selects the most recently unassigned variable, but if no improvement has occurred (in the number of assigned variables) after N backtracks then VAR selects a random unassigned variable. This produces a slowly-changing set of assigned variables.
- If $D = \{x\}$ then the value ordering rule VAL(D) returns x, otherwise it selects a value using a rule described below.
- A further heuristic is added: random restart. In case CLS becomes trapped in a deep local minimum, it is restarted at regular intervals (retaining the current E_{best} value). The interval used is 1.5^N backtracks.

Given a choice of values in D, VAL(D) selects as follows. It first tries to select a different value than the previous assignment for the given variable (previous assignments are stored in an array). On achieving this, future variables are assigned the same value as in their previous assignments, until backtracking next occurs. Then it tries to assign different values to variables again. The purpose of this heuristic is to reduce disruption to variable assignments as the set of assigned variables changes, while avoiding null local moves.

Figure 3 shows the results for the hybrid LABS algorithm: the sequence length N, the energy E, the merit factor F, the number of backtracks taken to find the sequence, the CPU time taken and an example of a sequence found by CLS. E_{best} was initialised to the known optimal energy plus 1 in each case. Mean times and backtracks were calculated over various numbers of runs: 10^6 (N=3–6), 10^5 (N=7–10), 10^4 (N=11–15), 10^3 (N=16–17), 10^2 (N=18–20), 10 (N=21–41) and 1 (N=42–48). Following convention, sequences are shown in *run-length notation*: each number indicates the number of consecutive elements with the same value. For example a sequence $(1, 1, -1, 1, -1, -1, -1, -1, 1)$ would be written 21141. For runs of length greater than 9, upper-case letters are used with A=10, B=11 etc. Note that 21141 could also represent the sequence $(-1, -1, 1, -1, 1, 1, 1, 1, -1)$. Sequences can have all their values inverted, or have alternate values inverted, or be reversed, without changing E.

The table shows that CLS is indeed able to find optimal sequences for $N \leq 48$, and it is the first stochastic search algorithm to do so. To estimate its scalability, execution times are plotted as a function of sequence length on a log-scale graph in Figure 5. Taking a least-squares fit, the estimated time taken to find an optimal solution is $O(1.698^N)$. Exhaustive search (without branch-and-bound) takes $O(2^N)$ and Mertens' algorithm takes $O(1.85^N)$ — that is to explore the *entire* search space, not simply to find the first optimal solution. However, the CSPLIB

N	E	F	backtracks	seconds	sequence
3	1	4.50	0	0.000008	12
4	2	4.00	0	0.000013	31
5	2	6.25	0	0.000026	311
6	7	2.57	0	0.000025	1131
7	3	5.44	5	0.00015	3211
8	8	4.00	4	0.00015	32111
9	12	3.38	4	0.00016	121113
10	13	3.85	4	0.00018	421111
11	5	12.10	15	0.0006	112133
12	10	7.20	40	0.0016	225111
13	6	14.08	75	0.0031	5221111
14	19	5.16	22	0.0011	42221111
15	15	7.50	360	0.0178	11213133
16	24	5.33	48	0.0042	11312143
17	32	4.52	11	0.0118	4221211112
18	25	6.48	1824	0.079	441112221
19	29	6.22	891	0.058	2122411114
20	26	7.69	9810	0.646	22124141111
21	26	8.48	52533	3.85	27221111121
22	39	6.21	8427	0.74	232212111115
23	47	5.63	28247	2.21	212121111632
24	36	8.0	114551	9.55	237111121221
25	36	8.68	10610	1.72	122121111733
26	45	7.51	36928	3.12	1122121111733
27	37	9.85	373197	33.9	34313131211211
28	50	7.84	407254	37.2	21211213131343
29	62	6.78	306246	43.3	212112131313431
30	59	7.63	53415	25.3	132311111212155
31	67	7.17	1135539	117	1112111122122337
32	64	8.00	3030725	319	12212233111121117
33	64	8.51	4322170	482	742112111111122221
34	65	8.89	3747743	422	842112111111122221
35	73	8.39	6100331	709	7122122111121111332
36	82	7.90	12207068	981	3632311131212111211
37	86	7.96	16596532	2096	122221111112112448
38	87	8.30	13033938	1679	22229421121121111111
39	99	7.68	40745979	5300	23241171111141122121
40	108	7.41	109581034	14305	111211211343143131312
41	108	7.78	38301376	21224	343111111222281211211
42	101	8.73	33446785	4890	211211211343143131313
43	109	8.48	324452495	46168	1132432111117212112213
44	122	7.93	166769694	27422	121112111222111311313525
45	118	8.58	367926334	52920	11111112343213212112128
46	131	8.08	35017866	5184	234232137111212212111111
47	135	8.18	164787014	26280	13211111111243212112A212
48	140	8.23	78278179	12096	244223212113212111111811

Fig. 4. Results on known optimal sequences

web site [8] contains a table of all optimal solutions for $N = 17 \ldots 50$, and in 23 out of 34 cases there is only one optimal solution (modulo symmetry); nor does the number of optimal solutions increase exponentially or even monotonically with N. We therefore expect Mertens' algorithm also to take approximately $O(1.85^N)$ to find a solution, though this remains to be tested. Hence it seems that CLS scales better than the best systematic algorithm, as might be expected from a local search procedure.

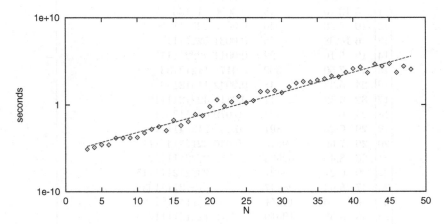

Fig. 5. Least-squares fit on known optimal sequences

The least-squares fit was made on the assumption that the curve has the form $a.b^N$ but this may not be the case. The graph has an interesting property: most of the points above the line occur in the middle of the graph, while those below the line occur mainly for low and high N. This *systematic variation* (to use statistics terminology) seems to indicate that execution time is a less-than-exponential function of N. If we estimate the scale factor based on $N \leq 25$ we obtain 1.887, for $N \leq 30$ we obtain exactly Mertens' factor of 1.850, and as we add the figures for larger N we obtain progressively smaller scale factors. As noted in Section 2, CLS and the local search algorithm WSAT exhibit similar sub-exponential scaling on hard random 3-SAT problems. The data is too noisy to draw a firm conclusion, but it would be remarkable if the same phenomenon occurs in LABS.

To investigate whether the algorithm is significantly slower when started from infinite energy, we repeated the experiment for $N \leq 30$. The least-squares fit to the formula $a.b^N$ gave a scale factor $b = 1.846$, which is very close to the factor for our original data for $N \leq 30$, and a coefficient a that is 2.29 times greater than before. In other words, the only effect of starting from infinite energy is to slow down the execution by a constant factor.

As a further experiment CLS was applied to sequences of length $N = 61$, which is currently too large for systematic search. de Groot et al [6] found sequences up to $F = 6.5$ using evolutionary strategies. Bernasconi [3] found $F \approx 6.8$ using simulated annealing, though with worse average-case behaviour over many runs. The best result obtained by CLS after 2 days of computation was the sequence

1222122211111111B3236411211211

with $F = 7.1$ and $E = 262$. This is easily verified to be non-skew-symmetric and is the best such sequence known. However, better skew-symmetric sequences have been found [2,6], and in future skew-symmetry will be added to CLS.

A note on symmetry breaking. This technique was not used because it is likely to be of little use for stochastic search. The reasoning is that stochastic search explores only part of the search space, so it is the density and distribution of solutions that are important. Symmetry breaking reduces the size of the search space by some factor (up to 8 in the case of LABS) but it also reduces the number of solutions by a similar factor, leaving the density unchanged. Symmetry breaking may even have a harmful effect on stochastic search: if it applies extra constraints, and if these constraints cannot be invoked until several variables are assigned, then stochastic search may be lured into regions of the search space whose solutions are forbidden by the extra constraints.

5 Related Work

CLS has much in common with Ginsberg's Dynamic Backtracking (DB) algorithm [11], both being able to backtrack to earlier variables without disrupting those in between. However, DB's completeness requirement restricts its choice of backtracking variable. Ginsberg notes that this restriction cannot be lifted without losing completeness. CLS ignores the restriction and is therefore incomplete, but this pays off in scalability. Another related algorithm is Ginsberg & McAllester's Partial-order Dynamic Backtracking (PDB) algorithm [12]. PDB is a hybrid of the GSAT local search algorithm [34] and DB. It is complete and has more freedom of movement than DB, though to achieve complete freedom it requires exponential memory in the worst case.

Other non-systematic backtracking algorithms have been described. Langley's Iterative Sampling [22] constructs a random consistent partial assignment until reaching a dead-end, then restarts. This is essentially CLS with maximum noise (B set to the number of variables) and randomised heuristics. Harvey's Bounded Backtrack Search [16] is a hybrid of Iterative Sampling and chronological backtracking, alternating a limited amount of chronological backtracking with random restarts. Gomes, Selman and Kautz [15] periodically restart systematic SAT algorithms with slightly randomised heuristics, obtaining improved scalability on some problems. Goldberg & Rivenburgh's Restricted Backtracking [14] constructs maximum cliques using a trade-off between solution quality and search completeness. Joslin & Clements' Squeaky Wheel Optimization algorithm [19] operates in two search spaces: a solution space and a prioritisation space. Both searches influence each other: each solution is analysed and used to change the prioritisation, which guides the search strategy used to find the next solution, found by restarting the search. Yokoo's Weak Commitment Search [39] (WCS) greedily constructs consistent partial assignments. On reaching a dead-end it randomly restarts, and it uses learning to maintain completeness. Richards & Richards [32] describe a SAT algorithm called learn-SAT based on WCS. None of these algorithms performs *random* backtracks on a *small* number of variables, and they therefore seem unlikely to behave as tunable stochastic local search algorithms.

An alternative hybrid approach is to augment local search with constraint propagation. Schaerf's timetabling algorithm [33], extended to constraint satisfaction problems, searches the space of *all* partial assignments (not only the consistent ones) using an objective function that includes a measure of constraint violation. Jussien & Lhomme's Path-Repair Algorithm [20] is designed for constraint satisfaction problems and applied to open shop problems. It is described as a generalisation of Schaerf's method. Besides not being restricted to consistent assignments it is different than CLS in detail: it uses learning (allowing complete versions to be devised) and it has heuristics such as clause weighting, a TABU list and greedy hill climbing. Pesant & Gendreau [27] apply systematic branch-and-bound search to efficiently explore local search neighbourhoods for scheduling and vehicle routing problems. Shaw [36] describes a vehicle routing algorithm that uses systematic search to test the legality of local search moves. Each of these algorithms permits constraint violation, implying (in the view of this author) that constraints are being under-used, which may be a drawback when solving structured problems.

There are several other hybrid approaches. Crawford [4] uses local search to select the best branching variable for a complete SAT algorithm. The two-phase algorithm of Zhang & Zhang [41] searches a space of partial variable assignments, alternating backtracking search with stochastic local search on the same data structure. It can be tuned to different problems by spending more time in either phase. A notable difference is that it *alternates* between constructive/systematic and non-constructive/non-systematic search, whereas CLS is *simultaneously* constructive/non-systematic. Kautz, McAllester & Selman's Dagsat algorithm [21] uses a special SAT problem representation (directed acyclic graphs) that makes variable dependencies explicit. Local search is then applied to the independent variables. Verfaillie & Schiex's Local Changes algorithm [37] is a complete search strategy used to solve dynamic and static constraint satisfaction problems. It extends a consistent partial assignment to a larger one by unassigning variables that are inconsistent with a new assignment, performing the new assignment then reassigning variables to the same values where possible. Experience with CLS suggests that forcing a new assignment in this way may be too disruptive for some problems.

6   Conclusion

This paper described the randomisation of the backtracking component of a systematic backtracker, with the aim of gaining scalability at the expense of completeness. The resulting algorithms can be viewed as hybrids performing stochastic local search in constrained spaces, and are therefore called Constrained Local Search (CLS) algorithms. The approach was shown to improve scalability on two very different classes of problem. A hybrid of local search and constraint propagation for SAT is the first constructive search algorithm to solve hard random 3-SAT problems with thousands of variables, and with almost identical scalability to the WSAT local search algorithm. A hybrid of local search with branch-and-bound for low-autocorrelation binary sequences (LABS) is the first stochastic search algorithm to find optimal solutions, and with improved scalability over the current best systematic backtracker. These results show that the hybridisation approach can be used to derive algorithms combining some of the best properties of stochastic and systematic search, and is applicable to both constraint satisfaction and optimisation problems.

The LABS search space topology is known to be hard for stochastic search. No stochastic algorithm has previously found optimal sequences (in the full aperiodic search space), and it has been suggested [23] that stochastic algorithms should be judged by the percentage of known optimal sequences they find. Because the CLS local search strategy is less sophisticated than most of the stochastic approaches used previously, its success on LABS is almost certainly due to the change in search space and objective function. A possible explanation is that the space of consistent partial sequences contains fewer local minima than the usual space of total sequences. The detection and characterisation of search space features detrimental to local search is a complex area of current interest (see for example [17,40]) but is beyond the scope of this paper.

This work is part of a series of studies on CLS, which has also yielded good results on graph colouring [29] and other SAT benchmarks [30]. The motivation behind CLS is to solve problems that are hard for pure stochastic search yet too large for systematic search. Its success in solving LABS problems is further evidence of its applicability to such problems. Future work will include applying CLS to skew-symmetric sequences and other combinatorial problems. Another possibility is the replacement of simple local search by evolutionary search to explore the space of partial solutions, an approach proposed in [31] for constraint satisfaction and optimisation problems. An intriguing possibility [4] is to remove the randomness from CLS in order to make it complete without losing scalability.

Acknowledgements

The author would like to thank the anonymous referees of this paper for their extremely helpful comments.

---

[4] Suggested by Ian Gent, personal communication.

References

1. R. J. Bayardo Jr, R. Schrag. Using CSP Look-Back Techniques to Solve Real World SAT Instances. *Proceedings of the Fourteenth National Conference on Artificial Intelligence and Ninth Innovative Applications of Artificial Intelligence Conference*, AAAI Press / The MIT Press 1997, pp. 203–208. 342
2. G. Beenker, T. Claasen, P. Hermens. Binary Sequences With a Maximally Flat Amplitude Spectrum. *Philips J. Res.* vol. 40, pp. 289–304. 338, 347
3. J. Bernasconi. Low Autocorrelation Binary Sequences: Statistical Mechanics and Configuration Space Analysis. *J. Physique*, vol. 48, pp. 559, 1987. 338, 347
4. J. M. Crawford. Solving Satisfiability Problems Using a Combination of Systematic and Local Search. *Second DIMACS Challenge: Cliques, Coloring, and Satisfiability*, October 1993, Rutgers University, NJ, USA. Available on: http://www.cirl.uoregon.edu/crawford/papers/papers.html 348
5. J. M. Crawford, L. D. Auton. Experimental Results on the Crossover Point in Random 3SAT. *Artificial Intelligence* vol. 81, nos. 1–2, March 1996, pp. 31–57. 341, 342
6. C. de Groot, D. Würtz, K. H. Hoffmann. Low Autocorrelation Binary Sequences: Exact Enumeration and Optimization by Evolutionary Strategies. *Optimization* vol. 23, Gordon & Breach Science Publishers S. A. 1992, pp. 369–384. 338, 346, 347
7. E. C. Freuder, R. Dechter, M. L. Ginsberg, B. Selman, E. Tsang. Systematic Versus Stochastic Constraint Satisfaction. *Proceedings of the Fourteenth International Joint Conference on Artificial Intelligence*, Morgan Kaufmann 1995, pp. 2027–2032. 341
8. I. Gent, T. Walsh. CSPLIB: A Benchmark Library for Constraints. Available on: http://csplib.cs.strath.ac.uk 338, 346
9. I. P. Gent, T. Walsh. Towards an Understanding of Hill-Climbing Procedures for SAT. *Proceedings of the Eleventh National Conference on Artificial Intelligence*, AAAI Press / MIT Press 1993, pp. 28–33. 341, 342
10. I. Gent, B. Smith. Symmetry Breaking During Search in Constraint Programming. Research Report 99.02, Department of Computer Science, University of Leeds, 1999. 338
11. M. L. Ginsberg. Dynamic Backtracking. *Journal of Artificial Intelligence Research* vol. 1, AI Access Foundation and Morgan Kaufmann 1993, pp. 25–46. 347
12. M. L. Ginsberg, D. A. McAllester. GSAT and Dynamic Backtracking. *Proceedings of the Fourth International Conference on Principles of Knowledge Representation and Reasoning*, Morgan Kaufmann 1994, pp. 226–237. 347
13. M. Golay. The Merit Factor of Long Low Autocorrelation Binary Sequences. *IEEE Transactions on Information Theory* IT-23, pp. 43–51. 337, 338
14. M. K. Goldberg, R. D. Rivenburgh. Constructing Cliques Using Restricted Backtracking. In [18] pp. 89–102. 347
15. C. Gomes, B. Selman, H, Kautz. Boosting Combinatorial Search Through Randomization. *Proceedings of the Fifteenth National Conference on Artificial Intelligence and Tenth Innovative Applications of Artificial Intelligence Conference*, AAAI Press / The MIT Press 1998, pp. 431–437. 347
16. W. D. Harvey. Nonsystematic Backtracking Search. PhD thesis, Stanford University, 1995. 347
17. H. Hoos. SAT-Encodings, Search Space Structure, and Local Search Performance. *Proceedings of the Sixteenth International Joint Conference on Artificial Intelligence (IJCAI'99)*, Morgan Kaufmann 1999, pp. 296–302. 349

18. D. S. Johnson, M. A. Trick (Eds). *Cliques, Coloring and Satisfiability: Second DIMACS Implementation Challenge, DIMACS Series in Discrete Mathematics and Theoretical Computer Science* vol. 26, American Mathematical Society 1996. 341, 350

19. D. E. Joslin, D. P. Clements. Squeaky Wheel Optimization. *Journal of Artificial Intelligence Research* vol. 10, 1999, pp. 353–373. 347

20. N. Jussien, O. Lhomme. The Path-Repair Algorithm. *Proceedings of the Workshop on Large Scale Combinatorial Optimization and Constraints*, Electronic Notes in Discrete Mathematics vol. 4, 1999. Available on: http://www.elsevier.nl/locate/disc 348

21. H. Kautz, D. McAllester, B. Selman. Exploiting Variable Dependency in Local Search. *Poster Sessions of the Fifteenth International Joint Conference on Artificial Intelligence*, Morgan Kaufmann 1997. 348

22. P. Langley. Systematic and Nonsystematic Search Strategies. *Artificial Intelligence Planning Systems: Proceedings of the First International Conference*, Morgan Kaufmann 1992, pp. 145–152. 347

23. S. Mertens. Exhaustive Search for Low-Autocorrelation Binary Sequences. *J. Phys. A: Math. Gen.* vol. 29 L473–L481, 1996. 338, 343, 349

24. S. Mertens, C. Bessenrodt. On the Ground States of the Bernasconi Model. *J. Phys. A: Math. Gen.* vol. 31, 1998, pp. 3731–3749. 338

25. P. Morris. The Breakout Method for Escaping Local Minima. *Proceedings of the Eleventh National Conference on Artificial Intelligence (AAAI'93)*, AAAI Press / MIT Press 1993, pp. 40–45. 341

26. A. J. Parkes, J. P. Walser. Tuning Local Search for Satisfiability Testing. *Proceedings of the Thirteenth National Conference on Artificial Intelligence and Eighth Innovative Applications of Artificial Intelligence Conference, (AAAI'96, IAAI'96)*, vol. 1, AAAI Press / The MIT Press 1996, pp. 356–362. 341

27. G. Pesant, M. Gendreau. A View of Local Search in Constraint Programming. *Principles and Practice of Constraint Programming, Proceedings of the Second International Conference*, Lecture Notes in Computer Science vol. 1118, Springer-Verlag 1996, pp. 353–366. 348

28. S. D. Prestwich. A Hybrid Local Search Algorithm for Low-Autocorrelation Binary Sequences. Technical Report TR-00-01, Department of Computer Science, University College, Cork, Ireland 2000. Available on: http://csplib.cs.strath.ac.uk 339

29. S. D. Prestwich. Using an Incomplete Version of Dynamic Backtracking for Graph Colouring. *Workshop on Large Scale Combinatorial Optimization*, Electronic Notes in Discrete Mathematics vol. 1, 1998. Available on: http://www.elsevier.nl/locate/disc 339, 340, 349

30. S. D. Prestwich. Stochastic Local Search In Constrained Spaces. *Proceedings of Practical Applications of Constraint Technology and Logic Programming, PACLP-2000*, Practical Application Company Ltd 2000, pp. 27–39. 339, 340, 341, 343, 349

31. S. D. Prestwich. A Generic Approach to Combining Stochastic Algorithms With Systematic Constraint Solvers. *Proceedings of Frontiers of Combining Systems 2 (FroCos'98)*, D. M. Gabbay and M. de Rijke (eds.), Research Studies Press/Wiley 1999, pp. 275–294. 349

32. E. T. Richards, B. Richards. Non-Systematic Search and Learning: an Empirical Study. *Principles and Practice of Constraint Programming, Proceedings of the Fourth International Conference*, Lecture Notes in Computer Science vol. 1520, Springer-Verlag 1998, pp. 370–384. 348

33. A. Schaerf. Combining Local Search and Look-Ahead for Scheduling and Constraint Satisfaction Problems. *Proceedings of the Fifteenth International Joint Conference on Artificial Intelligence*, Morgan Kaufmann 1997, pp. 1254–1259. 348
34. B. Selman, H. Kautz, B. Cohen. Noise Strategies for Improving Local Search. *Proceedings of the Twelfth National Conference on Artificial Intelligence*, AAAI Press 1994, pp. 337–343. 342, 347
35. Y. Shang, B. W. Wah. A Discrete Lagrangian-Based Global-Search Method for Solving Satisfiability Problems. *Journal of Global Optimization* vol. 10, Kluwer 1997, pp. 1–40. 342
36. P. Shaw. Using Constraint Programming and Local Search to Solve Vehicle Routing Problems. *Proceedings of the Fourth International Conference on Principles and Practice of Constraint Programming (CP'98)*, Lecture Notes in Computer Scienece vol. 1520, Springer-Verlag 1998, pp. 417–431. 348
37. G. Verfaillie, T. Schiex. Solution Reuse in Dynamic Constraint Satisfaction Problems. *Proceedings of the Twelfth National Conference on Artificial Intelligence*, AAAI Press 1994, pp. 307–312. 348
38. Q. Wang. Optimization by Simulating Molecular Evolution. *Biol. Cybern.* vol. 57, pp. 95–101, 1987. 338
39. M. Yokoo. Weak-Commitment Search for Solving Constraint Satisfaction Problems. *Proceedings of the Twelfth National Conference on Artificial Intelligence*, AAAI Press 1994, pp. 313–318. 348
40. M. Yokoo. Why Adding More Constraints Makes a Problem Easier for Hill-Climbing Algorithms: Analyzing Landscape of CSPs. *Proceedings of the Third International Conference on Principles and Practice of Constraint Programming (CP'97)*, Lecture Notes in Computer Science vol. 1330, Springer-Verlag 1997, pp. 357–370. 349
41. J. Zhang, H. Zhang. Combining Local Search and Backtracking Techniques for Constraint Satisfaction. *Proceedings of the Thirteenth National Conference on Artificial Intelligence and Eighth Conference on Innovative Applications of Artificial Intelligence*, AAAI Press / The MIT Press 1996, pp. 369–374. 348

Singleton Consistencies

Patrick Prosser[1], Kostas Stergiou[2], and Toby Walsh[3]

[1] Glasgow University, Glasgow, Scotland
pat@dcs.strath.ac.uk
[2] University of Strathclyde, Glasgow, Scotland
ks@cs.strath.ac.uk
[3] University of York, York, England
tw@cs.york.ac.uk

Abstract. We perform a comprehensive theoretical and empirical study of the benefits of singleton consistencies. Our theoretical results help place singleton consistencies within the hierarchy of local consistencies. To determine the practical value of these theoretical results, we measured the cost-effectiveness of pre-processing with singleton consistency algorithms. Our experiments use both random and structured problems. Whilst pre-processing with singleton consistencies is not in general beneficial for random problems, it starts to pay off when randomness and structure are combined, and it is very worthwhile with structured problems like Golomb rulers. On such problems, pre-processing with consistency techniques as strong as singleton generalized arc-consistency (the singleton extension of generalized arc-consistency) can reduce runtimes. We also show that limiting algorithms that enforce singleton consistencies to a single pass often gives a small reduction in the amount of pruning and improves their cost-effectiveness. These experimental results also demonstrate that conclusions from studies on random problems should be treated with caution.

1 Introduction

Local consistency techniques lie close to the heart of constraint programming's success. They can prune values from the domain of variables, saving much fruitless exploration of the search tree. They can also terminate branches of the search tree, again saving much fruitless exploration. But how do we balance effort between inference (enforcing some level of local consistency) and search (exploring partial assignments)? If we maintain a local consistency technique at each node in the search tree, then experience suggests that it must not be too expensive to enforce. We may, however, be able to afford a (relatively expensive) local consistency technique if it is only used for pre-processing or for the first few levels of search. We are then faced with a large number of choices as a vast menagerie of local consistencies have been defined over the last few years. Debruyne and Bessiere identified singleton arc-consistency as one of the most promising candidates [DB97]. This paper therefore explores its usefulness in greater detail, as well as that of other singleton consistencies.

R. Dechter (Ed.): CP 2000, LNCS 1894, pp. 353–368, 2000.

2 Formal Background

A constraint satisfaction problem (CSP) P is a triple (X, D, C). X is a set
of variables. For each $x_i \in X$, D_i is the domain of the variable. Each k-ary
constraint $c \in C$ is defined over a set of variables $(x_1, \ldots x_k)$ by the subset of the Cartesian product $D_1 \times \ldots D_k$ which are consistent values. Follow-
ing [DB97], we denote by $P|_{D_i=\{a\}}$ the CSP obtained by assigning value a to
variable x_i. An all-different constraint over the variables $(x_1, \ldots x_k)$ allows the
values $\{(a_1, \ldots a_k) \mid a_i \in D_i \, \& \forall u, v.a_u \neq a_v\}$. A solution is an assignment of
values to variables that is consistent with all constraints.

Many lesser levels of consistency have been defined for binary constraint
satisfaction problems (see [DB97] for additional references). A problem is (i, j)-
consistent iff it has non-empty domains and any consistent instantiation of i
variables can be extended to a consistent instantiation involving j additional
variables [Fre85]. A problem is strong (i, j)-consistent iff it is (k, j)-consistent
for all $k \leq i$. A problem is arc-consistent (AC) iff it is $(1, 1)$-consistent. A problem is path-consistent (PC) iff it is $(2, 1)$-consistent. A problem is strong path-
consistent iff it is strong $(2, 1)$-consistent. A problem is path inverse consistent
(PIC) iff it is $(1, 2)$-consistent. A problem is neighbourhood inverse consistent
(NIC) iff any value for a variable can be extended to a consistent instantiation
for its immediate neighbourhood [FE96]. A problem is restricted path-consistent
(RPC) iff it is arc-consistent and if a variable assigned to a value is consistent
with just a single value for an adjoining variable then for any other variable
there exists a value compatible with these instantiations. A problem is singleton
arc-consistent (SAC) iff it has non-empty domains and for any instantiation of
a variable, the resulting subproblem can be made arc-consistent.

Many of these definitions can be extended to non-binary constraints. For
example, a (non-binary) CSP is generalized arc-consistent (GAC) iff for any
variable in a constraint and value that it is assigned, there exist compatible
values for all the other variables in the constraint [MM88]. Regin gives an efficient algorithm for enforcing generalized arc-consistency on a set of all-different
constraints [Reg94]. We can also maintain a level of consistency at every node
in a search tree. For example, the MAC algorithm for binary CSPs maintains
arc-consistency at each node in the search tree [Gas79]. As a second example,
on a non-binary problem, we can maintain generalized arc-consistency (MGAC)
at every node in the search tree.

3 Singleton Consistencies

The notion of a singleton consistency is general, and can be applied to other
levels of local consistency than arc-consistency. For instance, a problem is singleton restricted path-consistent (SRPC) iff it has non-empty domains and for
any instantiation of a variable, the resulting subproblem can be made restricted
path-consistent [DB97]. As a second (and we believe previously undefined) example, a non-binary problem is singleton generalized arc-consistent (SGAC) iff it

has non-empty domains and for any instantiation of a variable, the resulting sub-problem can be made generalized arc-consistent. As generalized arc-consistency is itself a high level of consistency to achieve (see, for example, [SW99]), singleton generalized arc-consistency is a very high level of consistency to achieve. However, as our experimental results demonstrate, it can be very worthwhile enforcing it.

One advantage of singleton consistencies (which is shared with inverse consistencies like path inverse consistency and neighbourhood inverse consistency, as well as with restricted path-consistency) is that enforcing them only requires values to be pruned from the domain of variables. Enforcing path-consistency, by comparison, can change the constraint graph by adding new binary constraints. Note that a singleton consistency can be achieved using any algorithm that achieves the relevant local consistency. The definition of singleton consistency only insists we can make the resulting subproblem locally consistent. We are not interested in what values need to be pruned (or nogoods added) to make the subproblem locally consistent. We can therefore use a lazy approach to enforcing the local consistency. For example, we can use the lazy AC7 algorithm [SRGV96] when achieving SAC.

In this paper, we have used the algorithm proposed in [DB97] to achieve SAC and a simple generalization of this algorithm to $n-$ary CSPs to achieve SGAC. To achieve SAC (SGAC) in a CSP P, this algorithm first achieves AC (GAC) and then goes through each variable x_i in P. For every value a in the domain of x_i it checks if the subproblem $P|_{D_i=\{a\}}$ is AC (GAC). If it is not then a is removed from the domain of x_i and AC (GAC) is enforced. Failure to do so means that P is not SAC (SGAC). The process of going through the variables in the CSP continues while new inconsistent values are detected and deleted. In short, there is an inner loop that goes through the variables and an outer loop that keeps this process going while new values are deleted.

The worst-case complexity of achieving SAC is $O(en^2d^4)$, where e is the number of constraints, n the number of variables, and d the domain size. For non-binary constraints, if we assume that GAC-schema [BR97] is used to enforce GAC then the worst case complexity of achieving SGAC is $O(en^2d^{2k})$, where k is the arity of the constraints. For the specialized case of all-different constraints, taking advantage of Regin's algorithm means that SGAC can be achieved with $O(cn^4d^4)$ worst-case complexity, where c is the number of all-different constraints.

We can reduce the average cost of the above algorithm by making just one pass, i.e., going through the variables and deleting inconsistent values only once. This deletes less values and thus achieves a lesser level of consistency than SAC (SGAC), but as our experimental results show, is, in some cases, very cost-effective. We call this algorithm *restricted* SAC (SGAC).

4 Theoretical Results

Following [DB97], we call a consistency property A stronger than B ($A \geq B$) iff in any problem in which A holds then B holds, and strictly stronger ($A > B$) iff it is stronger and there is at least one problem in which B holds but A does not. We call a local consistency property A incomparable with B ($A \sim B$) iff A is not stronger than B nor vice versa. Finally, we call a local consistency property A equivalent to B iff A implies B and vice versa. The following relationships summarize the most important results from [DB97] and elsewhere: strong PC $>$ SAC $>$ PIC $>$ RPC $>$ AC, NIC $>$ PIC, NIC $\sim$ SAC, and NIC $\sim$ strong PC.

Our first result shows that a singleton consistency is stronger than the corresponding local consistency. A local consistency property A is monotonic iff when a problem is A-consistent then any subproblem formed by instantiating a variable is also A-consistent. Most local consistencies (e.g. all those introduced so far) are monotonic.

Theorem 1. *If A-consistency is monotonic then singleton A-consistency $\geq A$-consistency.*

Proof. Immediate from the definitions of monotonic and singleton consistency.

Note that it is possible to construct (admittedly bizarre) local consistencies which are not monotonic. For example, consider a weakened form of AC which is equivalent to AC on every arc except the arc between variables x_1 and x_2 when either are instantiated. If we take a problem in which the arc between x_1 and x_2 is not AC, then this weakened form of AC will detect the arc-inconsistency but the singleton consistency will not. On this problem, the singleton consistency is actually weaker than the corresponding local consistency. Note also that a singleton consistency is not necessarily *strictly* stronger than the corresponding monotonic local consistency. For example, on problems whose constraint graphs are trees, SAC is only equivalent to AC (since arc-consistency is already enough to guarantee global consistency).

Our next result allows us to map many previous results up to singleton consistencies. For example, as RPC is stronger than AC, singleton RPC is stronger than SAC.

Theorem 2. *If A-consistency $\geq B$-consistency then singleton A-consistency $\geq$ singleton B-consistency.*

Proof. Consider a problem that is singleton A-consistent, and a subproblem formed from instantiating a variable. Now this subproblem is A-consistent. As $A \geq B$, this subproblem is B-consistent. Hence the original problem is singleton B-consistent.

Note that we do not need A-consistency or B-consistency to be monotonic for this proof to work. Debruyne and Bessiere prove that SAC is strictly stronger than PIC [DB97]. We can generalize this proof to show that singleton

(i, j)-consistency is strictly stronger than $(i, j + 1)$-consistency. Debruyne and Bessiere's result is then a special case for $i = j = 1$. In addition, [DB97] does not give the proof of strictness, so for completeness we give it here for the case $i = j = 1$.

Theorem 3. *Singleton (i, j)-consistency $> (i, j + 1)$-consistency.*

Proof. Consider a problem that is singleton (i, j)-consistent, and the subproblem resulting from any possible instantiation. This subproblem is (i, j)-consistent. Hence, for any consistent instantiation for i variables in the subproblem, we can extend it to j other variables. That is, for any instantiation of i variables in the original problem, we can extend it to $j + 1$ other variables. Hence the original problem is $(i, j + 1)$-consistent. To show strictness, consider $i = j = 1$ and a problem in four 0-1 variables with the constraints $x_1 \neq x_2$, $x_2 \neq x_3$, $x_2 \neq x_4$, $x_3 \neq x_4$. This is path inverse consistent. However, enforcing SAC proves that the problem is insoluble since if we instantiate x_1 with either of its values, the resulting subproblem cannot be made arc-consistent.

Debruyne and Bessiere also prove that strong PC is strictly stronger than SAC [DB97]. We can also generalize this proof, showing that strong $(i + 1, j)$-consistency is strictly stronger than singleton (i, j)-consistency. Debruyne and Bessiere's result is again a special case for $i = j = 1$. As before, [DB97] does not give the proof of strictness, so for completeness we give it here for the case $i = j = 1$.

Theorem 4. *Strong $(i + 1, j)$-consistency $>$ singleton (i, j)-consistency.*

Proof. Consider a problem that is strongly $(i + 1, j)$-consistent. Any consistent instantiation for $i + 1$ variables can be extended to j other variables. As the original problem was strongly $(i + 1, j)$-consistent, it is (i, j)-consistent. Hence a subproblem formed by instantiating one variable is (i, j)-consistent, and any consistent instantiation of i variables can be extended to j other variables. Thus the original problem is singleton (i, j)-consistent. To show strictness, consider $i = j = 1$ and a problem in three 0-1 variables with $x_1 \neq x_2$ and $x_1 \neq x_3$. The problem is SAC. But it is not path-consistent since the consistent partial assignment $x_2 = 0$ and $x_3 = 1$ cannot be extended. Enforcing path-consistency adds the constraint $x_2 = x_3$.

The last two results show that singleton (i, j)-consistency is sandwiched between strong $(i + 1, j)$-consistency and $(i, j + 1)$-consistency. Finally, we give some results concerning SGAC. Whilst this is a very high level of consistency to achieve in general, our experiments show that it can be very worthwhile provided we have an efficient algorithm to achieve it (as we do for the all-different constraint). In [SW99], GAC was compared against binary consistencies (like SAC) on decomposable non-binary constraints. These are non-binary constraints that can be represented by binary constraints on the same set of variables [Dec90]. For example, an all-different constraint can be decomposed into a clique of not-equals constraints. Decomposable constraints are a special case of non-binary constraints where comparisons between the binary and non-binary representations are very direct. Constraints which are not decomposable (like parity constraints) require us to introduce additional variables to represent them using binary constraints. These additional variables make comparisons more complicated.

Theorem 5. *On decomposable non-binary constraints, singleton generalized arc-consistency is strictly stronger than singleton arc-consistency on the binary decomposition.*

Proof. The proof follows immediately from Theorem 1, and the result of [SW99] that GAC is strictly stronger than AC on the binary decomposition. To show strictness, consider three all-different constraints on $\{x_1, x_2, x_3\}$, on $\{x_1, x_2, x_4\}$, and on $\{x_1, x_3, x_4\}$, in which all variables have the domain $\{1, 2, 3\}$. The binary decomposition is SAC. But enforcing SGAC proves that the problem is unsatisfiable.

Though SGAC is a very high level of consistency to enforce, it is incomparable in general to both strong PC and NIC on the binary decomposition.

Theorem 6. *On decomposable non-binary constraints, singleton generalized arc-consistency is incomparable to strong path-consistency and to neighbourhood inverse consistency on the binary decomposition.*

Proof. Consider a problem with six all-different constraints on $\{x_1, x_2, x_3\}$, on $\{x_1, x_3, x_4\}$, on $\{x_1, x_4, x_5\}$, on $\{x_1, x_2, x_5\}$, on $\{x_2, x_3, x_4\}$, and on $\{x_3, x_4, x_5\}$. All variables have the domain $\{1, 2, 3, 4\}$. This problem is SGAC because any instantiation of a variable results in a problem that is GAC. Enforcing NIC, however, shows that the problem is insoluble. Consider a problem with three not-equals constraints, $x_1 \neq x_2$, $x_1 \neq x_3$, $x_2 \neq x_3$ in which each variable has the same domain of size two. This problem is SGAC but enforcing strong PC proves that it is insoluble.

Consider the following 2-colouring problem. We have 5 variables, x_1 to x_5 arranged in a ring. Each variable has the same domain of size 2. Between each pair of neighbouring variables in the binary decomposition, there is a not-equals constraint. In the non-binary representation, we post a single constraint on all 5 variables. This problem is NIC, but enforcing SGAC on the non-binary representation shows that the problem is insoluble. Finally, consider an all-different constraint on 4 variables, each with the same domain of size 3. The binary representation of the problem is strong PC but enforcing SGAC shows that it is insoluble.

5   Random Problems

These theoretical results help place singleton consistencies within the hierarchy of local consistencies. But how useful are singleton consistencies in practice? To explore this issue, we ran experiments first with random problems, then with problems that combine structure and randomness, and afterwards with more realistic structured problems. One of our intentions was to determine how well results from random problems predicted behaviour on more realistic problems. Our starting point is [DB97] which reports a set of experiments on random problems with 20 variables and 10 values. These experiments identify how well consistency techniques like SAC approximate global consistency, and give the ratio of the number of values pruned to the CPU times at different points in the phase space. Debruyne and Bessiere conclude that SAC is a very promising local consistency technique, removing most of the strong path-inconsistent values while requiring less time than path inverse consistency.

Debruyne and Bessiere's experiments suffer from two limitations. First, their experiments only measure the ability of singleton arc-consistency to approximate global consistency. They do not tell us if SAC is useful within complete search procedures like MAC. For instance, does pre-processing with singleton arc-consistency reduce MAC's search enough to justify its cost? Can we afford to maintain SAC within (a number of levels of) search? Second, their experiments were restricted to random binary problems. Do results on random problems predict well behaviour on real problems? What about non-binary problems? Can it pay to enforce the singleton version of non-binary consistencies like GAC? Our experiments tackle both these issues.

5.1   SAC and AC as a Pre-process

Mackworth's AC3 algorithm was encoded and used to implement the AC and SAC pre-processes and the domain filtering within the FC and MAC search algorithms. The reason AC3 was chosen is because it allows a standard measure of comparison between algorithms, namely the consistency check. FC was implemented as a crippled version of MAC, i.e. propagation within AC3 was disabled beyond the constraints incident on the current variable.

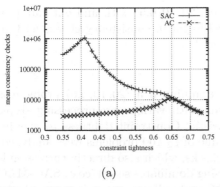
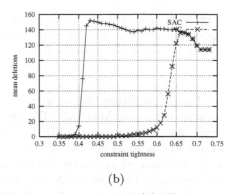

(a)   (b)

Fig. 1. SAC and AC pre-processing for $\langle 20, 10, 0.5 \rangle$: on the left (a) effort measured as mean consistency checks and on the right (b) values deleted

Figure 1a shows the mean pre-processing cost measured in consistency checks for AC and SAC over $\langle 20, 10, 0.5 \rangle$ model-B problems with a sample size of 500 (i.e. problems studied by Debruyne and Bessiere) at each value of constraint tightness p_2. Looking at the contours for SAC and AC we see that the two blend together at the arc-consistency phase transition ($p_2 \approx 0.65$). This is expected as the first phase of SAC is to make the problem arc-consistent. If this phase detects arc-inconsistency the problem is also SAC inconsistent and there is no more work to do.

Figure 1b shows the average number of values removed from the problem by pre-processing. Again, we see the SAC and AC contours blend together at the AC phase transition. About 80% of values are deleted in order to show SAC insolubility ($p_2 \approx 0.41$), and about 70% for AC insolubility. The solubility phase transition for this problem is round about $p_2 \approx 0.37$, and we see next to no values being deleted by SAC until $p_2 \approx 0.38$. This does not bode well for reduction in search effort for this problem.

5.2   Search after SAC

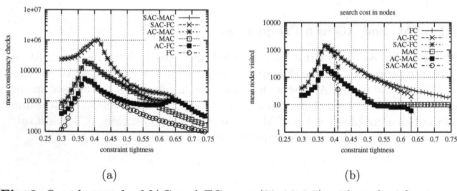

(a)   (b)

Fig. 2. Search cost for MAC and FC over $\langle 20, 10, 0.5 \rangle$ with and without pre-processing: on the left (a) effort measured as mean consistency checks and on the right (b) effort measured as nodes visited

Figure 2a shows the total cost of determining if a $\langle 20, 10, 0.5 \rangle$ problem is soluble using the MAC and FC algorithm with various pre-processing steps, both algorithms using the MRV dvo heuristic. Constraint tightness p_2 was incremented in steps of 0.01, and at each value of p_2 100 problems were analyzed. Cost is measured as average consistency checks, which also directly corresponds to cpu times. The cost of SAC pre-processing dominates search cost. SAC-MAC and SAC-FC compare poorly with their AC and null pre-processing equivalents. At the solubility phase transition, $p_2 \approx 0.37$, the average cost of SAC-MAC is 605K checks whereas MAC without any pre-process costs 198K checks. The cost of SAC pre-processing from Figure 1 is 432K checks at $p_2 = 0.37$. This suggests that in these problems SAC is an uneconomical overhead. In fact we see the solubility complexity peak dominated to such a degree that it appears shifted right to the higher value of constrainedness associated with the SAC phase transition. Around the solubility phase transition it was observed that for all algorithms studied soluble problems were easier than insoluble problems. This was most notable for SAC-FC, the reason being that SAC pre-processing frequently detected insolubility, but this was at the cost of deleting many values from variables, changing the problem and this in turn initiates more iterations of the outermost loop of the SAC algorithm. As an aside it should be noted that AC-FC exhibits a twin peaked complexity contour, the second (and lower) peak due to the AC phase transition.

Figure 2b shows cost measured in median nodes visited. SAC pre-processing makes no impact on the size of the search tree explored until it starts to delete values. As noted in Figure 1a, this does not begin to occur until just after the solubility phase transition. Consequently we see a reduction in nodes visited only as we approach the SAC phase transition, i.e. values of $p_2 > 0.4$.

5.3   Dense Problems and Large Sparse Problems

We investigated denser problems and large sparse problems. For the dense $\langle 20, 10, 1.0 \rangle$ problems search costs dominate pre-processing when problems are hard. At the solubility complexity peak $p_2 = 0.21$ the cost of SAC pre-processing was about 680K checks whereas SAC-MAC took 1835K checks, MAC alone took 1163K checks, SAC-FC took 931K checks, and FC alone took 258K checks. Therefore, although SAC pre-processing shows no advantage it is now substantially less effort than the search process on hard problems.

In the sparse $\langle 50, 10, 0.1 \rangle$ problems MAC and FC compete with each other over hard problems. Although the SAC pre-process continues to be uneconomic, it is just beginning to break even. In particular, on 100 (hard) instances of $\langle 50, 10, 0.1, 0.55 \rangle$ of the 26 insoluble instances 22 were detected by the SAC pre-process, and 23 of the 74 soluble instances were discovered without backtracking. In total 43 of the soluble instances took less than 100 search nodes. A study of $\langle 50, 10, 0.2 \rangle$ problems, i.e large but slightly denser, showed that SAC pre-processing was again uneconomical.

These experiments suggest that SAC pre-processing may be worthwhile on larger sparse problems with tight constraints, but uneconomical on dense problems with relatively loose constraints.

6   Small-World Problems

To test the efficiency of singleton consistency techniques on problems with structure, we first studied "small-world" problems. These are problems that combine structure and randomness. In graphs with "small world" topology, nodes are highly clustered, whilst the path length between them is small. Recently,

Watts and Strogatz have shown such graphs occur in many biological, social and man-made systems that are often neither completely regular nor completely random [WS98]. Walsh has argued that such a topology can make search problems hard since local decisions quickly propagate globally [Wal99]. To construct graphs with such a topology, we start from the constraint graph of a structured problem like a quasigroup. Note that a quasigroup can be modelled using either all-different constraints for each row and column or cliques of binary "not-equals" constraints. To introduce randomness, we add edges at random in the binary representation. Small world problems created in this way quickly become very hard when the order of the quasigroup is increased.

Figures 3a and 3b show the median number of branches explored and the cpu time used when GAC and SGAC are used for preprocessing small-world problems created by randomly adding edges to an order 6 quasigroup. GAC on the all-different constraints is maintained during search. The x-axis gives the percentage of added edges in the total number of edges left to turn the quasigroup into a complete graph. 100 problems were generated at each data point. We do not include SAC and AC preprocessing in Figures 3a and 3b because they have no impact as they do no pruning at all. This is not surprising, because of the nature of the constraints. AC on a binary "not-equals" constraint may delete a value from one of the variables only if the other one has a singleton domain. Likewise, when SAC reduces a variable x to a singleton value v then v is removed from the domain of all variables constrained with x, but no more filtering can be made. As a result, there can be no singleton arc-inconsistent values in problems with domain size 6.

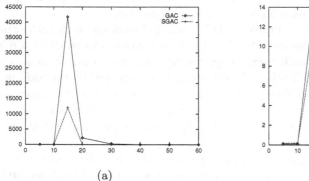
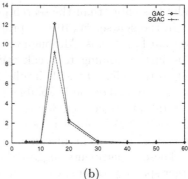

(a)   (b)

Fig. 3. Search cost for GAC and SGAC. On the left (a) effort measured as branches explored and on the right (b) effort measured as cpu time used (in seconds)

Preprocessing with SGAC is very efficient especially at the solubility complexity peak and in the insoluble region, where insolubility is detected without search for most insoluble instances. SGAC preprocessing is also cost-effective for soluble instances, especially for hard ones near the complexity peak, as it cuts down the number of branches explored significantly. CPU times are also reduced despite the cost of preprocessing. The presence of structure in the problems makes SGAC much more efficient than on purely random problems.

7   Problems of Distance

To test singleton consistency techniques on a class of structured, and non-binary problems, we ran experiments on a variety of *problems of distance*. This general class of problems is introduced in [SSW00], and models several challenging combinatorial problems including Golomb rulers and all-interval series. A problem of distances is defined by a graph in which nodes are labelled with integers, the edges are labelled by the difference between the node labels at either end of each edge, and there are constraints that all edge labels are different. As in [SSW00], we model such problems with variables for both the nodes and edges, ternary constraints of the form $d_{ij} = |x_i - x_j|$ that limit the values given to the edges, and a single all-different constraint on the edges.

7.1   Golomb Rulers

Peter van Beek has proposed the Golomb ruler problem as a challenging constraint satisfaction problem for the CSPLib benchmark library (available as prob006 at http://csplib.cs.strath.ac.uk). The problem specification given there is:

> "A Golomb ruler may be defined as a set of m integers $0 = x_1 < x_2 <$ ... $< x_m$, such that the $m(m-1)/2$ differences $x_j - x_i$, $1 \le i < j \le m$, are distinct. Such a ruler is said to contain m marks and is of length x_m. The objective is to find optimal (minimum length) or near optimal rulers."

Golomb rulers are problems of distance in which the underlying graph is complete. To turn optimization into satisfaction, we build a sequence of decision problems, reducing a_m until the problem becomes unsatisfiable. The longest currently known optimal ruler has 21 marks and length 333. Peter van Beek reports that even quite small problems (with fewer than fifteen marks) are very difficult for complete methods such as backtracking search, and that their difficulty lies both in proving optimality and in finding a solution, since the problems have either a unique solution or just a handful of solutions.

Table 1 shows the search cost in branches and cpu time for algorithms that preprocess with AC, SAC and restricted SAC, and maintain GAC during search. Although preprocessing with SAC deletes considerably more values than preprocessing with AC, this is not reflected in the search effort.

Table 2 shows the search effort for algorithms that preprocess with GAC, SGAC, and restricted SGAC, and maintain GAC on the all-different constraint during search. SGAC deletes a large number of values during preprocessing (more than 60% in some cases) and that has a notable effect on search. The number

Table 1. Branches explored and cpu time in seconds when trying to find a ruler of optimal length (F) or prove that no shorter exists (P). Preprocessing was done with AC, SAC and restricted SAC

Marks	Branches			CPU time		
	AC	SAC	restricted SAC	AC	SAC	restricted SAC
7-F	10	10	10	0.15	1.27	0.63
7-P	87	65	65	0.20	1.25	0.83
8-F	26	26	26	0.22	2.98	1.564
8-P	506	461	461	1.55	3.52	2.26
9-F	309	282	282	1.28	8.00	4.04
9-P	2489	2318	2318	8.44	13.73	10.30
10-F	1703	1692	1692	6.05	27.45	13.41
10-P	11684	9658	9665	56.18	68.16	54.17
11-F	7007	6584	6584	26.98	87.74	48.72
11-P	202137	193419	193498	1240.90	1170.77	1151.70

of explored branches is cut down, especially when trying to prove optimality, and despite the cost of preprocessing, there is a gain in cpu times for the harder instances. Restricted SGAC seems a better option than full SGAC since it deletes almost the same number of values and is more efficient in cpu times.

Given the good results obtained by preprocessing with SGAC, we investigated whether maintaining such a high level of consistency during search is worthwhile. Our results showed that maintaining SGAC even for depth 1 in search (i.e., at the first variable) is too expensive. When trying to find an optimal ruler, we enforced SGAC after instantiating the first variable. As a result, the number of branches was cut down (though not significantly), but runtimes were higher. When trying to prove optimality, we enforced SGAC after each value of the first variable was tried. Again there was a gain in branches, but runtimes were much higher than before.

7.2   2-d Golomb Rulers and All-Interval Series

A Golomb ruler is a problem of distance in which the underlying graph is complete (i.e. a clique). Our results with random problems suggest that singleton consistencies will show more promise on sparser problems. What happens then with problems of distance in which the underlying graph (and hence the associated constraint graph) is sparser? For example, in a 2-d Golomb ruler we have (2 or more) layers of cliques, with edges between node i in clique j and node i in clique $j + 1$. A 2-d Golomb ruler with k layers has a constraint graph with approximately $1/k$ the edges of that of a 1-d Golomb ruler of the same size.

Table 3 shows the search effort for algorithms that preprocess with GAC, SGAC, and restricted SGAC, and maintain GAC on the all-different constraint during search. SGAC preprocessing reduces the number of branches, and the

Table 2. Branches explored and cpu time in seconds when preprocessing with GAC, SGAC and restricted SGAC

Marks	Branches			CPU time		
	GAC	SGAC	restricted SGAC	GAC	SGAC	restricted SGAC
7-F	10	5	6	0.15	1.06	0.58
7-P	87	0	0	0.18	0.34	0.32
8-F	26	22	22	0.21	2.49	1.29
8-P	506	265	339	1.57	3.21	1.55
9-F	309	261	262	1.30	5.14	2.90
9-P	2489	1844	1862	8.64	8.56	5.92
10-F	1703	1592	1592	6.16	14.61	9.15
10-P	11684	7823	7924	56.35	37.65	30.77
11-F	7007	6464	6464	27.04	65.53	37.96
11-P	202137	98967	99602	1239.81	491.58	442.96

Table 3. Branches explored, and cpu time in seconds when GAC, SGAC and restricted SGAC are used for preprocessing 2-d Golmb rulers

Marks	Branches			CPU time		
	GAC	SGAC	restricted SGAC	GAC	SGAC	restricted SGAC
3-F	1	0	0	0.051	0.120	0.068
3-P	6	0	0	0.048	0.052	0.050
4-F	32	26	26	0.27	0.693	0.407
4-P	210	74	191	0.389	1.228	0.598
5-F	1404	1276	1276	2.552	3.767	3.111
5-P	8177	7521	7521	14.764	14.389	13.554
6-F	133010	113723	113723	376.23	321.553	317.033
6-P	433087	357320	357320	1420.63	1071.82	1067.32

cpu times in the harder instances (rulers with 6 marks), but the effect is not as significant as in the 1-d case.

An even sparser problem of distance is the all-interval series problem. This problem was proposed by Holger Hoos as a challenging constraint satisfaction problem for the CSPLib benchmark library (available as `prob007` at `http://csplib.cs.strath.ac.uk`). All-interval series are problems of distance in which the underlying graph is a simple ring. They therefore have an associated constraint graph which is very sparse compared to 1-d and 2-d Golomb rulers. In the case of all-interval series, preprocessing with SAC and SGAC had no effect as no values were pruned. Also, enforcing SAC (SGAC) at depth 1 had very little impact on the number of branches explored and increased runtimes.

8   Related Work

As mentioned briefly before, Debruyne and Bessiere compared the ability of a variety of different local consistencies (e.g. AC, RPC, PIC, SAC, strong PC, and NIC) at approximating global consistency on randomly generated binary problems with 20 variables and 10 values. [DB97]. In addition, they computed the ratio of CPU time to number of values pruned. They concluded that SAC and RPC are both promising, the first having a good CPU time to number of values pruned, and the second requiring little additional CPU time to AC but pruning most of the values of path inverse consistency. Debruyne and Bessiere also studied singleton restricted path-consistency (SRPC) but concluded that it is too expensive despite its ability to prune many values.

Closely related inference techniques have shown promise in the neighbouring field of propositional satisfiability (SAT). One of the best procedures to solve the SAT problem is the Davis-Putnam (DP) procedure [DLL62]. The DP procedure consists of three main rules: the empty rule (which fails and backtracks when an empty clause is generated), the unit propagation rule (which deterministically assigns any unit literal), and the branching or split rule (which non-deterministically assigns a truth value to a chosen variable). The effectiveness of DP is in large part due to the power of unit propagation. Note that the unit propagation rule is effectively the "singleton" empty rule. That is, if we assign the complement of an unit clause, the empty rule will show that the resulting problem is unsatisfiable; we can therefore delete this assignment. Other "singleton" consistencies (specifically that provided by the "singleton" unit rule) might therefore be of value. Indeed, some of the best current implementations of DP already perform a limited amount of "singleton" unit reasoning, having heuristics that choose between a set of literals to branch upon by the amount of unit propagation that they cause [LA97].

Smith, Stergiou and Walsh performed an extensive theoretical and empirical analysis of the use of auxiliary variables and implied constraints in models of problems of distance [SSW00]. They identified a large number of different models, both binary and non-binary, and compared theoretically the level of consistency achieved by GAC on them. Their experiments on 1-d, 2-d and circular Golomb rulers showed that the introduction of auxiliary variables and implied constraints significantly reduces the size of the search space. For instance, their final models reduced the time to find an optimal 10-mark Golomb ruler 50-fold.

9   Conclusions

We have performed a comprehensive theoretical and empirical study of the benefits of singleton consistencies. For example, we proved that singleton (i, j)-consistency is sandwiched between strong $(i + 1, j)$-consistency and $(i, j + 1)$-consistency. We also proved that, on non-binary constraints, singleton generalized arc-consistency (the singleton extension of generalized arc-consistency) is strictly stronger than both generalized arc-consistency and singleton arc-consistency (on the binary decomposition). Singleton generalized arc-consistency is, however, incomparable to neighbourhood inverse consistency and strong path-consistency (on the binary decomposition). Singleton generalized arc-consistency is a very high level of consistency to achieve. Nevertheless our experiments showed that it can be worthwhile if we have an efficient algorithm (as we do for all-different constraints). We ran experiments on both random and structured problems. On random problems, singleton arc-consistency was rarely cost-effective as a pre-processing technique. However, it did best on sparse problems. Results on problems with structure were quite different. On small-world problems, 1-d and 2-d Golomb rulers, singleton generalized arc-consistency was often cost-effective as a pre-processing technique, especially on large and insoluble problems. Unlike random problems, more benefits were seen on dense problems than on sparse problems. Our experiments also showed that restricting algorithms that enforce singleton consistencies to one pass only gave a small reduction in the amount of pruning.

What general lessons can be learned from this study? First, singleton consistencies can be useful for pre-processing but can be too expensive for maintaining, even during the initial parts of search only. Second, singleton consistencies appear to be most beneficial on large, unsatisfiable and structured problems. Third, limiting algorithms that enforce singleton consistencies to a single pass makes a small dent on their ability to prune values, and can thus improve their cost-effectiveness. Fourth, provided we have an efficient algorithm, it can pay to enforce consistencies as high as singleton generalized arc-consistency. And finally, random problems can be very misleading. Our experiments on random problems suggested that pre-processing with singleton consistencies was rarely cost-effective and that it was most beneficial on sparse problems. The results of our experiments on structured problems could hardly be more contradictory.

Acknowledgements

The third author is supported by an EPSRC advanced research fellowship. The authors are members of the APES (http://www.cs.strath.ac.uk/~apes) research group and thank the other members for their comments and feedback.

References

BR97.   C. Bessière and J. C. Régin. Arc consistency for general constraint networks: Preliminary results. In *Proceedings IJCAI-97*, pages 398–404, 1997. 355

DB97.   R. Debruyne and C. Bessière. Some practicable filtering techniques for the constraint satisfaction problem. In *Proceedings of the 15th IJCAI*, pages 412–417. International Joint Conference on Artificial Intelligence, 1997. 353, 354, 355, 356, 357, 359, 366

Dec90.   R. Dechter. On the expressiveness of networks with hidden variables. In *Proceedings of the 8th National Conference on AI*, pages 555–562. American Association for Artificial Intelligence, 1990. 357

DLL62.   M. Davis, G. Logemann, and D. Loveland. A machine program for theorem-proving. *Communications of the ACM*, 5:394–397, 1962. 366

FE96.   E. Freuder and C. D. Elfe. Neighborhood inverse consistency preprocessing. In *Proceedings of the 12th National Conference on AI*, pages 202–208. American Association for Artificial Intelligence, 1996. 354

Fre85.   E. Freuder. A sufficient condition for backtrack-bounded search. *Journal of the Association for Computing Machinery*, 32(4):755–761, 1985. 354

Gas79.   J. Gaschnig. Performance measurement and analysis of certain search algorithms. Technical report CMU-CS-79-124, Carnegie-Mellon University, 1979. PhD thesis. 354

LA97.   C. M. Li and Anbulagan. Heuristics based on unit propagation for satisfiability problems. In *Proceedings of the 15th IJCAI*, pages 366–371. International Joint Conference on Artificial Intelligence, 1997. 366

MM88.   R. Mohr and G. Masini. Good old discrete relaxation. In *Proceedings of the European Conference on Artificial Intelligence (ECAI-88)*, pages 651–656, 1988. 354

Reg94.   J-C. Régin. A filtering algorithm for constraints of difference in CSPs. In *Proceedings of the 12th National Conference on AI*, pages 362–367. American Association for Artificial Intelligence, 1994. 354

SRGV96.   T. Schiex, J. C. Régin, C. Gaspin, and G. Verfaillie. Lazy arc consistency. In *Proceedings of the 12th National Conference on Artificial Intelligence (AAAI-96)*, pages 216–221, Portland, Oregon, 1996. 355

SSW00.   B. Smith, K. Stergiou, and T. Walsh. Using auxiliary variables and implied constraints to model non-binary problems. In *To appear in Proceedings of the 17th National Conference on Artificial Intelligence (AAAI-2000)*, Austin, Texas, 2000. 363, 366

SW99.   K. Stergiou and T. Walsh. The difference all-difference makes. In *Proceedings of 16th IJCAI*. International Joint Conference on Artificial Intelligence, 1999. 355, 357, 358

Wal99.   T. Walsh. Search in a small world. In *Proceedings of IJCAI-99*, 1999. 362

WS98.   D. J. Watts and S. H. Strogatz. Collective dynamics of 'small-world' networks. *Nature*, 393:440–442, 1998. 362

Linear Formulation of Constraint Programming Models and Hybrid Solvers

Philippe Refalo

ILOG, Les Taissounieres
1681, route des Dolines, 06560 Sophia Antipolis, France
refalo@ilog.fr

Abstract. Constraint programming offers a variety of modeling objects such as logical and global constraints, that lead to concise and clear models for expressing combinatorial optimization problems. We propose a way to provide a linear formulation of such a model and detail, in particular, the transformation of some global constraints. An automatic procedure for producing and updating formulations has been implemented and we illustrate it on combinatorial optimization problems.

Keywords: linear formulation, global constraints, hybrid solvers

1 Introduction

Constraint programming (CP) offers a variety of modeling facilities, such as logical and global constraints, that lead to concise and clear models for expressing combinatorial optimization problems. CP models contain useful structural information permitting the development of dedicated and efficient domain reduction algorithms for high-level constraints and the design of efficient ad hoc solution search strategies. Industrial implementations (CHIP [4] and ILOG Solver [18], for instance) have shown the effectiveness of CP for solving problems in different areas.

Mixed integer programming (MIP) techniques are also an effective and widely used method for solving combinatorial optimization problems. With MIP, the model is limited to a set of linear constraints over binary, integer, or real variables. A MIP formulation is sometimes far from natural and contains little structural information. The emphasis is on having good linear relaxations of the problem. Consequently, MIP solvers maintain a relaxed optimal solution of the linear relaxation and generate cutting planes to strengthen the relaxation [22].

In this paper, we propose a way to provide a MIP formulation of a CP model. The aim of this transformation is threefold. First, it permits the use of a MIP solver for solving a CP model. This is for solving models where MIP techniques are effective, without having to give a linear formulation. Second, it permits the use of constraint programming capabilities for designing search strategies on the high level model together with linear relaxations. Solving the linear relaxation provides a lower bound that prunes the search space, while the relaxed optimal

R. Dechter (Ed.): CP 2000, LNCS 1894, pp. 369–383, 2000.

solution guides the search towards optimal solutions [2,13]. Third, it facilitates the use of hybrid solvers where domain reduction algorithms cooperate with a linear relaxation solver. This last approach has been shown to be promising (see [8,17,15,13]).

In the following we detail, in particular, the reformulation of the "all different" constraint [14]; constraints over occurrences of values such as "atmost", "atleast", and "among" [4]; constraints for variable indexing such as "element" [19]; and the "cycle" constraint [4]. The formulations presented can be viewed as an extension of the work done by Wallace et al. on the automatic transformation of a constraint logic program (including alldifferent constraints) to a MIP model [16] and of the work done on the transformation of logical formulas to MIP models [21,11] which is closely related to the seminal work of Balas and Jeroslow on disjunctive programming [3,10].

The linear formulation of a constraint is divided into two sets: the set of linear constraints that are *required* for the linearization and the set of linear constraints that are *delayed*. The latter are cutting planes that are added to the linear formulation when they are violated by the relaxed optimal solution. Cutting plane generation is embedded in the propagation process of the high-level constraint. Thus a global constraint can propagate not only new domains but also arbitrary constraints. Generating cutting planes from a global constraint by using the structure of the constraints is a clean integration of integer programming techniques into constraint programming which is related to the work of Bockmayer et al. [5]. However, this approach does not address the problem of systematically providing a linear formulation of models containing global constraints.

An automatic procedure for producing and updating formulations has been implemented and we illustrate it on problems such as the asymmetric traveling salesman problem, the facility location problem, and the quadratic assignment problem. Interestingly, our general reformulation of a natural CP model of a problem often gives a standard and even strong MIP formulation. Some experimental results are also given to illustrate the effectiveness of this method.

The rest of this paper is organised as follows. Section 2 gives details about how high-level constraints are reformulated in general. In Section 3 the reformulation of some global constraints is given. In Section 4, three applications are presented, and Section 5 concludes this article.

2   Constraint Reformulation

A constraint programming model is composed of variables and constraints. Constraints can be (1) domain constraints, (2) elementary constraints such as arithmetic constraints, and (3) high-level constraints which can be logical [20] or global constraints [4]. A linear formulation of these constraints needs to address two important issues. The first is the strength of the formulation that determines relevance of the linear relaxation; the second is maintaining this strength during the search.

2.1   Linear Reformulation

A linear reformulation of a set S of constraints over a set of variables V is a set S' of linear constraints over variables $V \cup V'$ such that both sets have the same solutions on variables V.

A set of linear constraints defines a convex set. Let Q be the solutions set of a high level constraint c. The strongest linear formulation of c represents the smallest convex set containing the solutions of Q. This set is called the *convex hull* of Q and the associated linear constraints represent a *sharp* formulation of Q [21]. The closer a formulation to a sharp one, the stronger it is.

Various sharp formulations can represent the same solution set. Moreover, in many cases the size of a strong formulation can be huge and it is desirable to avoid considering the whole reformulation at the same time. Therefore, the linear formulation $\mathcal{F}(c)$ of a constraint c is divided into two sets:

$$\mathcal{F}(c) = \mathcal{L}(c) \cup \mathcal{D}(c)$$

where $\mathcal{L}(c)$ is the set of linear constraints that are required in the reformulation and $\mathcal{D}(c)$ is a set of linear constraints whose addition is delayed. Constraints of $\mathcal{D}(c)$ are cutting planes that are not stored explicitly, but generated when needed. They are added when violated by the relaxed optimal solution. In the following, not specifying $\mathcal{D}(c)$ means that no constraint is delayed.

Constraints are not reformulated independently. Domain constraints are also considered. That is if S_D is the set of domain constraints of S, a formulation of $S_D \cup \{c\}$ is provided for c.

Since many logical conditions over linear constraints can be represented as a disjunction of convex sets, research in this field has focused on the linear representation of such disjunctions. A sharp formulation of $D = \{Ax \leq b \vee A'x \leq b'\}$ can have an exponential number of constraints when expressed on variables x. However, by introducing two new vectors of variables x^1 and x^2 and two binary variables γ_1 and γ_2, a sharp formulation of D is given by the system:

$$\mathcal{L}(D) = \begin{cases} Ax^1 \leq \gamma_1 b \\ A'x^2 \leq \gamma_2 b' \\ x = x^1 + x^2 \\ \gamma_1 + \gamma_2 = 1 \\ \gamma_i \in \{0,1\} \text{ for } i \in \{1,2\} \end{cases}$$

This fundamental result is known as the *disjunctive formulation*, which was developed by Balas and Jeroslow [3,10]. This transformation is applied in the following for constraints that can be restated as disjunctions of linear constraint sets.

2.2   Maintaining Sharpness under Domain Reduction

An important property of a linear formulation that is used together with a Branch and Bound search is *hereditary sharpness*, where the formulation remains sharp when variables are fixed from a parent node to a child node of the search tree [21]. In constraint programming with hybrid solvers, we need to go further. Since new domains are inferred when going down the search tree, we must maintain the sharpness under domain reduction. In [13] a general principle called *tight cooperation* is presented where linear formulations of high level structures are dynamically updated with variable fixing and cutting planes generation when domains are reduced. This goes beyond the classical solvers cooperation framework, where only bounds on variables are exchanged between the domain reduction solver and the linear optimizer [2,17].

The same approach is applied herein. For each constraint, the formulation is updated so that the modifications done during search on the (high-level) constraint programming model are reflected on the (low-level) linear formulation. As an example, suppose that in the disjunctive formulation above, the alternative $Ax \leq b$ becomes unsolvable w.r.t. new domains on variables x at a node of the search tree. Fixing the variable γ_1 to 0 maintains the sharpness of the formulation w.r.t to new domains. Conversely, if $Ax \leq b$ is entailed w.r.t domains of x, the variable γ_1 must be fixed to 1.

3   Reformulation of Constraint Programming Models

This section details the reformulation of domain constraints and some high-level constraints, such as the alldifferent constraint, constraints over occurrences of variables, variations of the element constraint, the cycle constraint, and unary meta constraints.

3.1   Domain Constraint

A sharp linear formulation of a domain constraint $x \in D$ is obtained by the disjunctive formulation of $\bigvee_{a \in D}(x = a)$. For writing ease, let's denote the variable introduced for the alternative $x = a$ by $v_{x=a}$. It is assumed that $v_{x=a} = 0$ when $a \notin D$. The linear formulation of a domain constraint is thus:

$$\mathcal{L}(x \in D) = \begin{cases} \sum_{a \in D} v_{x=a} = 1 \\ 0 \leq v_{x=a} \leq 1 \text{ for } a \in D \\ \text{integer}(v_{x=a}) \text{ for } a \in D \end{cases}$$

$$\mathcal{D}(x \in D) = \left\{ x = \sum_{a \in D} a \times v_{x=a} \right. \tag{1}$$

The addition of constraints linking the binary variables and the original variable is delayed, because the linear formulation of high-level constraints often concerns the binary variables only. This is the case for the constraints presented below. Thus, delaying these constraints significantly reduces the size of the linear problem solved in practice.

The impact of constraint propagation algorithms is reduced domains for variables. The linear formulation of a domain constraint can be updated when the domain D is reduced to a new domain D'. To maintain the sharpness of the formulation, variables are fixed depending on the values removed, according to the following propagation rules:

$$\forall \alpha \in D, \alpha \notin D' \iff v_{x=\alpha} = 0$$
$$D' = \{\alpha\} \iff v_{x=\alpha} = 1$$

Conversely, if some variables of the reformulation are fixed with an integer programming technique such as reduced cost fixing [22], the original domain is updated. Observe that variable fixing ensures that the value of x in the relaxed optimal solution stays between the lower and upper bound of its domain.

All linear formulations below reuse the variables introduced for the reformulation of the domain constraint. Therefore, these rules are sufficient to maintain sharpness of all global constraints presented in the following. Note also that, in many cases, these updating rules are sufficient to ensure that the delayed constraint is satisfied. Consequently, it may never be added.

3.2 Alldifferent Constraint

The constraint alldifferent$(x_1, \ldots, x_n)$ is satisfied if variables $x_1, \ldots, x_n$ have different values. A sharp formulation of this constraint is well-known: it is that of a bipartite matching [22].

Let $K = \bigcup_{i=1}^{n} D_i$ be the union of domains. The linearization of this constraint formulates that each value of K can be given at most once to any of the variables $x_1, \ldots, x_n$. Hence we have

$$\mathcal{L}(\text{alldifferent}(x_1, \ldots, x_n)) = \left\{ \sum_{i=1}^{n} v_{x_i=j} \leq 1, \ j \in K \right\}$$

Example 1 *Assuming that* $x_1, x_2, x_3 \in \{1, 2, 3, 4\}$ *and* $\gamma_{ij} = v_{x_i=j}$ *we have*

$$\mathcal{L}(alldifferent(x_1, x_2, x_3)) = \left\{ \begin{array}{l} \gamma_{11} + \gamma_{21} + \gamma_{31} \leq 1 \\ \gamma_{12} + \gamma_{22} + \gamma_{32} \leq 1 \\ \gamma_{13} + \gamma_{22} + \gamma_{33} \leq 1 \\ \gamma_{14} + \gamma_{24} + \gamma_{34} \leq 1 \end{array} \right\}$$

3.3 Constraint over Occurrences of Values

Many requirements in practical problems limit the number of values that a set of variables can have in a solution. This is the case for the *among* [4] constraint of CHIP and the *distribute* constraint of ILOG Solver [18].

The among constraint restricts the number of variables from a set having a given value. The constraint

$$\text{among}(y, [x_1, \ldots, x_n], [a_1, \ldots, a_k])$$

where x_i and y are variables and a_i are real numbers, is satisfied when exactly y variables among $x_1, \ldots, x_n$ have their value in the set $\{a_1, \ldots, a_k\}$. The formulation of this constraint specifies that each of the values a_i must be taken y times by variables x_i:

$$\mathcal{L}(\text{among}(y, [x_1, \ldots, x_n], [a_1, \ldots, a_k])) = \left\{ y = \sum_{i=1}^{n} \sum_{j=1}^{k} v_{x_i = a_j} \right\}$$

Without going into details, this formulation is obviously sharp since the associated one line matrix is totally unimodular (see [22]).

Example 2 *Assuming that $x_1, x_2, x_3 \in \{1, 2, 3, 4\}$ and $\gamma_{ij} = v_{x_i = j}$ we have*

$$\mathcal{L}(\text{among}(y, [x_1, x_2, x_3], [1, 3])) = \{y = \gamma_{11} + \gamma_{21} + \gamma_{31} + \gamma_{13} + \gamma_{23} + \gamma_{33}\}$$

The ILOG Solver constraint distribute($[x_1 \ldots, x_n], [a_1, \ldots, a_k], [y_1, \ldots, y_k]$) is satisfied if the number of variables among $x_1, \ldots, x_n$ having the value a_i is equal to the variable y_i. It has a sharp formulation when formulated as a conjunction of among constraints: among($y_1, [x_1, \ldots, x_n], [a_1]$) $\wedge \ldots \wedge$ among $(y_k, [x_1, \ldots, x_n], [a_k])\}$.

Note that the cardinality constraint atmost($\alpha, [x_1, \ldots, x_n], \beta$) and the constraint atleast($\alpha, [x_1, \ldots, x_n], \beta$) which require the number of variables from $x_1, \ldots, x_n$ that take the value β to be respectively atmost or atleast α, are also a special case of among constraints, and thus can be given a sharp formulation the same way.

3.4   Element Constraint

The constraint element was probably one of the first global constraints introduced in constraint logic programming systems [19]. The syntax is:

$$\text{element}(x, [a_1, \ldots, a_n], z)$$

where z is a variable, x is a variable whose domain D_x is a subset of $\{1, \ldots, n\}$, and a_i are real values. This constraint is satisfied if z is equal to the xth value of the array $[a_1, \ldots, a_n]$. In [9], this constraint is formulated by inequalities over x and z variables. Since we deal with domain constraints, we give a different formulation that has the advantage of being efficiently updated when domains are reduced.

Solutions of this constraint can also be represented by the disjunction $\bigvee_{i=1}^{n}(x = i \wedge z = a_i)$. Assuming that $D_x = \{1, \ldots n\}$, its disjunctive formulation gives the set:

$$\begin{cases} z = a_1 \gamma_1 + \cdots + a_n \gamma_n \\ x = \gamma_1 + \cdots + n \gamma_n \\ \gamma_1 + \cdots + \gamma_n = 1 \\ 0 \leq \gamma_i \leq 1 \text{ for } i \in D_x \\ \text{integer}(\gamma_i) \text{ for } i \in D_x \end{cases}$$

Since all constraints, except the first one, formulate the domain constraint on x, we have

$$\mathcal{L}(\text{element}(x, [a_1, \ldots, a_n], z)) = \left\{ z = \sum_{i \in D_x} a_i v_{x=i} \right\}$$

Example 3

$$\mathcal{L}\left(\begin{array}{l} x \in \{1,2,3\} \\ \text{element}(x, [7,8,12], z) \end{array} \right) = \left\{ \begin{array}{l} x = \gamma_1 + 2\gamma_2 + 3\gamma_3 \\ \gamma_1 + \gamma_2 + \gamma_3 = 1 \\ z = 7\gamma_1 + 8\gamma_2 + 12\gamma_3 \\ 0 \leq \gamma_i \leq 1 \; for \; i \in \{1,2,3\} \\ integer(\gamma_i) \; for \; i \in \{1,2,3\} \end{array} \right\}$$

Note that in this example, and in general, a compact reformulation is obtained if the variable $v_{x=i}$ is used for the alternative $y = a_i$. Consequently, the linear formulation of this constraint does not require any variables in addition to those that are introduced for domain constraints of x.

Element constraints can also be defined on higher dimensional arrays. Consider an element constraint $\text{element}(x, y, A, z)$ over an $m \times n$ matrix A where x and y are variables having domains $D_x \subset \{1, \ldots, m\}$ and $D_y \subset \{1, \ldots, n\}$, which is satisfied when z is equal to the element $A_{x,y}$. This constraint has the following disjunctive formulation:

$$\bigvee_{i=1,\ldots,m \;\; j=1,\ldots,n} (x = i \wedge y = j \wedge z = A_{ij})$$

Thus a sharp formulation is:

$$\mathcal{L}(\text{element}(x, y, A, z)) = \left\{ \begin{array}{l} v_{x=i} = \displaystyle\sum_{j=1,\ldots,n} (v_{z=A_{ij}}) \text{ for } i \in D_x \\ v_{y=j} = \displaystyle\sum_{i=1,\ldots,m} (v_{z=A_{ij}}) \text{ for } j \in D_y \end{array} \right.$$

The variables γ_{ij} can be reused for $v_{z=A_{ij}}$ provided that the value A_{ij} appears only once in the matrix.

Example 4

$$\mathcal{L}\left(\begin{array}{l} x \in \{1,2\} \\ y \in \{1,2,3\} \\ \text{element}\left(x, y, \begin{bmatrix} 7 & 8 & 4 \\ 3 & 1 & 2 \end{bmatrix}, z\right) \end{array} \right) = \left\{ \begin{array}{l} x = \gamma_1 + 2\gamma_2 \\ \gamma_1 + \gamma_2 = 1 \\ y = \delta_1 + 2\delta_2 + 3\delta_3 \\ \delta_1 + \delta_2 + \delta_3 = 1 \\ z = 7\lambda_1 + 8\lambda_2 + 4\lambda_3 + 3\lambda_4 + 1\lambda_5 + 2\lambda_6 \\ \lambda_1 + \lambda_2 + \lambda_3 + \lambda_4 + \lambda_5 + \lambda_6 = 1 \\ \gamma_1 = \lambda_1 + \lambda_2 + \lambda_3 \\ \gamma_2 = \lambda_4 + \lambda_5 + \lambda_6 \\ \delta_1 = \lambda_1 + \lambda_4 \\ \delta_2 = \lambda_2 + \lambda_5 \\ \delta_3 = \lambda_3 + \lambda_6 \\ 0 \leq \gamma_i \leq 1, integer(\gamma_i) \; for \; i \in \{1,2\} \\ 0 \leq \delta_i \leq 1, integer(\delta_i) \; for \; i \in \{1,2,3\} \\ 0 \leq \lambda_i \leq 1, integer(\lambda_i) \; for \; i \in \{1,\ldots,6\} \end{array} \right\}$$

This formulation can be easily extended to the case of an array of arbitrary dimensions.

3.5   Cycle Constraint

The constraint $\text{cycle}(k, [x_1, \ldots, x_n])$, where k is a positive integer and x_i are variables having domains $D_i \subset \{1, \ldots, n\}$, is mainly used to solve routing problems [4]. This constraint is satisfied when the values of the variables define k disjoint circuits in an directed graph such that each node is visited exactly once. Initially, a variable x_i is associated with the node i, the domain D_i corresponding to the set of possible nodes that can be visited from i.

A cycle in a set of variables $\{x_1, \ldots, x_n\}$ is a sequence of p indexes $C(1), \ldots, C(p)$ such that $C(i+1) \in D_{C(i)}$ for $i < p$ and $C(p) \in D_{C(1)}$. For instance if we have $x_1 \in \{2, 3\}$, $x_2 \in \{1, 3\}$, $x_3 \in \{2, 3\}$ the sequence $C(1) = 1$, $C(2) = 3$, $C(3) = 2$ is a cycle and thus the constraint $\text{cycle}(1, [x_1, x_2, x_3])$ is satisfied by the assignment $x_1 = 3$, $x_2 = 1$, $x_3 = 2$.

The formulation of the cycle constraint requires that each node must belong to a single circuit. This is equivalent to the formulation of an alldifferent constraint. To constrain the number of cycles to be at most k, the formulation also enforces connectivity on a partition of $k + 1$ subset of $\{1, \ldots, n\}$. There must be at least one variable having its index in one set and its value in another set. The number of constraints enforcing this is exponential, thus their addition to the linear model is delayed. To constrain the number of cycles to be atleast k, the formulation enforces that for each set of $k - 1$ disjoint cycles covering all nodes (called a $k - 1$ cycle-cover), one of the cycles must be broken.

$$\mathcal{L}(\text{cycle}(k, [x_1, \ldots, x_n])) = \mathcal{L}(\text{alldifferent}([x_1, \ldots, x_n]))$$
$$\mathcal{D}(\text{cycle}(k, [x_1, \ldots, x_n])) =$$
$$\begin{cases} \sum_{e=1}^{k+1} \sum_{i \in S_e} \sum_{j \in P \setminus S_e} (v_{x_i = j}) \geq 1 \\ \qquad \text{for all partition } (S_1, \ldots, S_{k+1}) \text{ of } \{1, \ldots, n\}, \ S_p \neq \emptyset \\ \sum_{e=1}^{k-1} \sum_{i \in C_e} (v_{x_{C_e(i)} = C_e(i+1)}) \leq n - 1 \\ \qquad \text{for all } k - 1 \text{ cycle-cover } (C_1, \ldots, C_{k-1}) \text{ of } \{1, \ldots, n\} \end{cases}$$

Observe that when $k = 1$, the set of delayed constraints represents the family of subtour elimination inequalities [22]. Consequently, this formulation is not sharp in general but, as it will be shown in the section of experimental results, it is strong enough to handle cycle constraints involving a few hundred variables. Stronger formulations could be obtained by generalizing stronger cuts for the case where $k = 1$; that is other strong cuts used to solve traveling salesman problems.

3.6   Higher-Order Expressions

Higher order expressions are arithmetic constraints that appear as terms in a constraint. For instance, $(x + y \leq 1) + (y = 5) = 1$ contains two higher-order expressions. The linear formulation of such constraints can be obtained by using the *big-M* formulation which introduces a binary variable for each constraint as a term [11]. It has been used in [16] for reformulating constraint logic programs as MIP models.

When using domain constraints, higher-order unary constraints must be handled differently. For instance, the occurrence of an expression $(x = 2)$ in a linear constraint should be replaced by the variable $v_{x=2}$ and not by the binary variable of the *big-M* formulation. More generally, here is how to reformulate unary higher order terms into linear terms in the general case.

$$\mathcal{L}'((x = a)) = (v_{x=a})$$
$$\mathcal{L}'((x \neq a)) = (1 - v_{x=a})$$
$$\mathcal{L}'((x \geq a)) = (\sum_{i \in D_x, i \geq a} v_{x=i})$$
$$\mathcal{L}'((x \leq a)) = (\sum_{i \in D_x, i \leq a} v_{x=i})$$

The mapping $\mathcal{L}'$ is an extension of the mapping $\mathcal{L}$ to the set of higher order terms. Note that, here again, the formulation does not introduce any new variables but reuses variables from the reformulation of the domain constraints.

4   Examples of Problem Solving Using Reformulation

A system has been implemented on the top of ILOG Planner/CPLEX [12] (for handling linear formulation) and ILOG Solver [18] (for domain reduction). It automatically reformulates a CP model into a MIP model. In this section, we detail the modeling of three classes of problems. For each of them we study the MIP formulation. To show the effectiveness of the method, some practical results are also given. In the following, all computation times are given in seconds on a Pentium II-300.

4.1   Facility Location Problem

This example illustrates the creation of a new global constraint. This is not for developing an efficient domain reduction algorithm, as is usually done in constraint programming, but to capture the structure of part of a model, whose sharp formulation must be delayed.

The facility location problem is to assign m clients to n depots that deliver to clients. A fixed cost f_j is associated with the use of depot j and a transportation cost c_{ij} if client i is delivered from depot j. A depot has a maximum number of clients w_j that it can serve. The problem is to decide which depots to open and which depot serves each client so as to minimize the fixed and transportation costs.

To model this problem, a binary variable y_j is introduced for each depot. It is equal to 1 if the depot j is open and to 0 otherwise. We also introduce for each client i, a variable x_i whose value corresponds to the depot that serves it. Thus

	Weak Model	Strong Model	
Problem	Time	Ch. Pts	Time
cap101	> 1000	0	3.9
cap102	> 1000	1	6.7
cap111	> 1000	2	11.0
cap112	> 1000	7	15.6
cap113	> 1000	14	21.8
cap114	> 1000	21	33.5
cap131	> 1000	0	21.3
cap132	> 1000	0	18.5
cap133	> 1000	0	20.7
cap134	> 1000	0	22.0

Fig. 1. Results on Facility Location Problems

we have the constraint $x_i \in \{1, \ldots, n\}$. The whole problem can be formulated in the following way:

$$\min \sum_{j=1}^{n} f_j y_j + \sum_{i=1}^{m} z_i$$

s.t.
$$\begin{cases} y_j \in \{0,1\} \text{ for } j \in \{1,\ldots,n\} & \text{(f1)} \\ x_i \in \{1,\ldots,n\} \text{ for } i \in \{1,\ldots,m\} & \text{(f2)} \\ \text{element}(x_i, [c_{i1},\ldots,c_{in}], z_i) \text{ for } i \in \{1,\ldots,m\} & \text{(f3)} \\ (x_1 = j) + \cdots + (x_m = j) \leq w_j y_j \text{ for } j \in \{1,\ldots,n\} & \text{(f4)} \end{cases}$$

The constraint element associates a cost z_i with a customer i, depending on the warehouse x_i that serves it. The last n higher-order constraints enforce that not more than w_j customers from $x_1,\ldots,x_m$ can be assigned to a depot j whose decision variable is y_j.

It is well known that this formulation can be strengthened by constraints $v_{x_i=j} \leq y_j$, whose logical meaning is to force y_j to be 1 if the jth depot serves customer i (see [22]). In fact, these constraints define the convex hull of the solution set of each constraint (f4). Since there are $n \times m$ strengthening constraints for a problem, it is efficient to delay their addition. To capture this structure, we introduce a new global constraint serve$(j, y, [x_1,\ldots,x_m], w)$ where j is a depot index, y is the binary variable associated with this depot, x_i are the variables associated with clients, and w is the depot capacity. This constraint is introduced in place of each constraint (f4). Its linear formulation is:

$$\mathcal{L}(\text{serve}(j, y, [x_1,\ldots,x_m], w)) = \left\{ \sum_{i=1}^{n} v_{x_i=j} \leq w \times y \right\}$$

$$\mathcal{D}(\text{serve}(j, y, [x_1,\ldots,x_m], w)) = \{ v_{x_i=j} \leq y \text{ for } i = 1,\ldots,m \}$$

To illustrate the effect of this new formulation, experiments were made on a list of problems from the OR Library[1]. The problems considered have from 25 to 50 facilities and 50 clients. Problems are solved using constraint programming and linear relaxations only. That is we use ILOG Solver to program the search over the linear optimizer ILOG Planner/CPLEX. The search strategy is based on the relaxed optimal solution. It chooses the expression $(x_i = j)$ whose relaxed solution is the closest to 0.5. This is to apply the first fail principle: these expressions are, a priori, the most difficult to instantiate. A binary choice point is created to explore either the subproblem when stating $x_i = j$ or the one when stating $x_i \neq j$. A solution is found when all variables have integer values.

The results are presented in figure 1. A comparison is made between solving the model with the constraints (f4) (Weak Model) and the one with the global constraint "serve" (Strong Model). The Strong model is solved in less than a minute for all instances considered, while no weak models were solved within the time limit of 1000 seconds.

4.2   Traveling Salesman Problem

The traveling salesman problem (TSP) is to visit a set of cities exactly once while minimizing the sum of the costs c_{ij} of going from a city i to a city j. The cost c_{ij} can be different from c_{ji}, in which case the problem is asymmetric. It can be modeled very concisely in constraint programming with the constraint cycle. For n cities to visit, n variables x_i are introduced, whose domain is included in $\{1, \ldots, n\}$ and that are assigned in a solution to the city to visit after i. A constraint programming formulation uses element constraints to associate a cost with each visit leaving a city and a cycle constraint for enforcing that visits must be done in one tour. The term to minimize is the sum of each visiting cost.

$$\min \sum_{i=1}^{n} z_i$$
$$\text{s.t.} \begin{cases} \text{element}(x_i, [c_{i1}, \ldots, c_{in}], z_i) \text{ for } i \in \{1, \ldots, n\} \\ \text{cycle}(1, [x_1, \ldots, x_n]). \\ x_i \in D_{x_i}, D_{x_i} \subset \{1, \ldots, n\} \text{ for } i \in \{1, \ldots, n\} \end{cases}$$

The linear constraints in the required part of the reformulation of this model define an assignment problem, which corresponds to the standard initial relaxation to solve this problem [22].

Two approaches to solve this model are compared. Some experimental results are given on small instances of symmetric and asymmetric traveling salesman problem (TSP) from the TSPLIB suite[2].

The first approach (Propag. + cost) uses the domain reduction techniques of ILOG Solver and, in addition, a constraint alldiff($[x_1, \ldots, x_n]$) that takes into account the objective function and performs pruning using an embedded assignment problem solver [7,6]. This approach outperforms previous pure constraint

---

[1] Problems are available at http://mscmga.ms.ic.ac.uk/jeb/orlib/capinfo.html
[2] Problems are available at http://softlib.rice.edu/softlib/tsplib/

	Asymmetric TSP				Symmetric TSP				
	Propag. + cost		Linear Relax.			Propag. + cost		Linear Relax.	
Problem	Fails	Time	Ch. Pts	Time	Problem	Fails	Time	Ch. Pts	Time
br17	-	-	9	0.3	gr17	646	0.7	0	0.3
ry48p	100000	248.0	40	12.2	gr21	31	0.1	0	0.2
ft53	6900	630.0	272	47.7	gr24	120	0.3	5	0.7
ft70	113	3.7	5	5.4	fri26	1600	2.9	1	0.7
ftv33	-	-	2136	195.2	bays29	8800	13.7	8	1.5
ftv35	-	-	5547	4137.2					
ftv38	-	-	36987	2697.3					
ftv44	-	-	841	116.1					
ftv47	-	-	27910	2730.6					
kro124p	121000	1321.2	46	58.2					

Fig. 2. Results on Traveling Salesman Problems

programming approaches and compares well with a dedicated approach. Several search strategies have been used and we give for each problem the time and number of fails obtained by the best approach. The results concern the proof time only, that is the time spent after having found an optimal solution because the method was not able to find rapidly optimal solutions. Entries are blank for problems that have not been tried.

The second approach (Linear Relax.) uses the formulation above. It solves the problem by using linear relaxations only. It uses ILOG Solver to program the search over the linear optimizer ILOG Planner/CPLEX. The search strategy used is the same as that used for the facility location problem. Here full computation times are given, that is the time for finding an optimal solution plus the time spent to prove optimality.

The results are presented in figure 2. The approach using linear relaxations often gives better results on larger problems. This is not very surprising, since the relaxation provided by the cutting planes added by the cycle constraint is tighter than that of the assignment problem. More important is to observe that the search strategy using the relaxed optimal solution allows us to find an optimal solution quickly. Appropriate choices are made for the variables, due to the tightness of the relaxation. It is interesting to note that the cutting planes are added locally to a node of the search tree and are removed when backtracking. This eliminates automatically irrelevant cuts, since those generated on one branch are mostly useless on other branches at the same level. Note also that many fewer choice points are needed to solve the problem. However, the time spent per node is larger since cutting plane generation is more time consuming than domain reduction.

Results obtained when using domain reduction in addition to linear relaxation are not presented here, because we uniformly obtained a slight reduction of search space together with a slight slowdown.

	Propagation		Linear Relax		Cooperation	
Problem	Ch. Pts	Time	Ch. Pts	Time	Ch. Pts	Time
7×7 (1)	9207	3720.1	51	15.1	49	17.2
7×7 (2)	11249	4261.2	37	13.3	32	12.1
8×8		> 5000	184	109.2	154	90.3
9×9 (1)		> 5000	652	780.6	295	580.5
9×9 (2)		> 5000	1183	2280.7	621	1780.1

Fig. 3. Results on Quadratic Programming Problem Instances

4.3   Quadratic Assignment Problem

The quadratic assignment problem (QAP) problem consists of locating n factories in n cities. There is a flow A_{ij} between factory i and factory j and there is a cost d_{lk} for each unit of flow transported from city l to city k. The problem is to determine where to locate the factories while minimizing the flow transportation cost, that is, $A_{ij} \times d_{loc(i)loc(j)}$ where $loc(i)$ is the location of factory i. This problem is strongly NP-Hard and instances having $n \geq 15$ are difficult to solve in practice.

A constraint programming formulation is possible by way of element constraints on matrices. For each city, a variable $x_i \in \{1, \ldots, n\}$ is introduced whose value is the factory number that is build in this city. These variables are constrained to take different values. Also, $n \times n$ variables y_{ij} are introduced. Each of them is assigned to the cost of transporting the flow from city i to city j. The constraint programming formulation is thus

$$\min \sum_{i,j=1,\ldots,n} d_{ij} \times y_{ij}$$

$$\text{s.t.} \begin{cases} x_i \in \{1, \ldots, n\} \text{ for } i \in \{1, \ldots, n\} \\ y_{ij} \in \{A_{uv} \mid u, v = 1, \ldots, n\} \text{ for } i, j \in \{1, \ldots, n\} \\ \text{alldifferent}(x_1, x_2, \ldots, x_n) \\ \text{element}(x_i, x_j, A, y_{ij}) \text{ for } i, j \in \{1, \ldots, n\} \end{cases}$$

where A is the matrix of flow between factories.

Interestingly, the reformulation of this problem gives the tight linear formulation introduced recently by Adams and Jonhson [1]. Several lower bounds introduced for solving QAP with a MIP solver can be considered as approximations of the lower bound given by this formulation. Unfortunately, the reformulation introduces a large number of binary variables and constraints, which create formulations having a large size for $n \geq 8$.

Nevertheless, we have solved problems having with up to 9 cities with this approach. The search strategy is the same as that used for previous examples. Note that only variables x need to be instantianted, since fixing these variables implies that variables y are also fixed. The results presented in figure 3 show the solving of the model with a pure CP approach (Propagation) using ILOG Solver, an approach using linear relaxation in constraint programming (Linear Relax.) and an approach using domain reduction together with linear relaxation (Cooperation).

We can observe that the pure domain reduction approach cannot solve problems having a size greater than 7. The approach using linear relaxations only finds optimal solutions rapidly thanks to the relaxed optimal solution. It is worth observing that the cooperative approach is faster than any of the others. This is mainly due to pertinent domain reduction done by global constraints that tighten the linear relaxation.

5   Conclusion

We have presented a linear formulation for commonly used global constraints like alldiff, atleast, among, element, cycle and meta constraints. Our linearization provides a set of required linear constraints and a set of delayed linear constraints added when violated. Specific formulations can also be defined to capture problem substructures having a strong linear formulation.

The first advantage is that the problem statement is more concise and expressive than in integer programming. Interestingly, formulations produced automatically are often standard and tight for the problem considered. Moreover, linear constraints and binary variables introduced can be fully ignored when designing search strategies. Practical results on combinatorial optimization problems show that this approach can be effective.

We believe that automatic reformulations will be a fundamental aspect of modeling systems since this allows the use of linear relaxations while avoiding the need to provide a linear formulation. Our current research is to experiment with more problems that can benefit from this approach, to identify useful substructures, and to provide a strong formulation for them.

References

1. W. Adams and T. Johnson. Improved linear programming based lower bounds for the quadratic assignment problem. In P. Pardalos and H. Wolkowicz, editors, *Quadratic Assignment and Related Problems*, number 16, pages 49–72. AMS, Providence, Rhode Island, 1994. 381
2. B. De Backer and H. Beringer. Cooperative solvers and global constraints: The case of linear arithmetic constraints. In *Proceedings of the Post Conference Workshop on Constraint, Databases and Logic Programming, ILPS'95*, 1995. 370, 372
3. E. Balas. Disjunctive programming and a hierarchy of relaxations for discrete optimization problems. *SIAM Journal Alg. Disc. Meth.*, 6(3):466–486, 1985. 370, 371
4. N. Beldiceanu and E. Contejean. Introducing global constraints in CHIP. *Mathl. Comput. Modelling*, 20(12), 1994. 369, 370, 373, 376
5. A. Bockmayr and T. Kasper. Branch and infer: A unifying framework for integer and finite domain constraint programming. *INFORMS Journal on Computing*, 10(3):287–300, 1998. 370

6. F. Focacci, A. Lodi, and M. Milano. Cost-based domain filtering. In *Proceedings of 5th International Conference CP 99*, Alexandria, Virginia, October 1999. Springer-Verlag. 379

7. F. Focacci, A. Lodi, M. Milano, and D. Vigo. Solving tsp through the integration of cp and or methods. In *Proceedings of the CP 98 Workshop on Large Scale Combinatorial Optimization and Constraints*, 1998. 379

8. J. N. Hooker and M. A. Osorio. Mixed logical / linear programming. *Discrete Applied Mathematics*, 1996. to appear. 370

9. J. N. Hooker, G. Ottosson, E. S. Thornsteinsson, and Hak-Jin Kim. A scheme for unifying optimization and constraint satisfaction methods. *Knowledge Engineering Review*, 2000. to appear. 374

10. R. Jeroslow. Logic based decision support: Mixed integer model formulation. *Annals of Discrete Mathematics*, (40), 1989. 370, 371

11. G. Mitra, C. Lucas, S. Moody, and E. Hadjiconstantinou. Tools for reformulating logical forms into zero-one mixed integer programs. *European Journal of Operational Research*, (72):262–276, 1994. 370, 377

12. ILOG Planner 3.3. *User Manual*. ILOG, S. A., Gentilly, France, December 1999. 377

13. P. Refalo. Tight cooperation and its application in piecewise linear optimization. In *Proceedings of 5th International Conference CP 99*, Alexandria, Virginia, October 1999. Springer-Verlag. 370, 372

14. J. C. Regin. A filtering algorithm for constraints of difference in csps. In *Proceedings of AAAI-94*, pages 362–367, Seattle, Washington, 1994. 370

15. R. Rodosek and M. Wallace. A generic model and hybrid algorithm for hoist scheduling problems. In *Proceedings of the 4th International Conference on Principles and Practice of Constraint Programming – CP'98*, pages 385 – 399, Pisa, Italy, 1998. Also in LNCS 1520. 370

16. R. Rodosek, M. Wallace, and M. T. Hajian. A new approach to integrate mixed integer programming with CLP. In *Proceedings of the CP'96 Workshop on Constraint Programming Applications*, Boston, MA, USA, 1996. 370, 377

17. M. Rueher and C. Solnon. Concurrent cooperating solvers over the reals. *Reliable Computing*, 3(3):325–333, 1997. 370, 372

18. ILOG Solver 4.4. *User Manual*. ILOG, S. A., Gentilly, France, June 1999. 369, 373, 377

19. P. van Hentenryck. *Constraint Satisfaction in Logic Programming*. MIT Press, Cambridge, Mass., 1989. 370, 374

20. P. van Hentenryck, H. Simonis, and M. Dincbas. Constraint satisfaction using constraint logic programming. *Artificial Intelligence*, 58(1–3):113–159, 1992. 370

21. H. P. Williams. *Model Building in Mathematical Programming*. Wiley, 1999. 370, 371, 372

22. L. A. Wolsey. *Integer Programming*. Wiley, 1998. 369, 373, 374, 376, 378, 379

A Global Constraint Combining a Sum Constraint and Difference Constraints

Jean-Charles Régin[1] and Michel Rueher[2]

[1] ILOG Les Taissounieres HB2
1681, route des Dolines Sophia Antipolis 06560 Valbonne
regin@ilog.fr
[2] Université de Nice–Sophia-Antipolis, I3S, ESSI
930, route des Colles - B.P. 145 06903 Sophia-Antipolis, France
rueher@essi.fr

Abstract. This paper introduces a new method to prune the domains of the variables in constrained optimization problems where the objective function is defined by a sum $y = \Sigma x_i$, and where variables x_i are subject to difference constraints of the form $x_j - x_i \leq c$. An important application area where such problems occur is deterministic scheduling with the *mean flow time* as optimality criteria. Classical approaches perform a *local* consistency filtering after each reduction of the bound of y. The drawback of these approaches comes from the fact that the constraints are handled independently. We introduce here a *global constraint* that enables to tackle simultaneously the whole constraint system, and thus, yields a more effective pruning of the domains of the x_i when the bounds of y are reduced. An *efficient algorithm*, derived from Dikjstra's shortest path algorithm, is introduced to achieve interval consistency on this global constraint.

1   Introduction

A great part of the success of *constraint programming* techniques in solving combinatorial problems is due to the capabilities of filtering algorithms to prune the search space. Roughly speaking, a filtering algorithm attempts to remove values from the domains of all variables occurring in a constraint whenever the domain of one of these variables is modified.

Arc consistency filtering algorithms on binary constraints are very popular but significant gains in performance have also been obtained during recent years with filtering algorithms associated with more complex constraints [Sim96]. These new filtering algorithms work on so–called "global constraints", e.g., cumulative constraint [BC94], edge-finder algorithm [CP94,Nui94], all–diff constraint [Rég94], cardinality constraint [HD91,Rég96]. They take into account the relations between the different occurrences of the same variable in a given set of constraints.

In this paper, we introduce a new global constraint that can achieve significant domain pruning in *constrained optimization problems* where the objective

R. Dechter (Ed.): CP 2000, LNCS 1894, pp. 384–395, 2000.

function is defined by a sum $y = \Sigma x_i$, and where the variables x_i are subject to difference constraints of the form $x_j - x_i \leq c$. Two important applications where such constraint systems occur are *minimizing mean flow time* and *minimizing tardiness* in deterministic scheduling problems. The following presentation of these applications is adapted from [BESW93].

The mean flow time is defined by $\overline{F} = \frac{1}{n} \sum_{j=1}^{n}(C_j - r_j)$ where C_j and r_j are respectively the completion time and the ready time of task T_j. Difference constraints are due to the precedence constraints and the distances between the tasks (and therefore between their completion times). The mean flow time criterion is important from the user's point of view since its minimization yields a minimization of the mean response time and the mean in-process time of the scheduled tasks set.

The mean tardiness is defined by $\overline{D} = \frac{1}{n} \sum_{j=1}^{n}(D_j)$ where $D_j = \max(C_j - d_j, 0)$, and where d_j is the due date of task T_j. Minimizing this criteria is useful when penalty functions are defined in accordance with due dates.

Both problems are NP-hard in most interesting cases [BESW93,DKD97].

Currently, in the constraint programming framework, such optimization problems are tackled by solving a sequence of decision problems: the solution of each decision problem must not only satisfy the initial constraint system but it must also provide a better bound than the best-known solution. In other words, each new decision problem must satisfy an additional constraint specifying that the value of y is better than the current bound. To take advantage of this additional constraint to cut the search space, and thus to avoid redoing almost always the same work for each decision problem, we introduce here a new global constraint.

In the remainder of this section we first detail the motivation of our approach before showing how it works on a short example.

1.1   Motivation

We consider the constrained optimization problem:

Minimize $f(x)$

subject to $p_i(x) \leq 0$ $(i = 1, \ldots, m)$

$q_i(x) = 0$ $(i = 1, \ldots, r)$

where f is a scalar function of a vector x of n components, $p_i(x)$ and $q_i(x)$ are functions which may be non-linear. We assume that an initial box D is given (i.e., the domains of x are bounded) and we seek the global minimum of $f(x)$ in D. For the sake of simplicity, we also assume in the rest of the paper that f is a sum of the form $y = \Sigma_{i=1}^{i=n} x_i$. Handling a sum of the form $y = \Sigma_{i=1}^{i=n} a_i x_i$ is straightforward as shown in Section 6.

Efficient filtering algorithms are available for sum constraints but in our case these algorithms are weakened by the fact that variables x_i involved in the objective function also occur in many other constraints. Among all these constraints, there is a subset of binary inequalities that only involve variables occurring in the objective function. Such inequalities may correspond to distance constraints as well as to constraints which have been introduced to break down symmetries of the problem to solve.

Note that the binary inequalities and the sum only model a sub–problem of a real application. Additional constraints are required to capture all the restrictions and features. So, what is needed is an *efficient filtering algorithm* for the conjunction of binary inequalities and the sum constraint.

Dechter et al [DMP91] have shown that shortest path algorithms can efficiently tackle such systems of inequalities in temporal constraint networks problems. The purpose of this paper is to introduce a new global constraint, named IS, which handles as a single global constraint the sum constraint and a system of binary inequalities. An efficient algorithm —using a shortest path algorithm on a graph of reduced costs— is introduced to achieve interval consistency (see definition 1) on this global constraint. Before going into the details, let us outline the advantages of this approach on a short example.

1.2   An Illustrative Example

Consider the constraint network $\mathcal{C} = \{C_1 : x_1 + x_2 = y, \quad C_2 : (x_1 \leq x_2 - 1)\}$ where $D(x_1) = [0, 6], D(x_2) = [1, 7]$ and $D(y) = [1, 13]$. Interval $[a, b]$ denotes the set of integer $S = \{k : a \leq k \wedge k \leq b\}$.

Constraint network $\mathcal{C}$ is arc consistent. Now, suppose that $\min(y)$ is set to 6. Arc consistency is unable to achieve any domain pruning. This is due to the fact that arc consistent filtering handles the constraints one by one. Now, let us examine what happens when constraints C_1 and C_2 are handled as a single constraint. To satisfy constraint C_2, the value of x_1 must be strictly less than the value of x_2, and thus, constraint C_1 cannot be satisfied when x_2 takes its values in $[1, 3]$. So, values $[1, 3]$ in $D(x_2)$ can be deleted. On this example, a global handling of C_1 and C_2 drastically reduces the search space.

1.3   A Brief Summary of Our Framework

The filtering process on C_1 and C_2 is exactly what will be performed on global constraint IS. More precisely, let:

- a sum constraint S_{um} defined by $y = \Sigma_{i=1}^{i=n} x_i$,
- a set of binary inequalities $\mathcal{I}_{neq} = \{x_i - x_j \leq c_{ji}, \quad (i, j \in [1, n])\}$,
- a set of domain constraints $\mathcal{D}_{om} = \{l_i \leq x_i \leq u_i, \quad (i \in [1, n])\}$.

The global constraint IS is defined by $\mathcal{I}_{neq} \cup \mathcal{D}_{om} \cup \{S_{um}\}$. Each time a bound of y is modified, the filtering on IS starts by performing the following operations:

1. Filtering $\{\mathcal{I}_{neq} \cup \mathcal{D}_{om}\}$ by interval consistency;
2. Filtering S_{um} by interval consistency;
3. Updating the bounds of every x_i with respect to constraint set $\mathcal{I}_{neq} \cup \mathcal{D}_{om} \cup \{S_{um}\}$.

Step 1 can be achieved with a shortest path algorithm on the graph associated with $\{\mathcal{I}_{neq} \cup \mathcal{D}_{om}\}$. (See Section 3.2.) Since the graph is likely to contain a negative cycle, this step can be achieved in $O(mn)$ running time.
It is also easy to show that step 2 can be performed with a simple algorithm that runs in $O(n)$ where n is the number of variables. (See Section 3.1.)
The contribution of this paper is an efficient *filtering algorithm* for step 3.

Outline of the paper: Section 2 introduces the notation and recalls the basics of CSP and of shortest paths that are needed in the rest of the paper. Section 3 successively shows how interval consistency can be achieved on a sum constraint and on binary inequalities. Section 4 defines interval consistency on the global constraint IS while Section 5 details the algorithm for finding a minimum value of x_i with respect to constraints $\mathcal{I}_{neq} \cup \mathcal{D}_{om} \cup \{S_{um}\}$.

2   Background

In order to make this paper self-contained, we now introduce the required background of CSP and of shortest paths.

2.1   Basics of CSP

A finite **constraint network** $P = (\mathcal{X}, \mathcal{D}, \mathcal{C})$ is defined by :

- a set of *variables* $\mathcal{X} = \{x_1, ..., x_n\}$;
- a set $\mathcal{D} = \{D(x_1), ..., D(x_n)\}$ of current *domains* where $D(x_i)$ is a finite set of possible values for variable x_i;
- a set $\mathcal{C}$ of constraints between the variables.

A total ordering $\prec$ can be defined on the domains without loss of generality. We will denote by $\min(x_i)$ and $\max(x_i)$ the minimal and the maximal value of $D(x_i)$ w.r.t. to $\prec$.
$|\mathcal{C}|$ denotes the number of constraints while $|X|$ denotes the number of variables. A **constraint** C on the ordered set of variables $X(C) = (x_1, ..., x_r)$ is a subset $T(C)$ of the Cartesian product $D(x_1) \times ... \times D(x_r)$ that specifies the *allowed* combinations of values for the variables $(x_1, ..., x_r)$. An element of $D(x_1) \times ... \times D(x_r)$ is called a *tuple* on $X(C)$ and is noted τ. $\tau[k]$ is the kth value of τ. $|X(C)|$ is the *arity* of C.
A value a for x is often denoted by (x, a) while $index(C, x)$ is the position of x in $X(C)$.
Let $P = (\mathcal{X}, \mathcal{D}, \mathcal{C})$ be a constraint network. The tuple $\tau = (v_1, ..., v_n)$ is a **solution** of P if the assignment $((x_1, v_1), ..., (x_n, v_n))$ satisfies all the constraints of $\mathcal{C}$. A value v is a **feasible value** for x if there exists a solution in which $x = v$. Let C be a constraint of $\mathcal{C}$. A tuple τ of $X(C)$ is *valid* if $\forall(x, a) \in \tau, a \in D(x)$. A value $a \in D(x)$ is *consistent with* C, either if $x \notin X(C)$, or if there exists a valid tuple $\tau \subset T(C)$ such that $a = \tau[index(C, x)]$. A constraint is **arc consistent** iff $\forall x_i \in X(C), D(x_i) \neq \emptyset$ and $\forall a \in D(x_i)$, a is consistent with C.

Filtering by arc consistency is often too costly for non-binary constraints and global constraints. **Interval consistency** [HSD98] can be achieved more efficiently. Interval consistency is derived from an approximation of arc consistency for continuous domains. It is based on an approximation of finite domains by finite sets of successive integers. More precisely, if D is a domain, interval consistency works on D^* defined by the set $\{\min(D), \ldots, \max(D)\}$ where $\min(D)$ and $\max(D)$ denote respectively the minimum and maximum values in D. A constraint C is interval–consistent [1] if for all x_i in $X(C)$, $\min(D(x_i)) \leq \max(D(x_i))$ and if both $\min(D(x_i))$ and $\max(D(x_i))$ are consistent with C.

2.2   Basics of Shortest Paths

We briefly recall here a few ideas about shortest paths that are needed in the rest of the paper. Most of the definitions are due to Tarjan [Tar83].

Let $G = (X, U)$ be a directed graph, where X is a set of nodes and U a set of arcs. Each arc (i, j) is associated with an integer called the cost of the arc and denoted c_{ij}. A *path* from node v_1 to node v_k in G is a list of nodes $[v_1, \ldots, v_k]$ such that (v_i, v_{i+1}) is an arc for $i \in [1..k-1]$. A path is *simple* if all its nodes are distinct. A path is a *cycle* if $k > 1$ and $v_1 = v_k$. The *length* of a path p, denoted by $length(p)$, is the sum of the costs of the arcs contained in p. A *shortest path* from a node s to a node t is a path from s to t whose length is minimum. A cycle of negative length is called a *negative cycle*. There is a shortest path from s to t iff no path from s to t contains a negative cycle. $d(u, v)$ denotes the shortest path distance from node u to node v in G while s denotes the source node.

G_{rc} is the graph derived from G by replacing, for each arc (u, v), c_{uv} with its reduced cost $rc_{uv} = c_{uv} + d(s, u) - d(s, v)$. The shortest path distance from node a to node b in G_{rc} is denoted by $d^0(a, b)$. The following properties [AMO93] hold in G_{rc}:

1. $\forall (u, v) \in G$: $rc_{uv} \geq 0$
2. $d(a, b) = d^0(a, b) - d(s, a) + d(s, b)$

3   Interval Consistency Filtering

This section successively shows how interval consistency can be achieved on a sum constraint and on binary inequalities.

---

[1] For specific constraint systems, interval consistency and arc consistency are equivalent. In particular, this is the case for constraints $\mathcal{I}_{neq} \cup \mathcal{D}_{om} \cup \mathcal{S}_{um}$ if the initial domains are finite sets of successive of integers (i.e., if $D_0^*(x_i) = D_0(x_i)$ for all variables). However, for more complex constraints this property does not hold. Consider for instance constraint $x^2 = 4$ and $D(x) = [-2, 2]$. This constraint is interval–consistent but not arc–consistent since $(x, 0)$ is not consistent with this constraint.

3.1 Sum Constraint

We will consider the following definition of a sum constraint:

Definition 1 *Let $X = \{x_1, ..., x_r\}$ be a set of variables. $S_{um} = SUM(X, y)$ is a sum constraint defined by the set of tuples $T(S_{um})$:*
$T(S_{um}) = \{ \tau$ such that τ is a tuple of $X \cup \{y\}$, and
$\qquad (\sum_{i=1}^{r} \tau[i]) - \tau[index(S_{um}, y)] = 0\}$

Proposition 1 *Let $X \cup \{y\}$ be a set of variables and let $S_{um} = SUM(X, y)$ be a sum constraint. S_{um} is interval–consistent if and only if the following four conditions hold:*

(1) $\min(y) \geq \sum_{x_i \in X} \min(x_i)$
(2) $\max(y) \leq \sum_{x_i \in X} \max(x_i)$
(3) $\forall x_i \in X : \min(x_i) \geq \min(y) - \sum_{x_j \in X - \{x_i\}} \max(x_j)$
(4) $\forall x_i \in X : \max(x_i) \leq \max(y) - \sum_{x_j \in X - \{x_i\}} \min(x_j)$

These conditions directly result from the definition of interval consistency. Interval consistency filtering of $SUM(X, y)$ can be achieved efficiently in an incremental way. The essential observation is that $\sum_{x_j \in X - \{x_i\}} \max(x_j)$ is equal to $\sum_{x_j \in X} \max(x_j) - \max(x_i)$. Since the sum over X can be computed only once, the above conditions can be checked in $O(n)$. Thus, the cost of updating the intervals after a modification of bounds of several variables is in $O(n)$. What is instructive with this complexity is the fact that it does not depend on the size of the domains of the variables.

3.2 Binary Inequalities

Arc consistency can be achieved on binary inequalities like $\mathcal{I}_{neq}$ by using specific filtering algorithms such as AC-5 [VDT92]. However, the complexity of such algorithms depends on the size of domains of the variables. Thus, they are rather ineffective for detecting inconsistencies. Interval consistency can be achieved in $O(mn)$ where n is the number of variables and $m = |\mathcal{I}_{neq}| + 2n$. This is due to a result of Dechter et al. [DMP91] on the "Simple Temporal Constraint Satisfaction Problem"(STCSP). Roughly speaking, interval consistency can be achieved by searching for shortest paths in a particular graph $G = (N, E)$, called the distance graph, where node set N represents the variables and arc set E stands for the inequality constraints.

More formally, let $P = (\mathcal{X}, \mathcal{D}^*, \mathcal{C})$ be a CSP such that $\mathcal{I}_{neq} \subset \mathcal{C}$ and where $\mathcal{D}^*$ denotes a set of continuous domains. The distance graph $G = (N, E)$ associated with P is defined in the following way:

– The node set N contains:
  • A special node s, named *source*, with a domain $D(s)$ that is reduced to a single value $\{0\}$.
  • One node for each variable x_i in $\mathcal{X}$.

- The arc set E contains:
    - An arc (x_j, x_i) with cost c_{ji} for each inequality $x_i \leq x_j + c_{ji}$.
    - An arc (x_i, s) with cost $-\min(x_i)$ for each variable x_i in $\mathcal{X}$.
    - An arc (s, x_i) with cost $\max(x_i)$ for each variable x_i in $\mathcal{X}$.

Arcs (x_i, s) and arcs (s, x_i) result from the definition of domain $D^*(x_i) = \{\min(x_i), ..., \max(x_i)\}$ by the inequalities: $0 \leq x_i - \min(x_i)$ (so $s \leq x_i - \min(x_i)$) and $x_i \leq \max(x_i)$ (so $x_i \leq s + \max(x_i)$).

This problem statement results from the following optimality condition of shortest paths: $d(s, x_j) \leq d(s, x_i) + c_{ij}$ for all $(x_i, x_j) \in N$. This inequality states that for every arc (x_i, x_j) in the network the length of the shortest path to node x_j is not greater than the length of the shortest path to node x_i plus the length of the arc (x_i, x_j). Dechter et al. have shown [DMP91] that :

a) **Theorem 1** *A STCSP is consistent iff its distance graph has no negative directed cycles.*

b) **Theorem 2** *Let G be the directed graph representation of a consistent STCSP $P = (\mathcal{X}, \mathcal{D}, \mathcal{C})$ where $\mathcal{C}$ is a set of binary inequalities. The set of feasible values for x_i is $[-d(x_i, s), +d(s, x_i)]$, where $d(x_i, x_j)$ denotes the shortest path from node x_i to node x_j.*

Theorem 1 states that the problem has no solution if G contains a negative cycle. Indeed, a negative cycle indicates that some of the inequalities are contradictory. The following property results from Theorem 2:

Proposition 2 *Let $P = (\mathcal{X}, \mathcal{D}, \mathcal{C})$ be a STCSP and let $G = (N, E)$ be the distance graph associated with $P^* = (\mathcal{X}, \mathcal{D}^*, \mathcal{C})$.*
$\forall x_i \in \mathcal{X} : (D^*(x_i) = \{-d(x_i, s), ..., +d(s, x_i)\}) \Rightarrow P$ *is interval–consistent*

Proof:
Assume that $D^*(x_i) = \{-d(x_i, s), ..., +d(s, x_i)\}$ and that G contains no negative cycles. From Theorem 2 it results that $-d(x_i, s)$ and $d(s, x_i)$ are feasible values. Thus, P is interval–consistent. ⊙

According to Theorem 2, interval consistency can be achieved by computing the shortest paths between s and the x_i, when G does not contain any negative cycle. Computing shortest paths when the problem graph is likely to contain a negative cycle can be achieved in $O(mn)$ running time [Tar83]. When the graph contains no negative arcs, Dijkstra's algorithm computes shortest paths in $O(m+n \log n)$. Of course, Dijkstra's algorithm can always be used on the graph of reduced costs. A nice property of the distance graph $G = (N, E)$ associated with $P^* = (\mathcal{X}, \mathcal{D}^*, \mathcal{C})$ is that the reduced costs can be derived from the minimal and maximal values of the domains.

Proposition 3 *Let $P = (\mathcal{X}, \mathcal{D}, \mathcal{C})$ be a CSP and let $G = (N, E)$ be the distance graph associated with $P^* = (\mathcal{X}, \mathcal{D}^*, \mathcal{C})$.*
$\forall x_i, x_j \in \mathcal{X} :$ $rc_{ij} = c_{ij} + \max(x_i) - \max(x_j)$
$\forall x_i, x_j \in \mathcal{X} :$ $d(x_i, x_j) = d^0(x_i, x_j) - \max(x_i) + \max(x_j)$

These properties trivially result from the definition of the reduced costs.

4   Global IS Constraint

Now, let us show how interval consistency of the global constraint IS can be achieved. A global constraint IS represents the conjunction of a sum constraint and a set of binary inequalities defined on variables involved in the sum constraint. More formally, we have:

Definition 2 *Let* $SUM(X, y)$ *be a sum constraint, and* $\mathcal{I}_{neq}$ *be a set of binary inequalities defined on* $X = (x_1, \ldots, x_r)$. *Global constraint* IS$(X, y, \mathcal{I}_{neq})$ *is defined by the set of tuples* $T(IS)$:
$T(IS) = \{ \tau \text{ such that } \tau \text{ is a tuple of } X(IS), \text{ and}$
$\qquad (\sum_{i=1}^{r} \tau[i]) - \tau[index(IS, y)] = 0, \text{ and}$
$\qquad \text{the values of } \tau \text{ satisfy } \mathcal{I}_{neq} \}$

Interval consistency for IS can be defined by extending inequalities of Proposition 1 in order to take into account the binary inequalities between the variables involved in the sum constraint.

Let us highlight this point by considering again the initial example. Now, the constraint network is expressed with one global constraint IS:
IS$(\{x_1, x_2\}, y, \{(x_1 \leq x_2 - 1)\})$ where $D(x_1) = [0, 6]$, $D(x_2) = [1, 7]$ and $D(y) = [1, 13]$. Suppose that min(y) is set to 6. Let us recall inequality (3) of Proposition 1: $\forall x_i \in X : \min(x_i) \geq \min(y) - \sum_{x_j \in X - \{x_i\}} \max(x_j)$. For x_2, this inequality states that $\min(x_2) \geq 6 - \max(x_1)$. Since $\max(x_1) = 6$ this inequality holds when $\min(x_2)$ is equal to 1 although the constraint $(x_1 \leq x_2 - 1)$ is violated for $x_2 = 1$ and $x_1 = 6$. Thus, inequality (3) must be modified in order to take into account the constraint $(x_1 \leq x_2 - 1)$. More precisely, $\max(x_1)$ must be compatible with the smallest value of $D^*(x_2)$ which is consistent with the constraint $(x_1 \leq x_2 - 1)$.

Let $\min_{(x_i \leftarrow a)}(x_j)$ and $\max_{(x_i \leftarrow a)}(x_j)$ respectively be the minimum and the maximum values of $D^*(x_j)$ which satisfy the binary inequalities $\mathcal{I}_{neq}$ when x_i is instantiated to a. Using this notation, inequality (3) can be rewritten in the following form:
$$\forall a \in D^*(x_i) : a \geq \min(y) - \sum_{j \neq i} \max_{(x_i \leftarrow a)}(x_j)$$
This new inequality does not hold for $x_2 = 1$ and $x_1 = 6$. The smallest value of $D^*(x_2)$ that satisfies this inequality is 4.

So, interval-consistency of IS can be defined in the following way :

Proposition 4 *Let* $X \cup \{y\}$ *be a set variables and let* IS$(X, y, \mathcal{I}_{neq})$ *be a global sum constraint.* IS *is interval-consistent iff the following conditions hold:*

(1b) $\min(y) \geq \sum_{x_i \in X} \min(x_i)$
(2b) $\max(y) \leq \sum_{x_i \in X} \max(x_i)$

$$(3b) \ \forall x_i \in X : \min(x_i) \geq \min(y) - \sum_{x_j \in X - \{x_i\}} \max_{(x_i \leftarrow \min(x_i))}(x_j)$$

$$(4b) \ \forall x_i \in X : \max(x_i) \leq \max(y) - \sum_{x_j \in X - \{x_i\}} \min_{(x_i \leftarrow \max(x_i))} (x_j)$$

Proof:
From inequalities (1b) and (2b) it results that constraint $SUM(X, y)$ holds
when y is set to $\min(y)$ and when y is set to $\max(y)$. Since y occurs only in
$SUM(X, y)$, it follows that IS is interval-consistent for y. Inequality (3b) ensures that both constraint $SUM(X, y)$ and the inequalities of $\mathcal{I}_{neq}$ hold when x_i
is set to $\min(x_i)$. This reasoning remains valid for inequality (4b).
Conversely, it is trivial to show that inequalities (1b), (2b), (3b), and (4b) hold
if IS is interval-consistent. ⊙

The general interval consistency filtering algorithm of constraint IS is given
in Figure 1. This algorithm is started whenever bounds of variables in $\mathcal{X} \cup \{y\}$
are modified. Note that steps 1 and 2 are systematically performed when interval
consistency on IS is achieved for the first time.
In the rest of this paper, we will only detail the search process of the minimum
value of a variable (step 3 in Algorithm 1) since the same kind of reasoning holds
for searching maximum values (step 4 in Algorithm 1).

Algorithm 1 Filtering IS by interval consistency

---

1. If a bounds of y have been modified, then interval consistency will be
   achieved on $SUM(X, y)$ with an algorithm derived from Proposition 1.
2. If a bound of some variable of X is modified, then interval consistency will
   be achieved on the conjunction of binary inequalities $\mathcal{I}_{neq} \cup \mathcal{D}_{om}$ with a
   shortest path algorithm.
3. For every variable $x \in X$, the minimum value of x satisfying inequality
   (3b) will be computed;
4. For every variable $x \in X$, the maximum value of x satisfying inequality
   (4b) will be computed.

---

5 Computing a New Minimum

The goal is to find the smallest value $\underline{x_i} \in [\min(x_i), \max(x_i)]$ such that inequality
(3b) of Proposition 4 holds. It follows from inequality (3b) that

$$\underline{x_i} = \min(y) - \sum_{x_j \in X - \{x_i\}} \max_{(x_i \leftarrow \underline{x_i})} (x_j) \tag{1}$$

The essential observation is that the value of $max(x_j)$ depends only on the
upper–bounds of the variables x_k that belong to a shortest path from s to x_j.

So, if the fact of assigning a to x_i—i.e., reducing the upper–bound of x_i to a—introduces x_i in a shortest path from s to x_j, then the length of this shortest path (i.e., $d(s, x_j)$) is the greatest value that is consistent with $\underline{x_i}$ for the computation of the sum y. So,

$$\max_{(x_i \leftarrow \underline{x_i})} (x_j) = \min(d(s, x_j), \underline{x_i} + d(x_i, x_j)) \tag{2}$$

We are now in a position to prove the following nice property:

$$\max_{(x_i \leftarrow \underline{x_i})} (x_j) = \underline{x_i} + d(x_i, x_j) \tag{3}$$

Proof:
First note that $d(x_i, x_j)$ is always finite since there exists at least one path from x_i to x_j which goes through s. So we can distinguish two cases :

1. x_i will belong to a shortest path from s to x_j when x_i is set to the value of $\underline{x_i}$ we are searching for. Then, $\max_{(x_i \leftarrow \underline{x_i})}(x_j) = \underline{x_i} + d(x_i, x_j)$;
2. x_i will never belong to the shortest path from s to x_j, even when x_i is set to $\underline{x_i}$. That is to say, $\max(x_j)$ does not depend on x_i. So $\underline{x_i} = \min(x_i) = -d(x_i, s)$.
   Since $\underline{x_i} + d(x_i, s) = 0$ we can rewrite $\max_{(x_i \leftarrow \underline{x_i})}(x_j)$ in the following way : $\max_{(x_i \leftarrow \underline{x_i})}(x_j) = d(s, x_j) = \underline{x_i} + d(x_i, s) + d(s, x_j)$. It remains to show that $d(x_i, s) + d(s, x_j) = d(x_i, x_j)$, i.e., that s belongs to a shortest path from x_i to x_j.
   Since x_i does not belong to a shortest path from s to x_j, we have $d(s, x_j) < d(s, x_i) + d(x_i, x_j)$. Suppose now that there is no shortest from x_i to x_j which contains s. Then $d(x_i, x_j) < d(x_i, s) + d(s, x_j)$ and thus, $d(s, x_j) < d(s, x_i) + d(x_i, s) + d(s, x_j)$. However, when x_i is set to $\underline{x_i}$, $d(s, x_i) = -d(x_i, s)$ yielding the following inconsistency $d(s, x_j) < d(s, x_j)$.

⊙

Substituting equivalence 3 in Equation 1, yields the following linear equation that gives the value of $\underline{x_i}$, i.e., the new lower bound of x_i:

$$|X| * \underline{x_i} = \min(y) - \sum_{x_j \in X - \{x_i\}} d(x_i, x_j) \tag{4}$$

The point is that the greatest value of x_j which is consistent with $\underline{x_i}$ can be determined by computing $d(x_i, x_j)$ on the graph of reduced costs. No propagation step is required: when $\min(x_i)$ is increased it is useless to reconsider $\min(x_j)$ if x_j has been updated before x_i during step 3 of the interval consistency filtering algorithm. (See Figure 1.) This results from Theorem 2 which states that $-d(x_i, s)$ is the lower bound of $D^*(x_i)$.

The shortest distance between x_i to all x_j can be computed with Dijkstra's shortest path algorithm on the graph of reduced costs in $O(m + n \log n)$. Then, the computation of $\underline{x_i}$ can be achieved in $O(n)$ time. So, the total complexity of the algorithm is $O(m + n \log n) * n$.

In many cases, it is useless to compute all $d(x_i, x_j)$ for checking property (3b). Indeed, the process can be speeded up by checking whether $\min(x_i)$ is greater than the difference

$$\Delta = \frac{\min(y) - \sum_{x_j \in X - \{x_i\}} d(x_i, x_j)}{|X|} \tag{5}$$

"while" computing the $d(x_i, x_j)$. To achieve such a check the essential point is the approximation of the $d(x_i, x_j)$ by their lower–bound. Since $d(s, x_j) \leq d(s, x_i) + d(x_i, x_j)$ we have $d(s, x_j) - d(s, x_i) \leq d(x_i, x_j)$ and thus $\max(x_j) - \max(x_i) \leq d(x_i, x_j)$. So, an upper-bound of Δ can be computed by replacing $d(x_i, x_j)$ with $\max(x_j) - \max(x_i)$ in Equation 5. Then, each time a node is scanned in Dijkstra's shortest path algorithm, we have just to subtract

$$\frac{1}{|X|} \left(d(x_i, x_j) - (\max(x_j) - \max(x_i)) \right)$$

from this upper bound. The shortest path algorithm can thus be stopped as soon as inequality (3b) of Proposition 4 holds.

6   Discussion

It is also instructive to remark that our algorithm still works when the function to be optimized is of the form $y = \Sigma_{i=1}^{i=n} \alpha_i x_i$ where the α_i are a non-negative real number. To capture the exact contribution of each x_i in the sum when the α_i are different from the value 1, we need only introduce the coefficient of x_i in Equation 1:

$$\underline{x_i} = \frac{1}{\alpha_i} \left(\min(y) - \sum_{x_j \in X - \{x_i\}} \alpha_j \max_{(x_i \leftarrow \underline{x_i})} (x_j) \right) \tag{6}$$

In Section 1, we defined $\mathcal{I}_{neq}$ as the subset of binary inequalities that involve only variables occurring in the objective function $f(x)$. However, $\mathcal{I}_{neq}$ could be extended to the subset of binary inequalities that involve either variables occurring in $f(x)$ or variables connected to variables occurring in $f(x)$. For instance, assume that x_1 and x_2 occur in the objective and let $\{x_1 \leq y_1 + c; y_1 \leq y_2 + c'; z_1 \leq z_2 + c''\}$ be the set of binary inequalities. Then, this extended set of inequalities would contain $\{x_1 \leq y_1 + c; y_1 \leq y_2 + c'\}$.

Let S_x be the set of variables occurring in $f(x)$. To capture this extension, we need only to replace X by S_x in $\sum_{x_j \in X - \{x_i\}}$ of Equations 1 and 3. Considering this extended set of inequalities may entail a better pruning of the domains.

7   Conclusion

This paper has introduced a new global constraint which handles as a single constraint a sum constraint and a system of binary linear inequalities. An efficient algorithm has been proposed to achieve an interval–consistent filtering of this new global constraint. The cost of this algorithm is not higher than the cost of a filtering algorithm which handles only the inequalities. A direct application of this constraint concerns optimization problems where it introduces a kind of "back" propagation process.

References

AMO93.   Ravindra K. Ahuja, Thomas L. Magnanti, and James B. Orlin. *Network Flows*. Prentice Hall, 1993. 388

BC94.   N. Beldiceanu and E. Contejean. Introducing global constraints in chip. *Journal of Mathematical and Computer Modelling*, 20(12):97–123, 1994. 384

BESW93.   J. Blazewicz, K. Ecker, G. Schmidt, and J. Weglarz. *Scheduling in Computer and Manufacturing Systems*. Springer Verlag, 1993. 385

CP94.   J. Carlier and E. Pinson. A practical use of jackson's preemptive schedule for solving the job-shop problem. *Annals of Operations Research*, 26(12):269–287, 1994. 384

DKD97.   Moshe Dror, Wieslaw Kubiak, and Paolo Dell'Olmo. Scheduling chains to minimize mean flow time. *Information Processing Letters*, 61(6):297–301, 28 March 1997. 385

DMP91.   R. Dechter, I. Meiri, and J. Pearl. Temporal constraint networks. *Artificial Intelligence*, 49(1-3):61–95, January 1991. 386, 389, 390

HD91.   Pascal Van Hentenryck and Yves Deville. The cardinality operator: A new logical connective for constraint logic programming. In *Proc. of ICLP'91*, pages 745–759, 1991. 384

HSD98.   Pascal Van Hentenryck, Vijay Saraswat, and Yves Deville. Design, implementation, and evaluation of the constraint language cc(FD). *Journal of Logic Programming*, 37(1-3):139–164, October 1998. 388

Nui94.   W. P. Nuijten. *Time and Resource Constrained Scheduling: A Constraint Satisfaction Approach*. PhD thesis, Eindhoven University of Technology, 1994. 384

Rég94.   J-C. Régin. A filtering algorithm for constraints of difference in CSPs. In *Proc. of AAAI94*, pages 362–367, Seattle, Washington, 1994. 384

Rég96.   J-C. Régin. Generalized arc consistency for global cardinality constraint. In *Proc. of AAAI-96*, pages 209–215, Portland, Oregon, 1996. 384

Sim96.   H. Simonis. Problem classification scheme for finite domain constraint solving. In *CP96, Workshop on Constraint Programming Applications: An Inventory and Taxonomy*, pages 1–26, Cambridge, MA, USA, 1996. 384

Tar83.   Robert E. Tarjan. *Data Structures and Network Algorithms*. CBMS 44 SIAM, 1983. 388, 390

VDT92.   P. Van Hentenryck, Yves Deville, and Choh-Man Teng. A generic arc-consistency algorithm and its specializations. *Artificial Intelligence*, 57(2-3):291–321, October 1992. 389

Efficient Querying of Periodic Spatiotemporal Objects*

Peter Revesz and Mengchu Cai

University of Nebraska-Lincoln
Lincoln, NE 68588, USA
{revesz,mcai}@cse.unl.edu

Abstract. In this paper we propose a new data model called periodic spatiotemporal objects (PSOs) databases. We show that relational algebra can be extended to PSO databases and any fixed relational algebra queries can be evaluated in PTIME in the size of any input database. We also describe a database system implementation of the PSO model and several sample queries.

1   Introduction

Many spatiotemporal objects change position or shape continuously and periodically. For example, suppose that a person A is swimming in a wavy sea. Figure 1 shows the positions of A at four different time instances.

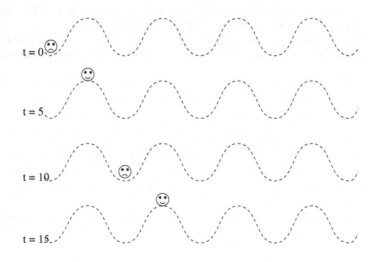

Fig. 1. Periodic Movements

* This work was supported in part by NSF grants IRI-9625055 and IRI-9632871 and by a Gallup Research Professorship.

R. Dechter (Ed.): CP 2000, LNCS 1894, pp. 396–410, 2000.

None of the existing spatiotemporal database models can represent continuous acyclic periodic movements like that in Figure 1. Worboys' spatiotemporal data model [32] can represent neither continuous movement nor periodicity. Linear and polynomial constraint databases [20,25] and the spatiotemporal data types of [14] can represent continuous change but not periodicity. Parametric rectangles [8] can represent continuous change and some limited periodicity but cannot represent acyclic periodic movements like that in Figure 1.

Much work in temporal databases aims to represent periodic time points, for example the fact that a class meets every Monday at 10:00 am. Proposals include periodicity constraints over the integers [4,30], linear repeating points [1,19], and an extension of Datalog with the successor function [10,11]. These data models, however, are not able to represent spatial dimensions or continuous movements of objects.

In this paper, we propose a new data model, called *periodic spatiotemporal objects* (PSOs), which is the first model that can represent the swimmer's movement in Figure 1.

In addition to a good representation, an easy and efficient way of querying the database is also important. For example, suppose that swimmer A tries to find another person B. Suppose also that they can see each other only when they are both on the top of the waves and are within 20 meters of each other. A possible query of the database is:

Q1: "Can A find B in 30 minutes?"

Suppose now that a ship moves toward some direction in that region and A and B can be discovered if they get within 100 meters of the ship. A natural query is:

Q2: "Can they be rescued by the ship?"

Another example from the area of physics is the following. Suppose that two photons travel in a reflecting path through an optical fiber cable as shown in Figure 2. A possible query is:

Q3: "Will the two photons collide and thereby cancel each other?"

As we show in this paper, all of the above sample queries can be expressed in an extension of relational algebra, which is a common query language within current database systems. Relational algebra contains the following basic operators: selection, projection, rename, intersection, union, difference and join. We generalize these operators for databases that contain a set of PSOs.

As is well-known in databases, each fixed query of standard relational algebra can be evaluated in polynomial time (PTIME) in the size of any variable relational database[1] This is an important result because in practice the size of the database is typically huge compared with the query size.

---

[1] Actually, it can be evaluated in LOGSPACE, which is included in PTIME.

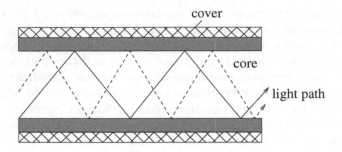

cover

core

light path

Fig. 2. Photons Travel through Optical Fiber

In this paper, we show that our extended relational algebra queries can also be evaluated in PTIME in the size of input databases with periodic spatiotemporal objects.

The paper is organized as follows. Section 2 describes the periodic spatiotemporal object data model and illustrates how to represent spatiotemporal objects in this model. It also defines the query language by generalizing relational algebra. Section 3 proves that the evaluation of queries is in PTIME in the size of the database. Section 4 presents implementation results. Section 5 covers related work. Finally, Section 6 lists some open problems.

2   Periodic Spatiotemporal Objects

By cyclic periodic movement, we mean that an object repeats its movement from the same position and with the same velocity every period as shown in Figure 3(a). Cyclic movement can be approximated by a function of time in the form of $a(t \ mod \ p) + b$, where a is speed of the object in each period, p is the period and b is the start position. Acyclic periodic movement is the composition of cyclic periodic movement and linear movement as shown in Figure 3(b), which can be represented by $g(t) + h(t)$, where $g(t)$ is a cyclic movement function and $h(t)$ is a linear function. Acyclic periodic movement is more general than cyclic periodic movement.

A periodic spatiotemporal object (PSO) is a periodically moving and growing or shrinking rectangle. The extent of a PSO in each dimension is represented by an interval whose lower and upper bounds are periodic functions of time. Figure 4 shows that the position and extent of a PSO in x_i dimension change over time. In $(x_i, \ t)$ space, the positions of the lower bound $X_i^{[}$ at the start times (or end times) of different periods are located on a line, which is called the lower bound start (or end) line. The belt between the lower bound start and end lines is called the lower bound belt. Similarly the positions of the upper bound $X_i^{]}$ at the start (or end) times of different periods are located on the upper bound start (or end) line, and the belt between them is called the upper bound belt.

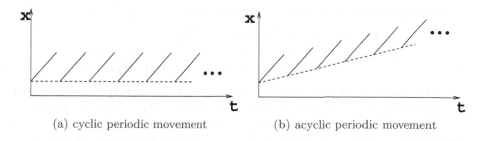

(a) cyclic periodic movement   (b) acyclic periodic movement

Fig. 3. Cyclic and Acyclic Periodic Movements

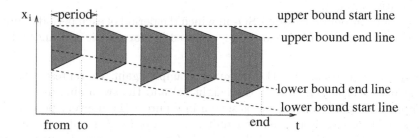

Fig. 4. The Projection of a PSO onto (x_i, t) Space

Formally, let $\mathbf{R}$ denote the set of real numbers, $\mathbf{R}^+$ the set of non-negative real numbers and $\mathbf{Z}$ the set of integers, $\mathbf{N}$ the set of non-negative integers and $\mathbf{N}^+$ the set of positive integers.

Definition 1. A periodic spatiotemporal object o is a tuple of the form

$$\langle X_1, \ldots, X_d, \ T, \ end \rangle$$

where for each $i = 1, \ldots, d$, the attribute X_i is a closed, open or half-open interval in the x_i dimension such that the lower and the upper bounds of X_i, denoted $X_i^{[}$ and $X_i^{]}$, are periodic functions ($\mathbf{R}^+ \rightarrow \mathbf{R}$) of time t, T is the union of a set of time intervals whose lower and upper bounds are constant rational numbers. The parameter end which represents the end time of the whole object is some constant or infinity.

The semantics of o, denoted by $sem(o)$ is a possibly infinite set of points defined in the following:

$$sem(o) = \{ \ (a_1, \ldots, a_d, t) \mid \forall \, i, \ 1 \leq i \leq d, \ a_i \in X_i(t), \ t \in T, \ t \leq end \}$$

where $X_i(t)$ is the interval obtained by substituting the value of t into the lower and the upper bound functions.

In this paper, we are looking at periodic functions of the form:

$$a((t - from) \bmod p) + b + c\lfloor \tfrac{t-from}{p} \rfloor$$

$$t \in T, \quad T = \begin{cases} [from, \, to] & \text{if } p = \infty \\ \bigcup_{k \in \mathbf{N}}\{[from + kp, \, to + kp]\} & \text{otherwise} \end{cases}$$

where mod is the modulus operator, p is the period p, $from$ and to are the start and the end times of the first period such that $0 \le (to - from) \le p$, a is the speed of the lower (or upper) bound in each period, b is the start position of the bound at time $t = from$, and c is the change of the start positions of two adjacent periods, we also call $s = \tfrac{c}{p}$ the slope of the lower (or upper) bound start line as shown in Figure 4. a, b, c, $from$ and to are constant rational numbers, p is a positive integer.

We call non-periodic those PSOs in which the period of each periodic function is $+\infty$. Non-periodic PSOs can be represented by parametric rectangles defined in [8].

Example 1. Let us consider the swimmer example again. We represent the head of the person A as one unit in the height (z) and the swimming direction (x). We approximate A's movement as shown in Figure 5 (1): in every period A first moves right in x with a speed of 1 unit per minute for 2 minutes, then A goes towards the top of the wave with a speed of 3 units per minute up in z and 1 unit per minute right in x, three minutes later A gets to the top, then A moves right in x with a speed of 1 unit per minute for 2 minutes, finally he falls down to the bottom with a speed of 3 units per minute down and 1 unit per minute right. The movement of A can be decomposed into four periodic pieces as shown in Figure 5 (2-5). Each piece can be represented as a PSO as shown in Table 1.

Table 1. Represent Swimmer A by PSOs

X	Z		T	end
$[f_1(t), \, f_1(t) + 1]$	$[0, \, 1]$		$[0, \, 2]_{10}$	∞
$[f_2(t), \, f_2(t) + 1]$	$[2(t - 2) \bmod 10, \, 2(t - 2) \bmod 10 + 1]$		$[2, \, 6]_{10}$	∞
$[f_3(t), \, f_3(t) + 1]$	$[9, \, 10]$		$[6, \, 8]_{10}$	∞
$[f_4(t), \, f_4(t) + 1]$	$[4((t - 8) \bmod 10), \, 4((t - 8) \bmod 10) + 1]$		$[8, \, 10]_{10}$	∞

$$\text{where } f_1(t) = (t \bmod 10) + 10\lfloor \tfrac{t}{10} \rfloor,$$
$$f_2(t) = \tfrac{1}{2}((t - 2) \bmod 10) + 2 + 10\lfloor \tfrac{t-2}{10} \rfloor,$$
$$f_3(t) = ((t - 6) \bmod 10) + 10\lfloor \tfrac{t-6}{10} \rfloor,$$
$$f_4(t) = 2((t - 8) \bmod 10) + 10\lfloor \tfrac{t-8}{10} \rfloor$$
$$[t1, \, t2]_{10} = \{[t1, \, t2], \, [t1 + 10, \, t2 + 10], \ldots\}.$$

Each PSO can be attached with any number of attributes to express other characteristics of the objects, which is called a PSO tuple. A *PSO relation* R is a finite set of PSO tuples. The semantics of R is the union of the semantics of each tuple in R. A *PSO database* is a finite set of PSO relations.

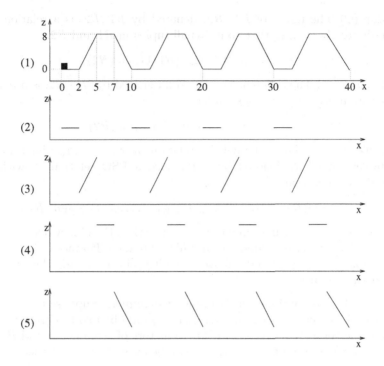

Fig. 5. Approximate the Swimmer's Movement as Four PSOs

Definition 2. Let $R1$ and $R2$ be two PSO relations over d dimensions $x_1, \ldots, x_d$ and k attributes $A_1, \ldots, A_k$.

- *projection* $(\hat{\pi}_Y)$ Let $Y \subseteq \{x_1, \ldots, x_d, A_1, \ldots, A_k\}$. The projection of $R1$ on Y, denoted by $\hat{\pi}_Y(R1)$, is a relation R over the attributes Y such that

$$R = \{r : \exists r_1 \in R1, \ \forall A \in Y, \text{ the values of } A \text{ in } r \text{ and } r_1 \text{ are equal}\}$$

- *selection* $(\hat{\sigma})$ Let E be the conjunction of a set of atomic comparison predicates in the form $A \theta c$ or $A \theta B$, where c is a constant, $A, B \in \{x_1, \ldots, x_d, A_1, \ldots, A_k\}$, $\theta \in \{=, \leq, \geq, >, <\}$ and each atomic comparison predicate contains at most one spatial dimension. The selection $\hat{\sigma}_E(R1)$ is a relation R containing the PSO tuples in $R1$ whose attribute values satisfy E.
- *rename* $(\hat{\rho})$ The rename operator, denoted by $\hat{\rho}_{R1'}(R1)$, changes the relation name and attribute names of $R1$ to that of $R1'$ with the same set of tuple as $R1$ has.
- *intersection* $(\hat{\cap})$ The intersection of $R1$, $R2$, denoted by $R1 \hat{\cap} R2$, is a relation R over attributes $A_1, \ldots, A_k$ such that

$$sem(R) = sem(R1) \cap sem(R2)$$

- *union* ($\hat{\cup}$) The union of $R1$, $R2$, denoted by $R1\hat{\cup}R2$, is a relation R over attributes $A_1, \ldots, A_k$ that contains all tuples in $R1$ and $R2$.

$$sem(R) = sem(R1) \cup sem(R2)$$

- *difference* ($\hat{-}$) The difference of $R1$, $R2$, denoted by $R1\hat{-}R2$, is a relation R over attributes $A_1, \ldots, A_k$ such that

$$sem(R) = sem(R1) \setminus sem(R2)$$

- *complement* ($\hat{\neg}$) Let R be a PSO relation over $x_1, \ldots, x_d$ dimensions. The complement of R, denoted by $\hat{\neg}R$ is also a PSO relation R' with the $\square$ attribute, such that

$$sem(R') = \{(a_1, \ldots, a_d, t) \mid (,_1, \ldots, a_d, \ t) \notin sem(R)\}$$

The unary operators have higher precedence than the binary operators. Intersection ($\hat{\cap}$) has higher precedence than union ($\hat{\cup}$) and difference ($\hat{-}$). A *relational algebra expression* over PSO databases is built up in the standard way, using the operators in Definition 2.

Example 2. Let us continue the example of swimmers. Suppose that the height of the wave is 8 meters. Let *RegionA* and *RegionB* be two PSO relations which represent the the moving region within 10 meters of swimmer A and B, respectively. Then the query **Q1** in Section 1 can be expressed as follows:

$$\hat{\sigma}_{z=8,\ t\leq 30} \ (RegionA \ \hat{\cap} \ RegionB)$$

Suppose also that the PSO relation *Ship* represents the region within 90 meters of the ship, then query **Q2** in Section 1 can be expressed as follows:

$$Ship \ \hat{\cap} \ (RegionA \ \hat{\cup} \ RegionB)$$

Example 3. Suppose that photons traveling in an optical fiber are represented by a PSO relation *Photons*. We first select from *Photons* the photons with $id = 1$ and $id = 2$, then we check whether their intersection is empty. This query can be expressed by the extended relation algebra as follows:

$$\hat{\pi}_{x,y,t}(\hat{\sigma}_{id=1}Photons) \ \hat{\cap} \ \hat{\pi}_{x,y,t}(\hat{\sigma}_{id=2}Photons)$$

3   Complexity of Relational Algebra Queries

Similarly to [30], we restrict the periods of the PSOs in a finite set K of natural numbers such that for any $k1, k2 \in K$, the least common multiple of $k1$ and $k2$, denoted by $lcm(K')$, is also in K. We also restrict the slopes of both the bound start lines and the bounds of the intervals in each period as follows: the difference any two different slopes is at least m and at most M, where m and M are two constants.

Lemma 1. *In any dimension, the "width" of any bound belt of a periodic spatiotemporal object o is at most a constant.*

Proof: Given $o = (X_1, \ldots, X_d, T, end)$. Without loss of generality, let us suppose that $T = [kp + from, \; kp + to]$ and $X_i^{\lceil} = sp\lfloor \frac{t}{p} \rfloor + a(t \bmod p) + b$ Then by Definition 1, the functions of the lower bound start and end lines of X_i are

$$st + b_1 \quad \text{and} \quad st + b_2$$

where $b_1 = (a - s) \cdot from + b$ and $b_2 = (a - s) \cdot to + b$. Since $to - from \leq period \leq \max(K)$, and $|a - s| \leq M$, hence $|b_1 - b_2| = |(a - s)(to - from)|$ is at most some constant. Similarly, we can prove that the "width" of the upper bound belt is at most some constant. □

Lemma 2. *In any dimension, if the bound belts of two PSOs intersect, then the time duration (intersection of the temporal projection) of the crossing part is at most some constant.*

Proof: Given two PSOs $o1$ and $o2$. Suppose that the functions of the lower bound start and end lines of $o1$ in the x_i dimension is: (1) $s_1 t + b_1$ and (2) $s_1 t + b_2$. And the functions of the lower bound start and end lines of $o2$ in the x_i dimension is: (3) $s_2 t + b_3$ and (4) $s_2 t + b_4$, where $s_1 \neq s_2$.

Let $t_{i,j}$ be the intersection time of line (i) and line (j) where i and j do not belong to the same PSO, we have :

$$t_{i,j} = \frac{b_i - b_j}{s_2 - s_1}$$

Then

$$\max(t_{i,j}) - \min(t_{i,j}) =$$
$$\max\left(\left| \frac{b_4 - b_3}{s_2 - s_1} \right|, \left| \frac{b_1 - b_2}{s_2 - s_1} \right|, \left| \frac{(b_1 - b_2) + (b_4 - b_3)}{s_2 - s_1} \right|, \left| \frac{(b_1 - b_2) + (b_3 - b_4)}{s_2 - s_1} \right| \right)$$

Since $|s_2 - s_1|$ is at least some constant $m > 0$, and by Lemma 1, the numerators are less than some constant, the time duration of the crossing part is at most some constant. □

Lemma 3. *The union of two linear PSO relations can be evaluated in PTIME in the size of the relations.*

Proof: By Definition 2, the union of two linear PSO relations computed as the regular set-union operation which can be done in PTIME in the size of the relation. □

Lemma 4. *The intersection of two linear PSO relations can be evaluated in PTIME in the size of the relations.*
(Sketch of proof see Appendix A)

Lemma 5. *The selection operation can be evaluated in PTIME in the size of the relations.*
(Sketch of proof see Appendix A)

Lemma 6. *The complement of a relation of PSOs can be evaluated in PTIME in the size of the relation.*

Lemma 7. *The difference of two PSO relations can be evaluated in PTIME in the size of the input PSO database.*

Theorem 1. *For any fixed d dimensions, any fixed relational algebra expression can be evaluated in PTIME in the size of the input PSO database.*

Proof: We prove by induction on the number of the operators in any relational algebra expression E that it can be evaluated in PTIME.

If there is only one operator, by Definition 2, E can contain selection, projection, rename, union, intersection, complement and difference. It is easy to see that projection and rename can be computed in PTIME. By Lemmas 3, 4, 5, 6, 7, selection, union, intersection, complement and difference can be evaluated in PTIME in the size of the input relations.

Induction Hypothesis: Assume that any relational algebra expression with equal or less than $k \geq 1$ operators can be evaluated in PTIME in the size of the input database and the result is a PSO relation.

Suppose now that E with $k+1$ operators. Then

1. there is E' with k operators such that $E = \hat{\sigma}_C E'$ or $E = \hat{\pi}_Y E'$ or $E = \hat{\rho}_Y E'$ or $E = \hat{\neg} E'$. Since E' contains only k operators, by the induction hypothesis, E' can be evaluated in PTIME in size of the input database. Let R be the result of E'. Since $\hat{\sigma}_C R$, $\hat{\pi}_Y R$, $E = \hat{\rho}_Y E'$ and $\hat{\neg} R$ can be evaluated in PTIME in size of R. E can be evaluated in size of the input database.
2. there is E_1 and E_2 such that $E = E_1 \hat{\cup} E_2$ or $E = E_1 \hat{\cap} E_2$ or $E = E_1 \hat{-} E_2$. Since E contain $k+1$ operators, the number of operators in E_1 or E_2 is less than k. By the induction hypothesis, both E_1 and E_2 can be evaluated in PTIME in size of the input database. And the result of E_1 and E_2 are two relations $R1$ and $R2$. By Lemmas 3, 4, 7, $R1 \hat{\cup} R2$, $R1 \hat{\cap} R2$ and $R1 \hat{-} R2$ can be evaluated in PTIME in size of $R1$ and $R2$. Therefore, E can be evaluated in PTIME in size of the input database.

$\square$

4   Implementation Results

We extended the PReSTO system [8] which is implemented in Windows NT platform, to represent and query acyclic periodic spatiotemporal objects. Table 2 shows the execution times for the evaluation of three different variants of the photon example in Section 2. In these variants, the number of possible intersections that the query had to test ranged from $4 \times 50 = 200$ to $4 \times 100 = 400$ and $50 \times 50 = 2500$. That is, it increased 2 and 12.5 folds, while the running time increased 2 and 6.4 folds respectively, hence the execution time seems to be linear in the product of the sizes of the two input relations.

Table 2. Query Evaluation Times

No. Tuples in Photon 1	No. Tuples in Photon 2	Running Time for Photon Query (seconds)
4	50	0.741
4	100	1.493
50	50	4.516

5   Related Work

Several proposals exist for representing continuous spatiotemporal objects. However, none of them can represent both cyclic and acyclic periodic movements. Constraint databases with rational linear or real polynomial constraints can be used to represent spatiotemporal objects with continuous change [20,25]. They can be queried by relational algebra, which is quite powerful, although they cannot express some queries like parity and transitive closure [3].

The parametric 2-spaghetti data model [12] generalizes the 2-spaghetti data model [24] by allowing the corner vertices to be represented as linear functions of time. The parametric 2-spaghetti data model cannot represent periodic spatiotemporal objects and cannot be queried by relational algebra, because it is not closed under intersection [12].

[13] represents spatiotemporal objects by a composition of a reference spatial extent at some reference time and various types of transformation functions. However, in some cases this model also may not be closed under intersection [13], and the query complexity may be high.

[14] defines continuously moving points and regions and an extended SQL query language on these objects. However, changing of object shape (shrinking and growing).

[32] can only represent spatiotemporal objects with discrete change. This model can be queried by an extended relational algebra. [17] proposes another spatiotemporal data model based on constraints in which, like in [32], only discrete change can be modeled. An SQL-based query language is also presented.

There are many data models to represent and query only temporal or only spatial data. These models can be queried by either relational algebra or Datalog. Some other purely temporal or purely spatial data models are reviewed in

[24,29,33]. We also did not deal with issues like visual query languages [6], indefinite information [23], query processing [7], nearest neighbor [22] and approximate queries [31]. We are currently investigating extensions in these directions.

6   Conclusion and Future Works

The periodic spatiotemporal database data model has great application potential in modeling physical processes, which we are currently exploring in more details. We are also developing additional operators to enhance the expressive power of the query language. Indexing is an important issue when we have a huge number of periodic spatiotemporal objects to be queried. Traditional stationary spatial object index structures like R-trees [18] and R*-trees [2] are inefficient for PSOs. Existing index structures for moving objects [21,26,28] are not efficient either since they are based on the moving points model and do not take periodicity into account. We are developing appropriate index structure for periodic spatiotemporal databases.

References

1. M. Baudinet, M. Niézette, and P. Wolper. On the Representation of Infinite Temporal Data and Queries. *Proc. 10th ACM Symposium on Principles of Database Systems*, pp. 280-290, 1991. 397
2. N. Beckmann, H.-P. Kriegel, R. Schneider, and B. Seeger. The R^*-tree: An Efficient and Robust Access Method for Points and Rectangles. *Proc. ACM SIGMOD International Conference on Management of Data*, pp. 322-331, 1990. 406
3. M. Benedikt, G. Dong, L. Libkin, and L. Wong. Relational Expressive Power of Constraint Query Languages. *Journal of the ACM*, 45:1, pp. 1-34, 1998. 405
4. E. Bertino, C. Bettini, E. Ferrari, and P. Samarati. An Access Control Model Supporting Periodicity Constraints and Temporal Reasoning. *ACM Transactions on Database Systems*, 23:3, pp. 231-285, 1998. 397
5. E. Bertino, B. Catania, and B. Shidlovsky. Towards Optimal Two-dimensional Indexing for Constraint Databases. *Information Processing Letters*, 64 (1997), pp. 1-8.
6. C. Bonhomme, C. Trépied, M-A. Aufaure, and R. Laurini. A Visual Language for Querying Spatio-Temporal Databases. *Proc. 7th ACM Symposium on Geographic Information Systems*, 34-39, Kansas City, MO, November 1999. 406
7. A. Brodsky, J. Jaffar, and M. Maher. Towards Practical Query Evaluation for Constraint Databases. *Constraints*, 2:3-4, pp. 279-304, 1997. 406
8. M. Cai, D. Keshwani, and P.Z Revesz. Parametric Rectangle: A Model for Querying and Animating Spatiotemporal Databases. In *Proc. of the 7th Conference on Extending Database Technology*, Springer LNCS-1777, pp. 430-444, Konstanz, Germany, March 2000. 397, 400, 404, 408
9. M. Casco Associates. *Linear Momentum and Collisions: A Mechanics Course*, available at http://www.mcasco.com/p1lmc.html.
10. J. Chomicki and T. Imieliński. Temporal Deductive Databases and Infinite Objects. In *Proc. of 7th ACM Symposium on Principles of Database Systems*, pp. 61-73, 1988. 397

11. J. Chomicki and T. Imieliński. Finite Representation of Infinite Query Answers. In *ACM Transactions on Database Systems*, (18) 2, pages 181-223, 1993. 397

12. J. Chomicki and P. Z. Revesz. Constraint-based Interoperability of Spatiotemporal Databases, *Geoinformatica*, 3:3, 1999. (Preliminary version In: *Proc. International Symposium on Large Spatial Databases*, Springer-Verlag LNCS 1262, pp. 142-161, Berlin, Germany, July 1997.) 405

13. J. Chomicki and P. Z. Revesz. A Geometric Framework for Specifying Spatiotemporal Objects. In: *Proc. International Workshop on Time Representation and Reasoning*, pp. 41-46, Orlando, Florida, May 1999. 405

14. M. Erwig, R. H. Güting, M. M. Schneider and M. Vazirgiannis. Spatio-Temporal Data Types: An Approach to Modeling and Querying Moving Objects in Databases. In: *Proc. ACM Symposium on Geographic Information Systems*, November 1998. 397, 405

15. A. U. Frank and M. Wallace Constraint Based Modeling in A GIS: Road Design as A Case Study. In: *Proceedings of Auto-Carto 12*, Charlotte, North Carolina, Vol. 4, pages 177-186, 1995.

16. R. Gonzalez, and R. Woods. *Digital Image Processing*, Addison-Wesley, 1998.

17. S. Grumbach, P. Rigaux, and L. Segoufin. Spatio-Temporal Data Handling with Constraints. In: *Proc. 6th ACM Symposium on Geographic Information Systems*, November 1998. 405

18. A. Guttman. R-Trees: A Dynamic Index Structure for Spatial Searching. *Proc. ACM SIGMOD International Conference on Management of Data*, pp. 47-57, 1984. 406

19. F. Kabanza, J-M. Stevenne, and P. Wolper. Handling Infinite Temporal Data. *Journal of Computer and System Sciences*, (51) 1, pages 26-52, 1995. 397

20. P. C. Kanellakis, G. M. Kuper, and P. Z. Revesz. Constraint Query Languages. *Journal of Computer and System Sciences*, 51:1, pp. 26-52, 1995. 397, 405

21. G. Kollios, D. Gunopulos, and V. J. Tsotras. On Indexing Mobile Objects. *Proc. 18th ACM Symposium on Principles of Database Systems*, pp. 261-272, 1999. 406

22. G. Kollios, D. Gunopulos, and V. J. Tsotras. Nearest Neighbor Queries in a Mobile Environment. In: *Proc. Workshop on Spatio-Temporal Database Management*, Springer-Verlag LNCS 1678, pp. 119-134, Edinburgh, Scotland, September 1999. 406

23. M. Koubarakis and S. Skiadopoulos. Tractable Query Answering in Indefinite Constraint Databases: Basic Results and Applications of Querying Spatio-Temporal Information. In: *Proc. Workshop on Spatio-Temporal Database Management*, Springer-Verlag LNCS 1678, pp. 204-223, Edinburgh, Scotland, September 1999. 406

24. R. Laurini and D. Thompson. *Fundamentals of Spatial Information Systems*. Academic Press, 1992. 405, 406

25. P. Z. Revesz. *Introduction to Constraint Databases*, Springer-Verlag, 2000. 397, 405

26. S. Saltenis, C. S. Jensen, S. T. Leutenegger and M. A. Lopez. Indexing the Positions of Continuously Moving Objects. In: *Proc. ACM SIGMOD International Conference on Management of Data*, pp. 331-342, 2000. 406

27. A. P. Sistla, O. Wolfson, S. Chamberlain, and S. Dao. Modeling and Querying Moving Objects. In *Proceedings of the 13th IEEE International Conference on Data Engineering*, pages 422-432, 1997.

28. J. Tayeb, O. Ulusoy, O. Wolfson. A Quadtree-Based Dynamic Attribute Indexing Method. *The Computer Journal*, 41(3):185-200, 1998. 406

29. A. Tansel, J. Clifford, S. Gadia, S. Jajodia, A. Segev, and R. T. Snodgrass. *Temporal Databases: Theory, Design, and Implementation.* Benjamin/Cummings Inc., Redwood City, California, 1993. 406
30. D. Toman and J. Chomicki. Datalog with Integer Periodicity Constraints. *Journal of Logic Programming*, 35(3), June 1998, pp.263-290. 397, 402
31. D. Vasilis and M. Christos and S. Spiros. A Provably Efficient Computational Model For Approximate Spatiotemporal Retrieval. In: *Proc. 7th ACM Symposium on Geographic Information Systems*, pp. 40-46, Kansas City, Missouri, November 1999. 406
32. M. F. Worboys. A Unified Model for Spatial and Temporal Information. *Computer Journal*, 37:1, pp. 25-34, 1994. 397, 405
33. M. F. Worboys. *GIS: A Computing Perspective*, Taylor & Francis, 1995. 406

A   Proofs

Proof of Lemma 4: Given two PSOs $o1$ and $o2$. For each dimension, there are at most four crossings between the lower and the upper bound belts of $o1$ and those of $o2$, as shown in Figure 6, where solid lines are the bound start and end lines of $o1$ and dashed lines are those of $o2$. There are $O(d)$ bound belt crossings for d dimensions. Projecting the crossings to the t-axis produces $O(d)$ time intervals. By Lemma 2, the size of each interval is at most some constant, hence the sum of the sizes of these intervals is $O(d)$. Since the period of $o1$ is at least some constant $min(K)$, where K is the set of all periods in the database, there are $O(d)$ periods of $o1$ falling in these intervals, which can be represented by a set of $O(d)$ non-periodic moving ractangles. Similarly, we represent $o2$ over these intervals by a set of $O(d)$ non-periodic PSOs. So the intersection of $o1$ and $o2$ over these intervals can be computed in $O(d^2)$ using the non-periodic parametric rectangle intersection algorithm [8].

Now let us consider the $O(d)$ gap intervals between two adjacent intervals discussed above. First we define a function $f1$ as always "smaller" (or "greater") than another function $f2$ over some time interval I, denoted by $f_1 << f_2$ (or $f1 >> f2$), if for any time $t \in I$, $f_1(t) \le f_2(t)$ (or $f1(t) \ge f2(t)$).

It is easy to see that within each gap interval $[t1, t2]$ and in each dimension x_i the lower and the upper bound start lines of $o1$ and $o2$ do not intersect. Let $f1$ be the "greater" function of the lower bound start lines of $o1$ and $o2$ over $[t1, t2]$, and $f2$ the "smaller" function of the upper bound start line of $o1$ and $o2$. If $f1 << f2$, then the intersection of $o1$ and $o2$ can be represented by a set of PSOs whose lower and upper bound start lines are $f1$ and $f2$ respectively, and whose period p is the least common multiple of the periods of $o1$ and $o2$.

Consider the first period $[t1, t1 + p]$. There are at most $\frac{p}{p1}$ periods of $o1$ and $\frac{p}{p2}$ periods of $o2$ falling in $[t1, t1 + p]$. Since $\frac{p}{p1}$ and $\frac{p}{p2}$ are at most $\frac{max(K)}{min(K)}$, we can reduce $R' = o1 \hat{\cap} o2$ over $[t1, t1 + p]$ to the intersection of two set of $O(1)$ non-periodic PSOs which can be computed in $O(d)$ time [8]. Each non-periodic PSO r in R' can be translated in $O(d)$ time to a PSO $(X_1, \ldots, X_d, T, t2)$ as follows:

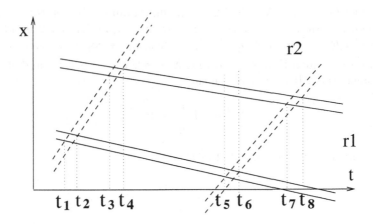

Fig. 6. Projection of a Periodic Spatiotemporal Object on (x_i, t) Space

For each dimension x_i, let $a_1 t + b_1$ and $a_2 t + b_2$ be the bound function of r,

$$X_i^[= s_1 p \lfloor \frac{t}{p} \rfloor + a_1 (t \bmod p) + b_1, \quad X_i^] = s_2 p \lfloor \frac{t}{p} \rfloor + a_2 (t \bmod p) + b_2$$

where s_1 and s_2 are the slopes of $f1$ and $f2$ respectively. And $T = [from + kp, \ to + kp]$, where $from$ and to are the lower and the upper bound of the time interval of r.

Since there are $O(d)$ gap intervals, $o1 \hat{\cap} o2$ over gap intervals can be computed $O(d^2)$ time. The intersection of $o1$ and $o2$ is the union of their intersections in all the intervals, which can be computed in $O(d)$ time. So the intersection of $o1$ and $o2$ can be computed in $O(d + d^2) = O(d^2)$ time.

Let $R1$ and $R2$ be two sets of at most n PSOs, since

$$R1 \cap R2 = \bigcap_{o1 \in R1, \ o2 \in R2} o1 \cap o2$$

the intersection can be evaluated in $O(d^2 n^2)$ time.   □

Proof of Lemma 5: Given $\hat{\sigma}_C R$, where R is a PSO relation with n tuples over $x_1, \ldots, x_d$ dimensions and $A_1, \ldots, A_k$ attributes, C is the selection conditions. We first write C as $C1$ and $C2$ where $C1$ is the conjunction of all the atomic constraints in C that contain one spatial dimension variable x_i, and $C2$ is the conjunction of those constraints that do not contain any spatial dimension. It is easy to see that $R' = \hat{\sigma}_{C2} R$ can be evaluated in PTIME by checking whether the tuples in R satisfy $C2$.

For each tuple o_j in R', we substitute the attributes in $C1$ with their values in r_j. For each dimension x_i, let $b1$ be the maximum of the set $B1$ of constants in all the constraints of the form $x_i \geq c$ or $x_i = c$ in $C1$ if $B1$ is not empty, otherwise let $b1 = -\infty$. And let $b2$ be the minimum of the set $B2$ of constants in all the constraints of the form $x_i \leq c$ or $x_i = c$ in $C1$ if $B2$ is not empty, otherwise let $b2 = +\infty$. Let $o'_j = (X_1, \ldots, X_d, T, +\infty, A_1, \ldots, A_k)$ be a PSO with period $+\infty$ such that $X_i^{[} = b1$ and $X_i^{]} = b2$, $T = [-\infty, \infty]$ and $A_1, \ldots, A_k$ are the same as o_j. It is easy to see that

$$\hat{\sigma}_C R = \bigcup_{o_j \in R'} o_j \hat{\cap} o'_j,$$

and by Lemma 4, it can computed in PTIME.   □

Arc Consistency for Soft Constraints

Thomas Schiex

INRA, Toulouse, France
Thomas.Schiex@toulouse.inra.fr
http://www-bia.inra.fr/T/schiex

Abstract. Traditionally, local consistency is defined as a relaxation of consistency which can be checked in polynomial time. It is accompanied by a corresponding "filtering" or "enforcing" algorithm that computes in polynomial time, and from any given CSP, an equivalent unique CSP which satisfies the local consistency property.

The question whether the notion of local consistency can be extended to soft constraint frameworks has been addressed by several papers, in several settings [4, 14, 12]. The main positive conclusion of these works is that the notion of local consistency can be extended to soft constraints frameworks which rely on an idempotent violation combination operator. However, the question whether this can be done for non idempotent operators as eg, in the MAX-CSP problem, is not clear and has lead to several different notions of arc consistency [14, 16, 1, 11, 10]. Each of these proposals lacks several of the original properties of local consistency.

In this paper, we show that using a small additional axiom, satisfied by most existing soft constraints proposals (including MAX-CSP), it is possible to define a notion of arc consistency that keeps all the good properties of classical arc consistency but the unicity of the arc consistent closure. We show that this notion directly provides improved lower bounds. Stronger alternative definitions, that allow partial inconsistencies to propagate are also considered.

1 Introduction

Compared to other combinatorial optimisation frameworks, the CSP framework is essentially characterised by the ubiquitous use of so-called local consistency properties and enforcing algorithms among which arc consistency is certainly the most preeminent one.

The notion of local consistency can be easily characterised by a set of desirable properties: local consistency is a relaxation of consistency: for any consistent CSP, there is an equivalent non empty locally consistent CSP. Finding this equivalent locally consistent CSP, which is unique, is achievable in polynomial time by so-called enforcing or filtering algorithms. Several papers have tried to extend the classical notion of arc consistency to weighted constraint frameworks. In such frameworks, the aim is to find an assignment that minimises combined violations. The first work in this direction is probably [12] which defined arc consistency filtering for fuzzy CSP.

R. Dechter (Ed.): CP 2000, LNCS 1894, pp. 411–425, 2000.
© Springer-Verlag Berlin Heidelberg 2000

This extension was rather straightforward and one could think that this would also be the case for other frameworks such as the MAX-CSP framework, introduced in [15, 9], where the aim is to find an assignment which minimises the (weighted) number of violated constraints. This was not the case. Later works tried to extend arc consistency in a systematic way using axiomatic frameworks to characterise the properties of the operator used to combine violations:

- the Semi-Ring CSP framework was introduced in [4, 5]. In this work, the extension of arc consistency enforcing is induced by a generalisation of the fundamental relational operators such as projection, intersection and join. The essential conclusion of this work is that extended arc consistency works as far as the operator used to combine violations is idempotent. This includes the case of fuzzy CSP and also some other cases with partial orders. For MAX-CSP and other related cases, the algorithm may not terminate and may also provide non equivalent CSP.
- the Valued CSP framework was introduced in [14]. Here, the extension of the arc consistency property is essentially based on the notion of relaxation. The same conclusion as in the Semi-Ring CSP framework is reached for idempotent operators. For other frameworks such as the MAX-CSP framework, it is shown that the problem of checking the extended arc consistency property defines an NP-complete problem.

Parallel to these tentative extensions of arc consistency, several works such as [16, 1, 11, 10] tried to offer improved lower bounds for the MAX-CSP. These works abandon the idea of extending arc consistency in order to simply offer the most important service i.e., the ability to detect that a CSP has no solution of cost below a given threshold.

Globally, each of these proposals violates some of the desirable properties of local consistency. In this paper we show that it is possible, by the addition to the Valued CSP framework of a single axiom, to define an extended arc consistency notion that has all the desirable properties of classical arc consistency but the unicity of the arc consistent closure. It has also the nice property that in the idempotent operator cases, it reduces to existing working definitions and unicity is recovered. We show that a lower bound can easily be built from any of the arc consistent closures and that this lower bound generalises and improves on existing lower bounds [16, 1, 11, 10]. Finally, in the last section we consider stronger enforcing algorithms that may further improve the lower bounds by propagating partial inconsistencies and not only value deletions as in [11, 10].

2   Notations and Definitions

A constraint satisfaction problem (CSP) is a triple $\langle X, D, C \rangle$. X is a set of n variables $X = \{1, \ldots, n\}$. Each variable $i \in X$ has a domain of values $d_i \in D$ and can be assigned any value $a \in d_i$, also noted (i, a). C is a set of constraints. Each constraint $c \in C$ is defined over a set of variables $X_c \subset X$ by a subset of the Cartesian product $\prod_{i \in X_c} d_i$ which defines all consistent tuples of values. The cardinality $|X_c|$ is the arity of the constraint c. k will denote the largest arity of a CSP. We assume, without loss of generality, that at most one constraint is defined over a given set of variables. The set C is partitioned in two sets $C = C^1 \cup C^+$ where C^1 contains all unary constraints. The unary constraint on variable i will be denoted c_i. The projection of a tuple of values t over a set of variables $V \subset X$ is denoted by $t_{\downarrow V}$. This is extended to constraints: the projection $c_{\downarrow V}$ of a constraint c on a set of variables $V \subset X_c$ is the constraint defined on V and equal to the set of the projections on V of all tuples in c. A tuple $t \in c$ such that $t_{\downarrow\{i\}} = (a)$ is a support for value (i, a) on c. A tuple of values t satisfies a constraint c if $t_{\downarrow X_c} \in c$. Finally, a tuple of values over X is a solution iff it satisfies all the constraints of the CSP.

2.1 Valued CSP

Valued CSP (or VCSP) have been initially introduced in [14]. A valued CSP is obtained by associating a mathematical object, called a valuation, to each constraint of an original CSP. The set E of all valuations is assumed to be completely ordered and its maximum element is used for the most important constraints, namely hard constraints. When an assignment violates a set of constraints, one can compute its valuation by combining the valuations of all violated constraints using a dedicated operator (noted $\oplus$). This operator must satisfy a set of properties that are captured by a set of axioms defining a so-called "valuation structure".

Definition 1. *A valuation structure is defined as a tuple $\langle E, \oplus, \succcurlyeq \rangle$ such that:*

- *E is a set, whose elements are called valuations, which is totally ordered by $\succcurlyeq$, with a maximum element noted $\top$ and a minimum element noted $\bot$;*
- *$\oplus$ is a commutative, associative closed binary operation on E that satisfies:*
  - *Identity: $\forall a \in E, a \oplus \bot = a$;*
  - *Monotonicity: $\forall a, b, c \in E, (a \succcurlyeq b) \Rightarrow ((a \oplus c) \succcurlyeq (b \oplus c))$;*
  - *Absorbing element: $\forall a \in E, (a \oplus \top) = \top$.*

This structure of totally ordered commutative monoid with a monotonic operator is also known in uncertain reasoning, E being restricted to $[0, 1]$, as a "triangular co-norm" [6]. In the rest of the paper, we assume that the computation of $\succ$ and $\oplus$ are always polynomial in the size of their arguments. We also assume E is countable.

It is now possible to define valued CSPs. For the sake of generality, rather than considering that a valuation is associated with each constraint, as in [14], we will consider that a valuation is associated with each tuple of each constraint. As it is observed in [3], the two approaches are essentially equivalent.

Definition 2. *A valued CSP is a tuple $\langle X, D, C, S \rangle$ where $S = \langle E, \oplus, \succcurlyeq \rangle$ is a valuation structure, X is a set of n variables $X = \{1, \ldots, n\}$. Each variable $i \in X$ has a set of possible values $d_i \in D$. $C = C^1 \cup C^+$ is a set of constraints. Each constraint $c \in C$ is defined over a set of variables $X_c \subset X$ as a function from $\prod_{i \in X_c} d_i$ to E.*

An assignment A of values to some variables $V \subset X$ can be simply evaluated by combining, for all assigned constraints, the valuations of the tuple used:

Definition 3. *In a VCSP $\mathcal{P} = \langle X, D, C, S \rangle$, the valuation of an assignment t over $V \subset X$ is defined by:*

$$\mathcal{V}_{\mathcal{P}}(t) = \bigoplus_{c \in C, X_c \subset V} [c(t_{\downarrow X_c})]$$

The problem usually considered is to find a complete assignment with a minimum valuation. Globally, the semantics of a VCSP is a distribution of valuations over the assignments of X. The choice of axioms is quite natural and is usual in the field of uncertain reasoning. The ordered set E simply allows various impact of violations to be expressed. The commutativity and associativity guarantee that the valuation of an assignment depends only on *the set* of the valuations combined. The monotonicity of $\oplus$ guarantees that assignment valuations cannot decrease when constraint violations increase. For a more detailed analysis and justification of the VCSP axioms, we invite the reader to read [14, 10] which also emphasise the difference between idempotent and strictly monotonic $\oplus$ operators.

Definition 4. *An operator $\oplus$ is idempotent if $\forall v \in E, (v \oplus v) = v$. It is strictly monotonic if $\forall a, b, c \in E$, s.t. $(a \succ c) \wedge (b \neq \top)$, we have $(a \oplus b) \succ (c \oplus b)$*

As shown in [14], these two properties are incompatible as soon as $|E| > 2$. The only valuation structures with an idempotent operator corresponds to classical and fuzzy CSP, which use $\oplus = \max$ as the combination operator. Other soft CSP frameworks such as MAX-CSP, lexicographic CSP or probabilistic CSP use a strictly monotonic operator.

Arc consistency enforcing must yield an equivalent problem, the so-called arc-consistent closure. Several notions of equivalence have been introduced in [14, 10] that enable to compare pairs of VCSP with different valuations structure. In this paper, the notion of equivalence will only be used to compare pairs of VCSP with the same valuation structure and can be therefore simplified and strengthened. Two VCSP will be said equivalent iff they define the same distribution over complete assignments:

Definition 5. *Two VCSP $\mathcal{P} = \langle X, D, C, S \rangle$ and $\mathcal{P}' = \langle X, D, C', S \rangle$ are equivalent iff for any complete assignment A, we have:*

$$\mathcal{V}_{\mathcal{P}}(A) = \mathcal{V}_{\mathcal{P}'}(A)$$

3   Arc Consistency Revisited

In this section we first give a slightly unusual and very naive definition of classical arc consistency which will make the extension to soft constraints easier. We consider that the final domains of the CSP are defined by the unary constraints $c_i \in C^1$.

Definition 6. *A classical CSP is arc consistent if for each constraint $c \in C^+$ and for each variable $i \in X_c$, we have $(c_i \subset c_{\downarrow\{i\}})$ and $(c_i \supset c_{\downarrow\{i\}})$.*

Traditionally, a CSP is said to be arc consistent simply when $(c_i \subset c_{\downarrow\{i\}})$. Our definition explicits the usual *implicit* assumption that tuples which use a deleted value are removed from the constraints i.e. that $(c_i \supset c_{\downarrow\{i\}})$ too. Except for the fact that a CSP with empty domains may be arc consistent using this definition, it is equivalent to the usual definition (we consider that the possible emptiness of the arc consistent closure is a separate property). The first condition guarantees that each value has a tuple supporting it while the second condition guarantees that all tuples are made of viable values. So, globally, each value is supported by a viable tuple.

A corresponding enforcing algorithm can be defined by the iterated application, until quiescence, of two procedures, each enforcing one of the two conditions above: Projection enforces the fact that $(c_i \subset c_{\downarrow\{i\}})$ by deleting values with no support. Extension enforces the fact that $(c_i \supset c_{\downarrow\{i\}})$ by deleting tuples that contain a deleted value. The unary constraints c_i are used to mark deleted values. Termination follows from the fact that each iteration of AC, but the last, removes at least one value or tuple and there is only $O(e.d^k)$ of them. In the binary case, since Projection and Extension are in $O(d)$, each iteration of AC is in $O(e.d^2)$ and this shows that our naive arc consistency enforcing algorithm is in $O(e^2.d^4)$.

Algorithm 1 – Naive Arc Consistency enforcing

```
Projection(c, i, a);
m ← 0;
if ∄t ∈ c s.t. t_{↓{i}} = (a) then
    Delete (a) from c_i;
    m ← 1;
return m;
```

```
Extension(i, a, c);
m ← 0;
if (a) ∉ c_i then
    foreach t ∈ c s.t. t_{↓{i}} = (a) do
        Delete t from c;
        m ← 1;
return m;
```

```
AC(X, D, C¹ ∪ C⁺);
m ← 1;
while (m) do
    m_c ← m_i ← 0;
    foreach c ∈ C⁺ do
        foreach i ∈ X_c do
            foreach a ∈ d_i do m_c ← (m_c∨ Projection(c, i, a));

    foreach i ∈ X do
        foreach c ∈ C⁺ s.t. i ∈ X_c do
            foreach a ∈ d_i do m_i = (m_i∨ Extension(i, a, c));
    m ← m_i ∨ m_c;
```

AC returns a CSP which is equivalent to the original CSP since Projection and Extension only remove values or tuples which cannot participate to a solution. The final CSP is arc consistent since it is closed under both Projection and Extension. The poor time complexity of this naive algorithm, compared to the optimal $O(e.d^2)$ time complexity first achieved by AC-4 on binary CSP should be considered as the consequence of its intended simplicity: the aim of this paper is (only) to show that arc consistency can be extended to eg. MAX-CSP. We have chosen to describe an enforcing algorithm that will be easy to extend to VCSP. To achieve this, we will mainly have to guarantee that the extended versions of the elementary operations Projection and Extension preserve the semantics of the problem.

3.1   Arc Consistency for Soft Constraints

We start with an introductory example. In the sequel of the paper, in order to illustrate the notions introduced on concrete examples, we will consider binary weighted MAX-CSP which correspond to valued CSP using the strictly monotonic valuation structure $\langle \mathbb{N} \cup \{+\infty\}, +, > \rangle$. To describe such problems, we use a graph representation where vertices represent values and weighted edges connect values from pairs of variables connected by a constraint. In this representation, we omit all edges weighted by 0 ($\bot$) and all weights equal to $+\infty$ ($\top$). Unary constraints (actual domains) are represented by weights associated with vertices, weights equal to 0 being omitted.

Let us consider the weighted MAX-CSP in figure 1(a). It has two variables called 1 and 2, each with two values a and b and a single constraint. The constraint forbids pair $((1,b),(2,b))$ with cost 1 and forbids pairs $((1,a),(2,a))$ and $((1,b),(2,a))$ completely (with cost $+\infty$). The pair $((1,a),(2,b))$ is authorised and the corresponding edge is therefore omitted.

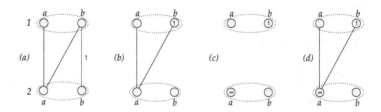

Fig. 1. Four equivalent MAX-CSP

If we assign the value b to variable 1, it is known for sure that a cost of 1 at least must be payed since the best support for $(1,b)$ has cost 1. Projection should make this explicit and induce a unary constraint on 1 that forbids $(1,b)$ with cost 1. However if we simply add this constraint to the MAX-CSP, as it has been proposed in [4] for those cases with an idempotent operator, the resulting CSP is not equivalent. The complete assignment $((1, b), (2, b))$ which has initially cost 1 would now have cost 2. In order to preserve equivalence, we must "compensate" for the induced unary constraint. This can be done by simply subtracting 1 from all the tuples that contain the value $(1, b)$. The corresponding equivalent CSP is described in figure 1(b): the edge $((1, b), (2, b))$ of cost 1 has disappeared (the associated weight is now 0) while the edge $((1, b), (2, a))$ is unaffected since it has an infinite cost. We can repeat this process for variable 2: all the supports of value $(2, a)$ have infinite cost. Thus we can add a unary constraint that completely forbids value $(2, a)$. In this specific case, and because the valuation $+\infty$ is such that $\forall v \in E, +\infty \oplus v = +\infty$, we can either compensate for this (figure 1(c)) or not (figure 1(d)). In both cases, an equivalent MAX-CSP is obtained. Actually, the weight associated with each of the edges connected to value $(2, a)$ cannot affect the semantics of the CSP since the value is completely forbidden. CSP 1(c) is interesting because it is is completely solved. However, we prefer the problem 1(d) because it makes the information explicit both at the domain and constraint level.

3.2   A New Axiom for VCSP

To generalise this idea to other possible valuation structures, we have to be able to "compensate" for the information added by projection. This is made possible by the following additional axiom:

Definition 7. *A valuation structure $\langle E, \oplus, \succcurlyeq \rangle$ is fair if for any pair of valuations $u, v \in E$, $v \preccurlyeq u$, there exist a valuation $w \in E$ such that $v \oplus w = u$. w will be called a difference of u and v. The unique maximum difference of u and v will be noted $u \ominus v$.*

This simple axiom is actually satisfied by most existing concrete frameworks, including concrete with idempotent or strictly monotonic $\oplus$ operators.

- classical CSP can be defined as VCSP using the valuation set $E = \{0, 1\}$, where $0 = \bot \prec 1 = \top$. The combination operator is max and we have $0 \ominus 0 = 0$, $1 \ominus 0 = 1$ and $1 \ominus 1 = 1$. So $\ominus = $ max too. Note that 0 is another difference between 1 and 1, but it is not the maximum one.
- possibilistic CSP, which define a min-max problem dual to the classical max-min problem of fuzzy CSP, can be defined using the valuation set $\mathbb{N} \cup \{+\infty\}$, ordered as usual and using $\oplus = $ max. Here again, differences exist and one can show that $\ominus = $ max.
- weighted MAX-CSP can be defined using the valuation set $\mathbb{N} \cup \{+\infty\}$, ordered as usual and using $\oplus = +$. Here again, differences exist and one can show that $u \ominus v = u - v$ on finite valuations. Else, for all $v \in E$, we have $+\infty \ominus v = +\infty$.

Note that other concrete frameworks such as probabilistic CSP [7] or lexicographic CSP [8] can be reduced to weighted MAX-CSP as shown in [14] and can therefore benefit from the results given in this paper. This is particularly important for lexicographic CSP for which difference is not always defined.

Theorem 1. *Let $S = \langle E, \oplus, \succcurlyeq \rangle$ be a fair valuation structure. Then $\forall u, v, w, \in E, w \preccurlyeq v$, we have $(v \ominus w) \preccurlyeq v$ and $(u \oplus w) \oplus (v \ominus w) = (u \oplus v)$.*

Proof. By definition, $(v \ominus w) \oplus w = v$. From the monotonicity of $\oplus$, this proves that $(v \ominus w) \preccurlyeq v$ (this inequality becomes strict if $\oplus$ is strictly monotonic and $v \neq \top$). The second property follows from the commutativity and associativity of $\oplus$: we have $(u \oplus w) \oplus (v \ominus w) = u \oplus ((v \ominus w) \oplus w) = (u \oplus v)$. $\square$

3.3   Soft Arc Consistency Enforcing

It is now possible to define an extended version of the AC enforcing algorithm presented before. Our aim is to define a generic algorithm that will consistently work in all fair valuation structures. Remember that c_i denotes the unary constraint on variable i in the current CSP. So, $c_i(a)$ is the valuation associated with value (i, a) in the unary constraint. Similarly to value removals in classical AC enforcing, we will also use statements such as $c(t) \leftarrow v$ which means that the valuation associated with the tuple t in c will be set to v. We also require the following definitions:

Definition 8. *Let $v, w \in E$, be two valuations. If $v \neq \perp$ and $v \ominus v = v$, we say that v is* absorbing. *If $v \oplus w \neq w$ we say that v* affects w.

We assume that these properties can be tested in constant time. This is the case in all the concrete valuation structures considered. Note that $\top$ is absorbing in all valuation structures. When $\oplus$ is idempotent, then all valuations but $\perp$ are absorbing. We are now ready to extend our elementary procedures Projection and Extension.

Algorithm 2 – Extended procedures for Soft AC enforcing

Projection(c, i, a);
$m \leftarrow 0$;
$v \leftarrow \top$;
foreach $t \in c$ s.t. $t_{\downarrow\{i\}} = (a)$ **do**
  $\lfloor\ v \leftarrow \min(v, c(t))$;
if v affects $c_i(a)$ **then**
  $\big|\ v' \leftarrow$ Choose(v);
  $\big|\ c_i(a) \leftarrow c_i(a) \oplus v'$;
  $\big|\ m \leftarrow 1$;
  $\big|\ $**foreach** $t \in c$ s.t. $t_{\downarrow\{i\}} = (a)$ **do**
  $\big|\ \ \lfloor\ c(t) \leftarrow c(t) \ominus v'$;
return m;

Extension(i, a, c);
$m \leftarrow 0$;
$v \leftarrow c_i(a)$;
if v is absorbing **then**
  $\big|\ v' \leftarrow$ Choose(v);
  $\big|\ $**foreach** $t \in c$ s.t. $t_{\downarrow\{i\}} = (a)$ **do**
  $\big|\ \ \big|\ $**if** v' affects $c(t)$ **then**
  $\big|\ \ \big|\ \ \lfloor\ c(t) \leftarrow c(t) \oplus v'$;
  $\big|\ \ \lfloor\ \ \ m \leftarrow 1$;
1 $\lfloor\ c_i(a) \leftarrow c_i(a) \ominus v'$;
return m;

Let analyse these procedures. Both use a function Choose(v) that takes a valuation as argument and returns a valuation. Assume for now that Choose(v)

is the identity function. In Projection, we first look for a cheapest support for the value (i, a) on constraint c and we keep its valuation in v. If (i, a) is used in an assignment, we will have to pay for this valuation at least. This gives a possible new unary constraint. Before adding this constraint, we first check if this would modify the CSP: we test if v affects the existing valuation $c_i(a)$ at the unary constraint level. If it does, we add the induced unary constraint to the CSP, we note that the CSP is modified and then we compensate for the addition by subtracting v from the valuations of all the supports of (i, a). This can always be done because the valuation structure is fair and by construction v is less than or equal to all the valuations of the supports.

In Extension, we first check if the valuation v of the value a is absorbing. This is needed for termination (see section 5). Then for each of the supports of (i, a) on c, we check if v can affect the valuation of the support and if so, we modify the tuple valuation. The line numbered 1 compensates for this at the unary level. This line is actually useless since v is absorbing but it will be useful in a later version of the procedure Extension where v may be non absorbing.

Theorem 2. *Given any fair VCSP $P = \langle X, D, C, S \rangle$, $i \in X$, $a \in d_i$ and $c \in C$ s.t. $i \in X_c$, the application of Projection(c, i, a) or Extension(i, a, c) to P yields an equivalent VCSP.*

Proof. Consider any complete assignment t. If $t_{\downarrow\{i\}} \neq (a)$ then the valuation of the assignment is unaffected by the application of Projection or Extension since these procedures only modify valuations of tuples containing value (i, a). If $t_{\downarrow\{i\}} = (a)$, we note $\alpha = c_i(a)$ and $\beta = c(t_{\downarrow X_c})$. The initial valuation of t can be written $\omega \oplus \alpha \oplus \beta$ where ω contains the combined valuations of all constraints except c and c_i. After the application of Projection, the valuation of t becomes $\omega \oplus (\alpha \oplus v) \oplus (\beta \ominus v) = \omega \oplus \alpha \oplus \beta$ by theorem 1 and is therefore unaffected. Similarly, the application of Extension yields a valuation of $\omega \oplus (\alpha \ominus v) \oplus (\beta \oplus v) = \omega \oplus \alpha \oplus \beta$ by theorem 1. □

Consider our initial AC algorithm using the new Projection and Extension procedures. If it terminates, it necessarily returns an equivalent problem. Termination is still unproved in the general case, however it is easy to prove it in the most important cases i.e. when $\oplus$ is either idempotent or strictly monotonic:

- Idempotent case: $\oplus$ is equal to max (see [14]) and obviously $\ominus$ = max too. The number of different valuations one may obtain by combining valuations with max is finite and equal to the number of different valuations that exist originally in the CSP. Then, each application of Projection or Extension may only increase valuations in domains or constraints. Since they can only take a finite number of values, the algorithm will stop.
- Strictly monotonic case: the only absorbing value is $\top$. For all other valuations $v \neq \top$, we have $v \ominus x \prec v$ for any $x \neq \bot$ (this follows from strict monotonicity). If we consider valuations inside constraints, each call to Projection may only reduce valuations while each call to Extension can only set constraint valuations to $\top$ which is the maximum element and as an absorbing value, cannot decrease. Globally, each iteration of the AC algorithm

can either lower constraint valuations or set them to $\top$. In the first case, the valuation cannot decrease below $\bot$ and in the second case they cannot be modified again. Termination is guaranteed because there is only a finite number of tuples inside constraints. Note that this proof is still valid if Choose returns any value which is smaller or equal to v and strictly larger than $\bot$.

So we now have an extended enforcing algorithm that terminates and yields an equivalent problem for all fair valuation structures with either an idempotent or strictly monotonic $\oplus$ operator. Note also that its specialisation to classical CSP described as VCSP corresponds to our classical AC enforcing algorithm. We can now define the corresponding arc consistency property as follows:

Definition 9. *A fair VCSP is arc consistent if for each constraint $c \in C^+$, for each variable $i \in X_c$, for each value $a \in d_i$ we have:*

- *the minimum valuation of the supports of (i, a) on c does not affect $c_i(a)$.*
- *if $c_i(a)$ is absorbing, then it does not affect any of the valuations of the supports of (i, a) on c.*

Our AC enforcing algorithm is correct by definition of the AC property which precisely corresponds to the properties enforced by Projection and Extension respectively. Note also that its specialisation to classical CSP described as VCSP corresponds to our classical AC definition.

We still have to prove that the algorithm is polynomial time. We haven't built a generic proof and have instead decided to limit ourself to the most significant case of binary weighted MAX-CSP. In this case, Projection is in $O(d)$ and Extension in $O(d)$ too. In AC each iteration performs $O(ed)$ calls to these procedures. Each iteration but the last either deletes a value, sets a tuple valuation to $0 = \bot$ or to $+\infty = \top$. There are only $e.d^2$ tuples and $n.d$ values so this naive AC enforcing algorithm is in $O(e^2.d^4)$ and is effectively polynomial time. Naturally, some work is needed to turn this theoretical result in a tuned time and space efficient algorithm.

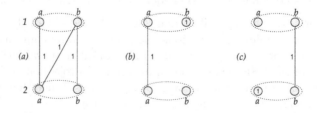

Fig. 2. A MAX-CSP and two different equivalent arc consistent closure

Finally, we observe that confluence of arc consistency enforcing is lost. This means that the arc consistent closure of a problem is not necessarily unique as the example of figure 2 shows. The MAX-CSP considered is similar to the problem of figure 1 except that non authorised tuples have all cost 1. If we start enforcing arc consistency by variable 1, we detect that $(1, b)$ has a minimum cost support of cost 1 and we obtain the CSP 2(b). This CSP is arc consistent and equivalent to the CSP 2(a). If we start by variable 2, we detect that $(2, a)$ has a minimum cost support of cost 1 and we obtain the CSP 2(c). This CSP is also arc consistent and equivalent to CSP 2(a) but is different from the CSP 2(b).

4   Lower Bounds and Comparison

In the VCSP framework, as in the CSP framework, each variable must be assigned a value. So, the following valuation is always a lower bound on the cost of an optimal solution:

$$\ell = \bigoplus_{i \in X} [\min_{a \in d_i} c_i(a)]$$

Computed after AC enforcing, this lower bound will be noted ℓ_{ac}. It depends on the arc consistent closure found which depends on the order in which constraints and variables are examined by AC enforcing. A CSP is said to be *maximally arc consistent* if it is arc consistent and if ℓ_{ac} is maximum over all equivalent arc consistent problems. The problem of enforcing maximum arc consistency is certainly important, but there are reasons to think that it is an NP-hard problem (see [13]). As an example, consider the CSP in figure 3. It has four variables with two values each and contains four constraints. Enforcing arc consistency of this problem yields the CSP on the right. The lower bound ℓ_{ac} is here equal to 4.

We now compare ℓ_{ac} to recent lower bounds for binary MAX-CSP. The first lower bound considered is the *reversible directed arc consistency counts* based lower bound (RDAC [11, 10]). It is parameterised by booleans indicating a direction per binary constraint. For each constraint c, and for each value a of the variable i indicated by the direction selected, the counter $w_{i,a}$ is incremented if the value has no support on the constraint. The induced lower bound is the sum of the minimum of the w_{ia} per variable. If we enforce AC and if we examine constraints in the same order as RDAC, always starting by the variable that RDAC examines, it is quite obvious that Projection will discover exactly the same counts as RDAC, as unary constraints. Additionally, it will examine the other side of each constraint and possibly infer more unary constraints which may lead to a strictly better lower bound. If we consider our example, exactly one value in each domain has a support of cost 0. So, RDAC will only be able to infer at most 4 counts of 1 for the eight values. Ideally, if the constraints are correctly oriented (eg. 2 constraints directed towards variable 1 and the 2 others towards variable 3), these 4 costs induce a lower bound of 2. However, a useless lower bound of 0 can also be inferred if the constraints are poorly oriented eg. if one constraint is oriented towards each variable.

The second lower bound considered is the *weighted arc consistency counts* based lower bound (WAC [1]). It is parameterised by one real number between 0 and 1 per constraint. It has been shown in [2] that it is a generalisation of RDAC.

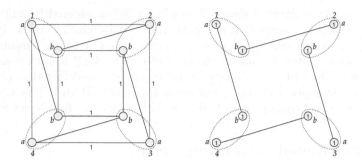

Fig. 3. A MAX-CSP, and its arc consistent closure

If α is the number associated with the constraint c, the counts inferred by WAC will be α times the counts that RDAC would have inferred in one direction and $(1 - \alpha)$ times the counts it would have inferred in the other direction. We can parameterise AC enforcing by modifying the Choose procedure so that instead of returning v it returns $\alpha.v$ on one side and $(1 - \alpha).v$ on the other side and conclude that AC can always yield a lower bounds that is at least as good as WAC: we start by applying Projection once on each constraint/variable with the Choose procedure parameterised by the α. The CSP obtained exhibits the same costs as WAC as unary constraints but may be non arc consistent. If we finish enforcing arc consistency using the standard Choose procedure, we only increase costs and therefore increase the lower bound. If we again consider the problem of figure 3, WAC can ideally infer a lower bound of 2, as RDAC, using eg. $\alpha = \frac{1}{2}$ for all constraints.

So, our AC enforcing algorithm provides stronger lower bounds than recent proposals. Furthermore, it preserves equivalence and is defined for non-binary constraints.

5   Propagating Local Inconsistencies

In this section we consider the possibility, for procedure Extension, of processing valuations that are not absorbing. The corresponding procedure is called Extension+ and is simply deduced from Extension by removing the test whether $v = c_i(a)$ is absorbing (see algorithm 2). Propagation of non absorbing valuations has been forbidden in the basic version in order to guarantee termination: for non absorbing valuations, the use of Extension+(i, a, c) exactly cancels the effect of a previous call to Projection(c, i, a) which my lead to infinite loops. However, termination can always be forced if it is not natural. We find agreeable, in this section, to consider AC enforcing as a local search process in the space of equivalent CSP. The criterion optimised is the lower bound ℓ. A first neighbourhood can be defined by all possible applications of Projection and Extension. Its use corresponds to the AC enforcing algorithm 2: a greedy local search process always terminates and the locally optimal CSP reached is arc consistent.

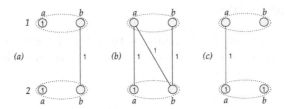

Fig. 4. Propagating non absorbing valuations may improve ℓ_{ac}

A second larger neighbourhood is defined by all possible applications of Projection and Extension+. It is particularly interesting in the context eg. of MAX-CSP where the propagation of non absorbing valuations may be the key to reach a maximum arc consistent closure. Consider the first MAX-CSP in figure 4. It includes one binary constraint that forbids pair $((1, b)(2, b))$ and two unary constraints that forbid values $(1, a)$ and $(2, a)$. The CSP is arc consistent and the corresponding lower bound ℓ_{ac} equals 0. If we apply Extension+ on value $(1, a)$ we get the equivalent CSP 4(b) which is not arc consistent. We can apply Projection on value $(2, b)$ and obtain the CSP 4(c) which is arc consistent with a corresponding lower bound $\ell_{ac} = 1$. The propagation of non absorbing valuations may allow the transport of local unary constraints from variable to variable. For some variables, this may be used to increase the minimum valuation $c_i(a)$ and therefore the lower bound ℓ_{ac}. The question whether a maximum arc consistent closure can always be reached from a given CSP using this second neighbourhood is open but obviously the first neighbourhood does not suffice. Further work is needed to determine if and how one could get similar results in an AC enforcing algorithm that always terminates.

6 Conclusion

In this paper, we have defined an extended version of arc consistency that applies to classical CSP, fuzzy CSP, weighted MAX-CSP and others. It extends the usual notion of equivalent arc consistent problem in a systematic way, including frameworks for which the notion was not available and this in the general case of non binary constraints. Several directions are still worth some attention. First of all, some work is obviously needed to turn our naive arc consistency enforcing algorithm in a tuned space and time efficient algorithm. This paper, combined with the existing arc consistency technology of AC-{6,7} should do the trick. The resulting algorithm should then be injected in tree-search algorithms for solving MAX-CSP such as PFC-MRDAC [11, 10]. More generally, the technique used in this paper to extend arc consistency should also allow the extension of most (if not all) existing local consistency properties of classical CSP to MAX-CSP and provide even stronger lower bounds.

424   Thomas Schiex

Acknowledgements

I want to sincerely thank G. Verfaillie for the stimulating discussions we always have and M. Lemaître for its comments on a first version of the paper.

References

[1] AFFANE, M. S., AND BENNACEUR, H. A weighted arc consistency technique for Max-CSP. In *Proc. of the 13th ECAI* (Brighton, United Kingdom, 1998), pp. 209–213. 411, 412, 421

[2] AFFANE, M. S., BENNACEUR, H., AND SCHIEX, T. Comparaison de deux minorants paramétriques pour Max-CSP. In *Actes de JNPC'99* (1999), pp. 95–102. 421

[3] BISTARELLI, S., FARGIER, H., MONTANARI, U., ROSSI, F., SCHIEX, T., AND VERFAILLIE, G. Semiring-based CSPs and valued CSPs: Frameworks, properties and comparison. *Constraints 4* (1999), 199–240. 413

[4] BISTARELLI, S., MONTANARI, U., AND ROSSI, F. Constraint solving over semirings. In *Proc. of the 14th IJCAI* (Montréal, Canada, Aug. 1995). 411, 412, 416

[5] BISTARELLI, S., MONTANARI, U., AND ROSSI, F. Semiring based constraint solving and optimization. *Journal of the ACM 44*, 2 (1997), 201–236. 412

[6] DUBOIS, D., AND PRADE, H. A class of fuzzy measures based on triangular norms. a general framework for the combination of uncertain information. *Int. Journal of Intelligent Systems 8*, 1 (1982), 43–61. 413

[7] FARGIER, H., AND LANG, J. Uncertainty in constraint satisfaction problems: a probabilistic approach. In *Proc. of ECSQARU '93, LNCS 747* (Grenade, Spain, Nov. 1993), pp. 97–104. 417

[8] FARGIER, H., LANG, J., AND SCHIEX, T. Selecting preferred solutions in Fuzzy Constraint Satisfaction Problems. In *Proc. of the 1st European Congress on Fuzzy and Intelligent Technologies* (1993). 417

[9] FREUDER, E., AND WALLACE, R. Partial constraint satisfaction. *Artificial Intelligence 58* (Dec. 1992), 21–70. 412

[10] LARROSA, J., MESEGUER, P., AND SCHIEX, T. Maintaining reversible DAC for Max-CSP. *Artificial Intelligence 107*, 1 (Jan. 1999), 149–163. 411, 412, 414, 421, 423

[11] LARROSA, J., MESEGUER, P., SCHIEX, T., AND VERFAILLIE, G. Reversible DAC and other improvements for solving max-CSP. In *Proc. of AAAI'98* (Madison, WI, July 1998). 411, 412, 421, 423

[12] ROSENFELD, A., HUMMEL, R., AND ZUCKER, S. Scene labeling by relaxation operations. *IEEE Trans. on Systems, Man, and Cybernetics 6*, 6 (1976), 173–184. 411

[13] SCHIEX, T. Maximizing the reversible DAC lower bound in Max-CSP is NP-hard. Tech. Rep. 1998/02, INRA, July 1998. 421

[14] SCHIEX, T., FARGIER, H., AND VERFAILLIE, G. Valued constraint satisfaction problems: hard and easy problems. In *Proc. of the 14th IJCAI* (Montréal, Canada, Aug. 1995), pp. 631–637. 411, 412, 413, 414, 417, 419

[15] SHAPIRO, L., AND HARALICK, R. Structural descriptions and inexact matching. *IEEE Transactions on Pattern Analysis and Machine Intelligence 3* (1981), 504–519. 412

[16] WALLACE, R. Directed arc consistency preprocessing. In *Selected papers from the ECAI-94 Workshop on Constraint Processing*, M. Meyer, Ed., no. 923 in LNCS. Springer, Berlin, 1994, pp. 121–137.   411, 412

Optimal Anytime Constrained Simulated Annealing for Constrained Global Optimization

Benjamin W. Wah and Yi Xin Chen

Department of Electrical and Computer Engineering
and the Coordinated Science Laboratory
University of Illinois, Urbana-Champaign
1308 West Main Street, Urbana, IL 61801, USA
{wah,chen}@manip.crhc.uiuc.edu
http://www.manip.crhc.uiuc.edu

Abstract. In this paper we propose an *optimal* anytime version of *constrained simulated annealing* (CSA) for solving constrained nonlinear programming problems (NLPs). One of the goals of the algorithm is to generate feasible solutions of certain prescribed quality using an average time of the same order of magnitude as that spent by the original CSA with an optimal cooling schedule in generating a solution of similar quality. Here, an *optimal cooling schedule* is one that leads to the shortest average total number of probes when the original CSA with the optimal schedule is run multiple times until it finds a solution. Our second goal is to design an anytime version of CSA that generates gradually improving feasible solutions as more time is spent, eventually finding a *constrained global minimum* (CGM). In our study, we have observed a monotonically non-decreasing function relating the success probability of obtaining a solution and the average completion time of CSA, and an exponential function relating the objective target that CSA is looking for and the average completion time. Based on these observations, we have designed CSA_{AT-ID}, the anytime CSA with iterative deepening that schedules multiple runs of CSA using a set of increasing cooling schedules and a set of improving objective targets. We then prove the optimality of our schedules and demonstrate experimentally the results on four continuous constrained NLPs. CSA_{AT-ID} can be generalized to solving discrete, continuous, and mixed-integer NLPs, since CSA is applicable to solve problems in these three classes. Our approach can also be generalized to other stochastic search algorithms, such as genetic algorithms, and be used to determine the optimal time for each run of such algorithms.

1 Introduction

A large variety of engineering applications can be formulated as constrained *nonlinear programming problems* (NLPs). Examples include production planning, computer integrated manufacturing, chemical control processing, and structure optimization. Some applications that are inherently constrained or have multiple

R. Dechter (Ed.): CP 2000, LNCS 1894, pp. 425–440, 2000.

objectives may be formulated as unconstrained mathematical programs due to a lack of good solution methods. Examples include applications in neural-network learning, computer-aided design for VLSI, and digital signal processing. High-quality solutions to these applications are important because they may lead to lower implementation and maintenance costs.

By first transforming multi-objective NLPs into single-objective NLPs, all constrained NLPs can be considered as single-objective NLPs. Without loss of generality, we consider only minimization problems in this paper. A general discrete constrained NLP is formulated as follows:

$$\text{minimize} \quad f(x)$$
$$\text{subject to} \quad g(x) \le 0 \quad x = (x_1, x_2, \ldots, x_n) \text{ is a vector} \quad (1)$$
$$h(x) = 0 \qquad \text{of discrete variables,}$$

where $f(x)$ is a lower-bounded objective function, $h(x) = [h_1(x), \cdots, h_m(x)]^T$ is a set of m equality constraints, and all the discrete variables in x are finite. Both $f(x)$ and $h(x)$ can be either linear or nonlinear, continuous or discrete (*i.e.* discontinuous), and analytic in closed forms or procedural. In particular, we are interested in application problems whose $f(x)$, $g(x)$, and $h(x)$ are non-differentiable. Our general formulation includes both equality and inequality constraints, although it is shown later that inequality constraints can be transformed into equality constraints. The search space (sometimes called solution space) X is the finite set of all possible combinations of discrete variables in x that may or may not satisfy the constraints. Such a space is usually limited by some bounds on the range of variables.

To characterize the solutions sought in discrete space, we define for discrete problems, $\mathcal{N}(x)$, the *neighborhood* [1] of point x in discrete space X, as a *finite* user-defined set of points $\{x' \in X\}$ such that x' is reachable from x in one step, that $x' \in \mathcal{N}(x) \Longleftrightarrow x \in \mathcal{N}(x')$, and that it is possible to reach every other x'' starting from any x in one or more steps through neighboring points. Note that neighboring points may be feasible or infeasible.

Point $x \in X$ is called a discrete *constrained local minimum* (CLM) if it satisfies two conditions: a) x is a feasible point, implying that x satisfies all the constraints $g(x) \le 0$ and $h(x) = 0$, and b) $f(x) \le f(x')$, for all $x' \in \mathcal{N}(x)$ where x' is feasible. A special case in which x is a CLM is when x is feasible and all its neighboring points are infeasible.

Point $x \in X$ is called a *constrained global minimum* (CGM) iff a) x is a feasible point, and b) for every feasible point $x' \in X$, $f(x') \ge f(x)$. According to our definitions, a CGM must also be a CLM.

In the next section we formulate the problem that we study in this paper. This is followed by a summary of the constrained simulated annealing algorithm (CSA) in Section 3 and a statistical model on the CSA procedure in Section 4. Finally, we present our proposed anytime CSA with iterative deepening in Section 5 and our experimental results in Section 6.

2   Formulation of the Problem

Constrained simulated annealing (CSA) [14] (see Section 3) has been proposed as a powerful global minimization algorithm that can guarantee asymptotic convergence to a CGM with probability one when applied to solve (1).

One of the difficulties in using CSA, like conventional *simulated annealing* (SA) [8], is to determine an *annealing schedule,* or the way that temperatures are decreased in order to allow a solution of prescribed quality to be found quickly. In general, the asymptotic convergence of CSA to a CGM with probability one was proved with respect to a cooling schedule in which temperatures are decreased in a logarithmic fashion [14], based on the original necessary and sufficient condition of Hajek developed for SA [6]. It requires an infinitely long cooling schedule in order to approach a CGM with probability one.

In practice, asymptotic convergence can never be exploited since any algorithm must terminate in finite time. There are two ways to complete CSA in finite time. The first approach uses an infinitely long logarithmically decreasing cooling schedule but terminates CSA in finite time. This is not desirable because CSA will most likely not have converged to any feasible solution when terminated at high temperatures.

The second approach is to design a cooling schedule that can complete in prescribed finite time. In this paper we use the following *geometric cooling schedule* with *cooling rate* α:

$$T_{j+1} = \alpha \times T_j, \qquad j = 0, \cdots, N_\alpha - 1, \tag{2}$$

where $\alpha < 1$, j measures the number of probes in CSA (assuming one probe is made at each temperature and all probes are independent), and N_α is the total number of probes in the schedule. A probe here is a neighboring point examined by CSA, independent of whether CSA accepts it or not. We use the number of probes expended to measure overhead because it is closely related to execution time. Given $T_0 > T_{N_\alpha} > 0$ and α, we can determine N_α, the *length of a cooling schedule,* as:

$$N_\alpha = log_\alpha \frac{T_{N_\alpha}}{T_0}. \tag{3}$$

Note that the actual number of probes in a successful run may be less than N_α, as a run is terminated as soon as a desirable solution is found. However, it should be very close to N_α, as solutions are generally found when temperatures are low.

The effect of using a finite α is that CSA will converge to a CGM with probability *less than one.* When CSA uses a finite cooling schedule N_α, we are interested in its *reachability probability* $P_R(N_\alpha)$, or the probability that it will find a CGM in any of its previous probes when it stops. Let p_j be the probability that CSA finds a CGM in its jth probe, then $P_R(N_\alpha)$ when it stops is:

$$P_R(N_\alpha) = 1 - \prod_{j=1}^{N_\alpha}(1 - p_j). \tag{4}$$

Table 1. An example illustrating trade-offs between the expected total number of probes in multiple runs of CSA to find a CGM, the cooling rate used in each run, and the probability of success in each run. The optimal cooling rate at $\alpha = 0.574$ leads to the minimum average total number of probes to find a CGM. Note that the probability of success is not the highest in one run using the optimal cooling rate. (The problem solved is defined in (6). Each cooling schedule is run 200 times using $f' = 200$.)

α	cooling rate in one run	0.139	0.281	0.429	**0.574**	0.701	0.862	0.961	0.990
N_α	avg. cooling schedule	99.8	148.0	207.5	**296.0**	434.5	798.0	2414.0	6963.5
T_α	avg. CPU time per run	0.026	0.036	0.050	**0.074**	0.11	0.18	0.54	1.58
$P_R(N_\alpha)$	succ. prob. of one run	1%	10%	25%	**40%**	55%	70%	85%	95%
$\frac{1}{P_R(N_\alpha)}$	avg. runs to find sol'n	100	10	4	**2.5**	1.82	1.43	1.18	1.05
$\frac{N_\alpha}{P_R(N_\alpha)}$	avg. probes to find sol'n	9980	1480	830	**740**	790	1140	2840	7330
$\frac{T_\alpha}{P_R(N_\alpha)}$	avg. time to find sol'n	2.6	0.36	0.20	**0.19**	0.20	0.25	0.64	1.7

Reachability can be maintained by keeping the best solution found at any time and by reporting the best solution when CSA stops.

Although the exact value of $P_R(N_\alpha)$ is hard to estimate and control, we can always improve the chance of hitting a CGM by running CSA multiple times, each using a finite cooling schedule. Given $P_R(N_\alpha)$ for each run of CSA and that all runs are independent, the expected number of runs to find a solution is $\frac{1}{P_R(N_\alpha)}$ and the expected total number of probes is:

$$\text{Expected total number of probes to find a CGM} = \sum_{j=1}^{\infty} P_R(N_\alpha)(1 - P_R(N_\alpha))^{j-1} N_\alpha j = \frac{N_\alpha}{P_R(N_\alpha)} \quad (5)$$

Table 1 illustrates trade-offs between N_α and $P_R(N_\alpha)$ in solving a constrained NLP with a 10-dimensional Rastrigin function as its objective:

$$\text{minimize} \quad f(x) = F\left(10n + \sum_{i=1}^{n}(x_i^2 - 10cos(2\pi x_i)), 200\right) \quad (6)$$

$$\text{subject to} \quad |(x_i - 4.2)(x_i + 3.2)| \leq 0.1 \quad \text{for } n = 10,$$

where F is the transformation function defined later in (11). A run of CSA is successful if it finds a feasible point with objective value less than or equal to 200 in this run, and the probability to hit a CGM is calculated by the percentage of successful runs over 200 independent runs.

Table 1 shows that $P_R(N_\alpha)$ increases towards one when α is increased. A long cooling schedule is generally undesirable because the expected number of probes in (5) is large, even though the success probability in one run of CSA approaches one. On the other hand, if the schedule is too short, then the success probability in one run of CSA is low, leading to a large expected number of probes in (5). An optimal schedule is one in which CSA is run multiple times and the expected total number of problems in (5) is the smallest.

Definition 1. *An optimal cooling schedule is one that leads to the smallest average total number of probes of multiple runs of CSA in order to find a solution of prescribed quality.*

Table 1 shows that $\frac{N_\alpha}{P_R(N_\alpha)}$ is a convex function with a minimum at $\alpha = 0.574$. That is, the average total number of probes of multiple runs of CSA to find a CGM first decreases and then increases, leading to an optimal cooling rate of 0.574 and an average of 2.5 runs of CSA to find a CGM.

This paper aims at determining an optimal cooling schedule that allows a solution of prescribed quality to be found in the shortest average amount of time. In order to find the optimal cooling schedule, users generally have to experiment by trial and error until a suitable schedule is found. Such tuning is obviously not practical in solving large complex problems. In that case, one is interested in running a single version of the algorithm that can adjust its cooling schedule dynamically in order to find a schedule close to the optimal one. Moreover, one is interested in obtaining improved solutions as more time is spent on the algorithm. Such an algorithm is an *anytime algorithm* because it always reports the best solution found if the search were stopped at any time.

The goals of this paper are two folds. First, we like to design cooling schedules for CSA in such a ways that the average time spent in generating a solution of certain quality is of the same order of magnitude as that of multiple run of the original CSA with an *optimal* cooling schedule. In other words, the new CSA is optimal in terms of average completion time up to an order of magnitude with respect to that of the original CSA with the best cooling schedule. Second, we like to design a set of objective targets that allow an anytime-CSA to generate improved solutions as more time is spent, eventually finding a CGM.

The approach we take in this paper is to first study statistically the performance of CSA. Based on the statistics collected, we propose an exponential model relating the value of objective targets sought by CSA and the average execution time, and a monotonically non-decreasing model relating the success probability of obtaining a solution and the average execution time. These models lead to the design of CSA_{AT-ID}, the anytime CSA with iterative deepening, that schedules multiple runs of CSA using a set of increasing cooling schedules that exploit the convexity of (5) and a set of improving objective targets.

Let $T_{opt}(f_i)$ be the average time taken by the original CSA with an optimal cooling schedule to find a CLM of value f_i or better, and $T_{AT-ID}(f_i)$ be the average time taken by CSA_{AT-ID} to find a CLM of similar quality. Based on the principle of iterative deepening [9], we prove the optimality of CSA_{AT-ID} by showing:

$$T_{AT-ID}(f_i) = O\left(T_{opt}(f_i)\right) \text{ where } i = 0, 1, 2, \cdots \tag{7}$$

Further, CSA_{AT-ID} returns solutions of values $f_0 > \cdots > f^*$ that are gradually improving with time.

There were many past studies on annealing schedules in SA. Schedules studied include logarithmic annealing schedules [6] that are necessary and sufficient for asymptotic convergence, schedules inversely proportional to annealing steps in FSA [13] that are slow when the annealing step is large, simulated quenching scheduling in ASA [7] that is not efficient when the number of variables is large, proportional (or geometric) cooling schedules [8] using a cooling rate between 0.8-0.99 or a rate computed from the initial and final temperatures [11], constant annealing [3], arithmetic annealing [12], polynomial-time cooling [2] adaptive temperature scheduling based on the acceptance ratio of bad moves [16], and non-equilibrium SA (NESA) [4] that operates at a non-equilibrium condition and that reduces temperatures as soon as improved solutions are found.

All the past studies aimed at designing annealing schedules that allow one run of SA to succeed in getting a desirable solution. There was no prior studies that examine trade-offs between multiple runs of SA using different schedules and the improved probability of getting a solution. Our approach in this paper is based on multiple runs of CSA, whose execution times increase in a geometric fashion and whose last run finds a solution to the application problem. Based on iterative deepening [9], the total time of all the runs will be dominated by the last run and will only be a constant factor of the time taken in the last run.

3   Constrained Simulated Annealing

In this section, we summarize our Lagrange-multiplier theory for solving discrete constrained NLPs and the adaptation of SA to look for discrete saddle points.

Consider a discrete equality-constrained NLP:

$$minimize_x \quad f(x) \tag{8}$$
$$subject\ to \quad h(x) = 0,$$

where $x = (x_1, \ldots, x_n)$ is a vector of discrete variables, and $f(x)$ and $h(x)$ are analytic in closed forms (but not necessarily differentiable) or procedural. An inequality constraint like $g_j(x) \leq 0$ can be transformed into an equivalent equality constraint $\max(g_j(x), 0) = 0$. Hence, without loss of generality, our theory only considers application problems with equality constraints.

A *generalized discrete Lagrangian function* of (8) is defined as follows:

$$L_d(x, \lambda) = f(x) + \lambda^T H(h(x)), \tag{9}$$

where H is a continuous transformation function satisfying $H(y) = 0$ iff $y = 0$.

We define a *discrete saddle point* (x^*, λ^*) with the following property:

$$L_d(x^*, \lambda) \leq L_d(x^*, \lambda^*) \leq L_d(x, \lambda^*) \tag{10}$$

for all $x \in \mathcal{N}(x^*)$ and all $\lambda \in R$. Essentially, a saddle point is one in which $L_d(x^*, \lambda)$ is at a local maximum in the λ subspace and at a local minimum in the x subspace. The concept of saddle points is very important in discrete problems because, starting from them, we can derive the first-order necessary and sufficient condition for CLM that lead to global minimization procedures. This is stated formally in the following theorem [15]:

1. **procedure CSA**
2.   set initial $\mathbf{x} = (x, \lambda)$ by randomly generating x and by setting $\lambda \leftarrow 0$;
3.   initialize temperature T_0 to be large enough and cooling rate $0 < \alpha < 1$
4.   set N_T (number of probes per temperature);
5.   **while** stopping condition is not satisfied **do**
6.   **for** $n \leftarrow 1$ **to** N_T **do**
7.   generate $\mathbf{x}'$ from $\mathcal{N}(\mathbf{x})$ using $G(\mathbf{x}, \mathbf{x}')$;
8.   accept $\mathbf{x}'$ with probability $A_T(\mathbf{x}, \mathbf{x}')$
9.   **end_for**
10.   reduce temperature by $T \leftarrow \alpha \times T$;
11.   **end_while**
12. **end_procedure**

Fig. 1. CSA: Constrained simulated annealing [15]

Theorem 1. *First-order necessary and sufficient condition for CLM. A point in the variable space of (8) is a CLM if and only if it satisfies the saddle-point condition (10).*

Figure 1 describes CSA [14] that looks for saddle points with the minimum objective value. By carrying out *probabilistic ascents* in the λ subspace with a probability of acceptance governed by a temperature, it looks for local maxima in that subspace. Likewise, by carrying out *probabilistic descents* in the x subspace, it looks for local minima in that subspace. It can be shown that the point where the algorithm stops is a saddle point in the Lagrangian space.

CSA differs from traditional SA that only has probabilistic descents in the x space, and the point where SA stops is a local minimum of the objective function of an unconstrained optimization. By extending the search to saddle points in a Lagrangian space, CSA allows constrained optimization problems to be solved in a similar way as SA in solving unconstrained optimization problems.

Using distribution $G(\mathbf{x}, \mathbf{x}')$ to generate trial point $\mathbf{x}'$ in neighborhood $\mathcal{N}(\mathbf{x})$, a Metropolis acceptance probability $A_T(\mathbf{x}, \mathbf{x}')$, and a logarithmic cooling schedule, CSA has been proven to have asymptotic convergence with probability one to a CGM. This is stated in the following theorem without proof [14].

Theorem 2. *Asymptotic convergence of CSA. The Markov chain modeling CSA converges to a CGM with probability one.*

Although Theorems 1 and 2 were derived for discrete constrained NLPs, it is applicable to continuous and mixed-integer constrained NLPs if all continuous variables were first discretized. Discretization is acceptable in practice because numerical evaluations of continuous variables using digital computers can be considered as discrete approximation of the original variables up to a computer's precision. Intuitively, if discretization is fine enough, the solutions found are fairly good approximations to the original solutions. Due to space limitations, we do not discuss the accuracy of solutions found in discretized problems [17]. In the rest of this paper, we apply CSA to solve constrained NLPs, assuming that continuous variables in continuous and mixed-integer NLPs are first discretized.

4   Performance Modeling of CSA

The performance of a CSA procedure to solve a given application problem from a random starting point can be measured by the probability that it will find a solution of a prescribed quality when it stops and the average time it takes to find the solution. There are many parameters that will affect how CSA performs, such as neighborhood size, generation probability, probability of accepting a point generated, initial temperature, cooling schedule, and relaxation of objective function. In this section, we focus on the relationship among objective targets, cooling schedules, and probabilities of finding a desirable solution.

4.1   Relaxation of Objective Target

One way to improve the chance of finding a solution by CSA is to look for CLM instead of CGM. An approach to achieve this is stop CSA whenever it finds a CLM of a prescribed quality. This approach is not desirable in general because CSA may only find a CLM when its temperatures are low, leading to little difference in times between finding CLM and CGM. Further, it is necessary to prove the asymptotic convergence of the relaxed CSA procedure.

A second approach that we adopt in this paper is to modify the constrained NLP in such a way that a CLM of value smaller than f' in the original NLP is considered a CGM in the relaxed NLP. Since the CSA procedure is unchanged, its asymptotic convergence behavior remains the same. The relaxed NLP is obtained by transforming the *objective target* of the original NLP:

$$F(f(x), f') = \begin{cases} f' & \text{if } f(x) \leq f' \\ f(x) & \text{if } f(x) > f' . \end{cases} \qquad (11)$$

Assuming that f^* is the value of the CGM in the original NLP, it follows that the value of the CGM of the relaxed NLP is f^* if $f' \leq f^*$ and is f' if $f' > f^*$. Moreover, since the relaxed problem is a valid NLP solvable by CSA, CSA will converge asymptotically to a CGM of the relaxed NLP with probability one.

As a relaxed objective function leads to a possibly larger pool of solution points, we expect CSA to have a higher chance of hitting one of these points during its search. This property will be exploited in CSA_{AT-ID} in Section 5.2.

4.2   Exponential Model Relating f' and N_α for Fixed $P_R(N_\alpha)$

In order to develop CSA_{AT-ID} that dynamically controls its objective targets, we need to know the relationship between f', the degree of objective relaxation, and N_α, the number of probes in one run of CSA, for a fixed $P_R(N_\alpha)$. In this section we find this relationship by studying the statistical behavior in evaluating four continuous NLPs by CSA.

Figure 2 shows a 3-D graph relating the parameters in solving (6), in which $P_R(N_\alpha)$ was obtained by running CSA 200 times for each combination of N_α and f'. It shows an exponentially decreasing relationship between f'

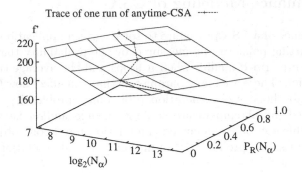

Trace of one run of anytime-CSA ······

Fig. 2. A 3-D graph showing an exponentially decreasing relationship between f' and N_α and a monotonically non-decreasing relationship between $P_R(N_\alpha)$ and N_α when CSA is applied to solve (6). The dotted line shows the trace taken in a run of CSA_{AT-ID}

Table 2. The averages and standard deviations of coefficient of determination R^2 on linear fits of f' and $log_2(N_\alpha)$ for fixed $P_R(N_\alpha)$

Benchmark	Mean(R^2)	Std. Dev.(R^2)
G1 [10]	0.9389	0.0384
G2 [10]	0.9532	0.0091
Rastrigin	0.9474	0.0397
Problem 5.2 [5]	0.9461	0.0342

and N_α at fixed $P_R(N_\alpha)$ and a monotonically non-decreasing relationship between $P_R(N_\alpha)$ and N_α at fixed f'. These observations lead to the following exponential model:

$$N_\alpha = ke^{-af'} \quad \text{for fixed } P_R(N_\alpha) \text{ and positive real constants } a \text{ and } k. \quad (12)$$

To verify statistically our proposed model, we performed experiments on several benchmarks of different complexities: G1, G2 [10], Rastrigin (6), and Floudas and Pardalos' Problem 5.2 [5]. For each problem, we collected statistics on f' and N_α at various $P_R(N_\alpha)$, regressed a linear function on f' and $log_2(N_\alpha)$ to find a best fit, and calculated the coefficient of determination R^2 of the fit. Table 2 summarizes the average and standard deviation of R^2 of the linear fit for each test problem, where R^2 very close to 1 shows a good fit. Since R^2 has averages very close to one and has small standard deviations, f' is verified to be exponential with respect to N_α at fixed $P_R(N_\alpha)$.

4.3 Sufficient Conditions for the Existence of $N_{\alpha_{opt}}$

In order for $N_{\alpha_{opt}}$ to exist at fixed f', $\frac{N_\alpha}{P_R(N_\alpha)}$ in (5) must have an absolute minimum in $(0, \infty)$. Such a minimum exists if $P_R(N_\alpha)$ satisfies the following

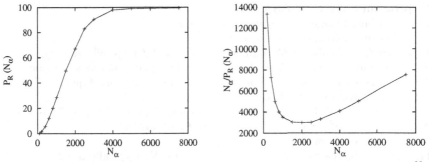

a) $P_R(N_\alpha)$ satisfies the two sufficient conditions   b) Absolute minimum in $\frac{N_\alpha}{P_R(N_\alpha)}$

Fig. 3. An example showing the existence of an absolute minimum in $\frac{N_\alpha}{P_R(N_\alpha)}$ when CSA was applied to solve (6) with $f' = 180$. ($N_{\alpha_{opt}} \approx 2000$)

sufficient conditions: a) $P_R(0) = 0$ and $\lim_{N_\alpha \to \infty} P_R(N_\alpha) = 1$, and b) $P_R''(0) > 0$. We do not show the proof of these conditions due to space limitation.

We collected statistics on $P_R(N_\alpha)$ and N_α at various f' for each of the four test problems studied in Section 4.2. The results indicate that $P_R(N_\alpha)$ satisfies the two sufficient conditions, implying that $\frac{N_\alpha}{P_R(N_\alpha)}$ has an absolute minimum in $(0, \infty)$. In other words, each of these problems has an optimal cooling schedule $N_{\alpha_{opt}}$ that minimizes $\frac{N_\alpha}{P_R(N_\alpha)}$ at fixed f'. Figure 3 illustrates the existence of such an optimal schedule in applying CSA to solve (6) with $f' = 180$. The experimental results also show that $P_R(N_\alpha)$ is monotonically nondecreasing.

Note that there is an exponential relationship between $P_R(N_\alpha)$ and N_α in part of the range of $P_R(N_\alpha)$ (say between 0.2 and 0.8) in the problems tested. We do not exploit this relationship because it is not required by the iterative deepening strategy studied in the next section. Further, the relationship is not satisfied when $P_R(N_\alpha)$ approaches 0 or 1.

It is interesting to point out that the second sufficient condition is not satisfied when searching with random probing. In this case, $P_R(N_\alpha) = 1 - (1 - \frac{1}{S})^{N_\alpha}$, and $P_R''(0) = -ln^2(1 - \frac{1}{S}) < 0$, where S is the number of states in the search space. Hence, $\frac{N_\alpha}{P_R(N_\alpha)}$ at fixed f' does not have an absolute minimum of N_α in $(0, \infty)$.

5   Anytime CSA with Iterative Deepening

We propose in this section CSA_{AT-ID} with two components. In the first component discussed in Section 5.1, we design a set of cooling schedules for multiple runs of the original CSA so that (7) is satisfied; that is, the average total number of probes to find a CLM of value f' or better is of the same order of magnitude as $T_{opt}(f')$. In the second component presented in Section 5.2, we design a schedule to decrease objective target f' in CSA_{AT-ID} that allows it to find f^* using an average total number of probes of the same order of magnitude as $T_{opt}(f^*)$.

1. **procedure anytime-CSA**
2.   set initial target of solution quality at $f' = \infty$;
3.   set initial cooling rate $\alpha = \alpha_0$;
4.   set K = number of CSA runs at fixed α and f (typically $K = 3$);
5.   **repeat** /* Lines 5-15 are for gradually improving solutions of value f' */
6.   **repeat** /* Lines 6-12 are for generating a solution of quality f' */
7.   **for** $i \leftarrow 1$ **to** K **do**
8.   evaluate CSA with transformed objective $F(f(x), f')$ and α;
9.   **if** CSA succeeded **then goto** 13; **end_if**
10.   **end_for**
11.   increase cooling schedule $N_\alpha \leftarrow \rho \times N_\alpha$ (typically $\rho = 2$);
12.   **until** number of probes in target f' exceeded 10 times
           the number of probes in previous target level;
13.   **if** ($f' == \infty$) **then** $f' = f_0$; **end_if** /* f_0 is first fesasible solution found */
14.   reduce target level $f' \leftarrow f' - c$;
15.   **until** no better solution was found in two successive decreases of f';
16. **end_procedure**

Fig. 4. CSA_{AT-ID}: Anytime-CSA procedure with iterative deepening. The only problem-dependent run-time information used is f_0.

CSA_{AT-ID} in Figure 4 first finds low-quality feasible solutions in relatively small amounts of time. It then tightens its requirement gradually, tries to find a solution at each quality level, and outputs the best solution when it stops.

It is important to point out that CSA_{AT-ID} does not use regression at run time in order to find the values of parameters of (12). One reason is that these problem-dependent parameters are hard to estimate. Rather, CSA_{AT-ID} exploits the exponential relationship between f' and N_α and the monotonically nondecreasing relationship between $P_R(N_\alpha)$ and N_α in order to derive a set of CSA runs with different parameters. The only run-time information used in CSA_{AT-ID} is f_0, the value of the first feasible solution found with an initial objective target of $f' = \infty$.

5.1   Finding a Solution Using Increasing Cooling Schedules

Lines 6-12 in Figure 4 are used to evaluate CSA using a set of cooling schedules, each involving multiple runs of CSA, in order to carry out iterative deepening [9] and to achieve geometric growth in the number of probes in successive schedules. By choosing an appropriate number of runs under each cooling schedule, we like to show that the total average overhead over all the schedules is dominated by that of the last schedule and is of the same order of magnitude as the average overhead of multiple run of the original CSA with the best cooling schedule.

Our approach in Lines 6-12 of Figure 4 starts with an objective target $f' = \infty$ and a cooling rate $\alpha = \alpha_0$, corresponding to a fast cooling schedule $N_0 = N_{\alpha_0}$. We propose to use a set of geometrically increasing cooling schedules:

$$N_i = \rho^i N_0, \qquad i = 0, 1, \ldots \tag{13}$$

where N_0 is the (fast) initial cooling schedule. Under each cooling schedule, CSA is run multiple times for a maximum of K times but stops immediately when a solution is found. For iterative deepening to work, $\rho > 1$.

Let $P_R(N_i)$ be the reachability probabilities of one run of CSA under cooling schedule N_i. Let $\beta(f')$ be the expected total number of probes taken by Lines 6-12 in Figure 4 to find a solution with objective target f' starting from schedule N_0, and $B_{opt}(f')$ be the expected total number of probes taken by the original CSA with optimal $N_{\alpha_{opt}}$ to find a solution of similar quality. According to (5),

$$B_{opt}(f') = \frac{N_{\alpha_{opt}}}{P_R(N_{\alpha_{opt}})} \tag{14}$$

The following theorem shows the sufficient conditions in order for $\beta(f')$ to be of the same order of magnitude as $B_{opt}(f')$. Due to space limitation, we do not show the proof here.

Theorem 3. $\beta(f') = O(B_{opt}(f'))$ *if*

a) $P_R(N_\alpha)$ *is monotonically non-decreasing for* N_α *in* $(0, \infty)$;
b) $P_R(0) = 0$, *and* $\lim_{N_\alpha \to \infty} P_R(N_\alpha) = 1$;
c) $P_R''(0) > 0$; *and*
d) $(1 - P_R(N_{\alpha_{opt}}))^K \rho < 1$.

The proof is not shown due to space limitations. Typically, $\rho = 2$, and in all the benchmarks tested, $P_R(N_{\alpha_{opt}}) \geq 0.25$. Substituting these values into the last condition in Theorem 3 yields $K > 2.4$. In our experiments, we have used $K = 3$. Since a maximum of three runs of CSA are done under each cooling schedule, $B_{opt}(f')$ is of the same order of magnitude as *one* run of CSA with the optimal cooling schedule.

5.2 Anytime Search Using Decreasing Objective Targets

After finding a solution of quality f' using Lines 6-12 in Figure 4, Line 14 adjusts f' to a new objective target so that better solutions will be found if more time is allowed. (If this were the first time that a feasible solution was found, then Line 13 updates f' to f_0, the value of first feasible solution with an initial objective target of $f' = \infty$.) Based on the exponential model in (12) and the principle of iterative deepening [9], the average number of probes to find a solution of value f' grows geometrically if f' is decreased using the following *linear schedule*:

$$f_{j+1} = f_j - c, \text{ where } c \text{ is a positive constant.} \tag{15}$$

In our experiments, we estimate c to be 10% of f_0.

Let $\gamma(f_n)$ be the expected total number of probes CSA_{AT-ID} takes to find f_n, using objective targets $f_0, f_1, \ldots, f_n$. The following theorem proves the relative complexities of $\gamma(f_n)$ and $B_{opt}(f_n)$.

Table 3. Comparison between $\overline{T}_{AT-ID}$ and $\overline{T}_{CSA}$ in solving four constrained NLPs with transformed objective $F(f(x), f')$. $\overline{N}_{\alpha_{succ}}$ is the average length of the cooling schedule when a desirable solution was found using Lines 6-12 of CSA_{AT-ID}. $N_{\alpha_{opt}}$ is the length of the optimal cooling schedule for the target objective

Problem ID	f^*	Target f'	CSA_{AT-ID}			CSA			$\frac{\overline{T}_{AT-ID}}{\overline{T}_{CSA}}$
			N_0	$\overline{N}_{\alpha_{succ}}$	$\overline{T}_{AT-ID}$	$N_{\alpha_{opt}}$	$P_R(N_{\alpha_{opt}})$	$\overline{T}_{CSA}$	
G2	-0.8036	-0.803	220	4640	9.176	5800	0.56	7.375	1.244
Rastrigin	162.6630	163.0	200	4560	3.964	3400	0.43	2.010	1.972
5.2	1.5670	1.7	2310	108100	595.662	136400	0.55	208.211	2.861
7.3	0.9705	1.3	450	515840	1105.948	829440	0.60	555.916	1.989

Theorem 4. $\gamma(f_n) = O(B_{opt}(f_n))$.

Proof. According to (12), and (14),

$$B_{opt}(f_i) = \frac{N_{\alpha_{opt}}}{P_R(N_{\alpha_{opt}})} = \Theta(e^{-af_i}). \tag{16}$$

Hence, using the result in Theorem 3,

$$\gamma(f_n) = \sum_{i=0}^{n} \beta(f_i) = \sum_{i=0}^{n} O(B_{opt}(f_i)) = \sum_{i=0}^{n} O(e^{-af_i})$$

$$= \sum_{i=0}^{n} O(e^{-a(f_0-ic)}) = O(e^{-a(f_0-nc)}) = O(B_{opt}(f_n)) \tag{17}$$

The theorem shows that, despite finding solutions of intermediate quality defined by a linear sequence of improving objective targets, the overall complexity is dominated by that in finding solutions to the last objective target f_n. In particular, we have established (7) by showing that $T_{AT-ID}(f^*) = O(T_{opt}(f^*))$.

6   Experimental Results

We tested CSA_{AT-ID} on four continuous constrained NLPs of different sizes and degrees of difficulty. G2 [10] and Rastrigin (6) are relatively easy NLPs with multiple feasible regions. In particular, (6) is characterized by a large number of deep infeasible local minima in the objective function. Finally, Floudas and Pardalos' Problems 5.2 and 7.3 [5] are large and difficult NLPs with many equality constraints. Although our experiments were on continuous NLPs, similar performance is expected for discrete and mixed-integer constrained NLPs.

Table 3 compares $\overline{T}_{AT-ID}$, the average time taken by Lines 6-12 in Figure 4 to obtain a CGM to the four benchmark NLPs with transformed objective

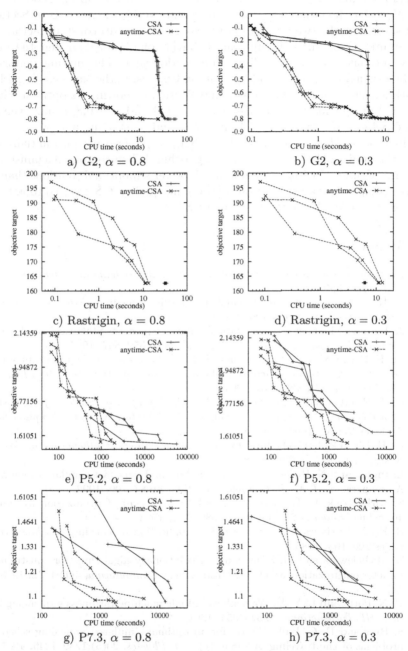

Fig. 5. Performance comparison of CSA_{AT-ID} and CSA in solving four continuous constrained minimization NLPs. CPU times were measured on Pentium 500-MHz computers running Solaris 2.7. α is the cooling rate of the original CSA

$F(f(x), f')$, and $\bar{T}_{CSA}$, the average time of CSA with an optimal cooling schedule $N_{\alpha_{opt}}$ for the objective target. The results verify the analysis in Section 5.1 and show that the two averages are related by a (small) constant factor.

Figure 5 compares the anytime behavior of CSA_{AT-ID} and the original CSA in terms of solution quality and execution time. The anytime performance of the original CSA was found by running CSA using the same cooling schedule multiple times until a CGM was found. Without knowing its optimal schedule, we tried two geometric schedules with $\alpha = 0.3$ and $\alpha = 0.8$, respectively. CSA and CSA_{AT-ID} were each ran from three random starting points.

In general, the results show that CSA_{AT-ID} performs substantially better than the original CSA as an anytime algorithm. When compared against a given amount of time, CSA_{AT-ID} found much better suboptimal solutions than CSA. When compared against solutions of the same quality, CSA_{AT-ID} took between one to two orders less CPU time than CSA.

References

1. E. Aarts and J. Korst. *Simulated Annealing and Boltzmann Machines*. J. Wiley and Sons, 1989. 426
2. E. H. L. Aarts. A new polynomial-time cooling schedule. *Proc. of the IEEE Int. Conf. on CAD-85*, pages 206–208, 1985. 430
3. J. Bernasconi. Low autocorrelation binary sequences: Statistical mechanics and configuration space analysis. *J. Physique*, 48(4):559–567, 1987. 430
4. M. F. Cardoso, R. L. Salcedo, and S. F. de Azevedo. Non-equilibrium simulated annealing: A faster approach to combinatorial minimization. *Industrial Eng. Chemical Research*, 33:1908–1918, 1994. 430
5. C. A. Floudas and P. M. Pardalos. *A Collection of Test Problems for Constrained Global Optimization Algorithms*, volume 455 of *Lecture Notes in Computer Science*. Springer-Verlag, 1990. 433, 437
6. B. Hajek. Cooling schedules for optimal annealing. *Mathematics of Operations Research*, 13(2):311–329, 1988. 427, 429
7. L. Ingber and N. Rosen. Genetic algorithms and very fast simulated re-annealing: A comparison. *J. Math. Comput. Modelling*, 16:87–100, 1992. 430
8. S. Kirkpatrick, C. D. Gelatt, Jr., and M. P. Vecchi. Optimization by simulated annealing. *Science*, 220(4598):671–680, May 1983. 427, 430
9. R. Korf. Heuristics as invariants and its application to learning. *Machine Learning*, pages 100–103, 1985. 429, 430, 435, 436
10. Z. Michalewicz and M. Schoenauer. Evolutionary algorithms for constrained parameter optimization problems. *Evolutionary Computation*, 4(1):1–32, 1996. 433, 437
11. C. N. Potts and L. N. V. Wassenhove. Single machine tardiness sequencing heuristics. *IIE Transactions*, 23:346–354, 1991. 430
12. S. Rees and B. C. Ball. Citeria for an optimal simulated annealing schedule for problems of the traveling salesman type. *J. Physics*, 20(5):1239–1249, 1987. 430
13. H. Szu and R. Hartley. Fast simulated annealing. *Phys. Lett. A*, 122(3-4):157–162, 1987. 430
14. B. W. Wah and T. Wang. Simulated annealing with asymptotic convergence for nonlinear constrained global optimization. *Principles and Practice of Constraint Programming*, pages 461–475, Oct. 1999. 427, 431

440   Benjamin W. Wah and Yi Xin Chen

15. B. W. Wah and Z. Wu. The theory of discrete Lagrange multipliers for nonlinear discrete optimization. *Principles and Practice of Constraint Programming*, pages 28–42, Oct. 1999. 430, 431
16. Y. Wang, W. Yan, and G. Zhang. Adaptive simulated annealing for optimal design of electromagnetic devices. *IEEE Trans. on Magnetics*, 32(3):1214–1217, 1996. 430
17. Z. Wu. *The Theory and Applications of Nonlinear Constrained Optimization using Lagrange Multipliers*. Ph.D. Thesis, Dept. of Computer Science, Univ. of Illinois, Urbana, IL, Aug. 2000. 431

SAT v CSP

Toby Walsh[*]

University of York, York, England
tw@cs.york.ac.uk

Abstract. We perform a comprehensive study of mappings between constraint satisfaction problems (CSPs) and propositional satisfiability (SAT). We analyse four different mappings of SAT problems into CSPs, and two of CSPs into SAT problems. For each mapping, we compare the impact of achieving arc-consistency on the CSP with unit propagation on the SAT problem. We then extend these results to CSP algorithms that maintain (some level of) arc-consistency during search like FC and MAC, and to the Davis-Putnam procedure (which performs unit propagation at each search node). Because of differences in the branching structure of their search, a result showing the dominance of achieving arc-consistency on the CSP over unit propagation on the SAT problem does not necessarily translate to the dominance of MAC over the Davis-Putnam procedure. These results provide insight into the relationship between propositional satisfiability and constraint satisfaction.

1 Introduction

Despite their proximity, there has been little direct comparison between propositional satisfiability and constraint satisfaction. One of the most immediate differences is that propositional satisfiability (SAT) problems have binary domains and non-binary constraints whilst constraint satisfaction problems (CSPs) typically have binary constraints and non-binary domains. However, a more intimate understanding of the similarities and differences between the two problem domains would aid research in both areas. For example, are local search procedures developed for SAT like WalkSAT and Novelty useful for CSPs?

One method for exploring the relationship between SAT problems and CSPs is to study mappings between them. As each problem class is NP-complete, we can reduce one into the other in polynomial time. However, the details of such reductions and the properties preserved can, as we show here, be very informative. Bennaceur previously looked at encoding SAT problems as CSPs [Ben96], whilst Génisson and Jégou looked at encoding CSPs as SAT problems [GJ96]. However, both these studies were limited to a single mapping. It is therefore instructive to study the range of mappings possible between SAT problems and CSPs. A more complete picture of the relationship between propositional satisfiability and constraint satisfaction then starts to emerge.

[*] The author is supported by an EPSRC advanced research fellowship. The author is a member of the APES research group (http://www.cs.strath.ac.uk/~apes) and wishes to thank the other members for their comments and feedback.

R. Dechter (Ed.): CP 2000, LNCS 1894, pp. 441–456, 2000.
© Springer-Verlag Berlin Heidelberg 2000

2   Formal Background

A constraint satisfaction problem (CSP) consists of a set of variables, each with a domain of values, and a set of constraints (relations) on the allowed values for specified subsets of the variables. A binary CSP has only binary constraints. A binary CSP is arc-consistent (AC) iff it has non-empty domains and every binary constraint is arc-consistent. A binary constraint is arc-consistent iff any assignment to one of the variables in the constraint can be extended to a consistent assignment for the other variable. A (non-binary) CSP is generalized arc-consistent (GAC) iff for any variable in a constraint and value that it is assigned, there exist compatible values for all the other variables in the constraint [MM88]. Algorithms for solving CSPs typically maintain some level of consistency at every node in their search tree. For example, the MAC algorithm for binary CSPs maintains arc-consistency at each node in the search tree [Gas79]. The FC algorithm (forward checking) for binary CSPs maintains arc-consistency only on those constraints involving the most recently instantiated variable and those that are uninstantiated. Finally, for non-binary CSPs, the nFC0 algorithm maintains generalized arc-consistency on those constraints involving one uninstantiated variable, whilst the nFC1 algorithm maintains generalized arc-consistency on those constraints and constraint projections involving one uninstantiated variable [BMFL99].

Given a propositional formula, the satisfiability (SAT) problem is to determine if there is an assignment of truth values to the variables that makes the whole formula true One of the best procedures to solve the SAT problem is the so-called Davis-Putnam (DP) procedure (though it is actually due to Davis, Logemann and Loveland [DLL62]). The DP procedure consists of three main rules: the empty rule (which fails and backtracks when an empty clause is generated), the unit propagation rule (which deterministically assigns any unit literal), and the branching or split rule (which non-deterministically assigns a truth value to a variable). As is often the case in implementations of DP, we will ignore the pure literal and tautology rules as neither are needed for completeness or soundness, nor usually for efficiency.

3   Encoding SAT into CSPs

There are several different ways that a SAT problem can be encoded as a binary or non-binary CSP.

Dual encoding: We associate a dual variable, D_i with each clause c_i. The domain of D_i consists of those tuples of truth values which satisfy the clause c_i. For example, associated with the clause $x_1 \vee x_3$ is a dual variable D_1 with domain $\{\langle T, F \rangle, \langle F, T \rangle, \langle T, T \rangle\}$. These are the assignments for x_1 and x_3 which satisfy the clause $x_1 \vee x_3$. Binary constraints are posted between dual variables which are associated with clauses that share propositional variables in common. For example, between the dual variable D_1 associated with the clause $x_1 \vee x_3$ and the dual variable D_2 associated with the clause $x_2 \vee \neg x_3$ is a binary constraint that the second element of the tuple assigned to D_1 must be the complement of the second element of the tuple assigned to D_2.

Hidden variable encoding: We again associate a dual variable, D_i with each clause c_i, the domain of which consists of those tuples of truth values which satisfy the clause. However, we also have (propositional) variables x_i with domains $\{T, F\}$. A binary constraint is posted between a propositional variable and a dual variable if its associated clause mentions the propositional variable. For example, between the dual variable D_2 associated with the clause $x_2 \vee \neg x_3$ and the variable x_3 is a binary constraint. This constrains the second element of the tuple assigned to D_2 to be the complement of the value assigned to x_3. There are no direct constraints between dual variables.

Literal encoding: We associate a variable, D_i with each clause c_i. The domain of D_i consists of those literals which satisfy the clause c_i. For example, associated with the clause $x_1 \vee x_3$ is a dual variable D_1 with domain $\{x_1, x_3\}$, and associated with the clause $x_2 \vee \neg x_3$ is a dual variable D_2 with domain $\{x_2, \neg x_3\}$. Binary constraints are posted between D_i and D_j iff the associated clause c_i contains a literal whose complement is contained in the associated clause c_j. For example, there is a constraint between D_1 and D_2 as the clause c_1 contains the literal x_3 whilst the clause c_2 contains the complement $\neg x_3$. This constraint rules out incompatible (partial) assignments. For instance, between D_1 and D_2 is the constraint that allows $D_1 = x_1$ and $D_2 = x_2$, or $D_1 = x_1$ and $D_2 = \neg x_3$, or $D_1 = x_3$ and $D_2 = x_2$. However, the assignment $D_1 = x_3$ and $D_2 = \neg x_3$ is ruled out as a nogood. Note that the literal encoding uses variables with smaller domains than the dual or hidden variable encodings. The dual variables have domains of size $O(2^k)$ where k is the clause length, whilst the variables in the literal encoding have domains of size just $O(k)$. This could have a significant impact on runtimes.

Non-binary encoding: The CSP has variables x_i with domains $\{T, F\}$. A non-binary constraint is posted between those variables that occurring together in a clause. This constraint has as nogoods those partial assignments that fail to satisfy the clause. For example, associated with the clause $x_1 \vee x_2 \vee \neg x_3$ is a non-binary constraint on x_1, x_2 and x_3 that has a single nogood $\langle F, F, T \rangle$.

4   Theoretical Comparison

We now compare the performance of the Davis-Putnam (DP) procedure against some popular CSP algorithms like FC and MAC on these different encodings. Our analysis divides into two parts. We first compare the effect of unit propagation on the SAT problem and enforcing arc-consistency on the encoding. We then use this result to compare DP (which performs unit propagation at each node in its search tree) with MAC (which enforces arc-consistency at each node) and FC (which enforces a limited form of arc-consistency). When comparing two algorithms that are applied to (possibly) different representations of a problem, we say that algorithm A dominates algorithm B iff algorithm A visits no more branches than algorithm B assuming "equivalent" branching heuristics (we will discuss what we mean by "equivalent" in the proofs of such results as the exact details depend on the two representations). We say that algorithm A strictly dominates algorithm B iff it dominates and there exists one problem on which algorithm A visits strictly fewer branches.

4.1   Dual Encoding

We first prove that enforcing arc-consistency on the dual encoding does more work than unit propagation on the original SAT problem. That is, if unit propagation identifies unsatisfiability then enforcing arc-consistency on the dual encoding also does (but there are problems which enforcing arc-consistency will show are insoluble that unit propagation will not). In addition, if unit propagation commits to particular truth assignments then enforcing arc-consistency on the dual encoding eliminates all contradictory values. To be more precise, if unit propagation assigns true (false) to some variable x_i, enforcing arc-consistency on the dual encoding removes those values from the domains of dual variables which correspond to assigning false (true) to x_i. When we come to assign these dual variables, the value chosen will correspond to assigning true (false) to x_i.

Theorem 1.

1. *If unit propagation commits to particular truth assignments, then enforcing arc-consistency on the dual encoding eliminates all contradictory values.*
2. *If unit propagation generates the empty clause then enforcing arc-consistency on the dual encoding causes a domain wipeout (but the reverse does not necessarily hold).*

Proof. 1. Suppose unit propagation makes a sequence of assignments: l_1, l_2, $\dots l_j$. The proof uses induction on j. Consider the final assignment l_j. Unit propagation makes this assignment because l_j occurs in a clause $l'_1 \vee \dots l'_k$ in which all the other literals l'_i ($\neq l_j$) have been assigned to false. Consider the dual variable associated with this clause. By the induction hypothesis, enforcing arc-consistency eliminates all values which assign any of the l'_i ($\neq l_j$) to true. Hence, the only value left in the domain of this dual variable assigns l'_i ($\neq l_j$) to false, and l_j to true. Enforcing arc-consistency on the dual encoding thus eliminates all contradictory values.

2. Unit propagation generates an empty clause if there is a clause, $l_1 \vee \dots l_k$ in which unit propagation assigns each literal l_i to false. Consider the dual variable associated with this clause. By the first result, enforcing arc-consistency on the dual encoding eliminates all contradictory values. Hence this dual variable has a domain wipeout. To show that the reverse may not hold, consider all possible 2-SAT clauses in 2 variables: $x_1 \vee x_2$, $\neg x_1 \vee x_2$, $x_1 \vee \neg x_2$, $\neg x_1 \vee \neg x_2$. This problem does not contain any unit clauses so unit propagation does nothing. However, enforcing arc-consistency on the dual encoding causes a domain wipeout.

There are difficulties in extending this result to algorithms that maintain (some form of) arc-consistency at each node of their search tree (like FC and MAC) and those that perform unit propagation at each node (like DP). One complication is that branching in DP can instantiate variables in any order, but branching on the dual encoding must follow the order of variables in the clauses. In addition, branching on the dual encoding effectively instantiates all the variables in a clause at once. In DP, by comparison, we can instantiate a strict subset of the variables that occur in a clause. Consider, for example, the two clauses $x_1 \vee \ldots x_k$ and $y_1 \vee \ldots y_k$. DP can instantiate the x_i and y_j in any order. By comparison, branching on the dual encoding either instantiates all the x_i before the y_j or vice versa. Similar observations hold for the literal encodings. In the following results, therefore, we start from a branching heuristic for the dual encoding and construct an "equivalent" branching heuristic for DP. It is not always possible to perform the reverse (i.e. start from a DP heuristic and construct an equivalent heuristic for the dual encoding).

Theorem 2. *Given equivalent branching heuristics, DP strictly dominates FC applied to the dual encoding.*

Proof. We show how to take the search tree explored by FC and map it onto a proof tree for DP with no more branches. The proof proceeds by induction on the number of branching points in the tree. Consider the root. Assume FC branches on the variable D_i associated with the SAT clause $l_1 \vee l_2 \vee \ldots \vee l_k$. There are $2^k - 1$ children. We can build a corresponding proof subtree for DP with at most $2^k - 1$ branches. In this subtree, we branch left at the root assigning l_1, and right assigning $\neg l_1$. On both children, we branch left again assigning l_2 and right assigning $\neg l_2$ unless l_2 is assigned by unit propagation (in which case, we move on to l_3). And so on through the l_i until either we reach l_k or unit propagation constructs an empty clause. Note that we do not need to split on l_k as unit propagation on the clause $l_1 \vee l_2 \vee \ldots \vee l_k$ forces this instantiation automatically. In the induction step, we perform the same transformation except some of the instantiations in the DP proof tree may have been performed higher up and so can be ignored. FC on the dual encoding removes some values from the domains of future variables, but unit propagation in DP also effectively makes the same assignments. The result is a DP proof tree which has no more branches than the tree explored by FC. To show strictness, consider a 2-SAT problem with all possible clauses in two variables: e.g. $x_1 \vee x_2$, $\neg x_1 \vee x_2$, $x_1 \vee \neg x_2$, $\neg x_1 \vee \neg x_2$. DP explores 2 branches showing that this problem is unsatisfiable, irrespective of the branching heuristic. FC, on the other hand, explores 3 branches, again irrespective of the branching heuristic.

Theorem 2 shows that DP, in a slightly restricted sense, dominates FC applied to the dual encoding. What happens if we maintain a higher level of consistency in the dual encoding than that maintained by FC? Theorem 1 shows that enforcing arc-consistency on the dual encoding does more work than unit propagation. This would suggest that MAC (which enforces arc-consistency at each node) might outperform DP (which performs unit propagation at each node). DP's branching can, however, be more effective than MAC's. As a consequence, there are problems on which DP outperforms MAC, and problems on which MAC outperforms DP, in both cases irrespective of the branching heuristics used.

Theorem 3. *MAC applied to the dual encoding is incomparable to DP.*

Proof. Consider a k-SAT problem with all 2^k possible clauses: $x_1 \vee x_2 \vee \ldots \vee x_k$, $\neg x_1 \vee x_2 \vee \ldots \vee x_k$, $x_1 \vee \neg x_2 \vee \ldots \vee x_k$, $\neg x_1 \vee \neg x_2 \vee \ldots \vee x_k$, $\ldots \neg x_1 \vee \neg x_2 \vee \ldots \vee \neg \neg x_k$. DP explores 2^{k-1} branches showing that this problem is unsatisfiable irrespective of the branching heuristic. If $k = 2$, MAC proves that the problem is unsatisfiable without search. Hence, MAC can outperform DP. If $k > 2$, MAC branches on the first variable (whose domain is of size $2^k - 1$) and backtracks immediately. Hence MAC takes $2^k - 1$ branches, and is outperformed by DP.

4.2   Hidden Variable Encoding

We first prove that enforcing arc-consistency on the hidden variable encoding does the same work as unit propagation on the original SAT problem. In particular, unit propagation identifies unsatisfiability if and only if enforcing arc-consistency also does, whilst unit propagation commits to particular truth assignments if and only if enforcing arc-consistency on the hidden variable encoding eliminates all contradictory values.

Theorem 4.

1. *Unit propagation commits to a particular truth assignment if and only if enforcing arc-consistency on the hidden variable encoding eliminates all contradictory values.*
2. *Unit propagation generates the empty clause if and only if enforcing arc-consistency on the hidden variable encoding causes a domain wipeout.*

Proof. 1. Suppose unit propagation makes a sequence of assignments: l_1, l_2, $\ldots l_j$. The proof uses induction on j. Consider the final assignment l_j. Unit propagation makes this assignment because l_j occurs in a clause $l'_1 \vee \ldots l'_k$ in which all the other literals l'_i ($\neq l_j$) have been assigned to false. Consider the hidden variable encoding. By the induction hypothesis, enforcing arc-consistency reduces the domain of each l'_i ($\neq l_j$) to false. Enforcing arc-consistency therefore removes any value from the domain of the dual variable associated with the clause $l'_1 \vee \ldots l'_k$ which assigns l'_i ($\neq l_j$) to true. Hence, the only value left in the domain of this dual variable assigns l'_i ($\neq l_j$) to false, and l_j to true. Enforcing arc-consistency on the constraint between this dual variable and l_j reduces the domain of l_j to true. Hence, enforcing arc-consistency on the hidden variable encoding eliminates all contradictory values. The proof reverses in a straightforward manner.

2. Unit propagation generates an empty clause if there is a clause, $l_1 \vee \ldots l_k$ in which unit propagation assigns each literal l_i to false. Consider the dual variable associated with this clause. By the first result, enforcing arc-consistency on the

hidden variable encoding reduces the propositional variable associated with each literal l_i to the appropriate singleton domain. Hence enforcing arc-consistency between these propositional variables and the dual variable in the hidden variable encoding causes a domain wipeout for the dual variable. The proof again reverses in a straightforward manner.

This result can be extended to algorithms that maintain (some level of) arc-consistency during search, provided we restrict ourselves to branching heuristics that instantiate propositional variables before the associated dual variables. It is then unproblematic to branch in an identical fashion in the hidden variable encoding and in the SAT problem.

Theorem 5. *Given equivalent branching heuristics, MAC applied to the hidden variable encoding explores the same number of branches as DP.*

Proof. We show how to take the search tree explored by DP and map it onto a proof tree for MAC with the same number of branches (and vice versa). The proof proceeds by induction on the number of propositional variables. In the step case, consider the first variable branched upon by DP or MAC. The proof divides into two cases. Either the first branch leads to a solution. Or we backtrack and try both truth values. In either case, as unit propagation and enforcing arc-consistency reduce both problems equivalently, we have "equivalent" subproblems. As these subproblems have one fewer variable, we can appeal to the induction hypothesis.

What happens if we maintain a lower level of consistency in the hidden variable encoding that that maintained by MAC? For example, what about the FC algorithm which enforces only a limited form of arc-consistency at each node? Due to the topology of the constraint graph of a hidden variable encoding, with equivalent branching heuristic, FC can be made to explore the same number of branches as MAC.

Theorem 6. *Given equivalent branching heuristics, FC applied to the hidden variable encoding explores the same number of branches as MAC.*

Proof. In FC, we need a branching heuristic which chooses first any propositional variable with a singleton domain. This makes the same commitments as unit propagation, without introducing any branching points. By Theorem 4, unit propagation is equivalent to enforcing arc-consistency on the hidden variable encoding. Hence, FC explores a tree with the same number of branches as MAC.

4.3   Literal Encoding

As with the hidden variable encoding, enforcing arc-consistency on the literal encoding does the same work as unit propagation on the original SAT problem. In particular, unit propagation identifies unsatisfiability if and only if enforcing arc-consistency on the literal encoding also does, whilst unit propagation commits to a particular (partial) truth assignment if and only if enforcing arc-consistency on the literal encoding eliminates all contradictory values.

Theorem 7.

1. *Unit propagation commits to particular truth assignments if and only if enforcing arc-consistency on the literal encoding eliminates all contradictory values.*

2. *Unit propagation generates the empty clause if and only if enforcing arc-consistency on the literal encoding causes a domain wipeout.*

Proof. 1. Suppose unit propagation makes a sequence of assignments: l_1, l_2, ... l_j. The proof uses induction on j. Consider the final assignment l_j. Unit propagation makes this assignment because l_j occurs in a clause $l'_1 \vee \ldots l'_k$ in which all the other literals l'_i ($\neq l_j$) have been assigned to false. Consider the literal encoding. By the induction hypothesis, enforcing arc-consistency removes l'_i ($\neq l_j$) from the domain of the variables D_i associated with the clause $l'_1 \vee \ldots l'_k$. D_i therefore has the singleton domain $\{l_j\}$. Enforcing arc-consistency with any constraint between this dual variable and another that contains $\neg l_j$ removes $\neg l_j$ from the domain. Hence, enforcing arc-consistency on the literal encoding eliminates all contradictory values. The proof reverses in a straightforward manner.

2. Unit propagation generates an empty clause if there is a clause, $l_1 \vee \ldots l_k$ in which unit propagation assigns each literal l_i to false. Consider the variable D_i associated with this clause. By the first result, enforcing arc-consistency on the literal encoding eliminates each literal from its domain. This causes a domain wipeout. The proof again reverses in a straightforward manner.

When we consider algorithms that maintain arc-consistency at each node, we discover that DP can branch more effectively than MAC on the literal encoding (as we discovered with the dual encoding). Since unit propagation in the SAT problem is equivalent to enforcing arc-consistency on the literal encoding, DP dominates MAC applied to the literal encoding.

Theorem 8. *Given equivalent branching heuristic, DP strictly dominates MAC applied to the literal encoding.*

Proof. We show how to take the search tree explored by MAC and map it onto a proof tree for DP with no more branches. The proof proceeds by induction on the number of branching points in the tree. Consider the root. Assume MAC branches on the variable D_i associated with the SAT clause $l_1 \vee l_2 \vee \ldots \vee l_k$. There are k children, the ith child corresponding to the value l_i assigned to D_i. We can build a corresponding proof subtree for DP with k branches. In this subtree, we branch left at the root assigning l_1, and right assigning $\neg l_1$. On the right child, we branch left again assigning l_2 and right assigning $\neg l_2$. And so on through the l_i until we reach l_k. However, we do not need to split on l_k as unit propagation on the clause $l_1 \vee l_2 \vee \ldots \vee l_k$ forces this instantiation automatically. Schematically, this transformation is as follows:

$$node(l_1, l_2, \ldots, l_k) \Rightarrow node(l_1, node(l_2, \ldots node(l_{k-1}, l_k) \ldots)).$$

In the induction step, we perform the same transformation except: (a) some of the instantiations in the DP proof tree may have been performed higher up and so can be ignored, and (b) the complement of some of the instantiations may have been performed higher up and so we can close this branch by unit propagation. The result is a DP proof tree which has no more branches than the tree explored by MAC. To prove strictness, consider a k-SAT problem with all 2^k possible clauses where $k > 2$. DP explores 2^{k-1} branches showing that this problem is unsatisfiable irrespective of the branching heuristic. However, MAC takes $k!$ branches whatever variable and value ordering we use.

4.4   Non-binary Encoding

If the SAT problem contains clauses with more than two literals, the non-binary encoding contains non-binary constraints. Hence, we compare unit propagation on the SAT problem with enforcing generalized arc-consistency on the non-binary encoding. Not surprisingly, generalized arc-consistency on the non-binary encoding dominates unit propagation.

Theorem 9.

1. *If unit propagation commits to particular truth assignments then enforcing generalized arc-consistency on the non-binary encoding eliminates all contradictory truth values.*
2. *If unit propagation generates the empty clause then enforcing generalized arc-consistency on the non-binary encoding causes a domain wipeout (but the reverse does not necessarily hold).*

Proof. 1. Suppose unit propagation makes a sequence of assignments: l_1, l_2, ... l_j. The proof uses induction on j. Consider the final assignment l_j. Unit propagation makes this assignment because l_j occurs in a clause $l'_1 \lor \ldots l'_k$ in which all the other literals l'_i ($\neq l_j$) have been assigned to false. Consider the non-binary encoding. By the induction hypothesis, enforcing generalized arc-consistency removes those values which assign l'_i ($\neq l_j$) to false. Enforcing generalized arc-consistency on the non-binary constraint involving l'_i eliminates the truth value that assigns false to l_j. Hence, enforcing generalized arc-consistency on the non-binary encoding eliminates all contradictory values.

2. Unit propagation generates an empty clause if there is a clause, $l_1 \lor \ldots l_k$ in which unit propagation assigns each literal l_i to false. By the first result, enforcing generalized arc-consistency on the non-binary encoding eliminates each truth value which assigns l_i to true. Consider the non-binary associated with this clause. Enforcing generalized arc-consistency on this constraint causes a domain wipeout. To show that the proof does not reverse even if we are in a polynomial subclass of SAT, consider a 2-SAT problem with all possible clauses in two variables: e.g. $x_1 \lor x_2$, $\neg x_1 \lor x_2$, $x_1 \lor \neg x_2$, $\neg x_1 \lor \neg x_2$. Enforcing (generalized) arc-consistency shows that this problem is insoluble, whilst unit propagation does nothing.

With equivalent branching heuristics, DP explores the same size search tree as nFC0, the weakest non-binary version of the forward checking algorithm. DP is, however, dominated by nFC1 (the next stronger non-binary version of forward checking) and thus an algorithm that maintains generalized arc-consistency at each node.

Theorem 10. *Given equivalent branching heuristics, DP explores the same number of branches as nFC0 applied to the non-binary encoding.*

Proof. We show how to take the proof tree explored by DP and map it onto a search tree for nFC0 with the same number of branches. The proof proceeds by induction on the number of propositional variables. In the step case, consider the first variable branched upon by DP. The proof divides into two cases. Either this is a branching point (and we try both possible truth values). Or this is not a branching point (and unit propagation makes this assignment). In the first case, we can branch in the same way in nFC0. In the second case, forward checking in nFC0 will have reduced the domain of this variable to a singleton, and we can also branch in the same way in nFC0. We now have a subproblem with one fewer variable, and appeal to the induction hypothesis. The proof reverses in a straightforward manner.

Theorem 11. *Given equivalent branching heuristics, nFC1 applied to the non-binary encoding strictly dominates DP.*

Proof. Trivially nFC1 dominates nFC0. To show strictness, consider a 3-SAT problem with all possible clauses in 3 variables: $x_1 \lor x_2 \lor x_3$, $\neg x_1 \lor x_2 \lor x_3$, $x_1 \lor \neg x_2 \lor x_3$, $\neg x_1 \lor \neg x_2 \lor x_3$, $x_1 \lor x_2 \lor \neg x_3$, $\neg x_1 \lor x_2 \lor \neg x_3$, $x_1 \lor \neg x_2 \lor \neg x_3$, $\neg x_1 \lor \neg x_2 \lor \neg x_3$. DP takes 4 branches to prove this problem is unsatisfiable whatever branching heuristic is used. nFC1 by comparison takes just 2 branches. Suppose we branch on x_1. The binary projection of the non-binary constraints on x_1, x_2 and x_3 onto x_1 and x_2 is the empty (unsatisfiable) constraint. Hence, forward checking causes a domain wipeout.

5 Encoding CSPs into SAT

We now consider mappings in the reverse direction. There are two common ways to encode a (binary) CSP as a SAT problem.

Direct encoding: We associate a propositional variable, x_{ij} with each value j that can be assigned to the CSP variable X_i. We have clauses that ensures each CSP variable is given a value: for each i, $x_{i1} \lor \ldots x_{im}$. We optionally have clauses that ensure each variable takes no more than one values: for each i, j, k with $j \neq k$, $\neg x_{ij} \lor \neg x_{ik}$. Finally, we have (binary) clauses that rule out any (binary) nogoods. For example, if $X_1 = 2$ and $X_3 = 1$ is not allowed then we have the clause $\neg x_{12} \lor \neg x_{31}$.

Log encoding: We have $n\lceil \log_2(m) \rceil$ propositional variables. The propositional variable x_{ij} is set iff the CSP variable X_i is assigned a value in which the j-th bit is set. We have a clause for each (binary) nogood. For example, if $X_1 = 2$

and $X_3 = 1$ is not allowed, and each CSP variable has the domain $\{0, 1, 2, 3\}$ then we have the clause $x_{10} \vee \neg x_{11} \vee x_{20} \vee \neg x_{21}$ (which is logically equivalent to $(\neg x_{10} \wedge x_{11}) \rightarrow \neg(\neg x_{20} \wedge x_{21})$). Note that we do not need clauses to ensure that each CSP variable is given a value, nor to ensure that each CSP variable is given only one value (any complete assignment for the propositional variables corresponds to an assignment of a single value to each CSP variable). If $\lceil \log_2(m) \rceil > \log_2(m)$ then we also have clauses that rule out (spurious) values at the top of each domain. For example, if variable X_i has only 3 values, then we have a clause $\neg x_{30} \vee \neg x_{31}$ which prohibits us assigning a fourth value to X_3.

5.1   Direct Encoding

We first prove that enforcing arc-consistency on the original problem does more work than unit propagation on the direct encoding.

Theorem 12.

1. *If unit propagation commits to particular truth assignments on the direct encoding, then enforcing arc-consistency on the original problem eliminates all contradictory values.*
2. *If unit propagation generates the empty clause in the direct encoding then enforcing arc-consistency on the original problem causes a domain wipeout (but the reverse does not necessarily hold).*

Proof. 1. Suppose unit propagation makes a sequence of assignments: l_1, l_2, ... l_j. The proof uses induction on j. Consider the final assignment l. Unit propagation makes this assignment because l occurs in a clause in which all the other literals have been assigned to false. The proof divides into three cases. If the clause is of the form $x_{i1} \vee \ldots x_{im}$ then, by the induction hypothesis, enforcing arc-consistency eliminates from the domain of X_i all but the value assigned by l. Hence all contradictory values have been eliminated for X_i. If the clause is of the form $\neg x_{ij} \vee \neg x_{pq}$ and (without loss of generality) $l = \neg x_{ij}$ then, by the induction hypothesis, enforcing arc-consistency eliminates the value q from the domain of X_p. Hence, enforcing arc-consistency on the constraint associated with the clause $\neg x_{ij} \vee \neg x_{pq}$ eliminates j from the domain of X_i. Hence all contradictory values have been eliminated for X_i. Finally, if the clause is of the form $\neg x_{ij} \vee \neg x_{ik}$ where $j \neq k$ and (without loss of generality) $l = \neg x_{ij}$ then X_i has been assigned the value k (and so cannot be assigned the contradictory value j).

2. Unit propagation generates an empty clause if there is a clause, $l_1 \vee \ldots l_k$ in the direct encoding in which unit propagation assigns each literal l_i to false. The proof divides into three cases. If the clause is of the form $x_{i1} \vee \ldots x_{im}$ then, by the first result, enforcing arc-consistency on the direct encoding eliminates all contradictory values. Hence X_i has a domain wipeout. The other two cases are similar. To show that the reverse may not hold, consider a CSP in two variables and two values in which there is a binary constraint ruling out every possible assignment. The direct encoding of this problem does not contain any unit clauses so unit propagation does nothing. However, enforcing arc-consistency causes a domain wipeout.

With equivalent branching heuristics, DP applied to the direct encoding explores the same size search tree as the forward checking algorithm FC applied to the original problem. DP is, however, dominated by MAC. Given equivalent branching heuristics, DP applied to the direct encoding also explores the same size search tree as the nFC0 algorithm applied to a non-binary problem. DP is again dominated by nFC1.

Theorem 13. *Given equivalent branching heuristics, DP applied to the direct encoding explores the same number of branches as FC applied to the original problem.*

Proof. We show how to take the proof tree explored by DP and map it onto a search tree for FC with the same number of branches. The proof proceeds by induction on the number of propositional variables. In the step case, consider the first variable branched upon by DP. The proof divides into two cases. Either this is a branching point (and we try both possible truth values). Or this is not a branching point (and unit propagation makes this assignment). In the first case, we can branch in the same way in FC. In the second case, forward checking in FC will have reduced the domain of this variable to a singleton, and we can also branch in the same way in FC. We now have a subproblem with one fewer variable, and appeal to the induction hypothesis. The proof reverses in a straightforward manner.

Theorem 14. *Given equivalent branching heuristics, MAC applied to the original problem strictly dominates DP applied to the direct encoding.*

Proof. MAC trivially dominates DP applied to the direct encoding since MAC dominates FC which itself dominates DP applied to the direct encoding. To show strictness, consider again the CSP in two variables and two values in which each possible assignment is ruled out. MAC solves this without search whilst DP takes two branches on the direct encoding.

5.2   Log Encoding

We first prove that unit propagation on the log encoding is less effective than unit propagation on the direct encoding. As enforcing arc-consistency on the original problem is more effective than unit propagation on the direct encoding, it follows by transitivity that enforcing arc-consistency on the original problem is more effective than unit propagation on the log encoding.

Theorem 15.

1. *If unit propagation commits to particular truth assignments on the log encoding, then unit propagation commits to the same truth assignments on the direct encoding.*
2. *If unit propagation generates the empty clause in the log encoding then unit propagation generates the empty clause in the direct encoding then (but the reverse does not necessarily hold).*

Proof. 1. Suppose unit propagation makes a sequence of assignments in the log encoding: l_1, l_2, ... l_j. The proof uses induction on j. Consider the final assignment l. Unit propagation makes this assignment because l occurs in a clause in which all the other literals have been assigned to false. By construction, this will assign $\lceil \log_2(m) \rceil$ (i.e. all) bits associated with one CSP variable and $\lceil \log_2(m) \rceil - 1$ (i.e. all but one) bits associated with another. That is, one variable will have a value assigned, By the induction hypothesis, unit propagation will have assigned the propositional variable associated with this value to true. Hence, unit propagation on the clause associated with this nogood will set the other variable (and thus its last bit).

2. Unit propagation generates an empty clause in the log encoding if there is a clause, $l_1 \vee \ldots l_k$ in which unit propagation assigns each literal l_i to false. This means that two CSP variables are effectively assigned values which contradict the nogood associated with this clause. By the first result, enforcing arc-consistency on the direct encoding makes the same assignments. Hence unit propagation on the direct encoding also generates an empty clause. To show that the reverse may not hold, consider a CSP in two variables, the first with one value, the second with four values, all o incompatible with the first value. Then unit propagation on the direct encoding generates the empty clause, but not on the log encoding.

With equivalent branching heuristics, the forward checking algorithm FC applied to the original problem strictly dominates DP applied to the log encoding. To simplify the proof, we assume that the branching heuristic in FC enumerates values in (numerical) order. The ability of FC to assign values in any order gives it an even greater edge over DP applied to the log encoding.

Theorem 16. *Given equivalent branching heuristics, FC applied to the original problem strictly dominates DP applied to the log encoding.*

Proof. We map the search tree explored by FC onto a proof tree for DP with at least as many branches. The proof proceeds by induction on the number of CSP variables. In the step case, consider the first variable x_1 branched upon by FC. We assume FC orders the values for this variable numerically. We branch in DP on x_{i0} then x_{i1}, ... $x_{i\lceil \log_2(m) \rceil}$. We now have a CSP subproblem with one fewer variable, and appeal to the induction hypothesis. To show strictness, consider a CSP in two variables, both with 3 values, in which all pairs of assignments are nogood. FC will take 3 branches to show that the problem is insoluble. DP on the log encoding will take 8 branches since both bits for one variable and one bit for the second variable must be set before we generate the empty clause.

6 Related Work

Bennaceur studied the literal encoding for encoding SAT problems as CSPs [Ben96]. He proved that enforcing arc-consistency on the literal encoding is equivalent to unit propagation. We re-prove this result and extend it to arc-inconsistency. Bennaceur also proved that a CSP is arc-consistent iff its literal encoding has no unit clauses, and strong path-consistent iff it has no unit or binary clauses. The direct encoding of a CSP into a SAT problem appears in [dK89]. Génisson and Jégou proved that, with suitable branching heuristics, DP is equivalent to FC applied to the direct encoding [GJ96].

Apt has also looked at propagation rules for Boolean constraints [A99]. He proves an equivalence between Boolean constraint propagation and unit propagation, and between Boolean constraint propagation and generalized arc-consistency. Our results complete the triangle, characterizing the relationship between generalized arc-consistency and unit propagation.

Frisch and Peugniez studied the performance of local search procedures like WalkSAT on encodings of non-Boolean formulae into propositional satisfiability [FP99]. The unary and binary encodings studied there are closely related to the direct and log encodings of CSPs into SAT problems studied here.

Bacchus and van Beek present a study of encodings of non-binary CSPs into binary CSPs [BvB98]. The dual and hidden variable encodings studied here can be constructed by composing the non-binary encoding of SAT problems into non-binary CSPs, with the dual and hidden variable encodings of non-binary CSPs into binary CSPs. Bacchus and van Beek's work is limited to the FC algorithm and a simple extension called FC+. Stergiou and Walsh look at the maintenance of higher levels of consistency, in particular arc-consistency within these encodings [SW99]. They prove that arc-consistency on the dual encoding is strictly stronger than arc-consistency on the hidden variable, and this itself is equivalent to generalized arc-consistency on the original non-binary CSP.

7   Conclusions

We have performed a comprehensive study of mappings between constraint satisfaction problems (CSPs) and propositional satisfiability (SAT). We analysed four different mappings of SAT problems into CSPs: the dual, hidden variable, literal and non-binary encodings. We proved that achieving arc-consistency on the dual encoding does more work than unit propagation on the original SAT problem, whilst achieving arc-consistency on the hidden variable and literal encodings does essentially the same work. We then extended these results to algorithms that maintain some level of arc-consistency during search like FC and MAC, and DP which performs unit propagation at each search node. DP strictly dominates FC applied to the dual encoding, is incomparable to MAC applied to the dual encoding, explores the same number of branches as MAC applied to the hidden variable encoding, and strictly dominates MAC applied to the literal encoding. We also analysed two different mappings of CSPs into SAT problems: the direct and log encodings. We proved that unit propagation on the direct encoding does less work than achieving arc-consistency on the original problem, but more work than unit propagation on the log encoding. DP on the direct encoding explores the same size search tree as FC applied to the original problem, but is strictly dominated by MAC. By comparison, DP on the log encoding is strictly dominated by both FC and MAC applied to the original problem.

What general lessons can be learned from this study? First, the choice of encoding can have a large impact on the level of consistency achieved. For instance, the dual encoding allows us to achieve higher levels of consistency than the literal encoding. Second, the choice of encoding also has a large impact on the branching structure of our search trees. In particular, the dual and literal encodings require us to branch using a variable ordering based upon the clauses. DP applied to the original SAT problem can therefore sometimes beat MAC applied to the dual encoding. Fourth, whilst a clearer picture of the relationship between SAT problems and CSPs is starting to emerge, there are several questions that remain unanswered. For example, how do local search methods like GSAT and Min-Conflicts compare on these different encodings?

References

A99.   K. Apt. Some Remarks on Boolean Constraint Propagation. In New Trends in Constraints, Papers from the Joint ERCIM/Compulog-Net Workshop. Springer, 1999. 454

Ben96.   H. Bennaceur. The satisfiability problem regarded as a constraint satisfaction problem. In W. Wahlster, editor, *Proc. of the 12th ECAI*, pages 155–159. European Conference on Artificial Intelligence, Wiley, 1996. 441, 453

BMFL99.   C. Bessière, P. Meseguer, E. C. Freuder, and J. Larrosa. On Forward Checking for Non-binary Constraint Satisfaction. In A. Brodsky and J. Jaffar, editors, *Proc. of Fifth International Conference on Principles and Practice of Constraint Programming (CP99)*. Springer, 1999. 442

BvB98.   F. Bacchus and P. van Beek. On the conversion between non-binary and binary constraint satisfaction problems. In *Proc. of 15th National Conference on Artificial Intelligence*, pages 311–318. AAAI Press/The MIT Press, 1998. 454

dK89.   J. de Kleer. A comparison of ATMS and CSP techniques. In *Proc. of the 11th IJCAI*. International Joint Conference on Artificial Intelligence, 1989. 454

DLL62.   M. Davis, G. Logemann, and D. Loveland. A machine program for theorem-proving. *Communications of the ACM*, 5:394–397, 1962. 442

FP99.   A. M. Frisch and T. J. Peugniez. Solving non-Boolean satisfiability problems with stochastic local search: A comparison of encodings., 1999. Unpublished manuscript, available from http://www.cs.york.ac.uk/aig/publications.html. 454

Gas79.   J. Gaschnig. Performance measurement and analysis of certain search algorithms. Technical report CMU-CS-79-124, Carnegie-Mellon University, 1979. PhD thesis. 442

GJ79.   M. R. Garey and D. S. Johnson. *Computers and intractability : a guide to the theory of NP-completeness*. W. H. Freeman, 1979.

GJ96.   R. Genisson and P. Jegou. Davis and Putnam were already forward checking. In W. Wahlster, editor, *Proc. of the 12th ECAI*, pages 180–184. European Conference on Artificial Intelligence, Wiley, 1996. 441, 454

MM88.   R. Mohr and G. Masini. Good old discrete relaxation. In *Proc. of the 8th ECAI*, pages 651–656, European Conference on Artificial Intelligence, 1988. 442

SW99.   K. Stergiou and T. Walsh. Encodings of non-binary constraint satisfaction problems. In *Proc. of the 16th National Conference on AI*. American Association for Artificial Intelligence, 1999. 454

Instruction Scheduling with Timing Constraints on a Single RISC Processor with 0/1 Latencies

Hui Wu, Joxan Jaffar, and Roland Yap

School of Computing
National University of Singapore
{wuh,joxan,ryap}@comp.nus.edu.sg

Abstract. In this paper, We propose a faster algorithm for the following instruction scheduling problem: Given a set of UET (Unit Execution Time) instructions with precedence constraints in the form of a DAG(Directed Acyclic Graph), latency constraints where latencies between any two instructions are restricted to be either 0 or 1, timing constraints in the form of individual integer release times and deadlines and a single RISC processor, find a feasible schedule which satisfies all constraints. The time complexity of our algorithm is $O(n^2 \log n) + min\{O(ne), O(n^{2.376})\}$, where n is the number of instructions and e is the number of edges in the precedence graph. Our algorithm is faster than the existing algorithm which runs in $O(n^3 \alpha(n))$ time, where $\alpha(n)$ is the inverse of Ackermann function. In addition, our algorithm can be used to solve the maximum lateness minimization problem in $O(n^2 \log^2 n + min\{ne, n^{2.376}\})$ time.

1 Introduction

Scheduling instructions in a basic block [8] on RISC processors is a classic problem in compiler optimization. A basic block consists of a set of instructions with precedence constraints, where precedence between two instructions denotes their data dependency. On RISC processors, an instruction is issued every machine cycle. However, there are often delays between instructions. These delays are called inter-instructional latencies, or latencies for short. They arise primarily because of off-chip communication and pipelining in the architecture. If the latency between instruction I_i and instruction I_j is k, then instruction I_j can be executed only after k time units has elapsed since I_i finishes. Throughout this paper, we assume that the time unit is one machine cycle. In the normal computation where no timing constraint exists, the objective of instruction scheduling is to find the shortest schedule. Even on a single processor with an arbitrary maximum latency, the problem of finding the shortest schedule for a basic block is hard. Hennessy and Gross [8] showed that finding the shortest schedule for a basic block on a single RISC processor with a maximum latency of $m - 1 (m \geq 2)$ is at least as hard as finding the shortest schedule on m identical processors without latency. If m is a part of the problem instance, then the problem is NP-complete [8,7,2]; for any fixed $m \geq 3$ the time complexity of finding the

R. Dechter (Ed.): CP 2000, LNCS 1894, pp. 457–469, 2000.

shortest schedule is still open. However, finding the shortest schedule on a single processor with a maximum latency of 1 can be solved in polynomial time. If all latencies are 1, then this single processor scheduling problem can be solved by Coffman and Graham's two processor scheduling algorithm [6,5,7]; if each latency is either 0 or 1, then this problem can be solved by the modified Coffman and Graham's algorithm [5]. Since Coffman and Graham's algorithm works on transitively closed or transitively reduced DAG (Directed Acyclic Graph) and it takes $O(min(en, n^{2.376}))$ time to compute the transitive closure [18,16], where n is the number of instructions and e is the number of edges in the precedence graph, these algorithms runs in $O(min(en, n^{2.376}))$ time.

Recently, RISC processors are being used more and more in embedded systems such as automobile brake systems. In embedded systems, computation is subject to timing constraints. Typical timing constraints are in the form of individual release times and deadlines. The release time of an instruction specifies the earliest time at which the instruction can start. The deadline of an instruction specifies the latest time by which the instruction must finish. In the presence of timing constraints, the objective of instruction scheduling is to find a feasible schedule which satisfies all constraints. In the case that no feasible schedule exists, the scheduling objective is to minimize the maximum lateness of all instructions over all schedules σ, i.e. minimize $max\{\sigma(I_k) - d_k\}$, where d_k is the preassigned deadline of instruction I_k and $\sigma(I_k)$ is the start time of instruction I_k in schedule σ. Palem and Simon proposed an approximation algorithm for scheduling instructions with deadline constraints in a basic block on multiple RISC processors [2]. The time complexity of their algorithm is $O(ne + e' \log n)$, where e' is the number of edges in the transitively closed precedence graph. Their algorithm can find a feasible schedule whenever one exists in the case of a single processor with a maximum latency of 1. Bruno et al [6] proposed an $O(n^3)$ algorithm for scheduling instructions with precedence constraints, individual integer release times and deadlines on a single pipelined processor with two stages(all latencies are 1). Leung, Palem and Pnueli [1] studied instruction scheduling in a basic block with both release time constraints and deadline constraints on multiple RISC processors. They proposed an approximation algorithm with time complexity of $O(n^3\alpha(n))$, where $\alpha(n)$ is the functional inverse of Ackermann function. Their algorithm can find a feasible schedule whenever one exists in the case of a single processor with a maximum latency of 1.

In this paper, we propose a faster algorithm for scheduling instructions with arbitrary precedence constraints, 0/1 latencies, individual integer release times and deadlines on a single RISC processor. The time complexity of our algorithm is $O(min(ne, n^{2.376}) + n^2 \log n)$. Our algorithm is based on computing *successor-tree-consistent deadline* for each instruction. The successor-tree-consistent deadline of each instruction is tighter than its preassigned deadline. We show that by using successor-tree-consistent deadline of each instruction as its priority, list scheduling [19] will find a feasible schedule whenever one exists. To make the computation of successor-tree-consistent deadlines faster, our algorithm uses a number of techniques such as *forward scheduling*, *backward scheduling* and binary search. Our algorithm can be used to solve the maximum lateness minimization problem in $O(n^2 \log^2 n + min\{ne, n^{2.376}\})$ time by using binary search.

2   Model and Definitions

The instruction scheduling problem studied in this paper is described as follows. Given a problem instance P: a set $V = \{I_1, I_2, \cdots, I_n\}$ of UET(Unit Execution Time) instructions, a set of precedence constraints in the form of a DAG $G = (V, E)$, where $E = \{(I_i, I_j) : I_j$ can start only after I_i completes $\}$, a set $L = \{l_{ij} : l_{ij} \in \{0, 1\}$ and $(I_i, I_j) \in E$ and instruction I_j can be executed only after l_{ij} time units has elapsed since I_i finishes$\}$ of latency constraints, a set $RT = \{r_i : r_i$ is a non-negative integer and I_i cannot start earlier than $r_i\}$ of release time constraints and a set $D = \{d_i : d_i$ is a natural number and I_i must finish before $d_i\}$ of deadline constraints, compute a feasible schedule on a single RISC processor whenever one exists. A schedule $\sigma : V \rightarrow \{0, 1, 2, \cdots\}$ on a single processor is called a *valid schedule* if it satisfies both constraints $C1$ and $C2$.

$C1$ Resource constraint: $\forall t \in [0, \infty)(|\{I_i \in V : \sigma(I_i) \leq t < \sigma(I_i) + 1\}| \leq 1)$, i.e. at most one instruction can be executed at any time.

$C2$ Precedence and latency constraints: $\forall (I_i, I_j) \in E(\sigma(I_i) + 1 + l_{ij} \leq \sigma(I_j))$.

$C3$ Release time and deadline constraints: $\forall I_i \in V(r_i \leq \sigma(I_i) < d_i)$

σ is called a *feasible schedule* if $C3$ is also satisfied.

Given a DAG G and two instructions I_i and I_j in V, if there is a directed path from I_i to I_j, then I_i is a *predecessor* of I_j and I_j is a *successor* of I_i. Especially, if $(I_i, I_j) \in E$, then I_i is an *immediate predecessor* of I_j and I_j is an *immediate successor* of I_i. If instruction I_i has no immediate successor, then I_i is a *sink instruction*; if I_i has no immediate predecessor, I_i is a *source instruction*. A successor I_j of I_i is called   1-*successor* if (i) I_j is an immediate successor of I_i and $l_{ij} = 1$; or (ii) I_j is a successor of some immediate successor of I_i. Throughout this paper, the set of all successors of instruction I_i is denoted by $Succ(I_i)$. The number of elements in a set U is denoted by $|U|$.

Definition 1. *Given a problem instance P, a set D of deadlines of all instructions is called* edge consistent *if $d_j \geq d_i + 1 + l_{ij}$ holds for each edge $(I_i, I_j) \in E$; a set RT of release times of all instructions is called* edge consistent *if $r_j \geq r_i + 1 + l_{ij}$ holds for each edge $(I_i, I_j) \in E$.*

Definition 2. *Given a DAG $G = (V, E)$ and an instruction $I_i \in V$, the successor tree of I_i is a directed tree $G(I_i) = (V, E(I_i))$, where $E(I_i) = \{(I_i, I_j) : I_j \in Succ(I_i)$ in $G\}$.*

The key idea of our algorithm is to compute the successor-tree-consistent deadline for each instruction. Given a problem instance P and an instruction I_i, its successor-tree-consistent deadline is an upper bound on the latest completion time of I_i in any feasible schedule for a relaxed problem instance $P'(i)$. One of the key differences between $P'(i)$ and P is that in $P'^{(i)}$ the new precedence constraints are the successor tree $G(i)$ instead of G in P. The complete definitions of the successor-tree-consistent deadline and $P'(i)$ will be given in Section 4. The successor-tree-consistent deadline of an instruction is tighter than its preassigned deadline. It is also tighter than the edge the consistent deadline.

To compute the successor-tree-consistent deadlines faster, our algorithm uses binary search. However, binary search is not applicable in a straightforward way. The preprocessing which involves *forbidden regions* must be performed before the binary search can be done.

Definition 3. *Given a feasible schedule σ for a problem instance P, an instruction I_i is called σ-rigid if $\sigma(I_i) = d_i - 1$ or the instruction scheduled in time slot $[\sigma(I_i) + 1, \sigma(I_i) + 2)$ is σ-rigid.*

Intuitively, if an instruction I_i is σ-rigid, it cannot be moved to any time slot after $\sigma(I_i)$ so that the resulting schedule is still feasible. When our algorithm computes the successor-tree-consistent deadline of an instruction I_i, σ-rigid instructions are used to determine all time slots in which I_i cannot be scheduled in any feasible schedule. If a time slot $[t, t + 1)$ cannot be used to schedule instruction I_i in any feasible schedule, it is called *forbidden slot*. In a schedule σ for P, a time interval $[t_1, t_2)$ is called a *forbidden region* if (i) all time slots $[t_1, t_1+1), [t_1+1, t_1+2), \cdots, [t_2 - 1, t_2)$ are forbidden slots, and (ii) neither $[t_1 - 1, t_1)$ nor $[t_2, t_2 + 1)$ is a forbidden slot. In a schedule σ for P, a time interval $[t_1, t_2)$ is called a *hole* if 1) for each time slot $[t_1, t_1 + 1), [t_1 + 1, t_1 + 2), \cdots, [t_2 - 1, t_2)$, no instruction is scheduled in it, and 2) there is an instruction scheduled in each of time slots $[t_1 - 1, t_1)$ and $[t_2, t_2 + 1)$.

3   Forward Scheduling and Backward Scheduling

In our algorithm, both *forward scheduling* and *backward scheduling* are used to compute the successor-tree-consistent deadline of each non-sink instruction. In both forward scheduling and backward scheduling, both precedence constraints and latency constraints are ignored. The forward scheduling is a greedy scheduling technique where each instruction is scheduled as early as possible. In contrast to forward scheduling, backward scheduling schedules each instruction as late as possible. Forward scheduling is performed in the increasing direction of time, while the backward scheduling is done in the decreasing direction of time. In forward scheduling, an instruction I_i is *ready* at time t if $t \geq r_i$. Whereas, an instruction I_i is ready at time t in backward scheduling if $t \leq d_i - 1$. In forward scheduling, we use *Earliest Deadline First* (EDF) strategy, i.e. among all ready instructions the instruction that has the earliest deadline will be scheduled. In backward scheduling, we ignore the release times. The reasons why we ignore the release times are that backward scheduling is used only to compute the successor-tree-consistent deadlines and ignoring release times will make it faster to compute the successor-tree-consistent deadlines. In backward scheduling, we use Latest Deadline First (LDF) strategy, i.e. whenever a processor is idle, the instruction which has the largest deadline among all ready instructions is scheduled. Ties are broken arbitrarily if there are multiple instructions whose deadlines are equal. The schedule generated by backward (forward) scheduling is called *backward schedule* (*forward schedule*).

The forward scheduling can be constructed in $O(n \log n)$ time by using a standard priority queue or in $O(n \log \log n)$ time by using a stratified binary tree [17]. However, if we keep two sorted arrays $L_{\bar{r}}^{\leq}$ and $L_{\bar{d}}^{\leq}$ of n instructions: $L_{\bar{r}}^{\leq}$ is sorted in non-decreasing order of release times and $L_{\bar{d}}^{\leq}$ is sorted in non-decreasing order of deadlines, then forward scheduling can done in $O(n)$ time by using Gabow and Tarjan's static tree union-find algorithm [12]. Since an $O(n \log n)$ algorithm for computing the forward schedule suffices for the time complexity of our scheduling algorithm, the forward scheduling algorithm with time complexity of $O(n)$ is omitted in this paper.

For backward scheduling, since all release times are ignored, the backward scheduling can be trivially done in $O(n)$ time if we have a sorted array in non-increasing order of deadlines. It is easy to show that forward scheduling and backward scheduling have the following properties.

Property 1. Given a set V of independent instructions with individual integer deadlines, backward scheduling will find a feasible schedule iff one exists. Furthermore, given a backward schedule σ_b for V, $t_{min}^{\sigma_b} = max\{t_{min}^{\sigma} : \sigma$ is a feasible schedule for $V\}$ holds, where $t_{min}^{\sigma} = min\{\sigma(I_i) : I_i \in V\}$.

Property 2. Given a set V of independent instructions with individual integer release times and deadlines, forward scheduling will find a feasible schedule iff one exists. Furthermore, given a forward schedule σ_f for V, $t_{max}^{\sigma_f} = min\{t_{max}^{\sigma} : \sigma$ is a feasible schedule for $V\}$ holds, where $t_{max}^{\sigma} = max\{\sigma(I_i) : I_i \in V\}$.

4   Scheduling Algorithm

The input of our algorithm is a problem instance P defined in Section 2. The output of our algorithm is a feasible schedule σ for P whenever one exists, or "No feasible schedule exists." if no feasible schedule exists. In our algorithm, the successor-tree-consistent deadlines of all instructions are computed backwards. For each sink instruction, its successor-tree-consistent deadline is equal to its edge consistent deadline. When computing successor-tree-consistent deadlines, we use the following rules to choose an instruction I_i: (i) The successor-tree-consistent deadlines of all successors of I_i have been computed, and (ii) among all instructions whose successors' successor-tree-consistent deadlines have been computed, I_i has the largest edge consistent release time. Ties are broken in arbitrary order. To follow these two rules, we sort all non-sink instructions in non-ascending order of their edge consistent release times. Our algorithm uses four arrays $L_{\bar{d}}^{\leq}$, $L_{\bar{d}}^{\geq}$, $L_{\bar{r}}^{\geq}$ and $L_{\bar{r}}^{\leq}$, where $L_{\bar{d}}^{\leq}$, $L_{\bar{d}}^{\geq}$ and $L_{\bar{r}}^{\leq}$ contain all instructions in V, and $L_{\bar{r}}^{\geq}$ contains all non-sink instructions in V. $L_{\bar{d}}^{\leq}$ and $L_{\bar{r}}^{\leq}$ are used in forward scheduling, $L_{\bar{d}}^{\geq}$ is used in backward scheduling and $L_{\bar{r}}^{\geq}$ is used to choose an instruction to compute its successor-tree-consistent deadline. Our algorithm consists of the following three main steps.

1. Preprocessing. It consist of the following computation:
   (a) Modify the release times and deadlines of all instructions so that they are edge consistent.
   (b) Sort $L_{\bar{d}}^{\leq}$ in non-decreasing order of edge consistent deadlines.
   (c) Sort $L_{\bar{d}}^{\geq}$ in non-ascending order of edge consistent deadlines.
   (d) Sort $L_{\bar{r}}^{\geq}$ in non-ascending order of edge consistent release times.
   (e) Sort $L_{\bar{r}}^{\leq}$ in non-decreasing order of edge consistent release times.
2. Computing successor-tree-consistent deadlines for all non-sink instructions. For each non-sink instruction $L_{\bar{r}}^{\leq}[i] (i = 0, 1, \cdots, n-1)$, do the following.
   (a) Compute the successor-tree-consistent deadline of instruction $L_{\bar{r}}^{\leq}[i]$.
   (b) Sort $L_{\bar{d}}^{\geq}$ in non-ascending order of deadlines.
   (c) Sort $L_{\bar{d}}^{\leq}$ in non-decreasing order of deadlines.
3. Construct a schedule σ by using list scheduling. If σ is not a feasible schedule, then no feasible schedule exists.

In list scheduling, priority of each instruction is its successor-tree-consistent deadline. List scheduling is greedy. Whenever a processor is idle, among all ready instructions, the one with the smallest successor-tree-consistent deadline is scheduled. An instruction I_i is ready at time t if 1) for each of its immediate predecessor I_j, I_j has finished before $t - l_{ji}$, and 2) $t \geq r_i$. Computing the successor-tree-consistent deadline for each non-sink instruction is the core of our scheduling algorithm. Next, we describe how to compute the successor-tree-consistent deadline for each non-sink instruction. In the rest of the paper, the successor-tree-consistent deadline of an instruction I_i is denoted by d'_i.

Assume that currently the successor-tree-consistent deadline of I_i is computed. To compute the successor-tree-consistent deadline of I_i in P, we first compute the latest completion time of I_i in all feasible schedules for the relaxed problem instance $P(i)$ of P: the same set $V = \{T_1, T_2, \cdots, T_n\}$ of instructions as in P, subject to precedence constraints in the form of the successor tree $G(i) = (V, E(I_i))$, release time constraints $RT' = \{r_j : r_j$ is the edge consistent release time of I_j [1]$\}$ and deadline constraints $D' = \{\bar{d}_j : \bar{d}_j$ is the edge consistent deadline d_j of I_j if I_j's successor-tree-consistent deadline has not been computed, or its successor-tree-consistent deadline d'_j otherwise $\}$. In this relaxed problem $P(i)$, all latencies and precedence constraints specified in the original problem instance P are ignored, and new precedence constraints in the form of the successor tree $G(i)$ are introduced.

Let σ_i^f be a forward schedule for $V - \{I_i\} - Succ(I_i)$, σ_i^{bo} a backward schedule for $Succ(I_i)$, $t'_{min} = min\{\sigma_i^{bo}(I_k) : I_k \in Succ(I_i)\}$ and $t_i^{max} = min\{d_i - 1, t'_{min} - 1\}$. Note that

1. I_i cannot be scheduled at any time before r_i, and
2. I_i cannot be scheduled at any time after t_i^{max}

---

[1] d_i and r_i will denote the edge consistent deadline and the edge consistent release time of I_i respectively in the rest of this paper unless their meanings are explicitly specified.

The possible start time for I_i in any feasible schedule must be within the time interval $[r_i, t_i^{max}]$. However, not every time slot can be used to schedule I_i. Specifically, for each time slot $[t, t+1)$ in $[r_i, t_i^{max} + 1)$, if the instruction scheduled in this time slot is a σ_i^f-rigid, then by Property 3.2 it is a forbidden slot. As a result, I_i cannot be scheduled in $[t, t+1)$. Otherwise, I_i could be scheduled in $[t, t+1)$ because the non-σ_i^f-rigid instruction in it can be scheduled at a later time slot.

By the greediness of forward scheduling, if I_i is scheduled at a time t, then all instructions which are scheduled no earlier than t in the forward schedule σ_i^f must be scheduled after I_i. Let $U_t = \{I_j : \sigma_i^f[I_j] \geq t$ and $I_j \in V - \{I_i\} - Succ(I_i)\} \cup Succ(I_i)$, σ_i^b be a backward schedule for U_t and $t_{min} = min\{\sigma_i^b(I_j) : I_j \in U_t\}$. To compute the latest completion time of I_i in all feasible schedules for $P(i)$, we have to find the latest time t such that $t \leq t_{min}$. Next, we describe how to find the latest completion time of I_i in all feasible schedules for $P(i)$ in $O(n \log n)$ time by using binary search.

Before the binary search is carried out, a preprocessing must be performed as follows. Let $A[1], A[2], \cdots, A[p]$ be all instructions scheduled in time interval $[r_i, t_i^{max} + 1)$ in forward schedule σ_i^f satisfying $\sigma_i^f(A[j]) < \sigma_i^f(A[j+1])(j = 1, 2, \cdots p - 1)$. For each instruction $A[j](j = 1, 2, \cdots, p)$, if it is σ_i^f-rigid, then I_i cannot be scheduled in time slot $[\sigma_i^f(A[j]), \sigma_i^f(A[j]) + 1)$. Otherwise, it could be scheduled in time slot $[\sigma_i^f(A[j]), \sigma_i^f(A[j]) + 1)$. Furthermore, in order not to miss out any feasible schedule, for each hole $[t_{j_1}, t_{j_2})$ in forward schedule σ_i^f which is fully or partially embedded in time interval $[r_i, t_i^{max} + 1)$, we have to create an unique empty instruction [2] I_j' such that $\sigma_i^f(I_j') = t_{j_1}$. We construct an array B for the binary search as follows:

1. Let $r = 1$. If there is a hole $[t_1, \sigma_i^f(A[1]))$ in forward schedule σ_i^f which is fully or partially embedded in $[r_i, t_i^{max} + 1)$, then create an unique empty instruction I_k', set $\sigma_i^f(I_k') = r_i$, $B[r] = I_k'$ and $r = r + 1$.

2. For each instruction $A[j](j = 1, 2, \cdots, p)$, do the following: 1) If it is not a σ_i^f-rigid instruction, set $B[r] = A[j]$ and $r = r + 1$; 2) if there is a hole $[\sigma_i^f(A[j]) + 1, t_2)$ which is fully or partially embedded in time interval $[r_i, t_i^{max} + 1)$, then create an unique empty instruction I_s', set $\sigma_i^f(I_s') = \sigma_i^f(A[j]) + 1$, $B[r] = I_s'$ and $r = r + 1$.

Obviously, the number of holes is less than $n - 2$. Therefore, the number of instructions in array B is less than $2(n-2)$. Once we have obtained array B, our task is to find the maximum index m to B such that $U_{min}(i) = \{B[m]\} \cup \{I_j : I_j \in V - \{I_i\} - Succ(I_i)$ and $\sigma_i^f(I_j) > \sigma_i^f(B[m])\}$ satisfies constraint C4.

$$\sigma_i^f(B[m]) \leq min\{\sigma_i^b(I_j) : I_j \in U_{min}(i) \cup Succ(I_i)\} \qquad \text{(C4)}$$

Where σ_i^b is a backward schedule for $U_{min}(i) \cup Succ(I_i)$. Given an instruction $B[j]$, we can trivially show that

---

[2] Empty instructions are used only to simplify the description of our algorithm and will be ignored in backward scheduling.

- if $U_{min}(i) = \{B[j]\} \cup \{I_r : I_r \in V - \{I_i\} - Succ(I_i)$ and $\sigma_i^f(I_r) > \sigma_i^f(B[j])\}$
  satisfies constraint C4, then for each natural number k with $k < j$, $U_{min}(i) = \{B[k]\} \cup \{I_r : I_r \in V - \{I_i\} - Succ(I_i)$ and $\sigma_i^f(I_r) > \sigma_i^f(B[k])\}$ also satisfies constraint C4.
- if $U_{min}(i) = \{B[j]\} \cup \{I_r : I_r \in V - \{I_i\} - Succ(I_i)$ and $\sigma_i^f(I_r) > \sigma_i^f(B[j])\}$
  does not satisfy constraint C4, then for each natural number k with $k > j$, $U_{min}(i) = \{B[k]\} \cup \{I_r : I_r \in V - \{I_i\} - Succ(I_i)$ and $\sigma_i^f(I_r) > \sigma_i^f(B[k])\}$ does not satisfy constraint C4 either.

Therefore, binary search can be applied on array B to compute the maximum index m. The procedure for computing the latest completion time t_{min} of I_i in all feasible schedules for $P(i)$ by binary search on B is as follows.

1. Let $l = 1$ and $r = $ the number of instructions in B.
2. While $l + 1 < r$ do the following.
   - Let $m = \lceil (l+r)/2 \rceil$ and $U_{min}(i) = \{B[m]\} \cup \{I_j : I_j \in V - \{I_i\} - Succ(I_i)$ and $\sigma_i^f(I_j) > \sigma_i^f(B[m])\}$. Compute a backward schedule σ_i^b for $U_{min}(i) \cup Succ(I_i)$. If constraint C4 is satisfied, then let $l = m$; otherwise let $r = m$.
3. Let $U_{min}(i) = \{B[r]\} \cup \{I_j : I_j \in V - \{I_i\} - Succ(I_i)$ and $\sigma_i^f(I_j) > \sigma_i^f(B[r])\}$ and compute a backward schedule σ_i^b for $U_{min}(i) \cup Succ(I_i)$. Consider the following cases.
   (a) Constraint C4 is satisfied. Then, $t_{min} = min\{\sigma_i^b(I_k) : I_k \in Succ(I_i) \cup U_{min}(i)\}$.
   (b) Constraint C4 is not satisfied. If $l = r$, then no feasible schedule exists for $P(i)$; otherwise, let $U_{min}(i) = \{B[l]\} \cup \{I_j : I_j \in V - \{I_i\} - Succ(I_i)$ and $\sigma_i^f(I_j) > \sigma_i^f(B[l])\}$ and compute a backward schedule σ_i^b for $U_{min}(i) \cup Succ(I_i)$. If the constraint C4 is satisfied, then $t_{min} = min\{\sigma_i^b(I_k) : I_k \in Succ(I_i) \cup U_{min}(i)\}$; otherwise, no feasible schedule exists for $P(i)$.

When the above procedure terminates, either no feasible schedule exists for $P(i)$ or the latest completion time t_{min} of I_i in all feasible schedules for $P(i)$ is found. Note that $P(i)$ is the relaxed problem instances of P. Hence, if there is no feasible schedule for $P(i)$, then there is no feasible schedule for P either.

Next, we compute the latest completion time in all feasible schedules for a stronger problem instance $P'(i)$ of $P(i)$. $P'(i)$ consists of $P(i)$ and the following latency constraints:

$$l_{ij} = \begin{cases} 1 \text{ if } I_j \text{ is a 1-successor of } I_i \text{ in } P \\ 0 \text{ otherwise} \end{cases}$$

Let $t'_{min}(i)$ be the latest completion time of I_i in all feasible schedules for $P'(i)$ and $U_{min}(i)$ be the one which leads to t_{min} in the procedure for computing the latest completion time of I_i in all feasible schedules for $P(i)$. Consider the following cases.

1. For each immediate successor I_j of I_i, the latency between I_i and I_j is 0. In this case $P'(i)$ is equivalent to $P(i)$. Therefore, $t'_{min}(i) = t_{min}$.

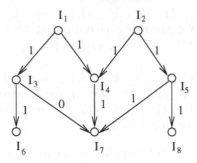

Fig. 1. The precedence and latency constraints in P

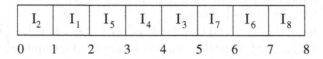

Fig. 2. A feasible schedule for P constructed by our algorithm

2. There is at least one immediate successor I_j of I_i such that $l_{ij} = 1$. Let $S(i) = \{I_j : I_j \in S_0(i)$ and $r_j \leq t_{min}\}$ and I_k be the instruction in $S(i)$ satisfying $\forall I_j \in S(i)(\bar{d}_k \leq \bar{d}_j)$, where $S_0(i) = \{I_j : I_j \in U_{min}(i)\} \cup \{I_j : I_j$ is an immediate successor of I_i in P and $l_{ij} = 0\}$. If $S(i) = \emptyset$, then one of the 1-successors of I_i must start no later than t_{min} in any feasible schedule for $P'(i)$. Therefore, $t'_{min}(i) = t_{min} - 1.^3$ In the case that $S(i) \neq \emptyset$, compute a backward schedule σ_b for $U_{min}(i) \cup Succ(I_i) - \{I_k\}$. Let $t = min\{\sigma_b(I_j) : I_j \in U_{min}(i) \cup Succ(I_i) - \{I_k\}\}$. There are only two possibilities.

(a) $t_{min} = t - 1$. Since instruction I_k can be scheduled at time t_{min} and all instructions in $U_{min} \cup Succ(I_i) - \{I_k\}$ can be scheduled no earlier than $t_{min} + 1$, $t'_{min}(i) = t_{min}$;

(b) $t_{min} = t$. In this case, in any feasible schedule for $P'(i)$, there must be a 1-successor I_j of I_i such that I_j must start no later than t_{min}. Therefore, $t'_{min}(i) = t_{min} - 1$.

Since $P'(i)$ is the relaxed problem instance of P, I_i must finish before $t'_{min}(i)$ in any feasible schedule for P. Therefore, $d'_i = t'_{min}(i)$. If $d'_i \leq r_i$, then no feasible schedule exists for P.

Example   Given a problem instance P: A set $V = \{I_i : i = 1, 2, \cdots, 8\}$ of 8 instructions with precedence and latency constraints shown in figure 1, release times $r_1 = r_2 = 0$, $r_3 = r_4 = r_5 = 1$, $r_7 = 4$ and $r_6 = r_8 = 6$, and

---

[3] In the case that $t'_{min}(i) = t_{min} - 1$, the latest completion time of I_i in all feasible schedules for $P'(i)$ could be less than $t_{min} - 1$ due to the forbidden slots caused by σ_i^f-rigid instructions. However, $t_{min} - 1$ is sufficient for the optimality.

deadlines $d_1 = d_2 = 3$, $d_3 = d_4 = 7$, $d_5 = 6$ and $d_6 = d_7 = d_8 = 8$, the successor-tree-consistent deadlines computed by our algorithm are $d'_1 = 2$, $d'_2 = 1$, $d'_3 = 5$, $d'_4 = d'_5 = 4$, $d'_6 = d'_7 = d'_8 = 8$. By using list scheduling, where the priority of each instruction is its successor-tree-consistent deadline, a feasible schedule on a single processor computed by our algorithm is shown in figure 2.

5   Correctness Proof and Complexity Analysis

From the description of our algorithm in the previous section, we can prove the following lemma.

Lemma 1. *Given a problem instance P, for each non-sink instruction, it must finish before its successor-tree-consistent deadline in any feasible schedule for P on a single processor.*

Theorem 1. *Given a problem instance P, our algorithm computes a feasible schedule whenever one exists.*

Proof Suppose that there is a feasible schedule σ for P and schedule σ' computed by our algorithm has at least one late instruction. Let I_k be the first late instruction and t be the earliest time which satisfies the following two constraints.

- There is no idle slot in time interval $[t, \sigma'(I_k))$.
- The successor-tree-consistent deadlines of all instructions scheduled in $[t, \sigma'(I_k))$ are less than or equal to d'_k.

Let $S = \{I_k\} \cup \{I_j : t \leq \sigma'(I_j) < \sigma'(I_k)\}$ and I_i be the instruction scheduled in time slot $[t-2, t-1)$. Consider all possible cases.

1. $t = 0$. By the pigeon hole principle, there must be a late instruction in any schedule for P, which contradicts the assumption.
2. No instruction is scheduled in time slot $[t-2, t-1)$ or $d'_i > d'_k$. In this case, by the greediness of list scheduling, the release times of all instructions in S must be greater than or equal to t. Therefore, by pigeon hole principle, at least one instruction must be late in any feasible schedule for P, which contradicts the assumption.
3. $d'_i \leq d'_k$. Consider the two possible cases.
   (a) The release times of all instructions in S is greater than or equal to t. By pigeon hole principle, there must be at least one late instruction in any feasible schedule for P, which contradicts the assumption.
   (b) There is at least one instruction whose release time is less than or equal to $t-1$. By our algorithm for computing successor-tree-consistent deadlines, the successor-tree-consistent deadlines of all instructions in S must have been computed when the successor-tree-consistent deadline of I_i is computed. Let $S' = \{I_j : d'_j \leq d'_k \text{ and } (I_j \text{ is a successor of } I_i \text{ or } r_j \geq t)\}$, then $S \subseteq S'$ must hold. Consider the case when I_i's successor-tree-consistent deadline $t'_{min}(i)$ is computed by our algorithm.

There are two possibilities: either $t'_{min}(i) = t_{min}$ or $t'_{min}(i) = t_{min} - 1$. If $t'_{min}(i) = t_{min}$, then all instructions in S' can be scheduled no earlier than $t_{min} + 1$ in the backward schedule. Therefore, $d'_i \leq d'_k - |S'| - 1$ must hold. If $t'_{min}(i) = t_{min} - 1$, then in any feasible schedule for $P'(i)$, there must be a 1-successor I_j of I_i such that I_j must start no later than t_{min}. Therefore, $d'_i \leq d'_k - |S'| - 1$ also holds. Furthermore, we have $d'_i \leq d'_k - |S'| - 1 \leq d'_k - |S| - 1 \leq \sigma'(I_k) - |S| - 1 = \sigma'(I_i)$. Therefore, I_i is also late in σ', which contradicts the assumption that I_k is the first late instruction.

Therefore, σ' has no late instruction and the theorem holds.

Theorem 2. *The space complexity of our algorithm is $O(n^2)$ and the time complexity of our algorithm is $O(n^2 \log n)$ if the transitive closure of the precedence graph is known, or $O(n^2 \log n) + min\{O(ne), O(n^{2.376})\}$ if the transitive closure is not known.*

Proof Obviously, the space complexity of our algorithm is $O(n^2)$. Next we analyze the time complexity of our algorithm. Our algorithm consists of three main parts: preprocessing, successor-tree-consistent deadline computation and constructing a schedule for P by using list scheduling. The time complexities of these three parts are analyzed as follows.

1. Preprocessing. Release time modifications can be done in $O(e)$ time by using forward breadth-first processing, where e is the number of edges in the precedence graph. Similarly, deadline modifications can be done in $O(e)$ time by backward breadth-first processing. In addition, sorting all arrays needs $O(n \log n)$ time. Therefore, preprocessing takes $O(e + n \log n)$ time.
2. Computing the successor-tree-consistent deadline of each non-sink instruction. It consists of the following two steps:
   - Determining the search domain for the binary search. This step is composed of following computation: 1) computing the forward schedule σ_i^f for $V - \{I_i\} - Succ(I_i)$, which takes $O(n \log n)$ time by using priority queue or $O(n)$ time by using Gabow and Tarjan's static tree union-find algorithm [12]; 2) computing the backward schedule σ_i^b for $Succ(I_i)$, which takes $O(n)$ time; 3) determining if each instruction scheduled is σ_i^f-rigid, which takes $O(n)$ time if there is an array [4] of instructions sorted either in ascending order or in decreasing order of their start times in forward schedule σ_i^f; and 4) constructing array B for binary search, which takes $O(n)$ time. Therefore, this step takes at most $O(n \log n)$ time.
   - Binary search. Since the time complexity for each backward scheduling is $O(n)$ and there are at most $2(n-2)$ instructions in array B, the binary search takes $O(n \log n)$ time.

---

[4] This sorted array can be obtained in the forward scheduling without affecting its time complexity.

468 Hui Wu et al.

After computing the successor-tree-consistent deadline of a non-sink instruction, our algorithm will sort $L_{\bar{d}}^{\geq}$ in non-ascending order of deadlines and sort $L_{\bar{d}}^{\leq}$ in non-decreasing order of deadlines. Since only one instruction's deadline is changed to it successor-tree-consistent deadline at a time, both sortings can be done in $O(n)$ time. Therefore, the time complexity for computing the successor-tree-consistent deadlines of all non-sink instructions is $O(n^2 \log n)$.

3. Constructing the final schedule by using list scheduling. This step takes $O(n^2)$ time [3].

Therefore, if the transitive closure of the precedence graph is known, the time complexity of our algorithm is $O(n^2 \log n)$. The transitive closure can be computed in $O(ne)$ time by n depth-first searches. Alternatively, it can be reduced to matrix multiplication [18], which takes $O(n^{2.376})$ time [16]. Therefore, the time complexity of our algorithm is $O(n^2 \log n) + min\{O(ne), O(n^{2.376})\}$ if the transitive closure is not known.

6 Conclusion

We propose a faster algorithm for scheduling instructions in a basic block with both release time constraints and deadline constraints on a single RISC processor with a maximum latency of one machine cycle. The key idea of our algorithm is to compute successor-tree-consistent deadlines. The successor-tree-consistent deadline of each instruction I_i is the upper bound on the latest completion time of I_i in any feasible schedule for the relaxed problem instance $P'(i)$. A number of techniques such as forward scheduling, backward scheduling and binary search are used to make it faster to compute the successor-tree-consistent deadlines. Our algorithm can find a feasible schedule whenever one exists.

Using our algorithm as a procedure, we can use binary search as in [3] to solve the maximum lateness minimization problem in $O(n^2 \log^2 n + min\{ne, n^{2.376}\})$ time. In addition, our algorithm can be generalized to be an approximation algorithm for the general case of multiple processors and arbitrary latencies.

An interesting open problem is in the case that the processing times of all instruction are equal to an arbitrary natural number, is there a polynomial algorithm for scheduling instructions with arbitrary precedence constraints, integer release times and deadlines on a single RICS processor with a maximum latency of one cycle?

References

1. Leung, Allen, Krishna V. Palem and Amir Pnueli. A fast algorithm for scheduling time-constrained instructions on processors with ILP. Proceedings of the 1998 International Conference on Parallel Architectures and Compilation Techniques. Paris, France, 1998. 458

2. Palem, Krishna. V. and Barbara B. Simon. Scheduling time-critical instructions on RISC machines. ACM Transactions on Programming Languages and Systems 15(4), Sept. 1993, 632-658. 457, 458

3. Garey, M. R. and D. S. Johnson. Two processor scheduling with start-times and deadlines. SIAM J. Comput. 6, 1977, 416-426. 468

4. Garey, M. R. and D. S. Johnson. Scheduling tasks with nonuniform deadlines on two processors. J. ACM 23, 1976, 461-467.

5. Bernstein, D. and I. Gertner. Scheduling expressions on a pipelined processor with a maximal delay of one cycle. ACM Transactions on Programming Languages and Systems, 11(1), 1989, 57-66. 458

6. Bruno, J. Jones and K. So. Deterministic scheduling with pipelined processors. IEEE Transactions on Computers, 29, April 1980, 308-316. 458

7. Finta, L. and Z. Liu. Single machine scheduling subject to precedence delays. Discrete Applied Mathematics 70, 1996, 247-266. 457, 458

8. Hennessy, J. and T. Gross. Postpass code optimization of pipeline constraints. ACM Transactions on Programming Languages and Systems 5(3), 1983. 457

9. Warren, H. Instruction scheduling for the IBM RISC system/6000 processors. IBM Journal of Research and Development, 1990, 85-92.

10. Coffman Jr, E. G. and R. L. Graham. Optimal scheduling for two processors. Acta Informatica 1, 1972, 200-213.

11. Gabow H. N. An almost linear-time algorithm for two processor scheduling. J. ACM 29, 1982, 766-780.

12. Gabow H.N and R. E. Tarjan. A linear-time algorithm for a special case of disjoint set union. Journal of Computer and System Sciences 30, 1985, 209-221. 461, 467

13. Tarjan, R. E. Efficient of good but not linear set union algorithm. J. ACM 22, April 1975, 237-246.

14. Radin, G. The 801 minicomputer. IBM J. Res. Dev. 27, 1983, 237-246.

15. Katevenis, M. Reduced instruction set Computer architecture for VLSI. MIT Press, Cambridge, Mass., 1984.

16. Coppersmith, D. and S. Winograd. Matrix Multiplication via Arithmetic Progressions. J. of Symbolic Computation, 9, 1990, 251-280. 458, 468

17. Boas P. V. E. Preserving order in a forest in less than logarithmic time. 16th Annual Symposium of Foundation of Computer Science, IEEE Computer Society, Long Beach, CA, 1978, 75-84. 461

18. Aho, A. V., J. E. Hopcroft and J. D. Ullman. The design and analysis of computer algorithms. Addison-Wesley, Reading, Mass., 1974. 458, 468

19. Coffman, E. G. Computer and Job-Shop Scheduling Theory. John Wiley and Sons, New York, 1976. 458

Arc Consistency on n-ary Monotonic and Linear Constraints

Zhang Yuanlin and Roland H. C. Yap

School of Computing, National University of Singapore
3 Science Drive 2, Republic of Singapore 119260
{zhangyl,ryap}@comp.nus.edu.sg

Abstract. Many problems and applications can be naturally modelled and solved using constraints with more than two variables. Such n-ary constraints, in particular, arithmetic constraints are provided by many finite domain constraint programming systems. The best known worst case time complexity of existing algorithms (GAC-schema) for enforcing arc consistency on general CSPs is $O(ed^n)$ where d is the size of domain, e is the number of constraints and n is the maximum number of variables in a single constraint. We address the question of efficient consistency enforcing for n-ary constraints. An observation here is that even with a restriction of n-ary constraints to linear constraints, arc consistency enforcing is NP-complete. We identify a general class of monotonic n-ary constraints (which includes linear inequalities as a special case). Such monotonic constraints can be made arc consistent in time $\mathcal{O}(en^3d)$. The special case of linear inequalities can be made arc consistent in time $\mathcal{O}(en^2d)$ using bounds-consistency which exploits special properties of the projection function.

1 Introduction

Arc Consistency (AC) is an important technique for solving Constraint Satisfaction Problems (CSPs) [17]. A large part of the literature is thus on efficient algorithms for enforcing arc consistency on CSPs. The focus is usually on binary CSP where each constraint involves at most two variables. The well-known algorithms for arc consistency in binary CSPs include Waltz's filtering algorithm [30], AC-3 [17], AC-6 [4], AC-5 [28] and many others.

Constraint programming has shown that consistency techniques, in particular, AC-based methods are effective and useful for solving practical problems [27]. However, many real-life problems can be modelled naturally as a non-binary CSP where a constraint involves more than two variables. We call a constraint which involves an arbitrary number of variables an n-ary constraint. An n-ary CSP is then one where the maximum number of variables in constraints is at most n. Some typical examples of n-ary constraints include the *all different* constraint, the *cardinality* constraint [24] and linear arithmetic constraints. Such n-ary constraints are provided by many constraint programming languages and libraries.

R. Dechter (Ed.): CP 2000, LNCS 1894, pp. 470–483, 2000.
© Springer-Verlag Berlin Heidelberg 2000

There are two main approaches to deal with n-ary CSPs. The first approach is to avoid altogether the question of an n-ary CSP. This is achievable since it is always possible to translate an n-ary CSP into a different binary CSP [10,25]. The standard techniques in binary CSP can be used to solve the transformed CSP thus solving the original n-ary CSP also. A recent paper [1] is a detailed examination of the translation approach.

The second approach is to develop consistency techniques directly applicable to n-ary constraints. One direction is to extend techniques developed in the binary case for general n-ary CSPs. The other is to develop specialised techniques which can exploit the semantics of the particular n-ary constraints. Some representatives of first direction are as follows. Mackworth [18] generalized AC-3 to NC to deal with n-ary constraints. This is improved by GAC-4 [19] which is a generalization of AC-4. GAC-4 improves the complexity of NC, at the cost of a higher space complexity and a bad average time complexity. The time complexity of GAC-4 is $\mathcal{O}(ed^n)$ where e is the number of constraints and d is the size of the domain. We see that in contrast to their binary CSP AC versions, NC and GAC-4 may not be practical due to their high time complexity. A more efficient approach is the GAC-schema [5] based on *single support* and *multidirectionality* but it has the same worst case time complexity as GAC-4. The second direction is consistency algorithms for particular classes of constraints which can lead to more efficient algorithms, for example the global *all different* constraint and *cardinality* constraint [24].

The main contributions of this paper are the following. We address the problem of efficient consistency enforcing for n-ary constraints. An observation here is that even with a restriction of n-ary constraints to linear constraints, arc consistency enforcing becomes intractable. We identify a general class of monotonic n-ary constraints (which includes linear inequalities as a special case). Such monotonic constraints can be made arc consistent in time $\mathcal{O}(en^3d)$. The special case of linear inequalities can be made arc consistent using bounds-consistency which exploits special properties of the projection function in time $\mathcal{O}(en^2d)$.

This paper is organized as follows. First, we present some background material for n-ary CSP and the generalization of AC used here. We then formalize bounds based propagation as bounds-consistency for linear constraints. We give an efficient bounds-consistency algorithm for linear constraints. In Section 4, we look at arc consistency for linear inequalities and define a new class of monotonic constraints which is tractable. We then examine arc consistency for linear equations. Finally, we discuss related work.

2   Preliminaries

In this section we will give some definitions and notation for general n-ary CSPs [17,19].

Definition 1. *An n-ary Constraint Satisfaction Problem (N, D, C) consists of a finite set of variables $N = \{1, \cdots, m\}$, a set of domains $D = \{D_1, \cdots, D_m\}$,* *where D_i is a finite set of values that i can take, and a finite set of constraints $C = \{c_X \mid X \subseteq N\}$, where each constraint c_X is a relation on variables of set X and thus c_X is a subset of $D_{i_1} \times D_{i_2} \times \cdots \times D_{i_l}$ where $i_k \in X, k \in \{1, \ldots, l\}$. The arity of the CSP is defined as $n = Max\{|X| \mid c_X \in C\}$.*

Throughout this paper, the number of variables is denoted by m, the maximum arity of constraints in the n-ary CSP is n, the size of largest domain is d, and the number of constraints is e. Thus, a binary CSP is simply a 2-ary CSP.

A constraint in an n-ary CSP may be defined and represented in a number of ways. It can be represented explicitly as a set of tuples (either allowed or disallowed), a conjunctive constraint, implicitly as an arithmetic expression, or by any predicate whose semantics is defined by a particular definition/program code. In this paper, we will use the notation c_X to represent both the form of a constraint and the set of tuples that satisfy the constraint.

Definition 2. *Given a CSP (N, D, C) and a constraint $c_X \in C$. We define a solution of constraint c_X to be any tuple $\langle v_{i_1}, \cdots, v_{i_n} \rangle \in c_X$. If c_X is empty, we say that there is no solution for c_X.*

We are now in a position to define arc consistency for n-ary CSPs. The following definition from Mackworth [17] is one natural generalization of arc consistency.

Definition 3. *Given an n-ary CSP (N, D, C), a constraint $c_X \in C$ is arc consistent with respect to D iff $\forall i \in X$ and $\forall v \in D_i$, v is a component of a solution of c_X in which case v is said to be valid with respect to c_X. A CSP (N, D, C) is arc consistent iff all $c_X \in C$ are arc consistent.*

In this paper, we will employ this particular definition of arc consistency for n-ary CSPS which is sometimes also called *hyper-arc consistency*. We remark that our definition of arc consistency is similar to relational arc consistency [26]. Enforcing higher consistency such relational path consistency on the n-ary CSPs is NP-complete in general (see Section 5).

The task of an arc consistency algorithm is then to remove those invalid values from the n variables in each constraint. In a binary CSP, the representation of a constraint may not be so important for this process. In the n-ary CSP case, the precise representation may fundamentally affect the efficiency of the arc consistency algorithm. For example, the *all different* constraint can be represented in a number of ways. Suppose that we represent the *all different* constraint using an explicit tuple representation as in GAC-4, the set of allowed tuples could be huge which may be impractical in terms of space and time. The GAC-schema of [5] is proposed to partly address this problem. However, GAC-schema is a general framework and does not address how to deal with special constraints such as linear arithmetic constraints efficiently.

3   Bounds Consistency on Linear Constraints

The first part of this section introduces the specialization of n-ary CSPs to linear arithmetic constraints and defines bounds-consistency on them. The second part presents bounds-consistency algorithms and their associated complexity analysis. We denote the set of integers by Z.

3.1   Linear Constraint and Bounds-Consistency

Definition 4. A linear arithmetic constraint $c_{\{x_1,\cdots,x_n\}}$ *is of the form*

$$a_1x_1 + a_2x_2 + \cdots + a_nx_n \diamond b$$

$$a_i, b \in Z \quad \diamond \in \{=, \leq\}.$$

where $vars(c)$ and $|c|$ is used to denote the set and the number of variables that occur in c respectively. A linear constraint system representing a n-ary CSP is one where all constraints are linear arithmetic constraint and all domains contain only integers. Other linear arithmetic constraints with $(<, >, \geq)$ can be rewritten in the above form.

Essentially, the problem of enforcing n-ary arc consistency is related to that of finding all solutions satisfying the given linear constraint. This may be quite expensive. One well known way to reduce this cost is to relax domains of the variables so that they form a continuous real interval bounded by the maximum and minimum values of the corresponding domains. Since variables can now take real values and are no longer discrete, it is easy to make the constraint arc consistent. We now make this precise. First, we introduce some basic interval arithmetic operations [20] which will simplify our presentation.

Assume that each variable x is associated with an interval $[l, u]$. We use $[x]$ and $\langle x \rangle$ to denote two kinds different kinds of operations: an interval operation; and a literal operation on x respectively. Let l, u denote the interval associated with x, we use the following notation:

$$[x] = [l, u] \qquad\qquad \langle x \rangle = \begin{pmatrix} l \\ u \end{pmatrix}$$

Given $[x] = [l_1, u_1]$ and $[y] = [l_2, u_2]$, the interval operations are defined in the usual fashion:

$$[x] + [y] = [l_1 + l_2, u_1 + u_2],$$

$$[x] - [y] = [l_1 - u_2, u_1 - l_2],$$

$$[x] - a = [l_1 - a, u_1 - a],$$

$$a[x] = \begin{cases} [al_1, au_1], a > 0 \\ [au_1, al_1], a < 0, \end{cases}$$

$$[x] \cap [y] = \big[\, max(l_1, l_2), min(u_1, u_2) \,\big].$$

The literal operations unlike the interval operations are defined as a pairwise tuple operation, which differs in subtraction from the interval counterpart:

$$\langle x \rangle \pm \langle y \rangle = \begin{pmatrix} l_1 \pm l_2 \\ u_1 \pm u_2 \end{pmatrix}.$$

We will for convenience also overload the [ ] and $\langle\ \rangle$ notation. We use $\langle[x]\rangle$ to mean a substitution of the literal operation for the interval operation.

The following example is now used to motivate the use of interval reasoning for consistency,

$$3x - 4y = 0, [x] = [y] = [1, 10].$$

Clearly, y cannot take the value 10 no matter what value x takes. More precisely, given any value of x in [1,10], y can only take a value in [3/4, 30/4]. So the set of valid values of y with respect to the above constraint is [3/4, 30/4] $\cap$ [1,10]=[3/4, 30/4]. The above process to remove invalid values can be formalized as follows.

Definition 5. *The* projection function π_i *of a constraint c on x_i is*

$$\pi_i(c) = \frac{-1}{a_i}(a_1 x_1 + \cdots + a_{i-1}x_{i-1} + a_{i+1}x_{i+1} + \cdots + a_n x_n - b).$$

Given intervals on all the variables, we can define the interval version of the projection of c on x_i as:

$$\Pi_i(c) = \frac{-1}{a_i}[a_1[x_1] + \cdots + a_n[x_n] - b].$$

We call $\Pi_i(c)$ the natural interval extension *of $\pi_i(c)$.*

We now define the function $Proj_i(c)$ as follows:

$$Proj_i(c) = \begin{cases} \Pi_i(c) & \text{if } \diamond' \text{ is } = \\ [-\infty, Ub(\Pi_i(c))] & \text{if } \diamond' \text{ is } \leq \\ [Lb(\Pi_i(c)), +\infty] & \text{if } \diamond' \text{ is } \geq \end{cases}$$

where

$$\diamond' = \begin{cases} \geq \text{ if } a_i \text{ is negative and } \diamond \text{ is } \leq \\ \diamond \text{ otherwise} \end{cases}$$

and $Ub([l, u]) = u, Lb([l, u]) = l$.

As a consequence of the intermediate value theorem from calculus, we have the following property.

Property 1. Given a constraint c with initial domains $([x_1], \cdots, [x_n])$, the constraint c is arc consistent with respect to the new domain $([x_1] \cap Proj_1(c), \cdots, [x_n] \cap Proj_n(c))$.

The relaxation of the domain of a variable from discrete to a continuous real interval allows efficient arc consistency enforcement for a single linear constraint in the time needed for computing n operations of $Proj_i(c)$. However for a system of constraints, this process may not terminate [13].

We now define bounds-consistency. Instead of using the real interval relaxation, we restrict the interval to the *Z-interval* whose upper bound and lower bound are integers. The Z-interval representation of a set $S \subset \mathcal{R}$ is $\Box S = [\lceil u \rceil, \lfloor v \rfloor]$ where u and v is the minimum and maximum real values in S respectively.

Definition 6. *A constraint* c *is* bounds-consistent *with respect to* $(\Box D_{x_1}, \cdots, \Box D_{x_n})$ *iff* $\forall x_i \in \text{vars}(c)$ $\Box D_{x_1} \subseteq \Box Proj_i(c_i)$. *A linear constraint system (N, D, C) is* bounds-consistent *with respect to* $(\Box D_1, \cdots, \Box D_m)$ *iff every* $c_i \in C$ *is bounds-consistent.*

3.2 Bounds Consistency Algorithm and Its Complexity

Although the definition of bounds-consistency holds for n-ary linear constraints, it fits well in an AC-3 style computation framework which is normally only used for binary constraints. We now describe a AC-3 like algorithm to achieve bounds-consistency on a system of linear constraints. We chose this presentation for two reasons. It is a simple and natural algorithm and for that reason would be similar to general propagation and filtering based algorithms as well. Unlike AC-3, the basic unit of manipulation here is a single constraint. A queue is employed to hold those constraints needing update when the domain of some of its variables is changed. The algorithm BC is listed in figure 1. The difference between BC and AC-3 is that the REVISE procedure is specialized for bounds-consistency and linear constraints.

Algorithm BC
begin
   $Q \leftarrow \{c_i | c_i \in C\}$;
   while (Q not empty)
   begin
     select and delete c_i from Q;
     REVISE(c_i, Q);
   end
end
procedure REVISE(c_j, Q)
begin
   for each $x_i \in vars$ (c_j)
   begin
     if $[x_i] \not\subseteq \Box Proj_i(c_j)$
       begin
1. $[x_i] \leftarrow [x_i] \cap \Box Proj_i(c_j)$;
2. $Q \leftarrow \{c_k \in C \mid x_i \in vars\ (c_k)\}$
     end
   end
end

Fig. 1. Algorithm BC

We point out that the operation in line 1 of BC is different from the *narrowing operation* [3] in that the Z-interval representation performs inward rounding while for continuous intervals represented by floating point numbers it an outward rounding operation. Note that the narrowing operation on c_j defined by REVISE is no longer idempotent given inward rounding.

Lemma 1. *Given a linear constraint system* (N, D, C), *the worst case time complexity of algorithm BC is* $\mathcal{O}(en^3d)$

Proof. The worst case complexity of BC depends on the number of constraints ever entering the Queue Q. A constraint c enters Q iff some value in some domain involved in c is deleted. For each variable $x_i \in N$, assume it appears in k_i constraints. In total, we have md values in the system where m is the number of variables in C. Thus the number of constraints ever entering Q is at most $\sum_{i=1}^{m} d \cdot k_i$. Let α be $\sum_{i=1}^{m} k_i$. A loose estimate of k_i can be simply e which means the variable can appear in any constraint in the system. However, a relatively tighter estimation for α is as follows. Consider the bipartite graph $G_{m,e}$ with vertices sets N and C. There is an edge between $x_i \in N$ and $c_j \in C$ iff x_i appears in c_j. α is exactly the number of edges of $G_{m,e}$. Since the degree of c_j is not more than n we have that the number of edges in $G_{m,e}$ is less than ne, that is $\alpha \leq ne$. The complexity of procedure REVISE is at most n^2. Therefore the complexity of BC is $\mathcal{O}(en^3d)$. $\square$

The naive algorithm can be improved by making REVISE more efficient using the following result.

Proposition 1. *Given an n-ary linear arithmetic constraint system* (N, D, C), *bounds-consistency can be achieved in time* $\mathcal{O}(en^2d)$

Proof. To improve the efficiency of BC, one way is to make REVISE faster. Let constraint c_j be

$$a_{j_1}x_1 + a_{j_2}x_2 + \cdots + a_{j_n}x_n \diamond b_j.$$

Let

$$f_j = a_{j_1}x_1 + a_{j_2}x_2 + \cdots + a_{j_n}x_n - b_j$$

Let F_j be the natural interval extension of f_j. Now, for any $x_i \in c_j$

$$\Pi_i(c_j) = -\frac{1}{a_{j_i}}[\langle F_j \rangle - \langle a_{j_i}[x_i] \rangle].$$

since we have that

$$\langle F_j \rangle - \langle a_{j_i}[x_i] \rangle = \langle [a_{j_1}[x_1] + \cdots a_{j_i}[x_i] + \cdots a_{j_n}[x_n] - b_j \rangle - \langle a_{j_i}[x_i] \rangle$$
$$= a_{j_1}[x_1] + \cdots + a_{j_{i-1}}[x_{i-1}] + a_{j_{i+1}}[x_{i+1}] + \cdots + a_{j_n}[x_n] - b_j$$

Note the f_j is not a projection function and the use of the literal $\langle \rangle$ operations in $\Pi_i(c_j)$. According to the definition of $Proj_i(c_j)$, REVISE can be implemented in linear time of n. So, the BC algorithm can be implemented in time of $\mathcal{O}(en^2d)$. $\square$

4   Linear Inequalities and Monotonic Constraint

We will now consider a system of linear inequalities. For a system of linear inequalities, we have the following result without any relaxation of the Z domain to Z-intervals.

Proposition 2. *Given an n-ary CSP (N, D, C) which consists only of linear inequalities, it will be arc consistent after bounds-consistency is enforced on it.*

Proof. Assume CSP (N, D, C) is bounds-consistent. Now we show that any constraint c_j is arc consistent with respect to D. Consider any variable x_i, $x_i \in vars(c_j)$, and any value v, $v \in D_i$. Let l and g be the least and greatest integers in D_i. Without loss of generality, assume that $a_i > 0$, we have $x_i \leq \pi_i$. Because the system is bounds-consistent, we have $[l, g] \subseteq \Box Proj_i(c_j)$, which means that $v \leq g \leq Ub(Proj_i(c_j))$ where $Ub(Proj_i(c_j))$ is obtained by letting $x_k = v_k, k :$ $1 \ldots n, k \neq i$ where v_k is either the lower bounds or the upper bounds of D_k depending on the interval operation. So, $(v_1, \cdots, v_{i-1}, v, v_{i+1}, \cdots, v_n)$ satisfies c_j. Similarly, when $a_i < 0$, we can prove v is part of a solution of c_j. $\Box$

It follows immediately that a system of linear inequalities can be made arc consistent in worst case time complexity of $\mathcal{O}(en^2 d)$.

This result can be generalized to a bigger class of n-ary constraints, the n-ary monotonic constraints. We begin by recalling the definition of binary monotonic constraint in [28]. From now on, we assume that all the domains D_i are finite and have a total ordering.

Definition 7. *[28] Given a binary CSP (N, D, C), a constraint $c \in C$ is monotonic with respect to domain $TD = \cup_{i=1}^{m} D_i$ iff there exists a total ordering on TD such that for all values $v, w \in TD$ and $c(v, w)$ implies $c(v', w')$ for all $v' \leq v$ and $w' \geq w$.*

An example of an arithmetic constraint which is monotonic under this definition is $x \leq y, [x] = [y] = [1, 10]$. However, with this definition, the linear inequality $x + y \leq 10, [x] = [y] = [1, 10]$ is *not* a monotonic constraint. For example, consider $x = 5, y = 5$ as an a valid pair, then $x' = 5, y' = 6$ is not consistent using the natural ordering. There is no total ordering on TD which makes this constraint monotonic.

However applying algorithm BC, a binary system of both kinds of constraints can be made arc consistent in time $\mathcal{O}(ed)$. Thus we see that this definition of monotonicity is stronger than necessary and does not fully exploit the special properties of inequalities which give more efficient arc consistency algorithms. We now give the following generalization of binary monotonic constraint which remedies this problem by relaxing the total ordering requirement on the union of all the domains.

Definition 8. *Given a binary CSP (N, D, C), a constraint $c_{\{i,j\}} \in C$ is monotonic iff there exists a total ordering on D_i and D_j respectively such that $\forall v \in D_i, \forall w \in D_j \ c(v, w)$ implies $c(v', w')$ for all $v' \leq v$ and $w' \geq w$.*

Consider again the example, $x + y \leq 10, [x] = [y] = [1, 10]$. This is now monotonic. A possible ordering is the natural one on x, and on y we have the reverse ordering. Now we have a natural extension of monotonicity to n-ary general constraints.

Definition 9. *Given an n-ary CSP (N, D, C), a constraint $c_X \in C$ is monotonic with respect to variable $i \in X$ iff there exists a total ordering on D_1 to D_n respectively such that $\forall v \in D_i, \forall v_j \in D_j \ c_X(v_1, \cdots, v_{i-1}, v, v_{i+1}, \cdots, v_n)$ implies $c(v_1', \cdots, v_{i-1}', v', v_{i+1}', \cdots, v_n')$ for all $v' \leq v$ and $v_j' \geq v_j$ for $j \in X, j \neq i$. A constraint $c_X \in C$ is monotonic iff c_X is monotonic with respect to all variables of X.*

It is easy to verify that any n-ary linear arithmetic inequality is monotonic. Another example of a monotonic constraint is, $x * y \leq z, D_x = D_y = D_z = \{1, \ldots, 100\}$. For finite domain constraints, our definition of monotonic constraints is more general than the monotonic functions defined in [11].

In order to achieve arc consistency on monotonic constraints, the REVISE in algorithm BC should be modified as in Figure 2. It is important to note that in the new algorithm, an explicit projection function is not required. At the initialization phase of BC, for any constraint c and $i \in vars(c)$, we explicitly store the particular ordering of each domain involved which makes c monotonic with respect to i.

Procedure REVISE(c_j, Q)
begin
   for each $x_i \in vars\ (c_j)$
   begin
      $\forall j, v_j \leftarrow$ the greatest value in D_j wrt x_i
      DELETE = 0;
1.   **while** (not $c(v_1, \cdots, v_n)$)
      begin
         remove v_i from D_i;
         DELETE = 1;
         $v_i \leftarrow$ the greatest value in D_i
      end
      if DELETE
         $Q \leftarrow \{c_k \in C \mid x_i \in vars\ (c_k)\}$
   end
end

Fig. 2. REVISE for monotonic constraint

Proposition 3. *Given a CSP (N, D, C) which contains only monotonic constraints, it can be made arc consistent in time complexity of $O(en^3d)$ if the complexity of evaluating $c(v_1, \cdots, v_n)$ is $O(n)$.*

The sketch of the proof is as follows. In a similar fashion to Proposition 2, we can show that arc consistency can be achieved on monotonic constraints. The complexity of the algorithm depends on the execution times of line 1 in the REVISE of Figure 2. If we expand one execution of the algorithm according to line 1, executions of line 1 can be separated into two groups. One group contains executions without any value removed and the other group contains executions with at least one value removed. Because REVISE can be executed at most $n^2 ed$ times, the complexity of executions of the first group is $n^3 ed$ according to the linear time evaluation of c. As for the second group, we cluster the computation around variables. Now the total computation is

$$\sum_{i=1}^{m} n \cdot (d_{i,1} + \cdots + d_{i,k}) \leq \sum_{i=1}^{m} n \cdot d \leq mnd$$

where $d_{i,l}(l : 1..k)$ denotes the number of elements removed from D_i in some execution of the while loop in line 1 on i. Because $m \leq ne$, the complexity of the second group will be smaller than the first group and thus the complexity of the algorithm is $\mathcal{O}(en^3 d)$. □

We remark that, as in proposition 1, by using the special semantics of monotonic constraint, it may be possible to decrease the complexity of the arc consistency algorithm by a factor n.

We now would like to briefly discuss how to embed the monotonic arc consistency algorithm into a general algorithm. AC-5 [28] does not discuss how this is to be done and leaves it as an implementation detail. The AC-6 algorithm is a suitable candidate for this. To simplify the discussion, we will illustrate the idea using a binary monotonic $c_{\{x,y\}}$ given in Figure 3.

In the initialization phase of AC-6 for $c_{\{x,y\}}$, we only need the least value in x and greatest value in y. The ordering used here gives a as the least value in x and g as the greatest value in y. In the implementation, we can easily associate the values a and g with the revision process for $c_{\{x,y\}}$. Now, any deletion of values of $b, c, e,$ or f by other constraints will not invoke the revision of constraint $c_{\{x,y\}}$. Only when a (or g) is removed will monotonic constraint revision be invoked. After the monotonic revision process finishes, it will associate the revision process again to the new least (or greatest) values left. This approach conforms to the *lazy* principle behind AC-6.

5   Linear Equations

We now consider n-ary CSPs where the constraints are linear equations. The importance of this section is that the complexity results are very different from the $\leq$ case. In the equation case when the domains are considered to be discrete, bounds-consistency does not imply arc consistency. It is only if we relax the domains to be Z-intervals that bounds-consistency implies arc consistency.

Unfortunately, the problem of enforcing arc consistency on a single linear equation is a very hard problem. Recall that arc consistency in the n-ary case

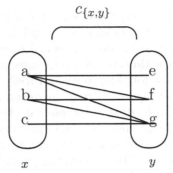

Fig. 3. A monotonic constraints embedded in AC-6

means that we need to show that single constraints are satisfiable by themselves. Consider the one-line integer programming problem: Is there a 0-1 n-vector x such that

$$a_1 x_1 + a_2 x_2 + \cdots + a_n x_n = b$$

where $b, a_1, \cdots, a_n$ are given positive integers? The above problem is NP-complete [23]. Obviously, enforcing arc consistency on a system of linear equations is also NP-complete. It is also immediate that enforcing arc consistency on any single arbitrary n-ary constraint is NP-complete in the worst case.

This observation highlights the computational difficulty with n-ary constraints and arc consistency. Arc consistency on linear inequalities (also monotonic constraints) is tractable, however generalizing to arbitrary linear constraints such as linear equations makes arc consistency intractable. This distinction can also be viewed as the difference in arc consistency between different representations. One can choose to represent linear equations as two inequalities per equation, eg. $exp = b$ as $exp \le b, exp \ge b$. In the continuous case, arc consistency on the original and double inequality representation gives the same resulting domains in the same time complexity. In the discrete case, the two inequality representation can be made arc consistent as in Section 4. It does not however make the original equations arc consistent since arc consistency treats each inequality separately.

Now consider relational consistency as defined in [26]. On a system of linear inequalities, relational arc consistency can be achieved in polynomial time, however enforcing relational path consistency is NP-complete.

6   Discussion and Conclusion

We now discuss the relationship of our work with that in the continuous domain. A substantial body of work in n-ary constraints comes from the continuous domain rather than the discrete domain. The early work [11,22] focused mainly on issues of correctness, convergence, searching strategy, etc. In more recent work the emphasis is on using numerical methods such as Newton methods [2] and Aitken acceleration [15] to speedup convergence. Our definition of bounds-consistency is similar to *arc B consistency* [16] and *interval consistency* [2,9] but differs in that bound-consistency uses an inward rounding operation. The time complexity of filtering algorithms in the continuous domain, on the other hand, is usually not treated for the following reasons. Firstly for real/rational intervals, the *interval Waltz filtering* algorithm may not terminate given arbitrary linear constraints [8]. Secondly for floating point intervals, the domain is huge and thus the worst case time complexity may not be of practical relevance and efficiency is gained not so much by reducing the time complexity, but by faster convergence using numerical methods. In [16], existing complexity results from general discrete arc consistency algorithm are used to bound their filtering algorithms. Thus, the work in the continuous case does not directly help in getting more efficient algorithms and their resulting time complexity analysis in the discrete case.

n-ary discrete constraints, including integer linear constraints [21], are widely used for modelling and solving many problems in systems for constraint programming using finite domain solvers [7,12,27]. Such solvers use various techniques based on the propagation of bounds for arithmetic constraints [14]. The use of bounds based propagation techniques is not new and originates as early as in 1978 [14]. However, the efficiency and level of consistency of such techniques is not studied and described in detail. In this paper, we address the question of what level of consistency can be achieved efficiently on n-ary linear constraints. The observation from Section 5 shows that arc consistency on n-ary linear equations is not tractable. We carefully introduce and formalize the notions of bounds-consistency in the context of discrete CSP. It is shown that arc consistency for linear inequalities system can be achieved with a simple AC-like algorithm in time complexity $\mathcal{O}(en^3d)$. Where an efficient implementation of REVISE is possible as is the case with the projection of linear inequalities, the time complexity is improved to $\mathcal{O}(en^2d)$.

Given that arc consistency on a single n-ary constraint can be NP-complete, we identify a general class of monotonic constraints (which need not be linear) for which arc consistency can be efficiently enforced. Monotonic constraints are actually a special case of *row convex constraints* [26]. [26] presents an algorithm achieving *relational path consistency* for row convex constraints but it behaves exponentially even for a system of two n-ary monotonic constraints (since it is an NP-complete problem).

The work in this paper also extends the results in [28] and complements the GAC-schema [5].

Some open questions suggested by the results here are the following. What are other general classes of n-ary constraints for which enforcing arc consistency is efficient. What is the optimal time complexity for arc consistency on linear inequalities and monotonic constraints?

References

1. F. Bacchus and P. van Beek, "On the conversion between non-binary and binary constraint satisfaction problems", *Proceedings of AAAI-98*, Madison, WI, 1998   471
2. F. Benhamou, D. McAllester, and P. van Hentenryck, "CLP(*intervals*) Revisited", *Proceedings of 1994 International Symposium on Logic Programming*, 124–138, 1994   480, 481
3. F. Benhamou and W. Older, "Applying Interval Arithmetic to Real Integer and Boolean Constraints", *Journal of Logic Programming* 32(1), 1997   475
4. C. Bessiere, "Arc-consistency and arc-consistency again", *Artificial Intelligence* 65:179–190, 1994   470
5. C. Bessiere and J. Regin, "Arc consistency for general constraint networks: preliminary results", *Proceedings of IJCAI-97*, Nagoya, Japan, 1997   471, 472, 481
6. C. Bessiere and J. Regin, "MAC and combined heuristics: two reasons to forsake FC(and CBJ?) on hard problems", *Proceedings of Principles and Practice of Constraint Programming*, Cambridge, MA. 61–75, 1996
7. P. Codognet and D. Diaz, "Compiling Constraints in CLP(FD)", *Journal of Logic Programming* 27(3), 185–226, 1996   481
8. E. Davis Constraint Propagation with Interval Labels *Artificial Intelligence* 32, 281–331, 1987   481
9. R. Dechter, I. Meiri and J. Pearl Temporal constraint networks *Artificial Intelligence* 49, 61–95, 1992   481
10. R. Dechter and J. Pearl, "Tree clustering for constraint networks", *Artificial Intelligence* 38:353–366, 1989   471
11. E. Hyvonen Constraint reasoning based on interval arithmetic: the tolerance propagation approach *Artificial Intelligence* 58, 71–112, 1992   478, 480
12. ILOG, *ILOG SOLVER Reference Manual*   481
13. Joxan Jaffar, Michael J. Maher, Peter J. Stuckey and Roland H. C. Yap Beyond Finite Domains *PPCP'94: Proceedings of the Second Workshop on Principles and Practice of Constraint Programming*, 1994, 86–94   474
14. J. Lauriere, "A language and a program for stating and solving combinatorial problems", *Artificial Intelligence* 10:29–127, 1978   481
15. Y. Lebbah and O. Lhomme Acceleration methods for numeric CSPs *Proc. of AAAI-98* 1998   481
16. Lhomme, Olivier, Consistency Techniques for Numeric CSPs, *Proceedings of IJCAI-93*,Chambery,France,232–238, 1993   481
17. A. K. Mackworth, "Consistency in Networks of Relations", *Artificial Intelligence* 8(1):118–126, 1977   470, 471, 472
18. A. K. Mackworth, "On reading sketch maps", *Proceedings of IJCAI-77*, 598–606, Cambridge MA, 1977   471
19. R. Mohr and G. Masini , "Good old discrete relaxation", *Proceedings of ECAI-88*, 651–656, Munchen, FRG, 1988   471
20. R. E. Moore, *Interval Analysis*, Prentice Hall, 1966   473
21. G. L. Nemhauser and L. A. Wolsey, *Integer and Combinatorial Optimization*, New York, Wiley, 1988   481
22. Older, W. and Vellino,A. Constraint Arithmetic on Real Intervals *Constraint Logic Programming:Selected Research*, Benhamou, F. and Colmerauer, A. (eds.), 175–195,1993   480
23. C. H. Papadimitriou, "On the complexity of integer programming", *J. of the ACM* 28(4):765–768, 1981   480

24. J. C. Regin, "Generalized arc consistency for global cardinality constraint", *Proceedings of AAAI-96*, 209–215, Portland, OR, 1996 470, 471
25. F. Rossi, C. Petrie, and V. Dhar, "On the equivalence of constraint satisfaction problems", *Proceedings of the 9th European Conference on Artificial Intelligence*, 550–556, Stockholm, Sweden, 1990 471
26. P. van Beek and R. Dechter, "On the minimality and global consistency of row-convex constraint networks", *Journal of the ACM* 42(3):543–561, 1995 472, 480, 481
27. P. van Hentenryck, *Constraint Satisfaction and Logic Programming*, MIT Press, Cambridge, 1989 470, 481
28. P. van Hentenryck, Y. Deville, and C. M. Teng, "A Generic Arc-Consistency Algorithm and its Specializations", *Artif. Int.* 58(1992):291–321, 1992 470, 477, 479, 481
29. P. van Hentenryck, L. Michel, and Y. Deville, *Numerica: A Modeling Language for Global Optimization*, MIT Press, Cambridge
30. D. L. Waltz, "Generating semantic descriptions from drawings of scenes with shadows", *MAC-AI-TR-217*, MIT, 1972 470

Some Observations on Durations, Scheduling and Allen's Algebra

` la Z ngelsmark* and ¨eter ´onsson**

Department of Computer and Information Science
Linköpings Universitet, S-581 83 Linköping, Sweden
{olaan,petej}@ida.liu.se

1 Introduction

Representing and reasoning about time has for a long time been acknowledged as one of the core areas of artificial intelligence and a large number of formalisms for temporal constraint reasoning (TCR) have been proposed in the literature. Important examples are the time point algebra [16], Z llen's algebra [1], simple temporal constraints [5] and the qualitative algebra [12]. These formalisms are almost exclusively dealing with the relative positions of time points (qualitaU tive information) and/or the absolute position of time points on the time line (quantitative or metric information).

Recently, the TCR community has shown an increasing interest in reasoning about the *distance* between time points on the time line. For example, suppose one wants to put a bound c on the distance between two time points x and y whose order is possibly unknown. This can be accomplished by imposing the constraint $abs(x - y) \leq c$ (where abs denotes the absolute value function). First studied in Kechter, Meiri & ¨ earl [5], recent examples of formalisms that can handle such constraints can be found in ı avarrete & Marin [13], Wetprasit & Sattar [17] and ¨ ujari & Sattar [15]. The full formalisms are ı ¨ Uhard in all cases but the authors have also identified nontrivial tractable subclasses.

Z n interesting variation on reasoning about distances is reasoning about *durations*, *i.e.*, reasoning about the length of intervals, see Cheng & Smith [3]. Such problems occur naturally in, *e.g.*, scheduling applications. In an (abstract) scheduling problem, we are given a collection of tasks of known durations and constraints on their relative order, say, in the form of limited resources and/or precedence relations, and the question is whether the tasks can be completed within a given time frame. Zs has been observed by Z nger & Rodriguez [2][1], many problems of this type can conveniently be expressed within an extended version of Z llen's interval algebra. Z nger & Rodriguez also presents two algoU rithms for solving this scheduling problem. The first solves the problem exactly

---

* This research has been supported by the Swedish Foundation for Strategic Research as part of the project "Computational Complexity of Temporal and Spatial Constraint Reasoning".

** This research has been supported by the Swedish Research Council for Engineering Sciences (TFR) under grant 97-301.

[1] Other authors, such as Belhadji & Isli [4], have made the same observation.

R. Dechter (Ed.): CP 2000, LNCS 1894, pp. 484–489, 2000.
© Springer-Verlag Berlin Heidelberg 2000

and in polynomial time when the only allowed relations are the basic relations of Zllen's algebra. The second algorithm is a heuristic algorithm for the general case. Clearly, the second algorithm cannot run in polynomial time since even the satisfiability problem is ι ¨Ućomplete when arbitrary relations are allowed.

In this paper we study complexity issues in Zllen's algebra extended for handling metric durations. 15 of the 1B known maximal tractable subclasses are shown to become intractable when metric durations are added, leaving only three for which the corresponding satisfiability problem is tractable. We also extend previous results regarding the scheduling problem and show that the only maximal tractable subclass of Zllen's algebra for which this problem is tractable is the ` RKŲ orn subalgebra, denoted $\mathcal{H}$.

See http://www.ida.liu.se/~olaan/publications.html for a full version of this paper with complete proofs and a more extensive discussion.

2   Metric Duration Information in Allen's Algebra

We extend Zllen's algebra to handle metric durations and the problem is formuU lated asL

Definition 1 (D-ISAT). *For an interval $I \in V$, we let d9I5 denote the duration of I, ie7, $I^+ - I^-$. An instance of the problem of interval satisfiability with metric duration information for a set $\mathcal{I}$ of interval relations, denoted D-ISAT$\mathcal{I}$5, is a tuple $Q = \langle V, E, X \rangle$ where X is a set of duration relations, expressed as Horn DLRs on d9I5.*

There are currently 1B known maximal tractable subclasses of Zllen's algeU bra [1I6 6]7 Three of them $9\mathcal{H}$ [1I]6 $\mathcal{S}9{\succ}5$ and $\mathcal{E}9{\prec}5$ [:]5 can be extended with metric constraints on durations without sacrificing tractability of the satisfiaU bility problem while the remaining 1q subclasses become ι ¨Ućomplete even if the only allowed duration information is the assignment of fixed lengths to the intervals7

$\mathcal{H}$ can easily be extended to handle durations7To see this6we note that ` RKU , orn is a subset of , orn KQRs and it is possible to add an arbitrary number of constraints of the form $I^+ - I^- = d_I$6 where I^+ and I^- are end points of an interval $I \in V$ and d_I is the required duration of this interval6 and still only deal with , orn KQRs7The problem of satisifiability for , orn KQRs is tractable6 see Xoubarakis [11] 9or ´onsson k Eäckström [18]Ƀ We denote this algorithm ALG-HORNDLRSAT7

That the subclasses $\mathcal{S}9{\succ}5$ and $\mathcal{E}9{\prec}5$ can be extended to handle metric duU ration information and still remain tractable follows from the correctness of the algorithm ALG-D-ISAT$_{\mathcal{S}(\succ)}$ in figure 17 9The algorithm for $\mathcal{E}9{\prec}5$ is gained by exchanging starting and ending pointsƀ ffor details on the subroutine ALG-ISAT$_{\mathcal{S}(\succ)}$ see Krakengren k ´onsson [:]7

Theorem 1. *$\mathcal{H}$, $\mathcal{S}9{\succ}5$ and $\mathcal{E}9{\prec}5$ are the only known maximal tractable subclasses of Allen's algebra for which the D-ISAT problem is tractable.*

Algorithm: ALG-D-ISAT$_{\mathcal{S}(\succ)}$
input: Instance $Q = \langle V, E, X \rangle$ of D-ISAT($\mathcal{S}(\succ)$)
```
 1  if not ALG-ISAT_{S(≻)}(⟨V, E⟩) then
 2     reject
 3  K := ∅
 4  for each ⟨I, r, J⟩ ∈ E do
 5     if not ALG-ISAT_{S(≻)}(⟨V, E ∪ {I¬{s, s⁻¹}J}⟩) then
 6        K := K ∪ {d(I) ≠ d(J)}
 7     if not ALG-ISAT_{S(≻)}(⟨V, E ∪ {I¬{≡, s}J}⟩) then
 8        K := K ∪ {d(I) ≤ d(J)}
 9     if not ALG-ISAT_{S(≻)}(⟨V, E ∪ {I¬{≡, s⁻¹}J}⟩) then
10        K := K ∪ {d(I) ≥ d(J)}
11  end for
12  X' := X ∪ {d(I) > 0 | I ∈ V}
13  if not ALG-HORNDLRSAT(X' ∪ K) then
14     reject
15  accept
```

Fig. 1. The ALG-D-ISAT$_{\mathcal{S}(\succ)}$ algorithm

Proof (Sketch). That the D-ISAT problem is tractable for $\mathcal{H}, \mathcal{S}9 \succ 5$ and $\mathcal{E}9 \prec 5$ follows from the previous discussion6 and it can be shown that the problem becomes ı ¨ ₵omplete for each of the remaining 1q classes7

3   The Scheduling Problem

We define the computational problem SCHED9$\mathcal{S}$5 as followsL

INSTANCE: Zn instance Θ of ₦ZT9$\mathcal{S}$5 with variable set V together with

17 a duration $d9I5 \in \mathbb{Z}^+$ for each $I \in V$ Rand
37 a *schedule length* $K \in \mathbb{Z}^+ 7$

QUESTION: ₦ there a model M of Θ such that

17 $M9I^+5 - M9I^-5 = d9I5$ for all $I \in V$ Rand
37 $K \geq 9\max_{I \in V} M9I^+55 - 9\min_{I \in V} M9I^-557$

Theorem 2. $\mathcal{H}$ *is the only known maximal subclass of Allen's algebra for which the scheduling problem is tractable.*

Proof (Sketch). The following shows that $\mathcal{H}$ really is tractable6 while the inU tractability of $\mathcal{S}9 \succ 5$ and $\mathcal{E}9 \prec 5$ can be shown using polynomialₜime reduction from the 3-COLORABILITY problem7

Ǫet Θ be an instance of SCHED9$\mathcal{H}$5 with schedule length K6 variable set V and constraint set E7 Ǫet $\nu = \{I^+ - I^- = d9I5 \mid I \in V\}$ where $d9I5$ is the duration of interval I7 Nonsider the relation $r = 9\equiv$ s f d5 $\in \mathcal{H}$7 This relation has the property that given $J_0 r J_1 6 J_0^- \geq J_1^-$ and $J_0^+ \leq J_1^+ 6 \, i.e.6 \, r$ expresses the fact that J_0 is inside J_1 71 ow add a fresh interval variable J together with the constraint $J^+ - J^- = K$ to ν6 and for each $I \in V$ add the constraint $I r J 7 \nu \cup E$ give us an instance Θ' of D-ISAT9$\mathcal{H}$56 which is tractable by the previous section7

Since the D-ISAT problem is intractable for the remaining 1q subclasses6 it follows that this also holds for the scheduling problem7

Thus $\mathcal{H}$ is the only known maximal subclass such that the scheduling problem is tractable7 This results extends Z nger and Rodriguez's [3] previously mentioned tractability result in at least two waysL915 we allow far more temporal relationsR and 935 we allow intervals with uncertain durations7

4 Summary

Table 1. The 1B known subclasses of Z llen's algebra7 Z ∘ marks a tractable problem7 $\mathbf{A}_{r,b}$ denotes the set of all A9r, b5 subclasses of Z llen's algebra

Subclass	ISAT	D-ISAT	SCHED
$\mathcal{H}$	∘	∘	∘
$\mathcal{S}(\succ)$	∘	∘	
$\mathcal{S}(\mathsf{d})$	∘		
$\mathcal{S}(\mathsf{o}^{-1})$	∘		
$\mathcal{E}(\prec)$	∘	∘	
$\mathcal{E}(\mathsf{d})$	∘		
$\mathcal{E}(\mathsf{o})$	∘		
$\mathcal{S}^*$	∘		
$\mathcal{E}^*$	∘		
$\mathbf{A}_{\equiv}$	∘		
$\mathbf{A}_{r,b}$	∘		

The results in this paper are summarized in table 17 ffor definitions of the respective classes6 see 1 ebel k Eürckert [1D] and Krakengren k ´onsson [: 6]7

5 Conclusion

While a complete classification of the subclasses of Z llen's algebra is yet to be made6 we know much about the 'undiscovered' classes7 $\mathcal{V}$ was shown in [M] that $\mathcal{S}$9$\succ$5 and $\mathcal{E}$9$\prec$5 are the only possible maximal tractable subclasses containing the relation 9$\prec$ $\succ$5 and thus can express *sequentiality*6 which is considered an important notion in many Z Vcontexts6 e.g.6 planning7 $\mathcal{V}$n the same paper it was shown that a new tractable subclass can contain at most the basic relations 9$\equiv$56 9b5 and 9b^{-1}56 where $b \in \{\mathsf{d}, \mathsf{o}, \mathsf{s}, \mathsf{f}\}$7 This quells most hope of finding a subclass more expressive than any known today while still retaining tractability7

It is important to note that while we have shown intractability of the schedul‑
ing problem for all but one of the known maximal tractable subclasses of Zllen's
algebra6this does not rule out the existence of interesting subclasses which are
not maximal7

References

1. J. F. Allen. Maintaining knowledge about temporal intervals. *Communications of the ACM*, 26(11):832–843, 1983. 484
2. F. D. Anger and R. V. Rodriguez. Effective scheduling of tasks under weak temporal interval constraints. In B. Bouchon-Meunier, R. R. Yager, and L. A. Zadeh, editors, *Advances in Intelligent Computing - IPMU'94*, pages 584–594. Springer, Berlin, 1994. 484, 487
3. C.-C. Cheng and S. F. Smith. Generating Feasible Schedules under Complex Metric Constraints. In *Proceedings of the 12th National Conference on Artificial Intelligence (AAAI-94)*, pages 1086–1091. AAAI Press, 1994. 484
4. S. Belhadji and A. Isli. Temporal constraint satisfaction techniques in job shop scheduling problem solving. *Constraints*, 3:203–212, 1998. 484
5. R. Dechter, I. Meiri, and J. Pearl. Temporal constraint networks. *Artificial Intelligence*, 49:61–95, 1991. 484
6. T. Drakengren and P. Jonsson. Eight maximal tractable subclasses of Allen's algebra with metric time. *Journal of Artificial Intelligence Research*, 7:25–45, 1997. 485, 487
7. T. Drakengren and P. Jonsson. Towards a complete classification of tractability in Allen's algebra. In IJCAI [9]. 487
8. T. Drakengren and P. Jonsson. Twenty-one large tractable subclasses of Allen's algebra. *Artificial Intelligence*, 1997. To appear. 485, 487
9. *Proceedings of the 15th International Joint Conference on Artificial Intelligence (IJCAI-97)*, Nagoya, Japan, Aug. 1997. Morgan Kaufmann. 488
10. P. Jonsson and C. Bäckström. A unifying approach to temporal constraint reasoning. *Artificial Intelligence*, 102(1):143–155, 1998. 485
11. M. Koubarakis. Tractable disjunctions of linear constraints. In *Proceedings of the 2nd International Conference on Principles and Practice for Constraint Programming*, pages 297–307, Cambridge, MA, Aug. 1996. 485
12. I. Meiri. Combining qualitative and quantitative constraints in temporal reasoning. *Artificial Intelligence*, 87(1-2):343–385, 1996. 484
13. I. Navarrete and R. Marin. Qualitative temporal reasoning with points and duarations. In IJCAI [9], pages 1454–1459. 484
14. B. Nebel and H.-J. Bürckert. Reasoning about temporal relations: A maximal tractable subclass of Allen's interval algebra. *Journal of the ACM*, 42(1):43–66, 1995. 485, 487
15. A. K. Pujari and A. Sattar. A new framework for reasoning about points, intervals and durations. In *Proceedings of the 16th International Joint Conference on Artificial Intelligence (IJCAI-99)*, pages 1259–1267, Stockholm, Sweden, 1999. 484
16. M. B. Vilain, H. A. Kautz, and P. G. van Beek. Constraint propagation algorithms for temporal reasoning: A revised report. In D. S. Weld and J. de Kleer, editors, *Readings in Qualitative Reasoning about Physical Systems*, pages 373–381. Morgan Kaufmann, San Mateo, Ca, 1989. 484

17. R. Wetprasit and A. Sattar. Temporal reasoning with qualitative and quantitative information about points and durations. In *Proceedings of the 15th National Conference on Artificial Intelligence (AAAI-98)*, pages 656–663. AAAI Press, 1998. 484

Using Randomization and Learning to Solve Hard Real-World Instances of Satisfiability

Luís Eaptista and João Marques-Silva

Department of Informatics, Technical University of Lisbon,
IST/INESC/CEL, Lisbon, Portugal
{lmtb,jpms}@algos.inesc.pt

Abstract. This paper addresses the interaction between randomization, with restart strategies, and learning, an often crucial technique for proving unsatisfiability. We use instances of SAT from the hardware verification domain to provide evidence that randomization can indeed be essential in solving real-world satisfiable instances of SAT. More interestingly, our results indicate that randomized restarts and learning may cooperate in proving both satisfiability and unsatisfiability. Finally, we utilize and expand the idea of algorithm portfolio design to propose an alternative approach for solving hard unsatisfiable instances of SAT.

1 Introduction

Recent work on the Satisfiability Problem (SAT) has provided experimental and theoretical evidence that randomization and restart strategies can be quite effective at solving hard satisfiable instances of SAT [4]. Indeed, backtrack search algorithms, randomized and run with restarts, were shown to perform significantly better on specific problem instances. Recent work has also demonstrated the usefulness of learning in solving hard instances of SAT [2,: ,8]. Learning, in the form of clause (*nogood*) recording, is the underlying mechanism by which non-chronological backtracking, relevance-based learning, and other search pruning techniques, can be implemented.

In this paper we propose to conduct a preliminary study of the interaction between randomization and learning in solving real-world hard satisfiable instances of SAT. Moreover, we propose a new problem solving strategy for solving hard unsatisfiable instances of SAT. Throughout the paper we focus on real-world instances of SAT from the hardware verification domain, namely superscalar processor verification [M][1]. These instances can either be satisfiable or unsatisfiable and are in general extremely hard for state of the art SAT solvers.

2 Randomization and Learning

A complete backtrack search SAT algorithm is *randomized* by introducing a fixed or variable amount of randomness in the branching heuristic [4]. The amount

---

[1] The superscalar processor verification instances can be obtained from the URL http://www.ece.cmu.edu/~mvelev.

R. Dechter (Ed.): CP 2000, LNCS 1894, pp. 489–494, 2000.

of randomness may affect the value of the selected variable, which variable is selected from the set of variables with the highest heuristic metric, or even which variable is selected from a set of variables within $x\%$ of the highest value of the heuristic metric. Morever, a *restart strategy* consists of defining a *cutoff* value in the number of backtracks, and repeatedly running a randomized complete SAT algorithm, each time limiting the maximum number of backtracks to the imposed cutoff value.

If randomized restarts are used with a fixed cutoff value, then the resulting algorithm is *not* complete. Even though the resulting algorithm has a non-zero probability of solving every satisfiable instance, it may not be able to prove instances unsatisfable. One simple solution to this limitation, that allows solving unsatisfiable instances, is to implement a policy for increasing the cutoff value. For example, after each restart the backtrack cutoff value can be increased by a constant amount. The resulting algorithm is complete, and thus able to prove unsatisfiability.

Clause (*nogood*) recording (i.e. learning) techniques are currently the foundation upon which modern backtrack search algorithms [2,:,8] build to implement different search pruning techniques, including non-chronological backtracking, relevance-based learning, among others. If an algorithm implements branching randomization and a restart strategy, then each time the cutoff limit on the number of backtracks is reached, new clauses are expected to have been identified. These clauses may either be discarded or kept for subsequent restarts of the algorithm. Clearly, one can limit the size of the clauses that are to be kept in between restarts. Eelow, we study how useful the different aspects of learning are when randomization with a restart strategy is used.

Next we compare GRASP [:] and SATZ [5] with randomization and restarts (results without restarts that involve these and other algorithms, as well as additional results with restarts, are analyzed in [1])[2]. For each instance and for each algorithm the number of runs was limited to 10. A significantly larger number would have required excessive run times.

Table 1 contains the results of running GRASP with chronological backtracking enabled (C), and with no clauses being recorded, and the results for the randomized version of SATZ [4,5]. For SATZ the cutoff values used were 20000, 1000 and 100 backtracks. For GRASP, the two inital cutoff and increment values considered were 100/0 and 500/250. As can be concluded, SATZ is only able to solve two instances for any of the cutoff values considered, and for these two instances, the CPU times decrease with smaller cutoff values. In addition, SATZ exceeds the allowed CPU time for all the other instances and for the different cutoff values considered. The results for GRASP depend on the cutoff initial and increment values. The utilization of the combination 100   /0 is clearly better for

---

[2] The results were obtained on a P-II 400 MHz Linux machine with 256 MByte of physical memory. The CPU time limit was set to 3,000 seconds. Column Time denotes the CPU time and column X denotes the number of times, out of the total number of runs, the algorithm was *not* able to solve the given instance.

Table 1. Results for Grasp with Restarts and without Learning and for SATZ

Instance	Grp 0/0C 100/0		Grp 0/0C 500/250		Satz 20000		Satz 1000		Satz 100	
	Time	X	Time	X	Time	X	Time	X	Time	X
2dlx_cc_bug1	790.0	1	2464.7	8	3000	10	3000	10	3000	10
2dlx_cc_bug105	7.3	0	120.2	0	3000	10	3000	10	3000	10
2dlx_cc_bug11	172.1	0	1702.4	4	3000	10	3000	10	3000	10
2dlx_cc_bug38	166.4	0	2121.8	6	3000	10	3000	10	3000	10
2dlx_cc_bug54	1322.2	3	2859.9	9	1208	2	359.0	1	142.2	0
2dlx_cc_bug80	397.5	0	1665.4	5	3000	10	3000	10	3000	10
dlx2_cc_a_bug5	1652.6	3	3000.0	10	3000	10	3000	10	3000	10
dlx2_cc_a_bug59	278.3	0	2099.0	6	657	0	79.4	0	41.4	0
dlx2_cc_bug02	1140.1	2	2768.2	8	3000	10	3000	10	3000	10
dlx2_cc_bug08	426.3	0	2852.8	9	3000	10	3000	10	3000	10

Table 2. Results with Restarts and Learning (cutoff/increment = 500/250)

Instance	Grasp 0/0		Grasp 0/10		Grasp 0/20		Grasp 10/20		Grasp 20/20	
	Time	X	Time	X	Time	X	Time	X	Time	X
2dlx_cc_bug1	57.0	0	67.0	0	105.9	0	66.3	0	196.2	0
2dlx_cc_bug105	19.6	0	22.2	0	25.5	0	33.7	0	51.4	0
2dlx_cc_bug11	240.4	0	338.8	0	399.1	0	168.5	0	226.9	0
2dlx_cc_bug38	44.4	0	54.4	0	50.3	0	73.6	0	100.4	0
2dlx_cc_bug54	252.6	0	228.1	0	198.1	0	166.8	0	143.3	0
2dlx_cc_bug80	127.3	0	54.7	0	50.5	0	41.5	0	59.8	0
dlx2_cc_a_bug5	133.9	0	121.9	0	206.1	0	151.0	0	204.4	0
dlx2_cc_a_bug59	33.2	0	14.2	0	24.3	0	17.8	0	17.3	0
dlx2_cc_bug02	147.6	0	49.9	0	47.0	0	42.9	0	91.9	0
dlx2_cc_bug08	48.8	0	27.0	0	19.8	0	25.7	0	29.8	0

these problem instances. Nevertheless, the algorithm quits in a few cases and for some runs.

Table 2 contains the results of running GRASP with non-chronological back-tracking enabled, using randomization and restarts, and with different clause recording arrangements. Each column is identified by two values ws/g, denoting the largest clause size that is kept in between restarts (ws), and the largest clause size that GRASP records during the search (g). For this experiment the initial cutoff value was set to 500, and the increment set to 250. The conclusions are clear. Branching randomization with a restart strategy allows solving *all* problem instances for *all* runs, provided learning is enabled. Moreover, and in most of the examples, recording clauses both during the search and in between restarts, can contribute to reducing the CPU times.

492   Luís Baptista and João Marques-Silva

3   Algorithm Portfolio Design

Recent work on algorithm portfolio design [3] has shown that a portfolio approach for solving hard instances of SAT can lead to significant performance gains. Basically, a set of algorithms is selected which is then used for solving each problem instance on different processors, or interleaving the execution of several algorithms in one or more processors. In this section we explore this idea with the objective of solving hard *unsatisfiable* instances of SAT. As before, the problem instances studied were obtained from hardware verification problems [7].

Our portfolio approach is somewhat different than what was proposed in [3], and targets proving unsatisfiability for hard instances of SAT. Instead of having fundamentally different algorithms, or several copies of the same algorithm running on different processors, our approach is to utilize randomization with a restart strategy, and each time the search is restart, a *different* algorithm is selected from a set of k different algorithms $\{A_1, \ldots, A_k\}$. Each algorithm $\{A_i\}$ has a given probability p_i of being selected.

The key aspects that characterize our portfolio approach are that the restart strategy used is to iteratively increase the cutoff limit, thus guaranteeing completeness of the algorithm, and that learning between restarts is used, thus reusing information from previously searched portions of the search tree to avoid subsequently searching equivalent portions.

In our current solution, instead of using significantly different search algorithms, we utilize instead significantly different configurations of the same algorithm, GRASP. Different configurations of GRASP basically allow different branching heuristics, different amounts of randomization in the branching heuristics, different learning bounds during the search, and different learning bounds in between restarts.

For the results presented below, the portfolio of configurations considered was the following:

- Four different configurations with similar probabilities are used.
- The limit on recorded clauses during search ranges from 30 to 40.
- Relevance-based learning ranges from 4 to 5.
- Recorded clauses in between restarts range from 10 to 15.
- The amount of randomization is fixed for all configurations.
- Three well-known and widely used branching heuristics are used (see [1]).

The experimental results for the unsatisfiable hardware verification instances [7] are shown in Table 3. For this experiment, we evaluated two portfolio organizations, i.e. pf1 and pf2, that differ in the initial cutoff and increment values. For pf1 the values were set to 500/250, and for pf2 the values were set to 100/50.

The results for the default GRASP algorithm results are shown in column Grasp, the results for the restart strategy in column Grasp (rst), and the results for the portfolio approach in columns Grasp (pf1) and Grasp (pf2). In addition, the results for rel_sat, SATZ and randomized SATZ (Satz (rst)) are

Table 3. Results on Unsatisfiable Instances

File	Grasp		Grasp (rst)		Grasp (pf1)		Grasp (pf2)		Relsat		Satz		Satz (rst)	
	Time	X	Time	X	Time	X	Time	X	Time	X	Time	X	Time	X
dlx1_c	1.9	0	2.2	0	3.6	0	3.7	0	7.0	0	7918.7	0	10000	10
dlx2_aa	1.8	0	2.7	0	17.5	0	9.5	0	23.7	0	10000	1	10000	10
dlx2_ca	2686.7	0	3006.1	0	631.3	0	758.2	0	10000	1	10000	1	10000	10
dlx2_cc	100000	1	10000	10	2032.1	0	2401.6	0	10000	1	10000	1	10000	10
dlx2_cl	100000	1	10000	10	1076.4	0	1077.9	0	10000	1	10000	1	10000	10
dlx2_cs	9598.1	0	8970.4	6	987.0	0	1263.3	0	10000	1	10000	1	10000	10
dlx2_la	6259.2	0	9617.4	7	307.7	0	382.0	0	10000	1	10000	1	10000	10
dlx2_sa	12.0	0	7.6	0	34.2	0	29.0	0	295.6	0	10000	1	10000	10

also shown. In all cases the CPU time limit was 10,000 seconds, with the exception of the default GRASP algorithm for which 100,000 seconds were allowed. Finally, and as in the previous section, the total number of runs was 10 for the algorithms using randomization with restarts.

As can be concluded, the portfolio approach, built on top of branching randomization with restarts, allows solving *all* instances with much smaller run times (for the harder instances more than 1 order magnitude faster). Of the two organizations evaluated, the best results were obtained with the initial cutoff and increment values set to 500/250, since on average this choice of values allows solving the harder instances faster. We should note that, to our best knowledge, no other SAT algorithm is capable of solving the harder instances, dlx2_cc and dlx2_cl, thus suggesting that an approach based on a portfolio of configurations may be crucial for proving unsatisfiability for some classes of instances.

4   Conclusions

This paper studies the interaction between randomization and learning in backtrack search SAT algorithms when solving real-world hard instances of SAT. Preliminary results indicate that both randomization and learning (in the form of non-chronological backtracking ability and recorded clauses) can be essential for solving the satisfiable problem instances studied. Moreover, and for unsatisfiable instances, we have provided empirical evidence that randomization and learning, when utilizing a portfolio of algorithm configurations, may solve problem instances that, to our best knowledge, no known SAT algorithm is otherwise able to solve. Finally, the experimental results obtained indicate that significantly different organizations (in terms of the initial cutoff and increment values) may be required for proving either satisfiability or unsatisfiability. Future work will necessarily address developing unified organizations for proving both satisfiability and unsatisfiability in classes of problem instances.

494   Luís Baptista and João Marques-Silva

References

1. L. Baptista and J. P. Marques-Silva. The interplay of randomization and learning on real-world instances of satisfiability. In *AAAI Workshop on Leveraging Probability and Uncertatinty in Computation*, July 2000. 490, 492
2. R. Bayardo Jr. and R. Schrag. Using CSP look-back techniques to solve real-world SAT instances. In *Proceedings of the National Conference on Artificial Intelligence*, 1997. 489, 490
3. C. P. Gomes and B. Selman. Algorithm portfolio design: Theory vs. practice. In *Proceedings of the Thirteenth Conference On Uncertainty in Artificial Intelligence*, 1997. 492
4. C. P. Gomes, B. Selman, and H. Kautz. Boosting combinatorial search through randomization. In *Proceedings of the National Conference on Artificial Intelligence*, July 1998. 489, 490
5. C. M. Li and Anbulagan. Look-ahead versus look-back for satisfiability problems. In *Proceedings of International Conference on Principles and Practice of Constraint Programming*, 1997. 490
6. J. P. Marques-Silva and K. A. Sakallah. GRASP-A search algorithm for propositional satisfiability. *IEEE Transactions on Computers*, 48(5):506–521, May 1999. 489, 490
7. M. N. Velev and R. E. Bryant. Superscalar processor verification using efficient reductions from the logic of equality with uninterpreted functions to propositional logic. In *Proceedings of Correct Hardware Design and Verification Methods*, LNCS 1703, pages 37–53, September 1999. 489, 492
8. H. Zhang. SATO: An efficient propositional prover. In *Proceedings of the International Conference on Automated Deduction*, pages 272–275, July 1997. 489, 490

Finding Minimal Unsatisfiable Subformulae in Satisfiability Instances

Renato Bruni and Antonio Sassano

Dipartimento di Informatica e Sistemistica, Università di Roma "La Sapienza"
via Buonarroti 12 - I-00185 Roma, Italy
{bruni,sassano}@dis.uniroma1.it

Abstract. A minimal unsatisfiable subformula (MUS) of a given CNF is a set of clauses which is unsatisfiable, but becomes satisfiable as soon as we remove any of its clauses. In practical scenarios it is often useful to know, in addition to the unsolvability of an instance, which parts of the instance cause the unsolvability. An approach is here proposed to the problem of automatic detection of such a subformula, with the double aim of finding quickly a small-sized one. We make use of an adaptive technique in order to rapidly select an unsatisfiable subformula which is a good approximation of a MUS. Hard unsatisfiable instances can be reduced to remarkably smaller problems, and hence efficiently solved, through this approach.

1 Introduction

We call minimal unsatisfiable subformula (MUS) of a logic CNF formula a set of clauses which is unsatisfiable, but becomes satisfiable removing any of its clauses (see sec. 2). An approach is here proposed to the problem of automatic detection of a MUS, with the double aim of finding it small, and of proving unsatisfiability faster. As for the first point, in fact, in practical scenarios it is often useful to know, in addition to the unsolvability of an instance, which parts of the instance cause the unsolvability. This expecially holds when the logic formula is obtained form the encoding of some other problem, and should be satisfiable. As for the second point, the task of proving unsatisfiability usually turns out to be computationally harder than proving satisfiability. Techniques to prove unsatisfiability by performing a fast complete enumeration are widely proposed in literature. Here, on the contrary, a technique is presented to reduce the set that enumeration works on.

We can, roughly speaking, classify the solution methods for the Satisfiability problem in exact and heuristic ones. The proposed procedure is a complete one. Most of complete methods are branching procedures based on case splitting. On the contrary, we use a new branching scheme, whose branching rule consists in trying to satisfy at first the hardest clauses while visiting a clause-based branching tree [1] (see sec. 3). Moreover, we use an Adaptive Core Search in order to rapidly select an unsatisfiable subformula, which is a good approximation of a MUS (see sec. 4). Small but hard unsatisfiable instances can be efficiently solved

R. Dechter (Ed.): CP 2000, LNCS 1894, pp. 495–499, 2000.

through this approach. More important, unsatisfiable subformulae are detected in all problems solved. Their size is often remarkably smaller than the original formulae. The proposed procedure is tested on a set of unsatisfiable artificially generated hard problems from the Dimacs collection.

2   Minimal Unsatisfiable Subformulae

Let A be the ground set of the literals a_i. Define $\neg a_l = a_{n+l}$ and $\neg a_{n+l} = a_l$.

$A \equiv \{a_i : a_i = \alpha_i \text{ for } i = 1, \ldots, n \; ; a_i = \neg \alpha_{i-n} \text{ for } i = n+1, \ldots, 2n\}$ Every clause is a set $C_j = \{a_i : i \in I_j \subseteq I \equiv \{1, \ldots, 2n\}\}$. A CNF formula is collection $\mathcal{F}$ of sets C_j over A: $\mathcal{F} = \{C_j : j = 1, \ldots, m\}$.

A truth assignment for the logical variable is a set $S = \{a_i : a_i \in S \Rightarrow \neg a_i \notin S\}$. It is partial if $|S| < n$, i.e. some variables are not assigned, and complete if $|S| = n$. Given a partial truth assignment S, the set of possible completion is $C(S) = \{a_i : a_i \notin S \wedge \neg a_i \notin S\}$. S satisfies C if and only if $S \cap C \neq \phi$. S falsifies C if and only if $C(S) \cap C = \phi$.

A minimal unsatisfiable subformula (MUS) is a collection $\mathcal{G} \subseteq \mathcal{F}$ of clauses of the original instance having the following properties:

1. $\forall S, \; \exists C_j \in \mathcal{G}$ such that $S \cap C_j = \phi$ (unsatisfiable)
2. $\forall \mathcal{H} \subset \mathcal{G}, \; \exists S$ such that $\forall C_j \in \mathcal{H}, \; S \cap C_j \neq \phi$ (every subset is sat.)

Of course, if any subformula is unsatisfiable, the whole problem is. On the other hand, an unsatisfiable formula always contains a MUS.

There are procedures that, given a set of clauses, recognize whether it is a MUS or not in polynomial time [3]. The key point is how to select a MUS. We propose a procedure to rapidly select a good approximation of a MUS, that means an unsatisfiable set of clauses having almost as few clauses as the smallest MUS.

3   The Branching Scheme

In order to reduce backtracks, it's clearly better to start assignment satisfying the more difficult clauses [1], i.e. those which have the fewest satisfying truth assignments, or, in other words, represent the more constraining relations. The point is how to find hardest clauses. An *a priori* parameter is the length: unit clauses are universally recognized to be hard, and the procedure of unit propagation, universally performed, satisfies them at first. Since hardness is due both to the clause itself and to the rest of the instance, a merely *a priori* evaluation is not easy to carry on.

Our evaluation of clause hardness is based on the history of the search, and keeps improving throughout the computation. We say that a clause C_j is *visited* when we make a truth assignment aimed at satisfying C_j, and that C_j cause a *failure* either when an empty clause is generated due to truth assignment made on C_j, or when C_j itself becomes empty. Visiting C_j many times shows that C_j

is difficult, and failing on it shows even more clearly that C_j is difficult. Counting visits and failures requires a very little overhead.

Therefore, we use the following branching rule:

1. Perform all unit resolutions.
2. When no unit clauses are present, make a truth assignment satisfying the clause C_{max} which maximizes our clause hardness measure φ (v_j is the number of visits, f_j the number of failures, p a parameter giving the penalty considered for failures, and l_j the length of the clause).

$$\varphi(C_j) = (v_j + pf_j) \,/\, l_j$$

To satisfy C_{max}, we add to the partial solution S a literal $a_l \in C(S)$ such that $a_l \in C_{max}$. If we need to backtrack, the next assignment is not just $\neg a_l$, because it does not satisfy C_{max}. Instead, we add another literal $a_k \in C_{max} \cap C(S)$ [1]. If $C_{max} \cap C(S)$ becomes empty, we obviously backtrack again to

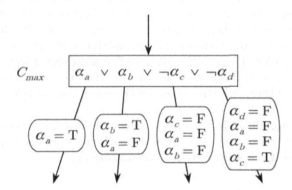

Fig. 1. Example of C_{max} with the consistent branching possibilities

the truth assignments made to satisfy the previous clause, until we have another choice. This is a complete scheme, because, if a satisfying truth assignment exists, it will be reached, and, if the search tree is completely explored, the instance is unsatisfiable.

4   Adaptive Core Search

By applying the above branching scheme, and φ to evaluate clauses hardness, we develop the following procedure of Adaptive Core Search.

0. (*Preprocessing*) Perform p branching iterations using just shortest clause rule (This gives initial values to φ). If instance is already solved, *Stop*.
1. (*Base*) Select an initial collection of hardest clauses whose cardinality is proportional to cardinality of $\mathcal{F}$:
$\mathcal{C}_1 = \{C_j : C_j \in \mathcal{F},\ \varphi(C_j) \geq \varphi(C_k)\ \forall C_k \in \mathcal{F},\ |\mathcal{C}| = c|\mathcal{F}|,\ c < 1\}$
This is our first core, i.e. candidate to be a MUS. Remaining clauses form another collection $\mathcal{O}_1 = \mathcal{F} \setminus \mathcal{C}_1$.

k. (*Iteration*) Perform h branching iteration on $\mathcal{C}_k$, ignoring $\mathcal{O}_k$. Obtain one of the following:

- $\mathcal{C}_k$ is unsatisfiable $\Rightarrow \mathcal{F}$ is unsatisfiable, then *Stop*.
- no answer after h iteration $\Rightarrow$ Re-start from (*Base*) selecting a new set of hardest clauses (allowed only a finite number t of times, in order to ensure termination: after t times, h is increased).
- $\mathcal{C}_k$ is satisfied by solution $S_k \Rightarrow$ Test S_k on $\mathcal{O}_k$. One of the following:
  - $\forall\, C_j \in \mathcal{O}_k,\ S_k \cap C_j \neq \phi \Rightarrow \mathcal{F}$ is satisfied, then *Stop*.
  - $\exists\, C_j \in \mathcal{O}_k,\mid C(S_k) \cap C_j = \phi$. Call this collection of falsified clauses $\mathcal{N}_k$. Add them to the core, obtaining $\mathcal{C}_{k+1} = \mathcal{C}_k \cup \mathcal{N}_k$, delete the partial solution S_k, and apply again (*Iteration*).
  - $\exists\, C_j \in \mathcal{O}_k,\mid S_k \cap C_j = \phi$ and $\nexists\, C_j \in \mathcal{O}_k,\mid C(S_k) \cap C_j = \phi$ Try to extend the partial solution S_k to $\mathcal{F}$ putting $\mathcal{C}_{k+1} = \mathcal{F}$ and apply again (*Iteration*).

The main idea is that we select the clauses that resulted hard during the branching phase, and try to solve them as if they were our entire instance. If they really are an unsatisfiable instance, we have done. If, after h branching iterations we cannot solve them, this means that our instance is still too big, and it must be reduced more. Finally, if we find a satisfying solution for the core, we try to extend it to the rest of the clauses. If some clauses are falsified, they are difficult (together with the clauses of the core), and therefore they should be added to the core.

The above algorithm is a complete one, and solves, in average case, smaller subproblems at the nodes of the search tree, hence operations performed, such like unit propagation, work only on current core $\mathcal{C}_k$.

5   Computational Results

Columns labeled n, m and *sol* show respectively number of variables, number of clauses and solution of the Satisfiability problem. Columns labeled 'branch', 'ACS sel', 'ACS sol', 'ACS tot' respectively are the running times for the branching procedure only (without Adaptive core Search), core selection, core solving, and total times of Adaptive Core Search. n_{core} and m_{core} are the number of variables and clauses appearing in the unsatisfiable subformula selected. Times are in CPU seconds.

The test problems (all unsatisfiable) are from the DIMACS. Four of them were used in the test set of the Second DIMACS Implementation Challenge [2]. Our running times on them are compared with those of the four faster complete algorithms of that challenge (C-sat , 2cl , TabuS and BRR). Times are normalized according to the DIMACS benchmark *dfmax*, in order to compare them in a machine-independent way.

6 Conclusions

An approach is here proposed to the problem of automatic detection of a MUS, with the double aim of finding a small-sized one, and of proving unsatisfiability faster. In particular, we present a clause based tree search paradigm for Satisfiability testing, a new heuristic to identify hard clauses, that are the clauses most likely to appear in a MUS, and the complete algorithm for approximating a Minimal Unsatisfiable Subformula.

Smaller unsatisfiable subformulae are detected in all the solved unsatisfiable instances. These can be remarkably smaller then the original formula, and give an approximation of a MUS in extremely short times.

Table 1. Results of C-SAT, 2cl(limited resolution), DPL with Tabu Search, B-reduction and ACS on the *aim* series: 3-SAT artificially generated problems. Times are normalized according to *dfmax* results, as if they were obtained on our same machine

Problem	n	m	sol	C sat	2cl	Tabu S	BRR	br.	ACS sel	ACS sol	ACS tot	n_{core}	m_{core}
aim-100-1_6-no-1	100	160	U					1.09	0.17	0.03	0.20	43	48
aim-100-1_6-no-2	100	160	U					0.67	0.54	0.39	0.93	46	54
aim-100-1_6-no-3	100	160	U					3.91	0.62	0.73	1.35	51	57
aim-100-1_6-no-4	100	160	U					0.52	0.61	0.35	0.96	43	48
aim-100-2_0-no-1	100	200	U	52.19	19.77	409.50	5.78	0.03	0.03	0.01	0.04	18	19
aim-100-2_0-no-2	100	200	U	14.63	11.00	258.58	0.57	0.38	0.05	0.04	0.09	37	40
aim-100-2_0-no-3	100	200	U	56.21	6.53	201.15	2.95	0.12	0.04	0.01	0.05	25	27
aim-100-2_0-no-4	100	200	U	0.05	11.66	392.23	4.80	0.11	0.04	0.01	0.05	26	32
Average (on last 4)				30.82	12.50	320.15	3.52	0.16	0.04	0.02	0.06		

Problem	n	m	literals	sol	branch	ACS sel	ACS sol	ACS tot	n_{core}	m_{core}
aim-200-1_6-no-1	200	320	959	U	5.02	0.12	0.09	0.21	52	55
aim-200-1_6-no-2	200	320	959	U	>600	14.04	32.31	46.35	76	87
aim-200-1_6-no-3	200	320	958	U	>600	10.80	35.87	46.67	73	86
aim-200-1_6-no-4	200	320	960	U	5.81	0.09	0.10	0.19	45	48
aim-200-2_0-no-1	200	400	1199	U	15.53	0.20	0.27	0.47	49	55
aim-200-2_0-no-2	200	400	1199	U	3.87	0.17	0.18	0.35	46	50
aim-200-2_0-no-3	200	400	1198	U	1.04	0.05	0.12	0.17	35	37
aim-200-2_0-no-4	200	400	1197	U	0.70	0.16	0.02	0.18	36	42

References

1. J. N. Hooker and V. Vinay. Branching Rules for Satisfiability. *Journal of Automated Reasoning*, 15:359–383, 1995. 495, 496, 497
2. D. S. Johnson and M. A. Trick, editors. *Cliques, Coloring, and Satisfiability*, volume 26 of *DIMACS Series in Discrete Mathematics and Theoretical Computer Science*. American Mathematical Society, 1996. 498
3. O. Kullmann. An application of matroid theory to the SAT Problem. *ECCC TR00-018*, Feb. 2000. 496

Branching Constraint Satisfaction Problems for Solutions Robust under Likely Changes

David W. Fowler and Kenneth N. Brown

University of Aberdeen, Aberdeen AB24 3UE, UK
{dfowler,kbrown}@csd.abdn.ac.uk

Abstract. Many applications of CSPs require partial solutions to be found before all the information about the problem is available. We examine the case where the future is partially known, and where it is important to make decisions in the present that will be robust in the light of future events. We introduce the branching CSP to model these situations, incorporating some elements of decision theory, and describe an algorithm for its solution that combines forward checking with branch and bound search. We also examine a simple thresholding method which can be used in conjunction with the forward checking algorithm, and we show the trade-off between time and solution quality.

1   Introduction

In this paper, we consider the problem of a solver that periodically receives additions to an existing problem, and must make a decision for each addition as it is received. We assume that there is a simple model of what additions are likely to occur. We believe that this knowledge can enable the solver to make decisions that will be robust under future events. The approach used here involves extending the framework of constraint satisfaction to include the model of future events to give a new form of CSP, called a *branching CSP* (BCSP). A detailed presentation can be found in [FB00].

As an illustration, consider a scheduling problem in which new tasks arrive during the process. The aim is to schedule as many tasks before their due date as possible. There are two identical resources that the tasks may use. The tasks for this problem are described in Fig. 1. We start with tasks A and B. We know that one of the other tasks will arrive at time 1. It will be C with probability 0.6, and D with probability 0.4. A final restriction (future work will look at how to overcome this) is that tasks A and B must be scheduled before it is known which of tasks C or D arrives next. How should we schedule tasks A and B?

There are three reasonable possibilities, shown in Fig. 2. Solution (a) allows C to be scheduled, but not D, whereas (b) allows D but not C. (c) allows both C and D to be scheduled, at the price of omitting B. Which is best depends on the probabilities and utilities. For this example, the expected utilities are (a) 3.8, (b) 5.2, and (c) 6.0. So it is best to schedule task A at time 0, omit B, and then schedule C at time 1 or D at time 2, depending on which arrives.

R. Dechter (Ed.): CP 2000, LNCS 1894, pp. 500–504, 2000.
© Springer-Verlag Berlin Heidelberg 2000

Task	Duration	#Resources	Due	Utility
A	2	1	4	1
B	2	1	4	1
C	3	1	4	3
D	1	2	4	8

Fig. 1. Tasks for Example Problem

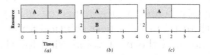

Fig. 2. Three Possible Solutions

2   Branching CSPs

The initial definition of a BCSP involves variables, constraints, and a state tree. The variables and constraints are as in standard CSPs, with the difference that each variable has an associated non-negative utility, which is gained if the variable has a value assigned to it. Variables can be left unassigned, in which case the utility gained from that variable is 0.

The state tree represents the possible development paths of the dynamic problem. Each edge in the tree is directed, and is labelled with a transition probability. Each node S_i has an associated variable X_{S_i}, with the restriction that a variable can appear at most once in any path from the root to a leaf node. There are transition probabilities p_{ij} labelling the edge (if it exists) between S_i and S_j. For any path through the tree from root to leaf node, a series of constraint satisfaction problems is produced, involving all variables that have been encountered at each node in the path so far. If a constraint involves variables that are all assigned values, then those values must satisfy the constraint.

A solution to a BCSP is a decision for each variable at each node in the state tree, so that on each path all relevant constraints (those that involve only variables that have been assigned values in the path) are satisfied. A solution is a plan for each possible sequence of variable additions, and we have assumed that the total utility of the solution can be found by summing the utilities of the assigned variables in the path that actually occurs. However, we must try to find a solution before we know which path will occur, and so we define the optimal solution to be the one with the highest expected total utility. For a solution, the expected utility from a node can be defined recursively as follows. The E.U. from a leaf node S_i is the utility of X_{S_i} if it is assigned a value, otherwise 0. For a nonleaf node S_i, the E.U. is the utility of X_{S_i} (or zero if it is unassigned) plus $\sum_j p_{ij} EU_j$, where the sum is over all the child nodes of S_i.

3   Solution Algorithms

Two complete algorithms have been implemented to solve BCSPs involving binary constraints on finite domains. These are: a straightforward branch and bound algorithm that examines each node in the state tree in a depth first order, and finds the value for the variable that maximises the expected utility from that node; and a forward checking algorithm that uses the constraints to prune the domains of variables lower down in the tree. As well as reducing the number of values that need to be examined, the propagation is used to calculate an upper bound on the expected utility from the current node. If this value is less than that of the best solution found so far, the effects of propagation can be undone, and the next value tried for the current variable immediately. Experiments show that FC is much faster than the basic branch and bound algorithm, so we concentrate on FC for the rest of this paper.

To test FC, we generated random problems as follows. The number of variables, n, was fixed at 10. Each variable had a domain with $m = 10$ values, and a utility which was an integer selected at random uniformly from the range [1,50]. The state tree was produced by the following branching process. For each node the probability of no children was 0.05, for one child 0.5, for 2 children 0.25, and for 3 children 0.2. The transition probabilities for each child node were then selected so that they summed to 1.0. We varied the density of the constraint graph p_1 and the tightness of constraints p_2. p_1 was varied from 0.1 to 1.0 in steps of 0.1, and p_2 from 0 to 1 in steps of 0.02. 100 problems were generated for each combination of p_1 and p_2, and the median number of constraint checks recorded. The results are shown in Fig. 3.

It is interesting to compare the hardness of BCSPs with that of static CSPs, where all variables must be assigned values (if this is possible). In Fig. 3 we have shown the curve for $p_1 = 0.6$ (other values of p_1 show similar behaviour). The static CSP also has $n = 10$ and $m = 10$.

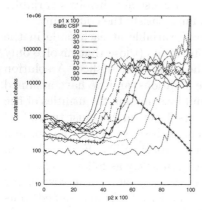

Fig. 3. FC Search

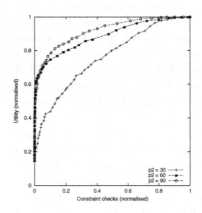

Fig. 4. Thresholding using FC

4   Thresholding

The algorithms presented above are complete, but may not have explored important branches by the time the first decision is required. In real world applications we usually prefer a slightly inferior result before a deadline has been reached, than an optimal result afterwards. It is also useful to be able to generate results that improve over time, instead of a single result at the end of the computation.

Thresholding is a simple method that can be used to implement either of the above. The idea is to ignore branches of the state tree that can not give a utility higher than a threshold value. For high thresholds, large sections of the tree will be pruned, giving a problem that can be solved much more quickly. For very low values the tree will be pruned only slightly, and for a threshold of 0 there will be no pruning at all.

The algorithm was tested on random problems generated as before. For each problem, the initial threshold was taken as an upper bound on the total expected utility, calculated by assuming that all variables could be assigned values. The threshold was reduced to zero in 50 evenly spaced steps, with the problem being solved with FC for each threshold. The last step (with the threshold equal to zero) corresponds to the full original problem. p_1 was fixed at 0.7, and three values of p_2 chosen to give underconstrained ($p_2 = 0.3$), hard ($p_2 = 0.6$), and overconstrained ($p_2 = 0.9$) problems. 100 problems were generated in each run. Fig. 4 shows how the expected utility increases with the number of constraint checks. For the hard problems, almost 80% of the achievable utility can be gained with 20% of the constraint checks needed to find the optimal solution. The overconstrained problems give similar results; for underconstrained problems the performance is poorer, but the time for solving these is not significant.

5   Related Work

Dynamic Constraint Satisfaction [DD88] models a changing environment as a series of CSPs. The emphasis in DCSPs has been on minimising the work needed to repair a solution when a change occurs. There is typically no model of the future, and thus no concept of solutions which are themselves robust to changes. Wallace and Freuder [WF97] do consider future events in their *recurrent* CSPs, and aim to find robust solutions, but they concentrate on changes which are temporary and frequently recurring. *Supermodels* [GPR98] are solutions which can be repaired in a limited number of moves, given a limited change to the original problem. This approach does not consider the likelihood of changes, nor does it take account of a sequence of changes. Fargier et al. [FLS96] propose *mixed* CSPs, in which possible future changes are modelled by uncontrollable variables. They search for conditional solutions, dependent on the eventual value of these variables, and thus the solutions are robust. However, they do not deal with sequences of events, but assume all changes occur at the same time. As a result, there is not necessarily any similarity between the different individual solutions derived from the conditional ones. Finally, it must be mentioned that the model of likely future events will occasionally be insufficient, and an unexpected event will occur. A practical solver will have to be able to fall back to existing DCSP methods in this case.

In addition to modelling changes, we also develop partial solutions to overconstrained problems. We choose to leave variables unassigned, and insist on all constraints being satisfied. Most work on partial CSPs, for example [FW92, BMR95], concentrates on finding solutions which violate the fewest constraints. Freuder and Wallace's [FW92] general scheme for solving PCSPs searches for variations on the problem which would allow complete solutions. It is possible to recast the unassigned variable approach in that scheme by creating new problems which retract exactly those constraints which involve the variables we leave unassigned. Our algorithms could be considered to be doing exactly that; however, we believe explicitly designating variables as being unassigned is a more natural representation for many applications.

6   Future Work

For the example problem of section 1, it can be seen that it would be better to schedule A, and delay a decision on B until we see whether C or D arrives. The expected utility is then 7.0. We have implemented an algorithm which allows such delays, but have yet to produce experimental results. At present, we can only postpone a variable until the next variable arrives; future work may consider how to relax this restriction. We intend to continue developing our understanding of the current model by more experimentation with the existing algorithms, developing the algorithms to include more propagation during search, and finding better anytime algorithms. We aim to extend the model to include explicit times for events, and to allow constraint violations as well as unassigned variables. We have started to compare our algorithms with CSPs that use 0/1 variables to signify that variables are unassigned. Early results indicate that our methods allow for both easier formulation of problems and more efficient solution. Finally we will compare our algorithms with existing methods of scheduling under uncertainty - for example, MDPs and Just-In-Case scheduling [DBS94].

References

[BMR95] S. Bistarelli, U. Montanari, and F. Rossi. Constraint solving over semirings. In *Proceedings of IJCAI-95*, pages 624–630, 1995. 503

[DBS94] M. Drummond, J. Bresina, and K. Swanson. Just-in-case scheduling. In *Proceedings of AAAI-94*, Seattle, Washington, USA, 1994. 504

[DD88]   R. Dechter and A. Dechter. Belief maintenance in dynamic constraint networks. In *Proceedings of AAAI-88*, pages 37–43, 1988. 503

[FB00]   D. W. Fowler and K. N. Brown. Branching constraint satisfaction problems. Technical report, Dept. of Computing Science, Univ. of Aberdeen, 2000. 500

[FLS96] H. Fargier, J. Lang, and T. Schiex. Mixed constraint satisfaction: a framework for decision problems under incomplete knowledge. In *Proceedings of AAAI-96*, Portland, OR, 1996. 503

[FW92]   E. C. Freuder and R. J. Wallace. Partial constraint satisfaction. *Artificial Intelligence*, 58:21–70, 1992. 503, 504

[GPR98] M. L. Ginsberg, A. J. Parkes, and A. Roy. Supermodels and robustness. In *AAAI-98*, pages 334–339, 1998. 503

[WF97]   R. J. Wallace and E. C. Freuder. Stable solutions for dynamic constraint satisfaction problems. In *Workshop on The Theory and Practice of Dynamic Constraint Satisfaction*, Salzburg, Austria, November 1997. 503

Constraint Propagation: Between Abstract Models and ad hoc Strategies

Laurent Granvilliers[1] and Eric Monfroy[2*]

[1] IRIN
B.P. 92208 – F-44322 Nantes Cedex 3 – France
Laurent.Granvilliers@irin.univ-nantes.fr
[2] CWI
Kruislaan 413 – 1098 SJ Amsterdam – The Netherlands
Eric.Monfroy@cwi.nl

1 Introduction

Constraint propagation [10,7,5] (CP) is a cornerstone algorithm of constraint programming, mainly devoted to the computation of local consistency properties of constraint satisfaction problems. The abstract formulation of CP is the combination of a set of reduction functions (black-box solvers) on a domain [8,9,2,1]. Intuitively, there is a dependence relation between functions and domains, such that a function must be applied if a domain it depends on is reduced. The essential property of CP is confluence or strategy-independence. In other words, the order solvers are applied does not influence the output characterized in terms of a common fixed-point of the solvers. Owing to this remark, several strategies based on heuristics, data structures, or knowledge of the solvers have been implemented.

Since there is no alternative between abstract models and *ad hoc* strategies, the design of a new strategy requires the program to be developed from top to bottom and to be proved confluent and terminating. We therefore design a generic algorithm called SCP3 (Strategies for CP, and 3 to recall it is an AC3-like algorithm) embracing a family of CP strategies. A set of specialized algorithms verifying some minimal properties can be plugged in SCP3. These software components must respectively implement the selection of a set of functions, application of these functions, a propagation method based on the dependence relation, and a stopping criterion. This software engineering approach to CP provides modularity, flexibility, re-use, easy prototyping, and efficiency. This results from the dissociation of the selection phase implemented by reasoning processes (based on some knowledge and heuristics), from the more basic application phase of the functions.

We illustrate this framework with a new strategy based on a strongness property of functions [6] combined with a CP fixed-point algorithm using the selection-intensification heuristics proposed in [3] (i.e., an adaptation of the heuristics of [4] for parallelism). Beside its design exposed here, its efficiency

---

* This research was carried out while Eric Monfroy was visiting IRIN.

R. Dechter (Ed.): CP 2000, LNCS 1894, pp. 505–509, 2000.
© Springer-Verlag Berlin Heidelberg 2000

has been proved in processing interval constraints by box consistency (but a lack of space does not allow to describe it here).

2   Constraint Propagation Strategies

2.1   Framework

We now present the main lines of the framework of finite chaotic iterations [1] (CI) on a partial order. Let us consider a set $\mathcal{D}$, and an $\sqcup$-po $(\mathcal{D}, \sqsubseteq)$ satisfying the finite chain property (every sequence $d_1 \sqsubseteq d_2 \sqsubseteq \cdots \sqsubseteq d_i \sqsubseteq \cdots$ is such that there exists $j \geqslant 1$ such that $d_{j+1} = d_j$).

Let n be a natural, and let us write $\mathcal{D}^n$ as $\mathcal{D}^{(1)} \times \cdots \times \mathcal{D}^{(n)}$, where each dimension is labelled by a natural. A *narrowing function* is an inflationary and monotonic function $f : \mathcal{D}^{(i_1)} \times \cdots \times \mathcal{D}^{(i_k)} \to \mathcal{D}^{(i_1)} \times \cdots \times \mathcal{D}^{(i_k)}$, *i.e.*, for all $x, y \in \mathcal{D}^{(i_1)} \times \cdots \times \mathcal{D}^{(i_k)}$, we have $x \sqsubseteq f(x)$ and $x \sqsubseteq y \Rightarrow f(x) \sqsubseteq f(y)$. Moreover, f is said *to depend on* each $i_1, \ldots, i_k$ (this means the application of f could possibly modify a corresponding domain). Given $d = d_1, \ldots, d_n \in \mathcal{D}^n$, let $f^+(d)$ denote $d'_1, \ldots, d'_n$ where $d'_j = f(d_{i_1}, \ldots, d_{i_k})_j$ if $j \in \{i_1, \ldots, i_k\}$, and $d'_j = d_j$ otherwise.

The main result is confluence of CI. Given $d \in \mathcal{D}^n$ and a set $\{f_1, \ldots, f_m\}$ of narrowing functions, every fair iteration (every function appears in it infinitely often) stabilizes and computes in d the least common fixed-point of $f_1^+, \ldots, f_m^+$. In other words, the order of application of the functions does not influence the output; this order and the mechanisms achieving it are called the *strategy*.

Several strategies have been proposed, most of them in the framework of constraint satisfaction by local consistency. In the next section, we propose a high-level algorithm representing a family of strategies parameterized by some component algorithms.

2.2   Between Abstract Models and Concrete Strategies

The SCP3 algorithm presented in Table 1 embraces a family of CP strategies parameterized by four component algorithms. More precisely, a CP strategy is given by a tuple of algorithms (SEL, CP, WAKE, STOP) such that each of them verifies some minimal properties to guarantee termination and confluence of the SCP3 algorithm. Those properties are the following:

- SEL (selection phase) outputs a non-empty subset S' of a set S of narrowing functions;
- CP (application phase) applies at least once all the narrowing functions in S' over the domains;
- WAKE (propagation phase) generates a new set S containing at least all the narrowing functions in F that modify the new domain d';
- STOP succeeds if $f(d) = d$ for every f in S.

Proposition 1 describes the invariant of the SCP3 algorithm.

Table1. Component-based software architecture for CP

```
SCP3(F : set of narrowing functions, d : 𝒟ⁿ) : 𝒟ⁿ
begin
    S := F
    repeat
        S' := SEL(S, d)
        d' := CP(S', d)
        if d' ≠ d then
            S := WAKE(F, S, S', d, d')
            d := d'
        else
            S := S \ S'
        endif
    until d₁ × ⋯ × dₙ = ∅ or STOP(F, S, d)
    return d
end
```

Proposition 1. *At the end of each step of the* **repeat** *loop in* SCP3, *every narrowing function* f *in* $F \setminus S$ *is such that* $f(d) = d$.

The confluence property of SCP3 trivially follows from Proposition 1 and the required property for the STOP algorithm. The termination property is addressed by Proposition 2.

Proposition 2. *The* SCP3 *algorithm terminates in finite time if so are its component algorithms* SEL, CP, WAKE, *and* STOP.

The classical CP strategy can obviously be described in this model. It suffices that SEL chooses only one narrowing function f in S, CP applies f on d, WAKE adds in S all the functions in F depending on a reduced domain and removes f from S if it is idempotent, and STOP checks if S is empty. Notice that WAKE depends on the CP algorithm, and in particular the set S' can be removed from S in the case CP implements a fixed-point strategy.

The design of SCP3 is quite trivial (only four instructions of standard algorithms are replaced with four algorithms), but the advantages with respect to the classical CP approach are significant. To sum up, we identify the following points:

- *generality*: SCP3 unifies several existing CP strategies, for instance, some strategies which only differ in using a stack or a queue [1];
- *re-use, modularity*: the component programs can be re-used by any strategy. This makes the framework very nice to quickly prototype new strategies;
- *flexibility*: each component program can be adapted to a specific computational model in order to gain in efficiency;
- *efficiency*: updating propagation structures after a long step of computation (and not after each application of a narrowing function) reduces the updating costs, as remarked in [4].

Table2. Intensification-based CP algorithm

```
ICP(F : set of narrowing functions, d : D^n) : D^n
begin
  S := F
  fixed-point := false
  repeat
    (S', d') := SELBEST(S, d)
    if d' = d then
      fixed-point := true
    else
      d'' := INTENSIFY(S', d')
      S := {f ∈ F | f depends on some i s.t. d_i ≠ d''_i}
      d := d''
    endif
  until fixed-point
  return d
end
```

2.3   An Example

The SCP3 algorithm is used here to design a new CP strategy which exploits a static partial order on narrowing functions with respect to their estimated reduction power, *i.e.*, their strongness [6]. A narrowing function f is said to be *stronger* than a narrowing function g if for all $d \in \mathcal{D}^n$, $g^+(d) \sqsubseteq f^+(d)$. Considering the classical version of WAKE (every function depending on a modified domain is added in S), the following are possible implementations of STOP and SEL:

- The STOP algorithm succeeds if either $S = \varnothing$ or for all $f \in S$, there exists $g \in F \setminus S$ such that g is stronger than f, *i.e.*, it is not worth applying f since there exists a stronger function that does not need to be applied.
- For convergence speed reasons, the SEL algorithm may select the narrowing functions from the weakest ones (which are generally the cheapest to apply) to the strongest ones. For instance, a possible strategy is to select only once each narrowing function such that there exists a stronger function in F. For this purpose, only a set of selected functions has to be stored and maintained in SEL.

Once a set of narrowing functions is selected, their application is managed by the CP algorithm. The ICP (see Table 2) algorithm is a possible efficient implementation of CP which iterates a selection phase (Algorithm SELBEST) of the most contracting narrowing functions, followed by an application phase (Algorithm INTENSIFY), until the fixed-point is reached. This algorithm has more "inherent parallelism" than the classical CP algorithm since SELBEST independently applies all the narrowing functions on the initial domain. Moreover, the INTENSIFY algorithm does not have to compute a fixed-point. This property permits the use of a large variety of algorithms.

3 Conclusion and Perspectives

This paper proposes a generic CP algorithm that is more general than the classical one but closer to practical requirements (re-use, prototyping, ...). A CP strategy is given by a set of four algorithms that are seen as black-boxes specified by some minimal properties to ensure termination and confluence. This framework is well-suited for the design of a CP library in which the components can be plugged in any new algorithm. Let us remark that in the framework of constraint satisfaction, the SCP3 algorithm can implement the AC1 and AC3 algorithms for arc consistency, and the BC3 algorithm for box consistency; nevertheless, the ACn (with $n > 3$) algorithms use particular data structures and then cannot be realized (except in the meaningless case where CP implements ACn).

The research reported in this paper may be extended in many ways, such as: design of new component algorithms, design of a CP library and its interface (specification of inputs and outputs of algorithms), implementation of new efficient strategies for particular classes of problems (it has already been done for interval constraints), and similar work for branch-and-prune algorithms.

Acknowledgements

The authors are grateful to Frédéric Benhamou, Frédéric Goualard, and Gaétan Hains.

References

1. Krzysztof Apt. The Essence of Constraint Propagation. *Theoretical Computer Science*, 221(1-2):179–210, 1999. 505, 506, 507
2. Frédéric Benhamou. Heterogeneous Constraint Solving. In *Proceedings of International Conference on Algebraic and Logic Programming*, volume 1139 of *LNCS*, pages 62–76, Aachen, Germany, 1996. Springer. 505
3. Laurent Granvilliers and Gaétan Hains. A Conservative Scheme for Parallel Interval Narrowing. *Information Processing Letters*, 74(3–4):141–146, 2000. 505
4. Olivier Lhomme, Arnaud Gotlieb, and Michel Rueher. Dynamic Optimization of Interval Narrowing Algorithms. *Journal of Logic Programming*, 37(1–2):165–183, 1998. 505, 507
5. Alan Mackworth. Consistency in Networks of Relations. *Artificial Intelligence*, 8(1):99–118, 1977. 505
6. Eric Monfroy. Using Weaker Functions for Constraint Propagation over Real Numbers. In *Proceedings of ACM Symposium of Applied Computing*, pages 553–559, San Antonio, USA, 1999. 505, 508
7. Ugo Montanari. Networks of Constraints: Fundamental Properties and Applications to Picture Processing. *Information Science*, 7(2):95–132, 1974. 505
8. Aleksandr Narin'yani. Sub-definiteness and Basic Means of Knowledge Representation. *Computers and Artificial Intelligence*, 5, 1983. 505
9. William Older and André Vellino. Constraint Arithmetic on Real Intervals. In Frédéric Benhamou and Alain Colmerauer, editors, *Constraint Logic Programming: Selected Research*. MIT Press, 1993. 505
10. David Waltz. Generating Semantic Descriptions from Drawings of Scenes with Shadows. In P. H. Winston, editor, *The Psychology of Computer Vision*. McGraw Hill, 1975. 505

How to Model and Verify
Concurrent Algorithms for Distributed CSPs*

Markus Hannebauer

GMD — German National Research Center for Information Technology FIRST
Kekuléstr. 7, D-12489 Berlin, Germany
markus.hannebauer@gmd.de

Abstract. Many recent systems tackling Distributed Constraint Satisfaction Problems (DCSPs) lack a theoretically founded specification and
safety or liveness property proofs. This may be due to the difficulty of
modeling and verifying concurrently running threads and their interaction. In this article we will briefly sketch an approach to the modeling
and verification of concurrent algorithms tailored to DCSP solving and
based on algebraic Petri nets. We will present a realistic case study on
distributed agreement finding and state according termination and consistency properties.

1 Introduction

Algorithms for solving DCSPs are mostly presented filling several pages of pseudo
code. Unfortunately, this kind of representation is not very intuitive and error-
prone. Therefore, we propose an approach to the modeling and verification of
concurrent algorithms specialized to DCSP solving and based on the suggestive
means of algebraic Petri nets.

Authors of DCSP algorithms often use sequential calculi, derivatives of the
Hoare calculus, to prove important properties of their algorithms, like (partial)
correctness, termination, and completeness. Yokoo et al. [5] prove the completeness of their algorithms by more or less verbal argumentation chains. Nguyen
and Deville [2] prove certain static assertions of single threads and combine them
to prove the overall system behavior. All these proofs run quite well since the
underlying algorithms contain some sequential aspects. The same holds for the
algorithms in [4]. Things are getting harder when one is trying to analyze the
behavior of fully detached concurrent threads. Zhang and Mackworth [6] for example describe a distributed algorithm with an endless loop but do not detail
on stabilization properties. The problem with using sequential proof methods
for concurrent algorithms is that in general the behavior of a system of threads
does not only depend on the behavior of the single threads but also on matters
like synchronization, interaction and so on. This is why we will briefly sketch an
alternative proof method tailored to concurrent DCSP algorithms.

---

* An extention of this paper can be found in [1]. Many thanks to Wolfgang Reisig,
Armin Wolf and Ulrich Geske for fruitful discussions on this paper.

R. Dechter (Ed.): CP 2000, LNCS 1894, pp. 510–514, 2000.

In the following, we will only consider decentralized variable-based algorithms on a shared search space using asynchronous message-passing. We will build upon a DCSP definition that is slightly more general than the classical one of Yokoo et al. [5]. It allows for complex constraints and additionally extends the notion of distribution to the constraints also.

Definition 1 (Distributed Constraint Satisfaction Problem). *A distributed constraint satisfaction problem is specified by* $\Pi = (X, D, C, A, \phi)$.

- $X = \{x_1, \ldots, x_n\}$ *is a set of* domain variables x_i *each ranging over its domain* D_i *from the set* $D = \{D_1, \ldots, D_n\}$.
- *A labeling* $\lambda : X \longrightarrow D_1 \cup \ldots \cup D_n, \lambda = (v_1, \ldots, v_n) \in D_1 \times \ldots \times D_n$ *assigns a value* $v_i \in D_i$ *to each domain variable* x_i. *A partial labeling* $\lambda' :$ $(\{x_{\lambda_1'}, \ldots, x_{\lambda_l'}\} = X' \subseteq X) \longrightarrow (D_{\lambda_1'} \cup \ldots \cup D_{\lambda_l'} = D')$ *assigns a value* $v_i \in D_i$ *to each domain variable* $x_i \in X'$.
- $C = \{C_1, \ldots, C_m\}$ *is a set of* constraints $C_i \subseteq D_{i_1} \times \ldots \times D_{i_k}$, *each of which is a relation of type* $2^{D_{i_1} \times \ldots \times D_{i_k}}$ *restricting the set of* feasible *(partial) labelings.*
- $A = \{(a_1, \kappa_1), \ldots, (a_p, \kappa_p)\}$ *is a set of* agents *each possessing a local consistency predicate* $\kappa_i : (X' \longrightarrow D') \times 2^C \longrightarrow \{\texttt{true}, \texttt{false}\}$ *over partial labelings and sets of contraints.*
- $\phi : X \cup C \longrightarrow A$ *assigns an agent to each domain variable and each constraint.* $\phi_X^{-1}(a) = \{x \in X \mid \phi(x) = a\}$. $\phi_C^{-1}(a) = \{c \in C \mid \phi(c) = a\}$.

Given this specification, the problem is to find a labeling $\lambda \in \Lambda(C) = \{(v_1, \ldots, v_n) \in D_1 \times \ldots \times D_n | \forall C_i \in C : (v_{i_1}, \ldots, v_{i_k}) \in C_i\}$ *from the* solution space Λ *defined by* C.

2   Modeling Concurrent DCSP Algorithms

Algebraic Petri nets satisfy the demand for an intuitive representation of concurrent control, a natural way to specify asynchronous behavior and so on. Additionally, they use a quite suggestive and nevertheless formally sound graphical notation. We cannot give a detailed introduction to algebraic Petri nets (refer to [3]). We will rather present a brief case study that consists of a simplified, yet realistic algorithm for finding agreement on the labeling of several variables among several agents. The result of the whole protocol is that if a variable x is labeled with a certain value v, then all neighbors $(N(x))$ have agreed on that labeling and have stored that information.

 In Petri nets local states are represented by *places* (ellipses) and *tokens* on these places (within ellipses). Atomic actions are represented by *transitions* (rectangles). Arcs connect places with transitions and model control and data flow. Under enactment, transition t consumes x from X and puts y on Y like shown by Fig. 1.

Fig. 1: Sample

We will follow exactly one instance of our protocol to exemplify the agreement protocol given by the Petri net model Σ_{af} in Fig. 2. The variable agent a

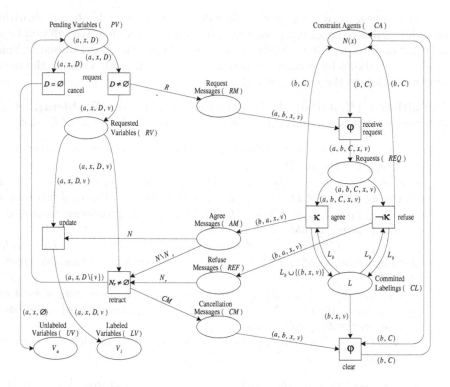

Fig. 2. Petri net model Σ_{af} of the labeling phase

selects a certain value v out of D to label x (D has to be non-empty for this) and sends request messages (set $R = \{(a, b, x, v) | (b, \cdot) \in N(x)\}$) to all neighboring constraint agents via the transition **request**. Based on the received request, its constraints C and its maximum set of already committed labelings $L_b = \{(b, \cdot, \cdot)\}$ each constraint agent b can decide to agree to the labeling or to refuse it by evaluating its consistency predicate $\kappa = \kappa_b(L_b \cup \{(b, x, v)\}, \phi_C^{-1}(b))$. In case of agreement the constraint agent adds the labeling (b, x, v) to its set of committed labelings L_b and sends an agree message. Otherwise, the set of committed labelings remains unchanged, a refuse message is sent to a and b returns to its idle state.

Agent a is blocked until all neighbors have answered. It can only update the requested variable (a, x, D, v) to the state **Labeled Variables** when all neighbors have sent agree messages. This full demanded set of agree messages is denoted by $N = \{(b, a, x, v) | (b, \cdot) \in N(x)\}$. The according incoming arc of the **update** transition ensures the desired behavior. A single refusing neighbor is enough to hinder firing of the **update** transition. But even if their is already a refusal, a will have to wait for all responds of its neighbors to inform the agreed neighbors on the failure of the agreement. This is realized by the transition **retract**. This transition can fire iff there is a set $N_r = \{(b, a, x, v) | (b, \cdot) \in N_r(x) \subset N(x)\} \neq \emptyset$ of refusal messages from some neighbors and exactly the complementary set of agreement messages $N \setminus N_r$ from the other neighbors. The transition `retract` deletes v from the domain of x and starts a new protocol instance. Additionally, all neighbors that have already agreed on the labeling v are informed by according cancellation messages (set $CM = \{(a, b, x, v) | (b, \cdot) \in N(x) \setminus N_r(x)\}$) to free them from their given commitments via the transition `clear`.

3 Verifying Concurrent DCSP Algorithms

Though desirable properties of concurrent algorithms for solving DCSPs are manifold, we will concentrate on two, namely *safety* and *liveness*. Safety properties are strongly related to assertions in sequential proof methods. A typical safety property is consistency. An algorithm represented by Σ preserves how-ever defined consistency iff in each reachable state of Σ the global state is consistent. We will use the following notion.

Definition 2 (ϕ-Consistency of a Partial Labeling). *Given a DCSP $\Pi = (X, D, C, A, \phi)$. A partial labeling $\lambda' : X' \subseteq X \longrightarrow D'$ is called ϕ-consistent, iff* $\forall (a, \kappa) \in A : \kappa \left(\lambda', \phi_C^{-1}((a, \kappa)) \right)$.

Techniques to verify safety properties include *place invariants*. In Petri nets, a set of places P defines a place invariant if any arbitrary enactment of any connected transition does not change the (local) system state represented by P and its tokens. In Fig. 2, places RV, RM, REQ, AM and REF define such a place invariant. The sum of all tokens on RM, REQ, AM and REF equals the sum of tokens on RV times $|N(x)|$. This can be formalized by introducing a special addition operation defined on multisets, counting instances in this case and stating linear equations. Such, the invariant is given by $RM + REQ + AM + REF = |N(x)| \cdot RV$. Fig. 2 contains further such invariants.

Unfortunately, there is no way to guarantee that an algorithm "does something reasonable" only by asserting safety properties. This is why we need the second class of properties, namely liveness. Termination and completeness belong to this second category. In [3] a concurrent temporal logic operator, called *causes* and denoted by $\hookrightarrow$, is introduced to prove liveness. $\Sigma \models p \hookrightarrow q$ ("in Σ holds p *causes* q") means that in Σ each reachable state in which p holds is always followed by a reachable state in which q holds. *Pick-up patterns* are used to derive liveness properties directly from the static structure of an algebraic Petri net.

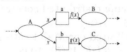

Fig. 3: Pattern 1

The pattern shown by Fig. 3 covers alternative forward branching while preserving any context α. Transitions a and b are in conflict for the tokens on A. Given that place A exactly hosts set U of tokens ($A = U$), these transitions can non-deterministically and concurrently consume a token x from A and produce $f(x)$ or $g(x)$, respectively. The final result of firing a and b as often as possible is that A is empty and the transformed tokens have been placed on B or C, respectively.

The set of tokens V consumed by a unified with the set of tokens W consumed by b again equals U. Hence, we can formally state $\alpha \wedge A = U \hookrightarrow \alpha \wedge A = 0 \wedge B.f(V) \wedge C.g(W) \wedge U = V \cup W$.

Theorem 1. *Given a DCSP $\Pi = (X, D, C, A, \phi)$. Then, each possible run of Σ_{af} is finite and will finally produce a ϕ-consistent partial labeling $\lambda' : X' \subseteq X \longrightarrow D'$ potentially trying each domain value of each variable $x \in X$.*

The essence of this theorem can be formalized by this *causes* proposition:

$$\Sigma_{\text{af}} \models PV.(a, x, D) \wedge CL = L \hookrightarrow \tag{1}$$
$$(LV.(a, x, D, v) \wedge CL = L + \{(b, x, v)|(b, \cdot) \in N(x)\} \wedge CM = 0) \vee \tag{2}$$
$$(UV.(a, x, \emptyset) \wedge CL = L \wedge CM = 0). \tag{3}$$

In words this proposition means that given a pending variable (a, x, D) under an existing partial labeling represent by L (1), every possible run of the protocol causes either that (a, x, D, v) has been successfully labeled and every neighbor has committed to it (2) or the domain of x has been traversed without success, $(a, x, \emptyset)$ is in state `Unlabeled Variables` and not a single neighbor is committed to the related requested labeling (3). This proposition can be proven using four place invariants and three pick-up patterns of the type presented above [1].

4   Conclusions

The purpose of this article has been to show how successful one can use algebraic Petri nets and according concepts, such as place invariants and *causes* deductions, as formal but suggestive means to model and verify concurrent algorithms for DCSPs. The algorithm presented in this paper does not guarantee completeness. Hence, it is part of our future work to augment it with concurrent backtracking facilities, model them appropriately and prove their validness using the proposed methods.

References

[1] M. Hannebauer. Their problems are my problems — The transition between internal and external conflict. In *Conflicting Agents: Conflict Management in Multi-Agent Systems*. Kluwer, 2000. 510, 514
[2] T. Nguyen, Y. Deville. A distributed arc-consistency algorithm. *Science of Computer Programming*, 30(1-2):227–250, 1998. 510
[3] W. Reisig. *Elements of Distributed Algorithms — Modeling and Analysis with Petri Nets*. Springer, 1998. 511, 513
[4] G. Solotorevsky, E. Gudes, A. Meisels. Modeling and solving distributed constraint satisfaction problems (DCSPs). In *Proc. of CP-96*, 1996. 510
[5] M. Yokoo, E. Durfee, T. Ishida, K. Kuwabara. The distributed constraint satisfaction problem: Formalization and algorithms. *IEEE Trans. KDE*, 10(5), 1998. 510, 511
[6] Y. Zhang, A. Mackworth. Parallel and distributed algorithms for finite constraint satisfaction problems. In *Proc. of the IEEE-Symposium on Parallel and Distributed Processing*, pages 394–397, 1991. 510

The Phase Transition in Distributed Constraint Satisfaction Problems: First Results

Katsutoshi Hirayama[1], Makoto Yokoo[2], and Katia Sycara[3]

[1] Kobe University of Mercantile Marine
5-1-1 Fukae-minami-machi, Higashinada-ku, Kobe 658-0022, Japan
hirayama@ti.kshosen.ac.jp
[2] NTT Communication Science Laboratories
2-4 Hikaridai, Seika-cho, Soraku-gun, Kyoto 619-0237, Japan
yokoo@cslab.kecl.ntt.co.jp
[3] The Robotics Institute, Carnegie Mellon University
5000 Forbes Ave., Pittsburgh, PA 15213, U.S.A.
katia@cs.cmu.edu

1 Introduction

For solving a distributed CSP by a distributed constraint satisfaction algorithm, since agents usually have *intra-agent constraints* (constraints which are defined over variables of one agent) and *inter-agent constraints* (constraints which are defined over variables of multiple agents), they have not only to perform local computation to satisfy their intra- and inter-agent constraints, but also to communicate with other agents to satisfy their inter-agent constraints. The efficiency of a distributed constraint satisfaction algorithm depends on its communication cost and computation cost, and both can vary with the numbers of intra- and inter-agents constraints. Therefore, it is important to know how the numbers of intra- and inter-agent constraints affect the communication and computation costs of a distributed constraint satisfaction algorithm because such an information may give us a hint to develop a more efficient distributed constraint satisfaction algorithm.

This paper presents first experimental results on the communication and computation costs of a distributed constraint satisfaction algorithm when we vary the numbers of intra- and inter-agent constraints for distributed graph 3-coloring problems. As we will show, both costs show an interesting pattern on the x-y plane (where the x-axis is the number of intra-agent constraints and the y-axis is the number of inter-agent constraints), and its pattern is closely related to the phase transition in the ratio of soluble problems. Since the pattern seems to be independent of algorithms and problem generation methods, we can expect that our first results can be the basis of theoretical analyses.

2 Distributed Constraint Satisfaction Problem

A distributed CSP[2] is a CSP where variables and constraints are distributed among multiple agents. It consists of:

R. Dechter (Ed.): CP 2000, LNCS 1894, pp. 515–519, 2000.

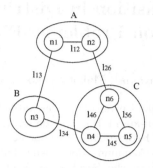

Fig. 1. Distributed graph coloring problem

- a set of agents, $1, 2, \ldots, k$
- a set of CSPs, $P_1, P_2, \ldots, P_k$, such that P_i belongs to agent i ($i = 1, \ldots, k$)

A solution to a distributed CSP is a set of solutions to CSPs of all agents.

Figure 1 illustrates an example of distributed CSP, a distributed graph coloring problem. A distributed graph coloring problem is a graph coloring problem where nodes and links of a graph are distributed among agents such that each agent has some nodes and all links that are connected to the nodes. In figure 1, there are three agents, A, B and C, and each of which has nodes in the corresponding ellipse and links that are connected to the nodes. For example, agent A has the nodes, n_1 and n_2, and the links, l_{12}, l_{13} and l_{26}. In other words, agent A has a CSP with the variables, n_1 and n_2, and the constraints, such as not_equal(n_1, n_2), not_equal(n_1, n_3) and not_equal(n_2, n_6). Note that there are 7 links (constraints) in this figure and among these constraints three are inter-agent constraints, l_{13}, l_{34} and l_{26}, and the other four are intra-agent constraints, l_{12}, l_{45}, l_{46} and l_{56}.

3   Experiments

3.1   Algorithm & Problem Generation

We used a simple backtracking type of algorithm in our experiments. It is basically the same one as the *asynchronous backtracking algorithm*[2] except that it is extended so that it can handle a situation where an agent has multiple local variables. We implemented this algorithm on a simulator of *synchronous distributed system*, which was implemented in C and ran on an Intel Celeron 333MHz processor, and measured the following as its communication and computation costs using this simulator.

Cycle : the number of cycles consumed until agents find one solution to a distributed CSP or the fact that no solution exists. This corresponds to the communication cost of an algorithm.

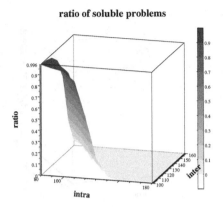

Fig. 2. Ratio of soluble problems (5 agents, 20 nodes each)

Maxcck : the total sum of the maximum number of consistency checks at each cycle until agents find one solution to a distributed CSP or the fact that no solution exists. This corresponds to the computation cost of an algorithm.

For generating a distributed graph 3-coloring problem, we used the following method.

1. Distribute 100 nodes among k agents ($k \in \{2, 5\}$ in our experiments) such that these agents have nodes as equally as possible.
2. Randomly define each of x intra-agent constraints and y inter-agent constraints.
3. Accept the graph if it is connected. If it is not connected, delete all the links and go to 2.

3.2   Results

We generated 500 problems at every combination of the number of intra-agent constraints, $intra \in \{80, 90, \ldots, 180\}$, and the number of inter-agent constraints, $inter \in \{100, 110, \ldots, 160\}$, and plotted the ratio of soluble problems among 500 problems at each data point. Figure 2 shows the ratio of soluble problems for 5 agents with 20 nodes each on the x-y plane (the x-axis is the number of intra-agent constraints and the y-axis is the number of inter-agent constraints). We should point out that the same pattern can be observed for 2 agents with 50 nodes each (the figure is omitted for lack of space). This figure clearly shows that when increasing the numbers of intra- and inter-agent constraints, we can observe a rapid drop from near one to zero in the ratio of soluble problems. The *phase transition region* where such a rapid drop is located lies around $210 \leq intra + inter \leq 240$ on the x-y plane.

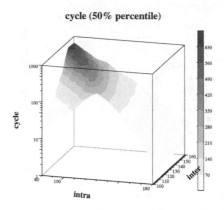

Fig. 3. Median cycle (5 agents, 20 nodes each)

We measured cycle and maxcck for each of 500 problems at every combination of *intra* and *inter*, and plotted the median cycle and maxcck of 500 problems at each data point. Figure 3 shows the median cycle for 5 agents with 20 nodes each. We should note that the similar patterns can be observed for other cases (the figures are omitted for lack of space). We can observe the following from these results.

- Both the median cycle and maxcck in the phase transition region are higher than those in the other regions. For this figure, we can see that there is a "ridge" along the phase transition region and the top of the ridge lies around $230 \leq intra + inter \leq 240$ on the x-y plane, which corresponds the region where the ratios of soluble problems are about between 0.3 and 0.
- When the number of intra-agent constraints decreases and the number of inter-agent constraints increases, the top of the ridge becomes higher.
- The top of the ridge has a steeper slope for 5 agents with 20 nodes each than for 2 agents with 50 nodes each. As a result, the case of 5 agents with 20 nodes each has a higher peak.

According to [1], for randomly generated (centralized) graph 3-coloring problems, the median computation cost of depth-first backtracking search with the Brelaz heuristic rises to the peak when the ratio of the number of links to the number of nodes is 2.3, and the location of the peak coincides with the point at which the ratio of soluble problems is 0.5. In our experiments, we can observe a basically similar result, where the top of the ridge of the median cost appears when the ratio of the number of links (*intra* + *inter*) to the number of nodes (100) is about 2.3 or 2.4. On the other hand, we should point out that its location does not coincide with the region where the ratio of soluble problems is 0.5.

We conjecture the reason why the top of the ridge becomes higher when the number of intra-agent constraints decreases and the number of inter-agent constraints increases as follows. When solving a distributed graph 3-coloring problem with a small number of intra-agent constraints and a large number of inter-agent constraints, an agent is likely to select a misleading color for its node. Once an agent (especially a higher priority agent) selects such a misleading color, other agents have to perform a lot of search to make the agent change that misleading color, and thus the communication and computation costs can be high for that kind of problems.

Although we are not able to show all the figures in this paper, the top of the ridge has a steeper slope for 5 agents with 20 nodes each than for 2 agents with 50 nodes each. For example, for 5 agents with 20 nodes each, the maximum and minimum cycles on the top of the ridge are 680 (at $intra = 80$ and $inter = 160$) and 232 (at $intra = 130$ and $inter = 100$), respectively, and for 2 agents with 50 nodes each, those are 200 (at $intra = 80$ and $inter = 150$) and 170 (at $intra = 130$ and $inter = 100$), respectively. We conjecture the reason is that a misleading color mentioned above can have a great impact on the entire performance if the number of agents increases or the number of nodes per agent decreases.

To confirm the generality of our findings, we should make more experiments using other problems and other distributed constraint satisfaction algorithms. For a preliminary report, we made experiments for the following combination of problems and an algorithm: 1) soluble distributed graph 3-coloring problems and the algorithm in section 3.1 and 2) soluble distributed graph 3-coloring problems and the *multi-AWC*[3]. Surprisingly, for each case, although there is no phase transition region because all problems are soluble, we can find a ridge almost at the same region as in figure 3, and its qualitative characteristics are consistent with our findings.

4   Conclusions

In this paper, we examine the communication and computation costs of a distributed constraint satisfaction algorithm when varying the numbers of intra- and inter-agent constraints for distributed graph 3-coloring problems.

From these results, we may say that a really hard distributed CSP is a problem in the phase transition region in which each agent has limited amount of knowledge about the problem, i.e., a small number of intra-agent constraints and a small number of variables per agent.

References

1. Hogg, T., Williams, C. P.: The hardest constraint problems: a double phase transition. *Artificial Intelligence*, Vol. 69 (1994) 359–377   518
2. Yokoo, M., Durfee, E. H., Ishida, T., Kuwabara, K.: The distributed constraint satisfaction problem: formalization and algorithms. *IEEE Transactions on Knowledge and Data Engineering*, Vol. 10, No. 5 (1998) 673–685   515, 516
3. Yokoo, M., Hirayama, K.: Distributed constraint satisfaction algorithm for complex local problems. *Proc. of the Third International Conference on Multi-Agent Systems* (1998) 372–379   519

Cooperating Constraint Solvers

Petra Hofstedt

Department of Computer Science, Berlin University of Technology

Abstract. We propose a general scheme for the cooperation of different constraint solvers. On top of a uniform interface for constraint we stepwise develop reduction systems which describe the behaviour of an overall combined system. The modularity of our definitions of reduction relations at different levels allows the definition of cooperation strategies for the solvers according to the current requirements such that our overall system forms a general framework for cooperating solvers.

1 Constraint Systems and Constraint Solvers

The combination of several constraint solving techniques enables to solve problems that none of the single solvers can handle alone (for examples see [2,4,5]). Thus, we developed an open and very flexible combination mechanism.

A *signature* $\Sigma = (S, F, R; ar)$ is defined by a set S of sorts, a set F of function symbols, a set R of predicate symbols, and an arity function $ar : F \cup R \to S^*$. A Σ-*structure* $\mathcal{D} = (\{\mathcal{D}^s \mid s \in S\}, \{f^{\mathcal{D}} \mid f \in F\}, \{r^{\mathcal{D}} \mid r \in R\})$ consists of 1. an S-sorted family of nonempty carrier sets $\mathcal{D}^s$, 2. a family of functions $f^{\mathcal{D}}$, and 3. a family of predicates $r^{\mathcal{D}}$, appropriate to F and R. $X = \bigcup_{s \in S} X^s$ is a many sorted set of variables. A *constraint system* is a tuple $\zeta = \langle \Sigma, \mathcal{D} \rangle$, a *constraint over* Σ is a string of the form $r \ t_1 \ldots t_m$ where $r \in R^{s_1 \times \ldots \times s_m}$ and $t_i \in \mathcal{T}(F, X)^{s_i}$ (, i.e. t_i is a term over F of sort s_i with variables from X). The set of constraints over Σ is denoted by $Cons(\Sigma)$. Let $\forall \psi$ resp. $\exists \psi$ denote the universal closure and the existential closure, respectively. $\exists_{-\tilde{Y}} \psi$ denotes the existential closure of formula ψ except for the variables occurring in the sequence $\tilde{Y}$ of variables. Let $\mathcal{D}$ be a Σ-structure, and let Φ be a constraint conjunction over Σ. Let $var(\Phi)$ denote the set of variables of Φ. A *solution* of Φ in $\mathcal{D}$ is a valuation $\sigma : V \to \bigcup_{s \in S} \mathcal{D}^s$ of a finite set V of variables, $var(\Phi) \subseteq V$, such that $(\mathcal{D}, \sigma) \models \forall \Phi$ holds. Solving Φ means finding out whether there exists a solution for Φ or not. A *constraint solver* consists of a collection of operations which can be used to solve and to transform constraints of a constraint system. A solver works on a constraint store $C \in CStore$ which, in the following, consists of a disjunction of constraint conjunctions. C has the property that it is satisfiable in the corresponding structure $\mathcal{D}$, i.e. $\mathcal{D} \models \exists C$ holds.

2 A Uniform Interface for Constraint Solvers

To enable a cooperation of constraint solvers to solve a given problem, the solvers need to exchange information. We want to enable them to communicate in such a way that a very tight cooperation is possible.

R. Dechter (Ed.): CP 2000, LNCS 1894, pp. 520–525, 2000.
© Springer-Verlag Berlin Heidelberg 2000

Let L be the set of indices of constraint systems, $\mu, \nu \in L$. Let to each constraint system a constraint solver be assigned. The following functions built our uniform interface for constraint solvers:

1. $tell$: $Cons(\Sigma_\nu) \times CStore_\nu \longrightarrow \{true_{changed}, true_{redundant}, false\} \times CStore_\nu$
2. $proj$: $\mathcal{P}(X) \times CStore_\nu \longrightarrow CStore_\nu$
3. $proj^{\nu \rightarrow \mu}$: $\mathcal{P}(X) \times CStore_\nu \longrightarrow CStore_\mu$

1. The (partial) function $tell$ is due to constraint satisfaction, i.e. an operation which is usually offered by constraint solvers. $tell$ adds a constraint $c \in Cons(\Sigma_\nu)$ to a constraint store $C \in CStore_\nu$ if the conjunction of c and C is satisfiable, i.e. if $\mathcal{D} \models \exists(C \wedge c)$ holds. We require $tell$ to be defined as follows:

if $tell(c, C) = (true_{redundant}, C)$,	then $\mathcal{D} \models \forall(C \longrightarrow c)$,
if $tell(c, C) = (true_{changed}, C')$, where $\mathcal{D} \models \forall((C \wedge c) \longleftrightarrow C')$,	
	then $\mathcal{D} \models \exists(C \wedge c)$,
if $tell(c, C) = (false, C)$	then $\mathcal{D} \not\models \exists(C \wedge c)$.

2. The function $proj$ is due to the operation constraint projection of constraint solvers. Usually, the aim of projecting a constraint store $C \in CStore_\nu$ wrt a sequence $\tilde{Y}$ (with $Y \subseteq X$) of variables which occur in C is to find a disjunction C' of conjunctions of constraints which is equivalent to $\exists_{-\tilde{Y}} C$ and where the variables which do occur in C but not in $\tilde{Y}$ are eliminated: $\mathcal{D}_\nu \models \forall(\exists_{-\tilde{Y}} C \longleftrightarrow C')$. However, since sometimes it is not possible to compute C' or it is not possible to compute it efficiently, we require $proj$ to be defined as follows:

$proj(Y, C) = C'$, where $Y \subseteq X$ and $\mathcal{D}_\nu \models \forall(\exists_{-\tilde{Y}} C \longrightarrow C')$.

3. Since we want to use projections for information exchange between the different constraint solvers, we need a function which projects a constraint store C^ν wrt another constraint system ζ_μ, $\mu \in L \backslash \{\nu\}$. $proj^{\nu \rightarrow \mu}$ can be defined by means of $proj$ and a conversion function. Thus each single constraint solver can be regarded as black box solver equipped with a projection function which allows the projection of the constraint store wrt a set of variables. These black box solvers are extended by functions for converting projections wrt other constraint systems.

Example 1. Consider a solver CS_{rat} for arithmetic constraints over rational numbers, and a solver CS_{FD} of a finite domain constraint system ζ_{FD}.
The projection functions $proj$ and $proj^{FD \rightarrow rat}$ of CS_{FD} could work as follows:
$proj(x, C^{FD}) = x \in_{FD} \{4, 5, 6\}$, and
$proj^{FD \rightarrow rat}(x, C^{FD}) = ((x \geq 4) \wedge (x \leq 6))$, where
$C^{FD} = ((y = 3) \wedge (x > y) \wedge (x \in_{FD} \{2, 3, 4, 5, 6\}))$.
The function $tell$ of CS_{rat} could yield the following results:
$tell((x = 4), C) = (true_{changed}, C')$, where $C = true$ and $C' = (x = 4)$,
$tell((x > 3), C') = (true_{redundant}, C')$, and $tell((x < 3), C') = (false, C')$. □

Clearly, the projection functions $proj$ and $proj^{\nu \rightarrow \mu}$, $\nu, \mu \in L$, must be defined in such a way that, first, projecting a constraint store wrt another constraint

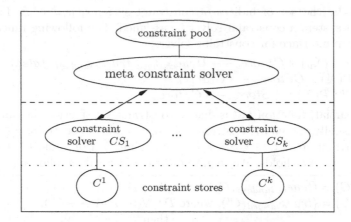

Fig. 1. Architecture of the overall system

system, no solutions of the constraints of the store are lost and, second, that a projection of a constraint store implies previous projections of this (at a previous time less restricted) store. We call these required properties *soundness* and *monotonicity*, a formal description is left out because of space limitations. We require the functions *tell*, *proj*, and $proj^{\nu \to \mu}$, $\nu, \mu \in L$, to be computable.

3   Combination of Constraint Solvers

The Architecture. Figure 1 shows the architecture of our overall system for co-operating constraint solvers. To every individual solver CS_ν a constraint store C^ν is assigned. The *meta constraint solver* coordinates the work of the different individual solvers. The meta solver manages the *constraint pool*. Initially, the constraint pool contains the constraints of the constraint conjunction Φ which we want to solve. The meta constraint solver takes constraints from the constraint pool and passes them to the constraint solvers of the corresponding constraint domains (step 1). Each of the individual constraint solvers is able to handle a subset of the set of constraints of the constraint pool independently of the other solvers, the individual solvers propagate the received constraints to their stores by *tell* (step 2). The meta constraint solver manages the exchange of information between the individual solvers. It forces them to extract information from their constraint stores by $proj^{\nu \to \mu}$. This information is added by the meta constraint solver to the constraint pool (step 3). The procedure of steps 1-3 is repeated until the pool contains either the constraint *false* or the constraint *true* only. If the constraint pool contains *false* only, then the initially given conjunction Φ of constraints is unsatisfiable. If the pool contains *true* only, then the system could not find a contradiction. Solutions of Φ can be retrieved from the current constraint stores. Using the described mechanisms, each individual solver deals with more information than only that of its associated constraints of Φ.

Syntax. To allow to solve a conjunction of constraints, where every constraint may contain function symbols and predicate symbols of different constraint systems, it is necessary to detect overloaded symbols by analysis and to convert the constraint conjunction into a conjunction such that every constraint is defined by symbols of exactly one constraint system (by flattening as usually).

Operational Semantics. We describe the operational semantics of our system by means of a reduction relation for *overall configurations*. An overall configuration $\mathcal{H}$ consists of a *formal disjunction* $\overset{.}{\bigvee}_{i \in \{1,...,m\}} \mathcal{G}_i$ of configurations $\mathcal{G}_i$. Formal disjunction $\overset{.}{\vee}$ is commutative. A *configuration* $\mathcal{G} = \mathcal{P} \odot \bigwedge_{\nu \in L} C^\nu$ corresponds to the architecture of the overall system (Fig.1). It consists of the constraint pool $\mathcal{P}$ which is a set of constraints which we want to solve and the conjunction $\bigwedge_{\nu \in L} C^\nu$ of constraint stores.

We lift the application of the functions *tell* resp. *proj*$^{\nu \to \mu}$ to the level of overall configurations and define the two *basic relations prop* resp. *put_proj* which are the basis of the stepwise definition of the operational semantics. We define *strategies for cooperating constraint solvers,* i.e. reduction systems for overall configurations using these basic relations. In general, in one derivation step one or more configurations $\mathcal{G}_i$, $i \in \{1, \dots, m\}$, are rewritten by a formal disjunction $\mathcal{H}\mathcal{G}_i$ of configurations:

$$OConf1 = \mathcal{H}_1 \overset{.}{\vee} \mathcal{G}_1 \overset{.}{\vee} \dots \overset{.}{\vee} \mathcal{H}_i \overset{.}{\vee} \mathcal{G}_i \overset{.}{\vee} \dots \overset{.}{\vee} \mathcal{H}_m \overset{.}{\vee} \mathcal{G}_m \overset{.}{\vee} \mathcal{H}_{m+1} \implies$$
$$OConf2 = \mathcal{H}_1 \overset{.}{\vee} \mathcal{H}\mathcal{G}_1 \overset{.}{\vee} \dots \overset{.}{\vee} \mathcal{H}_i \overset{.}{\vee} \mathcal{H}\mathcal{G}_i \overset{.}{\vee} \dots \overset{.}{\vee} \mathcal{H}_m \overset{.}{\vee} \mathcal{H}\mathcal{G}_m \overset{.}{\vee} \mathcal{H}_{m+1}$$

Thus, first, we define a derivation relation for configurations and, based on this, we define a derivation relation for overall configurations.

Step 1. Definition of a derivation relation for configurations (production level). The simplest possibility to define a derivation step $\mathcal{G}_i \to \mathcal{H}\mathcal{G}_i$ is to chose (nondeterministically) exactly one constraint $c \in Cons(\Sigma_\nu)$, $\nu \in L$, from the constraint pool of $\mathcal{G}_i$ and to propagate it to its associated constraint store C^ν building a new configuration $\mathcal{G}'_i$ (using the basic relation *prop*). This is followed by projections of the newly built constraint store C'^ν wrt other constraint systems building the new overall configuration $\mathcal{H}\mathcal{G}_i$ (using *put_proj*).

There are many other possibilities to define a strategy for the production level. We are able to let the solvers work in parallel as well as to fix the order of the constraint systems or constraints itself which are propagated next which enables to regard choice heuristics, for example to delay particular constraints, as naive solving nonlinear constraints.

Step 2. Defining a derivation relation for overall configurations (application level). A derivation step $OConf1 \implies OConf2$ for overall configurations is defined on the basis of the derivation relation for configurations (at production level). There are as well many possibilities: for example, we may define a derivation step such that the derivation of exactly one configuration or the derivation of several configurations in parallel or concurrently is allowed.

Using this *two-step frame* different reduction systems which realize different derivation strategies for the derivation of an *initial overall configuration* to normal form can be described. An initial overall configuration is a configuration $\mathcal{G}_0 = \mathcal{P}_\Phi \odot \bigwedge_{\nu \in L} C_0^\nu$, where the constraint pool $\mathcal{P}_\Phi$ contains the constraints of the conjunction Φ which we want to solve and all constraint stores C_0^ν, $\nu \in L$, are empty, i.e. they contain the constraint *true* only.

4   Conclusion and Related Work

We shortly presented a general scheme for cooperating constraint solvers. A uniform interface for the solvers allows to formally specify the information exchange between them. Because of this information exchange the overall combined system is able to solve constraint conjunctions which the single solvers are not able to handle. The modularity of our definitions of the basic relations and of the derivation relations at production level as well as at application level allows the definition of derivation strategies for cooperating solvers according to the current requirements, like properties of the particular constraint solvers as well as properties of the underlying software and hardware. Since our approach allows the integration of constraint solvers of very different constraint systems it is possible to integrate different host languages into the system by treating them as constraint solvers. In [1] we have shown the integration of a functional logic language. This new point of view on the host language of such a system and the possibility to define tight cooperation strategies according to the current requirements allow to specify a wide range of systems of cooperating solvers such that our overall system forms a general framework for cooperating solvers.

Cooperating solvers have been investigated from different points of view [2,3,4,5,6]. Usually this are very specialized approaches and their cooperation strategies are fixed. Our approach allows the definition of similar strategies and even a finer grained definition of strategies according to the current requirements. As far as for the mentioned approaches the form of constraints exchanged between the solvers is given, we are able to express this as well by means of our interface functions. For example, the main idea behind the combination approach in [6] is a mechanism which controls variable equality sharing which is an instance of information exchange by projections as done in our approach.

References

1. P. Hofstedt. A functional logic language as hostlanguage for a system of combined constraint solvers. In R. Echahed, editor, *8th International Workshop on Functional and Logic Programming*, pages 119–132. Grenoble, France, 1999. 524
2. H. Hong. Confluency of cooperative constraint solvers. Technical Report 94-08, Research Institute for Symbolic Computation, Linz, Austria, 1994. 520, 524
3. E. Monfroy. *Solver Collaboration for Constraint Logic Programming*. PhD thesis, Centre de Recherche en Informatique de Nancy. INRIA-Lorraine, 1996. 524
4. M. Rueher. An architecture for cooperating constraint solvers on reals. In A. Podelski, editor, *Constraint Programming. Châtillon Spring School 1994. Selected Papers*, volume 910 of *LNCS*, pages 231–250. Springer-Verlag, 1995. 520, 524
5. M. Rueher and C. Solnon. Concurrent cooperating solvers over reals. *Reliable Computing*, 3:3:325–333, 1997. 520, 524

6. C. Tinelli and M. T. Harandi. Constraint logic programming over unions of constraint theories. *The Journal of Functional and Logic Programming*, Article 6, 1998. 524

An Empirical Study of Probabilistic Arc Consistency as a Variable Ordering Heuristic

Michael C. Horsch and William S. Havens

Intelligent Systems Laboratory,School of Computing Science,
Simon Fraser University, Burnaby, B.C., Canada V5A 1S6
{mhorsch, havens}@cs.sfu.ca

Abstract. We report on an empirical evaluation of a new probabilistic heuristic for constructive search in constraint satisfaction problems. The heuristic is based on the estimation of solution probability. We show empirically that this heuristic is more accurate than related heuristics, and reduces the number of consistency checks and backtracks in constructive search by up to several orders of magnitude. Our results also show that the time required to estimate solution probabilities is less than the time required for search using other well-known heuristics as the problem size increases.

1 Introduction

The challenge in a constraint satisfaction problem (CSP) is to determine an assignment of values to variables that satisfies each of a given set of constraints, or otherwise, to conclude correctly that no such assignment exits. In a systematic constructive search process, it is well known that the order in which the variables are assigned can have a significant impact on the cost of the search.

In this paper we present a summary of our experiments using a heuristic for constructive search based on solution probability, i.e., the frequency with which each value is used in all solutions to the CSP. Solution probabilities for a CSP can answer such questions as "Which assignment appears most often in all solutions?" Solution probabilities can therefore provide an ordering to unassigned variables, as well as an ordering for the values for each variable.

We have developed a method for approximating solution probabilities for binary CSPs. We have shown elsewhere [6] that our method is a generalization of the arc consistency algorithm AC-3 [7] for general constraint graphs. We have also shown (op. cit.) that it is a specialization of probabilistic reasoning in Bayesian networks [9]. For this reason, we call our method *probabilistic arc consistency* (pAC).

Our method can compute exact solution probabilities for binary CSPs with tree-structured constraint graphs in time linear in the number of variables. Probabilistic arc consistency can also be used iteratively to provide a good approximation for CSPs of more general structure.

Probabilistic arc consistency is an extension of the techniques expressed in several previous proposals. Work by Dechter and Pearl [2], Meisels et al. [8],

R. Dechter (Ed.): CP 2000, LNCS 1894, pp. 525–530, 2000.

and Vernooy and Havens [13] is equivalent to pAC when the CSP's constraint graph is tree-structured. These proposals differ in their approach to more general CSPs. Peleg [10] developed a probabilistic relaxation method very similar to pAC that was intended to find a satisfying assignment to the variables in a CSP. The algorithm given by Shazeer et al. [12] on estimating posterior probability distributions over constraint problems is essentially the same as the pAC algorithm.

2   Probabilistic Arc Consistency

We briefly present the pAC algorithm which we use to compute or approximate the solution probabilities for every variable in a CSP. The formulation provided below is specific to binary CSPs with finite discrete domains. It is easily extended to deal with k-ary constraints. The claims in this section are stated without proof; proofs can be found in [5].

Let $< V, B >$ be a binary constraint satisfaction problem with variables V, and binary constraints B, such that the constraint graph $G =< V, B >$ is tree-structured. For every $X \in V$, let D_X be the domain of X, i.e., $D_X = \{x_1, \ldots, x_m\}$. For every pair of variables (X, Y) such that there is a binary constraint $C_{XY} \in B$, define the following:

$$C_{XY}(i,j) = \begin{cases} 1 \text{ if } (x_i, y_j) \in C_{XY} \\ 0 \quad \text{otherwise} \end{cases}$$

$$S_{XY}^{(k)}(i) = \sum_{j=1}^{m} C_{XY}(i,j) M_{XY}^{(k)}(j)$$

$$M_{YX}^{(0)}(i) = 1; \quad M_{YX}^{(k+1)}(i) = \begin{cases} \dfrac{F_X^{(k)}(i)}{S_{XY}^{(k)}(i)} \text{ if } S_{XY}^{(k)}(i) > 0 \\ \\ 0 \qquad \text{otherwise} \end{cases}$$

$$F_X^{(k)}(i) = \alpha \prod_{\{Y|(X,Y)\in B\}} S_{XY}^{(k)}(i) \quad \text{where } \alpha \text{ is such that } \sum_{i=1}^{m} F_X^{(k)}(i) = 1$$

These formulae define the pAC method. Each binary constraint in B is expressed numerically in C_{XY}. The value $F_X^{(k)}(i)$ represents the kth iterative approximation to the solution probability for $x_i \in D_X$. The value $S_{XY}^{(k)}(i)$ represents the kth approximation to the expected number of times value $x_i \in D_X$ is used consistently with values of neighbour Y; informally, it can understood as the support of X from Y. The value $M_{YX}^{(k)}(i)$ represents the kth estimate of the solution probability for $x_i \in D_X$, factoring out all effects of neighbour Y; informally, it can be understood as a "message" sent from X to Y, from which Y computes its support from X. This message is carefully constructed so that Y does not "double count" information it previously sent to X.

Theorem 1. *Let $G = <V, B>$ be a CSP such that the constraint graph for G is tree-structured, with diameter d. For any variable $X \in V$, the relative frequency that value $x_i \in D_X$ is used in all solutions of G is $F_X^{(d)}(i)$.*

For correctness, the computations described above require arbitrary precision floating point numbers. In our implementation, we use 64-bit floating point numbers, at the risk of a non-trivial loss of precision when the CSPs get very large.

When applied to CSPs with arbitrary topology, the theorem no longer applies. However, in many cases, pAC converges to a reasonable approximation of the solution probabilities. The accuracy depends on the degree to which the given CSP satisfies the assumption of independence of sub-graphs. This result is further explored in the next section. It is not too surprising in light of other recent results, wherein an algorithm for belief propagation in singly-connected Bayesian networks [9], has been shown to produce good results as an approximation method for probabilistic reasoning in networks of arbitrary topology (e.g., [3]). Elsewhere, we have shown that pAC is a special case of belief propagation in singly-connected Bayesian networks, and also a generalization of arc consistency [7].

We have no theoretical guarantees regarding convergence of our method. To limit computation, we use two parameters, ϵ and MaxIter; iteration continues while both of the following conditions are true: $\epsilon < \max_X \sum_i (F_X^{(k+1)}(i) - F_X^{(k)}(i))^2$ and MaxIter $> k$. When the change in solution probability is less than a given ϵ, the process is declared to have converged; when the number of iterations exceeds MaxIter, the process is halted without convergence.

3 Empirical Results

We performed three sets of experiments. The first examined the quality of the approximate probabilities that pAC returns, and showed that pAC performed very well as an approximation on many problems. Second experiment showed that pAC can reduce search compared to other heuristics for counting solutions (e.g., [2, 8, 13, 10]). The third experiment compared the use of pAC as a dynamic variable ordering heuristic against the variable ordering heuristics reported in the literature. We show that pAC reduced the number of consistency checks and backtracks by several orders of magnitude.

3.1 The Accuracy of pAC as an Approximation Method

To judge the accuracy of the approximate solution probabilities, we compared the distributions pAC determines against an exact frequency distribution, for a set of relatively small problems. We used a straightforward correlation computation to compare probability distributions.

We created three sets of 1000 random binary CSPs, with 20 variables with 10 values each. The p_1 values for these problems sets were $0.2, 0.5$ and 1.0 respectively. In our three sets of problems, we create 10 CSPs each for 100 values of p_2 starting at 0.01 and increasing by 0.01. We applied pAC to each problem using $\epsilon = 0.00001$, and MaxIter $= 1001$ iterations.

The approximate solution probabilities were strongly correlated with the exact distributions; the average correlation over the problem sets was determined to be 0.833, 0.771 and 0.788 resp., with standard deviations 0.16, 0.21 and 0.18. Many of the over-constrained problems were correctly identified as such: 75%, 95% and 96%, resp.

3.2   Using pAC as a Static Value Ordering Heuristic

We applied a constructive search algorithm to three sets of 2000 problems, each set having the same properties as in the previous experiment. The approximate solution probabilities were precomputed for each problem, and this static information was used to order values by decreasing solution probability. The variables were ordered lexicographically.

We compared the results of using pAC directly to the methods and results presented by Vernooy and Havens [13]. This also provided a basis for a comparison to Dechter and Pearl's method [2], Meisel et al.'s method [8]. We also implemented Peleg's method (Peleg) [10] for comparison. Using pAC as a static variable ordering heuristic substantially reduced the search cost in terms of the number of backtracks, compared to the other methods. We observed an order of magnitude improvement or higher in 80% of the problems for each of the problem sets.

3.3   Using pAC as a Dynamic Variable and Value Ordering Heuristic

The pAC method can be used as a dynamic variable ordering heuristic. After each assignment of a value to a variable, the pAC algorithm is run again, taking into account this assignment, and new heuristic information is computed. The approximate solution probabilities determined by pAC are used to order the variables as well as the values. While several choices are available, we ordered the (unassigned) variables so that the search proceed with the most certain assignments first.

In this experiment, hundreds of random problems were created, each with 20 to 70 variables, with 10, 20 or 30 values each. Each problem was created to be close to the phase transition region for its problem size. We compared the pAC heuristic to several well studied variable ordering heuristics Brelaz, FF, FFdeg, [1, 4] as well as a random selection criterion. The constructive search procedure was a highly optimized forward-checking back-jumping search algorithm [11], and each of the heuristics was employed using this search procedure.

We observed that the pAC heuristic required one to three orders of magnitude fewer consistency checks and backtracks than any of the other heuristics. This was uniformly observed across all problem sets. Computing the approximate solution probabilities can be very expensive, and for some problem sets, constructive search using pAC requires one to two orders of magnitude more time to find solutions, as compared to the other heuristics used in our experiment. However, as the problem size increased, we observed a decrease in the difference in time required to solve the problems. For the largest of the problem sets solved in our experiment, the median solution time using pAC was actually less than the median time for the other heuristics.

4   Discussion and Future Work

Our experiments have demonstrated that pAC is a valuable heuristic for solving CSPs by search. If the process converges, it usually converges to a good approximation to the relative frequency distribution of values in solutions to the CSP. When used as a dynamic variable ordering heuristic, failure to converge is not a serious issue: at worst, a search procedure will have to backtrack over an assignment made based on unreliable information returned when pAC is halted without convergence. We have found that since pAC identifies over-constrained problems quickly, the cost of the unreliable information is small. The approximations returned by pAC need not be accurate, as inaccurate results can still provide reliable value-ordering information.

We have shown that pAC can reduce search costs by orders of magnitude, depending on the difficulty of the problem, as compared to the heuristics found in the literature. However, when the problem is small enough, the cost of computation for pAC outweighs the benefit of reducing search costs. For larger problems, pAC's runtime is competitive or superior to the other heuristics used for comparison in this experiment.

We are currently investigating methods for reducing the computation costs of pAC. We are studying the effects of reducing the ϵ and MaxIter parameters, as well as the effects of limiting propagation to a subset of the CSP. We are also exploring the use of local propagation techniques in CSPs which have an optimization component, and how it might be used as a heuristic for local search.

References

[1] D. Brelaz. New methods to color the verticies of a graph. *JACM*, 22(4):251–256, 1979. 528

[2] Rina Dechter and Judea Pearl. Network-based heuristics for constraint-satisfaction problems. *Artificial Intelligence*, 34:1–34, 1988. 525, 527, 528

[3] Brendan J. Frey and David J. C. MacKay. A revolution: Belief propagation in graphs with cycles. In *Advances in Neural Information Processing Systems*, pages 479–485, 1998. 527

[4] Richard M. Haralick and Gordon L. Elliot. Increasing tree search efficiency for constraint satisfaction problems. *Artificial Intelligence*, 14(3):263–313, 1980. 528

[5] Michael C. Horsch and William S. Havens. How to count Solutions to CSPs. Technical report, School of Computing Science, Simon Fraser University, 2000. 526

[6] Michael C. Horsch and William S. Havens. Probabilistic Arc Consistency: A connection between constraint reasoning and probabilistic reasoning. In *Proceedings of the Sixteenth Conference on Uncertainty in Artificial Intelligence*, 2000. To appear. 525

[7] Alan K. Mackworth. Consistency in networks of relations. *Artificial Intelligence*, 8(1):99–118, 1977. 525, 527

[8] Amnon Meisels, Solomon Ehal Shimonoy, and Gadi Solotorevsky. Bayes Networks for Estimating the Number of Solutions to a CSP. In *Proceedings of the Fourteenth National Conference on Artificial Intelligence*, 1997. 525, 527, 528

[9] Judea Pearl. *Probabilistic Reasoning in Intelligent Systems: Networks of Plausible Reasoning*. Morgan Kaufmann Publishers, Los Altos, 1988. 525, 527

[10] Shmuel Peleg. A new probabilistic relaxation method. *IEEE Transactions on Pattern Matching and Machine Intelligence*, 2(4):362–369, 1980. 526, 527, 528

[11] P. Prosser. Hybrid algorithms for the constraint satisfaction problem. *Computational Intelligence*, 9:268–299, 1993. 528

[12] Noam M. Shazeer, Michael L. Littman, and Greg A. Keim. Solving crossword puzzles as probabilistic constraint satisfaction. In *Proceedings of the Sixteenth National Conference on Artificial Intelligence*, pages 156–162, 1999. 526

[13] Matt Vernooy and William S. Havens. An examination of probabilistic value-ordering heuristics. In *Proceedings of the 12th Australian Joint Conference on Artificial Intelligence*, 1999. 526, 527, 528

On Dual Encodings for Non-binary Constraint Satisfaction Problems

S. ı agarajan[1], S. Goodwin[1], Z. Sattar[2], and ´. Thornton[2]

[1] Department of Computer Science, University of Regina,
Regina, Saskatchewan, Canada
{shiv,goodwin}@cs.uregina.ca
[2] School of Information Technology,
Griffith University, Gold Coast, Queensland, Australia
j.thornton@gu.edu.au
sattar@cit.gu.edu.au

Abstract. In [Walsh and Stergiou, 1999] enforcing arc consistency (AC) in the dual encoding was shown to strictly dominate enforcing AC on the hidden or GAC on the original problem. We introduce a dual encoding that requires only a small subset of the original constraints to be stored in extension, while the remaining constraints can be stored intensionally. In this paper we present a theoretical comparison between the pruning achieved by enforcing AC on this dual encoding, versus enforcing GAC and dual arc consistency on the standard encoding. We show how the covering based encoding retains the dominance over enforcing GAC on the original problem, while using less space than the existing dual encoding.

1 Introduction

In this paper we present a new dual encoding that is based on the construction of constraint coverings from the original NS¨. We show how this covering based dual encoding can be used to address the space complexity issue of the dual encodings, while still retaining the soundness and completeness of the solution procedures. Z new form of local consistency based on this dual encoding called *covering arc consistency* (NZN), is defined. The amount of pruning achieved by enforcing NZN on the new encoding is compared theoretically to GZN on the original problem, ZN on the hidden encoding, and ZN on the standard dual encoding.

2 Preliminary Definitions

Given below are a few definitions. Qet $\langle V, D, C \rangle$ be a *CSP* where V is the set of variables, D are their domains, and C is the set of constraints. Furthermore, we can assume that each constraint $C_i = \langle V_i, S_i \rangle \in C$ consists of a list of variables $V_i = (v_{i1}, \ldots, v_{ik}) \subseteq V$ and a predicate on these variables,

R. Dechter (Ed.): CP 2000, LNCS 1894, pp. 531–536, 2000.
© Springer-Verlag Berlin Heidelberg 2000

$S_i \subseteq D_{v_{i1}} \times \cdots \times D_{v_{ik}}$. A binary *CSP* is one in which all the constraints are defined over pairs of variables. Associated with every binary *CSP* is a constraint graph with a node for every variable and an edge between two nodes if their variables share a constraint [36].

Definition 1. *Given a binary* NS", *the* **primal constraint graph** *associated with it is a labeled constraint graph, where* $N=V$, $\langle v_i, v_j\rangle \in A$ *iff* $\exists C_{ij} \in C \mid V_{ij} = \{v_i, v_j\}$. *Also the label on arc* $\langle v_i, v_j\rangle$ *is* C_{ij}. *Given an arbitrary* NS", *the* **dual constraint graph** *associated with it is a labeled graph, where* $N=C$, $\langle C_i, C_j\rangle \in A$ *iff* $V_i \cap V_j \neq \emptyset$. *Also the label on arc* $\langle C_i, C_j\rangle$ *is* $V_i \cap V_j$.

Definition 2. *If* V_i *and* V_j *are sets of variables, let* S_i *be an instantiation of the variables in* V_i. $S_i[V_j]$ *is the tuple consisting of only the components of* S_i *that correspond to the variables in* V_j. *This is also called the* **projection** *of tuple* S_i *on the variables in* V_j. *Let* C_i, C_j *be two constraints* $\in C$. *The* **join** *of* C_i, C_j, *denoted by* $C_i \bowtie C_j = C_{ij}$, *is the set* $\{t \mid t \in S_{ij} \wedge t[V_i] \in S_i \wedge t[V_j] \in S_j\}$.

Definition 3. *Consider a tuple* t_i *as a consistent instantiation of variables in* V_{t_i}. *An* **extension** *of* t_i *to variables in* $V_{t_i} \cup V_{t_j}$ *is a tuple* t_{ij} *where* t_{ij} *is an instantiation to variables in* $V_{t_i} \cup V_{t_j}$. *The two tuples* t_i *and* t_j *are* **compatible** *if* $t_i[V_{t_i} \cap V_{t_j}] = t_j[V_{t_i} \cap V_{t_j}]$, *i.e., the two tuples agree on values for all common variables.*[1] *The tuple* $t_{ij} = t_i \bowtie t_j$ *is a* **consistent extension** *of* t_i *iff* t_i *and* t_j *are* **compatible** *and* $\forall C_i$ *such that* $V_i \subseteq V_{t_{ij}}, t_{ij}[V_i] \in S_i$.

Definition 4. *Given a constraint* C_{ij}, *the value* b *in* D_j, *is called a* **support** *for value* a *in* D_j, *if the pair* $\langle a, b\rangle \in S_{ij}$. *A value* a *for a variable* i *is* **viable** *iff for every variable* j *such that a constraint* C_{ij} *exists,* a *has a support in* D_j. *The domain* D *of a constraint network, is* **arc consistent** *if for every variable* i *in the network, all the values in* d_i *are viable.*

Definition 5. *[5] A tuple* t *on* $\langle v_{i_1}, \dots, v_{i_q}\rangle$ *is valid iff* $t \in D\langle v_{i_1}\rangle \times \dots \times D\langle v_{i_q}\rangle$. *A CSP is said to be* **generalised arc consistent** *(GAC) if* $\forall v_i \in V, \forall val_i \in D\langle v_i\rangle, \forall C_j \in C, \exists t \in S_j$ *such that* t *is valid and* $t[v_i] = val_i$. *A CSP is said to be* **pair-wise consistent**, *iff* $\forall C_i, C_j, S_i[C_i \cup C_j] = S_j[C_i \cup C_j]$ *and* $\forall S_i, S_i \neq \emptyset$ *[4].*

The notion of arc consistency can be defined for tuples and dual variables in the dual encoding as follows.

Definition 6. *Given two constraints* C_i *and* C_j, *the tuple* $t_j \in S_j$ *is called a* **support** *for tuple* $t_i \in S_i$, *if* $t_i[V_i \cap V_j] = t_j[V_i \cap V_j]$. *A tuple* t_i *in a constraint* C_i *is* **viable** *iff for every constraint* C_j, *tuple* t_i *has support in* C_j. *A constraint network is* **dual arc consistent**, *if for every constraint* C_i, *all the tuples in* S_i *are viable.*

Definition 7. *Let* $C_{cover} = \{C_1, C_2, \dots, C_m\}$. *Also* $C_{cover} \subseteq C$. *Each* $C_i \in C_{cover}$ *is given as* $\langle V_i, S_i\rangle$, *where* $V_i \subseteq V$. C_{cover} **covers** V *iff* $\bigcup_{i=1}^{m} V_i = V$. C_{cover} *is a* **constraint cover** *of* V. *As well,* C_{cover} *is a* **minimal constraint cover** *of* V *if it is a constraint cover of* V *and no proper subset of* C_{cover} *is a constraint cover of* V. *If* C_{cover} *is a minimal constraint cover,* $|C_{cover}| \leq |V|$.

---

[1] If $V_{t_i} \cap V_{t_j} = \emptyset$, t_i and t_j are automatically compatible.

3 Covering Arc Consistency

Nonsider a dual encoding of a NS‥6where the nodes of the dual encoding are the constraints in a constraint cover of the given NS‥7We now define a new form of arc consistency based on this dual encoding known as *Covering Arc Consistency*6 which is defined on constraints in a cover7

Definition 8. *Let* $C_{cover} = \{C_1, C_2, \ldots, C_m\}$. *Given two constraints* $C_i \in C_{cover}$ *and* $C_j \in C_{cover}$, *the tuple* $t_j \in S_j$ *is called a* **covering arc support** *for tuple* $t_i \in S_i$, *if* $t_i[v_i \cap v_j] = t_j[v_i \cap v_j]$ *and* $\forall C_x \in \{C\text{-}\{C_i, C_j\}\}$, $\Re t_i \bowtie t_j 5[v_{ij} \cap v_x] \in S_x[v_{ij} \cap v_x]$. *A tuple* $t_i \in C_i \in C_{cover}$ *is* **viable** *iff for every constraint* $C_j \in C_{cover}$, *tuple* t_i *has covering arc support in* C_j. *A constraint network is* **covering arc consistent (CAC)** *w.r.t a covering* C_{cover}, *if* $\forall C_i \in C_{cover}$, *all the tuples in* S_i *are viable.*

Zn arc consistency algorithm removes all arc inconsistent values from the domains of the variables of the encoding7 The following theorems are proven in [ ]7

Theorem 1. *Achieving AC on the hidden variable encoding is equivalent to achieving GAC on the variables in the original problem.*

Theorem 2. *Achieving AC on the dual encoding is strictly stronger than achieving GAC on the original problem.*

Theorem 3. *Achieving AC on the dual encoding is strictly stronger than achieving AC on the hidden variable encoding.*

Vi the following we perform a similar theoretical comparison between enforcing covering arc consistency 9NZN56 ffiZN and dual arc consistency7 Nonsider the following example taken from [1]7 This NS‥ is already ffiZN6 while enforcing Kual ZN removes some values from the domains7 Onforcing NZN6 reduces the domains to singleton domains7

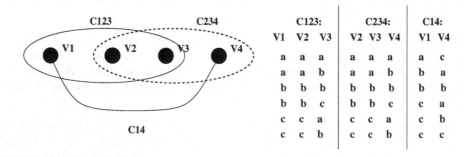

C123:			C234:			C14:	
V1	V2	V3	V2	V3	V4	V1	V4
a	a	a	a	a	a	a	c
a	a	b	a	a	b	b	a
b	b	b	b	b	b	b	b
b	b	c	b	b	c	c	a
c	c	a	c	c	a	c	b
c	c	b	c	c	b	c	c

Fig. 1. ı onŒinary NS‥ LZn example

Theorem 4. *Achieving CAC on the constraint covering based dual encoding is strictly stronger than achieving GAC on the original problem.*

Proof. Vf ffiZN on the original encoding removes a value val_i from the domain of variable v_i then there exists some constraint C_i that mentions variable v_i6and the assignment of val_i to v_i cannot be extended to a consistent assignment to the rest of the variables in C_i7Nonsider a covering based dual encoding7 Oither the cover contains the previously mentioned constraint C_i6or $C_i \in \{C\mathbb{C}_{cover}\}$7 Vf $C_i \in C_{cover}$6then we can derive the *nogood* that removes val_i from v_i 9since no tuple in C_i assigns val_i to v_i57` therwise6if $C_i \notin C_{cover}$6then there is some other constraint $C_j \in C_{cover}$ that mentions v_i 9since C_{cover} must cover all variables57 Vf C_j contains no tuple that assigns val_i to v_i6 then we can derive the same *nogood*7 Vf C_j contains some tuples that assign val_i to v_i6then these tuples will all be discarded when a consistent extension is verified against the constraint projection of C_i 9since $C_i \in C\mathbb{C}_{cover}$57 ˌ ence we can derive the *nogood* that val_i cannot be assigned to v_i7 To show strictness we can consider the example previously given in ffigure 17   □

Theorem 5. *Achieving CAC on the constraint covering based dual encoding is strictly stronger than achieving AC on the hidden variable encoding.*

Proof. ffrom Theorem 16enforcing ffiZN on the original problem and enforcing ZN on the hidden encoding are equivalent7 Using this and Theorem Ꭰ6if follows that enforcing NZN on the covering based dual encoding is strictly stronger than enforcing ZN on the hidden variable encoding7   □

Theorem 6. *Achieving CAC on the constraint covering based dual encoding is is incomparable to achieving AC on the standard dual encoding.*

Proof. To show that enforcing NZN on the covering based dual encoding and enforcing ZN on the standard encoding are incomparable6all that is required is to show a5 a problem where enforcing NZN on the covering based dual encoding prunes more than ZN on the standard dual encoding6 and b5 another problem where ZN on the standard dual encoding prunes more than NZN on the covering based dual encoding7 To show a5 we can consider the example in ffigure 17ffor b5 consider a NS¨ with : variables with binary domains7 The : constraints are $C_{a,b} = \{98, 85\}$6$C_{b,c} = \{98, 85\}$6$C_{d,e} = \{98, 15\}$6$C_{e,f} = \{91, 85\}$
$C_{a,b,c,d,e} = \{98, 8, 8, 8, 15\}6C_{a,b,c,d,f} = \{98, 8, 1, 8, 85, 98, 8, 8, 1, 85, 91, 8, 8, 8, 85\}$
Nonsider a constraint covering $C_{cover} = \{C_{a,b}, C_{b,c}, C_{d,e}, C_{e,f}\}$7 This NS¨ is covU ering arc consistent w⅞⅞ the covering C_{cover}7 Eut enforcing ZN on the standard dual encoding6will prove that the problem is insoluble since pairᵾwise consistency between $C_{a,b,c,d,e}$ and $C_{a,b,c,d,f}$ will fail7   □

Theorem 7. *When $|C_{cover}| = |C|$, CAC on the covering based encoding prunes at least as much as AC on the dual encoding.*

Proof. When $C_{cover} = C$6 NZN on the covering based encoding enforces pairU wise consistency between all the constraints in the cover6and then verifies that the relational join of all pairs of consistent constraints6 satisfy all the other constraints6on all common variables6by projection7 ، ence the pruning achieved is at least as much as pair wise consistency or dual ZN7 □

Theorem 8. *If $\forall C_i \notin C_{cover}$, $\exists C_p, C_q \in C_{cover}$ such that $V_i \subseteq 9V_p \cup V_q 5$, pair-wise consistency prunes at most as much as CAC on the covering based dual encoding w.r.t C_{cover}.*

Proof. " air wise consistency find inconsistencies between pairs of constraints7 NZN performs pair wise consistency on all the pairs of constraints in the coverU ing7 ffiiven a constraint covering C_{cover}6 if $\forall C_i \notin C_{cover}$6 $\exists C_p, C_q \in C_{cover}$ such that $V_i \subseteq 9V_p \cup V_q 5$6the algorithm enforcing NZN will find all inconsistent tuples in all $C_i \notin C_{cover}$ by projection7 ، ence under this condition6 pair wise consisU tency prunes at most as much as NZN on the covering based dual encoding w 𝜋 𝜋 a given C_{cover}7 □

Theorem 9. *If $\forall C_i, C_j \notin C_{cover}$, such that $\exists C_p, C_q \in C_{cover}$, $9V_i \cap V_j 5 \subseteq 9V_p \cup V_q 5$, CAC on the covering based dual encoding w.r.t C_{cover} prunes at least as much as pair-wise consistency.*

Proof. ffrom the example in part b5 of Theorem : it is clear that there exists a problem that satisfies this condition where pruning using ZN on the dual encoding prunes more than NZN on the covering based dual encoding w 𝜋 𝜋 a given C_{cover}7 To show that is *precisely* the condition when dual ZN prunes more than NZN w 𝜋 𝜋 a C_{cover}6 can be done as follows7 ⋎ it is the case that $\forall C_i, C_j \notin C_{cover}$ if $\exists C_p, C_q \in C_{cover}69V_i \cap V_j 5 \subseteq 9V_p \cup V_q 5$6then NZN 𝜋w 𝜋 𝜋 C_{cover} derives all pair wise inconsistent tuples that ZN on the dual encoding would derive7 ، ence this is precisely the condition when NZN w 𝜋 𝜋 a cover is no worse than dual ZN7 □

4   Conclusions

This paper presents a new dual encodings for NS¨ s based on constraint coverings7 We introduce a new form local consistency that is defined on this dual encoding called covering arc consistency 9NZN57⋎ is shown that enforcing NZN dominates ffiZN and hidden variable ZN6 and is incomparable to standard Kual ZN7 We also present a precise characterisation of conditions under which the pruning achieved by NZN is comparable to the pruning achieved by dual ZN7

References

1. Bessiere C. Non-binary constraints. In *Principles and Practice of Constraint Programming, CP-99, Invited Lecture*, 1999. 533
2. R. Dechter. Constraint networks. In Stuart C. Shapiro, editor, *Encyclopedia of Artificial Intelligence*, pages 276–285. Wiley, 1992. Volume 1, second edition. 532
3. R. Dechter and J. Pearl. Tree clustering for constraint networks. *Artificial Intelligence*, 38:353–366, 1989. 532

4. Janssen P, Jegou P, Nouguier B., and Vilarem M.C. A filtering process for general constraint satisfaction problems: achieving pair-wise consistency using an associated binary representation. In *Proceedings of the IEEE Workshop on Tools for Artificial Intelligence*, pages 420–427, Fairfax, USA, 1989. 532
5. Mohr R. and Masini G. Good old discrete relaxation. In *Proceedings ECAI'88*, pages 651–656, 1988. 532
6. Kostas Stergiou and Toby Walsh. Encodings of non-binary constraint satisfaction problems. In *Proceedings of the 16th National Conference on Artificial Intelligence*, pages 163–168, 1999. 533

Algebraic Simplification Techniques for Propositional Satisfiability

João Marques-Silva

Department of Informatics, Technical University of Lisbon,
IST/INESC/CEL, Lisbon, Portugal
jpms@inesc.pt

Abstract. The ability to reduce either the number of variables or clauses in instances of the Satisfiability problem (SAT) impacts the expected computational effort of solving a given instance. This ability can actually be essential for specific and hard classes of instances. The objective of this paper is to propose new simplification techniques for Conjunctive Normal Form (CNF) formulas. Experimental results, obtained on representative problem instances, indicate that large simplifications can be observed.

1 Introduction

Recent years have seen the proposal of several effective algorithms for solving Propositional Satisfiability (SAT), that include, among others, local search and variations, backtrack search improved with different search pruning techniques, backtrack search with randomization and restarts, continuous formulations and algebraic manipulation. (These different algorithms are further described and cited in [3].) Moreover, these algorithms have allowed efficiently solving different classes of instances of SAT. It is generally accepted that whereas most algorithms for solving SAT can be competitive in proving satisfiability for different classes of instances, backtrack search is preferred when the objective is to prove unsatisfiability. Nevertheless, algebraic simplification solutions are also known to be competitive for proving unsatisfiability in specific contexts [2].

The main goal of this paper is to propose and categorize new simplification techniques, and illustrate the effectiveness of algebraic simplification as a preprocessing tool for SAT algorithms. Moreover, we illustrate the application of the proposed simplification techniques in real-world instances of SAT.

The paper is organized as follows. We start with a few definitions in Section 2. Next we address algebraic simplification, namely the techniques in this paper. Section 4 provides experimental results on applying the proposed simplification techniques on real-world instances of SAT. Finally, Section 5 concludes the paper.

2 Definitions

This section introduces the notational framework used throughout the paper. Propositional variables are denoted $x_1, \ldots, x_n$, and can be assigned truth values 0

R. Dechter (Ed.): CP 2000, LNCS 1894, pp. 537–542, 2000.

(or F) or 1 (or T). In addition to letter x, and whenever necessary, we will use letters y, w and z to denote variables. To denote specific variables we may also use $x_i, x_j, x_k, \ldots$. A literal l is either a variable x_i (i.e. a positive literal) or its complement $\neg x_i$ (i.e. a negative literal). A clause ω is a disjunction of literals and a CNF formula φ is a conjunction of clauses. When referring to specific clauses we will utilize subscripts $a, b, \ldots$, and when referring to sub-formulas of a CNF formula we will utilize subscripts $r, s, \ldots$. Disjunctions of literals, not necessarily representing clauses will be represented as $\alpha, \beta, \gamma, \delta, \epsilon$.

3 Algebraic Simplification

Different formula simplification techniques have been proposed over the years. A detailed account of these techniques if provided in [3]. In this section we concentrate on two new techniques, namely *support-set variable equivalence* and *inference of binary clauses*.

3.1 Support Set Variable Equivalence

In many practical situations, a sub-formula φ_s of a CNF formula φ actually describes a Boolean function $x_i = f(y_1, \ldots, y_k)$. For example, the sub-formula $\varphi_a = (y_1 \vee \neg x) \wedge (y_2 \vee \neg x) \wedge (\neg y_1 \vee \neg y_2 \vee x)$ describes the Boolean function $x = y_1 \wedge y_2$. More interestingly, if we have two sub-formulas $\varphi_a = (y_1 \vee \neg x) \wedge (y_2 \vee \neg x) \wedge (\neg y_1 \vee \neg y_2 \vee x)$ and $\varphi_b = (y_1 \vee \neg z) \wedge (y_2 \vee \neg z) \wedge (\neg y_1 \vee \neg y_2 \vee z)$, then we can conclude that $x = y_1 \wedge y_2$ and $z = y_1 \wedge y_2$. Hence, x and z are indeed *equivalent* and we can replace z with x and vice-versa. Observe that, by suitable resolution operations, we could easily derive the clauses $(x \vee \neg z) \wedge (\neg x \vee z)$, obtaining the same conclusion.

The previous example suggests a pattern-matching approach for identifying a set E of variables that can be expressed as a Boolean function f of some other set S of variables (i.e., *the support set*) and thus replace the variables in set E by a single variable. This approach is simply too time consuming for sets S of arbitrary size, and so we restrict S to be of size 2, i.e. we only consider Boolean functions of two variables.

If the support set S is restricted to be of size 2, it becomes feasible to enumerate all possible Boolean functions of 2 variables, and determine the *irredundant* CNF formulas associated with each Boolean function. This information is shown in Table 1. (Observe that the missing six boolean functions are either constant 0 or 1, the actual function of a *single* variable or of its complement.) We can now apply a straightforward pattern matching algorithm to a CNF formula, and identify sets E of variables with a common two-variable support set. These variables can then be replaced by a single variable. Clearly, after variable replacement we can apply well-known formula simplification techniques [3].

Other researchers [1] have observed the existence of variable equivalences based on support sets, but on arbitrary instances of SAT (i.e. not in CNF format). Moreover, the underlying approach of [1,4] is significantly more time consuming (indeed exponential in the worst-case) than the one proposed above.

Table 1. Two-variable CNF formulas

Boolean function	CNF formula
$x \equiv f_1(a, b) = a \wedge b$	$(a \vee \neg x) \wedge (b \vee \neg x) \wedge (\neg a \vee \neg b \vee x)$
$x \equiv f_2(a, b) = a \vee b$	$(\neg a \vee x) \wedge (\neg b \vee x) \wedge (a \vee b \vee \neg x)$
$x \equiv f_3(a, b) = a \leftrightarrow b$	$(a \vee b \vee x) \wedge (a \vee \neg b \vee \neg x) \wedge (\neg a \vee \neg b \vee x) \wedge (\neg a \vee b \vee \neg x)$
$x \equiv f_4(a, b) = \neg a \wedge b$	$(\neg a \vee \neg x) \wedge (b \vee \neg x) \wedge (a \vee \neg b \vee x)$
$x \equiv f_5(a, b) = a \wedge \neg b$	$(a \vee \neg x) \wedge (\neg b \vee \neg x) \wedge (\neg a \vee b \vee x)$
$x \equiv f_6(a, b) = \neg(a \wedge b)$	$(a \vee x) \wedge (b \vee x) \wedge (\neg a \vee \neg b \vee \neg x)$
$x \equiv f_7(a, b) = \neg(a \vee b)$	$(\neg a \vee \neg x) \wedge (\neg b \vee \neg x) \wedge (a \vee b \vee x)$
$x \equiv f_8(a, b) = \neg(a \leftrightarrow b)$	$(a \vee b \vee \neg x) \wedge (a \vee \neg b \vee x) \wedge (\neg a \vee b \vee x) \wedge (\neg a \vee \neg b \vee \neg x)$
$x \equiv f_9(a, b) = a \vee \neg b$	$(\neg a \vee x) \wedge (b \vee x) \wedge (a \vee \neg b \vee \neg x)$
$x \equiv f_{10}(a, b) = \neg a \vee b$	$(a \vee x) \wedge (\neg b \vee x) \wedge (\neg a \vee b \vee \neg x)$

Another interesting result, is that the equivalence reasoning conditions proposed by C.-M. Li in [2] are also superseded by support set equivalences and *selective resolution* (see [1,3] for a definition). We should observe, in particular, that the utilization of function f_3 on two variables $x = (a \leftrightarrow b)$ and $y = (a \leftrightarrow b)$, for deriving the equivalence between x and y, corresponds to Li's inference rule (5) [2], the other rules being superseded by selective resolution, unit-clause rule and two-variable equivalence.

Despite the potential interest of identifying support sets of variables in a CNF formula, in the next section a further generalization is proposed, that subsumes variable equivalences based on two-variable support sets.

3.2   Generalized Inference of Binary Clauses

In this section we propose to study subsets of clauses for inferring binary clauses, which not only identify support set equivalences, but also provide more general conditions for deriving binary clauses. In what follows, all proposed conditions can be explained by resorting to resolution. However, it is in general extremely hard to decide to which clauses the resolution operation should be applied to, being computationally infeasible to apply the resolution operation to all possible pairs of clauses. The objective of studying sets of clauses is to indirectly select to which sets of clauses the resolution operation should be applied to.

Moreover, the reasoning technique to be described below is categorized in terms of how many binary clauses and ternary clauses are involved. Clearly, the size and number of k-ary clauses involved could be made arbitrary, but the computational overhead could become prohibitive. In general each proposed condition is classified as being of the form mB/nT, meaning that m binary clauses and n ternary clauses are involved.

Let us start by considering an illustrative example. Let $\varphi_c = (y_1 \vee \neg x) \wedge (y_2 \vee \neg x) \wedge (\neg y_1 \vee \neg y_2 \vee z)$ be a sub-formula. The application of the resolution operation between the three clauses allows deriving $(\neg x \vee z)$. Similarly, for the sub-formula $\varphi_d = (y_1 \vee \neg z) \wedge (y_2 \vee \neg z) \wedge (\neg y_1 \vee \neg y_2 \vee x)$, the resolution operation

Table 2. Rules for Inferring Binary/Unit Clauses

Clause Pattern	Inferred Clause(s)
$(l_1 \vee \neg l_2) \wedge (l_1 \vee \neg l_3) \wedge (l_2 \vee l_3 \vee l_4)$	$(l_1 \vee l_4)$
$(l_4 \vee \neg l_2) \wedge (l_1 \vee \neg l_3) \wedge (l_2 \vee l_3 \vee l_4)$	$(\neg l_3 \vee l_4), (l_1 \vee l_4)$
$(l_1 \vee l_2 \vee l_3) \wedge (\neg l_1 \vee \neg l_2 \vee l_3) \wedge (l_1 \vee \neg l_2 \vee l_4) \wedge (\neg l_1 \vee l_2 \vee l_4)$	$(l_3 \vee l_4)$
$(l_1 \vee l_2 \vee \neg l_3) \wedge (l_1 \vee l_2 \vee \neg l_4) \wedge (l_1 \vee l_2 \vee \neg l_5) \wedge (l_3 \vee l_4 \vee l_5)$	$(l_1 \vee l_2)$
$(l_1 \vee l_2) \wedge (\neg l_1 \vee l_2 \vee l_3)$	$(l_2 \vee l_3)$
$(l_1 \vee \neg l_2) \wedge (l_1 \vee \neg l_3) \wedge (l_1 \vee \neg l_4) \wedge (l_2 \vee l_3 \vee l_4)$	(l_1)
$(l_1 \vee l_2 \vee \neg l_3) \wedge (l_1 \vee l_2 \vee \neg l_4) \wedge (l_3 \vee l_4)$	$(l_1 \vee l_2)$
$(l_1 \vee l_2) \wedge (\neg l_1 \vee l_3 \vee l_4) \wedge (l_2 \vee l_3 \vee \neg l_4)$	$(l_2 \vee l_3)$

allows deriving the clause $(x \vee \neg z)$. It is interesting to observe that we have just illustrated a different approach for proving x equivalent to z for the first example of the previous section.

In general, let us consider a sub-formula of the form $\varphi_s = (l_1 \vee \neg l_2) \wedge (l_1 \vee \neg l_3) \wedge (l_2 \vee l_3 \vee l_4)$, where $l_1, \ldots, l_4$ are any literals. The application of resolution allows deriving the binary clause $(l_1 \vee l_4)$. Since 2 binary clauses and 1 ternary clause are involved in deriving the resulting binary clause, we say that 2B/1T reasoning was applied. The other form of 2B/1T reasoning is the following. Let the sub-formula be $\varphi_t = (l_4 \vee \neg l_2) \wedge (l_1 \vee \neg l_3) \wedge (l_2 \vee l_3 \vee l_4)$. Then, application of resolution allows deriving the binary clauses $(l_3 \vee l_4)$ and $(l_1 \vee l_4)$.

Additional forms of mB/nT reasoning can be established. Due to efficiency concerns, our analysis will be restricted to 2B/1T, 1B/1T, 1B/2T, 3B/1T and 0B/4T. The resulting set of unit/binary clause inference rules is summarized in Table 2. Moreover, and from the previous examples and claims, we can readily conclude that support set variable equivalence (described in the previous section) is superseded by 2B/1T and 0B/4T reasoning.

4   Experimental Results

This section evaluates the practical application of the algebraic simplification techniques described in this paper. These techniques can be evaluated according to two main metrics:

- The ability to effectively simplify the original formula.
- The effective reduction in the amount of search, when using formula simplification techniques within a preprocessing engine for backtrack search SAT algorithms.

In this paper we concentrate on the ability to simplify the original formula. The reduction in the amount of search is analyzed in [3]. Moreover, the problem instances used in this section are also described in [3]

Table 3 shows the results, namely the number of variables and clauses before and after applying the simplification techniques. As can be concluded, for most of

Table 3. Formula Simplification

Instance	Initial Formula		Final Formula	
	Variables	Clauses	Variables	Clauses
bf1355-075	2180	6778	722	3075
bf2670-001	1393	3434	411	1252
ssa2670-130	1359	3321	440	1295
ssa2670-141	986	2315	283	883
barrel6	2306	8931	519	2209
barrel7	3523	13765	805	3467
longmult5	2397	7431	1483	5180
longmult6	2848	8853	1824	6376
queueinvar12	1112	7335	1049	9884
queueinvar16	1168	6496	1088	7114
c1908	1917	5096	658	2248
c1908_bug	1919	5100	659	2250
c2670	2703	6756	1220	3725
c2670_bug	2708	6696	1162	3553
dlx2_cc_bug02	1515	12808	1486	13965
dlx2_cc_bug08	1515	12808	1486	13890

the instances considered, large reductions in the number of variables and clauses can be achieved. In some cases (e.g. *barrel6* and *barrel7*) the final number of variables is one fourth of the original number. Similar reductions can be observed in the number of clauses. Nevertheless, for some instances (e.g. *queueinvar16* and *dlx2_cc_bug08*) the amount of simplification in the number of variables is negligible. In these cases, it is interesting to observe an increase in the number of clauses, due to the application of clause inference techniques (see Section 3.2).

5   Conclusions

This paper proposes new techniques for the algebraic simplification of propositional formulas. These techniques have been incorporated into a preprocessing system to be used with any SAT algorithm. Preliminary experimental results, obtained on real-world instances of SAT, clearly demonstrate the effectiveness of the proposed techniques, allowing significant reductions in the sizes of the resulting CNF formulas.

Despite the promising results obtained, and given the amount of simplification achieved on most problem instances, the next natural step is to incorporate the same algebraic simplification techniques into backtrack search SAT algorithms, to be applied during the search.

References

1. J. F. Groote and J. P. Warners. The propositional formula checker heerhugo. Technical Report SEN-R9905, CWI, January 1999. 538, 539
2. C.-M. Li. Integrating equivalency reasoning into davis-putnam procedure. In *Proceedings of the National Conference on Artificial Intelligence*, August 2000. Accepted for publication. 537, 539
3. J. P. Marques-Silva. Algebraic simplification techniques for propositional satisfiability. Technical Report RT/01/2000, INESC, March 2000. 537, 538, 539, 540
4. G. Stålmarck. A system for determining propositional logic theorems by applying values and rules to triplets that are generated from a formula, 1989. Swedish Patent 467 076 (Approved 1992), US Patent 5 276 897 (approved 1994), European Patent 0 403 454 (approved 1995). 538

An Original Constraint Based Approach
for Solving over Constrained Problems*

J.-C. Régin[1], T. Petit[1,2], C. Bessière[2], and J.-F. Puget[3]

[1] ILOG
1681, route des Dolines, 06560 Valbonne, France
{regin,tpetit}@ilog.fr
[2] LIRMM (UMR 5506 CNRS)
161, rue Ada, 34392 Montpellier Cedex 5, France
{bessiere,tpetit}@lirmm.fr
[3] ILOG S.A.
9, rue de Verdun, BP 85, 94253 Gentilly Cedex, France
puget@ilog.fr

Abstract. In this paper we present a new framework for over constrained problems. We suggest to define an over-constrained network as a global constraint. We introduce two new lower bounds of the number of violations, without making any assumption on the arity of constraints.

1 Introduction

Encoding real-world problems often leads to define over constrained networks, which do not have any solution that satisfies all the constraints. In this situation the goal is to find the best compromise. One of the most well-known theoretical frameworks for over constrained problems is the Maximal Constraint Satisfaction Problem (Max-CSP). In a Max-CSP, the goal is to minimize the number of constraint violations. Best algorithms for solving Max-CSP [4,5] are based on computation of lower bounds of the number of violations. All these algorihms are related to binary constraint networks. On the other hand, solving real-life problems requires the use of non binary constraints [6].

In this paper we present a new framework for over constrained problems. No hypothesis is made on the arity of constraints. We introduce two new lower bounds of the number of violations. The first one is a generalization of the previous studies for binary Max-CSP to the non binary case, through a variable-based partitioning of the constraint set. The second one is an original lower bound based on computation of disjoint conflict sets. Moreover, one advantage of our framework is that filtering algorithms associated with constraints can be used in a way similar to classical CSPs.

---

* The work of ILOG authors was partially supported by the IST Programme of the Commission of the European Union through the ECSPLAIN project (IST-1999-11969).

R. Dechter (Ed.): CP 2000, LNCS 1894, pp. 543–548, 2000.

544   J.-C. Régin et al.

2   Background

A *constraint network* $\mathcal{N}$ is defined as a set of n *variables* $X = \{x_1, \ldots, x_n\}$, a set of *domains* $\mathcal{D} = \{D(x_1), \ldots, D(x_n)\}$ where $D(x_i)$ is the finite set of possible *values* for variable x_i, and a set $\mathcal{C}$ of *constraints* between variables. A *constraint* C on the ordered set of variables $X(C) = (x_{i_1}, \ldots, x_{i_r})$ is a subset $T(C)$ of the Cartesian product $D(x_{i_1}) \times \cdots \times D(x_{i_r})$ that specifies the *allowed* combinations of values for the variables $x_{i_1}, \ldots, x_{i_r}$. An element of $D(x_{i_1}) \times \cdots \times D(x_{i_r})$ is called a *tuple on* $X(C)$. $|X(C)|$ is the *arity* of C. A value a for a variable x is often denoted by (x, a). A tuple τ on $X(C)$ is *valid* if $\forall (x, a) \in \tau, a \in D(x)$. C is *consistent* iff there exists a tuple τ of $T(C)$ which is valid. A value $a \in D(x)$ is *consistent with* C iff $x \notin X(C)$ or there exists a valid tuple τ of $T(C)$ in which a is the value assigned to x.

Definition 1 *Let x be a variable, a be a value of $D(x)$, $\mathcal{C}$ be a set of constraints, $\#inc((x,a), \mathcal{C}) = |\{C \in \mathcal{C} \text{ s.t. } (x,a) \text{ is not consistent with } C\}|$.*

3   Satisfiability Sum Constraint

Let $\mathcal{N} = (X, \mathcal{D}, \mathcal{C})$ be a constraint network. We suggest to integrate $\mathcal{C}$ into a single constraint, called the Satisfiability Sum Constraint (*ssc*):

Definition 2 *Let $\mathcal{C} = \{C_i, i \in \{1, \ldots, m\}\}$ be a set of constraints, and $S[\mathcal{C}] = \{s_i, i \in \{1, \ldots, m\}\}$ be a set of variables and unsat be a variable, such that a one-to-one mapping is defined between $\mathcal{C}$ and $S[\mathcal{C}]$. A* **Satisfiability Sum Constraint** *is the constraint $ssc(\mathcal{C}, S[\mathcal{C}], unsat)$ defined by:*

$$[unsat = \sum_{s_i=1}^{m} s_i] \wedge \bigwedge_{i=1}^{m} [(C_i \wedge (s_i = 0)) \vee (\neg C_i \wedge (s_i = 1))]$$

Notation 1 *Given a $ssc(\mathcal{C}, S[\mathcal{C}], unsat)$, a variable x, a value $a \in D(x)$ and $\mathcal{K} \subseteq \mathcal{C}$:*
$max(D(unsat))$ is the highest value of "current" domain of unsat;
$minUnsat(\mathcal{C}, S[\mathcal{C}])$ is the minimum value of unsat consistent with $ssc(\mathcal{C}, S[\mathcal{C}], unsat)$;
$minUnsat((x,a), \mathcal{C}, S[\mathcal{C}])$ is equal to $minUnsat(\mathcal{C}, S[\mathcal{C}])$ when $x = a$;
$S[\mathcal{K}]$ is the subset of $S[\mathcal{C}]$ equals to the projection of variables $S[\mathcal{C}]$ on $\mathcal{K}$;
$X(\mathcal{C})$ is the union of $X(C_i), C_i \in \mathcal{C}$.

The variables $S[\mathcal{C}]$ are used to express which constraints of $\mathcal{C}$ must be violated or satisfied: a null value assigned to $s \in S[\mathcal{C}]$ expresses that its attached constraint C is satisfied, whereas 1 expresses that C is violated[1]. The variable *unsat* represents the objective, that is, the number of violations in $\mathcal{C}$, equal to the number of variables of $S[\mathcal{C}]$ whose value is 1.

Through this formulation, a solution of a Max-CSP is an assignment that satisfies the *ssc* with the minimal possible value of *unsat*. A lower bound of

---
[1] The extension to valued CSPs [1] can easily be performed by defining larger domains for variables in $S[\mathcal{C}]$.

the objective of a Max-CSP corresponds to a necessary consistency condition of the ssc. The different domain reduction algorithms established for Max-CSP correspond to specific filtering algorithms associated with the ssc. This point of view has some advantages in regards to the previous studies:

1. Any search algorithm can be used. Since we propose to define a constraint we can easily integrate our framework into existing solvers.

2. In all this paper, no hypothesis is made on the arity of constraints C.

3. When a value is assigned to $s_i \in S[\mathcal{C}]$, a filtering algorithm associated with $C_i \in \mathcal{C}$ (resp. $\neg C_i$) can be used in a way similar to classical CSPs.

4 Variable Based Lower Bound

The results presented in this section are a generalization to non binary constraints of previous works for Max-CSP [2,7,4].

4.1 Necessary Condition of Consistency

If $minUnsat(\mathcal{C}, S[\mathcal{C}]) > max(D(unsat))$ then $ssc(\mathcal{C}, S[\mathcal{C}], unsat)$ is not consistent. Therefore, a lower bound of $minUnsat(\mathcal{C}, S[\mathcal{C}])$ provides a necessary condition of consistency of a ssc. A possible way for computing it is to perform a sum of independant lower bounds, one per variable:

Definition 3 *Given a variable x a constraint set $\mathcal{K}$,*
$\#inc(x, \mathcal{K}) = min_{a \in D(x)}(\#inc((x, a), \mathcal{K}))$.

The sum of these minima with $\mathcal{K} = \mathcal{C}$ cannot lead to a lower bound of the total number of violations, because some constraints can be taken into account more than once. For instance, given a constraint C and two variables x and y involved in C, C can be counted in $\#inc(x, \mathcal{C})$ and also in $\#inc(y, \mathcal{C})$. In this case, the lower bound can be overestimated, and an inconsistency could be detected while the *ssc* is consistent. Consequently, for each variable, an independent set of constraints must be considered. In the binary case, the constraint graph[2] has been used in order to guarantee this independence [4]. Each edge is oriented and for each variable x only the constraints out-going x are taken into account. This idea can be generalized to the non binary case, by associating with each constraint one and only one variable involved in the constraint: the constraints are *partionned* w.r.t the variables that are associated with.

Definition 4 *Given a set of constraints $\mathcal{C}$, a* **var-partition** *of $\mathcal{C}$ is a partition $\mathcal{P}(\mathcal{C}) = \{P(x_1), ...P(x_k)\}$ of $\mathcal{C}$ in $|X(\mathcal{C})|$ sets such that $\forall P(x_i) \in \mathcal{P}(\mathcal{C}) : \forall C \in P(x_i), x_i \in X(C)$.*

Given a var partition $\mathcal{P}(\mathcal{C})$, the sum of all $\#inc(x_i, P(x_i))$ is a lower bound of the total number of violations, because all the sets belonging to $\mathcal{P}(\mathcal{C})$ are disjoint:

Definition 5 $LB(\mathcal{P}(\mathcal{C})) = \sum_{x_i \in X(\mathcal{C})} \#inc(x_i, P(x_i)), P(x_i) \in \mathcal{P}(\mathcal{C})$

---

[2] The vertex set of the constraint graph is the variable set and there is an edge between two vertices when there is a constraint involving these two variables.

Property 1 $\forall \mathcal{P}(\mathcal{C})$ *a var-partition of* $\mathcal{C}$. $LB(\mathcal{P}(\mathcal{C})) \leq minUnsat(\mathcal{C}, S[\mathcal{C}])$

Corollary 1 *If* $LB(\mathcal{P}(\mathcal{C})) > max(D(unsat))$ *then* $ssc(\mathcal{C}, S[\mathcal{C}], unsat)$ *is not consistent.*

4.2   Filtering Algorithm

From definition of $minUnsat((x, a), \mathcal{C}, S[\mathcal{C}])$ we have the following theorem:

Theorem 1 $\forall x \in X(\mathcal{C}), \forall a \in D(x)$: *if* $minUnsat((x, a), \mathcal{C}, S[\mathcal{C}]) > max(D(unsat))$ *then* (x, a) *is not consistent with* $ssc(\mathcal{C}, S[\mathcal{C}], unsat)$.

Therefore, any lower bound of $minUnsat((x, a), \mathcal{C}, S[\mathcal{C}])$ can be used in order to check the consistency of (x, a). A first lower bound is $\#inc((x, a), \mathcal{C})$:

Property 2 $\#inc((x, a), \mathcal{C}) \leq minUnsat((x, a), \mathcal{C}, S[\mathcal{C}])$

This property leads to a first filtering algorithm. However, it can be improved by including the lower bound of Property 1. We suggest to split $\mathcal{C}$ into two disjoint sets $P(x)$ and $\mathcal{C} - P(x)$, where $P(x)$ is the subset of constraints associated with x in a var-partition $P(\mathcal{C})$ of $\mathcal{C}$. Consider the following corollary of Theorem 1:

Corollary 2 *Let* $P(\mathcal{C})$ *be a var-partition of* $\mathcal{C}$, *x a variable and* $a \in D(x)$,
if $minUnsat((x, a), P(x), S[P(x)])$
$+ minUnsat((x, a), \mathcal{C} - P(x), S[\mathcal{C} - P(x)]) > max(D(unsat))$
then (x, a) *is not consistent with* $ssc(\mathcal{C}, S[\mathcal{C}], unsat)$.

Note that $minUnsat(\mathcal{C} - P(x), S[P(x)]) \leq minUnsat((x, a), \mathcal{C} - P(x), S[P(x)])$. From this remark and Properties 1 and 2 we deduce the theorem:

Theorem 2 $\forall \mathcal{P}(\mathcal{C})$ *a var-partition of* $\mathcal{C}, \forall x \in X(\mathcal{C}), \forall a \in D(x)$, *if* $\#inc((x, a), P(x)) + LB(\mathcal{P}(\mathcal{C} - P(x))) > max(D(unsat))$ *then* a *can be removed from its domain.*

5   Constraint Based Lower Bound

An original lower bound of the number of violations in $\mathcal{C}$, corresponding to a lower bound of $minUnsat(\mathcal{C}, S[\mathcal{C}])$, can be obtained by successive computations of disjoint conflict sets of $\mathcal{C}$.

Definition 6 *A conflict set is a subset* $\mathcal{K}$ *of* $\mathcal{C}$ *which satisfies:* $minUnsat(\mathcal{K}, S[\mathcal{K}]) > 0$.

We know that a conflict set leads to at least one violation in $\mathcal{C}$. Consequently, if we are able to compute q disjoint conflict sets in $\mathcal{C}$ then q is a lower bound of $minUnsat(\mathcal{C}, S[\mathcal{C}])$. They must be disjoint to guarantee that all violations taken into account are independent. For each $C_i \in \mathcal{C}$ such that $D(s_i) = 1$, the set $\{C_i\}$ is a conflict set. Moreover, constraints C_i of $\mathcal{C}$ with $D(s_i) = 0$ are not interesting in the determination of conflict sets. Hence we will focus on the set of constraints C_i of $\mathcal{C}$ with $D(s_i) = \{0, 1\}$, denoted by $\mathcal{C}_?$.

Consider any ordering $\prec$ on $\mathcal{C}_?$. De Siqueira N. and Puget have shown that a conflict set of $\mathcal{C}_?$ can be simply computed by temporarily setting the variables of $S[\mathcal{C}_?]$ to 0 w.r.t. $\prec$ until a failure occurs. When a variable of $S[\mathcal{C}_?]$ attached to $C \in \mathcal{C}_?$ is set to 0 then values from domains of variables $X(C)$ that are not consistent with C are removed. When a failure occurs, then all the constraints C for which s has been set to 0 form a conflict set. Given a set of constraints Q, we call COMPUTECONFLICTSET(Q) the function which implements this algorithm.

A set of disjoint conflict sets can be easily computed by calling function COMPUTECONFLICTSET(Q) with $Q = \mathcal{C}_?$ and by iteratively calling it with $Q \leftarrow Q - \mathcal{K}$ each time a conflict set $\mathcal{K}$ is found. The algorithm stops when Q is empty or when no conflict set is detected in Q. The lower bound depends on the number of conflict sets, and, since they are disjoint, on the size of the conflicts sets.

Definition 7 *Let Q be a set of constraint. A minimal conflict set w.r.t.* COMPUTE-CONFLICTSET *is a subset $\mathcal{K}$ of Q such that $\forall C \in \mathcal{K}$,* COMPUTECONFLICTSET($\mathcal{K} - \{C\}$) *detects no conflict set.*

De Siqueira N. and Puget have suggested a simple algorithm for finding minimal conflict set from a conflict set $\mathcal{K}$ [3]. This algorithm calls at most $|\mathcal{K}|$ times the COMPUTECONFLICTSET function. COMPUTEMINIMALCONFLICTSET($\mathcal{K}$) denotes the function that returns a minimal conflict set of $\mathcal{K}$. We can now propose an original algorithm for computing a lower bound LB of $minUnsat(\mathcal{C}, S[\mathcal{C}])$:

Step 1: Let $LB \leftarrow |\{C_i \in \mathcal{C} \text{ s.t. } s_i = 1\}|$ and $Q \leftarrow \mathcal{C}$;
Step 2: $\mathcal{K} \leftarrow$ COMPUTECONFLICTSET(Q);
       if $\mathcal{K} = \emptyset$ then return LB else $\mathcal{K}_{min} \leftarrow$ COMPUTEMINIMALCONFLICTSET($\mathcal{K}$);
Step 3: $LB \leftarrow LB + 1$; $Q \leftarrow Q - \mathcal{K}_{min}$; goto Step 2.

Corollary 3 *If $LB > max(D(unsat))$ xthen $ssc(\mathcal{C}, S[\mathcal{C}], unsat)$ is not consistent.*

6   Conclusion

This paper presents a new framework for over constrained problems, which can be directly integrated into existing solvers. New lower bounds of number of violations are introduced without making any assumption on the constraints.

References

1. S. Bistarelli, U. Montanari, F. Rossi, T. Schiex, G. Verfaillie, and H. Fargier. Semiring-based csps and valued csps: Frameworks, properties, and comparison. *Constraints*, 4:199-240, 1999.   544
2. E. Freuder and R. Wallace. Partial constraint satisfaction. *Artificial Intelligence*, 58:21-70, 1992.   545
3. J. L. de Siqueira N. and J.-F. Puget. Explanation-based generalization of failures. *Proceedings ECAI*, pages 339-344, 1988.   547
4. J. Larrosa, P. Meseguer, and T. Schiex. Maintaining reversible dac for max-csp. *Artificial Intelligence*, 107:149-163, 1999.   543, 545

5. J. Larrossa and P. Meseguer. Partition-based lower bound for max-csp. *Proceedings CP*, pages 303-315, 1999. 543
6. H. Simonis. Problem classification scheme for finite domain constraint solving. *CP Workshop on C. P. Applications: An Inventory and Taxonomy*, pages 1-26, 1996. 543
7. R. Wallace. Directed arc consistency preprocessing as a strategy for maximal constraint satisfaction. *Proceedings' ECA I*, pages 69-77, 1994. 545

An Efficient Approximate Algorithm for Winner Determination in Combinatorial Auctions

Yuko Sakurai, Makoto Yokoo, and Koji Kamei

NTT Communication Science Laboratories,
2-4 Hikaridai, Seika-cho, Soraku-gun, Kyoto, 619-0237, Japan
{yuko,yokoo,kamei}@cslab.kecl.ntt.co.jp

1 Introduction

Auctions on the Internet have become especially popular in Electronic Commerce. Among the various studies on the Internet auctions, those on combinatorial auctions have lately attracted considerable attention. Combinatorial auctions simultaneously sell multiple items with interdependent values and allow the bidders to bid on any combination of items. Therefore, they tend to increase the buyers' utilities and the seller's revenue.

On the other hand, determining winners in combinatorial auctions intended to maximize the sum of the bids with disjoint sets of items is a complicated constraint optimization problem and shown to be NP-complete [4]. This problem has recently attracted the interest of the AI community as an application of search techniques [1,5]. Although the previous methods have significantly improved the efficiency of the optimal winner determination algorithms, to solve large-scale problems, we eventually need to give up the idea of achieving the optimality of the obtained allocation and try to find a semi-optimal solution within a reasonable amount of time.

In this paper, we introduce *limited discrepancy search* (LDS) techniques [2] to limit the search efforts to the part where good solutions are likely to exist. Experimental evaluations using various problem settings show that our algorithm finds the allocations that are very close to the optimal solutions (better than 95%) very quickly (in about 1% of the running time) and can be extended to large-scale problem instances.

2 Preliminaries

2.1 Winner Determination Problem

A winner determination problem can be formulated as follows [4,5]. Let $G = \{1, 2, \cdots, m\}$ be the set of items to be auctioned and A be a set of bidders.

Suppose a bidder $i \in A$ can submit any bid $b_i(S)$ for any combination of items $S \subseteq G$. Let $\bar{b}(S)$ be the the maximal bid for the bundle S, that is, $\bar{b}(S) =$

R. Dechter (Ed.): CP 2000, LNCS 1894, pp. 549–553, 2000.

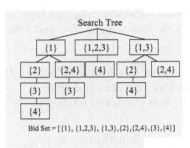

Fig. 1. Search Tree

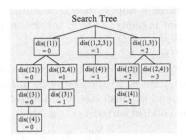

Fig. 2. Discrepancies of Nodes

$\max_{i \in A} b_i(S)$, and χ be the set of possible allocations, that is, $\chi = \{S \subseteq G | S \cap S' = \emptyset$ for every $S, S' \in \chi\}$. Then, the goal is to find an allocation χ such that

$$\arg\max_{\chi} \sum_{S \in \chi} \bar{b}(S). \tag{1}$$

2.2   Problem Formalization as Search Problem

We basically follow the problem formalization used in [5]. An example of a search tree is presented in Figure 1. Each node is associated with a bid, and a path from the root node to any other node represents one (partial) allocation, which consists of a sequence of disjoint bids. The child nodes of each node are limited to the nodes that include the item with the smallest index among the items that are not yet on the path but that do not include items that are already on the path. In [5], a search algorithm called IDA* [3] is used for searching this tree.

We introduce a special data structure called bins [1] to find quickly the children of each nodes. More specifically, we sort bids into bins, where a bin B_j contains all bids where j is the smallest index among the items in a bid.

The following heuristic function h is used to estimate the possible maximal revenue for the items not yet allocated on the path in [5].

$$h = \sum_{k \in \{\text{unallocated items}\}} r(k) \text{ , where } r(k) = \max_{\{S; k \in S\}} \frac{\bar{b}(S)}{|S|} \tag{2}$$

If we re-calculate h in IDA* whenever a bid is appended to the path, h becomes more accurate, but this re-calculation requires significant overhead. We found that this re-calculation is necessary in IDA* to decrease the number of visited nodes. On the other hand, we can avoid this re-calculation since LDS is less sensitive to the accuracy of heuristic evaluations.

We use an evaluation function $f(n) = g(n) + h(n)$ to estimate the best (highest) price of the solutions obtained from node n. $g(n)$ is calculated as the sum of the bids on the path appended to n. $h(n)$ is a heuristic function defined as (2). We use $f(n)$ used for ordering sibling nodes and for pruning.

1. If *stack* is empty, then terminate the algorithm, otherwise, pop *list* from *stack*.
2. If *list* is empty, go to 1, otherwise, set n_c to the first node in *list*, and remove n_c.
3. If $dis(n_c) > D_{max}$, then go to 1.
4. If $f(n_c) \leq f_{max}$, then go to 1.
5. If n_c is a leaf node, then record the current path as a best solution, set f_{max} to $f(n_c)$, set n_c to the first node in *list*, remove n_c from *list*, and go to 3.
6. Expand n_c. push *list* to *stack*, set n_c to the best child, and set *list* to the rest of the children sorted by f, go to 3.

Fig. 3. Pseudo Code of LDS Algorithm

2.3 Limited Discrepancy Search (LDS)

The original LDS algorithm was developed for searching a binary tree. As shown in [2], there are several alternative ways to modify LDS for a non-binary search tree. We define the discrepancy of node n (represented as $dis(n)$) as follows. The rank of node n (represented as $rank(n)$) is defined as the order among its siblings, i.e., the rank of the best child node is 0, the second-best node is 1, and so on. By representing the parent node as n_p, $dis(n)$ is defined as $dis(n_p)+rank(n)$, where the discrepancy of the root node $dis(root) = 0$.

Figure 2 shows the discrepancies of nodes of a search tree in Figure 1. Figure 3 shows the pseudo code of the LDS algorithm. We store a list of nodes, which are siblings sorted by f, into *stack*. f_{max} represents the highest price of the solutions found so far, and D_{max} is the maximal number of allowed discrepancies. Initially, the stack contains a list of the root node, and f_{max} is 0.

3 Experiments

We ran a series of experiments for several problem settings used in previous works [1,5] on a workstation (333 MHz Sun UltraSparc IIi with 512 MB) with a program written in C++. Due to space limitations, we only show the graphs of experiments on the following two distributions used in [5]. Let M be the number of items and N be the number of bids, where bids are different from one another. The trends of the obtained results on other problem settings used in [1] were also similar to the results described here.

Random Distribution The number of items in each bid is randomly chosen from $[1, M]$, and items included in a bid are also randomly chosen. The price is randomly chosen from $[0, 1]$.

Uniform Distribution The number of items is set to a constant k (we set $k = 3$). The items and the price are chosen in the same manner as above.

We generated 10 problem instances and calculated the average of them. To compare the results of LDS without re-calculation and the result of IDA* with re-calculation, we present (1) quality of obtained solution, i.e., the ratio of the

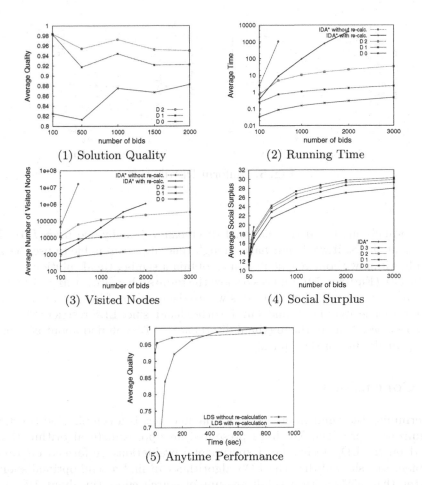

(1) Solution Quality

(2) Running Time

(3) Visited Nodes

(4) Social Surplus

(5) Anytime Performance

Fig. 4. Random Distribution

sum of the winning bids in LDS to the sum in IDA*, (2) running time, (3) number of visited nodes, and (4) social surplus, i.e., the sum of the winning bids, while varying the number of submitted bids, where we limit the maximal discrepancy to $i \in [0, 2]$ (represented as Di) in LDS.

Random (Figures 4): As a comparison, we also show the results of IDA* without re-calculation. Figures 4 show the running time and the number of visited nodes of IDA* increase exponentially (note that the y-axis is log-scaled) , while those of LDS increase rather slowly. LDS with $D2$ remains better than 95% even for lage-scale problem instances.

LDS can be considered an anytime algorithm. This property is desirable for winner determination problems. We illustrate (5) a comparison of the average anytime performance of LDS without re-calculation and with re-calculation. We generated 10 instances where $M = 400$ and $N = 1500$ and

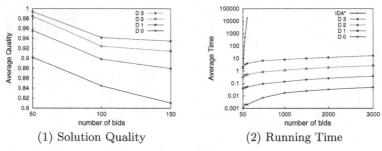

(1) Solution Quality   (2) Running Time

Fig. 5. Uniform Distribution

gradually increased the maximal discrepancy (one-by-one from $D0$). This result shows, if we do not have enough time, it is reasonable to use the LDS algorithm without re-calculation to obtain a semi-optimal solution.

Uniform (Figures 5): Figures 5 show the results where we set $M = 100$. IDA* can solve only problem instances where the number of bids is small within a reasonable amount of time. On the other hand, since LDS restricts the search space according to the maximal discrepancy, LDS can find about 95% of the optimal solution very quickly.

4   Conclusions

Determining the winners in combinatorial auctions is a complicated constraint optimization problem. We have presented an approximate algorithm that is based on the LDS technique. Experimental evaluations performed on various problem sets showed that the LDS algorithm can find a semi-optimal solution (better than 95%) with a small amount of search effort (in about 1% of the running time) compared with the existing optimal algorithm.

References

1. Fujishima, Y., Leyton-Brown, K., and Shoham, Y.: Taming the Computational Complexity of Combinatorial Auctions: Optimal and Approximate Approaches. *IJCAI-99* (1999) 549, 550, 551
2. Harvey, W. D. and Ginsberg, M. L.: Limited Discrepancy Search. *IJCAI-95* (1995) 549, 551
3. Korf, R. E.: Depth-first iterative deepening: an optimal admissible tree search. *Artificial Intelligence* **62** (1993) 43–78   550
4. Rothkopf, M. H., Pekeč, A., and Harstad, R. M.: Computationally Manageable Combinatorial Auctions. *Management Science* **44** (1998) 1131–1147   549
5. Sandholm, T.: An Algorithm for Optimal Winner Determination in Combinatorial Auction. *IJCAI-99* (1999) 549, 550, 551

Author Index